Trademark Acknowledgements

Wrox has endeavored to provide trademark information about all the companies and products mentioned in this book by the appropriate use of capitals. However, Wrox cannot guarantee the accuracy of this information.

Credits

Authors
John Kauffman
Brian Matsik
Kevin Spencer

Contributing Authors
Ian Herbert
Julian Skinner
Sakhr Youness

Technical Reviewers
Aaron Abdis
Maxime Bombardier
Beth Breidenbach
Robert Chang
Robin Dewson
Michael Erickson
Derek Fisher
Damien Foggon
Hope Hatfield
Ian Herbert
Jon Jenkins
John Kauffman
Don Lee
Gleydson de Macedo
Paul Morris
Scott Robertson
John Roth
Douglas Rothaus
Larry Schoeneman
Rick Tempestini
Gary Vartanoff
Helmut Watson
David West
Rory Winston

Additional Material
Alastair Ewins
Chris Ullman
Jerry Ablam

Category Manager
Kirsty Reade

Project Manager
Laura Jones

Technical Architect
Sarah Drew

Technical Editors
Claire Brittle
Alastair Ewins
Jake Manning

Production Manager
Simon Hardware

Production Coordinator
Mark Burdett

Figures
Shabnam Hussain
Mark Burdett

Proofreader
Christopher Smith
Agnes Wiggers

Index
Martin Brooks

Cover
Shelley Frazier

About the Authors

John Kauffman

John Kauffman has been teaching technology for eleven years in classrooms, on line and by writing books. His classrooms have ranged from Washington DC to the oil fields of Sichuan Province, China, from Amsterdam to the plains of Eastern Tanzania. He started teaching when the demand was for DOS and WordPerfect 5 and returned to the same clients to teach Windows3.1, dBase, MS Office and Windows 95. He now focuses on ASP, Visual Basic, Access and SQL. John keeps a logbook of students' questions and mistakes; those lists then form the basis for his new class materials and books.

My portions of this book are dedicated to the legions of students that have provided feedback on my past classes –
Thank You, Asanti, Thanks Mate, Xie Xie, Vous Remercie, Vielen Dank, RingraziarLo, Mange Takk, Obrigado,
Ddanken, Gracias, Nagyon Sszépen Köszönö , Doumoari Gatou and Cheers.

Brian Matsik

Brian Matsik is the President and Senior Consultant at OOCS in Charlotte, NC and is currently a Microsoft Certified Solution Developer and Microsoft Certified Trainer. His experience with Visual Basic, VBScript, and VBA goes back to the DOS days and VB 2.0. Brian currently specializes in ASP, SQL Server, ADO, and VB COM. When he is not coding, training or writing he is either in his scuba gear or in the garage trying to turn perfectly good oak into perfectly good kindling. Brian can be reached at brianmat@oocs.com.

I would like to dedicate this to my wife Tracy for having the patience of Job. Without her support, none of this
would have been possible. You are always there with me.

I would also like to thank Tony Profera, Bobby Allen, and Craig Tucker for everything. From helping me to keep
my sanity to the day-to-day "stuff", they have been there to lend a hand. I would also like to thank my Dad John
for helping me to remember all of the trigonometry that he taught me - and that I have since forgotten. Don't
worry Dad, it's coming back now - well, a little.

Kevin Spencer

Kevin Spencer began programming in the C language in the early 1990's, during which time he developed a number of shareware programs for BBS's (Bulletin Boards), using serial communications (modem) technologies, as well as custom-built relational databases. As the World Wide Web sprang into popular use, he shifted his emphasis to Internet programming. Microsoft was just beginning to release some of its' (now) most-popular Active Web programming technologies, such as ASP (Active Server Pages) and ADO (ActiveX Data Objects). Seeing the promise in these technologies, Kevin started his Internet Web application programming business, Site Design by TAKempis (http://www.takempis.com), in 1996.

By virtue of the fact that he had specialized in such a new technology, combined with his low-level C programming experience, he quickly became known as something of an expert regarding these technologies, and for his contributions to helping others to use these technologies, Microsoft has awarded him the MVP (Most Valuable Professional) award, starting in 1997.

Kevin's web site has carried a number of tutorials, articles, and Discussion Groups for learning about ASP and ADO for 4 years now. He has written for a number of online publications, including Wrox Press' ASP Today, as well as co-authoring Wrox Press' Beginning ASP Databases, with John Kauffman and Thearon Willis.

Kevin currently works and lives in Alabama with his wife (the Princess Dianne), Uncle Chutney, and Buffstrella the WonderDog.

Sakhr Youness

Mr. Youness is the lead architect of the Commerce One team in the Detroit area, Michigan. His work involves building business to business (b2b) applications and integration between Commerce One products and other products at the Covisint exchange, which facilitates the exchange of goods between the five largest auto makers in the World and their suppliers. Mr. Youness has extensive experience in database architecture, data modeling, web application architecture, design, and development, as well as experience with middleware products used to integrate different applications. Mr. Youness has many publications, including a book by Wrox on Microsoft data warehousing and OLAP *Professional Data Warehousing with SQL Server 7.0 and OLAP Services* published in 2000, and a book on SQL (*SQL Unleashed, Second Edition*), published by SAMS in 1999. Mr. Youness is also a speaker at many conferences, including the last two Wrox Web Developer Conferences in Las Vegas and Amsterdam.

Some of Mr. Youness' hobbies include swimming, and playing basketball. He enjoys going with his wife, Nada, and taking their 3-year old daughter on vacations. Mr. Youness would like to thank his wife for her patience with him working long nights and weekends on these writings, and would like to thank the Wrox team, for being the best editorial team he has ever worked with.

Ian Herbert

Ian is a director of Swifton Databases Limited (www.swifton.co.uk), based in Birmingham, UK. Swifton specializes in delivering database solutions for both small and large businesses, especially those operating in the chemical and chemical analysis sector.

I would like to thank John Kauffman for his excellent guidance at the start of this project. I am also indebted to the team at Wrox Press whose professionalism and support never fails to impress. Particular thanks here go to Sarah Drew, Laura Jones and Jake Manning.

Julian Skinner

Julian holds the position of Technical Architect at Wrox, helping to shape and guide the raw material of today into the books of tomorrow.

BeginningSQL
Dot
Dot
Dash
Dash
Dot
Dash
DotDot

Table of Contents

Table of Contents

Table of Contents

Table of Contents

Table of Contents

Table of Contents

Table of Contents

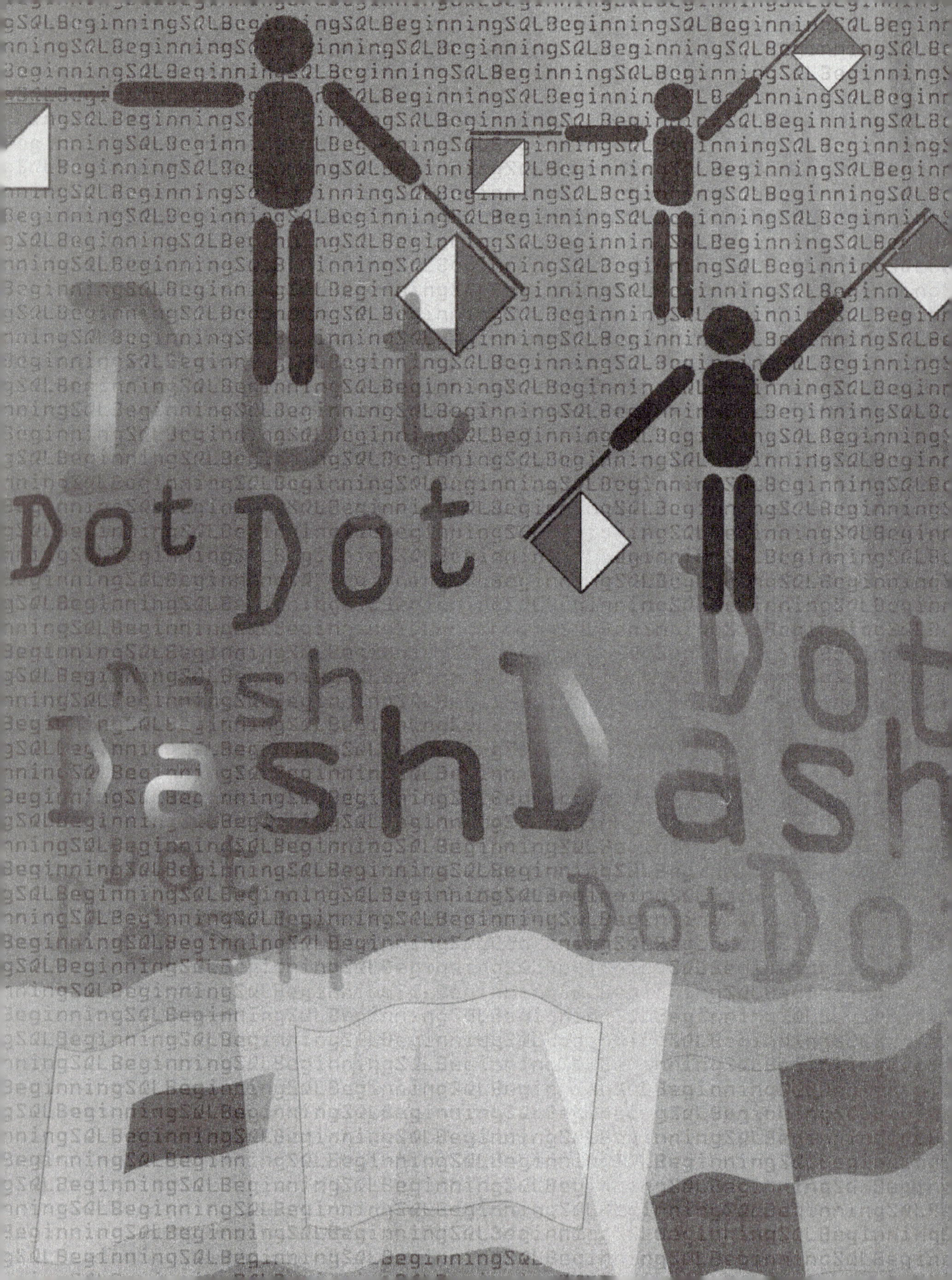

Dot Dot
Dash
Dot Dot

Introduction

SQL, or Structured Query Language, is the standard language programmers use to talk with databases through a Database Management System (DBMS). The SQL language is *open*, meaning it is not owned or controlled by any single company. The strength of SQL is its universal acceptance by database vendors; if you write a statement in SQL, it can be used in any database to get the information you want from the data it holds.

This book aims to teach you all you need to know to start experimenting with SQL – what it is, how it works, and what you can do with it. Starting from the basic syntax, you'll move on to learn how to create complex and powerful statements. Don't worry if you've never queried a database before – this book will teach you all you need to know, step by step. You'll find that SQL can be a great introduction into the world of database queries; with the knowledge and understanding that you'll gain from this book, you'll be able to move on to learn newer and more advanced technologies in the world of computing.

Who is This Book For?

This book is designed for novice database programmers or people familiar with a desktop solution such as Access who would like to scale up to a relational database that requires SQL.

The book will also be a valuable learning tool for people with some knowledge of Visual Basic programming who would like to work with databases, and also for web developers who have wandered into the world of dynamic page creation using databases.

What's Covered in This Book?

This book is intended to take you from knowing very little about SQL to being able to use it to formulate complicated queries to retrieve the information you need. With this in mind, the book starts off with **Chapter 1**, an introduction to SQL, including a bit of history about it, and bringing to your attention the terminology you will encounter in this book.

Chapter 2 tells you everything you need to know about getting your particular system up and running for using the examples in this book. Throughout, we use the Northwind database to demonstrate the capabilities of SQL – this chapter tells you how to setup Northwind on your system. Also, in this chapter you will learn about the different interfaces that you can use to formulate your SQL queries.

Chapter 3 covers an introduction to relational databases. There are many issues that it is important to understand, not least how the data is organized within. It is imperative that the basics of databases are understood, so that SQL can be used effectively to retrieve the correct information from them. This chapter therefore covers the structure of a relational database, and also what relationships are and how to form and understand them.

Chapters 4 and 5 look at the most frequently used SQL keyword: SELECT. This is used to retrieve data from the database – in its most basic form, covered in Chapter 4, it is still quite powerful, and when coupled with filtering and calculated conditions, it helps to return the information we need. Chapter 5 takes this further and looks at the intricacies of using some of the more advanced conditions with the SELECT statement, providing plenty of examples to show you how it all works.

The next three chapters, **Chapters 6, 7, and 8**, deal with tables. Chapter 6 starts the ball rolling with information on how we can create our own tables using SQL, looking carefully at what data type to use, or modify existing tables if the information is incorrect. Chapter 7 looks at data constraints – what they are, why you should enforce them, and also how to enforce them. Chapter 8 finishes off this idea by showing how tables are related in the database, and how you can JOIN them, based on their data type, constraints and other issues.

Now that we have our tables, we will need to populate them with records, and this is exactly the topic of **Chapters 9 and 10**. Chapter 9 leads with a discussion on how to create records and put them into the correct table. Chapter 10 continues the theme, with a look at how we can delete the data that we no longer need, for whatever reason, and shows how to delete just one part of the information, or a lot of information at one time. However, if deleting seems a little too drastic, Chapter 10 also covers how to update the data in a record – while still a form of deletion (as the old data will no longer exist when replaced with the new data), it is a much less frightening thought than getting rid of whole tables at a time!

Chapters 11, 12, and 13 then shift the focus to look at SQL functions. Date, Time and String functions are covered in Chapter 11, with Math and data type conversion functions covered in Chapter 12. Chapter 13 looks at using aggregate functions, which are used to group the returned data so that it is easier to understand.

Chapter 14 turns its attention to Stored Procedures, which are chunks of code that are frequently used, stored in such a way that they can be used over and over again in different databases and circumstances, simply by changing the parameters given to them. **Chapter 15** looks at Views – again, these are statements stored in the database that, when executed, present a virtual table. A view can draw data from any of the tables in the database, making them a powerful way to present often-used information without having to rewrite the SQL statement every time.

Chapter 16 covers the idea of a schema, such as what it is, when we need to use it, and what the various objects within it are. This chapter also looks at the INFORMATION_SCHEMA, which allows us to view information about a database and its objects.

Chapters 17 and 18 present two real world case studies, bringing together everything we have learned about SQL in this book. Chapter 17 presents a sports league database, showing us how we create a database and its schema, populate it with data and build queries to get useful and timely information out of it. Chapter 18 combines our knowledge of SQL with ASP to build an online Northwind Product Catalog – this chapter serves well to show just how powerful SQL can be when joined with the right tools and knowledge to get the best out of it.

What You Need to Use This Book

Ideally you will be running one of the following:

❑   Windows 2000 (Professional)

❑   Windows NT Workstation 4.0 with SP 5

❑   Windows 2000 Server

❑   Windows 2000 Advanced Server

❑   Windows NT Server 4.0 with SP5

If so, everything you need is on the CD included at the back of the book. The CD contains an 120 day Evaluation edition of Microsoft SQL Server 2000 (enterprise version). Steps and information on how to install this software and get started can be found in Chapter 2 ("Getting Started With SQL").

If you're running Windows 98, you will need the following:

❑   Microsoft Access (with the Northwind sample database).

❑   MSDE (Microsoft Data Engine) – This is the stripped and scaled down version of a SQL Server database engine. It comes with Microsoft Office 2000 Premium or Developer editions or can be freely downloaded from www.Microsoft.com if you have a license for Microsoft Visual software, such as Visual Studio, Visual Basic, Visual C++ etc.

If you are unable to obtain MSDE, you can still follow most (although not all) of the examples in this book using purely Microsoft Access.

If you have an Oracle, MySQL or IBM DB2 system, and either Microsoft SQL Server or Access, you can download a migration tool from www.wrox.com which will allow you to import the Northwind database into any of these systems. Instructions for how to perform this migration can be found in Appendix D.

For the case studies, you will also need Personal Web Server (PWS) if you are using Windows 98. This should be available on your original Windows installation disk.
If you are running NT 4.0 Workstation or Server, you will need the NT 4 Option Pack which can be downloaded from the Microsoft website. This will install PWS on Workstation and Internet Information Server (IIS) 4.0 on Server.

If you're running Windows 2000 Professional, Server, or Advanced Server, IIS version 5.0 will be included on your installation disks.

> **One final note: Appendix A provides an introduction and a short case study to familiarise you with the Northwind database in Access, with a useful refresher.**

Conventions

To help you understand what's going on, and in order to maintain consistency, we've used a number of conventions throughout the book:

When we introduce new terms, we **highlight** them.

Advice, hints, and background information comes in an indented, italicized font like this.

Try It Out

After learning something new, we'll have a *Try It Out* section, which will demonstrate the concepts learned, and get you working with the technology.

How It Works

After a *Try It Out* section, there will sometimes be a further explanation within a *How It Works* section, to help you relate what you've done to what you've just learned.

Words that appear on the screen in menus, like the File or Window menu, are in a similar font to what you see on screen.

Keys that you press on the keyboard, like *Ctrl* and *Enter*, are in italics.

We use two font styles for code. If it's a word that we're talking about in the text, for example, when discussing `functionNames()`, `<ELEMENTS>`, and `ATTRIBUTES`, it will be in a fixed pitch font. URLs and file names are also displayed in this font.

If it's a block of code that you can type in and run, or part of such a block, then it's also in a gray box:

```
SELECT EmployeeName
FROM Employees
```

Sometimes you'll see code in a mixture of styles, like this:

```
SELECT DISTINCT
    ShipCity,
    ShipRegion,
    ShipCountry
FROM
    Orders
WHERE
    ShipCountry = 'USA'
    OR ShipCountry = 'Canada'
```

In this case, we want you to consider the code with the gray background in particular, for example to modify it. The code with a white background is code we've already looked at, and that we don't wish to examine further.

Downloading the Source Code

As we move through the chapters, there will be copious amounts of code available for you, so that you can see exactly how the SQL principles being explained work. We'll also be stopping frequently to try it out, so that you not only see how things work, but can make them work yourself.

The source code for all of the examples is available for download from the Wrox site (see below). However, you might decide that you prefer to type all the code in by hand. Many readers prefer this, because it's a good way to get familiar with the coding techniques that are being used.

Whether you want to type the code in or not, we have made all the source code for this book available at our web site, at the following address:

```
http://www.wrox.com
```

If you're one of those readers who likes to type in the code, you can use our files to check the results you should be getting – this should be your first stop if you think you might have typed in an error. If you're one of those readers who does like typing, then downloading the source code from our web site is a must!

Either way, it'll help you with updates and debugging.

Tell Us What You Think

We've worked hard to make this book as relevant and useful as possible, so we'd like to get a feel for what it is you want and need to know, and what you think about how we've presented things.

If you have anything to say, let us know at:

```
feedback@wrox.com
```

Errata & Updates

We've made every effort to make sure there are no errors in the text or the code. However, to err is human, and as such we recognize the need to keep you informed of any mistakes as they're spotted and amended.

More details on obtaining support, finding out about errata, and providing us with feedback, can be found in Appendix F.

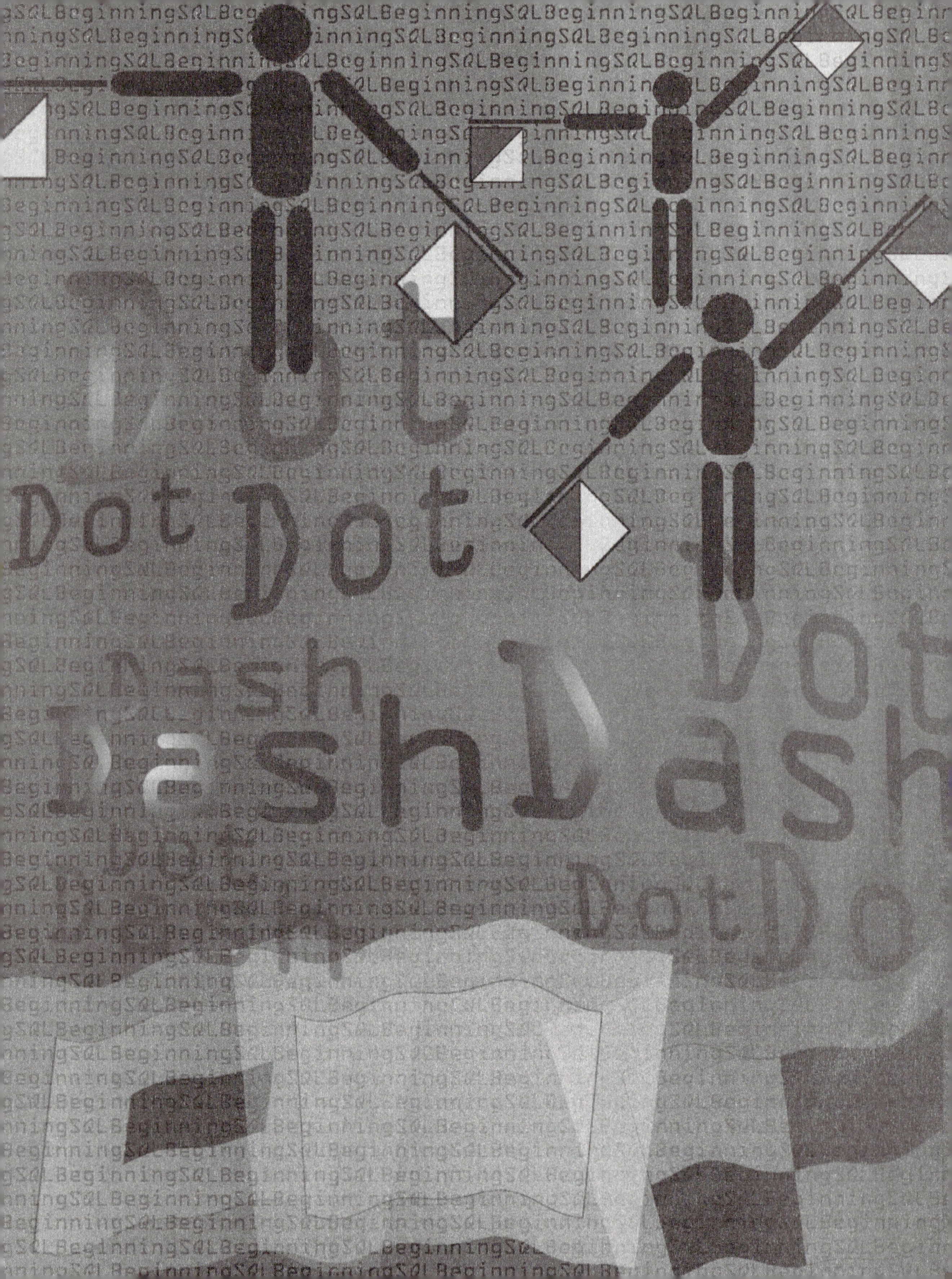

Introduction to SQL

The computer industry is criss-crossed with languages and standards, most of which are unintelligible to each other. Here and there, true standards have emerged, and in these cases it is well worth the time of any programmer to learn them. **Structured Query Language**, or **SQL** as we commonly call it, has, over the last ten years, emerged as the standard language for programmers to talk with databases through a Database Management System (DBMS). Oracle, Microsoft SQL Server, Microsoft Access, IBM's DB2, Sybase, and virtually every other DBMS sold in the last five years use SQL. Knowledge of SQL is becoming necessary for almost every IT professional. And as the development of basic web sites becomes common among non-programmers, a grasp of SQL will help them to integrate data into their HTML pages.

This introductory chapter covers topics that students usually ask in the first hour of classes; essentially, just what do we mean by SQL? We start by explaining what SQL is and also what it is not, and we provide a brief overview of the history of the language. We'll also clarify some confusing terminology at this point. Next we look at the types of system set-up in which SQL may be used; discussing front ends, back ends and how they connect. We then demonstrate some common implementations. We spend some time explaining why SQL, as a declarative language, is so different from procedural languages like Visual Basic, C++ or COBOL. We analyze when to move to using SQL, and finally we examine the human roles within a large data center. So in this chapter we will:

- ❑ Learn exactly what SQL is, and its history
- ❑ Understand the term ANSI-SQL
- ❑ Learn how SQL is implemented via a connection and how this is configured
- ❑ Know when to use SQL as a solution
- ❑ Understand the human roles in the data center

What is SQL & What Does It Do?

Structured Query Language (abbreviated SQL, pronounced to rhyme with *equal*) is a computer language for communication with databases. The communicating parties are typically a "front end" which sends a SQL Statement across a connection to a "back end" that holds the data. That statement contains instructions to create, read, change or delete data. The universal rules of the language have been established by ANSI (American National Standards Institute); a standards committee composed of database experts from industry, academia and software vendors. Therefore the SQL language is *open*, meaning it is not owned or controlled by any single company.

> **SQL is a non-proprietary (open) language whose rules have been set by a standards committee.**

The strength of SQL is its universal acceptance by database vendors. By learning SQL you have a language that can be used in Visual Basic or C++ to talk to an Oracle database. You can use SQL in an ASP page to talk to Microsoft SQL Server. You can send a request for data from IBM's DB2 to a Sybase datastore. You can even use SQL within Access to describe the items you want to include in a form's list box. There has been a lot of talk and marketing about "write once, run anywhere" languages like Java. For database programmers, understanding SQL is the ticket to "learn once, profit anywhere."

SQL has many capabilities, but the most common needs in business are to:

- ❑   Read existing data
- ❑   Create new records holding data
- ❑   Change existing data
- ❑   Delete data

SQL contains key words or parts to perform these basic tasks. Learning the basics and embellishments of those commands will consume most of this book. But before we begin to look at the syntax and lists of common mistakes, we'll look at some examples of each these operations in the next few paragraphs.

Reading data is the most common task. An ANSI-SQL statement requesting a list of names of all members of your society that live in New York, can be sent from a Visual Basic application to an Oracle database. If the database is later changed to IBM's DB2, the SQL statement is still valid. The SQL language offers many permutations of the request, including the ability to return the names in various orders, only the first or last few names, a list of names without duplicates and various other requests where people require specific information from their database.

Records can be created in a datastore using SQL. A form page on a web site can gather information from a visitor and then put that data into a SQL statement. The SQL statement will instruct the datastore to insert a new record into a Microsoft SQL Server database. Since SQL is universally accepted, the same SQL statement could, for example, be used for clerks that create new records from, say, a Visual Basic application on their local network.

Data can also be changed using SQL. As in the examples above, a front end user interface such as a web page can accept changes to data and send them via a SQL statement to the datastore. But there does not have to be direct user interaction. A DB2 database running on an IBM mainframe could have a procedure to connect to another corporate mainframe running Sybase. The IBM can generate and send a SQL statement to modify the data in certain records in the Sybase database. Although the systems are from different vendors and have different ways of storing and using data, they both understand the SQL statement.

Deleting data can be performed using SQL statements. In fact SQL can accommodate very complex sets of conditions for which records to delete and which to leave intact. Portions of data within a record can be deleted.

What Does SQL Not Do?

First, SQL is not a program or a development environment such as Access or VB. SQL is a pure language. There is no front end built into SQL, that is, the language does not have user forms like an Access application or Visual Basic, and SQL has no intrinsic way to talk with web pages. SQL statements are mainly generated by a separate front-end product. Many SQL-enabled DBMS do have a tool that allows you to type a SQL statement and run it against the data. But these tools are only for design time, not deployment.

Second, SQL does not have a back end. There are no tools intrinsic to the language that can actually store data. SQL is only a standard means of communicating with software products that can hold data (a DBMS as we will see later). In other words, the data itself is contained within a DBMS such as Oracle or SQL Server. You will also need a front end, such as VB or C++. Then you can use SQL as the language for the front end to send instructions to the DBMS.

To take these first two points together, SQL is a language and not a software product. Consider a spoken language; the language itself does not contain a speaker or a listener. The language only contains the vocabulary, grammatical rules and idioms to be used by speakers and listeners. The people are not part of, or specified in any way, by the language. SQL is like a spoken language in another way. The listener and speaker can have any mother tongue, as long as they can translate that to SQL. So a computer can use any operating system and any database software, as long as the software can translate from its internal language to SQL.

> **SQL is a language, not a software product. Front-end software interfaces with the user. Back-end software holds data. SQL is the standard language for the two pieces of software to communicate with each other.**

Third, SQL is not a procedural programming language. We will discuss the concepts of declarative versus procedural languages shortly. SQL is a set-based language, which communicates in statements that define an outcome. This is very different to procedural languages that instruct the computer how to proceed step by step to reach an objective.

Fourth, SQL does not have its own specific development environment. When you work with Access or Power Builder, for example, you have a highly evolved set of tools for:

❑   laying out your user interface

❑   troubleshooting

❑   rapid entry of code

❑   code reuse

But pure SQL does not include any of those tools (although most vendors include some tools in their products, they are not part of pure SQL). To go back to our spoken language analogy, SQL is the language. It is not a dictionary, grammar guide, printing press, loudspeaker, postal service, filing cabinet or any of the other tools we use to work with human languages. In the sense that "English" does not include these tools, neither does the SQL language.

Last, SQL is not network-aware. In the same sense that written English is not dependent on or aware of being used in telephones or e-mails, neither is SQL. Whenever a SQL statement is issued there must be a way for it to be conveyed, or connected, to its destination. Programmers create, maintain and fine-tune those connections with code in the front and back ends.

A Brief History of SQL

In this chapter we want to emphasize that SQL is both deep and wide. Deep in the sense that it is implemented at many levels of database communication, from a simple Access form list box right up to high-volume communications between mainframes. SQL is widely implemented in that almost every DBMS supports SQL statements for communication. The reason for this level of acceptance is partially explained by the amount of effort that went into the theory and development of the standards.

Early History

The father of relational databases, and thus SQL, is Dr. E.F. "Ted" Codd who worked for IBM. After Codd described a relational model for databases in 1970, IBM spent a lot of time and money researching how to implement his ideas. IBM came to market with a product named System/R in 1978.

But other companies had formed and created relational database products before IBM was ready to release System/R. The first to market was Relational Software's product named Oracle and the second was Relational Technology's Ingres. IBM then released improved products in 1982 named SQL/DS and DB2. Oracle (now from Oracle Inc.) and DB2 are still available today in nth generation forms while the Ingres technology was bought by Computer Associates.

Standards

As we said at the beginning, SQL is a standard, open language without corporate ownership. The commercial acceptance of SQL was precipitated by the formation of SQL Standards committees by the American National Standards Institute and the International Standards Organization in 1986 and 1987. Two years later they published a specification known as SQL-89. An improvement and expansion (to some 600 pages) to the standard gave the world SQL-92. We now have the third generation standard, SQL 99. The existence of standards is important for the general portability of SQL statements.

Who is ANSI? The American National Standards Institute is an administrator and coordinator of voluntary systems of standardization for the United States private sector. About 80 years ago a group of engineering societies and government agencies formed the institute to enhance the "quality of life by promoting and facilitating voluntary consensus standards and conformity." Today the Institute represents the interests of about 1,000 companies, organizations and government agencies. ANSI does not itself develop standards; rather it facilitates development by establishing consensus among qualified groups.

Current State

So the ANSI-SQL group has published three standards over the years:

- ❑ SQL89 (SQL1)
- ❑ SQL92 (SQL2)
- ❑ SQL99 (SQL3)

The vast majority of the language has not changed through these updates. We can all profit from the fact that almost all of the code we wrote to SQL standards of 1989 is still perfectly usable. Or in other words, as a new student of SQL there is over ten years of SQL code out there that needs your expertise to maintain and expand.

Most DBMS are designed to meet the SQL92 standard. Virtually all of the material in this book was available in the earlier standards as well. Since many of the advanced features of SQL92 have yet to be implemented by DBMS vendors, there has been little pressure for a new version of the standard. Nevertheless a SQL99 standard was developed to address advanced issues in SQL. All of the core functions of SQL, such as adding, reading and modifying data, are the same. Therefore, the topics in this book are not affected by the new standard. As of early 2001, no vendor has implemented the SQL99 standard.

There are three areas where there is current development in SQL standards. First entails improving Internet access to data, particularly to meet the needs of the emerging XML standards. Second is integration with Java, either through Sun's Java Database Connectivity (JDBC) or through internal implementations. Last, the groups that establish SQL standards are considering how to integrate object-based programming models.

Flavors of SQL

The computer industry (like most industries) both benefits and suffers from standards. We said that SQL is an open standard, not owned by a company, and the standard comes from ANSI. Therefore the SQL standard from ANSI is considered the "pure" SQL and called ANSI-SQL.

Two problems emerge to sully this pureness. First is that every DBMS vendor wants to differentiate their DBMS products. So if you look at the feature set of each DBMS product you see that not only does the product support ANSI-SQL but it also offers extra features, enhancements or extensions that are available only from individual vendors. For example, most vendors offer a field type which auto-increments even though this is not described in the SQL standards. These additions to ANSI-SQL are generally proprietary and will not work if you try to use them on competitor's SQL products. At the level we discuss in this book there are only very minor differences between the vendors that we will note throughout the book.

Many of these features are powerful and robust, but since they vary from vendor to vendor, programmers should use them with caution. It is always safest to stick with pure SQL whenever possible; if you stray it should be with full knowledge that you are losing the portability of your statements (and perhaps even your data).

Such enhancements are not all bad because these extensions are very useful. For example, ANSI-SQL does not contain an automatic way to assign a serial number to each new record but most DBMS sold today have added this feature. Since serial numbering is so common programmers are happy to have the enhancement. However, the method of implementation is not uniform, so code written to get the serial number from data in one DBMS may not work when used with another vendor's DBMS.

> **In this book we are helping people that use all of the flavors of SQL. As a beginner most of what you learn is pure ANSI-SQL and thus is consistent across all vendor's products. When we talk about vendor-specific features in this book we note it. Certainly as a student, not knowing what DBMS you will be using in a job, it is best to study the purest form of the language. Learning the extensions available in T-SQL, PL/SQL, Access SQL and others will come later. For an introduction to some of these variations see our Appendix D.**

Terminology

Structured Query Language and the science of databases is no different from other highly-evolved schools of thought, in that there are many words which are specific to the discipline. In the case of SQL some of these words are similar but actually refer to entirely different concepts. For example we use several words and phrases that contain the term "data." There are some shades of meaning to these terms that involve what layer of information or processes we are discussing.

❑   **Data:** A set of information with some aspect in common

For example data for employees might include social security numbers: "123-45-6789 Abe Adams, 234-56-7890 Beth Barrett, 345-67-8901 Chris Cao"

❑   **Metadata:** Information about the structure and organization of data in a database

In database terms (which we will cover in Chapter 3), metadata typically contains descriptions of the tables and their constraints, the fields and their sizes and rules, and the relationships between the tables. Some people have phrased metadata as "data about the data". An example of metadata for an employee database would be something like:

```
Table #1  name= Employees    field count = 3

Field #1     name= EmployeeID   type=integer    size= 9 digits (exactly)
Field #2     name= NameFirst    type= string    size <=15 characters
Field #3     name= NameLast     type=string     size <=30 characters
```

This metadata describes that we have a set of data about employees that is organized into a table. Within that table we hold three kinds of information about each employee, their ID number, and their first and last names. The metadata goes on to describe how each type of information is maintained. By the end of Chapter 7, you will have a lot of experience with these terms, but for now note that the metadata does not include the data, only a description of how the data is organized.

❑   **Database** A database is the data and the metadata

In other words a database is a set of related information as well as a description of how that information is organized. A database for employees would be the metadata we just looked at, plus the information described above under Data.

Employee ID	NameFirst	NameLast
12345	Abe	Adams
56789	Beth	Barrett
01234	Chris	Cao

> **Note that we frequently display data as being in a table. The table is only a logical structure, not a representation of exactly how the data sits on the disk. Different DBMS will physically store the data in different configurations, usually associated with the order that the records were added. As you will see later, the storage methodology is of no concern to us.**

❑   **Datastore:** A source of data

(for our purposes, a source of data that has a way of responding to SQL statements)

Since about 1985, the dominant form of database has been of a type called *relational.* We will study this term later in the book, but for now it is enough to understand that relational databases follow the rules for data organization established by Dr. E.F. "Ted" Codd. However, in the past few years more and more data has accumulated in non-relational forms, primarily hierarchical forms. Think, for example, of the amount of information in word-processing documents stored on your company's desktop hard drives. Clearly your company has data in those documents, but it is organized into drives, folders, subfolders and files; a hierarchical system with no rules about the data contained at each level. In an effort to emphasize data techniques that work with any source of data (relational or not), the term Datastore can be used instead of Database. The term datastore also includes older databases (generally called "*flat file*") that predate the relational rules of Dr. Codd. In summary, whereas the term *database* today generally means a modern relational database, the term *datastore* is much broader, including information contained in non-relational databases. Software companies have created many tools to allow SQL to talk with all types of datastores as well as proper relational databases.

❑ **Data Server:** A Data Server manages data and is typically one or more of many servers in an environment

Modern business computing relies on one or more central servers to hold data and handle centralized processing. In the past a single machine might perform data storage, security, print services and all other functions of the office. But as the number of computing jobs has increased (e-mail, Web Site Support, etc.), IT departments have split the job across multiple servers, each optimized to perform a very specific job. There may also be servers handling the business rules, web or network services and other functions. Any of the other servers can pass a SQL statement to the Data Server, which will execute the statement and then pass the results back to the requesting server. In simpler cases Data Servers pass information directly to clients such as desktop PCs.

The other point to note here is that a Data Server differs from a File Server. The latter holds files organized into folders and subfolders, with the intention of keeping employee's documents on one central server. A Data Server generally abandons the folders in favor of a disk organization scheme more efficient for relational data. In a small shop a single machine may function as both a file and data server by using different organization schemes on different disk areas.

> Note that the terms "server" and "client" are relative in multiple server environments. When a web server sends a SQL statement to a data server the web server is considered to be the "client." However the web server is then considered the "server" in relation to the browser. In other words, we refer to the client as the machine or software that sent the SQL statement to the DBMS and we refer to the server as the machine (or group of machines) that receives the statement and processes it.

❑ **Database Management System (DBMS):** Software which handles most aspects of data management including physical storage, reading and writing data, security, replication, error correction and other functions

Common DBMS include IBM DB2, Microsoft SQL Server, Oracle, Sybase and Informix. Although it is not a true DBMS and isn't designed for large numbers of users, Microsoft Access can also accept SQL statements. Each DBMS has a way of receiving a SQL statement and forwarding the statement to its Database Engine. The DBMS will then have a way to take a result from the engine and send it back out to the requester. Larger and more complex DBMS will be closely integrated with a specific Operating System and some actually contain an OS optimized for data management.

❑ **Database Engine:** The part of the DBMS that works with the data

An engine typically has code that can search, read, write, index and otherwise execute the actual interaction with the information. A database engine performs the largest share of work in most databases and thus it is the subject of an intense optimization effort by the DBMS creators. Some of the most advanced DBMS have engines which can self-optimize after monitoring the actual conditions after deployment. A DBMS will have additional features that are not part of the data engine, including query analyzing, replication and back-up tools, user management, security tools and performance monitoring.

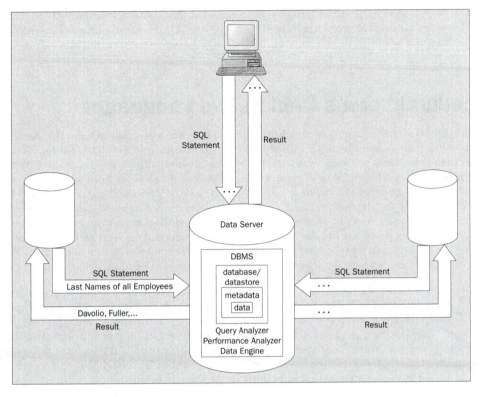

❑ **Results:** The term "Result" frequently confuses folks learning SQL because the term can be used in three ways:

  ❑ First, and most common, we mean a set of data that is returned after a front end sends a SQL statement to a DBMS. You ask for "The first and last names of all the employees that started after 1995" and you get back a block of characters (a recordset) containing those names.

  But what if the SQL statement instructs the DBMS to modify data rather than just read it?

  ❑ The second case is when the "result" refers to a change in the data. We do not necessarily receive any characters back from the DBMS although we may get a status message noting that the operation was successful.

  ❑ Third, we may make changes to the data and have the DBMS report back to us on the changes. Frequently this is a notice of how many records were changed or what errors arose or a `True/False` that the SQL statement was executed successfully. In this case we get a result back, but it is not actual data; it is a message or code indicating the number of records changed, an error or success.

  In this book we use the term all three ways since there is no common alternative vocabulary.

❑ **"SQL" and "SQL Server":** SQL is the name of an open-standard language for communicating with databases. Microsoft SQL Server and Sybase SQL Server are proprietary DBMS products that can handle SQL statements. Microsoft SQL Server is popular, but it is only one of many DBMS that can handle your data and your SQL statements.

Procedural Versus Declarative Languages

We mentioned at the beginning of the chapter, that SQL is not a procedural language. Before we move on to look at how we can actually implement SQL, we'll first see exactly what we mean by a declarative rather than procedural language. Many readers will have experience in languages like Visual Basic or C++ in which they mastered how to write a series of statements in order to achieve a goal. You have probably even used these commands to "walk through" a set of data checking to see if each item is the item of interest. If you wanted to change data you wrote a series of steps that somehow opened up the datastore, then put a pointer in the correct location, modified the data, moved to the next bit of data (all the while checking if you were at the end of the data yet), modified the next record and finished by closing the datastore. In a procedural language we tell the computer each step to perform. The computer performs those steps and, if they are well written, we will end up with our desired result.

SQL is not a procedural language but a declarative language. You write a single SQL declaration and hand it to the DBMS. The DBMS then executes internal code, which is hidden from us. The DBMS returns a set, which is a group of data that is somehow defined. For example, we write a SQL statement that would translate as something like Give me the last names of all the employees. The DBMS will work away for a few milliseconds and then produce a set that contains Adams, Barrett, Cao, etc. In a declarative language, we carefully phrase what we want and then let the DBMS get it for us. If we have written a good SQL statement then the resulting set of data will be correct.

> **Procedural languages result in many lines of code.**
>
> **Declarative languages result in one statement of the desired result.**

The distinction between these classes of languages drives the entire way that we think about database programming. Many of the mistakes that I see are a result of thinking in a procedural way when writing SQL statements. In this book we will show you hundreds of examples of good SQL statements that will help you on your way to thinking declaratively.

Languages in a Taxi Ride

A good analogy exists between these types of languages and different types of taxi rides. When I get in a taxi I can give a direction to the driver in one of two ways. If the driver looks and sounds like he knows what he is doing then I just give him the address. If the driver looks like he just moved to town yesterday, then I talk him through the directions to get to my destination.

If I give the driver an address I am communicating like a SQL statement, it is a clear description of the result and the driver carries it out as he or she sees fit. We may go south then east or we may go east then south. The driver is free to adapt to local conditions like a closed road or a traffic jam. It doesn't really matter to me; a good taxi driver will get me to my stated destination in the best way the driver knows. During the trip I just sit still and wait for the result. If the address is written on a piece of paper then I can show that same card to any good driver.

If I give the driver exact directions then I am communicating in a procedural language. I tell the driver to head south four blocks then turn left at the Luck Hunan Restaurant. Procedural languages work fine when the taxi driver is not too experienced and when the situation is very uniform. But I must constantly interact with the driver. If I get involved in a book we are likely to overshoot our destination. Likewise, if I tell the driver to turn left at the Luck Hunan Restaurant and the name has changed to the Lucky Duck Bar, then the communication will fail.

In this analogy we see a number of important points that apply to SQL. First, a declarative language only works when you have a strong, SQL-enabled DBMS (taxi driver). Second, procedural languages can fail when there are unexpected changes in the situation (changes in the city's landmarks). Third, procedural languages require interaction during the task (like me instructing the driver at every turn) whereas declarative languages only require that the requester wait for the process to finish. And fourth, a well-written SQL statement will work with any SQL-enabled DBMS (like an address on a paper will work with any good taxi driver).

Comparing Procedural and Declarative Languages

Procedural (Basic, C++, Cobol, etc.)	Declarative (SQL)
Most work done by interpreter of the languages	Most work done by Data Engine within the DBMS
Many lines of code to perform a task	One SQL statement to perform task
Programmer must be skilled in translating the objective into lines of procedural code	Programmer must be skilled in clearly stating the objective as a SQL statement
Requires minimum of management around the actual data	Relies on sophisticated, SQL-enabled DBMS to hold the data and execute the SQL statement against the data
Programmer understands and has access to each step of the code	Programmer has no interaction with the execution of the SQL statement
Data exposed to programmer during execution of the code	Programmer receives data at end as an entire set
More susceptible to failure due to changes in the data structure	More resistant to changes in the data structure
Traditionally faster, but that is changing	Originally slower, but now setting speed records
Code of procedure tightly linked to front end	Same SQL statements will work with most front ends
	Code loosely linked to front end.
Code tightly integrated with structure of the datastore	Code loosely linked to structure of data; DBMS handles structural issues
Programmer works with a pointer or cursor	Programmer not concerned with positioning
Knowledge of coding tricks applies only to one language	Knowledge of SQL tricks applies to any language using SQL

To summarize this table, declarative languages are quite different from the procedural languages you may be using now. Procedural languages like C++ place an emphasis on the programmer writing many lines of code to describe the exact steps of obtaining a result. Declarative languages like SQL place an emphasis on the programmer writing an exact description of the desired result. The DBMS then handles the task of obtaining the result. A good SQL programmer becomes very skilled at carefully describing the result but remains blissfully ignorant of the internal code of the DBMS that executes the result.

SQL's Place in the Data Center

So how does SQL actually fit into the solution to my data management problems? We discussed earlier that SQL did not have a front end (user interface) or a back end (DBMS). So in the next few sections we will discuss some "ends" that we can use as well as the protocols that create a bridge across which the SQL statements flow.

"How Do I Get SQL? "

You need a front end that can **connect** to a SQL-enabled DBMS and can pass a SQL statement. We will talk more about connections in Chapter 2, but for now consider a **connection** to be a conduit for carrying SQL statements between the front and back ends. A connection is like the apparatus of the telephone company that connects your handset to your friend's handset – it allows a language to be used to communicate. Third, you need a SQL-enabled DBMS. You probably already have a SQL-enabled front end and a DBMS in one form or another (see the sections below). And if you don't you can get an inexpensive version or a trial version that will allow you to get started learning SQL for free.

Keep in mind that since SQL is a standard in the public domain, you do not need software or a license to use the language. You can acquire SQL by simply learning the syntax of how to write the SQL statements. But in order to practice creating and running SQL statements you will need three parts:

- ❑   a front end
- ❑   a connection
- ❑   a back end

We will look in detail at various options for each of these, but let us start with a quick overview.

The **front end** provides a means to send a SQL statement. Usually the front end includes an interface to users with a form to gather data and buttons to carry out tasks. The front end may contain a fixed SQL statement or it may use code to create a statement on the fly using the data provided by the user. The most common type of front end is the web browser.

The **connection** provides a conduit to get the SQL statement to the back end and then to return results to the front end. The connection is like a telephone connection over which a spoken language travels, although the language itself is free. A common connection today is ADO (Activex Data Objects) but there are many other options.

The **back end** is a DBMS that accepts and can act on SQL statements. Usually the back end has two parts, the actual store of data and a database engine, which can carry out the SQL statement. The most common back ends are the major database products such as Oracle and Microsoft SQL Server.

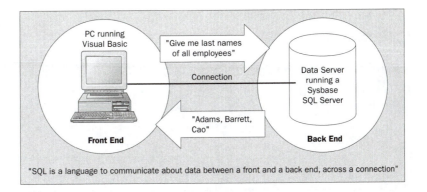

"SQL is a language to communicate about data between a front and a back end, across a connection"

The included CD contains a front end, connection and back end, but in a less conventional arrangement than the one we have just described. The CD is a 120-day trial version of Microsoft SQL Server 2000. SQL Server provides a very strong back end, but it does not come with front end or connection software. However, there is a utility called Query Analyzer which comes with SQL Server. This tool provides a front end optimized for developers that want to *test* SQL statements. It is a very simple front end that allows you to type a SQL Statement, run it and then view the results. A normal front end would have tools for creating a polished interface for users, but Query Analyzer is aimed at developers that are testing. Built into Query Analyzer is connection software that automatically creates a connection when the developer selects which database to work with.

Front Ends

In this book we will use different front ends in chapters in order to help you become more versatile. The differences are not very great; the SQL statements remain the same regardless of the front end. In Chapter 2 we will talk you through setting up various combination of front ends and back ends as well as showing samples of code.

The syntax of how each front end sends those SQL statements may vary occasionally. Likewise, each front end has its own syntax or tools for handling the data that is returned when a SQL statement asks for information. We will point such differences out where they may occur.

Access

Microsoft's desktop database uses SQL in many places. You can write and store queries as SQL statements. You can use SQL to define the source of a report or form. One option puts the actual SQL statement into the report as the value of the Record Source property. A second option stores the statement in a query and uses the query name as the value for the Record Source. SQL statements are also valid sources for list boxes on Access forms. Although Access never requires a user to employ SQL, in many places SQL can be used instead of Access object names.

The query grid contains a very powerful feature for students of SQL with Access experience. You can use the drag and drop interface of the grid to create a query, the same as you have already done many times in the past. But you can then click on View/SQL and see that visual interface expressed as a SQL statement, ready to cut and paste. Similarly a query can be created as a SQL statement and then viewed as a grid. At any time the query can be run to check the results.

You may be familiar with the Access Query Grid view:

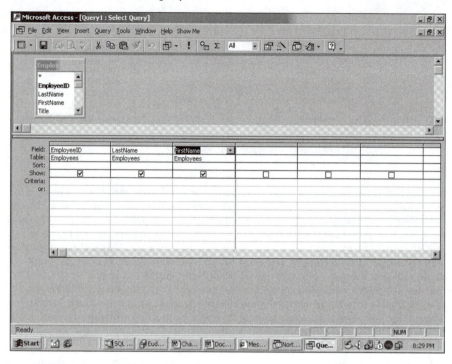

We can click on Menu:View | SQL View to see the same request written as a SQL statement:

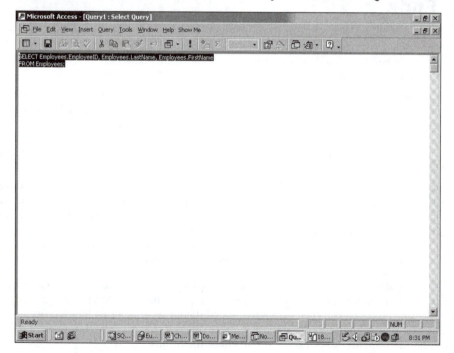

ASP

Active Server Pages, Microsoft's technology for server-side building of dynamic web pages, has the ability to use the ADO component (more on ADO in Chapter 2). The ADO Object allows a programmer to connect an ASP page to a datastore and then send a SQL command to that datastore and receive information back. For example, a web page visitor could enter her membership number into an ASP page and then click Submit. The responding ASP page could use that membership number to look up her account in the corporate database and return appropriate information in a table, text, or list box. ASP is not limited to reading data; it can use SQL statements to instruct the data store to add, change or delete data as per the web visitor's instructions.

> *For further information regarding Active Server Pages, you can visit http://msdn.microsoft.com/library/backgrnd/html/msdn_aspfaq.htm. You will find an introductory tutorial in ASP in Appendix E at the back of this book.*

Visual Basic

Visual Basic, from Microsoft, offers an easy-to-learn front end for Windows applications. It comes with a rich, graphical developer's environment, which allows quick prototyping and easy revisions. The finished product can then be compiled and deployed to any PC running Windows. The chief disadvantage of Visual Basic is that the features that speed up development also cause the applications to be slightly slower and less robust when deployed. The disadvantages will be largely eliminated with the .NET release of Visual Basic. Even though Visual Basic clocks a few percent slower than C++, it is still much faster than scripting languages used in ASP.

Visual Basic includes a DataGrid, which can be filled by the results of a SQL statement; other data–linked interfaces, like list boxes and text boxes, can also be filled from a datastore using SQL. Changes made to data on forms can be written to the database, either automatically or through specific SQL statements. Several third parties offer even more sophisticated controls that produce slick data-linked interfaces with minimal coding.

> *See Chapter 2 for code specifics of working with VB and SQL and www.vbextras.com for listings of third party products.*

In addition to using the controls, you can build and use SQL statements in any VB code. For example, a button on a form might fire an event containing code to send a SQL statement that will change data in certain records. Likewise, data returning from a SQL statement can be accepted into VB code and then manipulated.

> *For further information regarding Visual Basic & Visual Studio visit http://msdn.microsoft.com/vstudio/prodinfo/overview.asp..*

C++

Like ASP and VB, C++ can use ADO to connect to a DBMS and pass a SQL statement. The results are returned and can be used in an array, as variables or in expressions. Code that uses ADO, particularly the recent versions, is both efficient and flexible.

Besides ADO, C++ Programmers have an additional option of using connection technologies such as ODBC or OLEDB (covered in Chapter 2) to pass SQL statements to the DBMS. This procedure involves creating and managing Data Classes. Although more intensive, you can exert a finer level of control than using ADO.

Other Front Ends

Almost every other front end can process a SQL statement to a DBMS. For example, using Visual Basic for Applications (VBA) you can have Microsoft Word (including Mail Merge) use SQL to access data. Likewise, Excel VBA can connect your spreadsheet to a datastore and pass SQL statements to it.

PowerBuilder and Delphi are tools similar to Visual Basic that can create a user interface. That interface can also communicate with data stores via SQL statements.

Visit http://www.sybase.com/products/powerbuilder/ *to learn more about PowerBuilder.*

Cold Fusion can use proprietary tags to send SQL statements to a DBMS. DBMS vendors such as Oracle offer other packages for front-end development.

Both Java and JDBC can also create front ends that will both send and receive the results of SQL statements.

Back Ends

The front end will contain or create a SQL statement and have a way in which to connect to a back end, as we discussed in the sections above. We noted that virtually every front end can send a SQL statement. Likewise, virtually every DBMS sold in the last ten years can receive and process SQL statements. The heavy-duty products designed to support enterprises generally have the term "Server" in their product title in some way. Lightweight back ends are typically desktop applications, which also contain code to support receiving SQL Statements. They can all be used as back ends to receive and process a SQL statement.

Microsoft

The flagship database management system from Microsoft is SQL Server (versions 7 and 2000). The product is optimized to run on Windows NT (or Windows 2000) and has done well in speed test against competing products. Microsoft SQL Server is often less expensive to deploy than competing DBMS. Furthermore, an aggressive training and certification program is increasing the number of professionals qualified to program and run Microsoft SQL Server.

For product information on Microsoft SQL Server 7 or 2000, visit http://www.microsoft.com/sql/productinfo/prodover.htm.

Although SQL Server is Microsoft's enterprise scale DBMS product (it falls under the umbrella of their .Net enterprises servers), there are many other Microsoft products that can use SQL.

> Two DBMS products have similar names: Microsoft SQL Server and Sybase SQL
> Server are both specific DBMS products. These are two of many products that can
> receive SQL statements and thus function as back ends.

Oracle

Oracle offers one of the world's most widely deployed DBMS, currently named Oracle9i. The Oracle
product has proven itself in many of the largest datastores supporting entire corporations. Oracle has
established itself as a leader for web sites with very high traffic. The explosion of data access requests
from the web has pushed Oracle to further increase speed, capacity and reliability.

> *To check out Oracle DBMS products see*
> http://www.oracle.com/ip/deploy/database/index.html.

Sybase

Sybase currently offers three DBMS products. Adaptive Server Enterprise is optimized for enterprise
computing and web site support. SQL Anywhere Studio provides a suite of tools for rapid development
and deployment of business solutions. Adaptive Server IQ provides improved support for the analysis
of data and ad hoc queries.

> *Information about Sybase products can be found at*
> http://www.sybase.com/products/databaseservers/.

IBM

IBM offers the DB2 family of products, which run on the hardware and operating systems of both IBM
and non-IBM machines, including a developers kit for their products on Linux platforms. The *DB2
Universal Version 7* includes features that move more operations to memory and thus improve
performance.

> *Go to* http://www-4.ibm.com/software/data/db2/ *for information on IBM's DB2.*

Desktop DBMS

You do not need to buy and maintain a Data Server in order to have a back end. Several desktop
applications can support SQL requests and will run in memory space on your laptop.

Oracle offers an 8i Personal Edition that can be installed on a desktop. This version is fully capable of
storing data and then accepting SQL statements against that data. However, it is not intended to scale to
many simultaneous users. As of early 2001, a free trial download is available from www.oracle.com.

Microsoft also offers products for the desktop. First is Access, a DBMS that is easy to learn and powerful
but was not designed to scale to more than a few users at once. Access has a drag and drop interface
which translates to SQL, and displays both translations on the monitor for most points in the design
screens. Note that Access can function as both a front end with the forms and reports objects and as a
back end with its table and query objects.

Note that we have mentioned Access under both a front and back end. Some of Access's tools such as forms and reports function as a front end. Other tools such as queries and Tables function as back ends. For people using Access as an entire desktop database solution the distinction is not important. But the front and back end tools can be used separately in conjunction with products from other vendors. For example, an Access front end can connect to an IBM DB2 datastore. Or to switch hands, an ASP page can connect to Access queries and Tables offered as backends. In the case of these cross-software connections, SQL is the language for communication.

There are several places within Access where you can use SQL statements instead of using the names of objects like tables or queries. We discuss these in Chapter 2.

Microsoft also offers the MSDE (Microsoft Data Engine) which is essentially the Microsoft SQL Server data engine without the rest of the DBMS features (such as Query Analyzer), and without the ability to scale beyond a few users. You can use MSDE to manage your data and to run SQL statements against that data, but you do not have the tools for performance monitoring, replication, security and other features found in SQL Server. MSDE is, at the time of this writing, a free download from www.microsoft.com. It also ships with editions of Microsoft Office 2000 which include Access (Microsoft Office 2000 Premium or developer editions).

Connecting the Front and Back Ends

Having established a front end and a DBMS back end, we then need to connect them through some type of software. The connection functions include: defining which datastore to use, how to transfer SQL statements and results, and a host of settings that control the above processes. For example, in VB we may want to work with data in an Access database. We need to establish a connection to pass SQL statements to Access. We will want to establish how to handle multiple-user conflicts as well as whether to read the data as fast as possible or with more flexibility. Once these parameters are set for the data communication, we then need a way of actually sending our SQL statement to the DBMS.

By analogy, if the front and back ends are like telephone handsets, then the connection is like the telephone company equipment and wires. When starting a call we first establish a connection by dialing the other party and waiting for the phone company to connect the correct wires. Then we can begin using English across the connection. In the same way, we create a connection between our front- and back-end software, then we use SQL statements to communicate across that connection.

In this section we present an overview of four connection methods. We then move on to demonstrate the actual code for creating a connection (with tricks and traps) in Chapter 2.

An older and lower-level connection is ODBC (Object Database Connectivity), which was a result of collaboration throughout the industry in the early 1990s. Although not optimized for any particular database, it has enjoyed widespread use up until the late 90s. ODBC is not well suited to non-relational data. ODBC uses a driver for each type of datastore to hold communication specifics.

Chronologically next came OLEDB, a set of COM (Component Object Model) interfaces that can interact with most data stores.

> **COM objects are packages of code that have a standard interface for interacting with other code. Instead of thousands of programmers writing and troubleshooting duplicate code to achieve the same objectives, the task can be solved once by some experts and the result encapsulated into a COM object. The object can then be used by anyone that buys the object. You can think of COM objects as mini-applications that are available to programmers.**

COM depends on an Application Programming Interface (API) optimized for talking with C++. OLEDB uses providers to connect directly to the datastore. Alternatively, OLEDB can connect through the older ODBC and use the ODBC Drivers.

> **ODBC uses *Drivers* while OLEDB uses *Providers*.**
> **Both are "middleware" that contain instructions for how to talk to a specific kind of datastore.**

Now Microsoft offers the ActiveX Data Objects (ADO), which are COM objects for talking with data. In a sense, ADO encapsulates OLEDB into an object-based model. Instead of writing lengthy (and difficult) code in OLEDB, a programmer can simply instantiate one of the ADO objects and then set its properties to make a connection. An ADO object can send a SQL statement through that connection and receive back results.

For more information on ADO see the ADO 2.6 Programmers Reference (ISBN 186100463x) by David Sussman from Wrox Press.

Another popular technique to connect front and back ends is using the JDBC (Java Database Connectivity) object. As with ADO, experts have encapsulated into a set of classes and interfaces all the Java code needed to pass SQL statements from a front end to a back end. JDBC allows developers to create connections entirely within a pure Java API. With a JDBC solution you not only have the ability to use SQL to access any back end, but you write in Java so you can run the code on most front ends.

Other software vendors have solutions for connecting the front and back ends. Allaire's Cold Fusion uses a proprietary set of HTML tags. Some DBMS vendors have developed specialized connections specific to front ends and DBMS that they offer.

The techniques discussed in this section offer many connection options in order to satisfy a wide range of users. Some situations justify writing a custom coded connection. Although expensive and difficult to create, these custom connections can gain in performance by eliminating features that are not used.

Configurations for Using SQL

Before we move on we want to demonstrate some typical installations that use SQL. These drawings demonstrate a range of situations which you might encounter (or design), from a simple desktop to a complex multi-server environment.

How to Study These Configurations

Note that each section has a SQL requester, a back end and a connection. In many cases the requester is a front end (user interface) but not always. Consider the case where there are several servers between the user and the DBMS. In those scenarios, an intermediate server is the SQL requester.

Note the difference between a front end and a SQL requester. The front end deals with humans. The SQL requester is software that generates a SQL statement. Generally the requester uses information from the front end, such as which records to read or what data to write.

In most cases the back end is a DBMS, but not always. Datastores like Microsoft Exchange can also speak the SQL Language.

For most of these scenarios there are certain tasks that must be performed:

- ❑ user interface
- ❑ business logic (which may produce the SQL statement)
- ❑ data storage
- ❑ physical connections and
- ❑ logical connections

However, in each scenario these functions are divided differently across machines and locations. Having a clear image in your mind of where various tasks are performed is particularly useful in troubleshooting. It is useful to be able to follow mentally the path of information from the user all the way through to the data store and back out again. Frequently the first step in solving problems is to isolate which step in the process is creating the problem.

Access

Access, as we have discussed, has objects that function as parts of a front end (forms and reports) and table objects that function as a back end. In a sense Access query objects function like SQL statements, as they are one way to communicate between the front and back end objects. In addition to the query objects, any Access object property that accepts a SQL statement for a value is a SQL Requester, as is Access VBA code that executes a SQL statement. Unlike the other scenarios, Access is able to perform a connection internally between a form and a table without any external coding such as ADO or OLEDB.

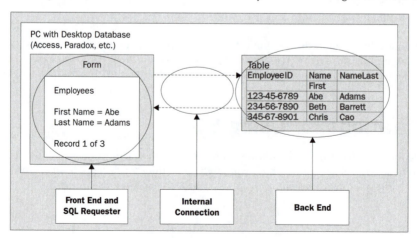

Two Tier Architecture on a LAN

A very simple system for smaller offices involves just user's desktop PCs, a server and a Local Area Network. The server performs the services of managing network traffic, security and holding the data. For example an office of 20 people may have an Intel-based server running Windows 2000 Server and SQL Server 2000. The front end could be an application created in Visual Basic, which runs on the user's desktop. In response to the user entering some parameters and clicking on a button, the VB code creates a request containing a SQL statement and sends it to the server via a connection such as ADO. The server receives the request and routes it to the DBMS. The DBMS executes the statement and then returns the data to the VB application for display.

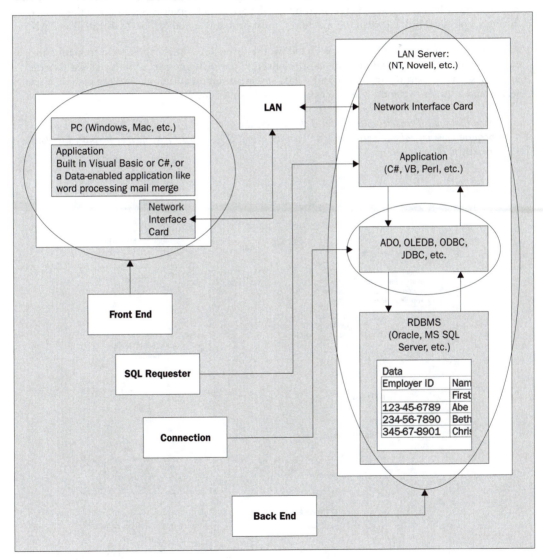

Three Tier Architecture on a LAN

As the complexities and security requirements of a company increase the IT department will move to a three (or more) tier architecture. The front end will still be the user's desktop PCs. But now the server function has been divided into two (or more) parts.

- ❑ A data server that runs the DBMS or other data store.
- ❑ A departmental server that usually routes traffic, controls security and does some business processing.

One of those business processes is the generation of SQL statements to communicate with the data server. Now, when the request is received by the departmental server it is sent on to the data server through a physical link between the machines, most probably a 100 Mb or 1 Gb Ethernet LAN.

As we will see in an example on the Web below, the three-tier model can expand to many more levels, called *n*-tier. Each additional machine is specialized to perform one part of the business process. Adding to the base of a departmental server and a data server, common additional servers include a security server and a server to handle the processing of the business logic.

> *Note that not all requests will be routed through all the servers. For example, a security server may perform some initial authentication and then the actual SQL requests may then be permitted to flow directly to the data server.*

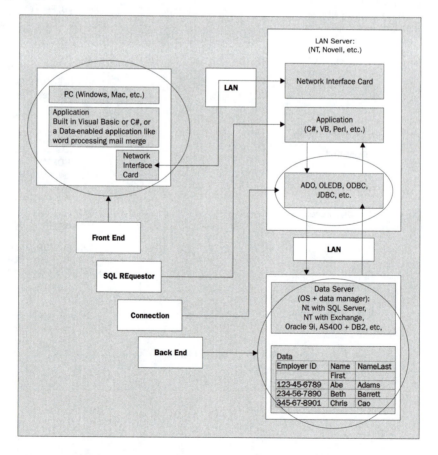

Two-Tier Architecture on the Web

Here we have the user's PC running a browser, which is connected via the web to a server. This is a lightweight website because the web server, the script processor and the database software are all held on one machine. Thus we have a two-tier system: PC/Browser and Web Server. In this case, the connection is between the script interpreter and the database.

Note that the way we use the word "connection" in this scenario is not the connection from the browser to the web site. In a two-tier system both the SQL requester and the datastore ends of the connection are on the same machine. The connection here is only a logical channel through the server's memory; there is no need for an external physical connection as in some other scenarios.

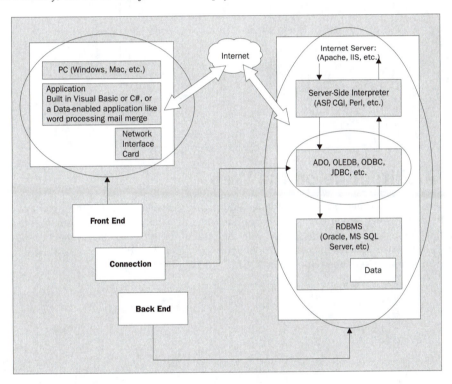

Three-Tier Architecture on the Web

As with a web server, the datastore may be on the same server or a separate machine(s). This architecture is the logical next move when the two-tier system (above) becomes overloaded. Just as with the 3-tier LAN system, we have moved the DBMS to another physical machine and have thus been able to optimize the hardware and OS to support reliability, security and scaling of a data store. The web server can also then be re-optimized for serving pages and executing scripts without having to accommodate a data service.

The front end shifts further from the SQL requester in a three-tier system. The front end (point of user interface) becomes the PC running a Browser. The SQL requester is the business logic software on the web server, not the user's PC. The web server will then pass information back and forth to the end user's PC.

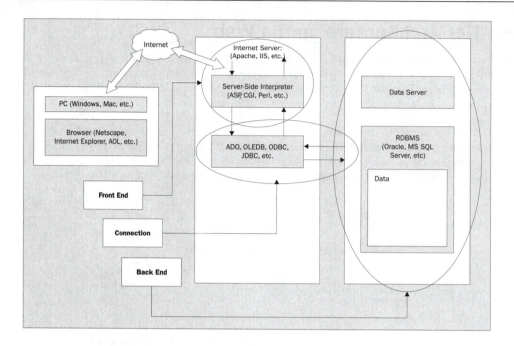

n-Tier Architecture on the Web

An *n*-tier system has the server tasks divided among more servers than the three-tier system. Now we have divided the web server into three parts, one to handle the web services, one to handle the sessions and a third to perform the business logic (run the bulk of the scripts). Our connection now links the business logic layer and the data store. As in every case in a "tiered" system (2-, 3-, and n-tier) the connection runs between the data server (DBMS) and the next layer up.

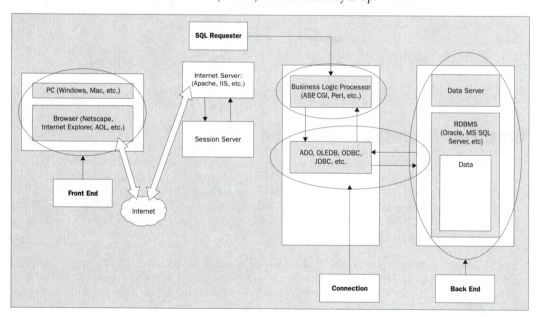

In the graphic below, the hardware and software is the same, but we see that more than one server in an *n*-tier system can establish connections and pass SQL statements to the Data Server (DBMS). Here the session server passes and receives data via SQL statements. Thus within one site we may have two or more servers creating connections and passing SQL statements to a DBMS. We expand further on this idea in the section titled *Data Warehousing* below.

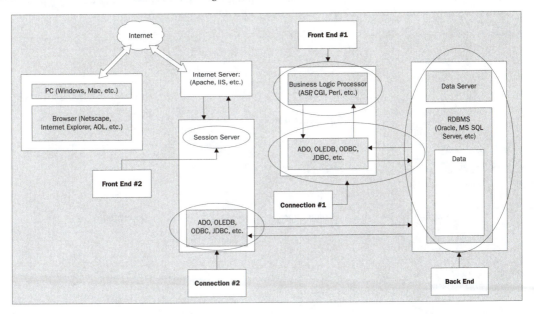

Mainframe and Terminals

A mainframe/terminal system resembles the two-tiered system described earlier. However, the terminals and mainframe are usually in one facility and thus the connection is normally through dedicated wiring and not through the Internet. Second, the terminal has a minimum of processing power, so it is controlled by the mainframe. As of 2001, this system is mostly limited to older installations or high security systems.

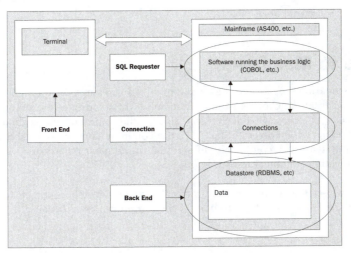

Mainframe and Terminals with a Separate Datastore

A mainframe can split off the data server in the same way that our LAN and website examples did when moving from two- to three-tier architectures. In this scenario we see that the mainframe handles the business logic but for data it sends a SQL statement out to a data server running a DBMS. The connection is from the business logic mainframe to the Data Server.

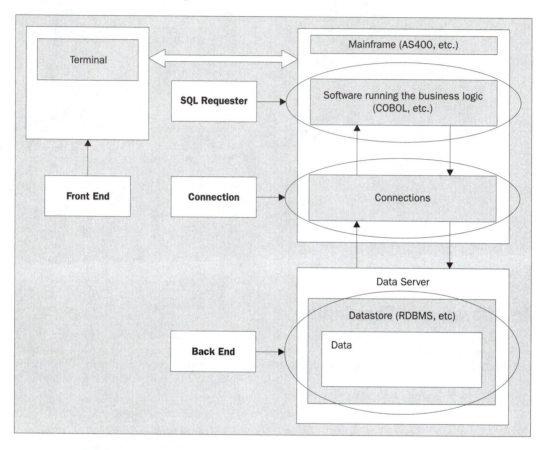

Mainframe to Mainframe

In each of the scenarios above there is a person involved. An employee (hopefully smiling and fully vested) sits at the desktop PC or a customer (hopefully with a loose wallet) sits at the other end of the Internet on a PC with a browser. But SQL can also handle communications about data between machines with no person involved. In fact SQL is a common language to establish communication between legacy systems with completely different hardware, operating systems and software (and probably incompatible administrators to boot).

In this graphic we see that an IBM mainframe is able to get information on customers from a VAX mainframe. Although there is a SQL Requester there is no front end because there are no humans involved.

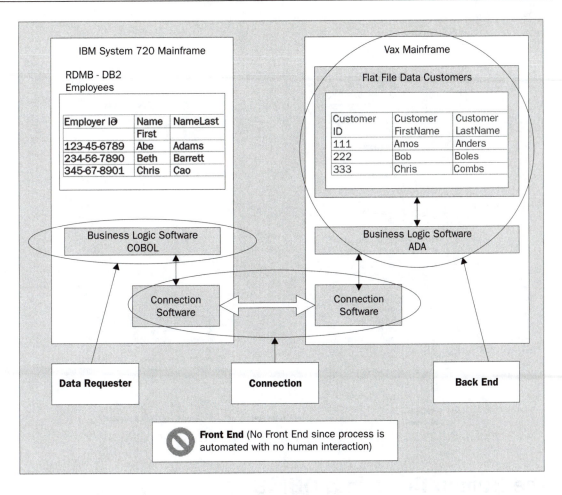

Data Warehouse with Multiple SQL Requesters

Last, let us look at an example that is probably realistic for most businesses. We have one datastore for the enterprise that consists of several data servers and a mainframe, collectively called a Data Warehouse or a **Distributed Data Processing system**. That conglomerate of a datastore receives SQL requests for internal business operations from a business logic server. The business logic server is processing operations as directed by employees using PCs and front-end software on their desks.

The company also has a website serviced by a web server. The web server interacts with visitors and then sends SQL requests to the same enterprise data warehouse. Although there are many brands of software involved and many platforms they are all able to speak and understand SQL.

We can trace the information flow in this graphic by starting with the PCs on the right. They are connected to either the Department Server or the Web Server. These servers can then create a SQL request using their business logic software and pass the request to one or more of the Data Servers. This is usually done through a high-speed LAN which only connects servers (represented on the far left). After the SQL Request has been processed the results can return from left to right through the servers and to the PCs.

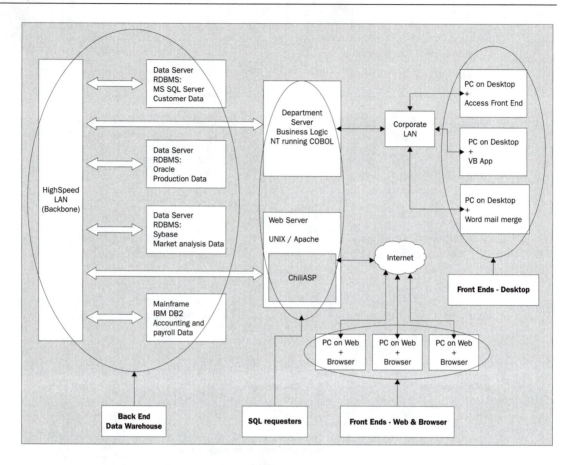

The Human Roles in a DBMS

With the increasing size and complexity of computing tasks, IT departments frequently grow to have several specialists contributing to the database solutions of the company. If you are coming from a background in desktop databases you may not have a clear idea of the titles and roles of the players. Obviously, in a small company one person may have more than one of these roles – as a SQL programmer you may even be expected to cover responsibilities beyond just programming.

The **DataBase Administrator** (**DBA**) specializes in installing and maintaining the DBMS, including the physical devices, backups and recoveries. Frequently the DBA is the person responsible for maintaining the security scheme as well as troubleshooting the DBMS. Note that the DBA is not usually specifically responsible for any given database. Rather, the DBA keeps the DBMS running as a service for all the users that have databases on that DBMS. Each DBMS vendor has training and certification programs for its particular systems.

The **Systems Administrator** (sometimes called the System Operator or "SysOp") specializes in the Operating System (OS) and connectivity of the servers, both data servers and others. "SysAdmins" perform back-ups of the OS and monitor the traffic load between servers. "SysAdmins" are likely also to be involved in the security settings of servers needed by SQL programmers.

A newer position is the **Security Administrator**. Valuable corporate data is now exposed through the web to a degree that would horrify the last generation of IT professionals. As hackers improve their sophistication and means of collaboration, IT shops have responded by hiring individuals with specific training in establishing hardware and software safeguards and in monitoring the servers for signs of intrusion. SQL programmers may have to work closely with a Security Administrator to develop ways of using data that minimize risk, for example, creating Views rather than permitting full table access (see Chapter 16).

A **Database Designer** creates the overall scheme of the datastore, generally using specialized database design tools. The designer will not only understand the principles of databases but also the client's business model. The result from the designer's desk will be a layout of tables, relationships and queries needed to satisfy the client's needs.

The **Database Programmer** writes code and interfaces to implement the design. The programmer may be less familiar with the business rules and more familiar with how to write SQL statements and front ends to implement the design. Whereas Database Designers are more involved at the start of a project, programmers are involved for as long as the database is in use and changes and amendments need to be performed. Many programmers joining a team will have no contact with the designer who left after the database deployment. On legacy systems it may even be difficult to find any manuals regarding how the system was designed.

*Last, never forget the **user** who is, directly or indirectly, paying your fee.*

When to Use SQL

My students frequently ask, "When should I be using SQL?" They may have created a database in a lower level desktop system and are considering switching to a DBMS that will require SQL. SQL is a language, not a software product, so the real question is best phrased as "When do I need to use a heavy-duty DBMS, which would then require me to start communicating in SQL?" There are several factors to consider which we'll look at in turn in this section.

Scaling

Many small sites or applications start in desk top systems such as Access. As they grow, a number of problems become apparent with the Access JET database engine. The primary problem is that it was never designed to support many users at once. Database software designed for the desktop generally fails when more than a few people try to use the data at the same time. Microsoft Access will perform well if five users are on a LAN. When you get to ten or twenty concurrent users, problems begin. Obviously a desktop database cannot handle the problems introduced by large numbers of concurrent hits from a web site.

Second, the Access file-based system becomes fragile when the amount of data starts to climb into the gigabyte range. Lower scale systems like Access also lack the security that more powerful systems offer. Access databases, for example, are quite easy to copy and walk away with. The individual installations can also be readily accessed.

So for these reasons companies move from Access type desk top systems to a more robust DBMS. Almost all of these heavy duty DBMS rely on SQL as the main form of communication. In summary, although there is nothing about SQL itself that concerns scaling, there is a need to use SQL in order to communicate with DBMS that scale well.

Speed

When SQL-enabled DBMS first appeared they were slower than previous DBMS. However, as they have taken over the market during the last ten years, SQL data engines have been the focus of an intense effort to improve performance. There are heated contests between the major vendors for bragging rights to the fastest machine with the lowest transaction price. But the intense competition drives the vendors to produce faster, more robust DBMS that work at lower and lower costs per transaction.

When you consider your quest for improved speed, consider that pure speed problems will be evident at all times, not just at peak usage. They are usually the result of more complex queries, particularly with the advanced techniques we study later like multiple joins on data that cannot be indexed. Although SQL itself does not cure speed problems, the implementation of faster DBMS does, and those faster DBMS will probably require communications in SQL.

Price

It is more expensive to run a server-centric DBMS (that only speaks SQL) than it is to use a desktop system such as Paradox or Access (for which you do not necessarily need to use SQL). First, the software is more expensive. Second, in most cases you have to run more expensive operating systems in order to support the DBMS. Third, you have to tune the OS differently to optimize for a DBMS than for other applications, so you generally need a server dedicated to the DBMS. Last, you will need personnel with more expensive qualifications.

However, the price of hardware and software is frequently the smallest item in an IT budget. As your data center grows, at some point the reliability, performance and standardization benefits of a DBMS that uses SQL will outweigh the cost.

A note on price – you can get started on a SQL-centric DBMS for almost nothing. In fact, we have included the 120-day trial version of Microsoft SQL Server 2000 with this book. You can download other trial versions such as Oracle Personal Edition. But remember, that these are trial versions; when you are ready to build your business on a SQL-centric DBMS you will be paying a considerable amount more than you did for Access.

Universality

An alternative to using SQL statements is to write code in a procedural language like C++. The problem with this approach is that you are then closely tied to the procedural language, the metadata and the specific DBMS. If there is a change in the structure of the tables the code must change. If a new DBMS is installed, most of the code must be revised to mesh with the new DBMS system of pointers, recordset definitions, etc. But by using SQL statements almost all changes are handled by the DBMS, behind the scenes from the programmer.

Analytic Capabilities

An advanced feature of SQL (which is beyond the scope of this book) is the emergence of analytical tools that allow managers to extract business knowledge from large amounts of data. These tasks frequently require the constructions of multi-dimensional aggregates of data. These tools are referred to by the generic names of Online Analytical Processing (OLAP), Decision Support Systems (DSS) and Executive Information Systems (EIS). Each vendor then has proprietary trademarks for their version. All of these tools are only available in full-scale DBMS that require SQL for their means of communication.

When to Skip Moving to a SQL-Centric DBMS

As much as we have talked about the power of SQL, we must be honest in describing those situations where an alternative system would be better. You are probably better off staying with software that does not require SQL (like Access) in most of these situations:

❑   Only one or a few people will use the database at once.

❑   The data can be stored within 50% of the disk capacity available to you.

❑   You are comfortable with the amount of media and operator time required by your backup plan.

❑   You do not expect to significantly expand the quantity of data or number of users.

❑   You do not plan to make the database available on an Internet site.

❑   The vast majority of the data you use is in a form that is not relational, such as files in folders.

If you the answer is yes to all of the above then a desktop solution like Microsoft Access will be cheaper and easier to learn. Most of what you will need to do can be performed through wizards and the drag 'n' drop interface, thus avoiding the need to invest in the hardware, software and learning for a SQL implementation.

> **As we discussed earlier on in this chapter, you can still use SQL with Access even though the system does not require it. Hence why we can use a desktop system such as Microsoft Access in order to learn SQL.**

Development of a system in a SQL-centric, heavy-duty DBMS is more time-consuming than in a drag and drop DBMS like Access. You may consider prototyping in Access to get a set of forms and reports for the revision and approval process with your clients. Then with a model approved you can create the final product with far fewer hours spent in coding SQL. You may even find that a lot of the queries you made in Access can be cut and pasted into your final code.

Summary

Structured Query Language, tested and true over many years, is the standard way to communicate with a database. SQL is almost universally understood by both front ends and back ends. Front ends present a user interface such as Visual Basic, C++, ASP, and Microsoft Office applications. They have the ability to connect to a datastore and send it a SQL statement. Back ends are Database Management Systems such as Oracle, Microsoft SQL Server, Sybase and sometimes, desktop systems like Access. Back ends can accept a SQL statement and return a result. SQL is also used for communication directly between different DBMS without a user interface.

SQL is a set-based language rather then a procedural language. The programmer creates a single SQL statement describing the desired result and sends it to the DBMS. The DBMS then uses internal code to achieve that result. The internal code will vary among DBMS vendors, but that does not matter to the SQL programmer using ANSI-SQL. Regardless of the DBMS the result will be the same.

In the next chapter we will discuss the specifics of setting up several back ends and front ends. Then we study the code to create a connection and transport your SQL statements from front to back. We'll also cover how to handle the results when they return to the front end.

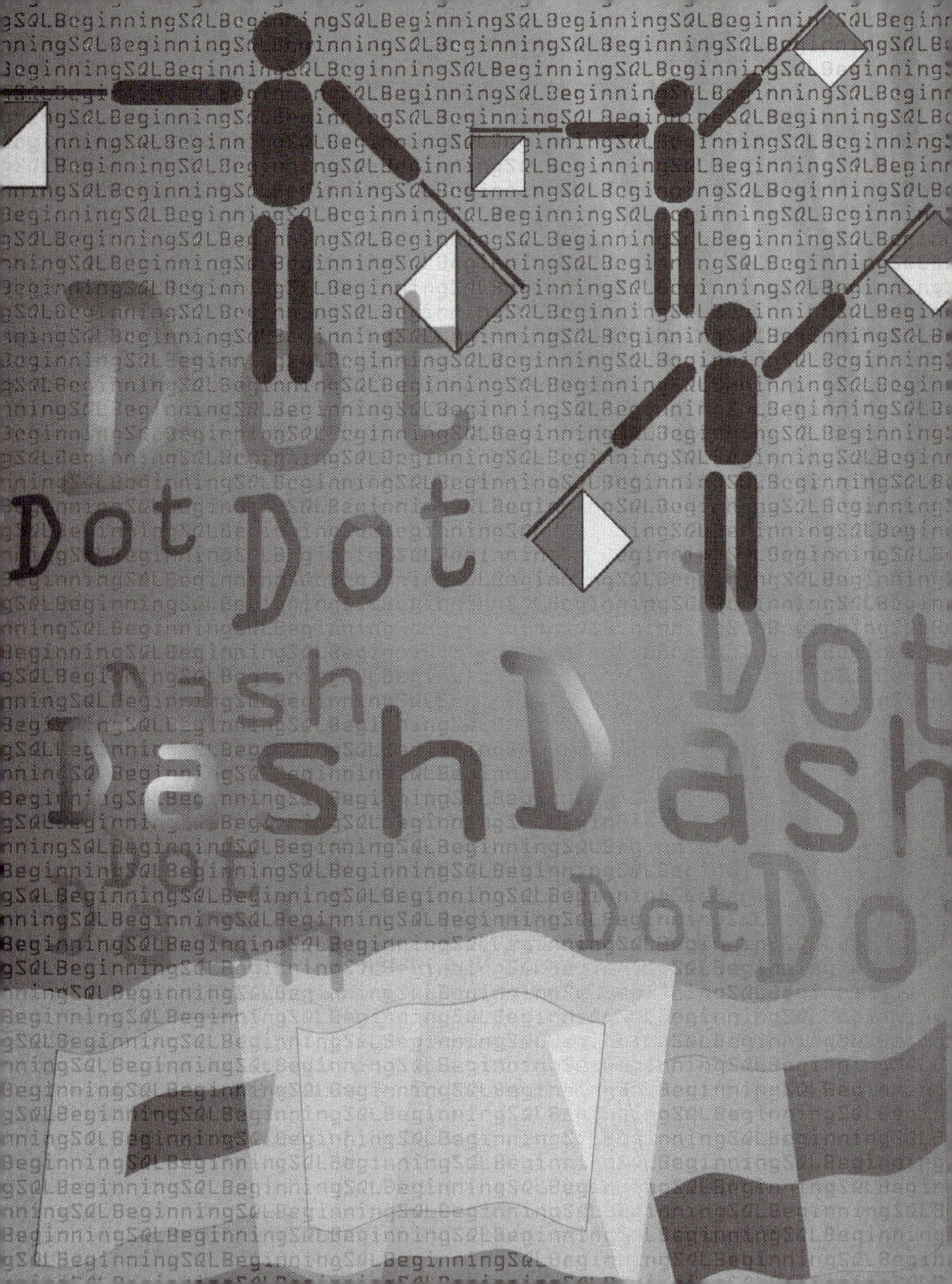

Getting Ready to Use SQL

We discussed in Chapter 1 that SQL is a universal language to communicate about data. This chapter covers how to obtain, install, and test some specific front- and back-ends so that you can get started on the examples in this book.

We begin by introducing the database that we'll be using throughout the book to test out our SQL examples, followed by a quick-start for using the tools that come on the CD provided with this book. Then we discuss several other backends that you could set up on your desktop for trying out the examples.

We also introduce the front-end interfaces where we can run our SQL statements including Microsoft Query Analyzer, a developer's tool that we will use in most of the examples of this book to test SQL statements.

We introduce our first SQL statement, an easy one-liner that we can use to test each of the tools we install in this chapter.

So the aims of this chapter are:

- ❑ To introduce the database we will be using throughout the book
- ❑ To introduce the software options for using this book
- ❑ To install your chosen software
- ❑ To execute a test SQL query to check that our software and database are running correctly

Getting Started

In Chapter 1 we discussed many configuration and software options for using SQL. Here we're going to focus directly on the software that you can use to work with the examples and case studies in this book.

We'll start by looking at the database that we'll be working with throughout.

Northwind

As we go through this book we need to use a database. In this book we will use a sample database created by Microsoft called Northwind that provides order-taking functions for a food wholesaler. Northwind is available in two forms, one for Access and the other for versions of SQL Server or MSDE (Microsoft Data Engine – see Chapter 1 if you need a refresher). The database is automatically installed during the setup of either product.

We've chosen to teach SQL using the Northwind database as it is easily obtainable from a number of sources and many of you will already have it available to you through your standard Microsoft Office suites. It also installs with the SQL Server 2000 evaluation edition that comes with this book.

> **We should point out that although we are using a Microsoft product to generate examples, this book is teaching ANSI SQL. We also provide the ability to migrate the sample database to other DBMS products; Oracle, MySQL, and IBM's DB2. Attention is paid throughout the book to any SQL variations occurring between vendor's products.**

So, the software options we could use in order to work with the Northwind database and the examples in this book are listed below.

Software Options

- ❑ **Microsoft SQL Server 2000**. An evaluation edition is included at the back of this book. This included evaluation version of SQL Server will run on the following platforms:

    - ❑ Windows 2000 Professional
    - ❑ Windows NT Workstation 4.0 with SP5 (or later)
    - ❑ Windows 2000 Server
    - ❑ Windows 2000 Advanced Server
    - ❑ Windows NT Server 4.0 with SP5 (or later)

    A full edition of SQL Server 2000 contains the Personal edition which can also be installed on Windows 98 platforms.

- ❑ **Microsoft SQL Server 7.0 (or Microsoft SQL Server 6.5)** Both products include the Northwind database. These products can be run on the following platforms:

    - ❑ Windows 2000
    - ❑ Windows NT
    - ❑ Windows 98 (desktop installation)

- ❑ **MSDE (Microsoft Data Engine)** MSDE is a cut-down version of SQL Server scaled for about 5 users and is a perfect learning facility. Essentially it is a SQL Server database engine stripped of all the additional functionality, scalability, client tools, and interfaces that SQL Server offers. As it doesn't come with a built-in interface of it's own, it is designed to utilize other front-end products. These include Access 2000 projects (`.adp` files), which seamlessly integrate SQL Server database objects (such as tables, views, and stored procedures) with an Access interface, and SQL Server's client tool, Query Analyser, which we can use to test SQL statements. MSDE doesn't include the Northwind sample database, but as it ships with Office 2000 it is easy to import the Northwind database into MSDE from Access. We'll cover steps for how we can do this later on in the chapter.

> So if you are running Windows 98 and Office 2000, you can install MSDE as your backend and install the Query Analyzer as your front end from the SQL Server 2000 evaluation CD included with this book

MSDE is included on the CD for both Office 2000 premium and Office 2000 Developer editions. It is also freely available for download from the Microsoft site if you have a license for any Microsoft Visual software such as Visual Basic, Visual C++, or Visual Studio; see http://msdn.microsoft.com/vstudio/msde/default.asp. You can install MSDE on:

- Windows 98 platforms
- Windows NT platforms
- Windows 2000 platforms

> MSDE does not install with the rest of the Office 2000 files. It has to be installed from the CD separately and manually. The steps for installation of MSDE will be covered later in this chapter.

- **Microsoft Access 2000 (or 97+)** Microsoft Access can be obtained as an individual product or more likely, as part of the Microsoft Office 2000 (or 97) suite. The Northwind database is included with the installation of Microsoft Access or Office. If you don't want to install MSDE or SQL Server, it is possible to follow most of the examples in this book using Access as both your front end interface and its Jet engine as the back-end. Access 2000 will run on:

  - Windows 98 platforms
  - Windows 2000 platforms
  - Windows NT platforms

> A note on Access and SQL:
> Access does not require the user or developer to use SQL. However, in many places within Access you can use SQL if you so desire. In this chapter we will discuss Access from three angles. First, we discuss how to use it as a back-end. Second, we will discuss Access again under Front Ends. Also under Front Ends we will discuss how to use the Access Query Window to help you learn SQL.

Once you've obtained Northwind, either from SQL Server or from Access, you can migrate the database objects for use in other systems. Appendix D provides instructions for how to migrate the database to Oracle, IBM DB2, and MySQL DBMS. We also provide a migration tool at www.wrox.com that allows you to perform the migration for use with this book.

> An introduction to the Northwind database including a case stzdy, which demonstrates how the Northwind schema works, can be found in Appendix A.

Starting with the CD in this Book

As you know, to get started with SQL you will need a front end, a connection, a back-end and a database. All four are included on your CD in the form of SQL Server 2000 and it's client tools. The back-end is a 120 day trial version of Microsoft SQL Server 2000 Enterprise Edition. Included in that is a developer's tool called the Microsoft Query Analyzer that can function as a front end for a developer or a student to test SQL statements. The Query Analyzer has a built-in connection to the engine. Last we have the NorthWind database on the disk – this will automatically be installed. To use this suite you will need 350 Mb disk space. Microsoft also recommends a minimum processor speed of Pentium 166 and minimum of 64 Mb of RAM.

Note that all of these minimum system requirements are to support an installation for you to work with SQL; they are too low for almost any "normal" database with multiple users and typical quantities of data.

Installation Steps for Microsoft SQL Server 2000 on the Enclosed CD

The CD enclosed in this book contains the 120 day trial version of Microsoft's SQL Server 2000 Enterprise Evaluation Edition. You get the DBMS and several utilities, including the Query Analyzer, which we will use with most of the examples in this book. The installation automatically copies to your hard drive a sample database called Northwind, which we will use throughout the book. This section of the chapter will talk you through installing and running the DBMS.

Several security settings may vary with your situation. The settings we suggest below are for installation on a user's PC or the server for a small group that includes one or more students. We do not guide you through the use of domain-level security or the SQL authentication settings. If there is some reason you want to protect the data on this trial version you can consult with your systems administrator for the specific settings for your server.

The product has a wizard which steps you through the installation. Even a slow (500MHz) server will finish the job in under fifteen minutes.

1. Close all applications, including screen savers.

2. Insert the enclosed CD into the drive and the installation should start automatically.

3. The install program will display a large graphic with several choices, as shown opposite. Click on **SQL Server 2000 Components**.

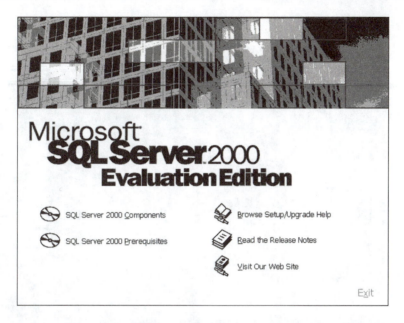

4. The same splash screen now offers additional choices, as below; click on Install Database Server.

5. The actual install wizard starts with a welcome screen as shown below. Click on Next.

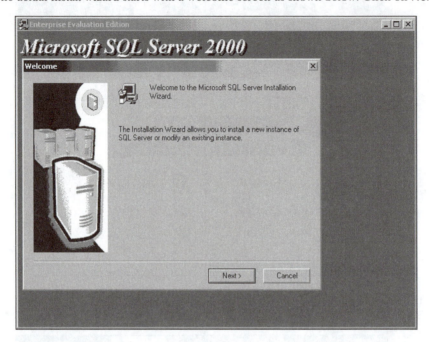

6. The wizard ask if you want to install locally or remote, select local, and click on Next.

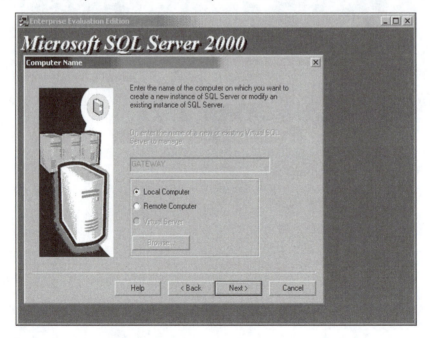

7. You must select from several instantiation options. Select Create a New Instance and click on Next.

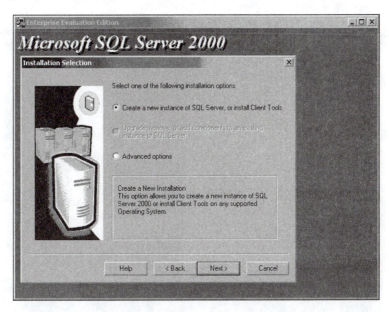

8. The wizard asks for some user information; accept the default or provide your name and company name and click on Next.

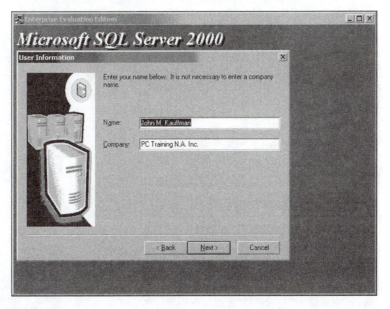

9. You must agree to the software license by clicking on Yes.

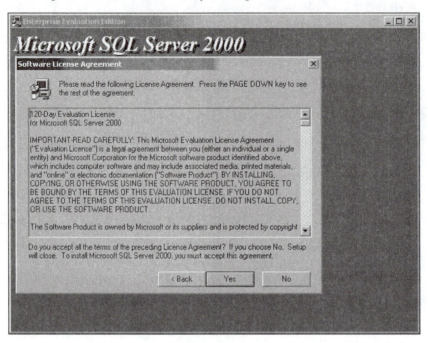

10. There are several groups of utilities that can be installed. Select Server and Client Tools and click on Next.

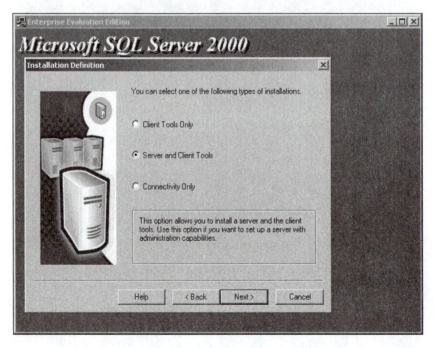

11. The wizard prompts you for the name of the instance of this installation. Turn the default ON. Alternatively you can use a name such as BegSQL (as we will do in these examples) or any other name. Avoid spaces and names of more than 16 characters, and start the name with a letter. Then click on Next.

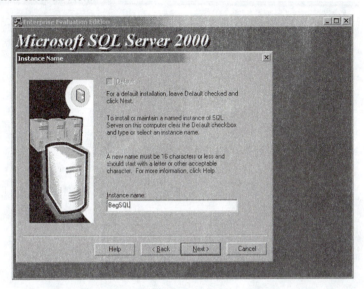

12. Select the several options from the Setup Type screen. First, select the Typical type of setup. Then check in the lower right corner that you have adequate space on your drives. Either accept the default folders or browse to a new folder. Then click on Next.

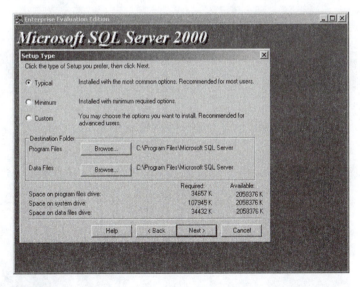

In a real installation you might choose to keep the data on another disk to ease backups. For our learning purposes (and remember that this install will only work for 120 days) the amount of data we will save in the exercises is minimal (under 50 megabytes including all overhead).

13. The wizard asks for some basic security information. Select Use the same account for each service and Use the Local System Account then click on Next.

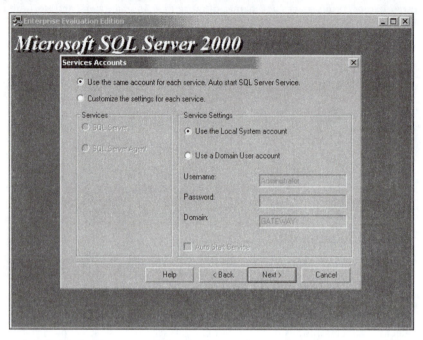

14. Select the Windows Authentication and click on Next.

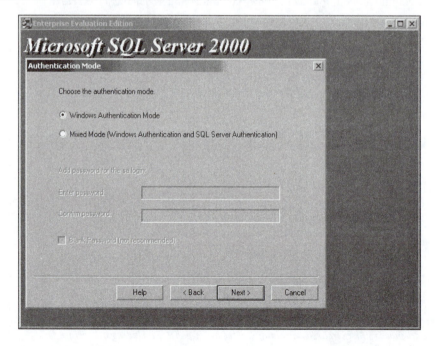

15. The wizard will notify you that it is ready to start copying files. Click on Next.

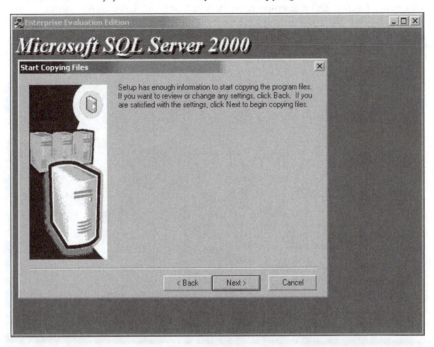

16. You then get a notice that the setup is complete; click on Finish.

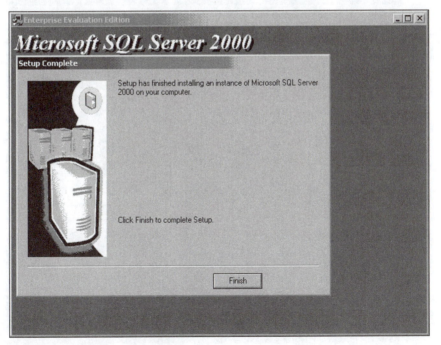

17. Start the server by clicking through: Start / Programs / Microsoft SQL Server/Service Manager. Then click on the green arrow Start button. After about a minute the service will be started. Within the Service Manager you can select to auto-start SQL Server when the OS starts. SQL Server takes up about 10 Mb of Ram when running in the background. Once the service is started you can close the Service Manager and the service will continue to run. You can reopen the service manager by double clicking the tray icon.

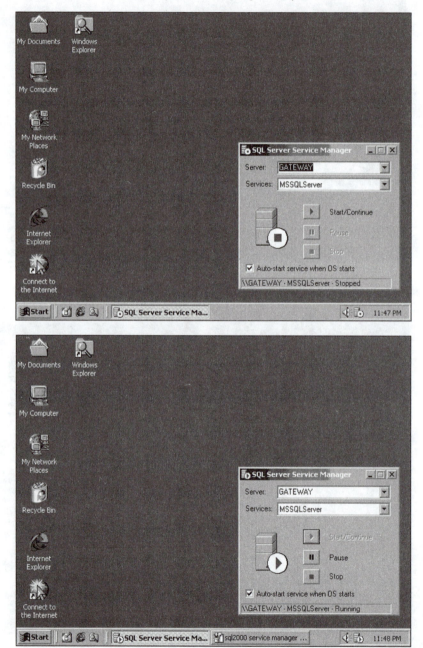

You can confirm your installation by taking note of a small server icon in the right end of your Windows system tray. The server should have a green triangle to indicate it is running. If you right mouse click on the server icon and select About you should see that you have version 8.00.194 running.

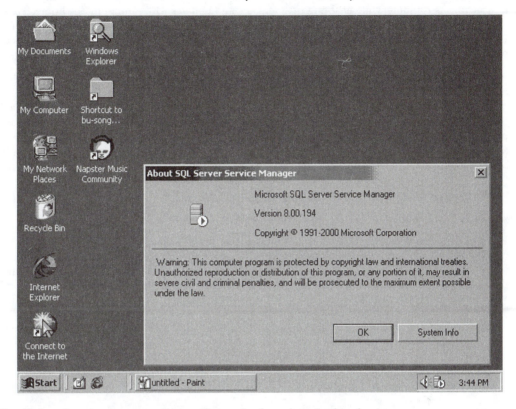

We will do a few tests in our section on Query Analyzer later in this chapter.

Back Ends

There are scores of Relational Database Management Systems (RDBMS) that can support SQL as a back end. In fact, virtually every RDBMS released in the last ten years supports SQL. The options range from inexpensive desktop solutions like Access, up through systems designed to handle tens of thousands of transactions per minute like Oracle and Microsoft SQL Server. Here we will provide you with setup instructions for the software that you can use with the examples in this book.

Microsoft SQL Server (other versions)

In the quick start section we discussed the installation and startup of the 120 day version of SQL Server. However, many people still use Microsoft SQL Server 7 or even 6.5. If you are not using Windows 2000 you could use an earlier version of MS SQL Server. Everything we do in this book is equally applicable to versions 6.5 and 7.0. They also include the Northwind database. The installation for these versions of SQL Server is very similar to the steps we've provided for installing SQL Server 2000 from the included CD so we won't repeat them here.

MSDE

The heavy-duty SQL DBMS like Oracle and Microsoft SQL Server can support tens of thousands of transactions per minute while enabling maintenance and updates with minimum downtime. They are a marvel of modern computing, but there are prices to be paid for this power. The first is the cost of the DBMS that starts at a few thousand dollars and goes up steeply for higher capacity. There is also the price of the memory, CPU power, and disk space required for an industrial-strength DBMS.

As developers, it can be prohibitive to install a full-blown system like this on our laptops in order to test SQL statements. As we said at the beginning of this chapter, Microsoft offers an alternative – it has taken the SQL Server product and stripped it of all the management and development tools, leaving just the data engine and then throttled it to a maximum of 5 users and 2 Gigabytes of data. The resulting product is called MSDE (Microsoft Data Engine). You can use it as a back end and then seamlessly attach the client tools from the SQL Server CD included with the book to create a smaller scale SQL Server installation.

Installing the Microsoft Database Engine (MSDE)

On the Office 2000 premium disks MSDE is on Disk One\SQL\x86\ SETUP\SetupSQL.exe.

If you have a license for one of the Visual Products you can download MSDE from http://msdn.microsoft.com/vstudio/msde/default.asp or, at the same location, request that a CD be sent to you. The install is straightforward and requires about 50 Mb of disk space plus your data. Although this is MSDE and not Microsoft SQL Server, the application will be installed in a C:\MSSQL7 folder. Within that folder is a Data folder where you can see the databases that are established by default.

1. The whole install process takes less then fifteen minutes. Start by shutting down all other applications.

2. Start/Run/browse to the SetupSQL.exe and select it. Click OK to leave the browse window and OK to run the setup file.

3. An install wizard starts and asks you to choose an install method. Select Local Install, and click on Next.

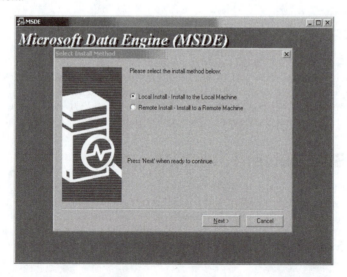

4. The wizard now gives you a welcome screen with a warning to exit all other applications and some copyright information. Click Next.

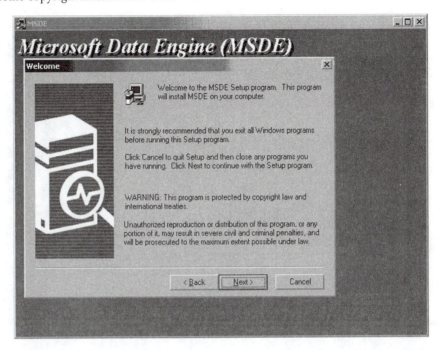

5. The wizard asks for the usual user information of name and company. Click Next.

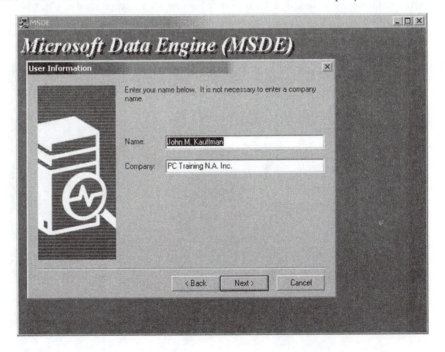

6. Your next choice is the Setup Type where you can only change the file locations. As with the full SQL Server product, you may choose to put your data on a drive other than the one holding your program files. Click Next.

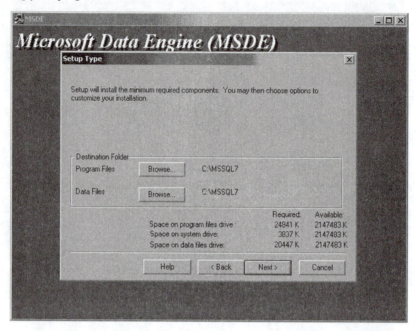

7. MSDE needs to know your default character set as well as some other language-specific settings. These are self explanatory. Normally you accept the defaults. Click Next.

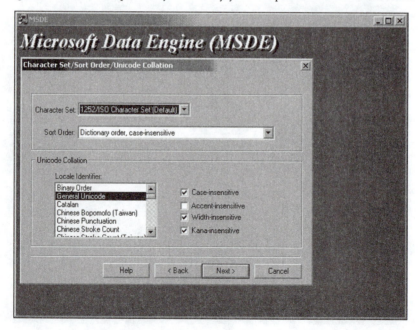

8. MSDE gives you options to install several network connection libraries. For the simplest case, accept the defaults of only installing TCP/IP Sockets and Multi-Protocol. Click Next.

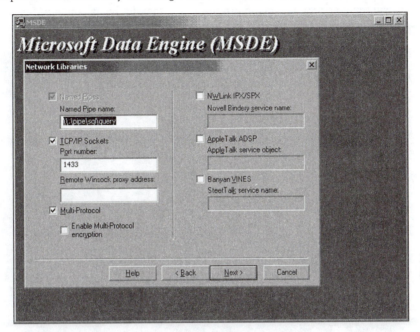

9. The wizard gathers information on what type of account management to use. For the simplest set up select Use the same account for each service and Use the Local System account. Click Next.

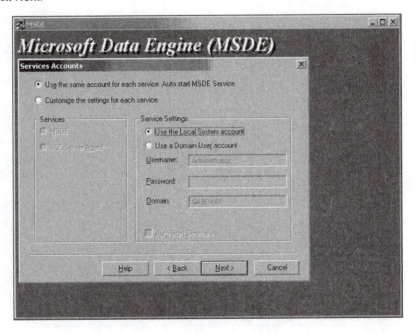

10. The wizard will now show a screen to begin copying; click Next.

11. You will then see message box informing you of the files being copied. After that you will get progress messages.

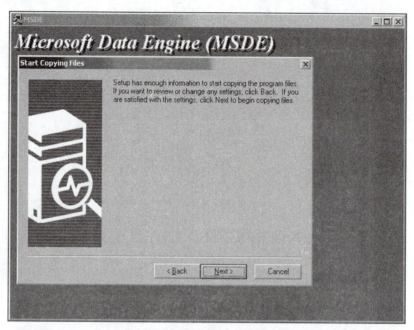

12. The Wizard displays a Setup Complete window. Click Finish.

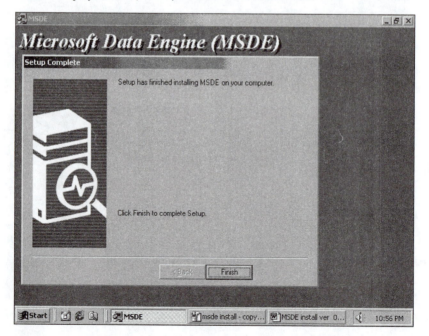

13. You can start MSDE by selecting: Start / programs / MSDE / Service Manager.

The service manager for MSDE is no different to the Service Manager for the complete SQL Server product.

14. Select autostart if desired.

MSDE takes about 5.3 Mb of RAM and the Service Manager another 2.3. So an autostart has some cost if you are not actually going to use it. You can always start by hand as needed.

15. Click the Start option with the green arrow to start the MSDE service.

When Service Manager is running there is a server icon in the right end of the system tray. When MSDE is running the icon will have a green arrow; when stopped it will display a red box.

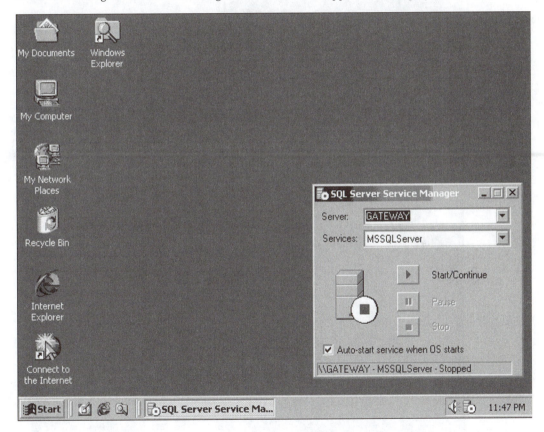

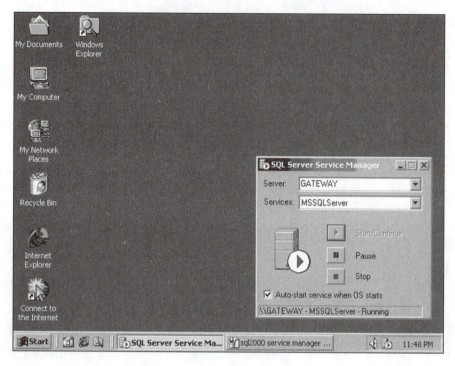

To check on your version you can right mouse click on the MSDE server icon in the system tray and select About. You should see that you have SQL Services Manager version 7.

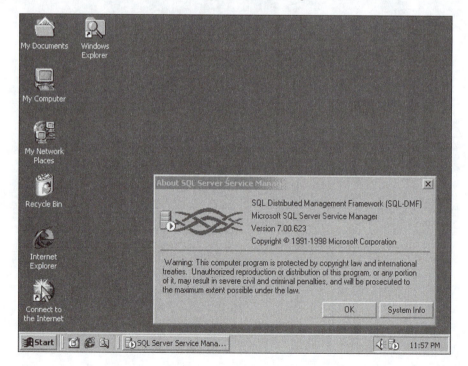

Importing Northwind into MSDE

If you are running a Windows 98 platform, you won't be able to install the SQL Server 2000 database engine on the included CD. Instead you will need to use MSDE and the client tools that come on the included CD. You can install the client tools (Query Analyzer is what we're actually interested in) by following the earlier installation steps for the included software, and opting to install the client tools when presented with the option.

> **You need to do this before you attempt to import the Northwind database from Access with the following steps.**

1. Search for the Northwind database by going to Start | Search | Files and folders | File and typing in Northwind.mdb in the Named: box. Copy (not move) the file to a folder called C:\BegSQL (which you will have to create).

2. Go to Start / Programs / MSDE or MS SQL Server/Import and Export Data. Observe the splash screen for the Data Transformation Wizard.

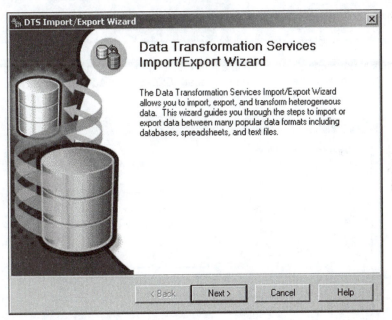

3. Click Next to move to the Source screen and set Data Source = Microsoft Access , File Name = Northwind (you will need to browse to Northwind, probably in C:\Program Files\Microsoft Office\Office\Samples).

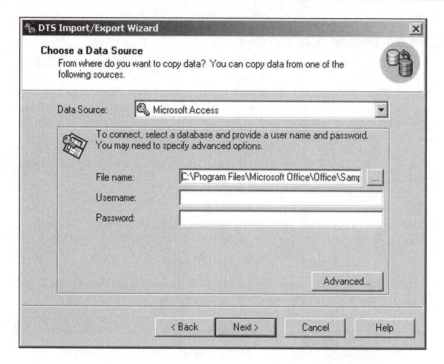

4. Click Next to move to the Destination screen and set Destination = Microsoft OLEDB Provider for SQL Server, Server = (local), SQL Server Authentication with sa as the Username (no password is needed).

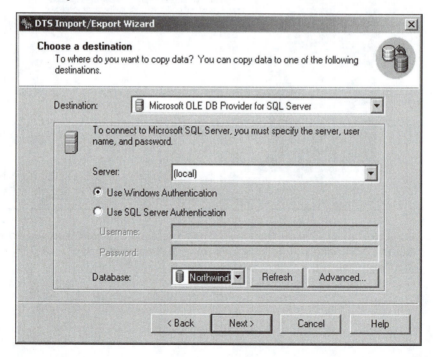

Database = New (enter the name, we will use "Northwind", Data file size = 4 Mb, Log file size = 1 Mb).

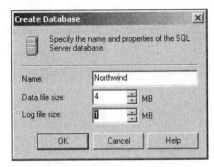

5. Click Next to move to the Method screen and select Copy table. Click Next and then select copy all on the next screen.

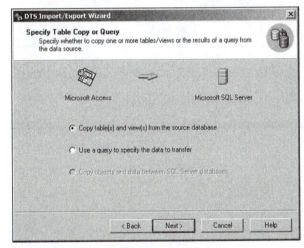

6. Click Next and select to run the DTS immediately.

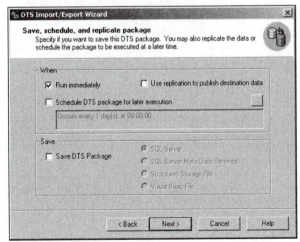

Click Next again, review the summary and click Finish.

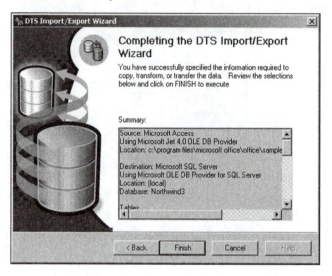

7. Watch for the notice of success, then click Done.

8. Note that the queries, reports, etc. were not copied.

9. Open Windows Explorer and note that in C:\MSSQL7\Data there is now a Northwind.mdf (not .mdb) file.

Access

Access can serve as both a front end and a back end. Although it does not scale well beyond a dozen or so simultaneous users, it is suitable for small groups. Access is also great for SQL students since many already own it.

Access is available from Microsoft as a standalone product, but it is more frequently sold as part of Microsoft Office. Before buying an Office license check that it includes Access; the cheapest versions do not. Access is easily set up using the Office Install wizard. There is no need to install any special options beyond the default options. The sample database, Northwind.mdb, is normally copied by the install wizard to C:Programs Files\Microsoft Office\Office\Samples.

> **Before we move on to front ends, we'll point out that some of the exercises later on in the book will involve changing and deleting data. Under those circumstances, it's best to perform that kind of modification on another copy of the sample database rather than on your original Northwind database. In SQL Server you can create a copy of Northwind by simply creating a new database and naming it something meaningful such as "Northwind2", for example. You then simply use the Data Transformation Wizard in Enterprise Manager to import the tables from your original Northwind database to your newly created database.**

> If you are using MSDE, the easiest method is to create a copy of the Access
> `Northwind.mdb` file that you originally imported into your database engine. Call it
> something meaningful like "Northwind2". You can then follow the steps that you used
> to import your Northwind database first time round, except this time import the copy
> of the Access database (`Northwind2.mdb`) that you created instead. You will then
> have a clean copy of the database, and a second version, which you can use when you
> want to modify or change the data that it contains.

Front Ends

In this section we will cover getting, installing and testing Front Ends.

Access Queries and Learning SQL from Access

The most obvious use of SQL in Access is to create queries. In many ways a SQL statement is
synonymous with an Access Query – both are a description of what we want the RDBMS to do. SQL
statements describe the results using English-like words while Access describes the result using a query
grid. The beauty of Access is that the query window's View will perform translations between grid view
and SQL Statements. Let's look at the basic example we are going to use in the rest of this chapter,
gathering the first and last names of all the employees.

A Test SQL Statement

We now need to perform tests of a SQL Statement but we haven't covered actually writing SQL
statements yet. So for this chapter we will test with one simple statement as follows:

```
SELECT LastName, FirstName FROM Employees
```

This statement is specific for the Northwind database. It simply obtains a set of the names for all the
employees (there should be nine employees, starting with Ms. Nancy Davolio).

> Since you probably haven't developed an eye yet for spotting SQL mistakes, I suggest
> you type the statement once into a Notepad file and check it carefully – then, each
> time you need to use it, cut and paste it into your test situations (thus reducing the
> chance of errors).

We will be using this test statement in several later sections of this chapter.

TRY IT OUT – Experiment with SQL in Access Queries

We will learn how to use the Access Query Window to convert between
a Query in Grid View and a SQL statement. The key is to change the
views by one of two ways. The first is to click on one of the View icons
at the far left of the standard tool bar; the second is to use the View
menu at the top of the screen.

1. Start Access and open `Northwind.mdb` (normally in C:\Program Files\Microsoft Office\Office\Samples) View the list of Query objects.

2. Open (in Datasheet View) the query named **Current Product List** and have a glance at the results. We see the Product ID and the Product Name for all of the products. Although we can not see it from the results, these are only the products that have not been discontinued.

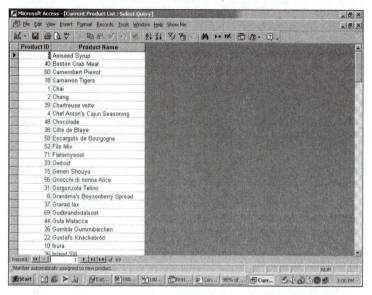

3. Switch to Design View by Menu:View | **Design View** and look over the grid design. Here we see that we use one table, `Products` and just three columns have been brought down to the grid. Two of those are shown and the third (Discontinued) is not shown. However, the third is used as the criteria.

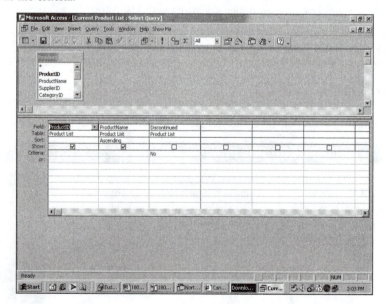

4. Switch to SQL View by Menu:View | SQL View Notice how the grid has been translated into SQL. We have not studied the syntax of SQL statements yet in this book, but we can sort of follow the basic English.

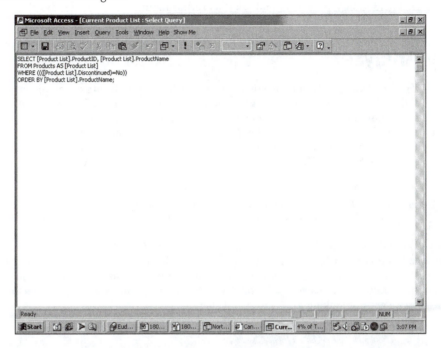

5. Switch back to the Design View and add the **Category ID** field to the grid by dragging it down to the fourth column.

6. Switch to the SQL View and note that addition to the end of the end of the first line.

7. Close the Query without saving it.

8. From the **Database** window create a new query in Design View using the single table `Employees`.

9. Add the `First` and `Last` name fields to the grid, then switch to SQL View and note how the result is the same as our sample statement.

10. Note that not all SQL statements can translate to a grid view. From the database window select the query named `Customers` and `Suppliers` by `City` and open in Design View. Access can only express this query in SQL because it is a UNION query.

How It Works – Experiment with SQL in Access Queries

There is not a lot of explanation needed here; Access is doing all of the work. Keep in mind for the future that you can easily have Access "translate" between the grid and the SQL statement views of a query. Students are familiar with creating a query by grid find it useful to get or check their SQL syntax by creating the query in the grid then converting to SQL View and then cutting and pasting the resulting syntax into their other Front End.

Note that there are some places where you may get a surprising result. The first case is if you write a SQL statement (such as a UNION) that cannot be represented by a grid. The second is if you include in a SQL statement a field that does not exist (like Hobby). In this case Access will consider the unrecognized field to be a parameter and ask the user for input.

Query Analyzer

The term *Front End* implies an interface that the users will see. But during development we would like to have a tool that allows us as programmers to send SQL statements like a front end, but with more flexibility and a minimum of setup. We don't care if it is pretty; we just want to know if our SQL statement works. Even better, when working with more complex statements we would like to get some clues about the speed and efficiency with which the DBMS executes the statement. Most DBMS offer such a tool. Included in your CD is the Microsoft version named Query Analyzer.

> **Be sure that SQL Server is started prior to using the Query Analyzer.**

When you start the QA (Start / Programs / MS SQL Server / Query Analyzer) you get a dialog box to specify which server you want to connect to. In the drop-down list will be the name you have given your server (or server & instantiation). For student installations the login has usually not changed from user = administrator and password = blank. Note that at this point we are not connecting to a particular database, so we are not looking for "Northwind" here.

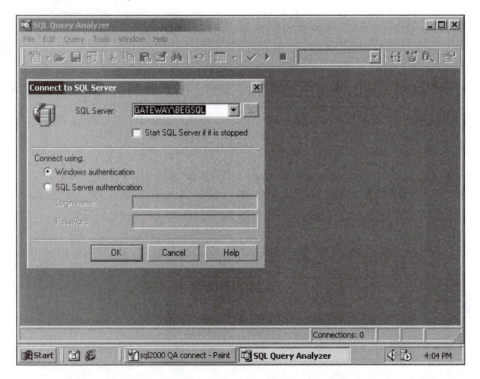

The screen is in a standard windows format with a menu and toolbar. The blank space in the center is like a text editor. You type the SQL statement that you would like to test.

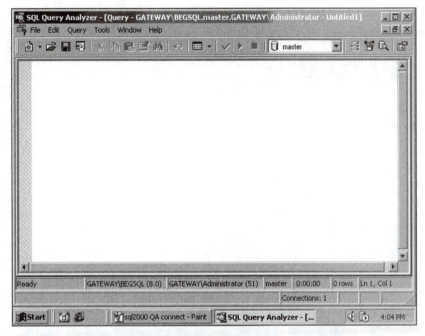

But before typing take a look on the toolbar at the list box named DB. That is set to master by default. You want to run your statement against Northwind, not master, so drop the list and change the database.

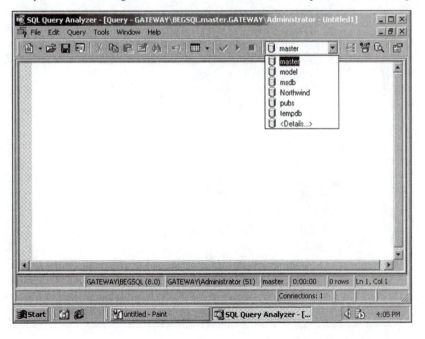

Now we can try our test statement. Type or paste the following:

```
SELECT LastName, FirstName FROM Employees
```

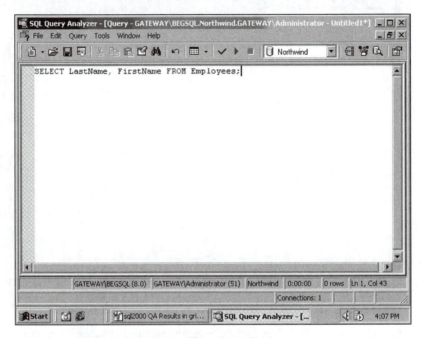

But before we run the statement select Query / Results in Grid.

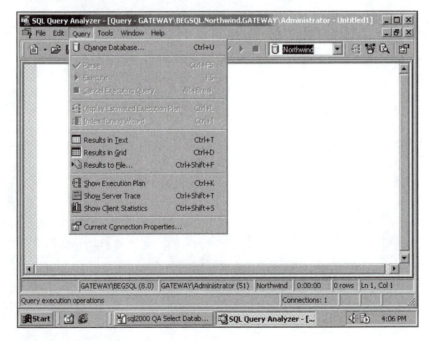

Then strike *F5* or click on the green triangle icon to execute the statement against Northwind. The window now divides in half (upper and lower panes) and the lower half holds the results generated by the SQL statement. You can adjust the columns like you can in Excel by dragging the dividers between the column headers or by double-clicking to auto-adjust. You can also select and copy results form the lower pane to other applications.

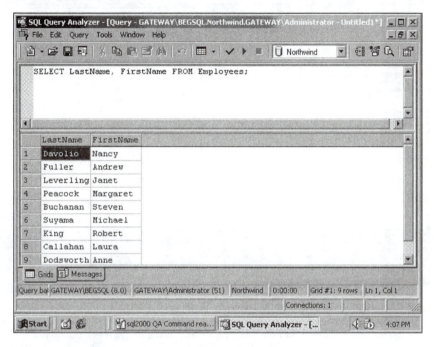

Common Mistakes When Using Query Analyzer

- ❑ Running a SQL statement against the wrong database.

- ❑ Not seeing results properly because of reading them in text view instead of grid view. If columns appear to be missing, scroll right in the results pane.

- ❑ Retyping statements instead of saving them.

- ❑ Failures because typographer's quotes were in a word processed document and then pasted into QA. QA requires true apostrophes.

- ❑ Wrong table or column names or typos.

When you get further in your understanding of how RDBMS work, and when you have more complex SQL statements you can begin to experiment with seeing the execution plan and estimated percent effort spent on each part of the plan. This information assists you in deciding which of multiple options you will use to achieve a given result. For now we can see the plan for our little test statement by *Ctrl+L* or Menu: Query / Display Estimated Execution Plan.

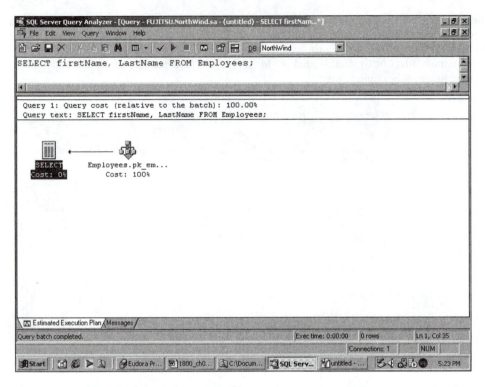

Last, notice a few items in the bottom status bar. There is an estimate of execution time for the statement that was last run. And on the far right side is an indicator of the cursor's line number location. This is very useful when you get an error on line xx and want to get there quickly.

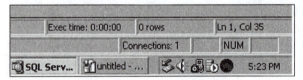

Let us wrap up this introduction to the Query Analyzer with some tips:

❑ You can save statements with File I Save As.

❑ Use the Edit's Replace to quickly find and replace multiple errors of the same type (like a wrong column name) or to change an existing statement into a new statement.

❑ You can enter more than one statement to run at once if you separate them by semicolons.

❑ You can use any formatting of tabs and enters that helps you to 'read' the statement. SQL does not care about whitespace.

❑ Next to the green "run" tool there is a check mark tool. This allows you to check the SQL statement without running it. If there are syntactical errors they will probably be caught by the check. *CTRL+F5* does the same thing.

❑ Strike *Ctrl +G* and enter a number to jump to that line number.

ASP

The most universal front end is a Browser calling World Wide Web pages. In fact for many people the potential for high numbers of users and database transaction loads drive the migration from a simple desktop or LAN DBMS to SQL. One solution for connecting your web site to a database is Active Server Pages. ASP, like Visual Basic and C++, allows the use of COM, a Microsoft technology for creating and using blocks of code. One such block is ADO, ActiveX Data Objects. ADO Objects can be used in ASP to connect your HTML pages to SQL Statements and then handle the SQL results. Since we will be using ASP in one of our case studies we will give you an introduction here.

> We have provided a short primer on ASP in Appendix E or you can read a more complete treatment in *Beginning Active Server Pages 3.0* (ISBN 1-861003-38-2) also from Wrox Press.
>
> You may want to return to this section before you tackle the case studies at the end of this book.

To send a SQL statement you need to perform six steps in your code:

❑ Start by creating some constants that will translate numeric values into English words

❑ Create `Connection` and `Recordset` objects

❑ Open a connection to the datastore

❑ Fill a recordset with the results of a SQL statement sent to the datastore

❑ Write from the recordset onto the web page

❑ Clean up the objects

Try It Out – Employees Table in an ASP Page

Your boss would like a new web page on your site listing the names of the employees of Northwind Traders. The data is contained in an Access database. We will send a SQL statement through a connection object to get the recordset of names. Then we will use VBScript to go walk through the names and put them into the table.

> If you have already switched to using ASP.NET you will be using VB instead of VBScript.

1. Create a new ASP page on your web site (or in the web folder of your hard drive for a local server) named `SQL-EmployeesTable.asp`.

2. Add the following code to the page (we will discuss what it does in a moment):

```
<%@ Language=VBScript %>
<%Option Explicit%>
<HTML>
<HEAD>
```

```
<META NAME="GENERATOR" Content="Microsoft Visual Studio 6.0">
<TITLE>BegSQL ch02 TIO Employees Table</TITLE>
</HEAD>
<BODY>
<H1>NorthWind Employees</H1>
<%
'establish some variables
'useful for Open method of the RecordSet object
'list of all constants available in adovbs.inc file
Dim adOpenForwardOnly, adLockReadOnly, adCmdText
adOpenForwardOnly = 0
adLockReadOnly = 1
adCmdText = 1

'Create and Instantiate Connection and Recordset objects
Dim strConn     'connection string listing provider, etc.
Dim oConn       'our connection object
Dim oRS         'our recordsetobject
Dim strSQL      'Will hold our SQL statement
Set oConn = server.CreateObject("ADODB.Connection")
Set oRS = server.CreateObject("ADODB.Recordset")

'Open the connection by creating a connection string then opening
strConn = "Provider=Microsoft.Jet.OLEDB.4.0; "
strConn = strConn & "Data Source=C:\BegSQL\Northwind.MDB; "
strConn = strConn & "Persist Security Info=False"
oConn.Open strConn

'Fill a recordset with the results of a SQL statement sent to the datastore
strSQL = "SELECT FirstName, LastName "
strSQL = strSQL & " FROM Employees"
oRS.Open strSQL, oConn,adOpenForwardOnly,adLockReadOnly,adCmdText

'Write from the recordset to the page by loop
Response.Write "<TABLE BORDER=1>"
While NOT oRS.EOF
    Response.Write "<TR><TD>" & oRS("FirstName") & "</TD>"
    Response.Write "<TD>" & oRS("LastName") & "</TD></TR>"
    oRS.MoveNext
Wend
Response.Write "</TABLE>"

'Clean up the objects to improve performance
oRS.Close
oConn.Close
set oRS=nothing
set oConn=nothing
%>
</BODY>
</HTML>
```

3. Be sure that your local server is running or connected to you external host. Test the code in your browser by typing its path and name into the URL address or double-clicking on it in Windows Explorer.

How it Works – Employees Table in an ASP Page

There are five blocks of code to get the job done.

```
<%
'establish some constants
'useful for Open method of the RecordSet object
'list of all constants available in adovbs.inc file
Dim adOpenForwardOnly, adLockReadOnly, adCmdText
adOpenForwardOnly = 0
adLockReadOnly = 1
adCmdText = 1
```

In the first section of code as listed above we create some constants. It is easier to work with these terms than it is to remember the numeric codes for the ADO parameters. Alternatively you can include a file named adovbs.inc (included with ADO; search your server's drive) that will establish about 140 constants. However, that is a lot of overhead if you only need three of them.

```
'Create and Instantiate Connection and Recordset objects
Dim strConn    'connection string listing provider, etc.
Dim oConn      'our connection object
Dim oRS        'our recordsetobject
Dim strSQL     'Will hold our SQL statement
Set oConn = server.CreateObject("ADODB.Connection")
Set oRS = server.CreateObject("ADODB.Recordset")
```

In the second section, above, we create and instantiate the two objects we will use to send our SQL statement. The first is the connection object, which provides a conduit to the datastore. The second is the recordset, which will hold the information that comes back from the execution of the statement.

```
'Open the connection by creating a connection string then opening
strConn = "Provider=Microsoft.Jet.OLEDB.4.0; "
strConn = strConn & "Data Source=C:\BegSQL\Northwind.MDB; "
strConn = strConn & "Persist Security Info=False"
oConn.Open strConn
```

Now in the third section, above, we can actually open the connection to the datastore. The syntax for the connection string is derived from the ADO documentation. This is a generic example for Access databases. If you are using Microsoft SQL Server or MSDE use the following string:

```
strConn = "Provider=SQLOLEDB; Data Source=MyServerName; "
strConn = strConn & "Data Source=MyServerName; Initial Catalog=MyDatabaseName; "
strConn = strConn & "User Id=MyUserName; Password=MyUserPassword"
```

The fourth section, below, creates the SQL statement and sends it as the source for the opening of a recordset:

```
'Fill a recordset with the results of a SQL statement sent to the datastore
strSQL = "SELECT FirstName, LastName "
strSQL = strSQL & " FROM Employees"
oRS.Open strSQL, oConn,adOpenForwardOnly,adLockReadOnly,adCmdText
```

Here we use the constants we created to inform ADO how to create the recordset. The last parameter, adCmdText, indicates that we are providing a SQL statement as opposed to the name of a query, stored procedure, or table.

```
'Write from the recordset to the page by loop
Response.Write "<TABLE BORDER=1>"
While NOT oRS.EOF
    Response.Write "<TR><TD>" & oRS("FirstName") & "<TD>"
    Response.Write "<TD>" & oRS("LastName") & "<TD><TR>"
    oRS.MoveNext
Wend
Response.Write "</TABLE>"
```

In the fifth section, above, we actually get the data out onto the page. We can refer to a field of data by putting its name inside quotes inside parentheses and after the name of the recordset object.

```
'Clean up the objects to improve performance
oConn.Close
set oRS=nothing
set oConn=nothing
%>
```

In the final section of code, above, we close our objects to release their memory. Freeing resources is important to allow the site to scale well.

Common Mistakes When Using SQL Statements in ASP Pages

❑   Pointing to a datastore that does not exist

❑   Wrong syntax in the Provider string (watch the punctuation)

❑   Forgetting a RecordSet.MoveNext in the loop

❑   Putting the <Table> tags within the loop or misplacing the <TR> or <TD> tags

❑   Not releasing the resources, that is, missing using CLOSE and SET Object = Nothing

For more examples, theory, shortcuts, syntax for connections and tips on ASP, ADO and SQL see *Beginning ASP Databases* – ISBN 1-861002-72-6.

Summary

So in this chapter, we have seen how to set up software to be able to start using the SQL examples that will follow in this book. We have been introduced to the Northwind database and we have tested our software configurations using a sample SQL statement. We have also seen how we can use ASP as a front end for real-world scenarios, in preparation for the case studies that appear at the end of the book.

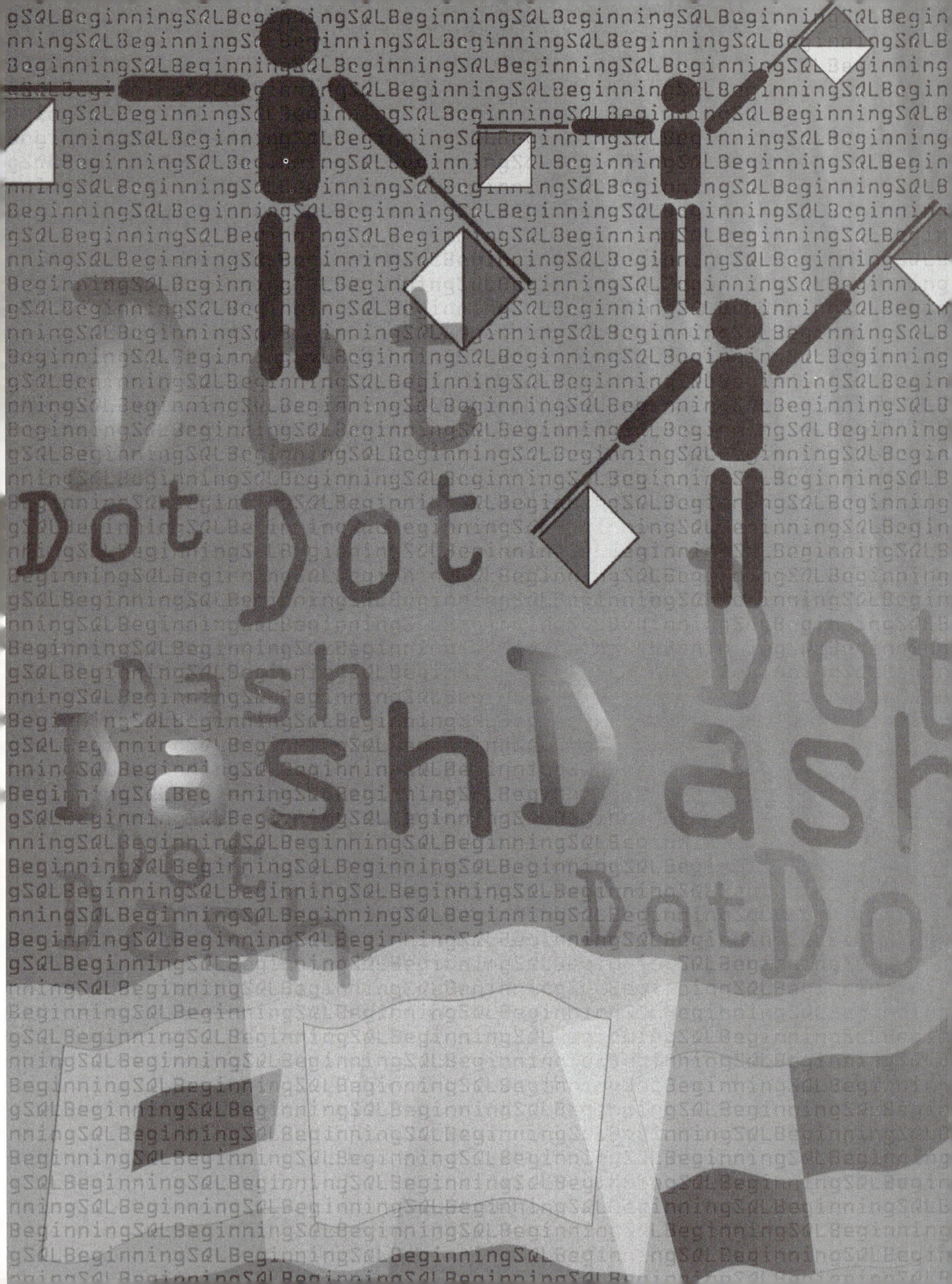

Introduction to Relational Databases

Computers have been available to the commercial world for about 50 years. During that time the greatest computing contribution to business, by far, has been the database. All of our accounting systems, inventory control, record keeping, and scheduling are based on databases. As a result many of the brightest minds in computer science have spent their careers refining the principles of good database design. It behooves us to learn and benefit from their research.

In this chapter we quickly run through the major points of those ideas as they apply to designing databases and writing SQL statements. If you have extensive experience of designing relational databases, you may want to skim this chapter. If your experience is with non-relational databases then there are some important new concepts to pick up in this section. Some of you may have a lot of practical experience with desktop systems like dBase, Paradox, or Access, but never had a good chance to study the theory. This chapter may help you understand some of the logic underneath the Access interface.

Parts of an Application that Use Data

In Chapter 1 we talked about the several components that part of an application that uses data. Let's give them a quick review before we begin discussing some principles of database design. There are, fundamentally, three parts to a data application: the first is the user interface, or the front end; second is the connection to the backend – across the connection travels a SQL Statement and data to the Relational Database Management System (RDBMS) – and the third is the RDBMS itself, which contains the data and the metadata about how the data is organized.

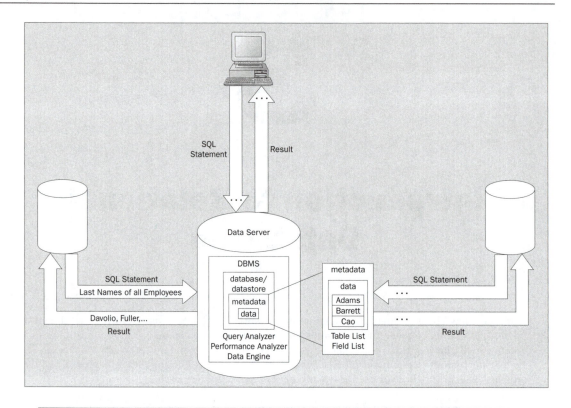

You will find that Relational Database Management Systems are commonly referred to as plain Database Management Systems with the shorter abbreviation DBMS. Generally, in this book you will see the DBMS abbreviation being used to refer to relational databases. We will explicitly say if we are using the term DBMS with reference to a non-relational database.

The front end can be C++, Visual Basic, Access, a web page, or virtually any other user interface created in the last ten years. They all have a way of sending a SQL statement to a DBMS and then displaying or otherwise handling the data that the DBMS returns. For those of you familiar with n-tier systems, one or more middle tiers can act as the conduit between the front and back ends.

The DBMS accepts your SQL statements and applies them to the database. The way that the DBMS executes the SQL statement is not of concern to us; they all react to a SQL statement in the same way, as defined in the SQL standards. Most DBMS can handle multiple databases: for example we may have a single installation of an DBMS like Oracle 9i that manages one database for the order taking process and another database to handle the factory production functions.

The next lower level, the metadata, describes the structure established for the data. The metadata and the data together are called the database. The lowest level is the data – although generally the largest in size, the data itself is the simplest element. As a programmer you have little control over how the DBMS physically organizes the data on the disk – in fact, that is one of the niceties of a DBMS: SQL hides the gritty details of how the data has been abstracted for you.

What is a Database?

Many computer scientists (and a few philosophers) have taken a stab at defining a database. We like a definition that covers enough of the ideas to get started, and so prefer:

An organized collection of information with a common purpose.

Note first that there is nothing in the definition that indicates it must be in a computer. A telephone book is a perfectly functioning database, albeit not one we will discuss in this book. Second, the value comes not in the information, but in the organization of the information. Having all the information about our business on bits of paper strewn around the office is neither a database nor valuable.

We can dissect this definition by using an example; we may run a Tulip-breeding business that has a collection of information such as:

- ❑   The color of Tulip breed number 1
- ❑   The color of Tulip breed number 2
- ❑   The identification number of the parents of Tulip breed number 3
- ❑   The address of the breeder that sold us Tulip breed number 3

This information must be organized before it becomes a database. We need to group all the information from one breed and then group all the information for the second breed. Last, this information must all, in one way or another, be related to a common purpose: in this case it is our Tulip Breeding business.

As we work our way through this chapter there will be many places where you must make a judgment call. Here we must decide what pieces of information should be included in the database, that is what is contained within our "common purpose". Each of the above bulleted items can be seen as part of our purpose of breeding and selling bulbs – but what about the telephone number of the local fire department? They are not customers, vendors, or employees and so would probably not fit into your database. On the other hand, if your database will be generating phone lists to hang by the telephones you might want the emergency number on the list and thus include the fire department as a miscellaneous contact. This is your judgment call.

There are tools other than a database that organize a collection of information. Spreadsheets do a fine job of holding information but they are usually limited in their theoretical and practical size. The spreadsheet's user interface also suffers when the amount of data grows above several thousand pieces of information. Word processor tables can also hold a lot of information, but are even more limited in size. Overall, you must move to a database in one of two cases: the first is when you move beyond a few thousand items with ten or more pieces of information each; the second is when you move beyond the simplest relationships between the pieces of information.

Let us look at an example of spreadsheets and databases from our Tulip business. Perhaps in the beginning of the business a batch of bulbs of one breed was produced each spring and the entire crop sold to the single buyer for a chain of flower shops. In this case there would be only one or a few sales each year and so several years' worth of sales data fit into a single spreadsheet quite well. It was certainly easy to set up such a spreadsheet, but as the company grew thitey began to produce many breeds of Tulips and sell them to many different customers. Now we have a case where there are more pieces of data than a spreadsheet can support efficiently. Furthermore, we start to have some relationships that are not so simple, for example the connection between an order, the many different boxes of bulbs in the order and the information about the customer for that order. In order to support this volume and complexity of data we must move the information from a spreadsheet to a database.

79

However, the basic definition does not give us much help in designing a good database. In the next few sections we will discuss the basic organizational structures used in a modern database, namely tables, records, and columns.

Tables

Tables are structures that are designed to hold the information in an organizational form that is optimized for the computer. The information is rarely stored in a format that is best for human interaction; rather it is optimized for speed and reliability on the hardware and DBMS. Other database tools, such as SQL statements, are then applied to tables to gather or change the stored data into a form that is optimized for human interaction.

Keep in mind that in a relational DBMS a table is not a file like it is in dBase or other "flat file" database systems. Rather, think of a SQL table as a single set of information out of the total information held in the database. Also remember that a table is not necessarily in any particular order in a relational DBMS: the order of information is generally the order in which the information was entered or in some order that was created by the self-optimizing schemes internal to the DBMS. When you retrieve information the DBMS will send your requested data in the order of your specification; however, note that the DBMS will not reorder the information as it is stored in the tables.

A good name for a table is the plural noun of what the table contains. In our Tulip business we would have tables with names like `Bulbs`, `Customers`, `Vendors`, and `Orders`; these nouns are short and clear, which helps to improve readability of SQL statements that refer to the tables. The DBMS could not care less what you name tables (within some basic naming rules), but when you go to work with the data in your SQL Statements it is much easier to maintain code that refers to logical names of objects.

Records

A record is one instance of a physical or conceptual object (or a single piece of information) within a table. If you think of the table as a collection of objects (`Customers`, `Bulbs`, or `Vendors`) then a record is one member of that collection. In a table of `Customers` one record will be one customer. In a rough analogy, a record in a table is like a row in a spreadsheet. In some vendor's terminologies a record is called an **instance** or a **row**.

Records are not exactly named in the sense that a table is named, but they do need to have the ability to be uniquely identified. We will discuss this in more depth later in the chapter, but the idea is that by looking at one or a combination of attributes of a record we can find that specific record out of the entire table.

Columns (Fields)

Within a table we will hold a series of descriptors about the records; each of these descriptors concerns an attribute or property of the record. For example, in our table of bulbs we will have columns for `Name`, `Color`, and `Parent`. Each record will have a piece of data for each column (albeit with some data possibly missing). Spreadsheets use the same terminology, that is each column holds the descriptors for the rows. Other database systems use the term **Fields** or **Attributes** for columns.

As with tables, a wise programmer will use names that convey the meaning of the contents.

An Example (and its Problems)

A simple example illustrates the above ideas (and sets up some problems that we will solve later). Here are two tables from our Tulip-breeding business database:

Breeds   ver01

Breeds.BreedID	Breeds.Name	Breeds.Color	Breeds.Parent	Breeds.SupplierCo
1	PAK's Pride	Blue	Gorgeous	RJ Farms
2	Gorgeous	Orange	Americana	RJ Farms
3	Sylvania	Yellow	Sebetha	Angelica Inc.
4	Millette	Red	Sebetha	Angelica Inc.

Customers   ver01

Customers.CustID	Customers.Name	Customers.Telephone	Customers.Fax
1	FlowerCity	456-7890	567-8901
2	FlowerTown	(86-10) 6789-0123	
3	FlowerWorld	890-1234	901-2345

Note that in each table we have records (four for `Breeds`, three for `Customers`). The tables also have columns holding descriptors such as the name of the breed or the telephone number of the customer. Note how each piece of data "fits" its column in the sense that it follows the pattern for that column. Even though a customer has two phones we would not enter data like

```
"123-4567 or 234-5678"
```

in the `Customers.Telephone` column, as every column should only contain a single piece of information, and the above example has two pieces of information. We have met the minimal requirements for a database in that we have organized the set of information that is for the common purpose of running our Tulip business.

However, if you take the above sample tables and begin to think about a real business you can imagine some very serious problems with the structure of these tables. For example, in the `Breeds` table we might want to add the telephone number of the company that supplied the parent. So we could modify the table to be as follows:

Breeds   ver02

Breeds.BreedID	Breeds.Name	Breeds.Color	Breeds.Parent	Breeds.SupplierCo	Breeds.SupplierTel
1	PAK's Pride	Blue	Gorgeous	RJ Farms	123-4567
2	Gorgeous	Orange	Americana	RJ Farms	123-4567
3	Sylvania	Yellow	Sebetha	Angelica Inc.	987-6543
4	Millette	Red	Sebetha	Angelica Inc.	987-6543

However, we have now introduced **redundancy** into the data because the telephone number of our suppliers is in the database twice. This can lead to a host of problems, including:

- It will take twice as much work by clerks to update our database if and when RJ Farms changes their telephone number

- We are using twice as much disk space when we keep two copies of the telephone numbers

- If the two numbers for RJ Farms do not match we cast doubt on each of the data

- If a clerk accidentally enters "JR Farms" for the supplier of breed number two then we will think we have three suppliers (RJ Farms, JR Farms, and Angelica Inc.) when we actually only have two

As you can imagine, these problems become exponentially worse as we start to have hundreds and thousands of records.

A second problem is obvious in the Customers table: we have a hole in our data matrix, because FlowerTown does not have a fax number. This does not create an integrity problem like duplicate data would, but it does have an effect on performance. Any time you have tables that look like Swiss cheese you will pay some performance penalty because the DBMS is maintaining structure for which there is no data. You will also leave yourself, as the data user, wondering whether any given piece of data will be present; if you have many missing fax numbers it is wasteful to rely on using fax number as a column in a report or a means to contact customers.

Less obvious is a third problem in the Customers table. What if FlowerCity has three telephone numbers? We could add columns for Customer.Telephone2 and Customer.Telephone3 but then we would be introducing holes for those records (customers) that have only one phone.

Relational Databases

The solution to all three problems was described by Dr. E.F. Codd in his concept of the Relational Database. In a nutshell, his ideas were twofold:

- As much as possible, divide data into smaller tables with strict rules for what data they can contain.

- Create relationships between the tables that allow the DBMS to look from one table to another to assemble the complete set of results.

To demonstrate, let us revise the tables of our database as follows:

Breeds   ver03

Breeds.BreedID	Breeds.Name	Breeds.Color	Breeds.Parent	Breeds.SupplierID
1	PAK's Pride	Blue	Gorgeous	1
2	Gorgeous	Orange	Americana	1
3	Sylvania	Yellow	Sebetha	2
4	Millette	Red	Sebetha	2

Suppliers   ver01

Suppliers.ID	Suppliers.Name
1	RJ Farms
2	Angelica Inc.

SupplierContacts   ver01

SupplierContacts.SupplierID	SupplierContacts.Type	SupplierContacts.Number
1	Voice	123-4567
2	Voice	987-6543

Customers   ver01

Customers.ID	Customer.Name
1	FlowerCity
2	FlowerTown
3	FlowerWorld

CustomerContacts   ver01

CustomerContacts.ID	CustomerContacts.CustomerID	CustomerContacts.Type	CustomerContacts.Number
1	1	Voice	456-7890
2	1	Fax	567-8901
3	2	Voice	6789-0123
4	3	Voice	890-1234
5	3	Fax	901-2345
6	3	Voice	012-3456
7	3	Voice	123-4567

Now we can add the relations as follows:

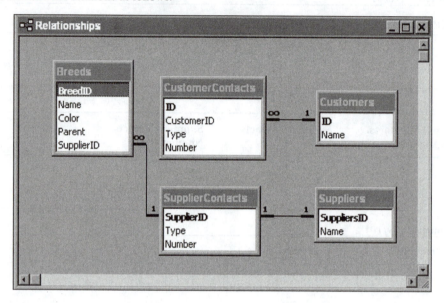

So what exactly do these relationships do? They allow the DBMS to point from one table to another for the purpose of looking up information. For example, we may need to get the voice number of the supplier of the Sylvania breed. We can specify the Sylvania record of the Breeds table and the DBMS will find out that the value for Breeds.SupplierID = 2. The DBMS will then follow the relation to the SupplierContacts table and go down to the record where SupplierContacts.SupplierID = 2. The DBMS can then read across to the SupplierContacts.Number and report back to us that the answer is 987-6543.

> Take another look at the CustomerContacts table and note that we still have a data redundancy problem. Our type of contact includes multiple instances of Voice and Fax. This is probably OK for most uses, but we run the risk of a clerk entering "Telephone" or "Tel" or "voice1" or some other descriptor of what we are calling Voice. Then if we did a search for Voice numbers, the records with errant data would not be found. The problem can be solved by creating a one column table of contact descriptors and only allowing the use of data that was in that descriptor list.

Have We Solved our Three Problems?

Problem one was that we had redundancy in the telephone numbers of our suppliers; this has been solved by moving data on suppliers to their own table and having each datum recorded only once. Only an identifier column, Breeds.SupplierID, remains in the Breeds table. The DBMS can look up the telephone number twice if we want to retrieve the data for both the Sylvania and Millette breeds. If there is a change to the telephone number, we only need to make the change in one place, thus eliminating our problems stemming from redundant data.

Problems two and three were too few and too many telephone numbers for our customers. We removed the `Voice` and `Fax` numbers from the `Customers` table; in a new `CustomerContacts` table we pair up the Customer ID and one of their telecomms numbers. Again, the DBMS will use the relationship to look up and join together information as frequently as needed. We have solved this as well by moving those numbers to their own `CustomerContacts` table. Now we can add as many telephone and fax numbers as we want for each customer.

Before we move on let me give you a preview of some thoughts we will cover later in the book that embellish these techniques for relating tables. The theory of the relational database and the language of SQL go hand in hand. So, SQL has additional tools to speed the process of matching up records: the most valuable is the index, as we will cover in Chapter 15. An index makes a tool that can rapidly find a record when you have data for one column of that record. In the case of relations we can quickly find a customer's record if we have an index on the `CustomerID` column. SQL also offers many tools to ensure that the matching process works smoothly (see Chapters 9 and 10).

> **What should be grouped in a table? Database designers tend to be divided into schools of "lumpers" and "splitters."**
> The solution we gave is of the splitter school in that customers and suppliers are in separate tables. However, they could both be contained in a "Companies" table. After all, we may find ourselves selling prize bulbs of our own creation to suppliers, thus making them customers.
> However, we have taken the lumper approach when it came to the fax and voice numbers – they are in the same table. We have included an extra field to differentiate them at the time we need to retrieve only voice numbers.
>
> There is no simple formula to give a definite answer in a given case, but here are some guidelines:
> First and foremost is the ability to generate the needed results and to protect the integrity of the data. You must split at least to the level where the metadata can achieve your goals.
> If you are in an IT group that favors one school then conform (at least until you are the senior designer, fully vested, and you can argue for a change).
> As you build more databases and can think through the consequences you will spot reasons to lump or split.
> Note that performance degrades from too much splitting because the DBMS must work harder following the relations and looking up the data in more than one table.
> Also note that performance degrades from too much lumping because your DBMS must do searches through larger blocks of data held by enlarged tables.
>
> This book will give you a good start on learning the science and the techniques of database design, but it will be with practice that you master the art of representing real-world data in suitable and efficient forms.

Matching Records – The Role of Key Fields

We have seen that an DBMS can relate one table to another and perform the lookups needed to associate the proper records in each table. This ability allows us to eliminate both redundant data and large areas of missing values. Let us look more closely at how we must design tables in order for the DBMS to perform these lookups.

It is important to understand that the DBMS does not keep track of which records group together. There is no metadata that says record number 45 of one table matches with record number 22 of another table. The DBMS makes matches at the time results are requested by looking at actual data in the columns. Therefore we must ensure that we have columns that will contain data that can make a correct and unambiguous match. The concept and rules for these columns is ensconced in the concepts of *keys* or *key fields*.

> **Key fields are not more important than other fields (like a key player on a team) – rather they are "key" because they provide the solution to matching records.**

Primary Key Fields

A primary key is a column, or group of columns, that uniquely identifies each record of a table. For example, in a table of citizens of the United States the column holding the social security number (SSN) could be a primary key. Since no two citizens have the same SSN, this key column would uniquely identify each record. However, frequently we do not have a natural piece of data that we can be sure will be unique; certainly not names, since, for example, there are likely to be at least two guys named James Smith out of any thousand English speakers. Without a natural primary key field (unique column) we can easily create a primary key field by including an ID column in our table. This field will get a unique serial number for each record added. As long as we do not make mistakes on assigning the number, we can be sure that the ID field is a primary key. I like to call the field *TableNameID* such as `EmployeesID` or `ContactsID`. In Chapter 9 we discuss various methods of assigning a unique number in an ID field to each new record.

Foreign Key Fields

A foreign key is a column holding data that is able to point to a unique column in another table. So, if we want our Order records to be linked to our Customer records, the `Orders` table will need a foreign key field that contains a valid `CustomerID`. The DBMS can then read data in the `CustomerID` field of the `Orders` table and go over and match the Order record to one, and only one, Customer record using the `Customers` table's Primary key field of `CustomerID`. If you are used to the terms "One-to-Many" in relationships, the Foreign Key will be a field on the Many side of the relationship.

Note the differences in the basic rules between primary and foreign keys. Primary keys must be unique within their own table. Foreign keys must be able to correctly match with a primary key in another table. In most cases the data in a foreign key will be duplicated from row to row since we will have more then one record (like Orders) in one table pointing to only one record (like a Customer) in the second table.

Keys in Action

Let's apply these ideas about key fields to our Tulip example. For example in our `Customers` and `CustomerContacts` table we have to have to provide key fields to the DBMS to match up a `CustomerContacts` record with a `Customers` record. The `Customers` table has a primary key field named `CustomersID` which holds a value unique for each customer. My `CustomerContacts` table has a foreign key field named `CustomerID`, which matches with one, and only one, of the records in the `Customers` table. With these two key fields the DBMS can correctly match each of the contact numbers to one and only one customer.

Now that you have the idea, let us provide two notes on key fields. First, the more alike you can keep the data in the primary and foreign key fields, the fewer problems you will have with the relationship. Try to have both columns have the same data type, size, constraints, etc. If they are different the DBMS will have to take its best guess at doing a conversion or inexact match and that can create problems. Second, more advanced database designs will try to optimize performance by not creating a serial-numbered ID field for a primary key and instead create a primary key from combinations of columns holding data. In this sense the primary key is not exactly a column, but rather a concept of two or more columns, which together provide a unique identification for each record.

We'll now summarize Key Fields by noting the important ideas.

❑   Key fields enable a DBMS to match up records between two related tables.

❑   Key fields are always one or more fields; there is no metadata that holds the relating information.

❑   Primary key fields hold unique values for each record in their table.

❑   Foreign key fields hold values that match values in the primary key of another table.

❑   Generally in a "One-to-Many" relationship the "One" side has a primary key field and the "Many" side has a foreign key field.

❑   When a match is needed, the DBMS will read the information from the foreign key, find the matching record in the primary key, and use that match to relate the two records.

Many students have experience with large data sets and understand how easy it is to have inconsistencies and problems in data. They ask: how can a programmer ensure that primary key values are unique and that foreign key values correctly match values in the other table's primary key? What happens, for example if a Customer is deleted and records in `CustomerContacts` are then left without a match? We discuss some techniques to solve these problems in Chapter 9. SQL contains the concepts of triggers, which we do not discuss in this book. A trigger can be set to alert or carry out actions whenever a key violation occurs. In addition, constraints can be set on the addition of new data, which ensure that it meets the needs of keys. Lastly, most DBMS vendors have tools that can check for violations and help to automate solutions to violations.

Another Way to Describe Relationships

The two most common goals of breaking up (normalizing) tables are:

❑   Reduce data redundancies and gaps.

❑   Reduce the number of columns in a table

The solutions give rise to terms that describe the relationship between the tables as "One-to-Many" or "One-to-One".

One-to-Many

Consider the example where we divided the customer contacts away from the `Customers` table. Recall that when we retrieve data we will ask the DBMS to match up the contacts records with Customers' records based on a value in the `CustomerContacts.CustomerID` matching a value in `Customers.CustomerID`. In the `CustomerContacts` table there are many (well, a few) records that match one record in the `Customers` table; this is because a Customer has several phone or fax lines and each of these lines must match back to its rightful owner in the `Customers` table. Therefore this relationship is called One-to-Many. In this case one `Customer` record matches many `CustomerContacts` records.

Most of the time that you create a One-to-Many relationship your objective is to eliminate data redundancy or data gaps. The Many side can grow and retract according to the amount of data without affecting the number of records or columns required in the One side. We discussed this in detail above as the solution to our Tulips company problem.

One-to-One

The second case did not arise in our example. So let us say we did a marketing survey and wanted to add a lot of the gathered information about our customers to the database. We could add columns to the `Customers` table for data like:

- ❑ Number of Employees
- ❑ Neighborhood Type (urban, suburban, rural)
- ❑ Square footage of retail space
- ❑ Type of computer accounting system
- ❑ Number of certified horticulturalists on staff

The problem is that our `Customers` table begins to get pretty large, and that means slow. The speed problem is particularly frustrating because we probably use the table most frequently for orders that just need some basic Customer data like the name and address. The survey data mostly sits around until our marketing department has a research request.

Note that in this case we probably have one value for each survey column for each record. So this example is not like the first case where we split tables to reduce redundancy and gaps. In this case our objective is to get our frequently used data (customer name and address) in the slimmest, fastest format we can in order to quickly process orders. We want to keep the survey data, but we don't want it to interfere with the columns that support order processing.

To solve the efficiency problems in the second case we split the table into two: the first remains `Customers` and contains the `CustomersID` and information, like address columns, that is needed for orders. The new table, which we could name `CustomersSurvey`, holds a `CustomersSurveyID` and the survey data fields. The ID numbers in `CustomersSurvey.CustomersSurveyID` exactly match, one for one, the ID numbers in `Customers.CustomerID`. We now have a second table that can be thought of as an extension of five extra columns added to the right side of the first table. The DBMS can link up a record of the new table to the correct record in the old table through the `CustomersID` and `CustomersSurveyID` fields.

This type of relationship is named "One-to-One." The net effect of this relationship is to split a table with many columns into two tables with fewer columns each. The main characteristic is that there should be about the same number of rows in each table and the rows should have a common ID number (primary key). The number may not be exactly equal, because the second table usually gets records as data is obtained, for example when the customers complete the survey. However, there should never be more than one row in the second table that matches a record in the first table.

There are several other types of relationships that can quickly become very complex. One type is used for cases where there may be many matches on both sides and is called a Many-to-Many relationship, but we won't go into that here.

Here is a comparison of One-to-One and One-to-Many relationships:

	One-to-One	One-to-Many
Purpose	Create tables with fewer columns so that frequently used tables are smaller and faster	Eliminate redundancy and gaps in data
Number of Records	Both tables have a similar number of records	Generally one table (Many) has far more records then the other
Duplication of data in primary key fields	Each table has primary key with unique values	"One" side has primary key with unique values; "Many" side has foreign key field with duplicated values

Normalization

Dr Codd and his followers went far beyond simply splitting up tables and creating relationships: they developed rules for how to define tables, columns, and records so that there cannot be a duplication of information or a failure in the logical relationships. The rules are named "Normal Forms" and are numbered from 0 upwards; in one version the numbered rules went past 300 but the most common lists are either 3 or 13 items. Explaining each of the rules and implications is outside the scope of this book, but let us look at how we have applied a few of the rules to our sample Tulip Business:

❑ All data is presented in the form of tables, records and columns, as per Normal Form Rule One. There is no data sitting out in extraneous structures (which might be inaccessible to SQL).

❑ There is a separate table for each set of related columns; that is, we do not have columns about Breeds mixed in with columns for Customers. This segregation satisfies another of the requirements for First Normal Form.

❑ The order of the records is not important: the DBMS will handle re-ordering to fit our requests (also First Normal Form).

❑ The first column of each table is an ID field with a number that is unique to each record. Using this number we can unambiguously identify any one record. First Normal Form requires this ability to identify a record. There are more complex ways to achieve this goal by making composites from multiple columns, but including an incrementally numbered field is one sure way to meet the requirement.

❑ There is no unnecessary repetition of data, such as the same supplier telephone number listed for many breeds (part of Normal Form 2). This does not preclude having a supplier code that is the same for several breeds from the same supplier; that is necessary to describe the relationships around the breed.

❑ Each piece of data is granular (as small as possible); in other words we do not have a company name and telephone number in one field (elements of First and Third normal form).

There are occasionally cases for de-normalizing data. For example there may be a nightly report that uses data from four different tables. Your analysis indicates that the relating of these tables is the bottleneck for your DBMS. You may choose to consciously duplicate some data in one table in order to reduce the amount of relational look-ups between tables. This is a common practice, but it is almost always done with extreme caution and after the database starts in compliance with as many normal forms as possible. Frequently there is a procedure to temporarily de-normalize (by introducing copies of data) to perform a certain task, then immediately re-normalize (delete the copies) after the task is complete. Stray from normalization only when there is a compelling reason to do so; understand the potential problems and you can control the source of conflicts.

The Normalization rules are critical for developing bullet-proof databases, but in their original language they are difficult to understand and not completely in a logical order that applies to the task of building a database. Nevertheless, it is worth reading an interpretation of them every six months or so and as your experience increases, so will your understanding of these rules. Hopefully your understanding will stay one step ahead of your needs.

> **Learning about Dr. Codd's Normal Forms:**
> The original paper is *A Relational Model of Data for Large Shared Data Banks* in the *Communications of the Association for Computing Machinery* 13(6):377. A good synopsis can be found in Robert Vieira's *Professional SQL Server 7.0 Programming*, ISBN 1-861002-31-9. Another good treatment lies in Joe Celko's book *SQL for Smarties: Advanced SQL Programming, 2nd Edition* ISBN 1-55860-576-2.

What is a NULL?

There is one empty spot in our discussion of database design – the NULL. There is no small amount of discussion on this topic, but here is a starting definition:

A NULL represents a value that we currently do not know.

Some people add that a NULL could mean "not applicable", "not known", or "undecided." Let's consider the wide range of cases where the above definition might apply:

❑ NULL for the value of yearly percent growth – does that mean that it is not yet the end of the year, so you cannot calculate the value? Perhaps it is for the first year of the company, so there is no previous year with which to compare. Or maybe some records were destroyed in a fire and one year can't be calculated.

❑ NULL for the date of birth of a person – does that mean they were not born, and how does that differ from a fetus for which we may have lots of data, but not yet a date of birth?

❑ NULL for the balance of a bank account – does that mean the balance is zero? Or does it mean the account was never opened? Perhaps it means there was a conflict that made it impossible to calculate a balance because of an error or inconsistency. Perhaps there is a balance, but you do not know what it is. Perhaps there is a value that is out of the range allowed for that column.

❑ NULL for a person's last name – does that mean you don't know the name? Could it be a person from Indonesia where last names are rarely used?

❑ NULL for the EmployeeID value in a column holding the ID of the employee's boss – is the person in training and not yet assigned to a boss? Is it the CEO who does not have a boss? Is it an outside consultant whose boss is in another company?

❑ NULL for the date that a warranty expires – does that mean the warranty does not exist? Is it a guarantee that lasts forever?

❑ NULL for a person's age – could that mean the person just doesn't want to tell the data clerk? Even though a value clearly exists and we have the value for most people, for some people we may never get a value.

NULL is the Only Way?

SQL does not have differing variations of NULL to address each of these possibilities. We are forced to use NULL as the only way to represent many sources of unknown or missing values. The rules of your business will differ according to why a value is missing, but SQL cannot differentiate among different causes of the gap in knowledge.

NULLs are a necessary evil. They consume more storage space than values and retard indexing and searching. However, most of the problems are logical – trying to properly guess and then handle which (one or more) of the meanings of NULL might currently apply. To make matters worse, NULLs propagate; that is, when you add, subtract, multiple, or divide numbers and one is NULL, the answer is NULL. Calculations involving dozens of numbers have an increased chance of at least one being NULL and thus making the overall answer NULL.

Equating NULL to a Value

Instead of living with uncertainty, many students try to mentally equate a NULL to a value. This is wrong – a NULL is not a zero, not is it an empty string of characters that we can indicate with a pair of double quotes.

Since NULLs are such a problem, there are some solutions, both within pure ANSI-SQL and from vendors of DBMS. First, ANSI-SQL specifies that NULLs are ignored in aggregate functions, such as finding the highest, lowest, or average values from a set of data. This topic is discussed further in Chapter 13. Second, many vendors have functions that allow you to substitute a default value for a NULL on a case-per case basis; in other words you may have one request for data within which you want any NULL value in a particular column to be changed to a zero. The NULL will remain in the table but the set of results will show a zero. These proprietary tools are covered in vendor-specific texts. Lastly, all SQL flavors support "three value logic" which standardizes the results of truth tables when the results of a NULL are compared to TRUE and FALSE. Three value logic is discussed in more advanced SQL texts.

General Advice on NULL

We will finish our NULL discussion (not that we feel this discussion was value-less!) by offering some general advice on working with NULLs:

❑ Make as many columns as possible NOT NULL in constraints; by making a column NOT NULL, each field in that column must contain a value.

❑ When possible use default values when values are not known; frequently zero or blank can be used.

❑ Never use a NULL in a primary key column (like the ID column in each of the tables of our Tulip example). Most DBMS will prevent you from using a NULL in a primary key field, but to be sure never design your front end to allow a NULL to be passed to a primary key field.

❑ Where possible and logical add an additional column to store a more specific value for NULL information. For example you can add a column that notes (TRUE/FALSE) that a person withheld their age. Later, when you understand how to make complex selections (Chapter 5), you will be able to handle the NULL properly by referencing the extra value.

❑ Be careful when doing calculations on nullable columns, because NULLs propagate.

❑ If NULL can have more than one meaning for the column then consider using a dummy value for one or more of the meanings. For example, if there's a difference between unknown and not applicable, you can enter "N/A" for the not applicable cases.

❑ Avoid using relational operators (=, >,<) with NULL values.

❑ If you are sure you can avoid the use of NULLs in a field then add a constraint (Chapter 7) that prevents them.

❑ Avoid NULLs in a foreign key field. If a record has a NULL in such a field then it cannot match with its counterpart record in the other table.

❑ Be careful of code schemes that do not cover all cases and thus lead clerks to enter a NULL.

So Where do SQL Statements Fit in with All This Theory?

The ANSI SQL standards actually define three subsets of the SQL language:

❑ The Data Definition Language (DDL) allows us to create data structures. Most of the principles of database design discussed in this chapter would be implemented when using DDL. We will explain and practice using DDL in Chapters 6 through 8.

❑ The most frequently used commands are of the Data Manipulation Language (DML), which covers all additions of data as well as the modifying and deleting of data (Chapters 8 to 10). All of the statements that read data (Chapters 4 and 5) also belong to the DML.

❑ The last language, Data Control Language (DCL), maintains security in a multi-user application. DCL commands include those to create users and allow them specific permissions. We provide an introduction to DCL in Appendix B.

These distinctions are not particularly important in daily life since you do not need to specify which language you are using; they all have the same grammar rules for syntax. As a programmer you focus on the construction of the actual commands rather than the command's sub-language type. By dividing the commands into these sub-types the SQL standard simplifies the setting of permissions. For example, all commands that can change database structure can be easily placed off-limits while still allowing changes to data.

Comparison of SQL Terminology with Other Data Systems

As a final approach to understanding the concept of a SQL database, let me present some comparisons of terminology used by SQL and used by other systems of working with information.

With a Paper System

For a person who still keeps their clients' information on paper cards, the whole file box would be like a table. Each file card would be a record and columns in SQL would correspond to spaces where the person writes the telephone number, city, and so on. A SQL Statement that selects data would be like a system where personal friends are marked with a notch in one corner, allowing easy separation from the other cards.

The great theoretical difference (we will not discuss speed) is that a paper system is very flexible. If you have an extra idea or note you can scribble it in the margins, or you can tape a business card or a Zip disk to a sheet of paper. However, in a normalized relational database no data can exist other than in the column's value space for a given record.

With a Spreadsheet

The analogies with a spreadsheet are easy but dangerous. An entire database would be like a multi-sheet workbook; tables like worksheets, a record like a row, and a SQL column like a spreadsheet column. The danger comes in thinking of a SQL table as being anywhere as flexible as a spreadsheet. In a spreadsheet you can put a formula in a cell, but in SQL you only keep raw data in tables: calculations (like a discount price) are calculated by a SQL statement at the moment before delivery to a user. Furthermore, a spreadsheet does not enforce a regime on the cell grid – you can mix numbers, words, and dates as you go across the cells of a row or down the cells of a column. In a SQL table, that flexibility is strictly forbidden in order to maximize the overall performance of the database.

Databases offer many advantages over spreadsheets. First, databases have the ability to create relations between tables and thus greatly reduce data redundancy and gaps. Solving those data problems is much more cumbersome in a spreadsheet. Second, databases have the capacity to handle huge amounts of information whereas spreadsheets are limited. Third, SQL statements offer the ability to describe much more complicated types of searches and aggregations then a spreadsheet. Lastly, SQL offers better tools for maintaining integrity of data between tables.

With Desktop Database Solutions (dBase, Access, Paradox)

Many readers will be coming from experience with a desktop database. They are generally not designed to scale to more than ten or so simultaneous users. Moving to a heavy-duty DBMS (that communicates in SQL) is a logical progression as you deploy your database to a greater number of internal users or incorporate your data into a web site (for specifics on integrating databases into a web site follow this book with a read of *Beginning ASP Databases*, ISBN 1-861002-72-6).

There is some variation among desktop database vendors in the terminology of objects. Most are very similar to SQL in that you have a database composed of tables that hold records and columns. dBase actually used files for each table. Some use the term fields instead of columns. SQL refers to requests for data as Statements where desktop systems sometimes use queries. The other major difference is that desktop systems are designed to keep all of their structure and data in files, whereas the interaction of the DBMS and the disks is managed in different ways by industrial-strength DBMS. None of them work with an Access-like file system because the concepts of file ownership and locking are not compatible with a DBMS designed to accommodate thousands of simultaneous users. Lastly, desktop systems actually combine a front end, connection, and backend into one package. Although you can create a form for user interaction in Paradox, the SQL language has no provision for a user interface.

Summary

Modern databases are a tribute to human analytical thought. The most widely utilized techniques for database design adhere to the principles of relational databases. Within each relational database are one or more tables that hold information about a collection of similar objects or concepts. Common examples of tables include Employees, Customers, Orders, Items, and Cities. Within each table are one or more columns that are descriptors of the items in the table. Columns for a Cities table might include Name, Population, Area, and CenterPointName.

Database designers should follow the rules of Normalization. Although the rules are complex the basics include:

❑   Keeping data in its smallest logical parts (separate first and last name)

❑   Tables should have only columns that contribute to the purpose of that table

❑   Each record in a table should be uniquely identifiable

You can hardly live with NULLs but you also can't live without them. A NULL means a value that you don't know, but that could mean you will learn it later, that it does not apply, or that you don't know an underlying value, which has propagated a NULL. Treat the use and interpretation of NULLS with caution.

DBMS based on SQL have both similarities and differences with the vocabulary and theory of older data storage techniques and desktop databases. Most theoretical differences exist to allow SQL the power to support thousands of simultaneous users interacting with the data. In particular SQL-based systems are characterized by ease and efficiency in supporting complex relationships and their ability to support very complex searches and selections of data.

We have spent three chapters without actually building SQL statements other than our practice statement for the setup chapter. In Chapter 4 we will start with the most basic of statements, the SELECT statement. You will learn how to read many permutations of data from a database that is already created and stocked with data (in our case Northwind).

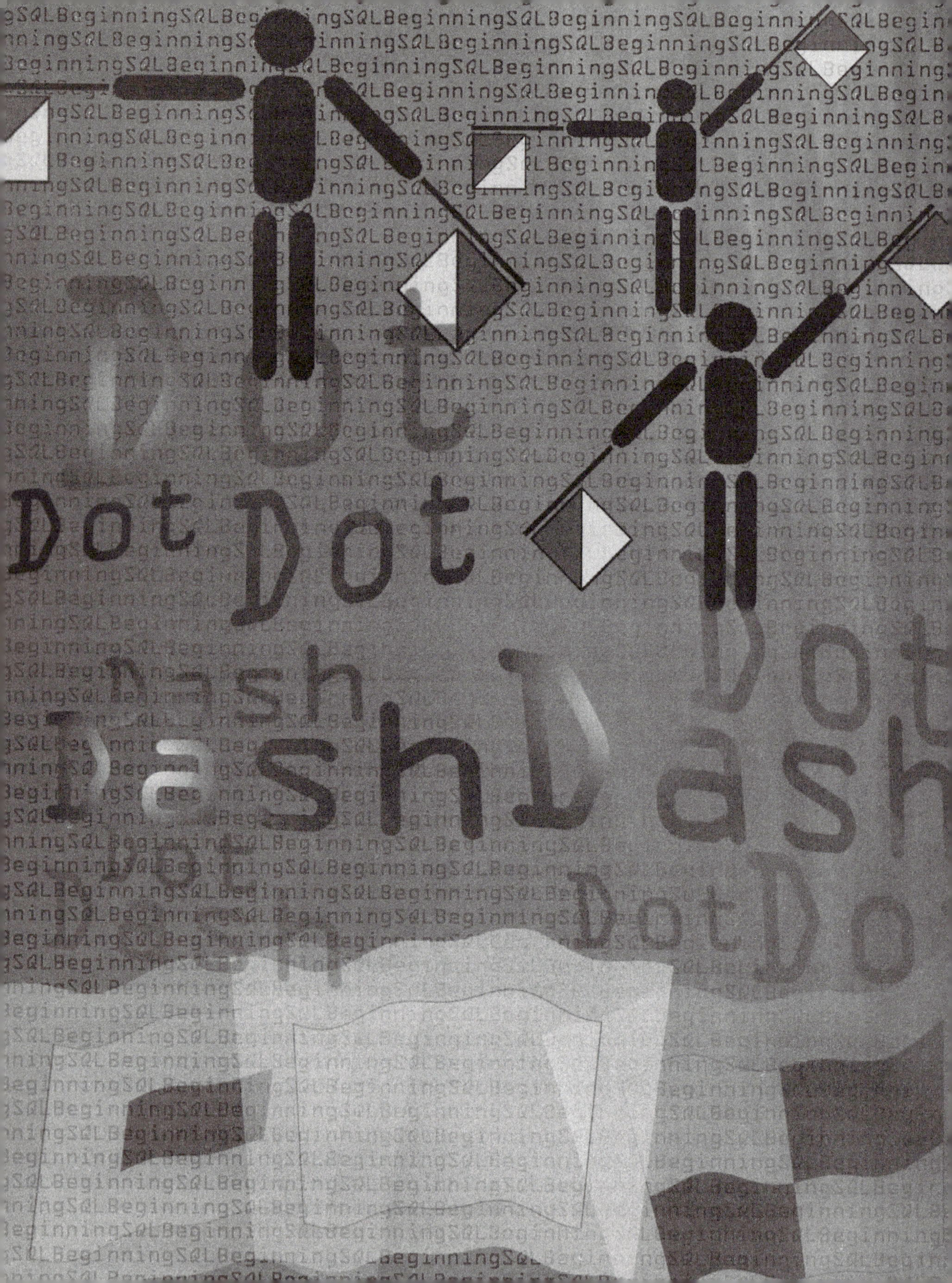

SQL Syntax and SELECT

The main purpose of a database is to store information in such a way that relevant information may be retrieved easily. Storing information about customers, contacts, or orders in one place is very handy, but only if there is a systematic way to retrieve this information. We also need to be able to take advantage of relationships that may exist between different types of data (for instance, the relations between customers and orders, students and classes, authors and books).

As we already know, relational databases expose the SQL, which enables us to work with our data in these ways. It provides ways of retrieving, modifying, and performing complex calculations on our data. In this chapter we will look at ways to get our data out of our database using SQL.

> It is very important to note that the SQL language is a standard that database providers have agreed to and support. Though the various vendors level of support varies according to how far they have implemented the standard, and enhanced it, the SQL that we look at here will work in any ANSI SQL-compliant database such as SQL Server, Access, Oracle, DB2, and MySQL.

In this chapter we will:

- ❑ Introduce ourselves to the basic principles of SQL

- ❑ Look at the basic syntax of SQL, and the most fundamental SQL statement, the SELECT statement

- ❑ Look in some depth at the WHERE clause and several of the logical operators that can be used with this to effectively filter data retrieved by the SELECT statement

- ❑ Look at the meaning and usage of NULL

- ❑ Look at how we can order our information with the ORDER BY function

The General Syntax of SQL

SQL is an easy language to learn since it contains a limited number of **keywords**, which are very English-like in their makeup. We will be looking at the fundamental SQL keywords throughout Chapters 4 and 5.

> **Keywords – Special words or phrases that are reserved by a language. Also known as "Reserved Words".**

SQL, by default, is not case sensitive, although some databases can be configured to be so. *Please check with your DBA or through your database configurations to see if the DBMS has been set for case sensitivity.*

The following queries are both treated in exactly the same way:

```
select * from Authors
```

```
SELECT * FROM Authors
```

> **Note that SQL statements in Oracle and MySQL's 'Command Prompt' interface must end with a semicolon as follows:**
>
> **SELECT * FROM Authors;**
>
> **MySQL's 'Admin' interface does not require the semicolon.**

Throughout this book, the keywords for SQL will be capitalized in examples and source code. The names of fields and tables will use initial capital letters throughout our source code as well. While this is not necessary, it is good programming practice since it provides a convenient way of highlighting keywords, thus making our queries more readable.

Spaces

SQL is not sensitive to spaces or whitespace in general, for eaxample, statements can span multiple rows and can be formatted with whitespace. When the statement is executed, SQL will ignore the extra whitespace in the command. For instance, the two SQL statements listed here are equivalent:

```
SELECT * FROM Jobs
```

```
SELECT
   *
FROM
Jobs
```

> **Whitespace – extra spaces, return characters and tab characters used for formatting purposes. Using whitespace makes code much more readable and clear.**

Since SQL ignores extra whitespace, we can use tabs, return characters, and spaces to make our statements much more readable. A SQL statement that uses several tables at once can easily become half a page long, so formatting becomes very important, especially if other people will be modifying or looking at our code.

Quotations and Special Characters

Text and dates in SQL Server, are enclosed in single quotation marks, although double quotation marks may also be used. The date 3/27/2000 can be written as "3/27/2000" or '3/27/2000'. SQL Server will then properly interpret the delimiters to the proper format. Depending on how the data is used, SQL Server will either treat this as a date or as a string. In order to be consistent in SQL, we should stick with one delimiter. Throughout the book we will use single quotes for all strings and dates.

> **Different providers will implement their own rules for strings and dates. Access, for example, uses double quotes for strings and pound signs (#) for dates. Check with your DBMS to verify the correct delimiters for strings and dates.**

Double quotations or brackets can be used when accessing tables or fields that have reserved words (words that have a particular function within SQL), contain special characters (characters that have a specific function within SQL), or contain spaces. Generally quotation marks are used, but SQL Server accepts brackets as well. As we're using a version of SQL Server (that comes on the CD with this book), we will be using brackets in our examples, but if you are using a different vendor product, please use double quotations for the SQL code examples here. For example, the following SQL statements are equivalent. Don't worry about what this statement actually does at the moment; we will soon be investigating this:

```
SELECT
  [Insert],
  [Update]
FROM
  [Employee Table]
```

```
SELECT
  "Insert",
  "Update"
FROM
  "Employee Table"
```

The double dash (--) is used for comments (descriptions of tables and fields that you can store in your queries). Documentation is very important in writing SQL queries since they can become very large and complex. The double dash must be used on each comment line to denote the text as a comment.

If you are writing a lot of comments or adding headers to your queries, then it is possible to use the block comment syntax of /* */. This will denote all of the text within the delimiters as comments, regardless of the number of lines. This is a quick way to comment blocks of statements or for headers (general information about the SQL code).

Both of the following are equivalent:

```
/*
Filename: GetEmployees.sql
 Author: Brian Matsik (OOCS)
 Date: 3/15/2000
 Purpose: This query returns all of the employees from
   the employees table.
*/
```

```
-- Filename: GetEmployees.sql
-- Author: Brian Matsik (OOCS)
--  Date: 3/15/2000
-- Purpose: This query returns all of the employees from
--   the employees table.
```

Once again, personal preference may dictate which comment delimiter to use. One thing to remember is that the block comments (/* */) may be used within a line of code to comment out pieces of a line, whereas the line comment (--) comments everything from the comment character to the end of the line.

Introducing SELECT

Let's take a look at the workhorse of all SQL queries, the SELECT statement.

The Basic Syntax

The SELECT statement is the most important keyword used in SQL statements. A SELECT statement is necessary in order to tell the database what data to return. The most basic SQL statement that we can write contains only two elements:

```
SELECT [field]
FROM [table]
```

The SELECT portion of the statement includes a list of fields that we would like to display. If we want to retrieve data from more than one field, then each field in the list must be separated by a comma, thus:

```
SELECT [field], [field2], [fieldn]
FROM [table]
```

Once we have defined the field list, we must provide the name of the table or tables that contain the fields. The table name follows the FROM clause.

There is a special field selector that you can use if you want **all of the fields in a table**: the * character. This will return every field in the order that they are defined within the structure of the table. It is fine to use this character for testing, but this should be avoided in a production environment since the use of the * is cumbersome and inefficient.

When we use the * the query processor must open the table and determine what the field list is before executing the statement. The other reason why we should avoid the * is that it makes reading a query much more difficult, since we would not typically know which fields are actually being returned, or their names. As we will see in later chapters, we must know the field names in order to calculate, sort, or filter information from your table.

Try it Out – Running a Simple Query

In order to execute a SQL statement, we must first open an appropriate interface. For SQL Server, this is called Query Analyzer, but if you are using another type of database, you will use a different interface that fits your particular DBMS.

1. Launch Query Analyzer by going to Start | Programs | Microsoft SQL Server | Query Analyzer.

2. Select the appropriate database from the drop-down list. In our case, we will be using the Northwind database:

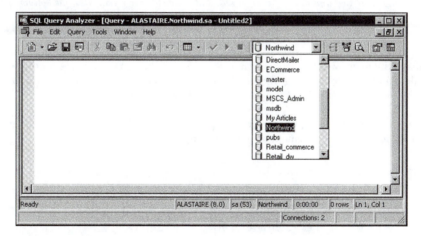

3. Enter the following SELECT statement in the query editor: the top textbox within the window. In this case we will be executing a SQL statement to return the employee names from the employee table:

```
SELECT FirstName, LastName
FROM Employees
```

4. Execute the statement by pressing the *F5* key or pressing the execute query button (the button showing the green triangular arrow). You should then see the following result:

If this is the first time that you have used Query Analyzer then there are a few things that you may have noticed. First, Query Analyzer uses color to delimit certain words or items. Reserved words are in blue or gray, strings and dates appear in red, and comments are green. Also, the bottom of the screen will show the results in a grid format (default) or as a plain text by pressing Ctrl+T. You can change back to the grid display by pressing Ctrl+D.

The results of the query will be displayed in the bottom window. You may see a grid or a text result window, depending on your configuration. To change between the grid and text window, right click in the edit window and select either Results in Grid or Results in Text.

Remember that if you are using Oracle or MySQL's Command Prompt interface, you must include a semicolon at the end of the statement as in this example:

```
SELECT Firstname, LastName
FROM Employees;
```

How it Works

Remember that our SQL statements can be translated back into normal requests. What have we asked SQL to do? "Show me the first and last names of all of the people". The SQL statement literally reads "Show me the first and last name of all of the data in the `People` table". Learning how to read a SQL statement and translate from an English language request to SQL statement will be very valuable later when you see items such as the following:

"Show me the top five salespeople for the southeast region in the last quarter. Let me see the results by individual state as well as a grand total.

The above statement will be a type of request that you will be able to translate by the end of this book. Throughout this chapter the request will be included with the query. This should help us in analyzing the SQL that we are adding and avoid some of the confusion about what we are trying to do with SQL.

> **Select only the data that is needed: queries will run faster!**

Sometimes, rather than receiving the results we might expect from a query, we might encounter an error message. With a bit of close attention, and double-checking of syntax, this can usually be quickly resolved. Have a look at the following table to see how mistakes are expressed in error messages:

Common Errors

Problem	Sample Message
Incorrect field name (misspelling, does not exist, etc.)	Server: Msg 207, Level 16, State 3, Line 1 Invalid column name 'Name'.
Incorrect table name	Server: Msg 208, Level 16, State 1, Line 1 Invalid object name 'Employee'.

Defining Fields

There may be many times that we will want to rename the fields so they make more sense for the developers using our databases, or when doing calculations and string manipulation in our queries, as we shall see. Other times we may want to rename the field to make the output more readable; to provide a common field name independent of the underlying table structure.

Suppose we had a field name `emp_Name_First` that we want to call `FirstName`. This would be an example of renaming the fields within a query.

SQL has a keyword, `AS`, for just this purpose. *Some databases (such as Oracle) do not require the use of AS and simply need a space between the field and the alias name.* We can use `AS` to rename fields that may not be clear to the consumers or to allow us to name fields that would not have a name (for instance a field constructed to contain the results of a calculation is not given a name). Instead of referring to `CustomerName` and `ContactName` in our queries, suppose that we want to call them `Customer` and `Contact` instead.

The original query – without renaming the fields – would simply be:

```
SELECT CompanyName, Contact Name
FROM Customers
```

and would return the following results:

But if we rewrite the query to rename the fields, then we use the AS operator to perform the rename:

```
SELECT CompanyName AS Company,
ContactName AS Contact
FROM Customers
```

Note that the field names have now changed in the output window:

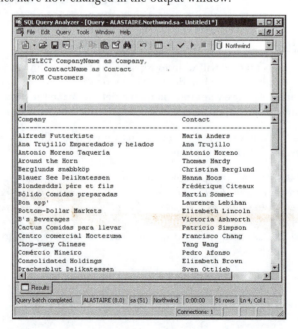

Notice that the resultset is now different. We have changed the names of the fields so that they are more suitable for reading. However, we haven't changed the actual field names, as stored in the database. For this reason, this technique is known as **aliasing**. The screenshot below shows how MySQL presents the results from this query:

We can also alias tables in the same fashion as with fields. Table aliasing will be handy when we start dealing with multiple tables in our SQL statements. Have a look at Chapter 8 for queries dealing with multiple tables.

> **Aliasing – Referencing an item (field or table) with a different name.**

How it Works

When we use the AS operator, we instruct the query that the field from which data is to be retrieved should be given another name once the query is complete and the resultset is passed back from the query. The calling application can now use the alias rather than the name of the underlying field.

The AS operator is very useful when we output fields based on a conditional statement, or when calculating the value of a field. *We'll begin looking at conditional statements in the next section, and we'll look closer at calculating fields later on in the chapter.* In these cases, the returned fields have no name since the value is calculated rather than pulled directly from a named field, and you need to give the 'result' a new field name. This is completed with the AS operator as well.

Renaming fields using the AS operator can assist us in writing cleaner queries, and can help to clear up any confusion over fields that look similar or have unfriendly naming conventions. We can also alias fields that contain spaces by using brackets ([ ]) or single quotes (' ') to surround the name with the space. In Oracle we must use double quotes (" ") to contain spaces. We could alias FirstName as [First Name] or 'First Name', or "First Name" in Oracle, and our query would display the field name with a space included.

> **Using field and table names with spaces is possible in some databases, but it is not recommended since some database interfaces may have difficulty dealing with spaces in the names. As a general rule, use long names, but with mixed case as one word. For instance, FirstName is preferred over "First Name" as is FederalTaxRate over "Federal Tax Rate".**

Filtering Data

We now know how to query a table for records using the SELECT statement. You may have noticed that, to this point, whenever we have run a query, we have returned all of the records in the table. If the table is small, say thirty records, then this may not be a big problem. But what if the table contains a million records? Running a query against such a table will take time and monopolize resources. We will probably still need some way to filter for the specific information that we want.

SQL provides a way for us to filter our data to produce smaller result sets. The WHERE clause is used in a SQL statement to specify that we want all of the records that fit specific criteria.

Syntactically, the WHERE clause comes after the FROM clause:

```
SELECT
  Field1, Field2, Field3, Fieldn
FROM
  Table
WHERE
  Condition
```

The condition statement, known as the search criteria, in the WHERE clause can include any logical operator, string comparison, or other type of criteria that we will look at in later chapters.

A very simple example of using a WHERE clause here where we want a list of all the employees that live in Washington.

> *The Customer table has a field called* Region. *This field is used for state information that only US and Canada customers use.*

```
SELECT
  EmployeeID,
  LastName,
  FirstName
FROM
  Employees
WHERE
  Region = 'WA'
```

This would produce the following result set of Washington employees:

```
EmployeeID   LastName               FirstName
-----------  --------------------   ----------
1            Davolio                Nancy
2            Fuller                 Andrew
3            Leverling              Janet
4            Peacock                Margaret
8            Callahan               Laura

(5 row(s) affected)
```

There are several comparison operators that you can use in search criteria. Below is a list of valid operators that we can use in the WHERE clause of a SQL statement:

Operator	Purpose	Example
=	Equality	NAME = 'SMITH'
<>	Inequality	STATE <> 'CA'
<	Less than	SALARY < 20000
>	Greater than	AGE > 21
>=	Greater than or equal to	Price >= 2.00
<=	Less than or equal to	Quantity <= 100
IS NULL	Tests for an empty value (NULL values*)	FaxNumber IS NULL
BETWEEN	Searches between values	ID BETWEEN 2 AND 10

NULL is used to describe a value which is unknown, as in the gender of an un-born baby. We'll discuss this operator further a little later in the chapter.

Let's look at a practical example of using the WHERE clause. Suppose we have been asked to find the first and last name of everyone in the Employee table who was hired after 1/1/1994.

We already know how to construct the SQL statement to get the names of everyone:

```
SELECT FirstName, LastName, HireDate
FROM Employees
```

Now, let's add the WHERE clause to meet our hire date criteria. In order for this query to work properly we need to be sure that we use the proper operator. Since we are looking for everyone hired after 1/1/1994 we will use the greater than operator (>):

```
SELECT FirstName, LastName, HireDate
FROM Employees
WHERE HireDate > '1/1/1994'
```

107

Note that we need to enclose the date in single quotes. If we were working in another database such as Microsoft Access we might need to use other delimiters. Access, for instance, uses the pound symbol (#) for enclosing dates. Check with your individual provider to determine which delimiters you should use. If you're working in Oracle, this date format will not work. The single quotes are fine, but you will have to write `'1-JAN-1994'` as in the following example, as this is how Oracle recognizes dates:

```
SELECT FirstName, LastName, HireDate
FROM Employees
WHERE HireDate > '1-JAN-1994';
```

When we run this query, we will have fewer records returned than are actually in the table:

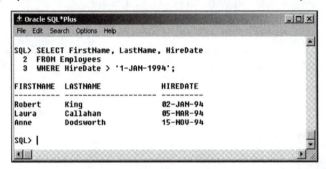

> **Remember that we need to enclose dates in single quotation marks in SQL Server and in the pounds (#) in Microsoft Access.**

Try It Out – Using the WHERE Clause

Suppose we have been asked to produce a report of the customer ID and name of all customers from the state of Washington.

1. We know that we need the `Customers` table as the basis for our query. We also know that we need the ID and name fields (`CustomerID` and `CompanyName`). With this information we can write the base query:

```
SELECT CustomerID, CompanyName
FROM Customers
```

This query returns all of the customers in the table.

2. Now, we want to filter our data so that we only display the Washington customers. We will need to filter on the `Region` field in the database for all values of `'WA'`. Since we are looking for an exact match, we should use the equals operator in our `WHERE` clause. With this information, we can now finish our query:

```
SELECT CustomerID, CompanyName
FROM Customers
WHERE Region = 'WA'
```

When we execute this query we get our filtered result set:

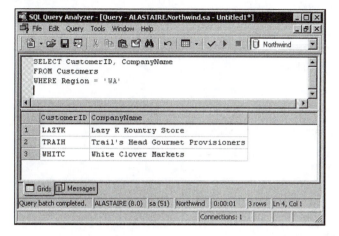

How it Works

When we use the WHERE clause in a query, we instruct SQL to filter the records based on the criteria in the WHERE clause. In our example, we are telling the query to filter for all of the records where the Region field contains only the string 'WA'. All other rows will be ignored. Each condition in a WHERE clause acts as a filter on the records from a field. WHERE clauses can be as complex as we need them to be, and we will be exploring their use throughout the book.

Following are some errors and error messages you may come across when constructing some of these statements:

Common Errors

Problem	Sample Message
Incorrect field name	Server: Msg 207, Level 16, State 3, Line 1 Invalid column name 'CompnayName'.
Criteria do not return any data	No error message
Use of the wrong delimiters; for instance, do not enclose strings and dates in single quotes	Server: Msg 207, Level 16, State 3, Line 1 Invalid column name 'WA'.

NULL Values

A NULL value in SQL represents an unknown entity. This is significantly different from an empty value. An empty value tells us that we **know** that there is no data, but a NULL value means that we **don't know** what value should be in the field, thus NULL is considered to be an unknown value. NULL values are treated as special items in SQL. We can see this in the following simple comparison between NULL and empty in SQL Server.

First, let's test to see if an empty value equals another empty value:

```
IF '' = ''
  PRINT 'TRUE'
ELSE
  PRINT 'FALSE'
```

The result in query analyzer is:

```
TRUE
```

Now, if we do the same test with NULL values:

```
IF NULL = NULL
  PRINT 'TRUE'
ELSE
  PRINT 'FALSE'
```

We get in the result window:

```
FALSE
```

So while an empty value is the same as another empty value, a NULL is not the same as another NULL value, because NULL means 'unknown value'; two unknown values will not necessarily be the same! Keep this definition in mind during all of the SQL queries that we write. NULL values are special and are treated differently from other values. The WHERE clause has a special condition just for NULL values: IS NULL. Let's try using the IS NULL operator with the WHERE clause.

Try it Out – Working with NULL Values

We would like to find a list of all of our customers that are not located in the US and Canada.

1. Remember the Region field that holds state information for only US and Canada customers? Well in the Northwind database, all other international customers have a NULL value in this field. Using this as the basis of our query, we know that we want the company name from the Customers table filtered where the Region field is NULL as this would output the names of customers outside the US and Canada.

2. Enter the following SQL statement:

```
SELECT CompanyName
FROM Customers
WHERE Region IS NULL
```

This will return the following results:

The following screenshot shows the resultset in MySQL:

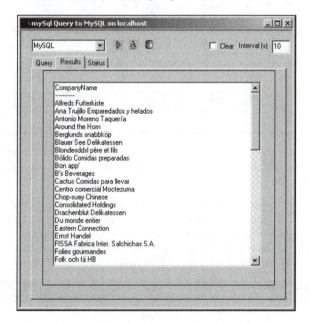

How it Works

When looking for NULL values, we must use the IS keyword. As our second example, above, showed, NULL does not equal anything, including other NULLs. We cannot run a calculation against a NULL, nor can we perform standard comparisons. This is the only context in which we will encounter the IS operator, since its only purpose is to look for NULL values.

We have seen how the NULL operator is a special type. We can use the IS NULL operator to test for NULL values, but you cannot use the = operator on NULL fields.

Calculating in WHERE Clauses

The search criteria in a WHERE clause may contain calculations on fields. For example, we can find all of the products that we have more than $3000 of in inventory with this statement:

```
SELECT ProductName, UnitsInStock * UnitPrice
FROM Products
WHERE UnitsInStock * UnitPrice > 3000
```

This results in only a few records:

SQL Server has a set of routines to handle date calculations such as the number of days between dates and other important functions. These will be covered in detail in Chapter 11, but the concepts here apply to any type of field.

Using the WHERE clause to filter calculated values will provide a lot of power to our queries. One of the more powerful aspects of SQL is its ability to calculate values either on a row-by-row basis or on an entire table. For example, we could use the WHERE clause to filter each customer order or we could filter based on the average customer order (after requesting a table-wide calculation to find the average customer order). We will look at calculating values in more detail in later sections.

Try it Out – Filtering Based on Calculated Values

We would like to know the orders where a customer bought more than $10,000 worth of an individual item.

1. The details for the order are stored in the Order Details table. Notice that there is a space in the name of the table. When we refer to this, we will need to use square brackets to enclose the table name or we will get an error. Remember to use quotation marks if you are using a different vendor product.

2. Note that we can calculate the total amount of money spent by a customer on a single order by simply multiplying the `Quantity` and the `UnitPrice` fields.

3. We can therefore construct a query that involves the multiplication of two columns where the result of this multiplication is larger that $10,000. Construct and enter the following query:

```
SELECT OrderID, UnitPrice * Quantity
FROM [Order Details]
WHERE UnitPrice * Quantity > 10000
```

As you can see in the result set we get, the column containing the calculated values has no name:

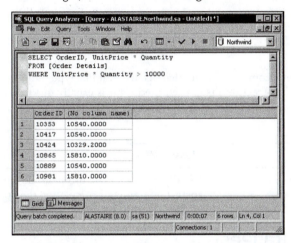

If we wanted to give the column a name, we could simply use the `AS` operator, in the following way:

```
SELECT OrderID, UnitPrice * Quantity AS LineItemTotal
FROM [Order Details]
WHERE UnitPrice * Quantity > 10000
```

We now have a column name for our results column. Note that the example below is taken from Oracle's SQL+ interface and that therefore, `OrderDetails` appears as one word rather than [`Order Details`], as Oracle does not accept brackets:

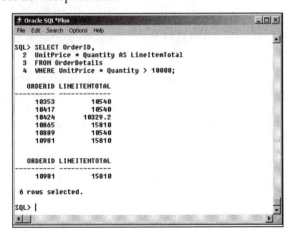

113

How it Works

When this query executes, a calculation is performed on each row, generating the total for each line item. Once the new row is generated, then it is evaluated to see if it's greater than 10,000. If it is, then it is added to the result set.

Remember that these calculations are performed on each row of data. We should exercise caution when using very complex calculations as they can run very slowly if there is a large amount of data. If we want to run the same calculations on data that will not change often (such as purchase data) then it may be to our advantage to create an additional table to hold these calculated values. We will look at how to create tables in Chapter 6.

Let's look at another table of examples, this time of filtering based on calculated values, and how such requests translate into SQL.

Common Errors

There is really only one common "error" that occurs with this type of query. More often than not, the problem will be that incorrect results are returned. This is usually due to a logic error or some calculation error. Double check your logic within the statement to be sure that you are actually filtering on the correct data.

Error	Message/Reason
Incorrect result set	Usually due to a logic problem. Be sure that you are using the correct operators or calculating the correct fields.

Working with Ranges

The BETWEEN operator allows us to search for a **range** of values in a WHERE clause. It provides a means of restricting the scope of the WHERE clause. For instance, we could use the BETWEEN operator to look for all part numbers between the values of 100 and 200.

The syntax for the BETWEEN operator is as follows:

```
BETWEEN <Start Value> AND <End Value>
```

> **The start and end values in a BETWEEN statement are inclusive.**

We can use the BETWEEN operator to find information such as date ranges or string ranges. The AND part of the BETWEEN statement is required since the BETWEEN statement requires the start **and** end of the range for the statement. For instance, if we would like to know all of the orders placed on or after 7/1/1996 and on or before 7/15/1996, then we could write the following query:

```
SELECT OrderID, OrderDate
FROM Orders
WHERE OrderDate BETWEEN '7/1/1996' AND '7/15/1996'
```

This would result in nine rows of data:

Again, remember that if you're using Oracle, you must write the dates as `1-JULY-1996` and `15-JULY-1996` as Oracle will not accept the American standard format.

Now, the `BETWEEN` operator is really nothing special. We could write our query another way to achieve the same results. We could simply use our standard `>=` and `<=` operators in the following way:

```
SELECT OrderID, OrderDate
FROM Orders
WHERE OrderDate >= '7/1/1996' AND
OrderDate <= '7/15/1996'
```

This is a good example of where the SQL language provides many ways to get to the same data. We will be seeing more examples of this as we progress.

Adding Logical Operators to WHERE Clauses

There are several **logical operators** in SQL. The operators are used to perform logical comparisons between groups of search conditions. If you have never worked in a programming language before then much of this may be new to you.

Boolean logic is a system of ascertaining the truth or falsity of sets of sentences, given certain relationships between those sentences. The main logical operators for Boolean statements are AND, OR, and NOT. In the context of programming languages, Boolean logic can be confusing at first glance, since it is not always obvious how we should apply the various logical operators – specifically, it is not always obvious what internal order of operations within a statement should have.

We will be looking at ways to make queries minimally complicated and easy to read.

SQL supports the following logical operators:

Operator	Result
ALL	If all of the statements evaluate to TRUE, then the statement is TRUE.
AND	If all of the expressions evaluate to TRUE then the entire expression is TRUE. If one of the expressions is FALSE then the entire expression is FALSE regardless of any other evaluation.
ANY	If any expression is TRUE then the entire expression is TRUE.
EXISTS	If a subquery that is the target of the EXISTS statement contains any rows then this evaluates to TRUE (this operator is covered in Chapter 5).
IN	If the value is in the given list of values then the expression evaluates to TRUE (this operator is covered in Chapter 5).
LIKE	If the pattern matches a value then the expression is TRUE. For instance, LIKE Sm% would find Smith, Smalls, and Smythe; all words beginning with Sm.
NOT	If the inverse is TRUE then the expression evaluates to TRUE. If x = 1 then NOT X = 2 would be TRUE.
OR	If any of the expressions evaluate to TRUE, then the entire expression evaluates to TRUE.
SOME	If some from a set of comparisons evaluate to TRUE, then the entire expression evaluates to TRUE.

Let's take a look at how such operators affect the truth of conjunctions of sentences: for this we will look at the President of the United States and the British Prime Minister – at the time of writing, these are George W Bush and Tony Blair, respectively.

```
George Bush IS President AND Tony Blair IS Prime Minister - True

Al Gore IS President AND Tony Blair IS Prime Minister - False

Al Gore IS President OR Tony Blair IS Prime Minister - True

Al Gore NOT President and Tony Blair IS Prime Minister - True
```

Ordering can be an issue when using multiple statements. Take, for example, the case where we want to know parts that are made by BobCo or JamesInc that have a weight of less than 10 pounds. We could write the statement in the following way:

```
WHERE
  Manufacturer = 'BobCo'
  OR Manufacturer = 'JamesInc'
  AND Weight < 10
```

This may appear to be correct, but the order of evaluation, or **precedence**, in SQL could catch us out here. The way that SQL evaluates operators is in the following order, that is it evaluates those functions in step one before those in step two, and so on:

1. + (Positive), – (Negative), ~ (Bitwise NOT)

2. *(Multiply), / (Division), % (Modulo)

3. + (Add), + (Concatenate), – (Subtract)

4. =, >, <, >=, <=, <>, !=, !>, !< (Comparison operators)

5. ^ (Bitwise Exlusive OR), & (Bitwise AND), | (Bitwise OR)

6. NOT

7. AND

8. ALL, ANY, BETWEEN, IN, LIKE, OR, SOME

9. = (Assignment)

This list may be a bit confusing, but here is the way that it works. We work from left to right on the statement. It helps at this point to dust off the cobwebs and remember the old algebra. If we have the following:

$(3 * 2 + 6 / 2) <= (4 / 2 + 6 * 1)$

We would evaluate using the above rules. Order number 2 would be first (multiplication and division):

$(6 + 3) <= (2 + 6)$

We would then use order number 3 to add and subtract:

$9 <= 8$

Finally, order 4 would be used to perform the logical evaluation. This would obviously evaluate to FALSE since 9 is not less than or equal to 8.

It is the same with SQL statements. Just follow the order of operations above from left to right and this is how SQL will evaluate a function.

So, we can see that the AND operator gets evaluated before the OR operator. Therefore, our WHERE clause is actually saying that we are looking for parts that weigh less than 10 pounds that are made by JamesInc and all parts made by BobCo. We could rewire the order to correct this, but this would be tedious and error prone. Instead, we can use an algebraic grouping. This is not to be confused with the SQL GROUPING function, which we will look at primarily in Chapter 13. 'Grouping' here refers purely to an algebraic grouping of data which will make our above SQL statement run as we would like. Algebraic grouping in SQL allows us to use parentheses to tell SQL how to evaluate a series of operators. We could rewrite the WHERE clause to read:

```
WHERE
  (Manufacturer = 'BobCo'
  OR Manufacturer = 'JamesInc')
  AND (Weight < 10)
```

This ensures that the conditions *within* parentheses are evaluated independently of the main condition. Thus, the weight condition is applied to parts made by both `BobCo` and `JamesInc`.

Try It Out – Using Multiple Filters

We would like to find all of the customers in either Washington or Oregon.

1. We have seen the query to find all of the Washington customers:

```
SELECT CustomerID, CompanyName
FROM Customers
WHERE Region = 'WA'
```

2. What we need to do is add the criterion to also find the `Oregon` customers. We can use the OR logical operator to add the additional filter, like this:

```
SELECT CustomerID, CompanyName
FROM Customers
WHERE Region = 'WA'
OR Region = 'OR'
```

As you can see, this gets us the correct list of customers:

How it Works

When applying multiple WHERE clauses, SQL must evaluate each row based on the criteria. In our example, we were looking for rows of data that had a region of 'WA' or a region of 'OR'. All other fields will fail the search criteria and will not be displayed.

We do not have to use the same fields for the filter. Our filter can contain multiple criteria, such as customers that spent more than $10,000 on a single line item or had a discount of more than 20%:

```
SELECT OrderID
    UnitPrice * Quantity as LineItemPrice,
    Discount
FROM [Order Details]
WHERE UnitPrice * Quantity >= $10000
    OR Discount > 0.20
```

This will result in a mixed set of records:

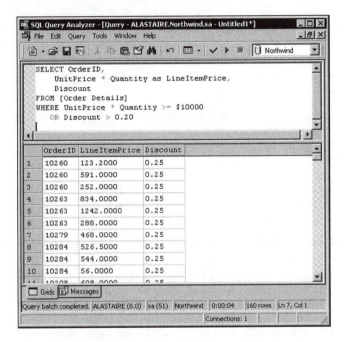

This list includes both rows where the `LineItemPrice` is more than $10,000 and where the discount was better than 20%.

It is important to note here, that if you're working with MySQL, aliases must be declared at the first point at which the relevant field is mentioned. Therefore, the above statement must be modified for MySQL, thus:

```
SELECT OrderID AS LineItemPrice,
    UnitPrice * Quantity as Discount
FROM Order Details
WHERE UnitPrice * Quantity >= 10000
    OR Discount > 0.20
```

Note also that the $ sign is missing. Both MySQL and Oracle cannot process the dollar sign, so simply leave it out when working with these products.

Our queries will get much more complicated as we add groupings to our `WHERE` clause, or multiple operators such as `AND` and `OR` in the same criteria.

Remember that we cannot use <field> = NULL because the NULL operator requires the use of the IS keyword. Using <field> = NULL will result in no records being returned, since nothing equals NULL, not even another NULL.

Following are some errors you may encounter when executing statements similar to those above:

Common Errors

Problem	Error Message/Reason
Incorrect records returned	Check the logic of the WHERE clause. Incorrectly grouping items or using the wrong logical operators will change the interpretation of the statement.
Use of the = when searching for NULL values	Use the IS keyword when dealing with NULL records.
Incorrect delimiters	Dates and strings (in SQL Server) should be in single quotes.

Using LIKE

So far we have learned how to find exact matches with SQL. However, there are likely to be many times that we may need to search for partial strings. Maybe we want to find everyone that has a first name starting with C or a book with "computer" in the title. SQL provides a LIKE operator for just this type of query.

> The **LIKE** operator can only be used on fields that have one of the string types set as their data type. **LIKE** cannot be used on dates or numbers.

LIKE is used when searching for inexact string matches in a table. It is used within the WHERE clause, and uses the following format:

```
WHERE
    field LIKE expression
```

The field can be any field in a table, and the expression is the type of comparison being used. The most common comparison operator is the percent symbol (%), or the asterisk (*) in Access. This is the wildcard character used for pattern matching within the LIKE operator. For example, we may want to find everyone with a first name that begins with C, so we would use the wildcard operator in the following way:

```
WHERE
    FirstName LIKE 'C%'
```

This will return everyone with a name starting with C. We can also use the wildcard at the beginning of a clause. If we were looking for a street address that includes 'Ave.', we could write our WHERE clause as follows:

```
WHERE
    Address LIKE '%Ave.'
```

We can go one step further and look for substrings in a field. If we have a jobs table that has a `JobDescription` field, then we can use the wildcard to search for the string 'SQL' anywhere in the text:

```
WHERE
   JobDescription LIKE '%SQL%'
```

The `LIKE` operator will prove to be very useful as we write more complex SQL statements, since it enables us to find partial matches without performing any complicated string manipulation. We should keep in mind that the `LIKE` operator is not the most efficient SQL command, and will degrade overall performance. If we know the exact string that we are looking for in a field, then we should use the = operator instead of `LIKE`. Adding an index on a field that is often searched using the `LIKE` operator may increase the system performance.

In addition to the `%` wildcard, there are two other important wildcards used with the `LIKE` operator:

❑   the underscore (_)

❑   square brackets ([])

Whereas the `%` wildcard is used to find a string with any number of characters before and/or after the specified string, the underscore is used to limit the search to a single leading or trailing character. A search of '%mith' would return `Smith` and `Johnsmith`. Changing our expression to '_mith' would limit the return values to just `Smith`, since we are now looking for any **single** character followed by the string 'mith'.

We can combine the operators to further refine searches. For instance, if we were looking for last names that started in a similar way to Smith, but don't care about the length, then we could use both the _ and the % to find the appropriate records:

```
WHERE
   LastName LIKE '_mith%'
```

This would return names such as Smith and Smithfield.

Additionally, we can use the brackets ([]) to further limit ranges of characters. With the brackets, we can specify particular characters that must appear in a particular position. For instance, if we were looking for words like night, light, and fight, but we only want to return night and light, then we need to modify our criteria since:

```
WHERE
   Word LIKE '_ight'
```

will return 'fight' as well as 'night' and 'light'. We want to limit our search to words that start only with n or l, so we specify this by putting these characters within brackets, in the appropriate place:

```
WHERE
   Word LIKE '[nl]ight'
```

This search criteria will only look for words that end in 'ight' and begin with an n or an l. Keep in mind that the brackets may only contain single characters, so we cannot use them for lists of substrings. This is the biggest limitation to the bracket wildcard, but there are still a large number of possibilities for expression searching in strings.

121

Try It Out – Using LIKE

Suppose we wanted to find all of the products where the product name starts with 'Chef'.

1. We start with our base SELECT statement to return the records from the Product table:

```
SELECT ProductName
FROM Products
```

2. We now need to add the filter to find the products that start with Chef:

```
SELECT ProductName
FROM Products
WHERE ProductName LIKE 'Chef%'
```

And we get the information we wanted:

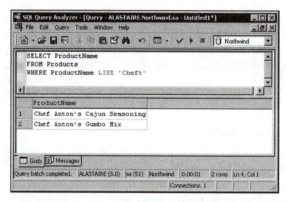

The results in MySQL look like this:

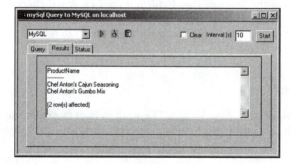

This query uses the % operator and the LIKE statement to check the first four letters of each product name. When we run this query, we get two records.

How it Works

The percent operator is a wildcard that says "any number of characters." Had we asked for any product name with 'Chef' anywhere in the string, we could have used %chef%. Likewise, we could look for words ending in chef by using %chef.

As with our other examples, this is performed on a row-by-row basis. The use of this operator is also inefficient in large tables, due to the fact that string comparisons take a bit of time. If we need to do this type of search on a large table, then we should see if there are ways to filter the records down a bit before searching the string.

Sorting the Records

At this point we can retrieve records from a table and filter the records from the table. We will be looking at an additional SQL keyword in this section that is designed to sort the records returned by our query. The ORDER BY clause is designed to sort data and, as we will see, is a very flexible keyword.

The ORDER BY clause is typically the last clause in a SQL statement. It has a special syntax, since this clause, like the SELECT statement, can operate on multiple fields. It also allows fields to be sorted in both ascending and descending order:

```
ORDER BY field1 [ASC/DESC], field2 [ASC/DESC], …, fieldn [ASC/DESC]
```

The optional ASC/DESC parameter on each field specifies the sort order of the specific column. ASC sorts the column in ascending order (smallest to largest) and DESC sorts in descending order (largest to smallest). If we do not specify a sort order in our ORDER BY clause, then ascending will be used as a default. The columns will be sorted in the order specified in the ORDER BY clause even if the SELECT list is in a different order. If you have NULL values then they will be interpreted as the lowest values.

If we do not specify an ORDER BY clause, then the query will display in the table order.

Try It Out – Ordering Records

Sort the employee table by the employee last name, then the first name.

1. We know we need to return the EmployeeID, FirstName, and LastName fields from the employee table, which would do with a query like this:

```
SELECT EmployeeID, LastName, FirstName
FROM Employees
```

However, this results in an unsorted result set:

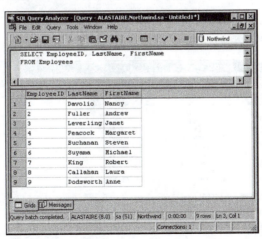

*Strictly speaking we don't need to return the Employee ID, but it is always good practice to do so because the employee ID number is a unique way of identifying each record. With this in our possession, we can use the results of our statement in much more diverse ways (for example, we could find out exactly when Robert King joined the company by searching on his Employee ID number rather than his name. This will ensure we reference the records of the particular Robert King we're interested in, and not another Robert King who could join the company at any moment). This unique identifier is called a **primary key**, and we will discuss the importance of these further in Chapter 7. For now, suffice to say this is just a good habit to get into.*

2. Now, add the ORDER BY clause to sort the columns. Since we want to sort multiple columns, we need to separate the list with commas. By default, the sort order will be ascending, so we do not need to explicitly state the order:

```
SELECT EmployeeID, LastName, FirstName
FROM Employees
ORDER BY LastName, FirstName
```

Now the result set displays the records in the properly sorted order:

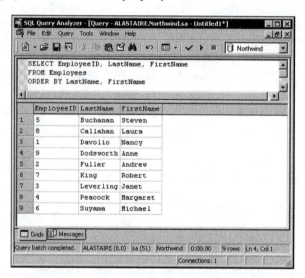

The result set in Oracle looks like this:

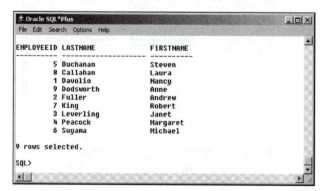

How it Works

ORDER BY is processed after the results have been built, and sorts your results into ascending or descending order, depending on what you specify. By providing a comma separated list we are applying multiple sorts to one result set.

Summary

In this chapter, we have learned how to extract information from individual tables using SQL statements. We began with the basic SELECT statement and practiced re-naming fields for clearer management of information in our returned data. We learned how to filter information using the WHERE clause and several of its conditions and logical operators. We progressed to using multiple filters in our statements, and calculating using the WHERE clause to locate more specific data. We discussed the order in which SQL statements are processed to help us create efficient and accurate statements. We also defined and practiced using the important NULL. We ended with a look at the LIKE operator which gives us more freedom in our statements, and the ORDER BY function, which helps in our presentation of data.

The next chapter will look at more techniques with the SELECT statement to work with individual tables, and other chapters will cover more advanced topics that build on the information presented here, but the techniques mentioned in this chapter make up most of the workhorse of SQL programming. It is important to understand these topics from a fundamental standpoint or you can easily get lost in the world of SQL.

One of the best approaches to learning SQL this early is to look at other SQL. The Northwind database contains several items that you can view. Look at how the SQL is structured and ordered. Copy this into Query Analyzer and pick it apart. Sometimes it helps to see how others do things because it can help you to better understand the fundamentals and you get an idea about some of the other approaches to problems in SQL. Like other languages, SQL has many ways to solve a problem. The approach that you take may be different from other approaches, so learn other ways to tackle problems.

All of the techniques covered so far will play an integral role in the chapters to follow. As the book progresses, we will see that the SELECT statement is very powerful and flexible. It is also fundamental to SQL programming. Many of the queries that you write will be SELECT statements.

Remember, when in doubt take it in steps. Do not try to write the entire query in one pass. Write part of the query and test. Write the next piece and test. This will reduce your debugging time and increase your overall knowledge of basic SQL.

The next chapter will build on more ways to use the SQL statement. As we take these steady steps, you will see how all of the pieces fit together. By the end of this book you will have a strong grounding in SQL – but basics first.

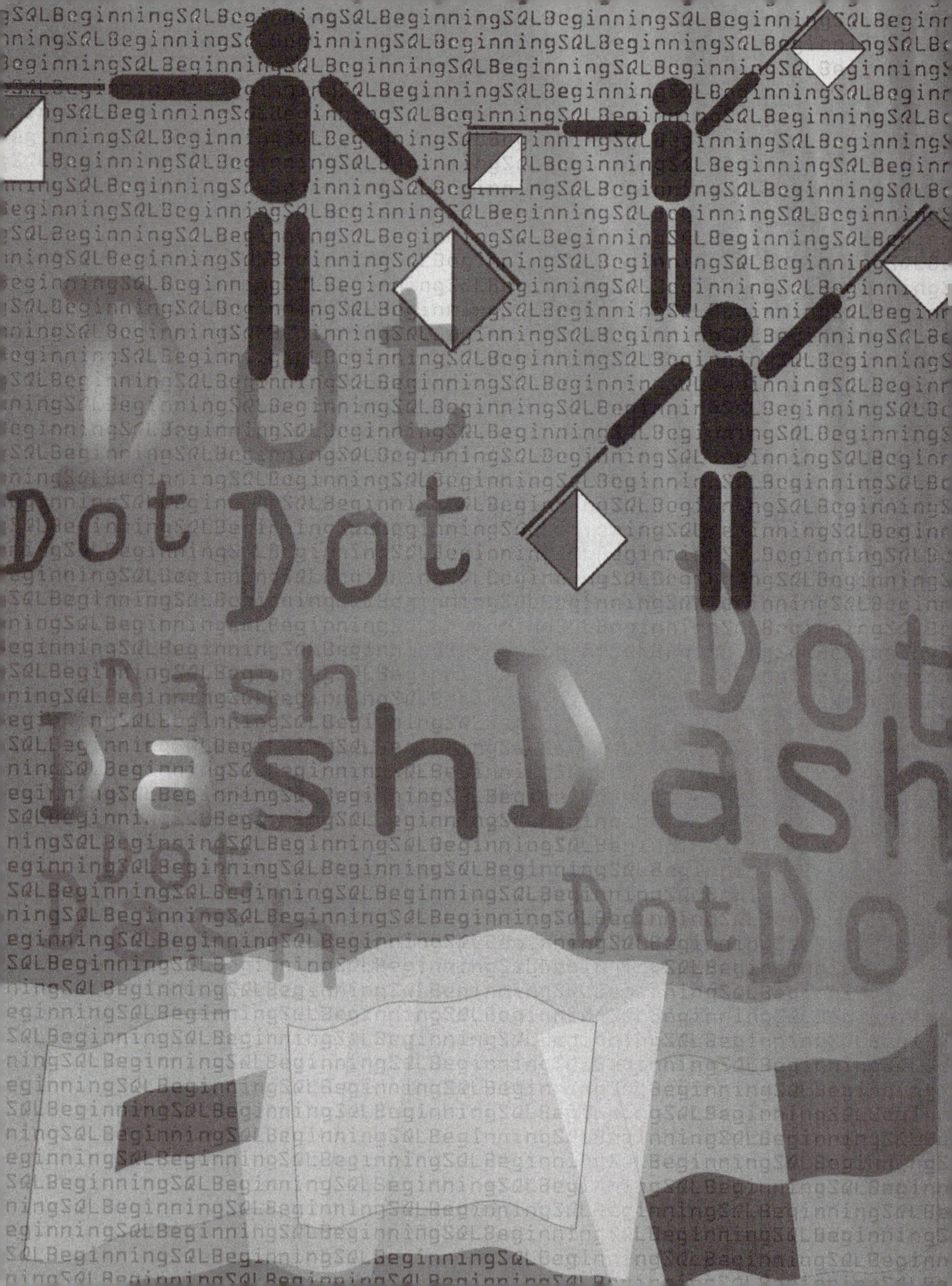

More Techniques with SELECT

The previous chapter introduced you to the SELECT statement, which is the most important one for you to understand in SQL since the majority of the queries and statements that you execute will be SELECT statements. Our last chapter covered many operations within SQL, but we fall a bit short of being able to handle more complex queries.

The things we will learn in this chapter are:

❑   The different ways to limit the rows that a query will return

❑   How to filter queries with calculated values

❑   How to execute nested queries

❑   How to utilize ranges and lists to select our data

Don't worry; each function will be covered by itself at first, and, working our way through the chapter, we will know how to answer questions such as:

❑   Who are the top 5 sales people?

❑   What are our top 10% selling items?

❑   Which customers are in the same state as an employee?

❑   What products have been ordered before?

❑   What products have never been ordered?

So, let's start with the TOP operator.

TOP *N* Queries

A very common query is a top *N* query. These types of queries should be familiar to you from everyday life: for instance: the weekly top 40 music hits, the top 5 cars sold, or the upper 20% of a group. There is really nothing new or special here, but how do we do this in SQL?

> **Not all databases support the `TOP` operator. Check with your documentation to see if your database supports this operation. SQL Server and Access do support the `TOP` operator.**

SQL includes a `TOP` keyword that you use with the `SELECT` section of your query. The `TOP` function gives you the ability to filter only the specified number from your result set or a specific percentile ranking of your result set. You can ask, for example, for the top 10 or the top 5% since both ranges are acceptable. The syntax for this is very simple:

```
SELECT TOP N [PERCENT] field1, field2, …, field n
FROM tablename
```

The `TOP` operator can specify a number or a percentage, but not both, and works best when you use the `ORDER BY` clause to first sort your data properly. You specify the `TOP` operator after the `SELECT` statement and before the field list of the `SELECT` statement.

Let's take a closer look at how the `TOP` operator functions. In the Northwind database there is a 'thing' called a View. A View is basically a `SELECT` statement that has been saved for later use. We will look at Views in a lot of detail in Chapter 15, so you really do not need to worry about them now. This is mentioned here just so you realize that a view is not a real table.

The view we are looking at is called `Sales by Category`. We start off by selecting all of the data from the view in Query Analyzer. Remember that this view has a name with spaces, so we need to enclose the name in brackets ([ ]) in order for this to work.

```
SELECT
   CategoryID, CategoryName, ProductName, ProductSales
FROM
   [Sales By Category]
```

If we execute this `SELECT` statement, we get an idea of what our data looks like:

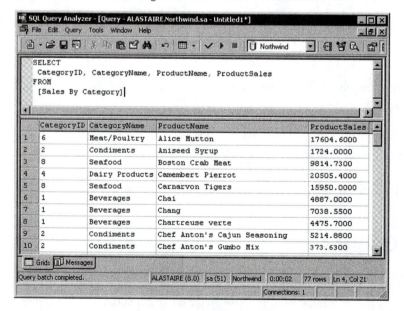

Notice that the **ProductSales** category is not formatted like a number as you may expect. Rather, the number is in the correct decimal format. It is up to the front end or the query designer to specifically format the number to look like a dollar amount.

When we execute our query, we receive CategoryID, CategoryName, ProductName, and TotalSales columns. What we want to do is generate a list of the top 5 products according to the sales. If we add TOP 5 to our query then it should return the top 5 sales:

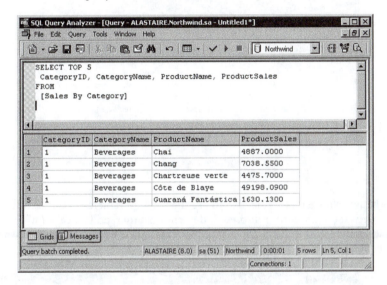

However, this doesn't look quite right. We added the TOP 5 predicate, but we did not order by any column. Since we excluded an ORDER BY clause, the database presented the table in the current sort order. In order to do a correct TOP n query, we need to order our data based on the column that will represent the top data:

```
SELECT TOP 5
    CategoryID, CategoryName, ProductName, ProductSales
FROM
    [Sales By Category]
ORDER BY
    ProductSales DESC
```

This will return the following results:

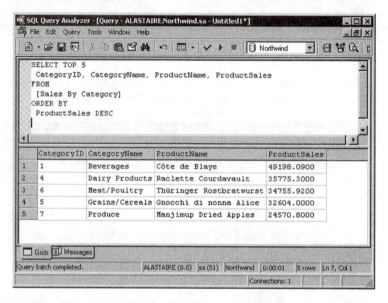

There, that's better. Notice that we needed to use the DESC parameter of the ORDER BY clause. This specifies that we want our records returned in descending order, and since we wanted the top figures, it is necessary to include it. If we eliminated this parameter, then we would have returned the bottom five sales since the default sort is ascending:

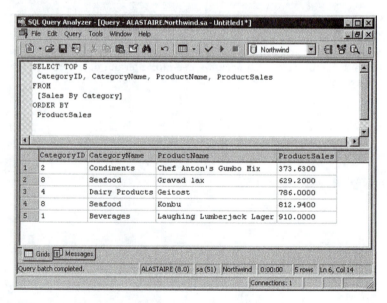

Note that, as it stands, this SELECT statement will not take into account situations where there are numerous results sharing the same ProductSales values. That is, if there were numerous records with a ProductSale value of 24570, only one of them would be shown, as we have only specified that 5 records should be returned.

There is a simple way to get around this: using the WITH TIES operator. WITH TIES will ensure that the query will continue to output rows until either the specified number of rows has been reached, or all the results sharing the same value as the last specified record have been returned. This may be a bit difficult to understand straightaway, so let's take a look at an example.

The best table to use for this example is our Order Details table. If we sort the results by Quantity and take the top 3 quantities, then we get three records:

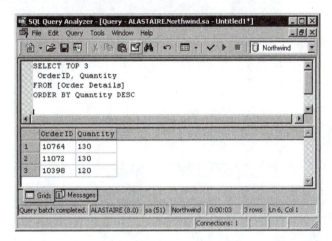

However, if we add WITH TIES then we get ten rows:

It has returned all the records that share the same Quantity value as the third record.

In order to further demonstrate, if we take the top 11 then you will see that the tenth row is the last value of 120 and the next value of 110 is displayed:

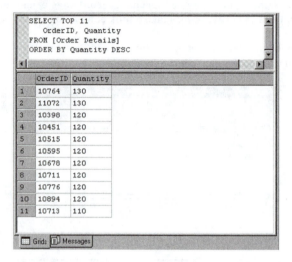

The bottom line when using WITH TIES is that you do not know how many records or even how may distinct values you will get.

We can also use a PERCENT operator to display a percentile ranking. There are many times where we want to generate statistics from our data using percentile operations. Let's say that we have been asked to display the top 10% of all sales:

If the WITH TIES operator was used as it was in the previous WITH TIES example, and there were any ties in the data, then the number of rows returned would vary.

When using the TOP operator you must use either PERCENT or leave it as the default (the default is the top number), but you cannot use both.

Try It Out – Using the TOP Operator

Suppose we have been asked to display the top 10% of the orders from the Sales Totals By Amount view. We want to know the company name and the order total.

1. Start a new query in the Northwind database.

2. First, define the SELECT statement that returns the fields of data that we want from the table that we need:

```
SELECT
    CompanyName,
    SaleAmount
FROM
    [Sales Totals By Amount]
```

Your data should look like this:

	CompanyName	SaleAmount
1	Save-a-lot Markets	2556.9500
2	Save-a-lot Markets	2505.6000
3	Eastern Connection	3063.0000
4	Rattlesnake Canyon G...	3868.6000
5	Ernst Handel	2713.5000
6	Simons bistro	11188.4000
7	Mère Paillarde	9194.5600
8	Ernst Handel	4899.2000
9	Save-a-lot Markets	4924.1400
10	QUICK-Stop	3849.6600
11	Wartian Herkku	2684.0000
12	Suprêmes délices	3891.0000
13	Vaffeljernet	2518.0000

Grids | Messages

3. We might now add our TOP predicate. Remember that we want a percentage, so we need to add PERCENT to the query, and, to properly order the data, we need to use the DESC operator.

```
SELECT TOP 10 PERCENT
    CompanyName, SaleAmount
FROM
    [Sales Totals By Amount]
ORDER BY
    SaleAmount DESC
```

	CompanyName	SaleAmount
1	Simons bistro	11188.4000
2	Rattlesnake Canyon G...	10495.6000
3	QUICK-Stop	10191.7000
4	QUICK-Stop	10164.8000
5	QUICK-Stop	9921.3000
6	Mère Paillarde	9194.5600
7	Ernst Handel	8623.4500

How It Works

When we use the TOP predicate, SQL Server takes the data requested by TOP from the results of the SQL statement. In our example above, we have an ORDER BY clause. This is processed before the TOP clause since we first need to build the results from which to take the TOP n. If we had more complex SQL then all of that would be executed prior to TOP.

TOP does not know anything about our data, so it will take the TOP from the results in order of the ORDER BY clause, otherwise it will use the default sort order. Be careful with this, since improper ordering of data is one of the biggest issues with incorrect results from a TOP clause.

Queries in English

In this section, we will look at some queries that deal with the top N items that we want. We will first see the query formulated in English, and then see how we would formulate the same query in SQL.

Display the 10 smallest orders that were placed with us.

```
SELECT TOP 10
    OrderID, Subtotal
FROM [Order Subtotals]
ORDER BY Subtotal
```

	OrderID	Subtotal
1	10782	12.5000
2	10807	18.4000
3	10586	23.8000
4	10767	28.0000
5	10898	30.0000
6	10900	33.7500
7	10883	36.0000
8	11051	36.0000
9	10815	40.0000
10	10674	45.0000

What were the top 10% of all products sold in 1997?

```
SELECT TOP 10 PERCENT
    CategoryName,
    ProductName,
    ProductSales
FROM [Product Sales for 1997]
ORDER BY ProductSales DESC
```

	CategoryName	ProductName	ProductSales
1	Beverages	Côte de Blaye	46563.0900
2	Dairy Products	Raclette Courdavault	33616.5500
3	Meat/Poultry	Thüringer Rostbratwurst	33109.5100
4	Grains/Cereals	Gnocchi di nonna Alice	32604.0000
5	Produce	Manjimup Dried Apples	23550.0200
6	Confections	Tarte au sucre	20762.8200
7	Dairy Products	Camembert Pierrot	20652.2800
8	Meat/Poultry	Alice Mutton	16580.8500

What were the top 10 orders for 1997?

```
SELECT TOP 10
    OrderID, Subtotal, ShippedDate
FROM [Summary of Sales By Year]
WHERE
    ShippedDate BETWEEN '1/1/1997' AND '12/31/1997'
ORDER BY SubTotal DESC
```

	OrderID	Subtotal	ShippedDate
1	10417	11188.4000	1997-01-28 00:00:00.000
2	10479	10495.6000	1997-03-21 00:00:00.000
3	10540	10191.7000	1997-06-13 00:00:00.000
4	10691	10164.8000	1997-10-22 00:00:00.000
5	10515	9921.3000	1997-05-23 00:00:00.000
6	10424	9194.5600	1997-01-27 00:00:00.000
7	10514	8623.4500	1997-05-16 00:00:00.000
8	10776	6635.2700	1997-12-18 00:00:00.000
9	10607	6475.4000	1997-07-25 00:00:00.000
10	10612	6375.0000	1997-08-01 00:00:00.000

Show the top 10 orders placed

```
SELECT TOP 10
    OrderID, Subtotal
FROM [Order Subtotals]
ORDER BY Subtotal DESC
```

	OrderID	Subtotal
1	10865	16387.5000
2	10981	15810.0000
3	11030	12615.0500
4	10889	11380.0000
5	10417	11188.4000
6	10817	10952.8400
7	10897	10835.2400
8	10479	10495.6000
9	10540	10191.7000
10	10691	10164.8000

A number of errors can commonly occur when using the TOP operator:

❑ **More records are returned than are expected.**
This usually occurs when using the WITH TIES operator since more than the specified records will be returned. For example, if you want only the top 5 records, but end up with 15, it will probably be because WITH TIES is an unnecessary part of the statement.

❑ **Records stop returning at the limit even if there are more records with the same value.**
This error generally occurs because the WITH TIES operator has not been used to return all the records with the same value – all the tied records.

Using DISTINCT

There are many times when we want to look at the results of our data in particular ways. For example, we may want to get a list of all of the products that have ever been sold. The TOP operator provides one way of gaining particular types of results from our data. Another statement that provides a way of selecting records in a particular way is the DISTINCT operator.

The DISTINCT operator takes the results of our data and drops any duplicate data. The DISTINCT evaluates the entire SELECT list for duplicates, not just individual columns. This is a very handy operator since there are many times where we want to generate a simple list of items from a table, but simply want a list of unique items – such as a list of all customers that have placed orders. For example, if we wanted to list all of the categories in the Sales By Category view, then we would write a simple SELECT statement:

```
SELECT
    CategoryName
FROM
    [Sales By Category]
```

	CategoryName
1	Beverages
2	Beverages
3	Beverages
4	Beverages
5	Beverages
6	Beverages
7	Beverages
8	Beverages
9	Beverages
10	Beverages
11	Beverages
12	Beverages
13	Condiments
14	Condiments
15	Condiments

Grids | Messages

We can see that we do get a correct list, but it is mighty confusing. We just want a list of unique categories in the view. This problem is easily solved with the DISTINCT keyword:

Now our data looks much more manageable.

Remember that the DISTINCT operator works on entire rows of data. This is not the underlying table data, rather it is the row information that is contained within our SELECT list. Had we added the ProductSales field to our query then our results would have been significantly different:

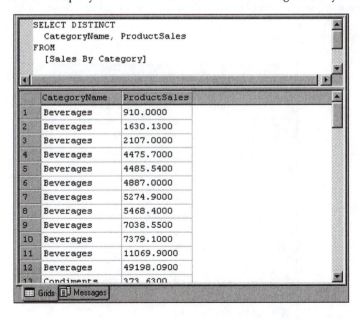

The fact that DISTINCT operates on a row level is very important to remember – especially when we start writing more complex SQL statements in later chapters and need to filter or manipulate the results of the data.

Try It Out – Using DISTINCT

Suppose we have been asked to create a simple report: what are all of the cities that we have shipped to in the US and Canada? We will use the data in the Orders table.

1. First, we start a new query.

2. We need to get the city information from the Orders table. We want a complete report of cities, so we will use the ShipCity, ShipRegion, and ShipCountry fields for our report (remember to use DISTINCT). We are using the ShipCity, ShipRegion, and ShipCountry to produce a unique list since a city may have the same name across multiple states. We also want to avoid a city/region conflict between countries. This is unlikely, but a situation that should be accounted for in any case.

Enter the following SQL statement:

```
SELECT DISTINCT
    ShipCity,
    ShipRegion,
    ShipCountry
FROM
    Orders
WHERE
    ShipCountry IN ('USA', 'Canada')
```

3. Execute the query and verify that your results match these below:

Insert 1800_Ch05_012.bmp

	ShipCity	ShipRegion	ShipCountry
1	Albuquerque	NM	USA
2	Anchorage	AK	USA
3	Boise	ID	USA
4	Butte	MT	USA
5	Elgin	OR	USA
6	Eugene	OR	USA
7	Kirkland	WA	USA
8	Lander	WY	USA
9	Montréal	Québec	Canada
10	Portland	OR	USA
11	San Francisco	CA	USA
12	Seattle	WA	USA
13	Tsawassen	BC	Canada
14	Vancouver	BC	Canada
15	Walla Walla	WA	USA

Note that the query in Step 2 could have also been written as follows:

```
SELECT DISTINCT
    ShipCity,
    ShipRegion,
    ShipCountry
FROM
    Orders
WHERE
    ShipCountry = 'USA'
    OR ShipCountry = 'Canada'
```

How It Works

As with the TOP operator, the DISTINCT clause operates on the result set of the SELECT statement. In our example, the SELECT statement is returning the ShipCity, ShipRegion, and ShipCountry fields where the country is the USA or Canada. Once we have this data then we can filter the results for all of the unique rows of data, thus returning to us our very short list in Step 3.

The TOP and DISTINCT clauses can be somewhat inefficient because you need to evaluate the final results against the entire result set from the SELECT statement. When possible, to speed up the process, we should index our tables on the rows that are frequently used with TOP and DISTINCT. We look at using indexes in Chapter 15. This will greatly improve performance because the indexes would be utilized for scanning the records.

Queries in English

In this section, we will look at some queries that need to use the DISTINCT keyword. As before, we will state our requirements in English, then see how we have to write the SQL to reflect this.

Find all of the customers that have placed orders.

```
SELECT DISTINCT CustomerID
FROM Orders
```

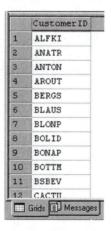

List all of the employees that have ever placed orders.

```
SELECT DISTINCT EmployeeID
FROM Orders
```

	EmployeeID
1	1
2	2
3	3
4	4
5	5
6	6
7	7
8	8
9	9

List all of the cities in the US that have at least one of our customers.

```
SELECT City, Region
FROM Customers
WHERE Country = 'USA'
```

	City	Region
1	Eugene	OR
2	Elgin	OR
3	Walla Walla	WA
4	San Francisco	CA
5	Portland	OR
6	Anchorage	AK
7	Albuquerque	NM
8	Boise	ID
9	Lander	WY
10	Portland	OR
11	Butte	MT
12	Kirkland	WA
13	Seattle	WA

Display all of the locations where we have shipped products.

```
SELECT DISTINCT
    ShipCity, ShipRegion, ShipCountry
FROM Orders
```

	ShipCity	ShipRegion	ShipCountry
1	Aachen	NULL	Germany
2	Albuquerque	NM	USA
3	Anchorage	AK	USA
4	Århus	NULL	Denmark
5	Barcelona	NULL	Spain
6	Barquisimeto	Lara	Venezuela
7	Bergamo	NULL	Italy
8	Berlin	NULL	Germany
9	Bern	NULL	Switzerland
10	Boise	ID	USA
11	Bräcke	NULL	Sweden
12	Brandenburg	NULL	Germany
13	Bruxelles	NULL	Belgium

Grids Messages

Using HAVING

Another way to narrow down the results that we want is to specify that the records we query meet certain criteria – this can be done by using the HAVING clause. The HAVING clause is almost the same as the WHERE clause, except that it can only be used with a GROUP BY clause as well, as the conditions it holds apply to groups. The HAVING clause also works on statistical data.

Say, for example, that we want to know how many orders have an order number higher than 10070 – this is because every order before that point has been paid, but every order after that point is outstanding. Our query would look like this:

```
SELECT OrderID
FROM Orders
GROUP BY OrderID
HAVING OrderID >= 11070
```

This should give us the following results:

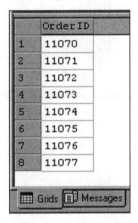

This is very simple, but it serves to show how, by using HAVING, we can specify criteria for our specified group of results to meet, to make sure that we get exactly the information we need.

Using Nested SELECT Statements

Up to this point, we have looked at some simple statements that only involve a single table. We will now start looking at instances and operators where we use multiple tables to retrieve data.

IN

We have seen the IN operator already, but it has been used to find matches in a defined list. The power of IN lies in its ability to work with a sub-SELECT statement, or nested SELECT statement. We may want to know the company names of all the companies that have a shipping address in the USA. We can get the company information from the Customers table and the order information from the Order table, but we do not yet have a way to get information from one table to match data in another table.

Enter IN. We know that IN can take a defined list of values (CustomerID for instance) and match against a field. If we knew that the companies that have US shipping addresses are 'GREAL', 'HUNGC', and 'LAZYK', then we could simply type the values in an IN clause and be done with the task. However, we usually do not have this type of information handy. We can get the company information from the Orders table:

```
SELECT DISTINCT
    CustomerID
FROM
    Orders
WHERE
    ShipCountry = 'USA'
```

	CustomerID
1	GREAL
2	HUNGC
3	LAZYK
4	LETSS
5	LONEP
6	OLDWO
7	RATTC
8	SAVEA
9	SPLIR
10	THEBI
11	THECR
12	TRAIH
13	WHITC

This would be a large number of items to type into an IN clause. Also, when using the IN clause you must know ahead of time what the values are. This forces the query to use a static list of items rather than a dynamic list. What if we had hundreds of companies? We would never be able to keep the list current. We can keep the list current by passing the list returned from this SELECT statement into an IN clause. Instead of typing the entire list, we can add the SELECT statement as the list:

```
IN
    (
    SELECT DISTINCT
        CustomerID
    FROM
        Orders
    WHERE
        ShipCountry = 'USA'
    )
```

This is our first example of a sub-SELECT. Notice that we put parentheses around the subquery. This is required in order to prevent the SQL parser from incorrectly executing the statement. Also, if we later wanted to add additional criteria such as an AND or OR operator, then the parentheses will correctly group the operations and evaluate properly. Otherwise, the AND or OR operation may become part of the subquery. We are able to take the output of one query and use it in other places in a parent query. If we wanted to go back to our example of getting the company names of all companies that have had a US shipping address then we can write the following query:

```
SELECT
    CompanyName
FROM
    Customers
WHERE
    CustomerID IN
    (
    SELECT DISTINCT
        CustomerID
    FROM
        Orders
    WHERE
        ShipCountry = 'USA'
    )
```

We get the following results:

	CompanyName
1	Great Lakes Food Market
2	Hungry Coyote Import...
3	Lazy K Kountry Store
4	Let's Stop N Shop
5	Lonesome Pine Restaurant
6	Old World Delicatessen
7	Rattlesnake Canyon G...
8	Save-a-lot Markets
9	Split Rail Beer & Ale
10	The Big Cheese
11	The Cracker Box
12	Trail's Head Gourmet...
13	White Clover Markets

We can use these types of nested SELECT statements in many places. Some examples would be to list the customer data of all customers that have placed orders – or those customers that have never placed an order. In later chapters we will see that there are other ways to join multiple tables like this, but using a sub-SELECT with certain clauses is a particularly useful technique, as some operations require this type of approach.

Just to add a little complexity to the picture, a subquery can also contain other subqueries; we are only limited by our imagination and the resources on the server.

The IN operator is not supported in MySQL; however, we can instead use:

```
SELECT table1.*
FROM table1,table2
WHERE table1.id=table2.id
```

An example would be:

```
SELECT *
FROM Customers, Orders
WHERE Customers.CustomerID = Orders.CustomerID
```

Try It Out – Using IN

We would like to find out if any of our customers happen to live in the same city as a supplier.

1. First, we want to generate the list of cities that our suppliers live in:

```
SELECT DISTINCT City
FROM Suppliers
```

This returns our list of lookup values that we will use in our comparison:

2. This will be used in our correlated subquery. Now, we can add this in to a main query that returns the customer information:

```
SELECT CustomerID, CompanyName
FROM Customers
```

3. We will compare the city to the list returned to us from the correlated subquery. We use the IN operator to compare to the list:

```
SELECT CustomerID, CompanyName
FROM Customers
WHERE City IN
    (
    SELECT DISTINCT City
    FROM Suppliers
    )
```

Now, when we run this query we get a small list of customers located near a supplier:

	CustomerID	CompanyName
1	ALFKI	Alfreds Futterkiste
2	AROUT	Around the Horn
3	BSBEV	B's Beverages
4	CONSH	Consolidated Holdings
5	EASTC	Eastern Connection
6	NORTS	North/South
7	SEVES	Seven Seas Imports
8	MEREP	Mère Paillarde
9	PARIS	Paris spécialités
10	SPECD	Spécialités du monde
11	COMMI	Comércio Mineiro
12	FAMIA	Familia Arquibaldo
13	QUEEN	Queen Cozinha
14	TRADH	Tradição Hipermercados

How It Works

The IN operator can accept either a list of values or a subquery that returns a value. We have generated a dynamic list of supplier locations to use in our comparison. We could have typed this list into an IN statement, but that would be time consuming, error prone, and would force us to update all of our queries once we add a new supplier. The query now generates the city list from the Suppliers table first. Then, as we navigate the rows, we compare the city in the Customers table to the list generated by the Suppliers table. If there is a match between the two, then the row is selected into the result set.

Queries in English

In this section, we look at some queries that rely on information from a number of different sources, that would require the use of the IN operator. We will look at these queries in English, and then see how we would have to formulate subqueries in SQL to get the exact information we want.

Are there any products that have never been sold?

```
SELECT ProductID
FROM Products
WHERE ProductID NOT IN
    (
    SELECT DISTINCT ProductID
    FROM [Order Details]
    )
```

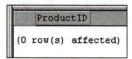

In this example, every product has been purchased at some point.

What products has the customer ALFKI never purchased?

```
SELECT ProductID, ProductName
FROM Products
WHERE ProductID NOT IN
   (
   SELECT DISTINCT ProductID
   FROM [Order Details]
   WHERE OrderID IN
      (
      SELECT DISTINCT OrderID
      FROM Orders
      WHERE CustomerID = 'ALFKI'
      )
   )
```

	ProductID	ProductName
1	1	Chai
2	2	Chang
3	4	Chef Anton's Cajun Seasoning
4	5	Chef Anton's Gumbo Mix
5	7	Uncle Bob's Organic Dried Pears
6	8	Northwoods Cranberry Sauce
7	9	Mishi Kobe Niku
8	10	Ikura
9	11	Queso Cabrales
10	12	Queso Manchego La Pastora
11	13	Konbu
12	14	Tofu
13	15	Genen Shouyu

Grids Messages

What were the sales of shipped items to our US customers in 1997?

```
SELECT OrderID, SubTotal
FROM [Summary of Sales by Year]
WHERE OrderID IN
   (
   SELECT OrderID
   FROM Orders
   WHERE CustomerID IN
      (
      SELECT CustomerID
      FROM Customers
      WHERE Country = 'USA'
      )
   )
   AND ShippedDate BETWEEN '1/1/1997' AND '12/31/1997'
```

	Order ID	SubTotal
1	10393	2556.9500
2	10394	442.0000
3	10398	2505.6000
4	10401	3868.6000
5	10415	102.4000
6	10432	485.0000
7	10440	4924.1400
8	10441	1755.0000
9	10452	2018.5000
10	10469	956.6800
11	10479	10495.6000
12	10482	147.0000
13	10483	668.8000

Grids Messages

Are there any shippers that the company ANATR does not use?

```
SELECT CompanyName
FROM Shippers
WHERE ShipperID NOT IN
    (
    SELECT DISTINCT ShipVIA
    FROM Orders
    WHERE CustomerID = 'ANATR'
    )
```

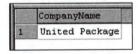

	CompanyName
1	United Package

An error occurs when our statements are written using the IN operator to return more than one field from the subquery. This is not allowed, unless we use EXISTS, which we will see in the next section. So, remember that, when using IN, you can only return one field, or column of data.

EXISTS

The EXISTS operator is very similar to the IN operator except that EXISTS tests for the existence of a row. For instance, we can see if the current CustomerID in the Customer table has a match in the Orders table by adding the EXISTS clause:

```
SELECT
    CompanyName
FROM
    Customers
WHERE
    EXISTS
        (
        SELECT DISTINCT
            CustomerID
        FROM
            Orders
        WHERE
            ShipCountry = 'USA'
            AND Orders.CustomerID = Customers.CustomerID
        )
```

147

> **The EXISTS operator is not supported in MySQL. Instead, we can use the following:**
>
> ```
> SELECT DISTINCT
>     CompanyName
> FROM
>     Customers, Orders
> WHERE
>     Customers.CustomerID=Orders.CustomerID
> AND
>     Orders.ShipCountry = 'USA'
> ```

What we get back is the same data that was returned in the IN example:

	CompanyName
1	Great Lakes Food Market
2	Hungry Coyote Import Store
3	Lazy K Kountry Store
4	Let's Stop N Shop
5	Lonesome Pine Restaurant
6	Old World Delicatessen
7	Rattlesnake Canyon Grocery
8	Save-a-lot Markets
9	Split Rail Beer & Ale
10	The Big Cheese
11	The Cracker Box
12	Trail's Head Gourmet Provisioners
13	White Clover Markets

> **Using EXISTS versus IN is much more efficient because EXISTS is a Boolean (True/False) test whereas IN has to evaluate each row in the query. EXISTS will terminate once it finds a match, thus reducing the processing required to execute the query.**

Notice that we have used several new techniques. First, we have used fully qualified field names.

Fully qualified field names are references to the table name and field name using the dot (.) operator. You can also specify additional information such as the database and user. If you would like to access the OrderID field in the Orders table then you can use Orders.OrderID. Additionally you can fully qualify all of the information such as dbo.Orders.OrderID or Northwind.dba.Orders.OrderID.

Orders.CustomerID tells the query processor that we want the CustomerID field from the Orders table. As our queries get more complex we will need to fully qualify the fields since the query processor may become confused and fail to execute since it cannot resolve the proper field names that exist in multiple tables.

Second, we have used the parent query information in the nested query – or more appropriately a correlated subquery. We are generating a SELECT statement based on the information of the current row of data in the parent query. It is important to note here that we can use the Customers.CustomerID information in the sub-SELECT, but we cannot use the Orders.CustomerID in the parent SELECT. This is because the child SELECT can see the parent SELECT information; the parent SELECT can only see the *results* of the child SELECT and cannot directly process the detail information contained in the child SELECT.

Try It Out – Using EXISTS

We want to display the contact information for any customer that has placed an order with us before.

1. First, we need to know who has placed an order:

```
SELECT DISTINCT CustomerID
FROM Orders
```

Use of the DISTINCT keyword assures us of a smaller result set since a customer can place many orders. A smaller result set, in turn, produces faster running queries.

2. We also need to display the contact information from the Customer table.

```
SELECT CustomerID, CompanyName, ContactName, Phone
FROM Customers
```

3. Using the EXISTS keyword we can check our subquery and test for any matches. Remember that the subquery must refer to a field in the parent query:

```
SELECT CustomerID, CompanyName, ContactName, Phone
FROM Customers
WHERE EXISTS
   (
   SELECT DISTINCT CustomerID
   FROM Orders
   WHERE CustomerID = Customers.CustomerID
   )
```

This results in our list of contacts:

	CustomerID	CompanyName	ContactName	Phone
1	ALFKI	Alfreds Futterkiste	Maria Anders	030-0074321
2	ANATR	Ana Trujillo Emparedados y helados	Ana Trujillo	(5) 555-4729
3	ANTON	Antonio Moreno Taquería	Antonio Moreno	(5) 555-3932
4	AROUT	Around the Horn	Thomas Hardy	(171) 555-7788
5	BERGS	Berglunds snabbköp	Christina Berglund	0921-12 34 65
6	BLAUS	Blauer See Delikatessen	Hanna Moos	0621-08460
7	BLONP	Blondesddsl père et fils	Frédérique Citeaux	88.60.15.31
8	BOLID	Bólido Comidas preparadas	Martín Sommer	(91) 555 22 82
9	BONAP	Bon app'	Laurence Lebihan	91.24.45.40
10	BOTTM	Bottom-Dollar Markets	Elizabeth Lincoln	(604) 555-4729
11	BSBEV	B's Beverages	Victoria Ashworth	(171) 555-1212
12	CACTU	Cactus Comidas para llevar	Patricio Simpson	(1) 135-5555
13	CENTC	Centro comercial Moctezuma	Francisco Chang	(5) 555-3392

Grids | Messages

4. Now, if we wanted to add a little twist to our query, we could use the NOT operator to see if there are any customers that have never made a purchase:

```
SELECT CustomerID, CompanyName, ContactName, Phone
FROM Customers
WHERE NOT EXISTS
    (
    SELECT DISTINCT CustomerID
    FROM Orders
    WHERE CustomerID = Customers.CustomerID
    )
```

Upon executing this we see that there are a few customers that have never ordered from us:

	CustomerID	CompanyName	ContactName	Phone
1	FISSA	FISSA Fabrica Inter. Salchichas S.A.	Diego Roel	(91) 555 94 44
2	PARIS	Paris spécialités	Marie Bertrand	(1) 42.34.22.66

How it Works

The EXISTS keyword checks for any rows returned by a subquery. The subquery typically refers to a parent row in a WHERE clause to help filter the records. We will see this technique in more detail when multiple table joins are covered later.

EXISTS is a Boolean check, so the existence of any rows in the subquery evaluates to TRUE. Contrast this to the IN clause where each of the rows in the subquery must be checked for matching records. For this reason EXISTS should be used when speed is important since EXISTS does not have to do row-by-row comparisons.

Queries in English

In order to demonstrate the similarities between the IN and EXISTS we will use the same English Query examples from the IN examples.

Are there any products that have never been sold?

```
SELECT ProductID
FROM Products
WHERE NOT EXISTS
    (
    SELECT DISTINCT ProductID
    FROM [Order Details]
    )
```

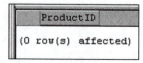

ProductID
(0 row(s) affected)

In this example, every product has been purchased at some point.

What products have the customer ALFKI never purchased?

```
SELECT ProductID, ProductName
FROM Products
WHERE NOT EXISTS
   (
   SELECT DISTINCT ProductID
   FROM [Order Details]
   WHERE EXISTS
      (
      SELECT DISTINCT OrderID
      FROM Orders
      WHERE CustomerID = 'ALFKI'
         AND [Order Details].OrderID = OrderID
      )
   AND ProductID = Products.ProductID
   )
```

	Product ID	ProductName
1	1	Chai
2	2	Chang
3	4	Chef Anton's Cajun Seasoning
4	5	Chef Anton's Gumbo Mix
5	7	Uncle Bob's Organic Dried Pears
6	8	Northwoods Cranberry Sauce
7	9	Mishi Kobe Niku
8	10	Ikura
9	11	Queso Cabrales
10	12	Queso Manchego La Pastora
11	13	Konbu
12	14	Tofu
13	15	Genen Shouyu

Grids Messages

What were the sales of shipped items to our US customers in 1997?

```
SELECT OrderID, SubTotal
FROM [Summary of Sales by Year]
WHERE EXISTS
   (
   SELECT OrderID
   FROM Orders
   WHERE EXISTS
      (
      SELECT CustomerID
      FROM Customers
      WHERE Country = 'USA'
         AND CustomerID = Orders.CustomerID
      )
   AND OrderID = [Summary of Sales by Year].OrderID
   )
AND ShippedDate BETWEEN '1/1/1997' AND '12/31/1997'
```

151

	Order ID	SubTotal
1	10393	2556.9500
2	10394	442.0000
3	10398	2505.6000
4	10401	3868.6000
5	10415	102.4000
6	10432	485.0000
7	10440	4924.1400
8	10441	1755.0000
9	10452	2018.5000
10	10469	956.6800
11	10479	10495.6000
12	10482	147.0000
13	10483	668.8000

Grids   Messages

Are there any shippers that the company ANATR does not use?

```
SELECT CompanyName
FROM Shippers
WHERE NOT EXISTS
    (
    SELECT DISTINCT ShipVIA
    FROM Orders
    WHERE CustomerID = 'ANATR'
    AND Shippers.ShipperID = ShipVIA
    )
```

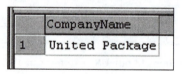

	CompanyName
1	United Package

A common error committed when using EXISTS is that a field name is written before the EXISTS keyword. This is a direct result of confusing the syntax of EXISTS with the syntax of IN – this is particularly easy, due to the two operators being so similar in functionality.

Summary

Over the last two chapters you have learned how to extract information from a relational database system. In this chapter we demonstrated some advanced techniques for answering several common business questions that we might need to address.

Firstly, we took a look at the TOP operator, which allows us to select either the top N items, or the top N percent of items. We also looked at using WITH TIES, which allows us to retrieve those records that have the same value as a record in our result set, otherwise known as tied records.

We moved on to look at the DISTINCT operator, which removes duplicated records from our result set, letting us better determine exactly how many individual and original records we have. For instance, there may be thousands of orders, but these are all made by only a third of your customers – using DISTINCT would let you identify your best, and worst, customers!

From there, we then looked at the more complex idea of nested SELECT statements, where the information we needed was located in a number of different tables rather than just one. There are two operators, similar in functionality, which allow us to nest our SELECT statements; these are IN and EXISTS.

The powerful techniques we have learned in this chapter will help us in later sections where we create even more powerful queries using calculations, string manipulations, and multiple table SELECT statements. For now, though, we move on to looking at creating and modifying tables.

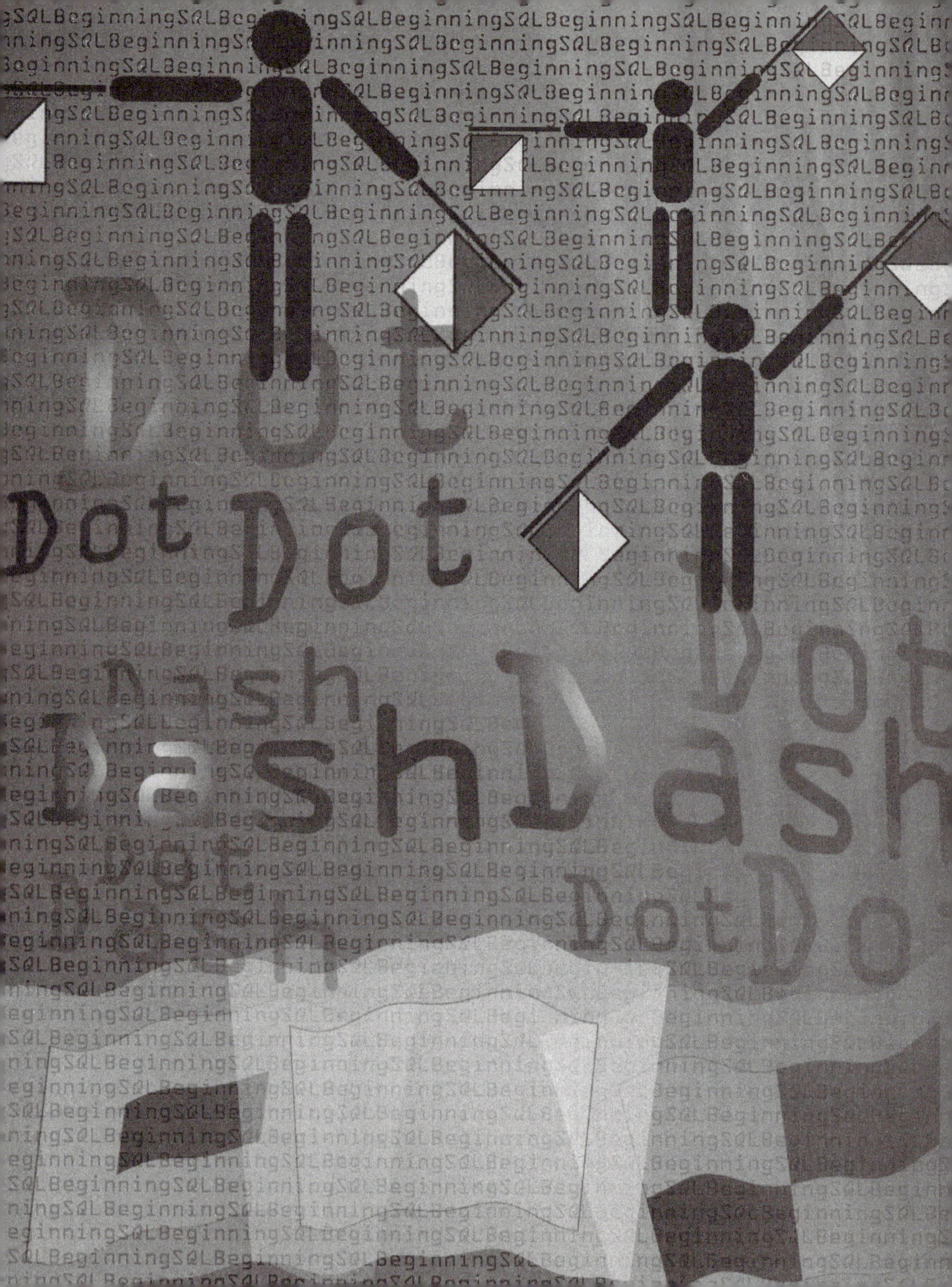

Creating and Modifying Databases and Tables

SQL programmers perform most of their work on existing databases, for example, we are working with Northwind in this book. But sometimes a programmer must create a database, either because the programmer is also the Database Administrator (DBA), a programming student, or wants to make a database for testing. In some cases programmers will write statements to modify the database structure during its use, for example creating and deleting temporary tables for certain reports. In this section we discuss how to **create**, **modify**, and **delete** databases and their tables using SQL statements.

Many books will show you the statements to create or drop a table, and those statements appear simple. But they actually support **parameters** that have important implications as to how data is handled during the structural change. In this chapter we will address how to use those parameters to insure a smoothly functioning system.

We will start by covering how to create a database, then cover how to create and delete a table within a database. After those basics we will cover the data types of the SQL language. Then we will circle back to making more complex tables to illustrate more accurate data typing. Finally, we will cover how to add, change, and delete existing fields (columns) in a table.

In this chapter we will look at:

- ❑ Creating, modifying, and deleting databases
- ❑ Creating, modifying, and deleting tables within databases
- ❑ Creating, modifying, and deleting fields within tables
- ❑ Adding and removing data types to fields

This will provide you with the tools to effectively create and manage databases from the base up. This chapter discusses and demonstrates actions at the most fundamental level, starting with how to create a database using SQL commands. The SQL standards are less specific at this level. Therefore the vendors are more free to introduce variations in the database creation methods. Because of these variations we suggest you check a reference for your particular DBMS so you can translate the statements described here to your environment. The statements have been tested on the following platforms and any differences have been noted: DB2, Microsoft SQL Server 2000, Oracle 8i, Microsoft Access, and MySQL. When we move to the second part of the chapter and discuss creating tables, vendor differences have much less significant impact.

A Quick Review

First let us review a few concepts from earlier chapters. Relational Database Management Systems (DBMS) hold all of the data in **tables**. Most vendor's DBMS run on a **data server,** which contains one or more databases, each of which contain one or more tables. Some vendors consider an entire installation of the server a "database" and thus go directly to the table level (review Chapter 2 for a discussion of the relationship between a server, a database and a table). The purpose of the table is to hold data in a construct within the DBMS that allows us to effectively and efficiently manipulate it. Records may be stored in any order, but generally in the order that they were added to the table. SQL tools, primarily the SELECT statement, **extract** the data and **arrange** it as desired prior to delivery to the requester.

Creating Databases – An Introduction

Usually, a DBA is given the responsibility of creating databases. By default only a Systems Administrator can create a database. However a SA can grant permission to create databases to others. In most IT shops that have a DBA this permission is denied to programmers.

Typically, the DBAs use their knowledge of servers' hardware (such as file locations) and the designer's specifications to create the database. Then the database designers create the table layouts and the relationships between the tables.

However, most programmers find that at some point they do have to create databases, especially if they are building Internet technologies. Also, in many smaller groups the programmer may also have DBA responsibilities. As a student you will want to try creating databases to achieve a broader understanding of the concept, or as a developer you may want to set up a database for testing.

CREATE DATABASE Command

The SQL standards avoid the use of the term "database" because the word has grown to have different meanings among various vendors. However, there is enough unification that most products can use a very simple statement to create a basic database. The ANSI SQL statement is as follows:

```
CREATE DATABASE MyDatabaseName
```

Most DBMS will then give you a database that is a copy of a **model** or **default** database. The model database usually contains settings for one or more of the following parameters:

- ❑ Size of the **database**
- ❑ Size of the **log files**
- ❑ List of **default users**
- ❑ List of **administrators**

In addition it will include **tables** that are required by the DBMS to maintain a database. DBAs have options to change the parameters or to add tables or users to the model.

You'll find parameters discussed in books on Database Administration for your specific DBMS.

Vendors use several variations on the above theme for creating a database.

- ❑ **IBM DB2** considers a database to be the entire instance of the DB2 software. All tables are stored within that one database.

- ❑ **Informix Universal Server** has options to CREATE in a *dbspace,* which is an area of one or more hard drives that is controlled by Informix independently of the operating system's file scheme. Informix allows the creation of many databases per server installation.

- ❑ **Ingress** uses the keyword CREATEDB instead of the CREATE DATABASE command discussed in this chapter, with which you can create several databases per installation.

- ❑ Older versions of **Oracle** were like IBM's DB2 in that tables were generally placed in a single database that was the installation of Oracle. More recent products have a CREATE DATABASE extension that allows multiple independent databases within the installation.

- ❑ **Microsoft Access** allows the creation of multiple "databases" within an installation. Each database has its own .MDF file to hold data, metadata, and front-end components like forms and reports. The databases are created by the Access Menu system (or wizards) rather then through SQL statements.

- ❑ **Microsoft SQL Server** supports the CREATE DATABASE command as described in this chapter. The databases created by DBAs are monitored by a *Master Database* of which there is one per installation.

- ❑ **Sybase Adaptive Server** is similar to the Microsoft products in that an installation can support multiple databases formed with the CREATE DATABASE command.

Note that almost all of these DBMS include tools that provide a graphic interface for the creation of databases. Included on this book's CD is the Microsoft SQL Server2000 Enterprise Manager, which contains a wizard to walk you through creating a database. To access the SQL Server 2000 Enterprise Manager go to:

Start | Programs | MS SQL Server 2000 | Enterprise Manager.

In the left pane expand Microsoft SQL Servers.

Expand SQL Server Group.

Expand your server.

Select Databases.

On the menu bar click Action and select New Database.

There are also third-party development tools that assist you to design and create databases.

Points to Be Aware of When Creating Databases

❑   Only those users specified in the model database can use a nascent database. For most products that is only the DBA or SA. The user(s) listed in the model database can then create permissions for others as per the security techniques discussed in Appendix B.

❑   There are a couple of pitfalls when creating databases. First, the database must have a name **unique** from all other databases in the installation of the DBMS. Second, a conceptual difference arises with IBM DB2 which considers a "database" to be a running installation of the DB2 software on one server. **Thus there is no need to "create" a database in DB2**.

❑   There are about a dozen parameters that affect a database that will actually be deployed. Most of these settings are determined by the DBA and will be covered in books for your specific DBMS. Here is a brief overview of some of the more widely implemented options; keep in mind that these ideas are fairly general because the commands are different between DBMS and because these settings are usually performed by DBAs, not by programmers.

  ❑   **Data file management** has many options in most DBMS. These are very specific to each manufacturer's product, so if you are creating a database and plan to use these parameters you must consult the references for your particular product. We will cover several of the most common here.

    ❑   The ON keyword usually contains several parameters that allow the database creator to define specific details about how and where the data will be stored. In some implementations you can spread the data across several files or file groups (and thus multiple disks) to improve speed and capacity, and assist backups. In other implementations you can specify both a shortcut NAME and a FILENAME that points to the actual location of the data.

    ❑   Parameters like FILESIZE and MAXSIZE allow the creator to limit the growth of the database on disk; most DBMS also have an UNLIMITED option.

    ❑   Parameters like FILEGROWTH or NEXT determine the size of the growth chunks the DBMS will give to the database as it grows from its FILESIZE up to its MAXSIZE. Most DBMS include tools that will calculate for you estimates of database size using your input of field types and number of records. As mentioned throughout this chapter, the creation of a database uses commands specific to each vendor. Although almost all of the rest of the book demonstrates generic SQL, coding the creation of a database will require you to check the specific syntax of your vendor.

❑ Almost all DBMS provide a **"logging" system** for transactions. Frequently the programmer wants to be sure an entire set of actions occurs and if there is a failure in any part then the entire set should not occur. The classic example is that prior to adding money to a receiver's account a bank wants to make sure the money exists in the giver's account. Neither the subtraction nor the addition should occur if the giver does not have the funds. The bank's DBMS can "test" a set of database actions in a transaction log rather than perform them directly on the database. After passing the tests for all of the actions then all parts of the transaction can actually be performed on the database. Most vendors create this transaction logging file at the same time as you create a database. The log file has parameters similar to the data file management parameters. The ON parameter can specify a log location and give it a name. Logs also have a MAXLOGSIZE, giving the database creator fine control over how the log files will consume disk space. More generally a log file can contain information about additions, deletions, and changes to your database data.

❑ The international scope of the Internet has forced database designers to include multiple language support at deeper and deeper levels of the enterprise. Most languages require (or at least appear better in) their own set of characters. Some DBMS establish character sets at the time the database is created. The most common setting is the CHARACTERSET which determines how data is stored. The NATIONAL_CHARACTER_SET determines the characters used by data stored in the NCHAR data type. Check the documentation for your specific product because some products (including older versions of Microsoft SQL Server and Sybase) handled character sets at the level of the entire server, not the database.

Modify and Drop Databases

The specifics of removing (dropping) a database vary among vendors because of the varying definition of a "database." In some systems like IBM, DB2, and Oracle the installation of the DBMS software creates one database. Users create multiple tables and groups of tables within that one database. In these cases there is no command to drop the database; instead programmers would drop all of the tables concerned with their project, leaving other projects' tables intact. In other systems an installation of the DBMS can hold more then one database and thus the following commands are used. Multiple-database systems include Ingres, Informix, Microsoft SQL Server, and Access. However, each of these vendors has a number of options and extensions, which you can learn from the Database Administrator's documentation for the product.

The command is simple but irrevocable:

```
DROP DATABASE DatabaseName
```

The DROP DATABASE command is available for DBMS that have multiple databases within one installation (for example Informix, Microsoft SQL Server, Sybase, and some installations of Oracle). The command is not available when the entire installation itself is considered a database (IBM DB2, older Oracle versions). In those cases you DROP the tables that are no longer wanted.

> **Be sure that you understand that** DROP DATABASE **(like** DROP TABLE**) removes the structure and the data and does so without a safety mechanism for you to recover the loss.**

Database parameters such as MAXSIZE and FILEGROWTH may need to be changed. These parameters are generally altered using a management tool provided by the vendor, such as Enterprise Manager included with SQL Server 2000.

Many DBMS can also handle ALTER commands on the database (ALTER DATABASE). These are, like the CREATE DATABASE commands, very specific to each vendor and thus require consultation with your vendor reference (we discuss the ALTER command as it applies to tables towards the end of the chapter in the *Adding Fields* section). Many DBMS include the following options with the ALTER command:

❑   Add a log file

❑   Chang the size of a log file

❑   Drop (Remove) a log file

❑   Rename a file

❑   Handle archiving of the log file

❑   Create, modify, and drop the data file(s)

> In most vendor's DBMS, the **ALTER** command can be used on many objects including database, index, and procedure. It is most frequently used on tables. It is the same command in every case, with a different object specified in the syntax and a different set of available parameters.

Creating and Modifying Tables – An Introduction

SQL supports three statements for working with tables: CREATE, ALTER, and DROP. CREATE TABLE is actually more complex than it appears because during the table creation you describe the **fields**. The field properties must include the **name** you choose for it, and the **data type** you want to include in it. You should also add **constraints** to the fields to restrict the data, as this will ensure you avoid storing nonsensical values. In this section we will describe the creation and typing of tables and fields, and then in the next chapter, we'll focus on constraints.

To illustrate our subject for the remainder of the chapter, we will add and modify tables in Northwind in order to track health insurance coverage. Northwind allows each employee to enroll in one of four plans offered by two insurance companies. The personnel department needs to know which plan each employee has selected and the date that they enroll. Northwind's accounting department will need to know the telephone number of the company's account manager. We have included some cookbook instructions on adding data to hold you over until you learn the details in Chapter 9.

The basic syntax to create a table is very simple. The statement must:

❑   Include the name of the table

❑   Include the name of at least one field

❑   Indicate the data type of the field

❑   Follow the rules for table naming as established in your DBMS

For most DBMS an identifier (name) must contain **less than 20 characters**, the first of which must be a **letter** (not a number or symbol). **Names must not include any SQL keywords**. Here is the pseudo-code to create three fields. The real code would have to use valid data type names, which we will cover shortly.

```
CREATE TABLE MyNewTable(
MyField1Name DataType,
MyField2Name DataType,
MyField3Name DataType
)
```

We will discuss data typing shortly, but for now let's add a new table to Northwind using the above code.

Try It Out – Create Table of Insurance Companies

Your boss has asked you to modify the Northwind database so you can store a list of insurance plans that are available to the employees. The information on the plans follows:

Company Name	Account Manager	Company Account Manager Phone
A-One	Adam Able	123-4567
Benchmark	Beth Bronson	234-5678

Those of you that have experience with normalization will know that this is traditionally done with two tables, but for now let us put the above information in one table to keep things simple. We'll discuss the best way of splitting the table later on.

1. Open your front end; in this case we will use the Query Analyzer that comes as part of Microsoft SQL Server on the CD in this book.

2. Connect to the Northwind database, and in this case, create a copy of the database for us to work on and call it BegSQLNorthwind.

It is wise at this point to keep the original, unedited copy of Northwind for use with the other examples throughout the book.

3. Type and then run the following SQL statement:

```
CREATE TABLE InsurCompanies
(InsurCompID Int,
InsurCompName VARCHAR(25),
InsurCompAcctManager CHAR(25),
InsurCompAcctManagerPhone CHAR(12),
);
```

4. If your front end has a developer's tool to list the tables then see if InsurPlans was added.

The procedure with Microsoft SQL Server (included on this book's CD) is:

Select Start | Programs | MS SQL Server | Enterprise Manager.

Expand MS SQL Servers, *then expand the* SQL server group.

Expand your machine then expand Databases.

Expand BegSQLNorthwind, *select* Tables.

Check the list in the right pane.

5. Last, we need to add some data to the table. We discuss this in depth in Chapters 9 and 10, but for now just run the following code, which is in the download for this chapter.

```
INSERT INTO InsurCompanies
     (InsurCompID,InsurCompName,
     InsurCompAcctManager,InsurCompAcctManagerPhone)
VALUES
     (1,'A-One','Adam Able','123-4567');

INSERT INTO InsurCompanies
     (InsurCompID,InsurCompName,
     InsurCompAcctManager,InsurCompAcctManagerPhone)
VALUES
     (2,'Benchmark','Bess Bronson','234-5678');
```

How it Works

We have now created a new table with the Name `InsurCompanies`. The nascent table has **four** fields, the first will hold an **identifying number** called the `InsurCompID`. Although there is nothing in this simple statement to designate it as such, you will know from chapter three that this is the kind of field which will hold numbers that are serial and unique and thus be used as a **primary key**. The second field will hold **text data**; the name of the insurance company. By making it a `VARCHAR` field instead of a `CHAR` field we have instructed the DBMS to minimize the field size when possible, thus we have limited the name to not exceed 25 characters. The last two fields are similar to the second and will hold the **name** and voice **telephone number** of the companies offering plans. We anticipate having companies from different nations, so we have chosen to hold the telephone number in a `CHAR` field so we can include the symbols.

> *Both* `VARCHAR` *and* `CHAR` *will be discussed in the section called* Character Datatypes *shortly, but for now just be aware that both data types specify that a string (characters, not numbers) must appear in the field, and that* `VARCHAR` *self-adjusts the size of your field to whatever string length you then input (as long as it doesn't exceed the maximum).*

Note that the `CREATE` statement is of the general form

```
CREATE ObjectType ObjectName
```

We will see this form frequently in later chapters as we look at creating indices and other objects.

Common Mistakes When Creating Tables

Mistakes with space characters. The key phrase "`CREATE TABLE`" must be two words with a space in the middle.

Mistakes with punctuation. Remember that all fields (columns) sit within one set of parenthesis. The fields names must be separated by commas.

Leaving off the right parenthesis at the end of the fields list.

Leaving out the semicolon at the end after the closing right parenthesis (some DBMS require the semicolon, some don't).

Omitting a data type for a field.

Not beginning the name of the table and of each field with a letter (not a number or symbol). The rest of the name may contain numbers or recognized symbols.

Drop Table

Before we go on we should try a removal of a table. The simplest syntax is direct:

```
DROP TABLE MyTableName
```

You will be losing not only the structure of the table (including all of the fields) but also the records within the table.

Try It Out – Remove and Recreate Table of Insurance Companies

1. Open your front end, in this case we will use the Query Analyzer that comes as part of Microsoft SQL Server on the CD in this book, and connect to BegSQLNorthwind or your equivalent.

2. Type and then run the following SQL statement:

```
DROP TABLE InsurCompanies
```

3. Use your facility to view the list of tables to check that InsurCompanies no longer exists.

4. Recreate and repopulate the table using the same SQL statement that you used in the last Try-It-Out.

How it Works

There is nothing to explain here, but there are two important notes:

❑ When you drop a table you are removing both the structure and the data – there is no "safety mechanism" that somehow keeps the data for you.

❑ Second, what will happen if other tables depend on the table you have just dropped? There are several options for handling dependencies which we will discuss later. For now, keep in mind that dropping a table may have consequences that flow out to other tables.

Data Types

One reason DBMS are so efficient is that, like many applications, they can utilize the minimum amount of resources needed to handle each field. A field containing a single-letter code for specifying gender can be handled with a much lower load on **memory**, **storage**, and **processing** than a field designed to hold a street address of 30 characters. However, to take advantage of this efficiency you must carefully select a data type that fits all of your needs but does not offer too much more than you actually need. If you pick a data type that is too limited you will have structural and integrity problems. If you pick a data type that is too large or cumbersome your performance will suffer and you will use more disk space then needed.

The explanation and selection of data types starts out fairly simply and then becomes more detailed as you start to apply the theory to real-world cases. Something to note here is that most DBMS vendors have added data types that are not compatible with each other, so keep an eye on your reference to your particular DBMS when working setting these up.

To start, then, the SQL standards describe three categories of data:

❑ **Character** – for data that is not to be used in arithmetic expressions

❑ **Numeric** – for data that can be used in arithmetic expressions

❑ **Time** – for data that can be used in time math

We will cover the theory and some specific advice for each group in the following sections.

Numeric Data Types

ANSI SQL specifies about a half dozen numeric types (depending on how you classify them). *Most DBMS have extended the list with another one or two types (check your particular references)*. All numeric types can be grouped into two sub-types: **exact** and **approximate**. Exact subtypes have a **size** and an **indicator** for the placement of the decimal point. Approximates have a size of **value** and a size of **exponent**. The accuracy will depend on the size of the value and the allowable range of data will depend on the size of the exponent.

Check your DBMS documentation for specific information on additional data types particular to your DBMS. Some common numeric types follow below. For many of these the same type has different names among vendors and thus multiple, synonymous terms are listed in the first field.

Name(s)	Size (Bytes)	Notes, Range and accuracy (approximate)
BIT	1	Usually limited to 1, 0, and NULL
SMALLINT	2	Only whole numbers (no decimal places)
		From –32,000 to plus 32,000 thousand
		Accuracy is exact
INT INTEGER	4	Only whole numbers (no decimal places) From –2,000,000 to plus 2,000,000 Accuracy is exact
DECIMAL DEC NUMERIC	Varies	The range will depend on the scale, precision, and number of bytes allocated by the programmer Accuracy is fixed
FLOAT	Varies	From about 2×10^{308} to -2×10^{308} Accuracy is variable

Two useful, but much less widely supported data types are:

TINYINT	1	Only whole numbers (no decimal places)
		From 0 to 255 Accuracy is exact. This datatype is specific to SQL Server. If you are using another DBMS, SMALLINT may be used for the same function.
MONEY	8	From about - 900 trillion to + 900 trillion
		(900,000,000,000,000)
		Accuracy of about +/- 0.0005. This datatype isn't supported in MySQL, DB2 or Oracle.

The various integer types do not need further specification, however, the decimal type requires that you provide values for the **precision** and **scale**. 'Precision' is the **total number of digits**, both right and left of the decimal point. The second value, scale, specifies the **maximum number of digits** to the right of the decimal point. For example DECIMAL(6,3) gives me a range of –999.999 up to 999.999 while DECIMAL(6,5) gives a range from essentially minus ten to plus ten, but with five digits of accuracy to the right of the decimal place.

Approximate Numeric Types: FLOAT

FLOAT is a SQL approximate numeric type and is used for numbers that are usually very large or very small, where the exact number is not very important. For example the distance from the earth to the sun is **about** 140 million kilometers; that is 1.4 times 10 to the 8th. The 1.4 is the mantissa of the number and the eight is the exponent.

For many situations we don't really care if the mantissa is 1.3 or 1.5 (in fact it varies through the year) but we care a lot whether the exponent is seven, eight, or nine.

The FLOAT data type (one of the most common SQL approximate numeric types) has two parts to its range:

❑   The first is the **number of zeros** that can be supported. This is **fixed** for the data type by the **vendor**, in conjunction with how the database server hardware handles floating point arithmetic. Typical values for the number of zeros supported range from 38 to 300.

❑   The second value is set by the **programmer** and determines **how many digits** can be accepted in the mantissa. In the case of the distance to the sun we would want two since our values would be numbers like "1.3." **Note that the number of digits is irrespective of the decimal place**. If we needed an accuracy like "1.345" then we would set the mantissa to be 4. So a field with a data types of FLOAT(2) in a DBMS that supports 78 zeros could handle positive or negative numbers with a mantissa from 0.0 to 9.9 with up to 78 zeros in the exponent. The value can have a plus or minus value for the zeros thus making the number very large or a very small fraction.

As a beginner using approximate numeric types, be aware of the following points:

❑   First, there are sudden changes in efficiency as you increase the number of characters in your fields, and the hardware must switch to using twice as much memory per value.

❑   Second, the FLOAT value has some advantages when moving data from one OS/hardware platform to another.

❑   Third, if you can, use the exact types since they give exact answers and are less demanding on the system. Move to FLOAT when your values exceed the range of the fixed types.

❑   Last, if you intend to use approximate data types and performance is a critical issue then you should read more advanced texts on typing or consult with an expert in the field.

> *Note that because a FLOAT value is not exact you may have problems using it in a WHERE clause with an equals comparator because database may not be able to find concrete results. Therefore remember to use greater than or lesser than with data of the FLOAT type.*

Choosing the Right Numeric Type

How do you pick the right Numeric type?

First ask yourself the **largest** number that may have to go into the field. Then ask how **accurately** you have to represent that number. Consider whether you might lose some information if you use approximate numeric types. Also, decide whether you will ever need a negative number. And remember, it is always easier (if not more efficient) to make your types slightly too large than too small. See the section on *Examples of Data types for Data*, below, for examples.

So to summarize, consider the range and accuracy needed for your expected values and compare those to the specifications for Data Types in your specific DBMS.

MONEY Data Type

Before moving on to character data types, let's look at some of the specifics of the MONEY data type as it is an interesting one.

Currency data is so widely used that you may wonder why a MONEY data type was not part of the original SQL standard. The purest answer (and the technique we used for years) was that everything that needs to be done with money can be done using one of the **pure number types**. After all, why should money be different than "count of apples in inventory" or "national population"?

The MONEY type was introduced in SQL92, later than the other data types. There is some variation among vendors, but generally the range is plus or minus 900 trillion units with an accuracy of a ten-thousandth of a monetary unit. The monetary unit is not defined so that the data type can be used with any currency. Output from this data type will not contain a currency symbol or commas, but can be formatted as specified in the local information and language settings of the server.

Currency data types are specific to the SQL vendor, so we will cover only the three main points: types by size, output, and input:

❑ They are usually of two types by size: **large** and **small**. In this case large (MONEY) covers amounts with up to 60 zeros and to four decimal places of accuracy. The (MONEY) datatype isn't supported in MySQL, DB2 or Oracle. The SMALLMONEY datatype is only supported in SQL Server. These amounts can be in any unit of currency; they are not nation specific.

❑ In terms of output, the DBMS will detect the server's default monetary settings from the locale settings and report the values with appropriate unit characters (like $, £, ¥) and appropriate use of commas and decimal points.

❑ When you input the values, they are entered **without** unit characters or commas. The decimal divider is, of course, required. Each vendor has its own nuances, but most support two sizes, autoformat of output and minimal input rules.

Character Datatypes

There are five data types for characters, varying mainly in the **flexibility of their length**.

❑ The fixed length type is called CHAR(length), with an argument of the maximum length. CHAR accepts characters from the ASCII set, and most DBMS default to sorting CHAR values according to the ASCII number order. If data is entered that is less than the stated size then the data is padded with spaces to make up the full size.

ASCII stands for American Standard Code for Information Interchange, and is merely a universally popular set of characters. It includes every character you are likely to use with the data types we discuss here and is thus of little concern.

❑ VARCHAR(length) creates a field with up to (length) characters, again from the ASCII set. The efficiency comes from the DBMS being able to **reduce the size of the field** to the minimum needed whereas CHAR fields will always remain the full specified size.

❑ For languages that require non ASCII character sets there is the NCHAR(length) which is fixed like CHAR but accepts characters as defined in ANSI standards.

❑ Some SQL implementations include a NVARCHAR, which is similar to NCHAR butcan vary in length. The maximum length for any of these CHAR types in most DBMS is 8,000 characters and for the VARCHAR types half that. See more on CHAR vs. VARCHAR in the section below on selecting a character data type.

❑ Most implementations of SQL have additional data types named something like TEXT or NTEXT. These are fields with a much larger capacity, in the range of **30 Kb to 1 Gb**. They can store résumés, publications, technical manuals, and other large chunks of data organized by byte (not by bits). Note that in the interest of performance most DBMS **exclude** these large fields from most types of queries.

The data within these fields is not organized in any way that is manageable by the database. In fact the inclusion of such fields is fraught with dangers because although information is there, it is not available in any unit less then the whole. In other words if all you will want to do is print an entire résumé then a TEXT field will work. But if you want to get the applicant's name from the résumé you will experience great difficulty.

TEXT and NTEXT also use space in large chunks; for most DBMS it is of the order of 8 Kb. So if you have a piece of data in a TEXT field that is 4 Kb it is using 8 Kb of storage. If you have a datum of 8,001 bytes you will need 16 Kb of storage because an entire additional 8 Kb chunk has been allocated for the byte that exceeded the space of the first 8Kb chunk.

Choosing the Right Character Type

How do you pick the right Character Type?

Consider the expected **size** and **character set** of the **values**. First, if it is larger then 8 Kb you will have to either **break it up** or use the TEXT or NTEXT types. If the size is under 8 Kb then you will have to decide whether to use a **fixed** or **variable** length character type. Fields that hold very uniform values such as the postal abbreviation for States and Provinces (2 characters in North America) should be set for CHAR type because there will be less overhead for the DBMS to figure out how long to make the field. If the length of values is going to vary, such as the street address, then go with a VARCHAR and set the maximum.

Temporal Data Types

Time data is more conceptual then the other data types because it must handle time calculations such as:

❑ Finding the number of days elapsed between two dates

❑ Find the number of hours and/or minutes between two times or

❑ Finding the date of today plus a number of days

In each of these cases we have to perform arithmetic that correctly handles numeric systems with bases other then base 10. **SQL can only support these types of calculations if the data is stored in a field of the Date/Time type**.

SQL specifies six data types for handling dates and time. The first three are available in most DBMS:

- ❑ DATE
- ❑ TIME
- ❑ TIMESTAMP

The other three have been implemented for very few of the DBMS and thus will **not** be covered in this book.

- ❑ TIME WITH TIME ZONE
- ❑ TIMESTAMP WITH TIME ZONE
- ❑ INTERVAL

INTERVAL describes the amount of time between two points in time and has not been introduced to any of the major DBMS. The vendors have preferred to offer proprietary extensions that solve the same problems.

Let's now look at the first three types, then:

- ❑ The DATE type stores **eight** digits that represent the year (four digits), month (two) and date(two). Since SQL has always held years with four digits there have been no problems with millennial roll-overs for the pure SQL part of information systems.

  The DATE type supports dates from 0001 to 9999 based on the Gregorian calendar. The Gregorian calendar offers few surprises for the last two hundred years. If you are working with data from before 1800 you will have to perform a complex set of adaptations for adjustments of about two weeks that were performed in different countries on different dates between 1582 and 1753 (with another adjustment for Russian dates in 1918).

- ❑ TIME data types contain **six or more** digits. The rigid part contains **two** digits each for hour, minute, and second. The flexible part is the precision of the fraction of a second. If you specify a data type as TIME then you get no fractions of a second (although some vendors automatically include some fractional digits in the default TIME type). TIME(n) allows you to specify the number of digits you require as fractions of a second.

- ❑ TIMESTAMP is both a favorite of programmers and a type that can create problems as systems increase in complexity. It is like a combination of DATE and TIME and thus contains **four** digits for year and **two** each for month, date, hour, minute, and second making a total of 14. SQL provides for a level of precision through the n of TIMESTAMP(n) although this is not implemented by all vendors. An of 3 provides millisecond precision, and 6 provides microsecond provision. TIMESTAMP is frequently used internally to handle some of the record keeping of transactions. Programmers like to use it as a unique number for primary keys. It is certainly much easier then writing code to calculate the next number in a series (see Chapter 9).

  However, TIMESTAMP can cause failures. The first problem comes when a TIMESTAMP datum is generated within a transaction. Transactions can take a relatively long time to complete and thus a timestamp may not contain the value that the programmer expected (it may be 'out of date' by the time the transaction is completed). Second, when more then one computer is involved (client/server, three tier, multi-server, etc.) you can not be sure that you will have unique values if you are getting time stamping from more than one machine. It is almost impossible to get two computer clocks exactly set to be equal and even harder to keep them synchronized.

169

Microsoft SQL Server, like most vendors, has its own way of handling temporal date. It has a single DateTime type that holds eight bytes to describe a point in time from 1753 to 9999 to an accuracy of three hundredths of a second.

Choosing the Right Temporal Type

Which temporal type should I use?

The selection of which of the three temporal types to use is easy because they do not overlap in the way that creates such problems for numeric types. The difficulty arises in how strictly you will follow the pure SQL standard for your time data. The temporal data types have been one of the stumbling blocks in complete portability of SQL code and data between DBMS. As the description of time is so complex (as shown below) programmers have actively sought extensions offered by DBMS vendors. Although many of these innovations are very valuable, they are rarely compatible with each other. Sacrificing compatibility for ease in getting work done, programmers rely more and more heavily on these extensions. When the SQL standards committee attempts to integrate these practices into the standard they find that the mutually incompatible techniques are so firmly entrenched that a compromise is impossible.

The take-home message is to carefully consider the most likely future path of your code and data. If you may be moving to new DBMS then you must make the effort to code completely within the rather limited options of the pure SQL standards. If you are sure that your project will remain on one platform then you can save considerable time and complexity by taking advantage of your platform's extensions.

Examples of Data Types for Data

Age	This could be an integer or it could be a decimal, indicating how far the value has gone into its next year. But wouldn't it be better to calculate the age based on the person or object's date of birth or creation? For large values (age of a fossil) an approximate subtype like DECIMAL would be most efficient.
Telephone numbers	Telephone numbers can be typed as numeric fields if you can be sure that all incoming data will be cleaned of symbols. But since we rarely do math on telephone numbers (what is the value of adding two phone numbers?) you may consider using a VARCHAR or CHAR type. If you are working with telephone numbers outside of your home country you may find some very different uses of symbols and your client may want those symbols as part of the output. It will be difficult to add the symbols to the data if the data is only stored as number, so VARCHAR would be appropriate.
Order Number	If the field contains your order number then you can ensure that you only use numbers, and an integer field would be most efficient. But if you are holding your client or vendor's order numbers then you may get hit with a system that contains letters or characters. In this case it would be better to use a VARCHAR field.

Rates and Percentages	These frequently have a fractional amount and thus must use a decimal type. You might consider a FLOAT, but that would be less efficient and probably not be needed for the typical number of digits used in exchange rates.
Scientific data of large values	Figures like the distance to the sun or the number of base pairs of DNA require the expression of a very large number, but not very accurately. The best bet is an approximate type such as Float.
Populations of countries	This is a little tricky. You might start by thinking of it as a scientific value where you want to describe big numbers like 250 million people in the USA but you don't have to be too accurate. But if you accept an accuracy of a million or even a couple hundred thousand then you will round off to zero the populations of Kiribati, Grenada, and Vanuatu. You probably don't want those countries to have a population of zero in your calculations. Even if the rounding error is not important, you will get errors when they are used as numerators in divisions. INTEGER (2 billion) would cover you just barely since China has 1.2 billion. Perhaps going to a decimal type with 10 places would be safest, covering you for even the total population of the earth.
Title	This is a text field and since we must accommodate different lengths of data (Mr., Ms., Reverend, Chief, Docent, Herr, Dr., Prof. etc.) we must use VARCHAR. If we intend to use non-ASCII characters in the data we will use NVARCHAR.
State or Province	Again a text field, but this time we can be sure that if our data is from North America it will always be two characters. With a known and consistent length of data we can improve performance with CHAR instead of VARCHAR.
Dates	Avoid the temptation to store dates or times as a character strings. Although easier to format you will find it more difficult to use the values to calculate an interval or perform date comparisons. Here we would use DATE, or TIMESTAMP as required.
Zip Codes	Remember that many postal codes outside of the US contain letters. Also keep in mind that full zip plus four uses 9 characters. If you make the data type CHAR you will be able to store the hyphen between the "zip" and the "plus four" but you will have a harder time using the data as a numeric for zip code statistics.

Although Access supports a NUMBER data type, in most SQL DBMS you have to select a more specific type within the numeric subtypes. On the other hand you can get by with a TEXT type in most DBMS but you may want to use CHAR instead.

Automating Serial Number Values (AUTOINCREMENT)

If you have worked with Access you will be familiar with the AUTONUMBER (or counter) field type. The DBMS will automatically fill the field with the next higher number from the last record's value. You can read values from an AUTONUMBER type, but not write to it. The writing is only done by the DBMS and only at the time that the record is created. Note that in some DBMS you can start at a number other then one and you can increment by a value other than one. Also, **numbers are never reused**. For example, if you have three records they will typically get 'autonumbered' 1, 2, and 3. If you delete record number 2 you will have two records left with data in the AUTONUMBER field of 1 and 3. If you then add another record it will get a value of 4 in the AUTONUMBER field. The value 2 is never reused.

> Not all DBMS use serial integers for values in an auto-incrementing field. For example, Microsoft SQL Server uses a **UNIQUEIDENTIFIER** data type, which contains a Globally Unique Identifier (GUID). This 16-byte binary string is guaranteed to be unique.

Another common misunderstanding about AUTONUMBER field types is that the DBMS somehow uses your AUTONUMBER values in its own internal management – not true. The DBMS will manage the records fine without an AUTONUMBER field. However, from the standpoint of the programmer, an AUTONUMBER field can be invaluable to Ensure that you can select one record from all others as per our discussion of Primary keys in Chapter 3. See Chapter 9 for details on autonumbering techniques.

Having expounded on the benefits and theory of AUTONUMBER fields I must warn you that they are not popular with everyone for both theoretical and practical reasons. Long essays have been written on how autonumbering types are not genuine SQL (true) and how they can not be relied upon (true in very rare cases). Furthermore, because they are a vendor implementation they are likely to fail when you move from one DBMS to another. For most programmers they are a welcomed convenience and used with many tables. But if you want to avoid them then you must generate your own serial number in the front end that prepares data prior to inserting it into the table. In Chapter 9 we discuss the specific procedures for working with serial numbered fields.

NULLs

When we are creating a table and considering data types we have to consider how to handle the absence of data. The absence of data is handled in SQL by the NULL value. A good test of students' worldly experience and creativity is to ask them to list situations that might be described by a NULL. The question is not trivial, it has vexed the experts since the beginning of computation. Here are some answers:

❑ *A value which is not known now but we expect to know in the future.* When I was a kid it was rare to know the gender of an unborn child. You could have a record for the unborn child in a database that might include information like the child's mother's name. But NULL could be for the baby's gender. We have a reasonable expectation that we will know the value in the future.

❑ *A value which is not known now and we probably will never know.* For example, whether my grandfather had the gene for red hair. My son's record can have a value since his grandfather could be tested. But my grandfather died before DNA sequencing was available.

- ❑ *An indicator that an underlying piece of information is* NULL *and therefore we are carrying the* NULL *forward through calculations.* If we had a NULL value for number of apples consumed in Pennsylvania and then tried to calculate the number of apples consumed per person we could call the result NULL.

- ❑ *An indicator that the field does not apply.* For example if a clinic had a field in a table of patients for "Number of Pregnancies" a male patient might have a NULL.

For SQL these four uses are valid. We can boil down the definition of NULL for our purposes to be as follows.

NULL is an indicator that the value is not now known.

> It is a very common misunderstanding to think of a **NULL** as a zero or an empty string. It is not. A **NULL** is an unknown value.

There are two places where NULLs can surprise you.

- ❑ The first is that they **propagate**. If you add two values and one is NULL the result is NULL, as in the Pennsylvanian apples example. Many vendor enhancements to the SQL standards will overcome the problem in aggregate functions like average. But they each do it in a specific way for their product.

- ❑ The second 'surprise' is that when comparing one or more NULLs in an expression you will get an answer of UNKNOWN, not a TRUE or FALSE.

An argument can be made that there should never be a NULL value in a database. The thinking is that if tables are perfectly **normalized** then a field that might hold a NULL (say fldN) will be in a **separate table** (say tblN) rather than with the other fields in the original table (say tblO) . For those records in tblO that have a value for fldN there will be a record in tblN and for those that have NULLs there will not be a record in tblN. With this system there will never be a record in tblO with a NULL.

For example we have an employees table. We could add a field for FavoriteSport. But maybe only half the employees like sport at all and so the field has half NULLs. We can create another field called EmployeeSports with fields called EmployeeID and FavoriteSport we only add records for those employees that have a favorite sport. So then the original employee table does not have a half-NULL Favorite Sports field and the Employee Sports table has no NULLs in its Favorite Sports fields. Conveniently, this would also accommodate employees who have more then one "favorite" sport.

Given the above argument, how should we handle missing data for a given field? Accept NULLs or normalize to the point where there are no NULLs? Consider two percentages.

- ❑ First, what percent of the records are going to have a NULL.

- ❑ Second, consider what percent of your NULLs will persist, that is not be temporary and soon replaced by real data?

If the percents are low then we can generally get better performance by accepting a few NULLs and not making the DBMS perform a join to gather data. If the percentages will be high, then we are better off moving the 'NULLy' field to another table and letting the DBMS perform the join on the occasion that it needs it.

Try It Out – Create Table of Insurance Plans Using Data Typing

You are now ready to add a table that uses a larger range of data types. Your business plan specifies that you need to hold the following information for each insurance plan. The specific details are included in the table below the list:

❑ Name of the plan

❑ The insurance company that provides the plan

❑ The plan's code as assigned by the insurance company

❑ StartDate – Date when plan was first offered to Northwind employees

❑ BenefitDeath – amount paid in case of death, ranging from $500,000 to 4 million dollars

❑ Pages in the contract – ranges from 1 to 24

❑ Monthly base premium

❑ Family plan available? – yes or no

	1	2	3	4
Name	American Plan	Bonus Plan	All Inclusive	Bounty Plan
InsurCompany	A-One	A-One	Benchmark	Benchmark
ProviderNumber	43N21-89	43N21-156	NW345	NW002
StartDate	1 Jan 1991	2 Feb 1992	3 Mar 1993	4 Apr 1994
BenefitDeath	$500,000	1 million	2 million	3 million
ContractPages	3	16	21	8
BasePremium	$110	$120	$330	$140
FamilyPlan	Yes	No	Yes	No

1. Start your SQL tool; in this book we use Microsoft Query Analyzer, which comes with the CD on the cover.

2. Connect to your copy of the Northwind database (BegSQLNorthwind).

3. Run the following SQL statement (remember that if you are not running SQL Server, use SMALLINT rather than TINYINT).

```
CREATE TABLE InsurPlans
    (InsurPlanID TinyInt,
    InsurPlanName VARCHAR(25),
    InsurCompany SMALLINT,
    ProviderNumber VARCHAR(15),
    StartDate DATETIME,
    BenefitDeath MONEY,
```

```
        ContractPages TINYINT,
        BasePremium SMALLMONEY,
        FamilyPlan BIT)
;
```

4. Check that the table has been created, using the techniques discussed in our earlier Try-It-Out.

5. Add data by running the following SQL statement. *Note that when we refer to the Insurance Company Name we use the values from the ID fields (the four numbers in the top row) of the Insurance Companies Table above.*

```
INSERT INTO InsurPlans
(InsurPlanID, InsurPlanName, InsurCompany, ProviderNumber,
 StartDate, BenefitDeath, ContractPages,
 BasePremium, FamilyPlan)
VALUES
        (1,'American Plan', 1,'43N21-89',
        01/01/1991, 500000,3,
        110,1)
;
INSERT INTO InsurPlans
(InsurPlanID, InsurPlanName, InsurCompany, ProviderNumber,
 StartDate, BenefitDeath, ContractPages,
 BasePremium, FamilyPlan)
VALUES
        (2,'Bonus Plan', 1,'43N21-156',
        02/02/1992, 1000000,16,
        130, 0)
;
INSERT INTO InsurPlans
(InsurPlanID, InsurPlanName, InsurCompany, ProviderNumber,
 StartDate, BenefitDeath, ContractPages,
 BasePremium, FamilyPlan)
VALUES
        (3,'All Inclusive',2, 'NW345',
        03/03/1993,2000000,21,
        330,1)
;
INSERT INTO InsurPlans
(InsurPlanID, InsurPlanName, InsurCompany, ProviderNumber,
 StartDate, BenefitDeath, ContractPages,
 BasePremium, FamilyPlan)
VALUES
        (4,'Bounty Plan',2,'NW002',
        04/04/1994,3000000,8,
        140,0)
;
```

How It Works

We start with our basic syntax for creating an object, in this case a table. Then we begin describing the **names** and **data types** of **fields** that we want in this table. Note that the first field will be an ID field that will probably be using as a primary key. We can be pretty sure that no two providers will have the exact same plan number, but it is safer to have the primary key data under our control. In Chapter 9 we will discuss automatically generating an autoincrementing datum. We can probably be sure that Northwind will never offer more than 255 plans, so TINYINT should work (see later Try-It-Out for a correction).

We continue listing fields with appropriate data types. Since plan names will vary in length we make that field a VARCHAR. The number of companies from whom Northwind offers plans will be under 32,000, so for that, we use SMALLINT. The number that the Provider assigns to its plan is out of our control and may well contain letters so that should be VARCHAR(25), and we hope that the size is large enough.

Microsoft SQL Server, the DBMS we included in the book, does not use separate data types for DATE and TIME, so we use the single DATETIME type for the first offering of the plan to Northwind employees. If your DBMS uses the standard SQL DATE then you could save space by using it. The benefit paid upon death will be money so we could use a MONEY or NUMERIC type. If we used numerics SMALLINT (32,000) would not be big enough, so we would go to INT which covers up to 2 billion. However, we will use MONEY, as this data type is supported in SQL Server. If your DBMS supports SMALLMONEY you will have to check that its range goes up to 10 million, which would be the upper limit we could expect on a death settlement. SQL Server SMALLMONEY only goes to 200 thousand, so we must use the larger MONEY.

The pages of the contract do not exceed 21 in our first few records, so TINYINT with a limit of 255 suffices. Our monthly premium will be under $200,000 so we can save space by using SMALLMONEY. The last field, FamilyPlan, will be either yes or no and so we can get by with just a BIT type with 1 representing "yes."

Modify tables

It would be a truly skilled database designer who could create all of his or her tables, load data, perform testing, and get client approval without having to make a revision to the table structure. Even if you could achieve that level, you will still have to modify existing tables to meet new demands of the business.

In this section we will cover Adding, Removing, and Changing fields of a table.

Adding Fields

Adding fields is performed by using the ALTER...ADD statement against the table. The syntax is simple, as follows:

```
ALTER TABLE TableName ADD FieldName FieldDataType
```

Some DBMS now include the option of using the syntax with an additional keyword, like so:

```
ALTER TABLE TableName ADD FIELD FieldName FieldDataType
```

Because tables can contain multiple constraints, key definitions, and other structures, maintainability improves when using the optional additional keyword FIELD. Microsoft SQL Server does not support the additional keyword.

Fields that are added to a table must be defined as a data type, the same as fields that are made using the CREATE TABLE command. The data of the new fields will be NULL unless a default is added to the definition as per techniques of Chapter 7.

Try It Out – Add Field to Table of Insurance Companies

Your boss has asked you to keep track of the city and state housing the headquarters of each insurance company.

1. Open your SQL testing tool and connect to your copy of Northwind.

2. Run the following code:

```
Alter Table InsurCompanies
     Add City VARCHAR(15)
;
Alter Table InsurCompanies
     Add State CHAR(2)
;
```

3. Check that the operation was successful by running the following command to see if the additional fields are displayed.

```
SELECT InsurCompName, City, State FROM InsurCompanies;
```

It is not necessary to add data to these fields; we just want to practice creating them.

How It Works

When we added the fields we immediately provided the field types. Since the city names could be of variable length we guessed the largest would be 15 characters and then used VARCHAR to allow the DBMS to shorten as possible. On the other hand we can be pretty sure that all North American states and provinces use a 2-character abbreviation and thus could set the STATE as a CHAR(2).

Note that when you ran the SELECT statement the nascent fields were filled with NULLs.

Removing Fields

Removing fields from a table using pure ANSI-SQL is not as easy as it might seem because there is no DROP FIELD syntax. However, many DBMS vendors have added a drop field extension. For example the DBMS on the disk with this book supports:

```
ALTER TABLE TableName DROP FIELD FieldName
```

Note that you cannot drop all the fields from a table. A table must contain at least one field, the same as table creation requires the definition of at least one field.

If your DBMS does not offer an enhancement to drop fields, then the most common technique is to:

1. CREATE a new table with fields the same as the existing (old) table, but **do not** include the fields you want to drop.

2. Copy data to the new table by INSERTing into the new table a SELECTion of records from the fields to keep from the old table.

3. DROP the old table.

4. RENAME the new table to the name of the old table.

The COPY step of this technique relies on creating records, which we will cover in Chapter 9. However, let's go through a COPY here to the extent of removing fields. Assuming that TableOld has Fields 1, 2 and 3 and we want to not copy Field 2 into the new table, the syntax is as follows.

```
INSERT INTO TableNew (Field1, Field3)
SELECT (Field1, Field3)
FROM TableOld;
```

Note that we have performed the INSERT INTO using only Fields 1 and 3 By leaving out the WHERE clause we get all of the records copied, but only Fields 1 and 3 from the old table.

There are two serious traps to removing fields. First, removing fields in a DBMS removes the fields and all of their data. There is no sense of "marking for removal" with an opportunity to unmark prior to actual removal. In this way, removing fields is like dropping tables. Second, and more important, is that it may be very difficult for you to know who else and how else the fields are being accessed. If there are other programmers involved they may not feel that the fields are no longer of use.

Changing Data Types

SQL allows the changing of the data type of an existing field, even it is already holding data. Not all data can be converted to another type and the allowable conversions vary among vendors. For example in most products you cannot convert from any numeric type to a TEXT type. Even for conversions that are allowed by all vendors, variation exists in how to handle sticky points in conversions. Each vendor has a listing of allowable conversions, generally in a table that indicates what is allowed and how the allowed conversions are performed.

The syntax to perform a conversion is not difficult:

```
ALTER TABLE TableName ALTER FIELD FieldName NewDataType
```

But there are some variations among vendors, particularly in the use of the keyword FIELD as a specifier. We shall see these differences in the following Try It Out.

Try It Out – Change Field Data Types

Your bosses have posted a B2B notice on the web calling for insurance companies to offer plans to Northwind employees. The response has been amazing, and there are now about 300 plans to add to the InsurPlans table. Also, as the applications are reviewed, it becomes clear that none of the plans' names exceeds 20 characters. Revise the InsurPlan table accordingly.

1. First, we need to change the data type of the `InsurPlanID` from `TINYINT` (max of 255) to `SMALLINT` (if you are not using SQL Server, you will already be using `SMALLINT`, but follow the example on paper to get a clearer understanding of changing data types) which allows us to hold values up to 32,000.

```
ALTER TABLE InsurPlans
ALTER FIELD InsurPlanID SMALLINT
;
```

2. Second, we can reduce the maximum number of characters of the InsurPlanName field to be 20 as follows:

```
ALTER TABLE InsurPlans
ALTER FIELD InsurPlanName VARCHAR(20)
;
```

How It Works

Changes to fields, like field creation, are done in SQL from the perspective of the Table object. We use the `ALTER TABLE` statement and then within that, specify that we want to change a field and finally which field to change. We do not need to state the data type that we are coming from, only the new data type that we want the field to have.

Summary

Normally DBAs create databases as per the request of the Database Designers. However, almost all database programmers end up creating databases at some time, particularly for learning and testing. The syntax to create a database in pure ANSI SQL is very simple, but most DBMS vendors have added **keywords** to set the database starting size, maximum size, and growth increments. Furthermore the creator can generally add specifications for how the data will be spread across one or more hard disks.

DBMS store all of the data in tables, as per the **normalization** rules of Dr. Codd. The table creation statement mostly focuses on the creation of the table's fields. There must be at least **one** field in each table.

SQL supports three families of data types: **Character, Numeric, and Temporal**. The character type can be fixed length (`CHAR`), variable length (`VARCHAR`) or can support large blocks of text. The Numeric family is most diverse, with the basic division between **exact types** (like `INTEGER` and `DECIMAL`) with ranges up to about 10^{38} and **approximate types** (like `FLOAT`) that support up to around 300 zeros behind the mantissa.

After a table is created (and possibly holding data) it can be **modified** with the `ALTER TABLE` statement. SQL has provisions to **add** or **change** a field. Most vendors include a provision to `DROP` a field, but in pure ANSI SQL this must be performed by copying the non-drop fields to a new table, then dropping the old table. In almost all situations, removal of data or structures supports **no recourse**. This includes dropping a table, removing records, and dropping fields.

> **Tables are removed with DROP.**
> **Records are removed with DELETE.**
> **Fields are removed with ALTER Table… DROP.**

In the next chapter we look at an important augmentation to the table structure – adding rules called constraints to reduce the chance that errant data will be stored or that fundamental inconsistencies will arise in the database scheme.

Data Constraints

A database is compromised when bad data percolates into the tables. SQL offers several techniques to avoid the problem, including the use of **constraints**. Constraints are like conditions that new data must be checked against to be accepted into the database. Whenever data is added or changed the DBMS will check the data against any constraints. If there are conflicts the data write will fail and a message is raised to the front end.

In this chapter we will:

- ❑ Examine the theory of constraints and compare them to other tools and techniques in performing the task of validating data and maintaining data integrity.
- ❑ Cover some general examples of constraints.
- ❑ Study specific cases for each of the major data types.
- ❑ Look at how to react to failures reported by constraints.

Why Do We Have Constraints?

The only thing worse than no data is bad data. In this case bad data means values that are clearly **inappropriate** or **invalid**. For example, we could have an employee's date of hire set as before the company was started, or we could have a negative number for the number of children a person has raised. We would like to avoid writing to our tables data such as ages of 200 years old or a professor teaching in the department "qwerty." Note also that bad data may not be immediately obvious, the problem may surface many years hence. For example a telephone number may be set as belonging to a customer #58. But there may not be a customer #58 and it is only when we try to associate the number and the customer do we discover the problem.

Defining and predicting bad data is an art developed from several sources:

- ❑ First is by making sure you're using appropriate **data types**.
- ❑ Second is by thinking through **logical ranges** for data.
- ❑ Third comes from your experience of looking at other programmer's code.

❑ A fourth and very important source is to analyze every piece of bad data that arrives in the testing phase.

❑ Fifth, talk to the users. If you have data entry clerks, find out what kind of data they get from the customers. It is amazing to list the variety of clearly wrong responses that arrive on forms.

❑ Last, it doesn't hurt to spend a few minutes hanging around the water cooler asking the old timers what kind of weird or bad data they have seen over the years. That's how I learned that some European professors actually use more than one Dr. in their title, along with the equivalent of "Mr." and possibly "Docent" added on. That is not bad data, but it certainly affects how we would build constraints for European clients.

SQL offers several techniques to assist a programmer in ensuring that only usable data enters a table. In this chapter we will cover constraints in detail and mention **rules**, **validation** and **triggers** for comparison. Note that no matter how accomplished you become with the SQL tools, you will still probably have your front end or SQL requestor doing some validation. In many cases the ability to catch and correct problems is easier when the processes are performed closer to the user. This is particularly true on the web where the time spent in a round trip from browser to server is very costly. Most systems we have worked on use a belt and suspenders approach where both front-end and 'internal' SQL validation is performed.

We have actually already discussed a technique that SQL considers, broadly, to be constraints: supplying a **default value** (data type) is a kind of SQL constraint. However, we are really interested in constraining the allowable values.

What Are We Constraining?

In this section we want to give you a heads-up on some of the many kinds of bad data that sneak into datastores. And to give you further leads on finding these problems, let's go through some sources of bad data.

A Rogue's Gallery of Bad Data

We cannot describe every kind of invalid data for every situation. But this list gives you a starting point for thinking through the potential problems for your applications.

Many kinds of columns should be limited to certain characters. Consider:

❑ Letters only

❑ Numbers only

❑ No symbols or only certain symbols

❑ Acceptance of letter characters above ASCII 122 (é, Æ, Ü, , etc.)

❑ Acceptance of ASCII versus UNICODE characters

❑ Acceptance of non-Western character sets like Japanese

❑ Acceptance of non-printing characters like CR and LF or the results of the Enter key

❑ Characters in a wrong pattern, like for a model number that has two letters then two numbers

Most Temporal columns can be checked for values that are out of an acceptable range, like:

❑ A date that is prior to the start of the company

❑ Dates which are clearly prior to the bounds of the data set

❑ Dates which are in the future for events that must be in the past

❑ Dates which are too close together, like a mother's age less then 10 at child's birth date

❑ Dates which are outside a range when events occur, such as end-of-quarter report which falls in the middle of a quarter

❑ Times that are outside the logical data range (sunset in Mexico is never at 11:00)

❑ Note that dates like "January 35th" are automatically rejected by the DBMS for columns of Date data type.

Sources of Bad Data

❑ Many errors are introduced in the data entry process. If it is done by hand it is a mind-numbing job and mistakes are inevitable, especially at the end of a shift, Friday afternoons, on days when people are ill, etc. In critical situations such as legal papers, data is often entered twice and then a computer compares the two and highlights differences for a third human to review and arbitrate.

❑ Errors arise when people are providing data. It is easy for a user to perceive a box for City to be for State. Asked for a "birthday" some user will put in a date and month while others will put in a date, month and year.

❑ In complex systems there may be many front ends, and they may not all be controlled by you. Other programmers may have misconceptions about the data, and their front ends may submit data in a form that you did not expect.

❑ Even when humans are not involved there are plenty of opportunities for mistakes to arise. When a comma delimited data file is being created by a computer there may be a comma missing or corrupted that throws off the phasing of the record and creates bad data.

As you can see there are many points in the system where an invalid piece of data can arise. Your two primary defenses are **front-end validation** and **database constraints**. We will primarily look at the latter in this chapter.

Terminology

Before we really get stuck into this chapter, let's look at some of the terminology you may encounter as you learn about, and begin implementing your own constraints. The majority of these are referred to in this chapter:

Domain – the set of all the values that are allowed in the column. The domain is defined by the data type of the column, plus its constraints. A domain contains definitions from both the DBMS and the programmer. Values that are allowed by the DBMS storage and processing specifications are derived from the data type. Values allowed by the programmer are established in the constraints.

Column Constraint – a clause that prevents certain values from being entered into a column. Constraints can be stated as exclusionary (such as "value cannot be over 100") or inclusionary (value must be in this list: Chicago, Paris, Eden).

Table Constraint – A table constraint is like a column constraint but it can involve values from multiple columns.

Rules – Rules are an older form of constraint, and perform some of the same functions as the CHECK constraint. Some DBMS allow rules only to permit backward compatibility (compatibility with older versions of software). Rules are objects that are bound to the table or column, whereas constraints are part of the table object. You can only have one rule per column, whereas you can have several constraints. Rules also suffer from performance problems relative to other constraints.

Trigger – A set of one or more SQL statements (a stored procedure) that is performed whenever the DBMS performs a specified task, generally updating or inserting records. Triggers are slower than column constraints.

Deferred Constraint – a type of constraint that improves performance by waiting to perform the constraint check until the end of a transaction (at the time of the COMMIT statement). We do not cover deferred constraints in this beginning book.

Business Model for 'Try it Outs' in this Chapter.

The Northwind company "enhances the employment experience" by offering a well-organized bowling league for its employees. Northwind pays the salaries of coaches and at the end of the season awards trophies. There are three trophies: "Best Bowler," Best Sport," and 'Most Improved." Coaches can nominate one employee for each trophy. Northwind has asked you to keep records on the coach's nominations so that later the trophy winners can be determined.

We will review Chapter 6 and set up for Chapter 7 by creating three tables, Coaches (holding names and ID numbers of coaches), Nominations (each record holding one nomination for one award) and Awards (the list of the three trophies). The Nominations table will contain **relationships** with employees, coaches and trophies. The pattern through the rest of this chapter will be to delete the existing forms of these tables and create better forms using the constraint techniques we will study. In a few cases we will modify the existing forms so you get practice in that syntax.

Try It Out – Set Up Tables for the Northwind Bowling Awards

1. Open your SQL tool (we use the Query Analyzer in this book) and prepare to work on your copy of the Northwind database (we have been using BegSQLNorthwind).

2. Run the following statement to create the table of coaches (remember that if you are using Oracle or MySQLs Command Prompt, you must add a semicolon at the end of each statement!):

```
CREATE TABLE Coaches
     (CoachID integer,
     CoachName VARCHAR(30)
     )
```

3. Run the following statement to create the table of awards:

```
CREATE TABLE Awards
    (AwardCode CHAR(2),
    Award VARCHAR(30)
    )
```

4. Run the following statement to create the table of nominations:

```
CREATE TABLE Nominations
    (NomID INTEGER,
    CoachID TINYINT,
    EmployeeID SMALLINT,
    AwardCode CHAR(2)
    )
```

At this point do not add data because later we will recreate these tables with constraints.

How It Works

This exercise reviews table creation from Chapter 6. We are using an integer type to identify the coaches and nominations. However, in our small list of awards we are using the AwardCode since that will be more intuitive and we do not expect to ever have more than a few more awards than our current three. Since we would not expect to have more than 255 coaches or 32,000 employees, we can use numeric data types smaller than INTEGER for our columns in the nominations table.

Nominations will be the central table. If we have two coaches each nominating one employee for each of three awards, we will have six records in this table. (Considering that the league will probably continue for many years we would add a year field, but let's keep it simpler for this chapter). Each nomination record will be related to one coach, one employee and one award. We will want to insure, through constraints, that the nomination records do not hold errant data that would lead to a broken relationship.

A Note on Adding Data

We have not formally covered how to add a new record to a table (see Chapter 9), but we would like to add some records in this chapter to test our constraints. The simplest syntax for adding a new record is as follows:

```
INSERT INTO TableName(FieldName1,FieldName2...)
VALUES (Value1, Value2...)
```

For example if Northwind hires a Mr. John Smith on January 3rd 2001 and gives him employee number 200 then the SQL statement to add the record would be:

```
INSERT INTO Employees(EmployeeID, LastName, FirstName, HireDate)
VALUES (200,'Smith','John',03/01/2001)
```

Some versions of Northwind will not allow you to assign an `EmployeeID`, rather Northwind does it itself. So if you get an error message that you cannot insert an explicit value for an identity column (`EmployeeID`) then use the following statement, which leaves out the `EmployeeID` column name and value:

```
INSERT INTO Employees(LastName, FirstName, HireDate)
VALUES ('Smith','John',03/01/2001)
```

Also note that you may have to change the way you type the date. For example, depending on your system, `03/01/2001` may record the date as March 1, 2001 rather than Jan 3, 2001. Whatever the case, use the same format as is in your OS settings. In the case of Windows that would be found in:

Start / Settings / Control Panel / Regional Options / Date tab.

If you are using Oracle you will have to change the way you type the date to: `3-JAN-2001` as Oracle will not accept the format we are using in our examples. Further, if you are using DB2, the dates will have to be entered in the following format `'2001-01-03-00.00.00'` (note the inverted commas). This is because the dates in the original Northwind database are in `DATETIME` format.

You can confirm your insertion by running a `SELECT` statement as we covered in Chapters 4 and 5, such as the following:

```
SELECT * FROM Employees
```

You should get a result set something like this:

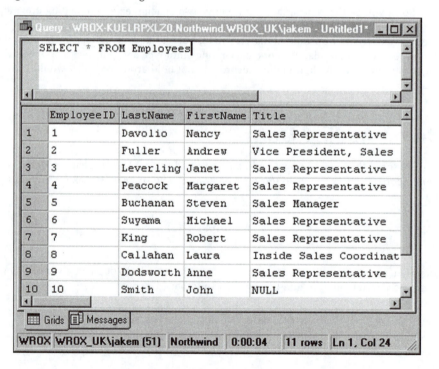

Your new entry for John Smith is now on the list.

> Note that the Northwind database, as it comes from Microsoft, requires that every record has an **EmployeeID**. The original employees use ID numbers 1-10.

We will present much more on creating records in Chapter 9 but for now this will allow you to test your constraints with some new data. If you have problems, take a look at the first few pages of Chapter 9.

NULL / NOT NULL

In Chapter 3 we discussed the necessity of being able to handle the fact that we "don't know" a value and thus handle the NULL. But we do not have to accept this uncertainty for every column. In fact for some tables we should not create a record if we can not provide a value for certain columns such as primary keys (identifier columns).

For example, when we create an order we should have an order number. If we can't create an order number then we shouldn't have an order. In other words, order number cannot be NULL. Likewise for the Coaches table we created in Northwind. If we can't give a value to the Coaches.CoachID then we should not be creating a record.

A constraint of NOT NULL is easy to add at the time a column is created, as follows:

```
CREATE TABLE TableName
    (ColumnName DataType NOT NULL,
    ColumnName DataType NULL)
```

Adding a NOT NULL constraint to an existing column is trickier. Generally (depending on the DBMS) you must re-specify the data type when you add a NOT NULL constraint as follows:

```
ALTER TABLE MyTestTable
    ALTER COLUMN ColumnName DataType NOT NULL
```

Even if there is no change to the data type you must still restate it.

You can check if you were successful by checking the metadata, as described in Chapter 17, specifically for NULLs as follows (In QueryAnalyzer be sure to use Menu: Query / Results in Grid):

```
SELECT Table_Name, Column_Name, Is_Nullable
    FROM Information_Schema.Columns
```

You will see a result set like this:

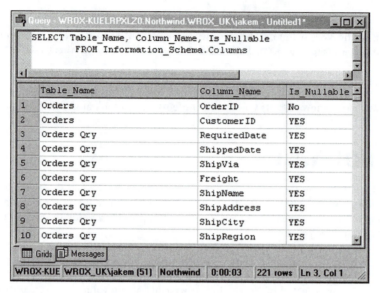

You can get a more specific list from the following statement:

```
SELECT Table_Name, Column_Name, Is_Nullable
    FROM Information_Schema.Columns
    WHERE Table_Name = 'TableName'
```

> **If a column is constrained as a primary key then it will not accept NULLS.**

Try It Out – Creating Columns with NOT NULL constraint.

We will eliminate our first tries at the `Awards`, `Coaches` and `Nominations` tables and re-create them to insure that the ID fields are not left empty for any records. Furthermore, we will require that the table of nominations and the coach, award and employee fields also contain data.

1. Open your SQL tool (we use the Query Analyzer in this book) and prepare to work on your copy of the Northwind database (we have been using BegSQLNorthwind).

2. Run the following statement to delete the old table of awards (since we have not entered data we are only losing the metadata, or structure, of the table):

```
DROP TABLE Awards
```

3. Now re-create the table with a NOT NULL constraint on the `AwardsCode` column:

```
CREATE TABLE Awards
    (AwardCode CHAR(2) NOT NULL,
    Award VARCHAR(30)
    )
```

4. Delete the other two tables we created:

```
DROP TABLE Coaches
DROP TABLE Nominations
```

5. And now recreate those tables with NOT NULL constraints:

```
CREATE TABLE Nominations
     (NomID INTEGER NOT NULL,
      CoachID TINYINT NOT NULL,
      EmployeeID SMALLINT NOT NULL,
      AwardCode CHAR(2) NOT NULL
     )
```

```
CREATE TABLE Coaches
     (CoachID integer NOT NULL,
      CoachName VARCHAR(30)
     )
```

6. Check your success by running:

```
SELECT Table_Name, Column_Name, Is_Nullable
FROM Information_Schema.Columns
WHERE Table_Name IN ('Coaches','Nominations','Awards')
ORDER BY Table_Name, Column_Name
```

As you can see, all the ID columns in our table are not nullable:

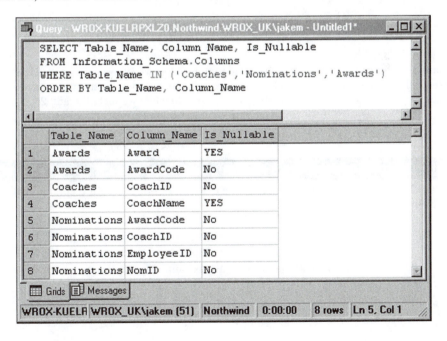

How It Works

In this TIO we deleted our first try at three tables and replaced them with improved table creation statements. The improvement of adding a NOT NULL constraint greatly reduces the possibility of the DBMS being unable to link a given nomination to its coach, award type and employee.

The most common mistakes that students make are with the location and spelling of the constraint. NOT NULL must come after the data type and before the comma that ends the description of the column. Also remember that NOT NULL is two words with a space between them.

When we check our success using the SELECT statement we are getting values from the metadata (we turn to the Schema techniques discussed in Chapter 17, which also discusses the differences among vendors). Of all the data, we want the DBMS to return values about columns. We are only interested in three columns of values (table name, column name and its nullability) and only from records that concern our three nascent tables.

CHECK Constraints - General Syntax and Examples

CHECK constraints limit values to a programmer-generated rule. For example they may limit invoice dates to be after the company was formed. Constraints are commonly created at the time when the columns are established in the CREATE TABLE statement. They can also be created when a column is added to an existing table or even be added to an existing column with data, as shown above.

The syntax is simple if the constraint is created at the same time as the column. After the data type, use the keyword CHECK and then the constraint, written in the same way as a WHERE clause.

```
CREATE TABLE TableName(
Field1 as DATA TYPE,
CHECK (expression)
)
```

For example, Northwind may want to track the number of years experience a coach has. It is logical that no coach will have more then 100 years of experience. So if we constrain the values to less than 100, then we will avoid accidentally adding a value of 220 when we meant to add 20.

MySQL does not currently support the CHECK keyword.

Try It Out – Create a Constraint for Max Years of Coaching

Drop the old Coaches table and add a new one that has a YearsCoached column that cannot accept values over 100.

1. Open your SQL Tool and begin to work on your copy of Northwind.

2. Remove the old table with the DROP TABLE command, as follows:

```
DROP TABLE Coaches
```

3. Create a better table with the following code:

```
CREATE TABLE Coaches
    (CoachID INT,
    CoachName VARCHAR(30),
    YearsCoached TINYINT CHECK (YearsCoached<100)
    )
```

Check your statements worked by getting a list of constraints from the schema.

If you are using Query Analyser we suggest that you turn on Menu: Query / View Results in Grid. If you view as text, the results columns of interest are way to the right of the scroll bar.

```
SELECT * FROM Information_Schema.check_constraints
    ORDER BY Constraint_Name
```

We can see that our new constraint has been created and stored:

How It Works

We want to be sure that spurious data such as 222 is not entered into our YearsCoached field. We can be quite sure that no coaches will have over 100 years experience, so we add a CHECK constraint. Note that the constraint is placed before the comma, which ends the description of the column. Also note that the entire expression to be checked goes inside a pair of parenthesis.

When we do our check at the end we again turn to the Schema described in Chapter 17. We perform a SELECT to get all the fields from a table described in the Owner.Object syntax of Information_Schema.Check_Constraints. This object uses underscores to indicate spaces. However, the statement we ran created a CHECK constraint without a recognisable name for that constraint. Later we will want to refer to that constraint in order to drop, override or modify the checking. The preferred syntax for creating a constraint name is as follows:

```
CREATE TABLE TableName(
Field1 as DATA TYPE,
CONSTRAINT ConstraintName CHECK (expression)
 )
```

Note that constraint names are held for the entire database, not just for individual columns. So if you choose to name the above constraint con_ExperinceUnder100 and you already have a con_ExperinceUnder100 in another table, you cannot add the second one.

Common Mistakes When Creating Constraints:

- ❑ Placing table constraint in location for a column constraint or vice versa
- ❑ Column constraint not located before the column definition closes, with a comma or right parenthesis
- ❑ Using functions that are vendor-specific to a different vendor
- ❑ Including logical errors in the expression, especially around boundary numbers and dates

Try It Out – Create a Constraint for Max Years of Playing Experience

We want to keep track of the number of years the coaches have played the game of bowling. These values will, logically, always be below 100. We want to name the constraint, con_YrsPlydUndr100.

Note that DB2 cannot accept constraint names longer than 18 characters. Our examples in this chapter account for this limitation, but be aware of it if you will be establishing your own constraints on a DB2 platform in the future.

1. Run a statement to create the column with a named constraint:

```
ALTER TABLE Coaches
    ADD YearsPlayed TINYINT
    CONSTRAINT con_YrsPlydUndr100
    CHECK (YearsPlayed<100)
```

2. Check your work by getting a list of constraints from the schema using the following statement:

```
SELECT * FROM Information_Schema.check_constraints
    ORDER BY Constraint_Name
```

We now have a recognizable name for our constraint:

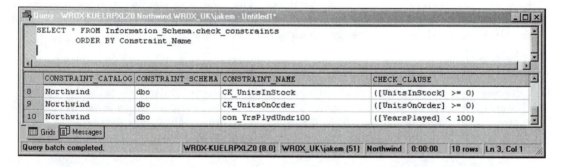

As mentioned above, the ALTER command allows constraints to be added to a table that already contains data. But what if existing data violates a new constraint which is being added to the table? The DBMS will check for existing data which violates the constraint. If violations would occur, the DBMS will raise an error message the same as if offending data was added to an existing constraint. Like other constraint violations, that message ends execution of the entire SQL statement so no bad data is added.

How It Works

This TIO is different from the last because we want a name for the constraint, so we add the terms
CONSTRAINT ConstraintName after the name of the table, but before the definition of the CHECK
expression.

The above examples are called column constraints because they have been added within the definition
of one column. You can also add constraints that perform a CHECK on more than one column. These
are called table constraints. The difference in the statements is the location within the CREATE TABLE
statement. Column constraints are located within the column definition; that is before the comma or
closing parenthesis that ends the description of the column. Table constraints are created after the last
column. The general syntax for creating table constraints at the time the table is created is as follows:

```
CREATE TABLE TableName(
Field1 as DATA TYPE,
Field2 as DATA TYPE
CONSTRAINT TableConstraintName CHECK (expression)
)
```

To return briefly to the Coaches table we have been constructing, it is reasonable that the coaches
should have been playing for more years than they have been coaching. With reference to the ALTER
command and the syntax above, we can add a table-level constraint, which checks this relationship in
the following way:

```
ALTER TABLE Coaches
    ADD CONSTRAINT con_CoachLessPlay
            CHECK (YearsCoached<YearsPlayed)
```

Constraints can be created at the same time a column is added to a table. However, you cannot add a
NOT NULL constraint on a new column because the existing rows would have NULL for data and there
would be an immediate constraint violation.

SQL allows multiple constraints, for example we could have the number of years played more than the
number of years coached, and also less than the coach's age, if we added an Age field to our Coaches
table. This would be a second table-level constraint and it is placed after the first, separated by a
comma.

We could test for a maximum and a minimum within one expression, but as you will learn later, when
there is a failure a constraint can report back the constraint name. Having separate constraints for
maximum and minimum violations will give us better feedback in an error message.

To date we have not discussed who can create constraints. As described in Appendix A, each object has
an owner. Most DBMS only allow an owner of the table to add a constraint unless specific permission
has been given by the owner to another user.

Disadvantages of Using Constraints

One experienced programmer observed that every time you fix a bug you introduce another. You may
have been thinking about how you can make your datastore foolproof by larding it with a layer of clever
constraints. It pays to keep in mind a few places where constraints can be unfavorable.

The most common mistakes we have observed are errors by the programmers in defining the domain of the constraint. In a business scenario, the data or business spec may seem to indicate that a range of 0 to 100 is correct, but the business might actually accept values of up to 200 in some rare cases. This type of problem often springs up late in the game when the largest sets of data are being tested and you finally hit values at the very extreme fringes. The best solution is to include ranges or other domain definitions in the specification that are approved by the client.

A second common problem arises when the programmer errs in the expression which defines the constraint's domain. Mistakes frequently arise in the boundary areas, like including or excluding the day at the end of a time period. A good practice for any programming is to intensively test data around all boundaries, including those for constraint domains.

We like to think that our programming work will endure. Unfortunately business rules are very rigid, so constraints that are perfectly valid today may cause havoc in the future. When I was growing up no one would have guessed that there was a need for five digits in the Dow Jones Industrial Average. Errors also arise from the past. The business may want to import historical data and find that old values are outside of the current acceptable range.

Always name constraints to help in future changes; all of these pitfalls can be more easily solved if you name your constraints. The errors raised will then include a logical clue to which constraint was offended, rather than being stuck with the DBMS crypto-names.

CHECK Constraints for Numeric Data Types

The simplest numeric CHECK is to confine the data to one side of a value. For example:

```
Constraint OrderQuantityMax50 CHECK OrderQuantity < 50
```

or

```
Constraint OrderQuantityMin1 CHECK OrderQuantity > 1
```

However, it is usually better to check both ends of the range. For example although OrderQuantity must be less than 50 it must also be at least one, as follows:

```
Constraint OrderQuantityRange CHECK ((OrderQuantity < 50) AND (OrderQuantity > 1))
```

Note that we are using an AND clause, as SQL does not support syntax like "1<value<50" as we would use in written algebra. Also note that each test should be in its own set of parentheses and that all the tests are within a set of parentheses for the CHECK as a whole. The above statement is easier to read if you type it in the following format:

```
Constraint OrderQuantityRange
   CHECK (
   (OrderQuantity < 50) AND
   (OrderQuantity > 1)
   )
```

SQL does support the BETWEEN clause which gives you code that is even easier to read such as the following:

```
Constraint OrderQuantityRange
    CHECK
    (OrderQuantity BETWEEN 1 AND 50)
```

When limiting a value to a range it is important to test the boundaries carefully. Many mistakes occur because of confusion between the programmer and business rules over whether a boundary number is inclusive or not. Further confusion arises from fractional values near a boundary.

You may want to check your columns against the following list of common mistakes.

- ❑ Value of zero

- ❑ Values near zero like 0.5 and –0.5

- ❑ Values within a fraction of the upper boundary, like 9.9 with an upper boundary of 10

- ❑ Values just over the boundary

- ❑ Values with the smallest allowed increment to the boundary, like a column with 4 decimals places allowed, test 9.9999 against a boundary of 10

Some data must be in multiples of a certain number; for example, your company may sell items in quantities of five. In this case you can use the MODULUS function built in to most SQL vendor's products. In many products it is represented by a percent sign, such as the following, which will only allow entry of numbers that are an even multiple of five.

```
Constraint OrderQuantityFive CHECK OrderQuantity % 5=0
```

SQL allows numeric data to be limited to values in a list. For example you may accept order quantities as 5, 10, 50 or 100 pieces. A constraint would be:

```
Constraint RightOrderQuantity CHECK OrderQuantity in (5,10,50,100)
```

CHECK Constraints for Temporal Data Types

The most basic temporal checks will be for dates that are before or after an event, such as the day a company was formed or the start date of production for a product. You may want to also constrain:

- ❑ Earliest possible date

- ❑ Events that must happen before date of record entry

- ❑ Events that are within a certain time frame, for example a Fiscal year

- ❑ Events that must happen in chronological order

- ❑ Dates that may occur earlier or later than expected due to time zone differences and the international date line

197

Try It Out – Constraints on Date Types

Northwind wants to keep track of when each bowling coach first started with the Northwind leagues. Based on values in the Order table it looks like Northwind started business in the summer of 1996, so let's make a constraint that coaches must have started after 01 January 1996

1. Using your SQL front end and working on your copy of Northwind, run the following statement:

```
ALTER TABLE coaches Add DateStart DATETIME CONSTRAINT con_DateStart1996
CHECK (DateStart>'01/01/1996')
```

2. Check your constraint with:

```
SELECT Constraint_Name,Check_Clause
    FROM Information_Schema.Check_Constraints
    ORDER BY Constraint_Name
```

3. And finish by testing both good and bad data

Good:

```
INSERT INTO Coaches
    (CoachID, CoachName, DateStart)
    VALUES
    (1,'Louie','1/1/2001')
```

Bad:

```
INSERT INTO Coaches
    (CoachID, CoachName, DateStart)
    VALUES
    (2,'Maxine','1/1/1990')
```

For the second INSERT INTO you should see something like:

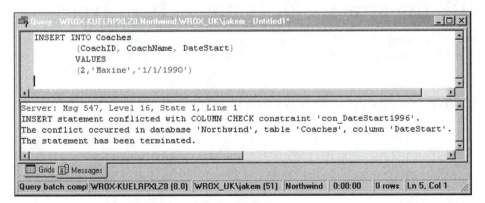

How It Works

We add this constraint to an existing table, but we are adding the constraint at the same time as a new column. The ALTER TABLE command has many uses. In this case we follow it with the ADD keyword, and then the name of a new column. New columns are always followed by their data type. In this case we use DATETIME. Following the data type we use the CONSTRAINT keyword followed by the name of the constraint. Every constraint gets named, but the choice is whether you want the name to be given by the DBMS (which will include some unintelligible string) or whether you want to give it a name that is clearly recognizable. We pick the latter. Now we define the constraint as a CHECK type followed by its expression. In this case we indicate that the DATESTART value must be after the first of January 1996. Note that this expression will not allow people who were hired on the first of January; it must be after the first.

We could see that the constraint addition was successful by listing all the constraints held in the Information_Schema.Check_Constraints collection.

Then we gave it a run by adding Louie, a person hired about 5 years after the cut-off and were successful. When we tried Maxine we got to see the error thrown by a constraint violation.

CHECK Constraints for Character Data Types

SQL allows you to constrain character data as well as numbers and dates: any valid SQL expression can be put within the parenthesis after the CHECK keyword.

Character constraints can be inclusive in the sense that only specified characters can be used. For example if we wanted to record either of two directions we could use the following:

```
ALTER TABLE TableName
    ADD ColumnName CHAR(16)
    CONSTRAINT con_MyCONstraintName
        CHECK (ColumnName IN ('clockwise','counterclockwise'))
```

SQL allows CHECK expressions to be any valid WHERE clause, including exclusions. For example you may want to prevent the word "white" in the data:

```
ALTER TABLE TableName
    ADD ColumnName CHAR(16)
    CONSTRAINT con_MyConstraintName
        CHECK (ColumnName NOT IN ('white'))
```

Try It Out – Constraints on Character Types

The league asks you to keep track of whether each coach is right- or left-handed.

1. Using your SQL Analyser or other tool, and working on your copy of Northwind, run the following statement:

```
ALTER TABLE coaches
    Add Hand CHAR(1)
    CONSTRAINT con_CoachHand
        CHECK (Hand IN('l','r'))
```

2. Check your constraint with:

```
SELECT Constraint_Name,Check_Clause
    FROM Information_Schema.Check_Constraints
    ORDER BY Constraint_Name
```

3. And finish by testing both good and bad data

Good (the last value is the lower case letter 'L', not a number one):

```
INSERT INTO Coaches
    (CoachID, CoachName, Hand)
    VALUES
    (5,'Lefty','l')
```

Bad:

```
INSERT INTO Coaches
    (CoachID, CoachName, Hand)
    VALUES
    (6,'Scooter','t')
```

You should see a similar error message we saw at the end of our previous TIO.

How It Works

When we added the constraint in the first statement we followed the syntax of using the word IN. Note that the acceptable list must have each character string in single quotes and separated by a comma. The entire list goes into parenthesis and then the entire expression goes into parenthesis. You will make less mistakes if you think of the IN as sort of an equal sign with the column name on the left and the list on the right.

Note that when you check the constraint SQL actually expands the short hand from

```
(Hand IN('l','r')) to ([Hand] = 'r' or [Hand] = 'l')
```

Overriding Constraints

One way to react to constraint violations is to instruct the DBMS to ignore the constraint. (I've been trying to figure out how to do this for my tax authority's expense deductions tables, but no success yet). Obviously you can end up shooting yourself in the foot with an override because the constraints have a purpose. But sometimes there will be a case where you want to force some values outside the column's domain. Overrides can't be done in response to an actual violation, but SQL does accept statements that override constraints. Note that in the following syntax for overriding constraints the term NOCHECK is one word:

```
ALTER TABLE TableName
    NOCHECK CONSTRAINT ConstraintName
```

Then we can reinstate the constraint with:

```
ALTER TABLE TableName
    CHECK CONSTRAINT ConstraintName
```

Remember two notes for working with constraint overrides:

❑ The technique is generally only usable when the constraint has been named.

You cannot disable unique or primary key constraints.

Try It Out – Add a Field Value Which Violates Existing Data

Remember that we added a constraint that bowling coaches had to have a start date after the company was formed? We named the constraint con_DateStart1996. Well it turns out that the Northwind founder (Mr. Windy) had Maxine for a coach since 1985 and Mr. Windy wants her in the database with the '85 start date.

1. Using Query Analyzer or another tool, open your copy of Northwind.

2. As a refresher, check the constraints as follows. We want to review the check expression for con_DateStart1996. To do this, type the following query:

```
SELECT Constraint_Name,Check_Clause FROM Information_Schema.Check_Constraints
ORDER BY Constraint_Name
```

3. Run the following statement:

```
ALTER table coaches
    NOCHECK CONSTRAINT con_DateStart1996
```

```
INSERT INTO Coaches
    (CoachID, CoachName, DateStart)
    VALUES
    (2,'Maxine','1/1/1985')
```

```
ALTER table coaches
    CHECK CONSTRAINT con_DateStart1996
```

4. Check your success with:

```
SELECT * FROM Coaches
```

Indeed, we can see that we were successful in by-passing our con_DateStart1996 constraint, and adding Maxine to our database:

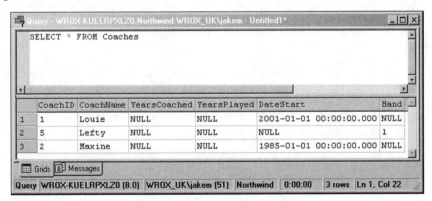

How It Works

In this TIO we added an illegal value to our `Coaches` table. But prior to that we reviewed the constraints using our `Check_Constraints` table owned by `Information_Schema` as per the techniques of Chapter 17.

First, we turned off the constraint that we intended to violate using the `NOCHECK` keyword. This was possible because we named the constraint at its creation. Second, we performed our `INSERT INTO` with the offending date (note that there was no error message). Last we turned the `CHECK` back on so that we can avoid writing values in the future that exceed the column's domain.

Key Constraints

Perhaps the most important constraint in a relational DBMS is the enforcement of key rules. The keys are the fields that provide the match in a join or relationship (as we will review below) and so any erroneous data in key fields will mean a match cannot be created and thus the relationship has been lost for the errant row.

To review relationships, recall that in our tulip company example of Chapter 3 (relational databases section) we ended with two tables for the vendors for our bulbs: `Suppliers` and `SuppliersContacts`, repeated below.

Suppliers

Suppliers.ID	Suppliers.Name
1	RJ Farms
2	Angelica Inc.

SupplierContacts

SupplierContacts.SupplierID	SupplierContacts.Type	SupplierContacts.Number
1	Voice	123-4567
2	Voice	987-6543

Within `Suppliers`, we had a field named `ID`, which was our primary key. The values in that column are unique for each record and thus identify each record separate from all other records. In our case we used a simple serial numbering system. Then in `SupplierContacts` we have a column called `SupplierID` that identifies which supplier matches with this record's telephone number. The DBMS is able to match the `SupplierContacts` record with its appropriate supplier record by matching these two values.

There are two problems that could occur to upset this flower basket. First, what if two suppliers were given the same `SupplierID` number, say number 58? Then the DBMS would not know which of the two #58 suppliers to match to a `SupplierContact` record with a value of 58 for `SupplierID`. Conversely, a problem arises if a record in `SupplierContacts` holds a value for `SupplierID` which does not exists in `Suppliers.SuppliersID`.

Case One: Duplicate Primary Key

Suppliers

Suppliers.ID	Suppliers.Name
1	RJ Farms
2	Angelica Inc.
58	Orlando Acres
58	Richland Rich Lands

SupplierContacts

SupplierContacts.SupplierID	SupplierContacts.Type	SupplierContacts.Number
1	Voice	123-4567
2	Voice	987-6543
58	Voice	585-8585

For the third record in the SupplierContact table, which arrow is the correct match-up? Due to a duplication in Suppliers.SupplierID, the DBMS can not know. The solution is to give Suppliers.SupplierID a primary key constraint.

Case Two: Erroneous Value in Foreign Key

Suppliers

Suppliers.ID	Suppliers.Name
1	RJ Farms
2	Angelica Inc.

SupplierContacts

SupplierContacts.SupplierID	SupplierContacts.Type	SupplierContacts.Number
1	Voice	123-4567
2	Voice	987-6543
58	Voice	585-8585

For the third record in the SupplierContact table there is no matching value in Suppliers.ID. Therefore, the DBMS cannot make a match and the third record of SupplierContacts is essentially lost. The solution is to add a REFERENCES constraint to SupplierContacts.SupplierID that only permits data that can be found in Suppliers.ID.

As we shall now see, both of these problems can be overcome by using constraints.

Primary Key Constraints

Primary keys require two types of constraints.

❑ First, they must be unique to avoid the problem in the first graphic above.

❑ Second, they must not have a value of NULL since it would be impossible to match the value of a foreign key to null.

The syntax for a primary key is actually simple.

When creating a primary key at the same time you create the table use:

```
CREATE TABLE TableName
     (ColumnPrimaryKeyName integer NOT NULL PRIMARY KEY,
     ColumnTwoName....)
```

The constraints added are NOT NULL and PRIMARY KEY.

If you already have a table, you can use the ALTER TABLE command as follows:

```
ALTER TABLE TableName
     ADD CONSTRAINT ConstraintName
     PRIMARY KEY (ColumnPrimaryKeyName)
```

Whether you are making the constraint at CREATE or ALTER keep in mind the limitations that most DBMS impose on the primary key constraints:

❑ A column constrained as a primary key must also be constrained as NOT NULL. If the NOT NULL constraint has not already been set then most DBMS automatically set the nullability to NOT NULL.

❑ A table can contain only one primary key constraint.

❑ The primary key constraint will automatically create an index; if there is a limit on indices per table there must be room for the new primary key index.

Try It Out – Add and Test Primary Key Constraint on Coaches, Awards

We know that we want both Coaches.CoachesID and Awards.AwardCode to be primary keys because the nominations table will be looking to those column's values to match up a coach, award and employee. In this TIO we will assign primary keys and then add some data (both good and bad).

1. Using Query Analyzer or another tool open your copy of Northwind.

2. Run the following code to make the Coaches.CoachID column NOT NULL:

```
ALTER TABLE coaches
     ALTER COLUMN CoachID Integer NOT NULL
```

3. Now we add the primary key constraint:

```
ALTER TABLE Coaches
     ADD CONSTRAINT con_CoachIDPK
     PRIMARY KEY (CoachID)
```

4. Let's add some data:

```
INSERT INTO Coaches
     (CoachID, CoachName)
     VALUES
     (3,'Buster')
```

5. At this point we will check if we can violate the nascent primary key by adding another coach with the same `CoachID` number:

```
INSERT INTO Coaches
     (CoachID, CoachName)
     VALUES
     (3,'Beatrice')
```

You should get a message like:

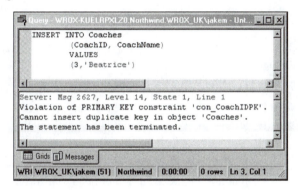

6. Now we will do the same thing for the `Awards` table, as follows:

```
ALTER TABLE Awards
     ALTER COLUMN AwardCode Char(2) NOT NULL
```

```
ALTER TABLE Awards
     ADD CONSTRAINT con_AwardCodePK
     PRIMARY KEY (AwardCode)
```

```
INSERT INTO Awards
     (AwardCode,Award)
     VALUES  ('bb','Best Bowler')
```

7. Finally we'll test that `PRIMARY KEY` by trying to add another record with a duplicate value (`'bb'`) for `AwardCode`:

```
INSERT INTO Awards
     (AwardCode,Award)
     VALUES  ('bb','Bounciest Ball')
```

We should get an error message similar to the last one.

How It Works

Primary key constraints must go on fields that cannot hold NULL values. Some DBMS will automatically create the NOT NULL when you create a primary key, we have done it by hand. Recall that when adding a NOT NULL constraint you must ALTER TABLE and you must provide the data type, even if it is the same data type as the column had to start with.

We then added the constraint, being careful to name it so that we will be able to modify or drop the constraint in the future. Last we did an INSERT INTO of data. If all went well you will find the second INSERT INTO is rejected because the primary key data is a duplicate.

Foreign Key Constraints

A serious problem arises if we add a SupliersContact with a value for SupplierID which is not found in the Suppliers table. In other words we have entered a telephone number as belonging to supplier #72 but there is no supplier #72. In the relationship between Suppliers and SuppliersContacts the SupplierContacts.SupplierID column is the foreign key. It references the primary key Suppliers.SupplierID.

SQL allows you to add a constraint named 'FOREIGN KEY', which only permits the addition of values that have a match with their corresponding column in the related table. The DBMS actually waits with changing a value in a foreign key until it looks up the new value in the related table. If the value is found then the addition or change is actually made. If the value is not found then the change is not made and an error message is returned. SQL also specifies that a column constrained with a foreign key can accept a NULL value. In most cases you will want to avoid that situation by using your front end or other software to prohibit NULL values prior to attempting a write to the data store.

We are limited to one primary key per table. But you can have many foreign keys per table. However, most DBMS do not allow a column to be involved in more than one foreign key constraint. Another limitation is that the column that you reference in the other table must have constraints of either UNIQUE or (better) primary key.

Implementing a foreign key is not difficult. If you have two tables named Suppliers and SuppliersContacts as in our Chapter 3 example that we revisited above, you can use:

```
CREATE TABLE SuppliersContacts
(SupplierID Integer
FOREIGN KEY SupplierID REFERENCES Supplier(SupplierID)
… more columns…
)
```

Normally we would want to avoid NULLs in the foreign key field, so we would use:

```
CREATE TABLE SuppliersContacts
(SupplierID Integer NOT NULL
FOREIGN KEY SupplierID REFERENCES Supplier(SupplierID)
… more columns…
)
```

The most common mistake here is to forget the syntax in the references clause. The other table is referred to with its name and then column in parenthesis, not in the usual form of being separated by a period.

Most DBMS also allow you to define a `foreign key` in an existing column as follows:

```
ALTER TABLE SuppliersContacts
    ADD CONSTRAINT c_ForKeySuppCont_SuppID
    FOREIGN KEY (SupplierID) REFERENCES Suppliers(SupplierID)
```

Try It Out – Create and Test Foreign Key Constraints

Your boss wants to make a table to hold the nominees for Northwind's Intramural Bowling League Athlete of the Year.

1. Start your SQL statement editor and open your copy of Northwind.

2. Run the following statement:

```
CREATE TABLE BowlNoms
    (BowlNomsID int NOT NULL PRIMARY KEY,
    EmployeeID int NOT NULL FOREIGN KEY REFERENCES Employees(EmployeeID),
    )
```

3. Try adding good data by creating nominations for employee #4 and employee #7:

```
INSERT INTO BowlNoms (BowlNomsID,EmployeeID) VALUES (4,4)
```

```
INSERT INTO BowlNoms (BowlNomsID,EmployeeID)VALUES (7,7)
```

4. Test with a SELECT on BowlNoms:

```
SELECT * FROM BowlNoms
```

You should see your new entries, as in the screenshot below:

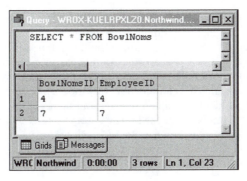

5. Do a SELECT on Employees, and while there check the highest Northwind EmployeeID number (it should be around 10).

```
SELECT EmployeeID, Lastname FROM Employees
```

6. Finally, try adding bad data by creating a nomination for employee #1234.

```
INSERT INTO BowlNoms (BowlNomsID,EmployeeID)VALUES (1234, 1234)
```

207

You should receive an error message similar to this:

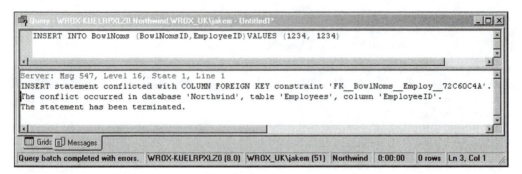

How It Works

We created a new table named `BowlNoms` which holds one record for each nomination. We just need two columns. The first is an ID column to be our primary key; we want to use it but it is good habit to have a primary key for every table, even if you're not immediately sure how you can use it. Our second column is the `EmployeeID` number of the nominee. These `EmployeeID` numbers must match up with the `EmployeeID` numbers in the `Employees` table. Our relationship here will be "bowling nominees are employees." That means that we want to make the `BowlNoms.EmployeeID` reference `Employees.EmployeeID`. We must be sure that `Employees.EmployeeID` can be referenced, as per the first code in the 'Try It Out'.

Once we established the table with its relationship we found that we could add nominations for real employees (matching values in `Employees.EmployeeID`. But we failed to add a record that used an invalid `EmployeeID` number.

A Few Notes on Problems with Key Constraints

Let us finish with a warning about foreign keys. They can be used when a person has a permission to create a foreign key to a table that they do not have permission to read. Say, for simplicity, that you have created a table called `WinEmployees` containing the names and employee numbers of the winners of the ten employees of the year awards. Many employees have access to a list of all the employees and their employee numbers, but the results of the awards must be secret for another week. Cris Cracker does not have rights to read the table of winners but she can create a new table called `CrackWinners` that will hold a list of all employees and their employee numbers. She adds the constraint of a foreign key from her `CrackWinners.EmployeeID` to your `WinEmployee.EmployeeID`. She then tries to add each of the employees. Only the winners will meet the foreign key criteria and succeed in being added. Cris now has a replica of your winners table. Although security schemes vary among vendors, most have a specific permission for allowing use by a foreign key.

There is another problem with having your table referenced by another table's `foreign key`. If a record is deleted from `Suppliers`, what happens to the corresponding records in `SuppliersContacts`? SQL offers options for handling this common situation and we will cover them in Chapter 10. Some of those options require you to get permission from the owner of the other table prior to dropping your table. Again, it behooves you to think carefully about whom you give permission to reference your table in a foreign key.

UNIQUE Constraint

Adding a UNIQUE constraint to a column insures that each record in a column can be identified from all the rest of the records. We have discussed a similar situation with primary keys where we need to be able to find a single specific column in order to match a record with records in a related table.

But there is a major difference in the number of columns that can have primary key and UNIQUE constraints. Only one column in a table can be a primary key. Many columns can be UNIQUE (up to limits set by the DBMS, usually far more than you will every need). So a primary key is generally used for the column that will be the main look-up in relationships. For example, this would be EmployeeID in the Employees table. UNIQUE is often used for columns that will hold values that will be looked up in additional relationships. For example if there were unique job titles for each employee, then the JobTitle column might be used to link to another table such as JobResponsibilities. Because of that relationship we would want uniqueness in the Employee.JobTitle.

When you first create a table (and before you create any records) you can use the following syntax:

```
CREATE TABLE MyTable
    (MyColumn1 Integer UNIQUE,
    MyColumn2 …
    )
```

What happens when I want to add a NULL to a column with a UNIQUE constraint? A NULL value is considered as any other value. You may have only one record with a NULL value. A second NULL value will be rejected since it is duplicating the first record with a NULL in the UNIQUE column. A common use of a NULL value in a UNIQUE column is to cover the cases where a related table may have a NULL value in the column used for look-up (for example you may be trying to find the CompanyName for an "Unknown Company" which has its value of NULL. The match will be made and the result will be an association which lacks information, but does not fail).

Adding a UNIQUE constraint to a table that already contains records requires that you think through the logic. If you are adding the constraint to a column which is already designated UNIQUE (including no more than one NULL, for example) then you will have no problems. But if you are adding a new column and want to have a UNIQUE constraint, you will have a problem with the new column being full of NULLs to start. The DBMS will not accept the constraint.

Constraints and Validation

Validation can be performed at the front end or user interface, generally with procedural code. There are strengths and weaknesses to performing validation checks at front end as opposed to creating constraints on the back end, which we'll briefly discuss here.

Please note that validation is purely a front end issue, and it is beyond the scope of this book to discuss the ways the numerous front ends deal with this function. Therefore, for an expansive understanding of validation, please consult texts relating specifically to your own front end.

Validation Advantages

It is usually easier to detect and resolve user's mistakes in the front end rather than send a write to the DBMS and then have to figure out what went wrong when the DBMS sends back a failure message. For example, front end validation can catch an invalid data entry and report to the user the problem and the acceptable range. A constraint failure only sends a message back to the front end that a failure occurred in a constraint.

Validation also offers the flexibility of different front ends having different rules. Perhaps for a bank kiosk you want a rule that no more than $400 can be withdrawn. However, for the front end at the bank teller's terminal you want to allow up to $4,000, and for automatic bank transfers that are done between bank's computers you may want to allow up to $40,000. Each of these requests will hit the same DBMS but will come from different front ends. A constraint on the column to handle all three situations would be difficult to build, but a different validation could easily be built in each of the three front ends.

Validation Disadvantages

One problem with validation arises when multiple front ends are running validations. Programmers end up writing and maintaining redundant code to cover each front end. On the other hand, with constraints they might have to write just as much code in the front end to handle constraint check failures.

Validation in the front end requires many more lines of code. Constraints are easy to implement – just add a few characters to the column definition. But as above, if the check is only performed at the DBMS, then failures will come back to the front end and code will have to be written to handle the failure.

Compromise

Validation at the front end works well with constraints to reduce the number of constraint failures. Constraints work well to create a final barrier to storing rotten data. In most systems both validation and constraints are used.

Summary

The column data types available to a SQL programmer define how the DBMS will store and process values within a table. Constraints are tools available to programmers to define what kind of values are allowed into the table. Constraints can be created at any time in the life of the database, including after data has been entered.

The basic syntax is to follow the column definition with a constraint name and CHECK expression. Those expressions can be any valid WHERE clause, including the use of AND, OR, vendor functions and column names. The location of the constraint in the syntax determines whether it applies to a single column or the table as a whole.

Each data type suggests its own kinds of constraints. Temporal data types are generally limited by start and end date or by validity in a look-up in a table of acceptable dates. Character data types are frequently limited in size or in a pattern of numbers and letters established for the field.

If a constraint is violated in a SQL statement the statement is not completed. A message is returned to the front end which includes the name of the violated constraint. The programmer has the option to override constraints by adding ## to the statement.

Constraints are not the only option for avoiding accession of bad data. SQL offers rules (an older technique), triggers and deferred constraints. Most programmers will also want to add validation code to their front ends in order to head off bad data as early as possible. Good validation schemes also catch data that would violate the DBMS data type restrictions.

In the next chapter we will discuss the importance of and the techniques for relating (joining) tables. The correct use of relational techniques creates a tight logical structure for the database. That structure ensures that the DBMS can work as efficiently as possible while providing answers to the questions that will be sought from the data.

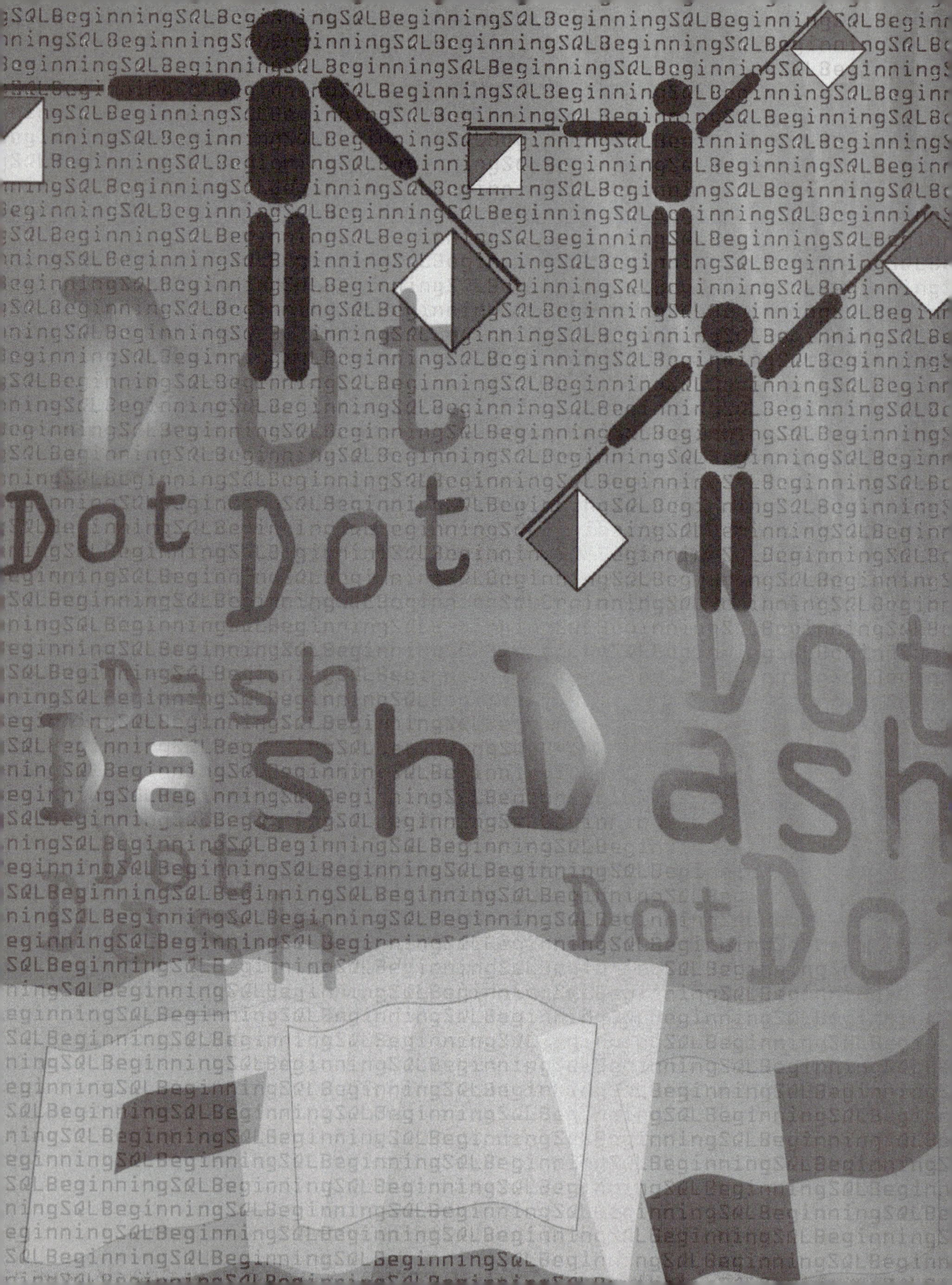
Dot
Dot
Dash
Dash
Dot
DotDot

Relating Tables

In the early years of computerized data storage, databases were very large and difficult to use. Many tasks were very difficult to achieve, and, if they could be solved, it was usually through the use of complex procedural code. Then came the theory of the relational database. In Chapter 3, when we used the Tulip Growers example, we introduced the idea of relating tables. Recall that we saw the inefficiency of having multiple copies of the same data. Likewise, we observed that having a lot of empty places in the data was problematic. We solved both of those problems by creating additional tables and relationships between them.

In this chapter we will:

❑   discuss the theory of relationships in more depth

❑   create tables to illustrate our ideas

❑   look at joining data

❑   look at the syntax of the JOIN statement and how to use it

Let's get started.

Basics of Relating Tables

As we begin to design and use tables in real business situations, we find logical situations where we think we need to have tables with one of two problems:

❑   The same data repeated in several places.

❑   Large regions of emptiness in tables.

For example, in a Students table we might want to add columns called MothersFirstName, MothersLastName, MothersWorkPhone and MothersCellPhone. If we had four students from one family, then we would have those same phone numbers listed in four places.

An example of empty areas is when we want to accommodate the possibility that an employee has two phone numbers at home, two phone numbers for work, and a cell phone. We could add these five columns to the Employees table, but for most employees, we would probably have half of the values as NULL. Note that this emptiness is not temporary in the sense that we just have not gathered the data yet – it is a structural emptiness that has been created in order to accommodate the needs of a few records.

In both of these cases there is a pattern that we need one copy of some of the data (the student's name, the employee's name) and a variable number of records from a second set of data (Mother's information or Employees' various phone numbers). In both cases we solve the problem by using more than one table so we can split the variable numbers of records away from the single copies of information.

Problematic Design

Students Table - weak

StudentID	LastName	FirstName	MotherName	MotherPhone	MotherFax
1	Adams	Ann	Abigail	111-1111	111-1000
2	Becket	Ben	Bonnie	222-2222	222-2000
3	Becket	Bill	Bonnie	222-2222	222-2000
4	Becket	Bob	Bonnie	222-2222	222-2000

Note how this data is duplicated.

Problematic Design

Employees Table - weak

EmployeeID	LastName	FirstName	Land1	Land2	Cell1	Cell2	Fax
1	Author	Allen	111-1111	222-2222	333-3333	444-4444	555-5555
2	Becket	Bob	666-66666				
3	Cathers	Chris	777-7777				

Note how this table has a region of emptiness.

Each of these situations creates problems. When the same data is repeated in multiple places we increase the cost of data entry and run the risk that not all of the values will be entered the same. Second, we must create processes that ensure that changes are made synchronously for all copies of the same data. Lastly, if the values do become unsynchronized then we have lost confidence in our data, because we have no idea what is the correct value. So for these reasons we seek a solution whereby we do not have the same piece of data stored in more than one place.

Regions of emptiness incur their own set of inefficiencies. First, we end up adding a load to the DBMS to have to maintain, search and parse regions of emptiness that we never expect to fill. Second, we waste time checking constraints and data integrity for values that we will probably never fill. So we want to avoid table designs that create regions of emptiness.

Understanding the relational database provides us with visible solution to both of these types of problem. Data is distributed over multiple tables, and the DBMS is designed to bring information contained in the columns of these tables back together when we need to provide answers to specific queries. When the columns are brought together, the DBMS can duplicate records, as necessary, for a particular request. A DBMS can simulate the copying of records multiple times, and this solves the problem of having to actually store the data multiple times. Also, a DBMS may skip records that do not have data, and this solves the problem of having structural emptiness.

The process of breaking up information into multiple tables is called **normalization**, and the process of bringing the information back together in a flexible fashion is called **joining**. Joins are performed as needed to carry out the *relationships* of the database design. Note that the normalization (splitting) is performed only once, and so becomes part of the permanent database structure. The joining (bringing columns back together) is performed as needed, and so repeated for each request . During a Join data is not actually copied in storage except in special cases.

> The terms `Relationship` and `Join` address the same concept, but one from the theoretical and one from the practical side.
> A `Relationship` is an English language *description* of how the records in two or more tables are associated.
> A `JOIN` is a SQL Keyword that describes *how* to actually associate the tables within a SQL statement.

For example, in our Students table we had the problem of the same information about the mother of four siblings having to be stored repeatedly. When we normalize the scheme, we can create a second table called Parents. In the Students table, we add just one column, called MotherID, instead of the multiple columns that contained information pertaining to the siblings' mother. We include in the Parent table a ParentID column.

We can now see that when we now enter the data about each sibling's mother, we only enter a single value (the ParentID) to represent their mother. Now, if we wish, the DBMS join will match up all the data on the mother with the first sibling student, then match it up again when we need information on the second sibling, and again for the third and fourth. Although we enter and store the parent's data only once, we can extract it via Joins as often as needed, thus solving the problem of having to have mother's data entered multiple times in the student table.

Problematic Design

Students Table - weak

StudentID	LastName	FirstName	MotherName	MotherPhone	MotherFax
1	Adams	Ann	Abigail	111-1111	111-1000
2	Becket	Ben	Bonnie	222-2222	222-2000
3	Becket	Bill	Bonnie	222-2222	222-2000
4	Becket	Bob	Bonnie	222-2222	222-2000

Note how this data is duplicated.

Better Design

Students Table - better

StudentID	LastName	FirstName	ParentID
1	Adams	Ann	1
2	Becket	Ben	2
3	Becket	Bill	2
4	Becket	Bob	2

Relationship from Students.MotherID to Parents.ParentID

Parents Table

ParentID	MotherName	MotherPhone	MotherFax
1	Abigail	111-1111	111-1000
2	Bonnie	222-2222	222-2000

Note that we would still have to enter the Mother's ID four times in the student table, once for each of the siblings. Isn't that redundancy? Not according to the Relational Model, because a single data identifying the mother of a student is the absolute minimum possible to describe the situation. There are many rules that determine what the minimum possible storage requirements are in complex cases, but in this simple case, we can see that this is true. In terms of efficiency in data entry and ease of maintenance (meaning where we change values in the database when they change in the real world), the storage of one value is far better than many.

There is a process called de-normalizing which merits a note here. For the most part normalizing speeds database performance and reduces costs. However, in some specific situations performance can be improved by actually de-normalizing some data. For example we may need to join many tables to create a recordset that will be used many times before the data changes. Normally the DBMS would have to perform the intense process of doing all the joins for each request of the recordset. If we broke the normalization rules by creating a temporary table with redundant or hole-y data, then the DBMS would not have to re-do the Joins for each request. This practice is very common, but extreme caution is urged with this procedure until you are very comfortable with the basics of normalization. Having redundant copies of data is very risky.

In earlier chapters we have covered the theory of designing a normalized database; that is, how to split data into multiple tables. In this chapter, we focus on the second half of the solution, how to bring data from normalized tables together in order to generate the answers our business needs. Once we see how the joining process works, it is much easier to design the normalization (splitting). Joining is so powerful and so fundamental to modern databases that many types of Joins have been developed. Furthermore, the terminology has evolved as the original idea of a Join has been refined, and various vendors seek to differentiate their products within the SQL standards. We will not cover all of the possibilities in this book, but we will cover those that are most commonly used..

Keys

If the DBMS is going to join tables then it needs a way to accurately match the records from one table to the other. As we will see shortly in our syntax examples, the JOIN specifies the columns to match. In order for the match to work those columns must be correctly prepared. A column that is used in Joins is called a key. Two types of keys are most common, the primary key and the foreign key.

A primary key is a column (or a set of columns) in a table that uniquely identifies records in the table. When the DBMS is looking for a certain value in a primary key, it will find only one record that matches that value. Common examples include the ID number for records in a table or an Order Number or a Social Security Number.

A foreign key is a column (or set of columns) in a table that is used in a Join to reference a primary key in another table. When the DBMS wants to match a record to another table it reads the foreign key and uses that value to find a match with the other table's primary key.

Let us look at an example already in Northwind, the inclusion of an Employee number.

Setting columns to be primary keys or foreign keys is not difficult, as we discussed at the end of Chapter 7 on Constraints. To review the syntax that was used for the Employee Table:

```
CREATE TABLE Employees
    (EmployeeID INT NOT NULL PRIMARY KEY,
    other columns…)
;
```

To establish a foreign key we must indicate what column holds acceptable values as in EmployeeID below, which holds the number of the employee who takes the order.

```
CREATE TABLE Orders
    (… other columns…
    EmployeeID INT FOREIGN KEY REFERENCES Employees(EmployeeID),
    other columns…)
;
```

Note that a foreign key can only point to (REFERENCE) a primary key or a UNIQUE column. In other words the DBMS will only let us create a foreign key that points to a column that is guaranteed not to have duplicates. It is not enough that the column does not currently contain duplicates; the DBMS requires that it be structurally impossible to ever add duplicates in the future. Finally, as we will see in the following Try It Out, if we have a table that already has records and those records have duplicate values in a certain column, we cannot put a primary key or UNIQUE constraint on that column.

These 'rules' that apply to the creation of primary and foreign keys are also known by another name – **Referential Integrity**. This is the term given to the idea of protecting the data so that it remains as current as possible. It also means that 'wrong' data cannot be inserted into the database and thus confuse and pollute the data we already have, and that a primary key field cannot be deleted if it still has records in other tables referencing it as a foreign key. This is to ensure that no related data becomes orphaned, and therefore useless because it can no longer be retrieved as it has no connection with the rest of the data.

We will get some more practice with creating keys and enforcing referential integrity in the rest of the chapter. Since keys are so important we will continue to explain them in the examples below.

Business Model for This Chapter

In this chapter we will add a new dimension to the Northwind Database. Suppose that employees reported to the marketing team that customers frequently ask for employee's advice on products, and that Northwind has decided to formalize this process by storing employees' reviews of products. As a protective measure, the actual names of the employees will not be known to the public: rather they will go by nicknames. To improve quality and consistency, employees that want to write reviews will have to complete a short seminar and be certified to write reviews. We can predict that some of the popular products will get lots of reviews while others will get few or no reviews. Some employees will actively participate, some will not. Reviews will be limited to 200 characters in length (3-4 sentences).

The requirements of the Northwind management have been encapsulated into the following list of objectives. We should be able to generate lists of:

1. All reviews for a product

2. All reviews that employees have written on all products

3. All the reviews from one reviewer (both with and without the reviewer's real name)

4. All the employees who are certified to be reviewers but have not written any reviews

5. All the employees that are not participating in the product review program

As we work through different types of joins, we will see how they are best applied to the requirements of the new Northwind employee reviews program.

How *Not* to Solve the Problem

One solution would be to add a review column to each product in the Products table, such as the review column below:

Product ID	Product Name	Supplier	Review
1	Chai	Exotic Liquids	Chai is one of the smoothest teas I have enjoyed.
2	Chang	Exotic Liquids	Chang has more bite than Chai, but I like the strength.
3	Aniseed Syrup	Exotic Liquids	Probably made from Canadian fennel, not the Asian variety.

However, we can expect products to get more than one review. This *could* be solved by adding multiple columns, such as `Review1` and `Review2`; however, the problem with this solution is that products that do not get reviewed would still have the overhead of carrying these multiple review columns, resulting in large regions of empty space. Furthermore, the number of extra columns would either have to be as many as the maximum number of reviews we expect, or we would have to limit the number of reviews to the number of columns added. Obviously, the solution of adding review columns to the products table is going to be problematic.

Before we look at a good solution, let us look at a second poor solution, one for registering the information about the employees as reviewers.

We could add columns to the `Employee` table that will contain the employees' nick names and the date they certified as reviewers. We could call them `NickName` and `DateCertified`. However, this solution will add an additional load to all operations involving the table, including looking up information about those employees that have nothing to do with reviewing. Even if an employee is a reviewer, many of the reads from this table will have nothing to do with reviewing, such as looking up the employee number for each order. Avoiding this type of inefficiency is another advantage to normalizing the tables. In the Try It Outs of this chapter we will discuss far better techniques to solve these problems.

Creating the Tables We Need

The solution to having multiple reviews for each product is to put all the reviews in their own table. A table containing the reviews should hold its own `ReviewID` as well as the `ID` of the employee reviewer as a foreign key and the product as a foreign key. Those constraints will ensure that the DBMS will only allow values in `Reviews.EmployeeID` that match values already existing in `Employees.EmployeeID` (and likewise for `ProductsID`). Including a column for date might be useful, and, of course, we would want a column for the actual text of the review.

Try It Out – Create Table of Reviewers

We have been asked to design and create a table that will hold information on those employees that have passed the reviewers course. This table will have records that match the `Employee` records; but not all employees will have a record in the `Reviewers` table. We discussed in the description of the problem that we wanted to keep these columns separate from the columns in the `Employee` table so that these extra columns (rarely used) would not slow down the DBMS in its frequent use of the `Employee` table columns.

In the future we will want to use the `EmployeeID` numbers in this table as a reference column for other foreign keys. So we will have to make `Reviewers.EmployeeID` a primary key.

1. There should be no duplicate values in `Employee.EmployeeID` in Northwind, but check that, in the course of adding records so far in the book, you do not have duplicate values for `Employee.EmployeeID`:

```
SELECT EmployeeID, LastName
FROM Employees;
```

2. If (and only if) you found any duplicates then delete them using the following statement, substituting for *duplicate value* the duplicate `EmployeeID` that you found.

```
DELETE FROM Employees
WHERE EmployeeID = duplicatevalue
```

3. Check your records again and repeat the DELETE statement as necessary to remove all records with duplicates in the `EmployeeID` field

4. Now we need to make the `EmployeeID` column a primary key as follows.

```
ALTER TABLE Employees
    ADD CONSTRAINT pk_EmployeeID
    PRIMARY KEY (EmployeeID)
;
```

5. Now we can create a table of reviewers that has a foreign key to `Employees.EmployeeID`.

```
CREATE table Reviewers
    (EmployeeID INTEGER
        NOT NULL
        PRIMARY KEY
        FOREIGN KEY REFERENCES Employees(EMployeeID),
    ReviewerNickName CHAR(20),
    ReviewerCertificateDate DATETIME)
;
```

> In DB2, the **TIMESTAMP** data type takes the place of the **DATETIME** data type we see here. However, the format of the **TIMESTAMP** datatype in DB2 takes the following form:
> **1900-01-01.00.00.00**
> so where we input dates, DB2 will only accept them as:
> **2001-01-01.00.00.00** rather than the **1/1/2001** format seen below.

6. Let us check this by adding some good data.

```
INSERT INTO Reviewers
    (EmployeeID, ReviewerNickName,
    ReviewerCertificateDate)
VALUES
    (1, 'Daisy ','1/1/2001')
;
```

7. We can confirm our success with a simple `SELECT` statement.

```
SELECT * From Reviewers
```

8. And now let's add some bad data in the sense that there is no `Employee 999` in the `Employees` Table.

```
INSERT INTO Reviewers
    (EmployeeID, ReviewerNickName,
    ReviewerCertificateDate)
VALUES
    (999, 'Darth Bambi','2/2/2002')
;
```

We should be happy to fail with something like:

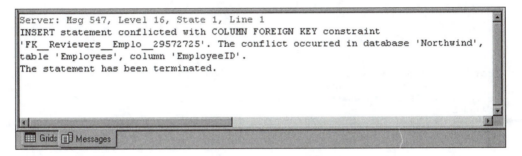

```
Server: Msg 547, Level 16, State 1, Line 1
INSERT statement conflicted with COLUMN FOREIGN KEY constraint
'FK__Reviewers__Emplo__29572725'. The conflict occurred in database 'Northwind',
table 'Employees', column 'EmployeeID'.
The statement has been terminated.
```

9. Our last test checks another kind of failure: a duplicate value in our primary key of `ReviewersID`. We added `Reviewer 1` above, let's try to add another.

```
INSERT INTO Reviewers
    (EmployeeID, ReviewerNickName,
    ReviewerCertificateDate)
VALUES
    (1, 'Daisy Two','3/3/2003')
;
```

We should be presented with something like:

```
Server: Msg 2627, Level 14, State 1, Line 1
Violation of PRIMARY KEY constraint 'PK__Reviewers__286302EC'.
Cannot insert duplicate key in object 'Reviewers'.
The statement has been terminated.
```

10. We finish by adding records for four more reviewers just so we have some data to work with in later chapters.

```
INSERT INTO Reviewers
    (EmployeeID, ReviewerNickName,
    ReviewerCertificateDate)
VALUES
    (2, 'Amazin Andy','3/3/2003')
;

INSERT INTO Reviewers
    (EmployeeID, ReviewerNickName,
    ReviewerCertificateDate)
VALUES
    (4, 'marGREAT','4/4/2002')
;

INSERT INTO Reviewers
    (EmployeeID, ReviewerNickName,
    ReviewerCertificateDate)
VALUES
    (6, 'Slick Suy','5/5/2002')
;

INSERT INTO Reviewers
    (EmployeeID, ReviewerNickName,
    ReviewerCertificateDate)
VALUES
    (7, 'Anaheim KINGSman','6/6/2002')
;
```

How It Works

In this Try It Out we had some preliminary steps prior to creating the table, so first let us list the salient points of the theory.

- ❑ In `Reviewers` we want a foreign key field for `EmployeeID` so that the values in `Reviewers.EmployeeID` match up with a value in `Employees.EmployeeID`.

- ❑ Foreign Keys can only reference columns that cannot have duplicates

- ❑ The way to not have duplicates in a column is to enforce either primary key or `UNIQUE` constraints.

A primary key constraint cannot be added to a column if the table already holds records with duplicates in that column.

Now we can go through the steps to implement those ideas. The steps we took work their way from the bottom to the top of the above list of points. The `Employees` table originally comes without a primary key constraint on `EmployeeID`. Considering that we have been using the `Employees` table we may have some duplicate `EmployeeIDs`. So first we looked at the `Employees` table and checked for any duplicates; if there were duplicates we deleted those records.

Next we added a primary key constraint to `Employees.EmployeID`, as we did in Chapter 7 with the following statement. Note that we named the constraint to make it easier to manipulate in the future.

```
ALTER TABLE Employees
    ADD CONSTRAINT pk_EmployeeID
    PRIMARY KEY (EmployeeID)
;
```

Now that Employees.EmployeeID can be used as a REFERENCE, we can create our Reviewers table. There is only one confusing point here: Reviewers.EmployeesID is both a primary key and a foreign key. It is a foreign key because we only want it to accept values that already exist in Employees.EmployeeID. And since other tables (like in the next Try It Out) will reference Reviewers.EmployeeID we need it to be a primary key.

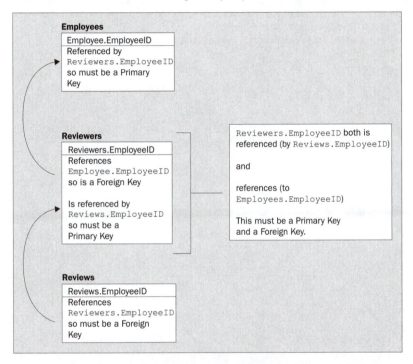

Try It Out – Create Table of Reviews

We have been asked to design and create a table that will hold the reviews. We will want to make this table have a foreign key named EmployeeID and another foreign key named ProductID. Foreign keys must point to columns that do not have duplicates, either by being primary keys or UNIQUE. So we will have to start with background work as in the last worked example.

1. Remember that in the last Try It Out we had to do some preparation to make Employees.EmployeeID usable as a reference for a foreign key. Now we need to do the same for the Products Table. Since Products.ProductsID does not have duplicates to start with and since we have not shown any examples that use the Products table, we will not go through the process of searching for and eliminating duplicates. If you have played with Products at all you may want to check for duplicates, in the same way as in Steps 1 and 2 of the last Try It Out. Knowing that there are no duplicates we can perform the following:

```
ALTER TABLE Products
    ADD CONSTRAINT pk_ProductID
    PRIMARY KEY (ProductID)
;
```

2. Now we are ready to create the `Reviews` table

```
CREATE TABLE Reviews
    (ReviewID INTEGER NOT NULL PRIMARY KEY,
    EmployeeID Integer NOT NULL
        Foreign KEY References Reviewers(EmployeeID),
    ProductID Integer NOT NULL
        Foreign KEY References Products(ProductID),
    Date Datetime,
    ReviewText VARCHAR(200)
    )
;
```

3. Test some good data. We added `Employee #1` as a reviewer in the last Try It Out and we can easily run a `SELECT` to find out that there is a `Product #5`

```
INSERT INTO Reviews
    (ReviewID, EmployeeID,
    ProductID, Date,
    ReviewText)
VALUES
    (1,1,
    1,'1/1/2001',
    'Chai is one of the smoothest teas I have enjoyed.')
;
```

And check it with

```
SELECT * FROM Reviews
```

4. Now add some bad data, a review from `Employee 999`, which neither exists as an `Employee` in the `Employees` table nor as a `Reviewer` in the `Reviewers` table.

```
INSERT INTO Reviews
    (ReviewID, EmployeeID,
    ProductID, Date,
    ReviewText)
VALUES
    (2,999,
    1,'2/2/2002',
    'Chai has a barnyard aroma')
;
```

We should get something like:

```
Server: Msg 547, Level 16, State 1, Line 1
INSERT statement conflicted with COLUMN FOREIGN KEY constraint
'FK__Reviews__Employe__2D27B809'. The conflict occurred in database 'Northwind',
table 'Reviewers', column 'EmployeeID'.
The statement has been terminated.
```

Grids Messages

5. Last, let us test a bad `Product ID`. To simulate a really bad mistake let us use the value `qwerty`

```
INSERT INTO Reviews
    (ReviewID, EmployeeID,
    ProductID, Date,
    ReviewText)
VALUES
    (2,1,
    'qwerty','2/2/2002',
    'Chai tastes like dirt')
;
```

In this case we don't even get to the constraint since the value 'qwerty' is the wrong data type.

```
Server: Msg 245, Level 16, State 1, Line 1
Syntax error converting the varchar value 'qwerty' to a column of data type int.
```

Grids Messages

However, if we try it with a reasonable but wrong number like 999 instead of qwerty in the statement above, we get the error message as expected, which should look something like the following.

```
Server: Msg 547, Level 16, State 1, Line 1
INSERT statement conflicted with COLUMN FOREIGN KEY constraint
'FK__Reviews__Product__2E1BDC42'. The conflict occurred in database 'Northwind',
table 'Products', column 'ProductID'.
The statement has been terminated.
```

Grids Messages

225

6. Let's finish by adding a few reviews so we have some data to work with in the future (we will discuss this shorter syntax in the How It Works section)

```
INSERT INTO Reviews VALUES
    (2,7,61,'2/2/2001',
    'Far too strong, should be named Sirop de irratable')
;

INSERT INTO Reviews VALUES
    (3,6,7,'3/3/2001',
    'Full of flavor, each one is like a pair of pears.')
;

INSERT INTO Reviews VALUES
    (4,4,14,'4/4/2001',
    'Good texture and rich flavor. I wish they made a Chou Tofu')
;

INSERT INTO Reviews VALUES
    (5,4,7,'5/5/2001',
    'Far too dry for my taste.')
;
```

How It Works

We may want to review the important points from the last How It Works. As with the last Try It Out we had to do some preparation work to insure that the REFERENCES column meets the criteria of Uniqueness. In this case we made ProductsID a primary key as follows.

```
ALTER TABLE Products
    ADD CONSTRAINT pk_ProductID
    PRIMARY KEY (ProductID);
```

Note that we named the constraint so that we could refer to it with a logical name in future statements.

After that groundwork was laid we could run the following statement, which actually created our new Reviews table. The first column is the identifier for this table. We may want to use it as a primary key for some other relationship some other day and so we make it a primary key from the start.

```
CREATE TABLE Reviews
    (ReviewID INTEGER NOT NULL PRIMARY KEY,
```

The next column instructs the DBMS to not allow any values except those that already exist in the Employees.EmployeeID column. This insures that when a JOIN goes to look up the EmployeeID it will, in fact, find a matching value.

```
EmployeeID Integer NOT NULL
    Foreign KEY References Employees(EmployeeID),
```

We do the same for the third column, ProductID

```
ProductID Integer NOT NULL
    Foreign KEY References Products(ProductID),
```

We finish with two simple columns as follows.

```
Date Datetime,
ReviewText VARCHAR(200)
)
;
```

We then did some checking by adding data. The first review used the syntax to add a record as we discussed in the last Try It Out. The next INSERT INTO failed because of the constraint that Reviews.EmployeeID is a foreign key related to Employees.EmployeeID and thus when the value 999 was looked up and not found, the INSERT INTO failed. We also failed in Step 6 when we gave unmatchable data for the other foreign key, namely Reviews.ProductID.

In the last step we added more records using an abbreviated syntax. We took advantage of a shortcut for INSERT INTO by not listing the column names. To do so we must meet two requirements:

❑   Provide values in the same order as the columns

❑   Provide a value for every column

We can get the columns' ordinal position by running this statement:

```
SELECT Table_Name, Ordinal_Position, Column_Name
FROM Information_Schema.Columns
ORDER BY Table_Name, Ordinal_Position;
```

Joining Data

Relational databases rely on two techniques: **normalization**, to divide the data into multiple tables; and Joins, to bring columns back together into a virtual table for use. During joining, the DBMS will repeat records from one or more tables in order to match the data properly as per the request. For example, if there are ten reviews from one reviewer, the DBMS will match all ten reviews to the one reviewer. In this section we look at the syntax of Joins.

The syntax for a simple Join specifies both of the tables that are to be joined and the columns that contain the data that will be matched up. As columns will come from more than one table, we must make sure we specify the relevant source tables in the SELECT clause.

Our query will be structured in the following way:

```
SELECT table1.columnname, table2.columnname
FROM table1 JOIN table2
ON table1.matchingcolumn = table2.matchingcolumn;
```

> **Oracle does not support the JOIN statement. Instead, you will have to use the following syntax:**
>
> ```
> SELECT table1.columnname, table2.columnname
> FROM table1, table2
> WHERE table1.matchingcolumn = table2.matchingcolumn
> ```

The SELECT clause is the same as we studied previously, except now we should identify the table providing the column (Table1.ColumnName) instead of just the column name. The FROM clause now lists two tables with the keyword JOIN. Then we specify the two columns, one from each table, that provide the matching data for the DBMS to use to synchronize the records.

Since JOINs are so important let us talk through exactly what happens when this statement is executed. The DBMS sees the JOIN and knows that it will be producing a result set that has values from more than one table. There may be many more records from one table than the other. The DBMS will look at the value of MatchingColumn in the first record in Table1 and match it with the value in MatchingColumn in Table2. The DBMS will add all of the values from the ColumnNames to the result set. Then the DBMS goes down to the second Table1 record and repeats the process. If there were three records in Table2 that matched a record in Table1, we will end up with three records in the result set with the data from the single matching record in Table1 repeated three times.

In our first exercise below, we look at the simplest type of Join where for each record in one table there exists only one match (or no match) in the second table. This is the case in joining the Reviewers table to the Employees table, since the columns of the Reviewers table can be looked at as essentially additional columns added to the side of the Employees table.

Try It Out – List Employee Reviewers

We are asked for a list of all of the reviewer's names, nicknames and certification dates.

This information is stored in two tables (Employees has the names and Reviewers has the other two items of data) so we must instruct the DBMS to do a Join to generate the results.

```
SELECT
    Employees.EmployeeID, Employees.FirstName,
    Employees.LastName, Reviewers.ReviewerNickName,
    ReviewerCertificateDate
FROM Employees JOIN Reviewers
ON Employees.EmployeeID = Reviewers.EmployeeID
;
```

We should get the following results:

	EmployeeID	FirstName	LastName	ReviewerNickName	ReviewerCertificateDate
1	1	Nancy	Davolio	Daisy	2001-01-01 00:00:00.000
2	2	Andrew	Fuller	Amazin Andy	2003-03-03 00:00:00.000
3	4	Margaret	Peacock	marGREAT	2002-04-04 00:00:00.000
4	6	Michael	Suyama	Slick Suy	2002-05-05 00:00:00.000
5	7	Robert	King	Anaheim KINGSman	2002-06-06 00:00:00.000

Grids Messages

How It Works

Notice that in the above type of Join we only get records where there is a match in both tables. We do not have any records from Employees that are not Reviewers. Employee 1 has a listing in both the Employees and Reviewers tables, so the Join creates a record for her. Employee 3 has not become involved in the reviewing program, so he does not have a record in the EmployeeReviewers table, and is thus not represented in the result of the Join. This type of Join is called an Inner Join.

> **`Inner Joins` produce only the records that have a match in both tables**

In fact, a more exact and more readable syntax specifies the `Join` type as follows:

```
SELECT
    Employees.FirstName, Employees.LastName,
    Reviewers.ReviewerNickName, Reviewers.ReviewerCertificateDate
FROM Employees INNER JOIN Reviewers
    ON Employees.EmployeeID = Reviewers.EmployeeID;
```

Let us look at the primary and foreign keys in our examples of `Employee` reviews of Northwind products. Recall that in our example we will `JOIN` the `Reviews.EmployeeID` to the `Employees.EmployeeID`. Since each reviewer will do many reviews our matches will join many records from `Reviews` to one record from `Employees`. We do not want any duplication in the `EmployeesID` column, as this would cause confusion for the DBMS; which of the duplicate `EmployeeIDs` would it match? So the `EmployeeID` column must have unique values and is assigned the role of primary key.

From the foreign key side, we do not want to have a value for `Reviews.EmployeeID` that points to an `Employee.EmployeeID` that does not exist. So we want to constrain the `Reviews.EmployeeID` column to only accept values that exist in the `Employees.EmployeeID` column. This restriction makes `Review.EmployeeID` a foreign key, accepting only values that is already in `Employees.EmployeeID`.

Some Common Cases Where Joins are Used

We have mentioned two cases where relational tables are beneficial. The first is to avoid adding a lot of extra columns that will end up mostly empty. The second is when we have many rows with the same values for a given column. There are many more. Generally, a good guide to follow when deciding whether to split a table is to see whether a variable number of columns are needed to hold the appropriate information.

A common case is the database to support a business' ordering process (for example, Northwind). Getting the information for one of Northwind's orders will require the joining of several tables. Here we can see a pattern that cries out for normalization: some data (like the customer names) is needed once and other data (like description of an ordered product) is presented more than once if they were ordered more than once. We have the `Customer` table to store the name, address, and other customer-specific details. We also have the `Orders` table for each order that comes in. Finally, we have the `Order Details` table that contains a record for each product (line) of the order. The DBMS matches up the appropriate customer and order and the correct details (however many) to that order number. The most important tools for the DBMS are the `Key` columns. The DBMS will read a record's value in a foreign key and then look that up in the second table's primary key in order to find a match.

For a more easily understandable example, let's take the case of a phone bill. Here is a case similar to `Orders` in that we have a set of data that is on each phone bill once (name, address, account number) and a second set of data that will be on each phone bill a varying number of times (date, number called and amount charged) depending on the number of phone calls made. The scheme for this database will have a table for `Customers` that includes the first set of data and a table for `Calls` that includes a `CustomerID` and the details of the call. The DBMS is able to match up all the calls for one `CustomerID` to the record for the `Customer`.

Theory of Joins

There are two basic ways in which records can match up between two tables:

- ❑ One to One
- ❑ One to Many

These terms describe the potential number of matches between two related tables. The concepts exist in the designer's mind and in the structure and data of the tables – there is no ONE TO ONE or ONE TO MANY keyword phrase in SQL. We will only see the matching type in diagrams or discussions and, of course, we will think of the relationships in our minds as producing one-to-one or one-to-many matches.

One to One Joins create a set of results with some columns from the first table and some columns from a second table. For example, we might have a table with ten fields of basic information on Employees, and want to add some more fields for all or some of the Employees. Only one record in the second table will apply to a given record in the first table, but the information in the second table will only be used occasionally. Rather than enlarge and burden the original table, we create a second table with a one to one Join to the first table. On the occasion that we need all the fields, we can join them, but most of the time we just use the leaner, faster original table.

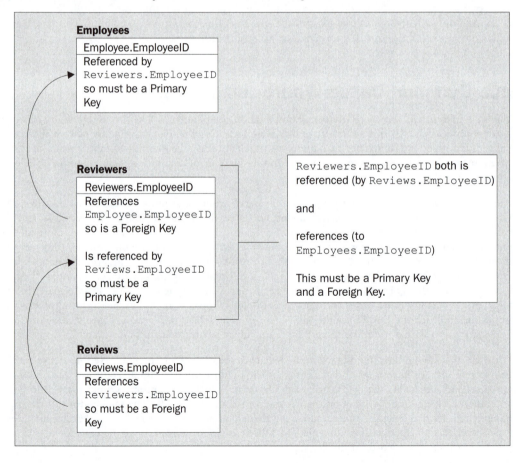

Another example is when we have a `Products` table that is being used for a large percent of the database's work – almost every enquiry and order is doing multiple look-ups on the table. For best performance, we want to limit this table to as few fields as needed to perform the task of accepting an order. Any fields that are not part of the ordering process (like the supplier's name) we split into another table. The second table will have exactly the same number of records as the first, one for each product. Both tables will start with a `ProductsID` field, and through this common ID number we can match up the records of the two tables in a `Join` to get access to all the fields regarding products.

The other basic type of relationship is a One-to-Many. In this case there will be many records from the second table that match up with a single record of the first table. For example each reviewer will write many reviews thus we describe a one-to-many relationship for reviewers to reviews.

Better Design

Students Table - better

StudentID	LastName	FirstName	ParentID
1	Adams	Ann	1
2	Becket	Ben	2
3	Becket	Bill	2
4	Becket	Bob	2

Relationship from Students.MotherID to Parents.ParentID

Parents Table

ParentID	MotherName	MotherPhone	MotherFax
1	Abigail	111-1111	111-1000
2	Bonnie	222-2222	222-2000

We can arrive at one-to-one and one-to-many relations through two ways in the design process. The first is to design a large table and then realize that performance may be improved by splitting off some of the fields. A common second scenario is to start with a table then find that we want to add more columns. If the new columns are not part of the most frequent processes carried out on the table then we may want to put the second batch of columns in a second table. There are two main advantages to using one-to-one relations. First, security is improved, since we can limit permissions at a table level for information in a second table and still allow table-level access to the first table. Second, performance is improved for those queries that do not need all of the fields. However, there will be a price paid for those operations that do involve a `Join`.

Joins

`Joins` define the rules for how to match the records of two tables. There are two basic types:

- ❑   `Inner`
- ❑   `Outer`

Then there are many variations that we will not cover in this book, including `Full Joins`, `Cross Joins` and `Theta Joins`. Intermediate and Advanced textbooks on database design discuss these options in great detail.

It is important to understand that descriptions of relationships such as one-to-one and one-to-many are independent of descriptions of `Joins` such as inner and outer. The relationship describes in words the way the records match. `Joins` describe in SQL statements which records to get by using the relationships.

Inner Joins

Inner Joins only produce records for which there is a match on both sides of the Join. Take for example the graph above for the one-to-many relationship for Reviewers and Reviews. An Inner Join will produce no records with Reviewer 3 because he has not done any reviews yet.

The syntax is not difficult. We just have to add two parts:

❑ The JOIN keyword and the table to which we want to join

❑ Which columns to match up.

The generic form follows.

```
SELECT ColumnNames
FROM TableOne
    INNER JOIN TableTwo
    ON TableOne.MatchingColumn = TableTwo.MatchingColumn
;
```

The above syntax will give us a result set of the ColumnNames listed. Only those records that have a match in TableOne and TableTwo will be listed. In more advanced cases we can use expressions in the ON clause that are inequalities like > or <.

Try It Out – Inner Join

We need to generate a list of Employees that are Reviewers along with their nicknames.

1. Run the following statement

```
SELECT
    Employees.EmployeeID,
    Employees.FirstName,
    Employees.LastName,
    Reviewers.ReviewerNickName
FROM Employees
    INNER JOIN Reviewers
    ON Employees.EmployeeID=Reviewers.EmployeeID;
```

The results should look like:

	EmployeeID	FirstName	LastName	ReviewerNickName
1	1	Nancy	Davolio	Daisy
2	2	Andrew	Fuller	Amazin Andy
3	4	Margaret	Peacock	marGREAT
4	6	Michael	Suyama	Slick Suy
5	7	Robert	King	Anaheim KINGSman

Grids Messages

Note that we do not get any records for Employees 8 and 9 because they have not joined the reviewing program and thus do not have a record in Reviewers.

232

2. Try an alternative syntax that uses shortcuts for table names.

```
SELECT
    e.employeeID, e.FirstName, e.LastName, r.ReviewerNickName
FROM Employees as e
    INNER JOIN Reviewers as r
    ON e.EmployeeID=r.EmployeeID;
```

3. Let us try another one. This time, we need to generate a list of product names and the reviews written about the products.

```
SELECT
    Reviews.ReviewID,
    Products.ProductName,
    Reviews.ReviewText
FROM Reviews
    INNER JOIN Products
    ON Reviews.ProductID = Products.ProductID
;
```

The results are as follows:

	ReviewID	ProductName	ReviewText
1	1	Chai	Chai is one of the smoothest teas I have enjoyed.
2	2	Sirop d'érable	Far too strong, should be named Sirop de irratable
3	3	Uncle Bob's Organic Dried Pears	Full of flavor, each one is like a pair of pears.
4	4	Tofu	Good texture and rich flavor. I wish they made a Chou Tofu
5	5	Uncle Bob's Organic Dried Pears	Far too dry for my taste.

4. Let us finish with a triple `Join` for when we need to see all of the reviews along with the product number and last name of the reviewer.

```
SELECT
    Employees.EmployeeID,
    Employees.FirstName,
    Products.ProductID,
    Reviews.ReviewText
FROM Employees
    INNER JOIN Reviews
    ON Employees.EmployeeID=Reviews.EmployeeID
    INNER JOIN Products
    ON Products.ProductID=Reviews.EmployeeID
;
```

And here are the results:

	EmployeeID	FirstName	ProductID	ReviewText
1	1	Nancy	1	Chai is one of the smoothest teas I have enjoyed.
2	4	Margaret	4	Good texture and rich flavor. I wish they made a Chou Tofu
3	4	Margaret	4	Far too dry for my taste.
4	6	Michael	6	Full of flavor, each one is like a pair of pears.
5	7	Robert	7	Far too strong, should be named Sirop de irratable

Grids Messages

How It Works

If we look at Step 1, the beginning is the same as the SELECT statements that we studied in Chapters 4 and 5 – we list the columns we want to be in the result set. The FROM statement starts the same but then we have the JOIN clause. We specify what kind of JOIN with INNER, meaning we want only records with a matching value in both tables. Then we state the table we want to match to, Reviews. We finish the JOIN clause by using an ON clause to state what columns the DBMS should match.

The results from Step 1 include columns from both Employees and Reviewers – that is the success of the JOIN. We only see columns where there is a match on both sides as a result of including the INNER specification.

Let us look at that shortcut syntax from Step 2. In Chapters 4 and 5 we discuss using an alias for columns names, such as:

```
SELECT EmployeeID AS id …
```

In Step 2 we used:

```
SELECT
    e.employeeID, e.FirstName, e.LastName, r.ReviewerNickName
FROM Employees as e
    INNER JOIN Reviewers as r
    ON e.EmployeeID=r.EmployeeID;
```

Using aliases for the tables in a JOIN clause can make it easier to refer to the table in the rest of the statement. The DBMS will interpret the aliases first, then they are available to the whole statement. However, it bothers many students that the aliasing instructions occur in the statement after the aliases are used in the column list. This is because SQL is a set language that produces results based on the entire statement.

The three places most common places where students get muddled are:

❑   When using shortcut syntax we cannot mix and match original and alias names. If we use FROM Employees as e then we cannot use Employees.FirstName; we must use e.Firstname. That rule of consistency holds for the entire SQL statement: column list, ON clause and any ORDER BY or GROUP BY clauses.

❑   When we create the alias the alias, name does not go in quotes.

❑   Be sure that aliasing actually simplifies the reading of the statement for a human. Too many times there are aliases like t1 and t2 for the two tables. The result is shorter but far more confusing than the original. We should always make our aliases clearly understandable.

There is another situation where aliases are used: we may inherit tables with lousy column names. We can use the alias to give the column a better name to use within this statement. The objective is not to make the code more compact, but rather more understandable.

Outer Joins

Recall that Inner Joins produce a set of results with only those records that have a match in both tables. Outer Joins produce a set of results where every record from one table is represented, even if there is no match in the other table. I once did some work for a company that made snow removal equipment. The client asked for a list of how many units had been sold to each state and province over the last year. We had a table of shipments with a state column and we had a table of states. Obviously there are no snow blowers sold in Hawaii, so Inner Joins do not produce a record for Hawaii, but the client wanted every state listed, even if sales equaled zero. So I did an Outer Join and then Hawaii showed up, albeit with no sales.

Which table has all of its records shown? There are two types of Outer Joins, *right* and *left*. The term indicates which side of the Join gets all records listed. The syntax is only slightly different to that for the Inner Join:

```
SELECT ColumnNames
FROM TableOne
    RIGHT JOIN TableTwo
    ON TableOne.MatchingColumn = TableTwo.MatchingColumn
;
```

The above syntax will give us a result set of the ColumnNames listed. All of the records of the right table (TableTwo) will be listed. Only those records from TableOne that have a match in TableTwo will be listed.

We see the opposite in the code below.

```
SELECT ColumnNames
FROM TableOne
    LEFT JOIN TableTwo
    ON TableOne.MatchingColumn = TableTwo.MatchingColumn
;
```

Here we would get in the result set all of the records in TableOne but only matching records from TableTwo.

Try It Out – Outer Join

We have to produce a list of all the product names and, if they have a review, the review's ID number and the actual review text.

1. Run the following SQL statement

```
SELECT
    Reviews.ReviewID,
    Products.ProductName,
    Reviews.ReviewText
FROM Reviews
    RIGHT JOIN Products
    ON Reviews.ProductID = Products.ProductID
;
```

We should get the following results:

	ReviewID	ProductName	ReviewText
1	1	Chai	Chai is one of the smoothest teas I have enjoyed.
2	NULL	Chang	NULL
3	NULL	Aniseed Syrup	NULL
4	NULL	Chef Anton's Cajun Seasoning	NULL
5	NULL	Chef Anton's Gumbo Mix	NULL
6	NULL	Grandma's Boysenberry Spread	NULL
7	3	Uncle Bob's Organic Dried Pears	Full of flavor, each one is like a pair of pears.
8	5	Uncle Bob's Organic Dried Pears	Far too dry for my taste.
9	NULL	Northwoods Cranberry Sauce	NULL
10	NULL	Mishi Kobe Niku	NULL
11	NULL	Ikura	NULL
12	NULL	Queso Cabrales	NULL
13	NULL	Queso Manchego La Pastora	NULL

Grids | Messages

2. Let's try another `Outer Join`. This time, we need a list of the names of all the `Employees`, and if they have reviewer nicknames, we need to return those as well. We will use a `LEFT JOIN`:

```
SELECT e.FirstName, e.LastName, r.ReviewerNickName
FROM Employees As e LEFT JOIN Reviewers As r
   ON e.EmployeeID = r.EmployeeID
;
```

	FirstName	LastName	ReviewerNickName
1	Nancy	Davolio	Daisy
2	Andrew	Fuller	Amazin Andy
3	Janet	Leverling	NULL
4	Margaret	Peacock	marGREAT
5	Steven	Buchanan	NULL
6	Michael	Suyama	Slick Suy
7	Robert	King	Anaheim KINGSman
8	Laura	Callahan	NULL
9	Anne	Dodsworth	NULL

Grids | Messages

3. As an aside, we can create the same results as Step 2 by using a RIGHT JOIN

```
SELECT e.FirstName, e.LastName, r.ReviewerNickName
FROM Reviewers As r RIGHT JOIN employees As e
   ON e.EmployeeID = r.EmployeeID
;
```

How It Works

Our objective in using the `Outer Join` is to include all of the records from one table, `Products`. The difference from our `Inner Join` Try It Outs is very small: we just switch the one key word from inner to outer. Let us examine the results set.

First, we get all products listed in the results. Second, most products do not have reviews. For non-reviewed products the values for `ReviewText` is NULL. Keep this in mind – when doing an `Outer Join` we will usually get lots of NULLs representing those records that are listed because of the `RIGHT` keyword, but do not have a match in the other table.

In Step 2 we did not introduce any new theory, but we did tighten up the code by using aliases and fewer line breaks. Again, we see the expected results: all employees, even those that don't review. In Step 3 we get the same results by reversing the left and right tables and then substituting the keyword `RIGHT` for `LEFT`.

Using Outer Joins to Find Non-Matching Records

Take a look at the following statement and result. We want to get a list of all `Employees` and if they have a nickname we want to see it.

```
SELECT e.FirstName, e.LastName, r.ReviewerNickName
FROM employees As e LEFT JOIN Reviewers As r
    ON e.EmployeeiD = r.EmployeeID
;
```

The above code produces the following result:

	FirstName	LastName	ReviewerNickName
1	Nancy	Davolio	Daisy
2	Andrew	Fuller	Amazin Andy
3	Janet	Leverling	NULL
4	Margaret	Peacock	marGREAT
5	Steven	Buchanan	NULL
6	Michael	Suyama	Slick Suy
7	Robert	King	Anaheim KINGSman
8	Laura	Callahan	NULL
9	Anne	Dodsworth	NULL

Grids Messages

Notice in the results of the `LEFT JOIN` that we have all `Employees`. Also notice that about half have a `NULL` value for `ReviewerNickName` because they are not in the reviewers program.

If we wanted to see the `Employees` that were not participating in the program we could add a `WHERE` clause to limit the results to the records with a `NULL` for `ReviewerNickName`, as follows.

```
SELECT e.FirstName, e.LastName, r.ReviewerNickName
FROM employees As e LEFT JOIN Reviewers As r
    ON e.EmployeeiD = r.EmployeeID
WHERE r.ReviewerNickName IS NULL;
```

The above code produces the following results:

	FirstName	LastName	ReviewerNickName
1	Janet	Leverling	NULL
2	Steven	Buchanan	NULL
3	Laura	Callahan	NULL
4	Anne	Dodsworth	NULL

However, in the real world, we probably wouldn't care about the `NULL`s that we used to get the list so we can get a neater result with the following code.

```
SELECT e.FirstName, e.LastName
FROM employees As e LEFT JOIN Reviewers As r
    ON e.EmployeeID = r.EmployeeID
WHERE r.ReviewerNickName IS NULL;
```

Try It Out – Outer Join to Find Non-Matching Records

We have been asked to produce the following two lists:

❑   Products that have been reviewed

❑   Products that have not been reviewed

1.   To find the `Products` that have been reviewed, use the following statement:

```
SELECT Products.ProductName
FROM Products INNER JOIN Reviews
    ON Products.ProductID = Reviews.ProductID
;
```

We should get the following results:

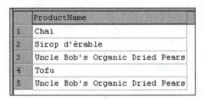

	ProductName
1	Chai
2	Sirop d'érable
3	Uncle Bob's Organic Dried Pears
4	Tofu
5	Uncle Bob's Organic Dried Pears

2.   To find the `Products` that have not been reviewed, use the following statement:

```
SELECT Products.ProductName
FROM Products
    LEFT JOIN Reviews
    ON Products.ProductID = Reviews.ProductID
WHERE Reviews.ProductID IS NULL
;
```

We should then get these results:

	ProductName
1	Chang
2	Aniseed Syrup
3	Chef Anton's Cajun Seasoning
4	Chef Anton's Gumbo Mix
5	Grandma's Boysenberry Spread
6	Northwoods Cranberry Sauce
7	Mishi Kobe Niku
8	Ikura
9	Queso Cabrales
10	Queso Manchego La Pastora
11	Konbu
12	Genen Shouyu
13	Pavlova

How It Works

In this series of statements we generate two lists. Our first list shows reviewed products – in other words we only want records with a match, so we use an INNER JOIN. In our second list we want to list all the products that have not been reviewed. We do this by specifying an OUTER JOIN (a LEFT in this case) to get records for all the products; but then we apply a WHERE filter that eliminates those records for which the DBMS found a match in the Reviews table. The records left are the un-reviewed products.

Preparation for Making Joins

Over the years we have observed that students are more successful if they are extra careful in the steps of preparation for the JOIN. Here is a short checklist that we can follow. We may not be able to perform or control every one of these steps when we are working with existing tables.

1. Have a column of the same data type in both tables

2. Have a column with the same name in both fields

3. Check that the data of these two columns is exactly equal

4. Determine the one and many sides

5. Write the query

Warnings and Reminders for Joins

Last, we want to leave you with some things to look out for when working with Joins.

❑ Joins do not establish or enforce the concepts of one-to-one and one-to-many. The concepts of One-to-Many and Many-to-Many exist because of the design of the tables, not because a JOIN statement is executed

❑ The more carefully normalization is performed (as described in Chapter 3), the more confidence we can have that our Joins will work as expected

❑ Specifying more columns than needed degrades performance for no benefit. The problem is even worse in a query that uses Joins.

❑ Performing a query with a Join consumes DBMS resources. If we can tightly confine the WHERE clause, then fewer records have to be joined and performance will be improved.

❑ The keywords LEFT and RIGHT are not absolute; they only operate within the context of the given statement: we can reverse the order of the tables and reverse the keywords, and the result would be the same.

❑ Consider whether it is worth using aliases for tables. Is it easier to read and understand a statement that has clear names and is very long, or one that has alias names and is shorter. Sometimes, however, using the original table names keeps code easier to maintain.

❑ LEFT and RIGHT only apply to outer Joins

❑ Be very careful to have matching data in the columns used in the Join. Data that doesn't match will result in the DBMS not being able to find records' counterparts in the other table.

❑ If possible, make the matching columns have the exact same data type.

❑ Once we are comfortable with Inner and Outer Joins consider reading a more advanced book on SQL to learn about the other types of Joins.

Summary

In this chapter we have looked at the idea of how tables are related and how the use of primary keys and foreign keys tells the DBMS how the data is related in the real world. For the sake of efficiency, many tables are split up into smaller tables, but sometimes we need to bring them together again to get the information we need. The way we have done this in this chapter is by using the JOIN keyword.

The JOIN statement allows us to use data from a number of different tables, as long as the primary key of one table is defined as a foreign key in another table. There are a number of different types of JOIN statements, but the ones we have covered here are:

- ❑ **Inner Join** – A SQL command that combines columns from two tables based on matching columns. An Inner Join results in only those records that have a matching value in both tables.

- ❑ **Outer Join** – A SQL command that combines columns from two tables based on matching columns. An Outer Join results in all of the records. We use the term OUTER to describe both LEFT- and RIGHT- JOINs in theoretical discussions. We actually specify RIGHT or LEFT in the code (most DBMS will not accept the term OUTER JOIN).

- ❑ **Right Join** – an Outer Join where the second table (the one listed to the right of the keyword JOIN) has all of its records included in the result. The other table will only have matching records in the result set.

- ❑ **Left Join** – an Outer Join where the first table (the one listed to the left of the keyword JOIN) has all of its records included in the result. The other table will only have matching records in the result set.

- ❑ **Simple Join** – If the type of join is not specified as inner or outer then it will be executed as an Inner Join

The ways that tables, and the data within them, relate to each other is important to understand – not only for the sake of performance and efficiency, but also for understanding how the data is related in the real world. This makes it easier to formulate relevant queries to get the information we need.

In the next chapter, we move on to creating our own records and cleaning the data within them.

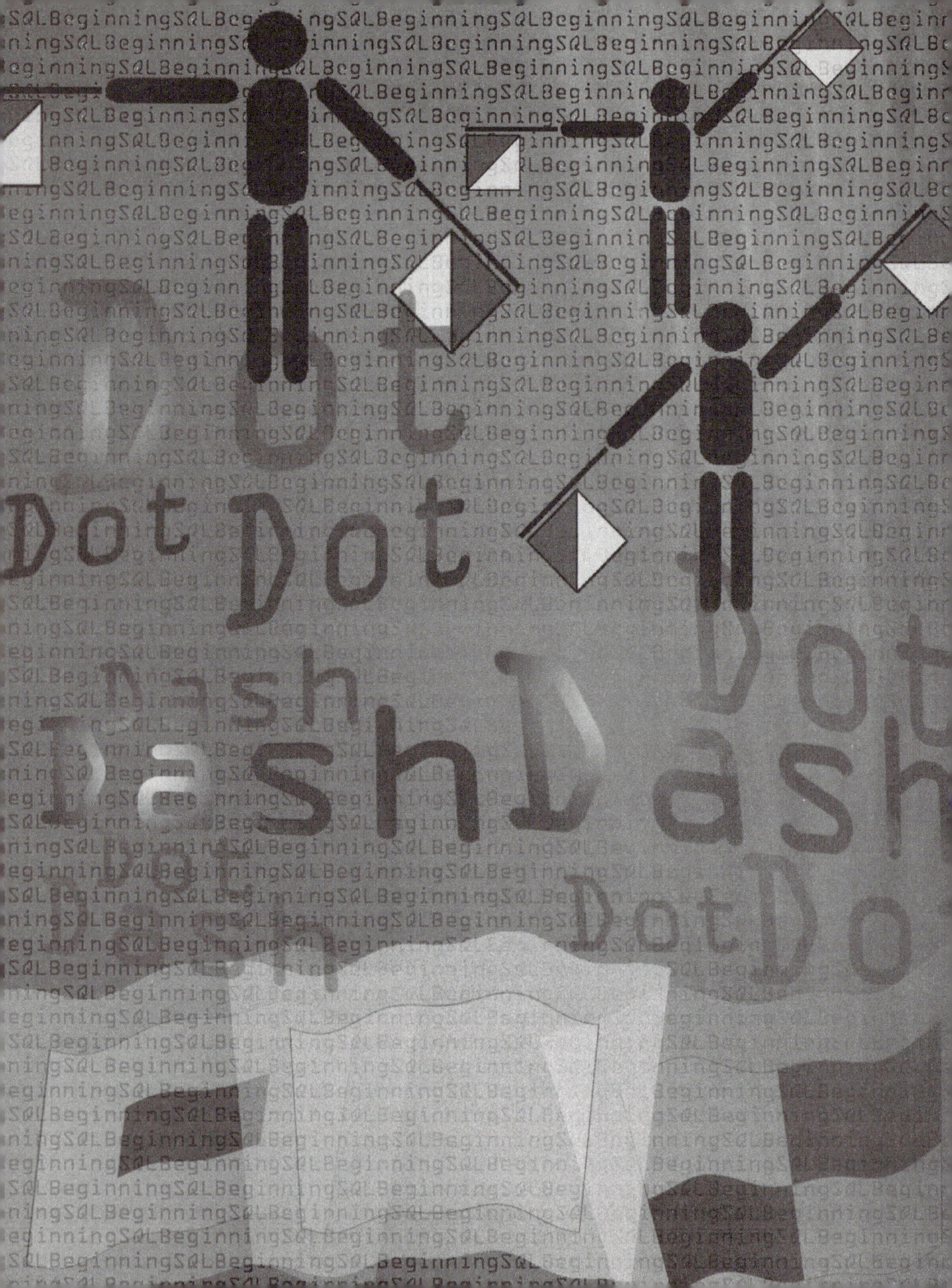

Creating New Records

We have looked in some depth at the theory of designing databases and creating an appropriate structure for data storage, and also at techniques for retrieving data that already resides in a database. We can now begin to focus on how to actually add data to a table.

The theory and practice of adding data to a database is quite simple, but, as we start to experiment with real-world data, we will see that there are many pitfalls that must be avoided.

In this chapter, we investigate techniques for:

- ❑ How to insert a single record into a table
- ❑ Ensuring that data is properly delimited
- ❑ Validating data
- ❑ Using numeric data
- ❑ Preparing Text Data
- ❑ Using Autonumber
- ❑ Adding Multiple Records

Introduction to INSERT

In several earlier chapters, we used cookbook code with which to add a few records to a database. In this chapter, we focus on the details of the process of creating one or more records in a table.

Tables are empty immediately after their creation. In other words, no data is automatically inserted into a table as part of the CREATE TABLE statement. And since SQL organizes data as sets, there are no place markers like BOF (Before Start of File) or EOF (End Of File).

Another characteristic of sets is that there is no sense of *where* within a table we insert a new record, in other words the records are not kept in a specific order in a set. A new record may be stored at the beginning, middle or end of the other records; the physical location of records is of no concern to us. We only care that the record is in the correct table and is uniquely identifiable. Of course there are ways to order a group of records that we read from tables, as we have learned using the ORDER BY clause. But that ordering is *ad hoc* for those records that were pulled out to the results.

SQL supports two basic varieties of statements to add records:

❑ INSERT INTO statements, with VALUES which allows us to enter one record at a time while providing the actual values in the statement.

❑ SELECT INTO, which allows us to add many records at once, using data from another table.

When adding information to a database, there are two general points that we need to bear in mind:

❑ In order to create a new record, we must have the right privileges. Privileges may be inherited with a role or they may be obtained explicitly.

❑ Most DBMS have a table locking system to ensure that two users do not attempt to create records at the same time. If one user is writing to the record all or part of the table may be locked, and the second user must wait until the initial procedure has finished and unlocked. Generally records are unlocked within milliseconds and a DBMS will automatically delay the write for that short time until the lock is released.

Adding One Record at a Time

In order to create a new record in a table, we use a statement of the following form:

```
INSERT INTO TableName(Column1, Column2, Column3)
VALUES (value1, value2, value3);
```

where column1, column2, and column3 identify the fields into which data is to be inserted, and value1, value2, and value3 specify the data that is entered into the fields. Note that we have to be careful to have the values presented in the same order as the list of column names. The order of the values is the only way the DBMS knows the association to the columns.

Although the order of columns must match the order for inserted values, we do not have to make those orders match any structure of the table. For example we can use:

```
INSERT INTO TableName(Column1, Column3, Column2…)
VALUES (value1, value3, value2);
```

As long as the order of columns and values matches within the statement, the DBMS will enter the values correctly.

Short Syntax to Add a Single Record

Let's now look at how we might want to vary this basic statement.

If we wanted to insert values into all the fields of a table, we could use the following:

```
INSERT INTO TableName
VALUES (value1, value2, value3);
```

Note that the values will have to be specified in the order of the fields in the table.

String Delimiters

We will look at preparing different types of data for insertion into tables a little later. But, to get us going, note that the following rules have to be respected when inserting data into a table:

- ❑ Strings for character type fields should be enclosed in single quotes.

- ❑ Numbers should be naked.

- ❑ Values for temporal data types are generally in single quotes, with one notable exception: Access requires hash marks around dates.

Common Errors

Errors when using INSERT INTO to insert new records into a table are frequently caused by one of the following:

- ❑ Missing commas in the list of column names or list of values

- ❑ Values list order does not agree with column list order

- ❑ Typos in column names or wrong column names

- ❑ Values in wrong order when columns not listed

- ❑ Columns names go in parentheses (as part of the table object)

- ❑ Values list goes within parentheses

- ❑ Incorrect formatting of temporal values

- ❑ Incorrect number of values (more or less than the number of columns)

Try It Out – Add Records to Reviews

Let's look at inserting records into the Review table of our database.

Suppose that some employees have sent us reviews, as summarized in the following table:

Reviewer ID	Product	Date of Review	Review text
1	10	6/6/2001	A good value on a commercial ikura.
2	11	7/7/2001	Just like my Mom used to make back in Tegoose
4	12	8/8/2001	Not quite as good as the Sonoran Brand
6	13	9/9/2001	Warning – this is the southern style of Konbu

1. Recall that we have a Review.ReviewID column in which we keep a serial integer. First let us find out the highest current value in this:

```
SELECT * FROM Reviews
```

Our highest number is 5, but you may have added more or less data. We'll want to use the next three higher numbers when inserting records into this table.

2. We will add the first review using the most basic syntax:

```
INSERT INTO Reviews
     (ReviewID,
     EmployeeID,
     ProductID,
     Date,
     ReviewText)
VALUES
     (6,
     1,
     10,
     '6/6/2002',
     'A good value on a commercial ikura.');
```

Check your results with the same statement we used in step one.

3. For the next record, we will change the order of presentation of the columns and values. We will also tighten up the layout of the statement by putting multiple columns and values on the same line.

```
INSERT INTO Reviews
   (ReviewText,Date,EmployeeID,ReviewID,ProductID)
VALUES
   ('Just like my Mom used to make back in Tegoose.','7/7/2002',2,7,11);
```

4. Our last addition will be the tightest yet because we will present the values in exact column ordinal position and thus avoid having to type the column names.

```
INSERT INTO Reviews
VALUES
(8,6,13,'9/9/2002','Warning - this is the southern style of Konbu');
```

How It Works

Later in the chapter, we will discuss automatic numbering of values in primary keys. For now, we just look at all the records and find the highest number used to date.

The INSERT statement that we used in step two is the most basic form of the syntax. Notice how we keep the numbers naked, but encapsulate the temporal and text data in single quotes. If you are using Access for a back end you should encapsulate the temporal values in hash marks (#). We must be careful to match the orders of the columns names and the values.

The second statement jumbles the order of the column/value pairs. They are in an odd order, but they are still synchronized with each other.

The last example demonstrates that if we are entering data in the order of the columns' ordinal positions, we do not have to explicitly list the column names.

Two Notes on Inserting Records

What happens when we don't want to enter a value for every column? Well, in one type of case, we might want to add a NULL value. In other words, we do not now know what the value should be. This is fairly straightforward.

For example, if we had no date value for a new record in our Reviews table, we could use:

```
INSERT INTO Reviews
VALUES (6,1,33,NULL,'I liked this food.');
```

In another type of case, we might want to use the default value for the column. In such a case, we would have to know that the field in question has been set up with a default value, but so long as it has, the DBMS will insert the approprate default value for us when we don't explicitly declare a value to insert. We'll see how to achieve this shortly.

Try It Out - Using NULL and Defaults

Supposing Northwind has added referees to the Bowling League. We need to track the referees' first and last name and their level of certification (master or senior). Almost all of the referees are certified at the Master level.

Here are details about our first four referees:

First Name	Last Name	Certification level
Sylvia	Venezia	Master
John	Millette	Master
?	Cooper	Master
Elizabeth	Annco	Senior

1. Create a table as follows. Note that the CertLevel field has a default value of 'master':

```
CREATE TABLE Refs
    (RefID INTEGER PRIMARY KEY,
    NameFirst VARCHAR(20),
    NameLast VARCHAR(20),
    CertLevel CHAR(6) DEFAULT 'Master');
```

2. Let's enter the first new referee:

```
INSERT INTO Refs
    (RefID,NameFirst,NameLast,CertLevel)
VALUES
    (1,'Sylvia','Venezia','Master');
```

3. We can check that this has been entered properly with:

```
SELECT * FROM Refs
```

4. Since we know that the default value for `CertLevel` is `Master`, we can leave that out of both the columns list and the values list when we insert the second record:

```
INSERT INTO Refs
    (RefID,NameFirst,NameLast)
VALUES
    (2,'John','Millette');
```

5. For the third referee, we will have to enter a `NULL` value:

```
INSERT INTO Refs
    (RefID,NameFirst,NameLast)
VALUES
    (3,NULL,'Cooper');
```

6. For the last referee, we have to be careful not to use the default for the certification level:

```
INSERT INTO Refs
    (RefID,NameFirst,NameLast,CertLevel)
VALUES
    (4,NULL,'Cooper','Senior');
```

How It Works

We created our table with a `DEFAULT` value for the level of certification since we know from our business description that most referees will have a value of `'master'` for their certification level. As usual, we include an `ID` field that is constrained as a primary key.

In inserting the first referee, we encountered nothing special. To insert the second referee, we take advantage of the default value for the column `CertLevel`. It is important that we remove the column from the list. Some people are tempted to try to use the default by changing the value list to use the word `DEFAULT`, or using nothing (just two adjacent commas). This would get us unexpected results. The way to use the default is to leave the column out of the column list and thus outside of the value list as well.

The third `INSERTION` requires us to use a `NULL` value. The only proper technique is to use the keyword `NULL`. Since it is a keyword, it is not encapsulated in single quotes. Our fourth referee is certified at the senior level. This requires us to add the `CertLevel` column back in to the column list so we can provide an explicit value rather than accept the default.

A Note on Validation

The SQL statement that performs the creation of a new record is not complex. Once we are mindful of the commas and the column order, we will have few problems with the syntax. However, a far more difficult problem will rear its head when we move from the theory to the real world: the data that will be provided to an `INSERT INTO` statement will frequently contain characters or syntax that are not acceptable to SQL. There are several classes of examples:

❑ Characters that will be interpreted as part of the SQL syntax rather than data. For example, single quotes.

❑ Values that are out of range of the data type. For example, a value of 300 for a `TINYINT`.

❑ Values that are out of range of the column constraints. For example, a value of 100 when the constraint limits values to 50 or less.

To prevent such problems occurring, it is useful to check input before it is submitted to a SQL statement. This is known as validation. This is generally done in the procedural language of your front end or business layer, not within the SQL language. However, validation may be done within SQL.

There are some tools which allow us to stretch SQL to perform validations within the DBMS, rather than in the front end. Functions such as CONVERT, CAST and the string manipulating functions can do some data cleaning and validating. We can also use stored procedures to create validation code. But most businesses rely on the other tiers of an application to provide the validations prior to sending data to the DBMS.

Numeric Data

Numeric data is generally easier to prepare than other data types. Numeric data should be presented in SQL statements without encapsulation. In other words, do not put apostrophes around numbers or currency.

Numeric data may be of the following data types:

❑   BIT – This can have the value of 1 or 0 (or NULL). Although this can be used as a Boolean, we cannot enter values like 'TRUE' or 'YES' as we can in some desktop database systems, such as Access. Likewise, use of negative numbers in bit fields will be ignored: a –1 will be stored as 1. Any number larger than 1 will be stored as a one, any fractional number will be stored as a 1. Remember: bit stores a zero as a zero and all other numbers as a one.

> **VB and VBA Programmers Beware - With SQL we cannot use a bit stored –1 as a TRUE as we can in VB and VBA.**

❑   INTEGER data types accept numbers within their range (the normal integer is from -2,147,483,648 to +2,147,483,647, but most DBMSs also have other Integer types). Never include commas as place markers in your numbers because SQL will think you are entering more than one value. Most DBMS accept numbers in engineering format such as 2E5 for 2,000. Although it depends on the vendor, fractions entered in integer types will get truncated to an integer, so 1.0, 1.5, 1.9 and 1.999 will all be stored as 1. Numbers that are too high or too low will generate an arithmetic overflow error.

❑   DECIMAL or NUMERIC values require adherence to two factors. Recall from chapter 3 that when we created a DECIMAL type, we had to provide two parameters: the first was the total number of digits available for both the right and left of the decimal point combined, and the second was the maximum number of digits that can be used to the right of the decimal place. So when we pass DECIMAL type values in an INSERT INTO, we merely provide the number with a correctly placed decimal point.

If the left side is too large, we will get an arithmetic overflow error. On the right side any digits more than the range are rounded to the nearest (up or down) integer off. Therefore a DECIMAL(4,2) column will store 1, regardless of whether we enter a value of 1, 1.00 or 1.009. We will get an error for 100, 100.0 and 100.00, because we only have space for two digits on the left side of the number.

Try It Out - Experimenting with Numeric Data

1. Create a table that will hold a text field and each of the numeric fields that your DBMS supports. For Microsoft SQL Server 2000, we could have:

```
CREATE TABLE TestNumbers
(MyText CHAR(20),
MyInteger INTEGER,
MySmallInteger SMALLINT,
MyTinyInteger TINYINT,
MyBit BIT,
MyMoney Money,
MyDecimal DECIMAL(4,2)
);
```

2. Now we will add some values and see the results. In each case we add the same values to all the columns. For the `MyText` column we put the value in single quotes so the DBMS stores the exact characters we entered.

```
INSERT INTO TestNumbers
(MyText,MyInteger,MySmallInteger,MyTinyInteger,MyBit,MyMoney,MyDecimal)
VALUES ('1',1,1,1,1,1,1);
```

3. Then we can run a `SELECT` and in the results see how the value in `MyText` was actually stored in each of the numeric columns.

```
SELECT * FROM TestNumbers
```

4. This example is fairly straightforward: we can predict that all of the results will be 1, but note the difference in `MONEY` and `DECIMAL` types.

5. Try using a value of 0.5 in each of the fields.

```
INSERT INTO TestNumbers
(MyText,MyInteger,MySmallInteger,MyTinyInteger,MyBit,MyMoney,MyDecimal)
VALUES ('0.5',0.5,0.5,0.5,0.5,0.5,0.5);
```

Continue entering interesting values, we suggest the following. Some may give you an error, in which case enter a `NULL` for the offending column:

0	0.1	-1	-0.1	1.1	1.5	1.9	1.99	1.999	1.9999	1.99999

How It Works - Experimenting with Numeric Data

Let's take a look at what happened to the various values we entered into our table, given the various numeric data types of the fields:

❑ Value = 1 : Note that 1 becomes `TRUE` as a `BIT` data type.

❑ Value = 0.5 : This fraction gets truncated to a zero for all the pure integer types. It is not zero, so it becomes 1 in the `BIT` data type. `MONEY` and `DECIMAL` hold the 0.5 without problem.

❑ Value = 0.1 : Like 0.5, fractions get truncated for integer types.

❑ Value = -0.1 : Here we encounter a problem, as TINYINT does not accept negative numbers. So when preparing numbers for TINYINT fields, we must validate that the value is greater than or equal to zero.

❑ Value = 1.1, 1.5, 1.9... 1.99999 : Real numbers get their fractional part chopped off when stored in any of the integer data types. Even when we get close to 2, the value remains 1 until we actually enter 2. However, the DECIMAL and MONEY types round up once the number of decimal places exceeds the data type's limit of exactness. For MONEY this is fixed at 4 decimal places. For the DECIMAL type we can set it as we did in the CREATE TABLE statement.

Preparing Text Data

Values as literal text should be presented within apostrophes. But a problem arises when there is an apostrophe within that text: for example the names O'Neil or O'Brian.

SQL will read two adjacent single apostrophes in a string and store a single apostrophe. In other words, the apostrophe is acting as an **escape** character.

Try It Out - Apostrophes in String Values

1. Create a table with one column called MyText of data types char(30):

```
CREATE TABLE TestText
    (MyText CHAR(30),
    MyNote VARCHAR(100));
```

2. Add a straightforward record as follows:

```
INSERT INTO TestText (MyText,MyNote)
VALUES ('Tom','No apostrophes');
```

3. Now lets add some tougher ones. Try entering the following records to test the effects of having the double quote character in various places:

MyText	MyNote	Result
'"Hi" he said'	Start with Single and double	Double saved without problem
'Say "Hi" quickly'	Double in middle	Double saved without problem
'He said "Hi"'	End with double then single	Double saved without problem

4. Try these two phrases that test a string that begins with a single apostrophe:

''nuff said'	Start with two singles	Failure
'''nuff said'	Start with three singles	One starting single apostrophe stored

5. Try three phrases that test a string with an ending single apostrophe:

`'CA Dreamin'`	`End with one single`	No apostrophes stored
`'CA Dreamin''`	`End with two single`	Error
`'CA Dreamin'''`	`End with three single`	One ending apostrophe stored

6. Try three phrases that test a string with a single apostrophe in the middle of the string:

`'Not 'till later'`	`Middle has a single`
`'Not ''till later'`	`Middle has two singles`
`'Not '''till later'`	`Middle has three singles`

7. We can see that to store a single quote we need the string to contain two adjacent single quotes. Let us check on last thing – what if the single quotes are not adjacent, but have a space between them?

`'Not ' 'till later'`	`Middle has two singles separated by a space`	Fails

How It works - Apostrophes in String Values

We can conclude from the first three examples that SQL does not care about a double quote character anywhere in a text string.

- ❑ In the remainder of the examples, we saw that to store a single apostrophe, we need to have it in the string value as two adjacent single apostrophes:

- ❑ To start a stored value with an apostrophe we must use two adjacent single apostrophes: we need the single apostrophe that encapsulates the whole string, so we end up with three at the beginning.

- ❑ In the middle of the string, we just need to put two adjacent singles to get one stored.

- ❑ When we want to store an ending apostrophe, we end up with three, because we need two to tell SQL to store a single apostrophe and then one to close the encapsulation of the string.

- ❑ In the last example we did a quick proof that the two adjacent single apostrophes must in fact be adjacent.

We can't very well tell our users to type in two apostrophes if they want one saved. Fortunately, SQL Server, has a function called `Replace` which is essentially the same as the VB function. This takes three arguments:

- ❑ The target string.

- ❑ The string to find within the target string (that is, the string we want to replace).

- ❑ The string to replace it with.

Let's look at how we could use this.

1. Continuing to use `TestText` (from the last Try It Out Section), try inserting a new record with the value *hot 'n' wild* in the `MyText` column:

```
INSERT INTO TestText (MyText,MyNote)
VALUES (REPLACE("Hot 'n' Wild" , " ' " , " ' ' " ) ,'Replace puts in two singles');
```

2. We've managed to store two single quotes. Let us try using a replacement string of just a single apostrophe:

```
INSERT INTO TestText (MyText,MyNote)
VALUES (REPLACE("Hot 'n' Wild","'","'"),'Replace puts in one singles');
```

We might be surprised, but this works!

How It Works - Using the REPLACE function

Well, the REPLACE function works just like we expect, it looks in the string and when it finds a string that matches the second argument it replaces it with the third argument.

But the stored result in the DBMS is surprising – we end up with two single apostrophes. The reason is that SQL handles the result of internal functions differently to literal values that we supply within single quotes.

Autonumber

In many situations, it is useful to have an automatic incremental field for use with an ID or RecordNumber field. This value would generally be an integer, is guaranteed to be unique, is ever increasing, and is provided automatically by the DBMS when a record is created. Even if records are deleted, their ID values are never reused.

In this section, we'll look at ways of using such a field.

The SQL standards do not provide for such a data type. However, most vendors have included this feature as a built-in function. SQL Server calls such a field an Identity Field.

In another solution to this problem, Oracle allows the user to access the ROWID of a record, which is a reference to the physical location on the storage.

Other vendors have functions such as NUMBER(*), which generates the next sequential number. Some versions of SQL have an AUTOINCREMENT available as a constraint when a column is created.

Although an autonumber field is convenient, these vendor solutions generate a number of problems:

❑   Under some very rare situations, we may get a duplicate value, possibly when using a UNION statement or when the next sequential value exceeds the range of the data type.

❑   Implementations vary from vendor to vendor, which makes it harder to transfer code or to write code prior to knowing which DBMS will be deployed.

❑   If the autonumber value or function is correlated to the physical drive, then when data is moved or restored from a back up, the ROWID may change.

❑   With some vendor solutions, it is difficult to get the ID number of a row that was just added.

Notwithstanding these problems, using vendor specific solutions for identity fields can still be a good idea. Lots of programmers use them because they are simple to use and are fairly robust. Also, the chances of the failures mentioned above actually happening are fairly slim.

However, let's take a look at how we could develop our own way of generating unique numbers using SQL.

One such solution would be based on simply adding one to the highest existing number in a column. Assuming we are holding the incremental values in a field called MyIDColumn, the basic syntax for such a function could be as follows:

```
(SELECT MAX (MyIDColumn) FROM MyTable) + 1
```

This code uses the MAX aggregate function (which we will look at in more detail in Chapter 16). Basically, this simply returns the highest existing value in a particular field.

This little function should give us the next highest number for any existing value. However, what if you and another user both read the MAX number at the same time, and thus both get the same number? Then, in the next instant, you both add a record with the same MAX + 1. Our identity column would break. Or, depending on circumstances, our DBMS would complain that we are trying to add a duplicate value in a Primary Key column.

To solve the problem, a transaction should be started which locks until the INSERT new record is performed.

This solution also requires us to enter the first record, to ensure that there is a value to increment. There is, however, a way of getting round this.

If there are no records in our incremental field, then the MAX() function will return a NULL. Recall from Chapter 3 that we cannot add anything to a NULL value. In order to ensure this doesn't happen, we can use the COALESCE function.

COALESCE requires two or more arguments, each of which is an expression, value or SELECT statement. COALESCE returns the first one that is not NULL. So, in our case, we use the above SELECT as the first argument. If that returns a value, then the value is used, but if the first argument (the above SELECT) returns a NULL, then we use the second argument (a zero) for the result. The following code would be used as the value for an INSERT INTO.

```
COALESCE ((SELECT MAX(MyIDColumn) FROM MyTable),0) + 1
```

Now, for our first record, SQL will have no problem incrementing to a zero.

Try It Out - Creating Primary Key Values in Alleys Table

Supposing Northwind wants to start keeping track of the bowling alleys in the area. For now, we just need a primary key, the alley's name and the number of lanes each alley has.

First, we create the table:

```
CREATE TABLE Alleys
    (AlleyID INTEGER PRIMARY KEY,
    AlleyName VARCHAR(20),
    Lanes INT);
```

Next, we add some values using our SQL statement to insure that we are getting auto incrementing integers starting at 1 for the ID. We start by determining the number to use for our AlleyID column. This should be 1, as returned by the following statement:

```
SELECT COALESCE ((SELECT MAX(AlleyID) FROM Alleys),0) + 1
```

And now we have the values to use in our INSERT INTO statement

```
INSERT INTO Alleys VALUES (1,'Ace Lanes', 11);
```

Let us try another to see if the incrementing is working correctly. First, we get the ID value:

```
SELECT COALESCE ((SELECT MAX(AlleyID) FROM Alleys),0) + 1
```

Then use that value to insert the second record:

```
INSERT INTO Alleys VALUES (2,'Beta Bowling',22);
```

We will also insert a third record, to use later in the book:

```
INSERT INTO Alleys VALUES ((3,'Charlie''s Bowl',33)');
```

How It Works

When we created the table, we utilized a PRIMARY KEY constraint on the ID column, as discussed in Chapter 7. Then the main piece of code in this returned the value we should use for our next record's ID column:

```
SELECT COALESCE ((SELECT MAX(AlleyID) FROM Alleys),0) + 1
```

The core of the statement is the MAX(), which finds the highest number that we have used so far. But if there are no records, then MAX() will return a NULL, which is of no use to us. So we used the COALESCE function.

Adding Multiple Records

In many cases, you will want to add many records to a table in one go. These records may come from another table, or they may come from outside the database.

There are two main techniques to insert multiple records at once:

- ❑ Use a SELECT within an INSERT INTO to transfer records from another table.
- ❑ Use a vendor-specific bulk data transfer utility.

In this chapter, we'll look at the first of these. Some information about vendor specific bulk data transfer may be found in Appendix D:

Copying Records Using a Nested SELECT

At times we may want to copy values from existing records in one table into new records in a second table. We will then be left with two copies of the data. If we are going to eliminate the old records, then we will have no problems with normalization. But if the old records will remain, then we have to ask ourselves if we are sure we want to de-normalize.

The two common cases when we can accept denormalization are:

❑ We want to make a temporary table to increase speed for a certain operation (and then will destroy the table).

❑ We want to archive some data into a duplicate table (removing the old records).

The syntax to copy records from one table to another is long but not complex. We start with our usual INSERT. However, instead of using the VALUES keyword, and providing literal values, we will provide a SELECT that will give a recordset containing the values:

```
INSERT INTO NewTable
    (Col1, Col2, Col3)
    SELECT Col1, Col2, Col3
        FROM OldTable
        WHERE expression;
```

The DBMS will take the results of the embedded SELECT statement, and insert them into the NewTable table.

Try It Out – Inserting Multiple Records With Nested SELECT

Suppose our boss thinks some of the reviews are getting stale. He wants everything from 2001 removed from the active review table and put into storage.

1. First of all, we want to create a table called ReviewsOld, that is just like Reviews:

```
CREATE TABLE Reviewsold
    (ReviewID INTEGER,
    EmployeeID INTEGER,
    ProductID INTEGER,
    Date DATETIME,
    ReviewText CHAR(200));
```

2. Now we can insert the old reviews into the ReviewsOld table:

```
INSERT INTO Reviewsold
    (ReviewID,EmployeeID,
    ProductID,Date,ReviewText)
    SELECT ReviewID,EmployeeID,ProductID,Date,ReviewText
        FROM Reviews
        WHERE Date < '01/01/2002';
```

3. Let's see that this has worked properly:

```
SELECT * FROM ReviewsOld
```

How It Works – Inserting Multiple Records With Nested SELECT

This process is not difficult, but we do have to keep an eye on the nested SQL statements. Indenting as shown will help.

There are three basic traps:

❑ When using this syntax, we must leave out the VALUES keyword.

❑ The columns list in INSERT is in parentheses, the columns list in SELECT is not in parentheses.

❑ We cannot have a different number of columns in the INSERT and SELECT parts of the statement. This is the same rule as for our simple INSERT statements.

Note how we used the WHERE clause in the SELECT clause. We can use all the tricks we studied in Chapters 4 and 5 to select only those records that we want to add.

There are some possibilities which can lead to trouble. Although allowed in SQL92 and SQL99, we caution beginners to avoid them:

❑ We should avoid an ORDER BY in the SELECT. After all, a sense of ordering does not exist within set logic as records are kept in an DBMS.

❑ Avoid doing a UNION in the SELECT.

In summary, the nested SELECT makes an excellent way to bring data from one table to another. The most important point is to understand the normalization implications of duplicating data within a database. In almost all cases either the copied or original data is destroyed as soon as appropriate.

SUMMARY

In this chapter, we have investigated various techniques for inserting data into tables. In particular, we have covered:

❑ How to insert a single record into a table

❑ Insuring that data is properly delimited

❑ Validating data

❑ Using numeric data

❑ Preparing Text Data

❑ Using Autonumber

❑ Adding Multiple Records

In the next chapter, we will look at techniques for removing records from tables.

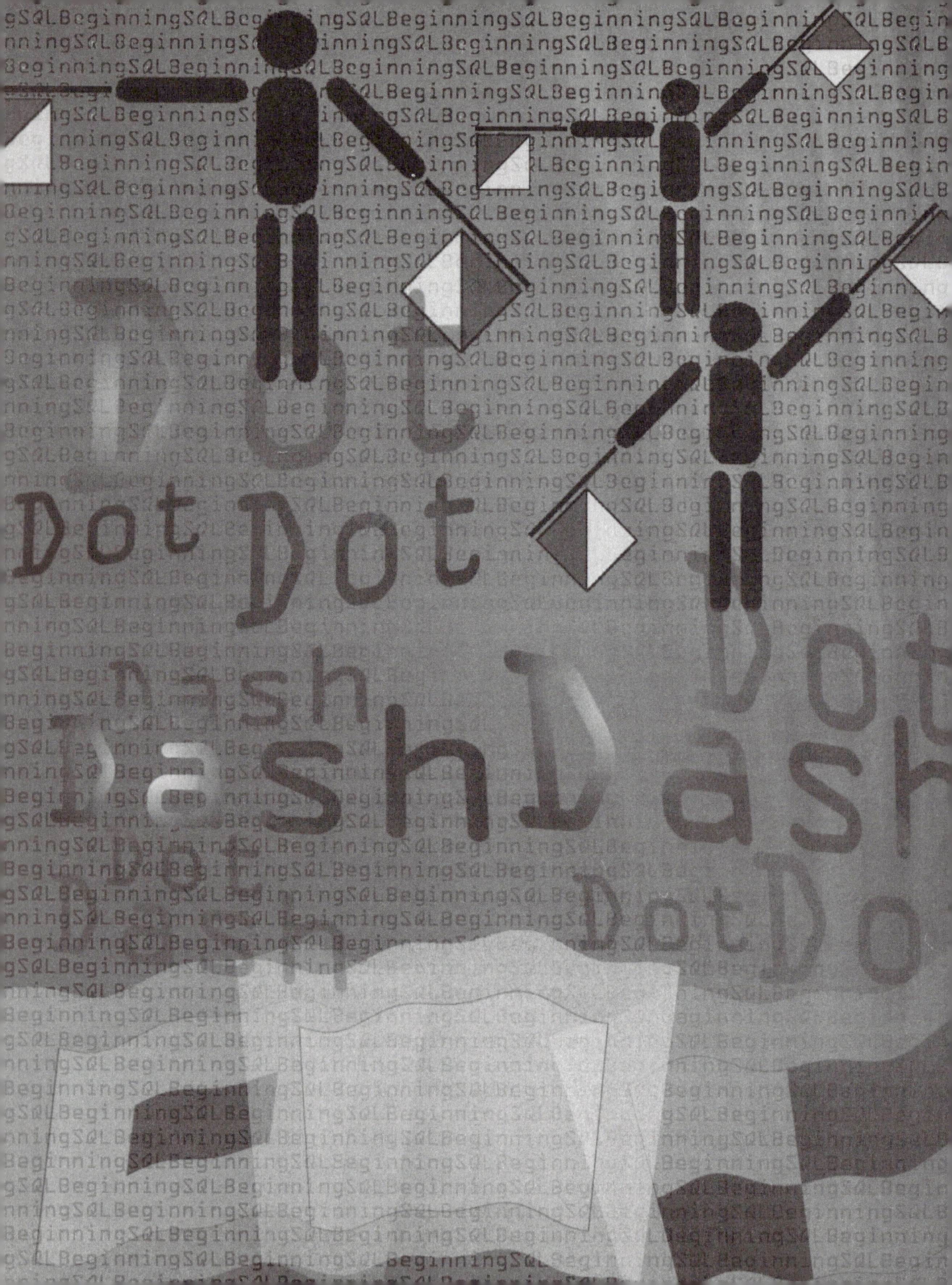

10

Deleting and Updating Records

Once, while on a nature walk with a scout troop, a scout asked why, if leaves keep falling from trees every autumn, and had been doing so for thousands of years, isn't the earth covered with hundreds of feet of leaves. Databases end up a lot like the forest floor: covered with the detritus of data left from the ongoing conduct of business. Without the ability to delete and archive data our DBMS would be covered in terabytes of dead data. We also need to be able to update information in our database. When performing updates, old data is deleted and replaced by the new information, so just as with a straight delete, the actions we take when updating records is irrevocable, so we have to be sure and exact in the way we write SQL statements.

In this chapter we cover:

- ❑ How to delete one or more records
- ❑ How we can avoid problems if the simple deletion runs into trouble
- ❑ Techniques to handle the elimination of duplicate records
- ❑ How to update records using the UPDATE command

The most important message in this chapter is that in a normalized database we can rarely just throw away data; we must be very careful to delete data in a way that will maintain the referential integrity of the data as a whole.

Thinking About Deleting

Before we discuss the techniques let us spend a few pages thinking about deleting. We want to consider why we are deleting data and whether an archiving solution might be better. We also want to cover some fundamental difference between how we may have been doing deletes on the desktop and how they work in a heavy-duty DBMS. Last we want to cover some confusing vocabulary about removing information from databases.

Deleting data is not for the faint of heart. It should certainly not be for the unauthorized. Almost all of the deletion techniques discussed in this chapter require specific permission from the DBA as discussed in Appendix B on security and discussed in the Database Administrator texts for your specific DBMS. In SQL Server 2000 we need to have DELETE permissions, which are given for the systems administrator account that you are probably using for learning SQL using the Query Analyzer.

When we delete data we may be removing records that are in the middle of a process: for example we may delete a receiver's account after the DBMS has already removed money from a payer's account. There are techniques to prevent things such as this from happening, but they are covered in more advanced texts. For now you will be able to learn the techniques of deleting from the relatively static Northwind.

Why Delete?

Unused or outdated data creates several problems for a business. Firstly, all data takes up space and space costs money. We are all aware that the cost of storage is falling rapidly so we may be able to overcome the raw cost of maintaining dead data by buying larger drives. However, drives can fail and one result of keeping more and more data on the drives is that we have a larger and larger egg in the basket. I agree that RAID (a disk system which increases performance and provides fault tolerance) solves most drive failures, but RAID demands a premium of 20% to 100% more capacity than is actually used. Then you must consider that some database operations require space available that is equal to the size of the database. So although drives may be cheap, are you prepared to be buying storage at a rate of two or three times that at which your data size is expanding?

Secondly, unused data mixed with useful data slows performance of frequently performed operations. The DBMS creates its sets based on all the records included in the SQL statement. SQL does not automatically bias or exclude based on whether a record is frequently used or not. As dead data piles up, deleting it, or moving it away from live data can be one of the most productive performance improvements.

Thirdly, the mixing of "live" and "dead" data can confuse the user. For example, we may have a vendor that our company no longer uses, but the vendor's record is still in a table. An unsuspecting buyer for our company may include the unused vender when sending a Request For Proposal.

Archiving as an Alternative to Deletion

Before we go further with deleting data, I suggest that you give consideration to a plan where you transfer data which is not needed to a cheap mode of storage. This process, called archiving, achieves most of the benefits of deleting data, but the information is still available, albeit more slowly or with inconvenience. Consider the following options:

- ❑ Move the data from an active table to an archive table within the database, thus improving the performance when searching through "live" records in the active table.

- ❑ Move the archive data to tables on your slower drives, perhaps using drives that were headed for retirement. Move the data to tables housed on slower servers or servers that have slower connections to your users. These archive tables would be created using the DBA's commands to locate the archive table on a specific disk.

- ❑ Move archive data to off-line media such as CDs or tapes.

This list moves the data through locations that are progressively slower and more difficult to access. In each case above we will have to access archived data through different SQL statements than we do "live" data, because we will work with different tables. We will have to either write front-end procedural code or SQL stored procedures or views that distinguish which table to use. One technique is to first look in the live table, then if the result is not found ask the user if he wants to wait while we search archived records.

What Should Be Deleted (or Archived)?

Many businesses approach the decision to delete by asking, "Do we need this data?" A more logical question is "Is this data worth saving?" That makes the decision a cost-to-benefit analysis. In many cases the costs of storage can be greatly reduced by the techniques described above, such as moving the data to older disks. On the benefits side, vendors are constantly providing more powerful analysis tools that can turn old data into justification for business decisions. Other types of data, such as financial records, may have to be kept for many decades after they are seemingly 'dead' in order to provide audit trails. It is hard to state that there will never be a call for a given set of data at some later point.

SQL DELETEs are Different to Many Desktop Database Systems

If you are coming from a background in desktop database systems like dBase or Paradox you will have to learn that in SQL DELETE means delete; it is permanent and immediate. Some systems execute a DELETE by just marking records as "to be deleted", while keeping the record in the database until a completion step such as a "compact" or "commit" command is issued. This is not the case for the kinds of true SQL-based DBMS that we discuss in this book. For these products, any two-step process of first flagging and then deleting is internal and occurs without opportunity to take action between the two steps.

SQL does not prompt the user for confirmation about deleting. After all, SQL usually receives a command from a front end and so a prompt would not be going back to a human for confirmation. Any prompting that you might wish to add should be handled in the procedural code of the front end.

Scope of Deletion

The DELETE keyword removes zero or more entire records. DELETE does not remove a value from one column of one record – it must remove entire records. An entire record means all the values from all the columns and leaving no space or marker or sense that the record existed. If you want to remove value(s) in one or more rows or columns then use UPDATE to replace them with a NULL or some marker value. In relation to the table, DELETE has no effect on the structure of a table's columns. DELETE does, of course, reduce the overall size of the table by removing records.

> There may be one artifact remaining to show that a deletion occurred. If you have a column with values from a serial numbering scheme then a delete will leave behind holes in the sequence. However, this is not a robust detection technique. Firstly, not every table has a serial number column. Secondly, the sequence may have been burdened with missing values from other operations. Therefore it is generally a weak technique to use sequence holes to indicate deletions.

A similar command to DELETE is TRUNCATE. Both remove all of the records from a table, but there are two differences:

❑ TRUNCATE has no option for specifying a sub-set of records to remove. By definition TRUNCATE removes all the records, leaving you a table with structure but no data.

❑ TRUNCATE is performed without an implicit transaction. That means that the DBMS does not record the steps of the delete (keep an internal transaction) to the extent that the DBMS could reverse the delete (perform a rollback).

Without the transaction overhead TRUNCATE can remove records much faster than DELETE, which does set up an internal action-tracking system. So if you are sure you want all records removed then TRUNCATE performs better than DELETE.

> The word *Truncate* has two meanings when working with databases. The **TRUNCATE** command removes all records from a table and recovers the storage space, without the opportunity to roll back the action. The term truncate can also describe the way that digits are removed from a number, namely by dropping the part of a number to the right of the decimal place, turning a mixed number into an integer.

The following table shows the techniques used to remove data from a database:

Keyword	Action	Effect on Data in Columns	Effect on Records	Effect on Tables
DELETE	Removes one or more entire records	Removes all data in all columns for affected record	Removes one or more	No effect on structure, size of data reduced
TRUNCATE	Removes all records from a table	Removes all	Removes all	No effect on table structure, size of data reduced to zero
DROP TABLE (Chapter 6)	Removes a table and all of its records	Removes all	Removes all	Removes data and structure
DROP *User* (Used by DBAs)	(Does not remove data, included for comparison) Users are removed with the DROP keyword in the Data Control Language.			
DROP *Object* (Chapter 6)	DROP is a way to remove any object, such as a procedure, index, view or even an entire database.			
UPDATE used to replace old values with a NULL	Removes values from specific columns of records	Effects only those columns where values change	Records remain, but contain NULL in one or more columns	No effect on table structure, size of data reduced
Editor-Specific Definitions of Delete	You may also use the term *delete* in commands or statements for your SQL editor, analyzer or other CASE tool. For example your editor may hold the last twenty SQL statements, and have a menu option to *delete* the first ten all at once.			

Basic Technique

The DELETE syntax is one of the most basic in SQL. Listing columns is not needed (or allowed) in a DELETE statement because the command deletes entire rows. Use UPDATE if you want to delete values from only some fields of a record and leave the rest of the record intact. The DELETE keyword removes one or more entire records. The basic form removes all of the records from a table, as follows.

```
DELETE FROM Employees
```

> **A DELETE without a WHERE clause will remove all of the records from the table.**

Usually a DELETE has a WHERE clause which causes only a specific record to be removed. For example in the Employees table we have unique values for the EmployeeID:

```
DELETE FROM Employees WHERE EmployeeID=11
```

The WHERE clause can specify more than one record, such as the following, where we probably had lots of customers who were from South Cape May:

```
DELETE FROM Employees WHERE City="South Cape May"
```

Notice an important point from this syntax: DELETE works on one table at a time. If you want to delete records from several tables then you must run several SQL statements.

Try It Out – Simple Deleting of Records

Here are some simple examples of deleting records, using the Alleys table from the previous chapter.

1. First of all we will demonstrate deleting specific records. Delete the alley named 'Charlie's Bowl':

```
DELETE FROM Alleys WHERE AlleyName = 'Charlie''s Bowl'
;
SELECT * FROM Alleys
;
```

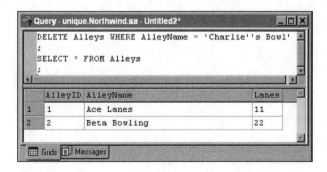

2. Delete only the alleys with less than 20 lanes:

```
DELETE FROM Alleys WHERE Lanes<20
;
SELECT * FROM Alleys
;
```

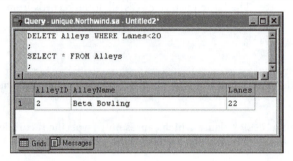

3. Delete any alleys whose name begins with a B:

```
DELETE FROM Alleys WHERE AlleyName Like 'B%'
;
SELECT * FROM Alleys
;
```

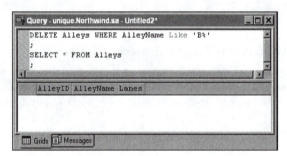

4. Now we will recreate the records so that we can demonstrate deleting all the records at one time:

```
INSERT INTO Alleys (AlleyID, AlleyName, Lanes)
VALUES
(1,'Ace Lanes',11)
;
INSERT INTO Alleys (AlleyID, AlleyName, Lanes)
VALUES
(2,'Beta Bowling',22)
;
INSERT INTO Alleys (AlleyID, AlleyName, Lanes)
VALUES
(3,'Charlie''s Bowl',33)
;
```

5. Now, delete all of the records in the `Alleys` table.

```
DELETE Alleys
```

6. Demonstrate that the `Alleys` table still exists by running the following:

```
SELECT * FROM Information_Schema.Columns
WHERE Table_Name='Alleys'
ORDER BY Table_Name, Column_Name
;
```

	TABLE_CATALOG	TABLE_SCHEMA	TABLE_NAME	COLUMN_NAME	ORDINAL_POSITION	COL
1	Northwind	dbo	Alleys	AlleyID	1	NUL
2	Northwind	dbo	Alleys	AlleyName	2	NUL
3	Northwind	dbo	Alleys	Lanes	3	NUL

7. Now reinsert the values again so that the table is back to normal:

```
INSERT INTO Alleys (AlleyID, AlleyName, Lanes)
VALUES
(1,'Ace Lanes',11)
;
INSERT INTO Alleys (AlleyID, AlleyName, Lanes)
VALUES
(2,'Beta Bowling',22)
;
INSERT INTO Alleys (AlleyID, AlleyName, Lanes)
VALUES
(3,'Charlie''s Bowl',33)
;
```

How It Works

In this Try It Out we experimented with several basic deletions, starting with specific deletions. In Step 4 we know the name of the alley and can thus find a match. Step 5 broadens the `delete` to remove all the alleys that meet an arithmetic expression, and in Step 6 we refresh our memory about using the `LIKE` keyword in an expression. We then removed all of the records from the table by not providing a `WHERE` clause on the `DELETE` statement. We then proved to ourselves that the structure of the table still existed by listing its columns from the `Information_Schema` (see Chapter 16 for more details). Note that there was no "Undo" or "Recover' command that could be used; we had to reinsert the values by hand just like we did when we first created the records in the last chapter.

Some Notes on the Basic Syntax

In Chapter 15 we will discuss views. For now, consider them to be a set of columns from one or more tables that are given a name. For example you may have a view that provides a `Salutation` field containing data like "Dear. Mr. Thomas Jefferson" or "Dear Tom." These fields are usually made from several fields in the underlying table such as `FirstName`, `LastName`, `Title`, `NickName`, `UseInformal`, and so on. A database administrator may give you the rights to see data in an `EmployeesBasic` view that contains columns of first and last name and company phone extensions. You might not be given rights to see the actual `Employees` table that holds more personal information. The columns of a view do not have to be exact columns from the underlying table: they can be constructed from the data of the table's columns. Therefore `DELETE`-ing from a view poses a few problems.

If the view is built from a single table you can usually delete a record from the view and the underlying record in the table will be deleted. So it is possible that you are deleting information that you cannot see. However, you cannot delete from a VIEW if it violates one of the following conditions:

❑   One or more columns in the view are created by an aggregate function such as TOP or AVERAGE (see Chapter 14)

❑   If the view's column list includes columns from more than one table

❑   A column in the view contains a GROUP BY clause.

In short, DELETE can delete records from one table at a time and that rule cannot be violated when deleting from views instead of directly from the table.

The way DELETE works in most DBMSs is to make one pass marking records to delete, then immediately making a second pass and actually deleting them. This means that while rows are being marked you can still use them in the WHERE clause of the DELETE statement that is being executed. If the deletion was made immediately, there would be problems doing DELETEs when the WHERE clause contained aggregate functions such as TOP or AVERAGE. If the DBMS did not do a two-pass execution, then as it deleted the first records it would be impossible to calculate TOP for the original set of records.

As a programmer, you can confirm a delete in two ways from your front end. The first is to check the message returned by the DBMS – most will return something like "x rows affected". The second technique is to re-run the same WHERE clause used in the DELETE, but now in a SELECT statement and the result should be zero rows. However, in a system where there are many new records being created all the time, you may find that the second technique returns a few records that were INSERTed between your DELETE and your SELECT.

Referential Integrity When Deleting Records

We have talked again and again in this book about the benefits and complexities of relationships. They will also have an impact on your DELETEs. Recall that relationships in their most common form have a referring table with a Foreign Key that has a value that matches a value in a Primary Key or Unique column of a referred table.

If we try to delete a record from a referred table and if that record actually is referred to by a related table, then the DELETE will fail. In other words our DBMS will not allow a referring record to be left "orphaned' by deleting the record it refers to. Trying to delete the record referred to will result in an error:

Message number 547 "DELETE statement conflict with COLUMN REFERENCE constraint."

Note that you are not prevented from deleting a referring record.

The solution is to first delete the record that is making the reference from the table holding the foreign key. If no other records refer to the referred record then you can delete it in a second statement.

> **If one row references another then we must delete the referencing row before the referenced row.**

Try It Out – Deleting Records That are Related

We will add some new Products and Reviews to Northwind, then delete them. Recall that:

❑ Employees has a Primary Key on EmployeeID

❑ Products has a Primary Key on ProductID

❑ Then Reviews has foreign keys on:

    ❑ Review.EmployeeID that references Employees.EmployeeID

    ❑ Reviews.ProductID that references Products,ProductID

So every record in Reviews has two values that must be found in records of other tables.

1. First let us add two new Products

```
INSERT INTO Products
    (ProductID,ProductName,Discontinued)
VALUES
    (1001,'Cooper Cactus Leaves',0)
;


INSERT INTO products
    (ProductID,ProductName,Discontinued)
VALUES
    (1002,'Dave''s Basement-Grown Shitakes',0)
;
```

2. Now let us create some reviews

```
INSERT INTO Reviews
    (ReviewID,EmployeeID,ProductID,Date,ReviewText)
VALUES
    (100,1,1001,'10/10/2003','Softer thorns than other brands')
;


INSERT INTO Reviews
    (ReviewID,EmployeeID,ProductID,Date,ReviewText)
VALUES
    (101,2,1002,'11/11/2003','These hold up very well in stir frying')
;
```

3. That gives us two new reviews that have foreign keys of Products.ProductsID and Employees.EmployeeID. Now let us say that Northwind decides to get rid of the cactus leaves product (the method designed into Northwind is to change the Discontinued value to 1, but we will actually delete the record for this Try It Out).

```
DELETE Products WHERE ProductID=1001
```

This gives us the following error message.

```
Server: Msg 547, Level 16, State 1, Line 1
DELETE statement conflicted with COLUMN REFERENCE constraint
'FK__Reviews__Product__2E1BDC42'. The conflict occurred in database
'Northwind', table 'Reviews', column 'ProductID'.
The statement has been terminated.
```

4. The solution is to first delete the product, then the review. So run the following code:

```
DELETE Reviews WHERE ProductID=1001
;
DELETE Products WHERE ProductID=1001
;
```

How It Works

Recall that when we created the `Reviews` table we made a constraint that the `Review.ProductID` `Foreign Key` referenced the `Product.ProductID Primary Key`. So now if we try to delete a record from `Products` the DBMS checks to see if there are any dependencies on that record from records in `Reviews`. There were, so our first attempt at deletion failed.

In our second attempt we first removed the referring record and then the referred record could be removed without throwing an error.

Deleting Duplicate Records

A business needs to remove duplicate records from a table; many of the mail-order companies that send out catalogs seem to have overlooked this bit of housekeeping! Obviously removing duplicate records improves performance. The results of using duplicated data costs as well, for example the printing and postage for the duplicate catalogs we all receive.

There are five basic steps to the duplicate record problem:

- ❑ Understand the source of the duplicates
- ❑ Define *duplicate* for this purpose
- ❑ Understand the relationships within the database
- ❑ Find the duplicates as per your definition
- ❑ Delete the duplicates without damaging the integrity of the database

Understanding the Source of Duplicates

How did the duplicates get there in the first place? The rules of normalization establish that each record in a table should be unique from all other records. The easiest way to ensure there are no duplicates is to have a `Primary Key` (usually an `ID` field). However, you could have two records that are alike in every column except for different `Primary Key` values. So the first step in deleting duplicates is to examine how they got there in the first place and correct the problems that introduce duplicates into your data.

Defining Duplicates

Duplicates can be of many types. You may have two mailing addresses for catalogs, which have the same values for last name, street, city, state and zip code but for first name one has 'T.' and the other has "Thomas". From a human point of view they are duplicates, but we would have to write some fancy code to get the DBMS to identify the pair as duplicates.

Generally when we talk about duplicates we do not mean two records with the exact same data. Rather we talk about deleting records that are duplicates according to some business rule, even though they are not true duplicates in a strict data comparison. The rule may be one or more of:

- ❑   Same street address, city, state and zip

- ❑   Same first, middle and last names

- ❑   Same identifier code (even if not the same serial ID number)

Then you must decide which duplicate to remove. In our example above, do you delete the "T. " or the "Thomas"? The SQL techniques provided in this beginner's book do not give us control over which is deleted. That may be acceptable, but if not we will have to write code to encapsulate our selection rules. If the data set is not large we may consider sending a recordset of duplicates to our front end and then have a human point out and mark which one is to be deleted. Based on those marks the actual `Deletion` statement is generated.

A last concern on duplicates is for pairs of tables in a one-to-one relation. This is the case where we use a second table to extend the number of columns that we keep on these records. Each record in the second table is a match to a record in the first table. Now what happens when we have duplicates, say A and B in the first table? The fact that A and B are duplicates in the first table does not guarantee that they are duplicates in the second table. If we delete A from table one are we sure that we eliminate the record for A in table two? We may eliminate the record that matches B and then we will be left with a mismatch.

As a theoretical aside, it is difficult to eliminate a true duplicate. After all, any conceivable WHERE clause that selects a duplicate will also select the original. Exact duplicates contain the same value in every column.

Finding and Deleting Duplicates

A strong technique to eliminate duplicates is to copy them into a new table using the DISTINCT keyword. Let us say we have a list of zip codes in a table called OldZip and feel we have accidentally entered two of the same zip code. We can use:

```
INSERT INTO CleanZip
    (SELECT DISTINCT Zip FROM OldZip)
```

Any duplicate will be eliminated by placing the DISTINCT keyword at the beginning of the column list.

Try It Out – Delete Duplicates

Northwind wants to have a post-awards celebration and asks a few employees to submit suggestions for a location.

1. We create a quick table to hold the suggestions:

```
Create table Bars
    (BarName varchar(30),
     BarAddress varchar (30))
;
```

2. An employee does some research one Friday afternoon and comes up with these records:

```
INSERT INTO Bars
    (BarName,BarAddress)
VALUES
    ('Joe''s','111 Main')
;

INSERT INTO Bars
    (BarName,BarAddress)
VALUES
    ('Freds','222 Railrod')
;

INSERT INTO Bars
    (BarName,BarAddress)
VALUES
    ('Ace ''s ','333 Carpenter')
;
```

3. Another employee bills the company for six hours of research on Saturday night and then adds these records:

```
INSERT INTO Bars
    (BarName,BarAddress)
VALUES
    ('Joe''s','111 Main')
;

INSERT INTO Bars
    (BarName,BarAddress)
VALUES
    ('Freds','222 Railrod')
;
```

4. Take a look at what we have with the following.

```
SELECT * FROM Bars ORDER BY BarName
```

	BarName	BarAddress
1	Ace 's	333 Carpenter
2	Freds	222 Railrod
3	Freds	222 Railrod
4	Joe's	111 Main
5	Joe's	111 Main

5. After reviewing the list you suspect that there are duplicates. So you decide to remove them by transferring them to an intermediate table and deleting duplicates in the transfer.

```
CREATE TABLE BarsNew
    (BarName VARCHAR(20),
    BarAddress VARCHAR(30))
;

INSERT INTO BarsNew
    (BarName, BarAddress)
    (SELECT DISTINCT * FROM Bars)
;
```

6. Check with a `SELECT` on `BarsNew` to see that there are no duplicates.

```
SELECT * FROM BarsNew ORDER BY BarName
```

	BarName	BarAddress
1	Ace 's	333 Carpenter
2	Freds	222 Railrod
3	Joe's	111 Main

7. Delete the old set of records from `Bars`, transfer back from `BarsNew` and then drop `BarsNew`:

```
DELETE FROM Bars
;

INSERT INTO Bars
    (BarName, BarAddress)
    SELECT BarName,BarAddress
    FROM BarsNew
;

DROP TABLE BarsNew
;

SELECT * FROM Bars ORDER BY BarName
;
```

If you want to repeat this Try It Out you can start by running DROP TABLE statements on Bars and then you will be back to the state before the first step.

How It Works

We start in Step 1 by creating a table; however, note that there is no primary key or mechanism to maintain a serial numbering of records. Then two employees enter sets of records, obviously with some duplication, which we can confirm in Step 3.

Our approach to deleting the duplicates was to create a new table named `BarsNew` that mimicked the structure of the `Bars` table. Then we used `INSERT INTO BarsNew` to insert the records from `Bars` using the nested `SELECT` method we discussed in the last chapter. However, instead of copying all of the records from `Bars` we will only copy `DISTINCT` records, which means that duplicates will not be `INSERT`ed into `BarsNew`.

We finish in Step 7 with three statements. First we get rid of all the records of `Bars`, the table with duplicates. Then we copy our records (now without duplicates) from `BarsNew` back into `Bars`. We finish by eliminating the temporary table `BarsNew`.

It is all well and good deleting records, but it is not a trivial matter. Sometimes, it is better to just update the records, and this is what we will look at next.

Updating Records

So far in this book, we've learned how to create a table for storing data, how to modify the properties of a table, fetch records from a table, insert data into a table, and delete data from a table. However, what if we already have a table with records in it, and we want to make a change to one of those records? Let's say, for example, that a customer in the Northwind `Customers` table has moved from his/her old address. We change the information in the record by using `UPDATE`.

The `UPDATE` statement is used to modify existing data in your database. The example above is just a single case where you would want to change data in your database. Most data is not static; it changes over time. Addresses, phone numbers, names, and statistics, are just a few examples of data that frequently changes.

As we said at the start of this chapter, deleting and updating records is an irrevocable act, so we have to be careful that we are only applying changes to the information that we really wish to alter. The considerations that apply to deleting data, such as maintaining the integrity of the database, which we've discussed throughout this chapter, also apply to updating records too. In the following section we'll look at the syntax of performing an `UPDATE` rather than a straight `DELETE`.

The UPDATE Statement

The syntax for an `UPDATE` SQL statement looks like this:

```
UPDATE <table>
SET <field> = <newvalue>
WHERE <criteria>
```

The syntax for your specific DBMS may differ slightly, but all major vendors support the ANSI SQL syntax we see here.

To perform an update we must supply the following information:

❑   The name of the table to update

❑   The name of the field, or fields, to update

❑   The new value to set in the specified field, or fields

> Sometimes the term scalar expression is used instead of the straightforward **<new value>**:
> **SET <field> = <scalar_expression>**
> A scalar expression is simply an expression that resolves to a single value; it can be a literal value, or an expression, such as a function or sub-query that returns a single expression.

We can also set some criteria to select the specific records that we would like to update, by using a WHERE clause. The WHERE clause in an UPDATE statement behaves in the same way as it does in a SELECT statement. The most basic UPDATE statement, however, requires only the three pieces of information we specified.

Basic UPDATE

So, for example, if the Northwind Trader management decided to implement a cost cutting exercise and drastically wanted to change the discounts on all orders, we could update the database to reflect this action with the following simple UPDATE statement:

```
Update "Order Details"
Set Discount = 0
```

This code would set the Discount field to 0 for *all* records in the Order Details table:

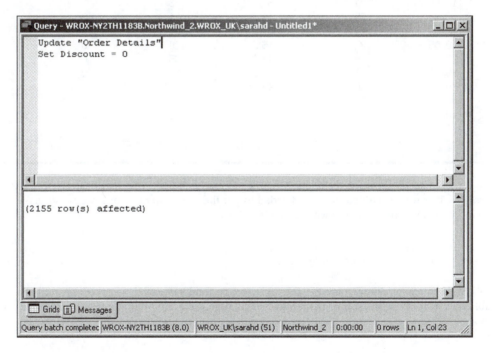

Notice that the UPDATE statement doesn't actually return a set of results; it just indicates the number of records affected by the command. If we refresh the database and check back with the Order Details table, we can see that the Discount field for all records in the table has been modified:

OrderID	ProductID	UnitPrice	Quantity	Discount
10248	11	14	12	0
10248	42	9.8	10	0
10248	72	34.8	5	0
10249	14	18.6	9	0
10249	51	42.4	40	0
10250	41	7.7	10	0
10250	51	42.4	35	0
10250	65	16.8	15	0
10251	22	16.8	6	0
10251	57	15.6	15	0
10251	65	16.8	20	0
10252	20	64.8	40	0
10252	33	2	25	0
10252	60	27.2	40	0
10253	31	10	20	0
10253	39	14.4	42	0
10253	49	16	40	0
10254	24	3.6	15	0
10254	55	19.2	21	0
10254	74	8	21	0
10255	2	15.2	20	0
10255	16	13.9	35	0
10255	36	15.2	25	0
10255	59	44	30	0
10256	53	26.2	15	0
10256	77	10.4	12	0
10257	27	35.1	25	0

We can use exactly the same technique to carry out mathematical type modifications to data. For example, if as well as cost cutting, we decided to put the prices up on goods, we could make a universal 5% increase on all our products with the code below:

```
UPDATE Products
    SET UnitPrice = UnitPrice * 1.05
```

This SQL statement simply increases the UnitPrice field values for every record in the Products table by 5% by doing the simple percentage calculation. So if the original prices were as they appear opposite:

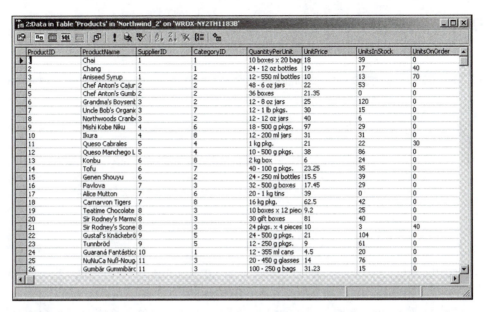

When we check back with the table, we can see the results in the `UnitPrice` field:

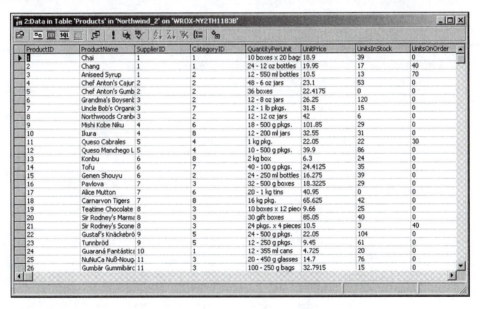

Every record in the table has been modified.

This is a very basic type of UPDATE statement because we don't apply any criteria for altering the data. Consequently we have to be extremely careful when executing this command, as it will irrevocably affect every row in an entire table.

Just as we saw with the DELETE statement, we would most likely wish to add some conditions to determine precisely which records the UPDATE statement will modify. As we mentioned earlier, we add a WHERE clause to the statement.

UPDATE Using a WHERE Clause

In most situations it is likely that we would only want to update a specific record or group of records rather than a whole table of them. Just as we do with a SELECT statement, we use WHERE to enable us to set conditions for performing the command.

```
UPDATE <table>
SET <field> = <newvalue>
WHERE <criteria>
```

So, for example, we may need to update the name of a customer who has recently been married. Victoria Ashworth, the Sales Representative for B's Beverages has become Victoria Richards. In order to update her record in the Customers table, we can use the following SQL statement:

```
UPDATE Customers
SET ContactName = 'Victoria Richards'
WHERE ContactName = 'Victoria Ashworth'
```

So, where the field ContactName has a value of Victoria Ashworth, the system will change the value to become Victoria Richards.

We can also update several fields with one UPDATE statement. Victoria Richards has received a promotion from Sales Representative to Sales Manager and the area code for her London telephone number has also changed, so we need to alter two pieces of information in her customer record which currently looks like this:

CustomerID	CompanyName	ContactName	ContactTitle	Address	City
ALFKI	Alfreds Futterkiste	Maria Anders	Sales Representati	Obere Str. 57	Berlin
ANATR	Ana Trujillo Empare	Ana Trujillo	Owner	Avda. de la Constit	México D.F.
ANTON	Antonio Moreno Ta	Antonio Moreno	Owner	Mataderos 2312	México D.F.
AROUT	Around the Horn	Thomas Hardy	Sales Representati	120 Hanover Sq.	London
BERGS	Berglunds snabbköj	Christina Berglund	Order Administrato	Berguvsvägen 8	Luleå
BLAUS	Blauer See Delikate	Hanna Moos	Sales Representati	Forsterstr. 57	Mannheim
BLONP	Blondesddsl père el	Frédérique Citeaux	Marketing Manager	24, place Kléber	Strasbourg
BOLID	Bólido Comidas pre|	Martín Sommer	Owner	C/ Araquil, 67	Madrid
BONAP	Bon app'	Laurence Lebihan	Owner	12, rue des Bouche	Marseille
BOTTM	Bottom-Dollar Mark	Elizabeth Lincoln	Accounting Manage	23 Tsawassen Blvd	Tsawassen
BSBEV	B's Beverages	Victoria Richards	Sales Representati	Fauntleroy Circus	London
CACTU	Cactus Comidas pa	Patricio Simpson	Sales Agent	Cerrito 333	Buenos Aires
CENTC	Centro comercial M	Francisco Chang	Marketing Manager	Sierras de Granada	México D.F.
CHOPS	Chop-suey Chinese	Yang Wang	Owner	Hauptstr. 29	Bern
COMMI	Comércio Mineiro	Pedro Afonso	Sales Associate	Av. dos Lusíadas, 2	Sao Paulo
CONSH	Consolidated Holdir	Elizabeth Brown	Sales Representati	Berkeley Gardens 1	London
DRACD	Drachenblut Delikat	Sven Ottlieb	Order Administrato	Walserweg 21	Aachen
DUMON	Du monde entier	Janine Labrune	Owner	67, rue des Cinqua	Nantes
EASTC	Eastern Connectior	Ann Devon	Sales Agent	35 King George	London
ERNSH	Ernst Handel	Roland Mendel	Sales Manager	Kirchgasse 6	Graz
FAMIA	Familia Arquibaldo	Aria Cruz	Marketing Assistan|	Rua Orós, 92	Sao Paulo
FISSA	FISSA Fabrica Inter	Diego Roel	Accounting Manage	C/ Moralzarzal, 86	Madrid
FOLIG	Folies gourmandes	Martine Rancé	Assistant Sales Age	184, chaussée de 1	Lille
FOLKO	Folk och fä HB	Maria Larsson	Owner	Åkergatan 24	Bräcke
FRANK	Frankenversand	Peter Franken	Marketing Manager	Berliner Platz 43	München
FRANR	France restauratior	Carine Schmitt	Marketing Manager	54, rue Royale	Nantes

We are able to make the changes to both the `ContactTitle` field and the `Phone` field with one simple SQL statement:

```
UPDATE Customers
SET ContactTitle = 'Sales Manager',
    Phone = (020)555 1212
WHERE ContactName = 'Victoria Richards'
```

When we consult her record now in the `Customers` table, we see that the values in both the `ContactTitle` and `Phone` fields have been updated.

Victoria Richards	Sales Manager	Fauntleroy Circus	London	<NULL>	EC2 5NT	UK	(020)555 1212

We can also use the `UPDATE` command with subqueries. Imagine that Northwind wants to consolidate their business relationship with Victoria Richard's Company, B's Beverages. To do that, they have decided to increase their discount on orders to 30 %. One of the tables that would need updating is `Order Details` to reflect the increased discount. We can write a subquery that will match up the `OrderID`s belonging to Victoria Richard's company as follows:

```
UPDATE "Order Details"
SET Discount = 0.3
WHERE OrderID IN
    (SELECT OrderID
     FROM Orders
     WHERE CustomerID IN
        (SELECT CustomerID
         FROM Customers
         WHERE ContactName = 'Victoria Richards'
        )
    )
```

If we check the `Order Details` table, we can see that a number of records are now displaying a discount of 30%:

The `Customer ID` for B's Beverages is `BSBEV`. If we run a simple `SELECT` statement against the `Orders` table which has both `Customer ID` and `OrderID` fields, we can obtain the list of `OrderID` numbers for B's Beverages:

```
SELECT OrderID
FROM Orders
WHERE CustomerID = 'BSBEV'
```

	OrderID
1	10289
2	10289
3	10471
4	10471
5	10484
6	10484
7	10484
8	10538
9	10538
10	10539

If we now query the Order Details table to obtain the OrderIDs for orders that have a discount of 30%, you should find that they match.

```
SELECT DISTINCT OrderID
FROM "Order Details"
WHERE Discount = '0.3'
```

You can see the list rendered is exactly the same as the list for B's Beverages orders.

	OrderID
1	10289
2	10289
3	10471
4	10471
5	10484
6	10484
7	10484
8	10538
9	10538
10	10539

Summary

We spent several pages discussing theories and considerations for deleting since the removal of data is not trivial. We wrote about considerations for archiving data rather than deleting it, particularly moving data to cheaper storage media, which would reduce the cost and make it worth saving for potential future use.

It is important to remember that DELETEs in almost all DBMS systems are immediate and complete. There is no flagging for later deletion like in some desktop databases. It is also important to remember the differences in terminology for various means of removing data. DELETE affects records whereas DROP affects entire tables. Last, keep in mind that a simple DELETE command removes all of the records; you will almost always use it with a WHERE clause that limits the statement to only deleting some records.

DBMSs will not allow you to delete a record if other records refer to it. You must first delete the referring record, and then you can delete the referred record. Deletion is a tool to remove duplicate records from a table. By specifying UNIQUE in a copy you can avoid bringing duplicates to a new table.

If deleting the data is a bit too drastic, maybe because most of the information in a record is actually still useable, then we can UPDATE a record, or just a few fields in that record instead. This means that we only have to get rid of the data that is no longer needed, rather than the whole record and reinsert every single field. Of course, updating itself is a form of deletion as data is removed in the same way but new data is also added; so the considerations we must apply to straight deletes must also be employed when using UPDATE. However, we can see that UPDATE can help us greatly: updating a few fields is a much more friendly prospect than deleting a whole record and ploughing through a complete reinsertion.

We have now covered the basic statements of SQL – in the next chapter, we move on to the slightly more complex idea of SQL Functions, specifically Date, Time and String.

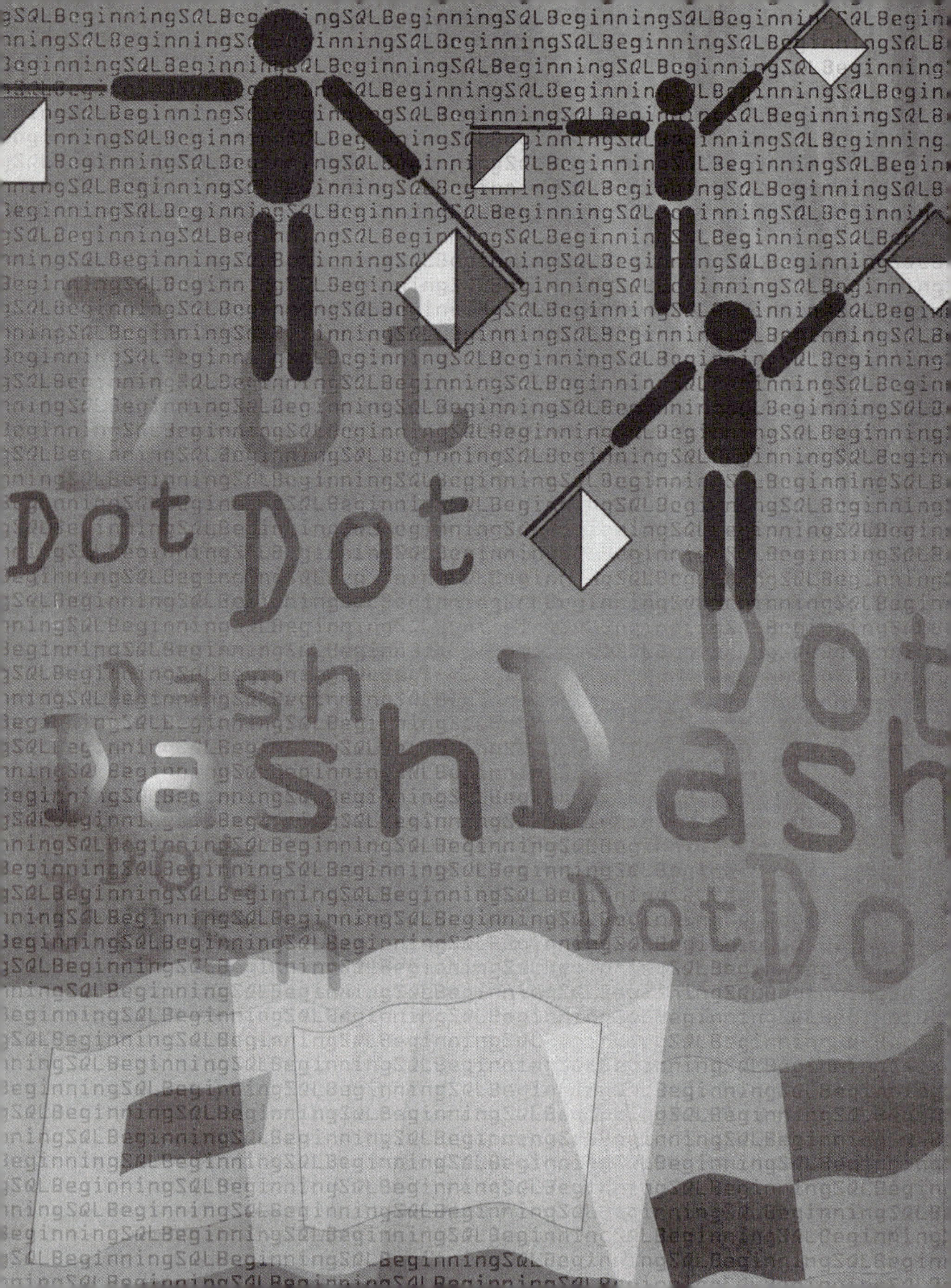
BeginningSQL
Dot
Dot
Dash
Dash
Dot
Dot

11

SQL Functions Date, Time, and Strings

In this chapter, we're going to discuss how to work with dates and times with SQL. We're also going to discuss some elements of ANSI SQL 99 that aren't supported by any DBMSs. As the Internet moves toward more cross-platform solutions, and cross-platform language specifications, like XML and .NET, compliance with the ANSI SQL Standard is going to become more and more important in database software, and my guess is that we *will* be able to use many of these elements in the near future.

We'll be covering the following topics:

❑   SQL and Date and Time data types

❑   Time intervals

❑   Using TIMESTAMP

❑   Data type conversions

❑   Date and Time functions

❑   String and character data types

❑   Converting between data types

❑   String functions

Let's start by looking at how times are handled in SQL.

SQL and Time

In order to work with time and date data with SQL, we can use two basic types of data:

❑   Dates/Times – specific points in time, specified in the familiar date and time notations.

❑   Intervals – measures of the elapsed time between two points in time.

Dates and times are familiar to us, but let's look in a little more detail at the notion of an interval.

Note that we will be using United States Date format (mm/dd/yyyy) in this chapter for our examples. Your DBMS might be configured to accept dates in a different format, in which case you will have to make appropriate changes where appropriate.

ANSI SQL provides for a data type called `Interval`. However, most databases don't, at this time, provide *direct* support for it, although all DBMSs use the interval data type at some level.

However, consider the following SQL statement:

```
SELECT EmployeeID, FirstName, LastName, HireDate
FROM Employees WHERE DateDiff("yyyy", HireDate, CURRENT_TIMESTAMP) >= 5
```

This query will return the ID, name, and the date on which a particular employee was hired only in cases where the employee in question has been with the company for at least 5 years. The `DateDiff` function takes three arguments: the type of interval required (in this case, years), and the two dates between which we want to measure (`Hiredate` and today's date, in this example). As it stands, this example will only work in SQL Server.

`Datediff` is not part of ANSI SQL. In MySQL, we could use the following to achieve the same results:

```
SELECT EmployeeID, FirstName, LastName, HireDate, HomePhone, Extension
FROM Employees WHERE EXTRACT(YEAR FROM CURRENT_TIMESTAMP) - EXTRACT(YEAR FROM
HireDate) >= 5
```

In DB2, the following:

```
select hiredate from employees where DATE(current timestamp) - DATE(hiredate) >= 5
```

And in Oracle, we could use the following to achieve the same results:

```
SELECT EmployeeID, FirstName, LastName, HireDate, HomePhone, Extension
FROM Employees WHERE ((SELECT SUBSTR(SYSDATE,8,9) FROM DUAL)+100) -
SUBSTR(HireDate,8,9) >= 5;
```

Note the different ways in which the current day is accessed in these different DBMSs.

All these queries produce the same results in the different DBMSs, and all show that, although none of the DBMSs support the `INTERVAL` data type, we can still work with intervals. In this case, the interval between the hire date and the current date.

Time Data Types

In the above example, we measured the interval between the two dates in years. However, there are numerous different data types that we can use to represent time intervals, although these differ from vendor to vendor. The following table gives a summary of the data types supported by SQL Server, MS Access, DB2, Oracle, and MySQL. We also show the ANSI SQL specified time data types:

ANSI SQL Start_datetime	SQL Server	MS Access	(Definition)
YEAR [(leading precision)] |	Year | yy | yyyy |	'yyyy' |	(Year)
MONTH [(leading precision)] |	Quarter | qq | q |	'q' |	(Quarter)
	Month | mm | m	'm' |	(Month)
DAY [(leading precision)] |	dayofyear | dy | y |	'y' |	(Day of Year)
	Day | dd | d |	'd' |	(Day)
	Week | wk | ww |	'w' |	(Weekday)
		'ww' |	(Week)
HOUR [(leading precision)] |	Hour | hh |	'h' |	(Hour)
MINUTE [(leading precision)] |	minute | mi | n |	'n' |	(Minute)
SECOND [(leading precision	second | ss | s |	's'	(Second)
[, (fractional seconds precision)])]	millisecond | ms		

Note: Access uses a *string expression* (e.g. 'yyyy') for date-time intervals, while ANSI SQL and SQL Server (which conforms very closely to the ANSI specification) use character tokens (e.g. yyyy). Remember to always enclose the Access tokens in quotes.

ANSI SQL Start_datetime	MySQL	Oracle
YEAR [(leading precision)] |	YEAR	N/A
MONTH [(leading precision)] |	MONTH	N/A
DAY [(leading precision)] |	DAY	N/A
HOUR [(leading precision)] |	HOUR	N/A
MINUTE [(leading precision)] |	MINUTE	N/A
SECOND [(leading precision	SECOND	N/A
[, (fractional seconds precision)])]		

Interval Literals

It is a shame that no DBMSs support the INTERVAL data type as, without it, calculating intervals between two points of time can be tricky.

In our earlier example, we had to specify that we wanted to calculate the interval between two times in years. However, without doing this, one can run into unexpected results. For instance, if we wanted to generate a list of employees in the Northwind database who were over forty years of age when first hired, we might try using the following:

```
SELECT birthdate, hiredate from employees where hiredate - birthdate > 40
```

However, we might be surprised to find that *all* our employees are returned:

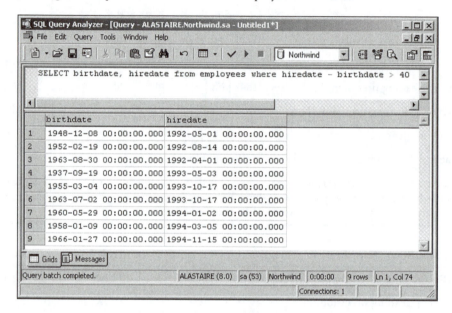

This has happened because, within SQL Server, the integer that we test our results against (the '40'), represents the interval between the dates in days. To see that this is in fact the case, we could query the database to see which employees were over forty when employed by selecting those queries where the difference between the birthdate and the hire date of particular employees is greater than 14,600 (the number of days in forty years – give or take a few days for leap years).

The results would be as follows:

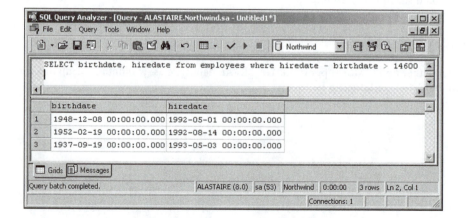

This shows how it might be possible to get caught out when dealing with time intervals. This is something that the INTERVAL data type would be useful in dealing with.

Although not yet implemented by any DBMS, it might be worth having a quick look at some **interval literals**. ANSI SQL provides for two different types of Interval Literals: the year-month literal, and the day-time literal.

A year-month literal can include YEAR, a MONTH, or both. It cannot contain any other date-time values. Here's an example of a year-month literal:

```
INTERVAL '10-00' YEAR TO MONTH
```

The value represented by this interval literal is 10 years exactly. We can also represent negative numbers as interval literals:

```
INTERVAL '-10-11' YEAR TO MONTH
```

This represents an Interval of –10 years and 11 months.

The day-time INTERVAL type cannot contain any YEAR or MONTH values, but can have any combination of DAY, HOUR, MINUTE, and SECOND intervals. As with the year-month INTERVAL, this value can either be positive or negative.

Let's look at a few examples of the day-time INTERVAL data type:

```
INTERVAL '20' MINUTE
```

This is fairly self-explanatory (20 minutes). The following is a little less clear:

```
INTERVAL '3 2' DAY TO HOUR
```

This represents an Interval of 3 days and 2 hours. Note the space between the day and hour value. The only space in such a literal is between the day and the first fractional portion of an hour. After that, the portions are separated by colons, except for the fractional part of a second, which comes after a decimal point:

```
INTERVAL '1 2:25:37.6789' DAY TO SECOND
```

This represents 1 day, 2 hours, 25 minutes, and 37.6789 seconds.

Do remember that such data types are not yet supported by any of the major DBMSs.

DATE

The DATE data type combines the date-time fields YEAR, MONTH, and DAY. The DATE data type will accept dates in the 'yyyy-mm-dd' format.

For example, the following will create a table of two columns, each of which will accept dates:

```
CREATE TABLE important_dates (
    entry_date    DATE,
    date_of_event DATE);
```

Once created, we can enter dates into this table in the following way:

```
INSERT INTO important_dates
(entry_date, date_of_event)
VALUES
('2001-06-07','2001-12-12')
```

> *Note that only DB2 and Oracle support the* DATE *data type, although Oracle's* DATE *data type is an implementation of the* DATETIME *data type – see below. For this reason, the code for inserting values into our table will only work with DB2.*

TIME

TIME represents a fraction of a day. It has three different elements: HOUR, MINUTE, and SECOND.

For example, to create a table containing one column that contains times, we could use the following:

```
CREATE TABLE important_times (
    times TIME);
```

We could insert times into this table with the following:

```
INSERT INTO important_times
(times)
VALUES
('09.30.00')
```

> *Note that, although part of the SQL 99 standards,* TIME *is only currently supported by DB2. The above examples will thus only work on DB2. If you're using another DBMS, you'll have to use* DATETIME *(see below).*

DATETIME

The DATETIME data type stores date *and* time information in the following format:

```
2001-12-31 11.45.30
```

Although not part of the SQL 99 standards, this is the most widely implemented date/time data type, and is the data type used in the Northwind database to store dates.

To create a table with one column containing date-time information, we could use the following:

```
CREATE TABLE important_date_times (
important_dates datetime);
```

And to insert information into this, we would use:

```
INSERT INTO important_date_times
VALUES ('2001-05-06 11:45:30');
```

Note that in Oracle, the DATE data type is equivalent to the DATETIME data type.

TIMESTAMP

The TIMESTAMP data type is very much the same as the DATETIME data type, and is supported in the SQL 99 standards. However, it will automatically store the current date and time, and is useful in recording the precise time at which a data entry is made.

For example, we might create a table containing two columns, the first of which uses the TIMESTAMP format, and the second of which simply stores an integer:

```
CREATE TABLE important_date_timestamp (
important_dates timestamp, info INT);
```

We can insert information into the info column:

```
INSERT INTO important_date_timestamp (info)
VALUES (1);
```

And the TIMESTAMP column should be automatically populated. We can see the contents of the table by using the following query:

```
SELECT * from important_date_timestamp;
```

This should give us the following results:

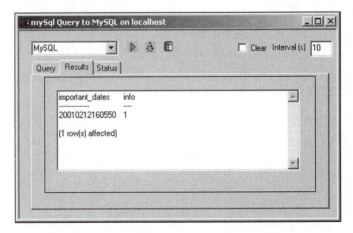

This screenshot was taken in MySQL. We can see that the information entered into the info column was entered on the twelfth of February, 2001, at five minutes and fifty seconds past four.

Using TIMESTAMP in SQL Server

In SQL Server, the TIMESTAMP data type deviates quite dramatically from the SQL 99 standards. If we use the code we used above in SQL Server, and look at the results, we will see the following:

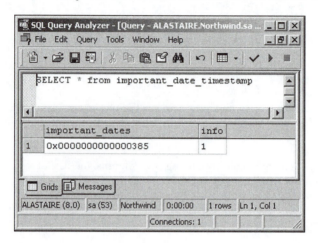

As we can see, the timestamp column does not store a date. Rather, it stores a number, which is guaranteed to be unique within the database.

> *In SQL Server 2000, a synonym for TIMESTAMP has been introduced, called ROWVERSION.*
> *Wherever possible, we should use this, as it is quite likely that the implementation of TIMESTAMP*
> *will, in future SQL Server releases, be changed to conform to the SQL 99 standards.*

Type Conversion

In many situations, we might want to compare dates. If the dates in question are stored in different date/time data types, then they cannot be directly compared. We need some way of converting the information into the same data type.

Alternatively, we might want to combine different data types in one column. To do both these things, we can use CAST.

For example, supposing we wanted to combine the birth date information and the name information of the employees in the Northwind database. We could use the following:

```
SELECT FirstName + ' ' + LastName
+ ' was born on '
+ CAST(BirthDate AS VARCHAR) FROM Employees;
```

Note how the BirthDate column (which is in the DATETIME data type) is converted to VARCHAR data type using CAST. This allows it to be combined with other character data.

We should receive the following results:

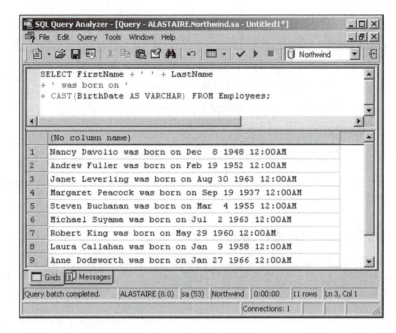

Not all conversions are possible. For instance, a TIME data type cannot be converted to a DATE data type – for obvious reasons.

Comparison

As you might imagine, the arithmetic operators (=, <>, <, >, <=, >=) are legitimate SQL Date comparison operators. In addition, three quantifiers (ALL, SOME, and ANY) can be used with date-time values. For example, the following will return the names of employees whose date of birth precedes all the hire dates in the table. The results aren't particularly interesting, as all the employees were born before the oldest serving member of the company was first hired:

```
SELECT FirstName,LastName, Birthdate, hiredate FROM Employees where Birthdate <
ALL (Select Hiredate from employees)
```

This example query shows the use of the ALL operator with a date-time query. It returns all records where the date is lower than ALL of the dates returned by the sub query.

Remember that date-time values must be compatible to be compared with one another. We can't compare a TIME field to a DATE field, for example. Of course, we can always CAST one or the other to make our comparison.

Arithmetic Functions, Dates, and Times

The standard SQL Arithmetic operators: +, -, *, and /, can be used with dates. However, they can't all be used in all cases.

Scalar Functions

A **scalar function** performs an operation on either a single value, multiple values, or no value whatsoever, returning a scalar value. The following are just a few examples of scalar functions provided by most DBMSs:

- ❑   ABS   Returns the absolute value of a number
- ❑   HEX   Returns the hexadecimal representation of a value
- ❑   LENGTH   Returns the number of bytes in an argument
- ❑   YEAR   Extracts the year portion of a datetime value

Scalar functions that take no parameters are known as **niladic functions**. Most date-time functions are of this kind. Let's take a look at how they function.

Niladic date-time Functions

A **niladic function** is similar to a scalar function, except that it doesn't work on a value passed to it. It simply returns a standard value (such as today's date) when invoked. There are 5 niladic functions for date-time values:

- ❑   CURRENT_DATE returns a result with a DATE data type, containing the current date. This is a date with no time value. It is represented in Access by the Date() function, and in Oracle by the DATE function. MySQL supports this directly.

- ❑   CURRENT_TIME returns a data type of TIME WITH TIME ZONE. It returns the current time, taking into account the default time zone offset.

  Access and SQL Server provide the DatePart() function to return the time part of the current date. In addition, with Access, we can use the Visual Basic Time Function to get the current time.

  In Oracle, the TRUNC() function can be used to extract the time part of a date. MySQL supports this directly *and* indirectly (the CURTIME() function returns the CURRENT_TIME).

- ❑   CURRENT_TIMESTAMP returns a data type of TIMESTAMP WITH TIME ZONE. It returns the current date and time taking into account the default time zone offset.
  This is actually the value returned by the Access Now() function, the Oracle SYSDATE, and the SQL Server GETDATE() function.
  MySQL supports this function directly and indirectly (via the SYSDATE and NOW() functions).

- ❑   LOCALTIME is the same as CURRENT_TIME, but with no TIME ZONE OFFSET. It returns the current time.

- ❑   LOCALTIMESTAMP is the same as CURRENT_TIMESTAMP, but with no time zone offset. It returns the current date and time.

The various DBMSs provide varied support for these functions. The following table presents the various levels of support provided by five major DBMSs:

ANSI SQL	SQL Server	MS Access
CURRENT_DATE	Not Supported	DATE
CURRENT_TIME (fractional seconds precision)	Not Supported	TIME
CURRENT_TIMESTAMP (fractional seconds precision)	GETDATE()	NOW
LOCALTIME (fractional seconds precision)	Not Supported	Not Supported
LOCALTIMESTAMP (fractional seconds precision)	Not Supported	Not Supported

ANSI SQL	MySQL	Oracle	DB2
CURRENT_DATE	CURRENT_DATE CURDATE()	DATE	Supported
CURRENT_TIME (fractional seconds precision)	CURRENT_TIME CURTIME()	Not Supported	Supported
CURRENT_TIMESTAMP (fractional seconds precision)	CURRENT_TIMESTAMP NOW SYSDATE	SYSDATE	Supported
LOCALTIME (fractional seconds precision)	Not Supported	Not Supported	Not supported
LOCALTIMESTAMP (fractional seconds precision)	Not Supported	Not Supported	Not Supported

Note that even though many of these functions are not directly supported in these DBMSs, equivalent functionality is provided, in many cases, in their provider-specific built-in functions. For example, the DATEPART() function in SQL Server allows us to extract the current date, current time, or current timestamp values from CURRENT_DATE.

EXTRACT Expression

The EXTRACT function extracts part of a date-time value. For instamce, we could extract the year or the time from a date-time value. The ANSI SQL EXTRACT expression is not directly supported in any database products except MySQL. However, in SQL Server it is provided via the DatePart() function. In Oracle, the TRUNC() function can be used. And MySQL, in addition to supporting this syntax, has a number of scalar functions for this purpose as well. In DB2, we can use DATE() or TIME() to extract the relevant parts of a date-time value.

For instance, in MySQL, we could use the following:

```
SELECT EXTRACT (YEAR FROM CURRENT_TIMESTAMP)
```

to return the current year.

We may select any of the following sections of a date-time data type:

- ❑ YEAR
- ❑ MONTH
- ❑ DAY
- ❑ HOUR
- ❑ MINUTE
- ❑ SECOND
- ❑ TIMEZONE_HOUR
- ❑ TIMEZONE_MINUTE

The temporal argument can be any of the following:

- ❑ DATE
- ❑ TIME
- ❑ TIMESTAMP
- ❑ INTERVAL

For example:

```
SELECT EXTRACT(YEAR FROM BirthDate) AS BirthYear FROM Employees
```

The above SQL Statement will return the date of birth of each employee in the Northwind database.

Interval Absolute Value Function (ABS())

The ABS() function takes an argument and returns a positive integer of the same data type.

The ABS() function is implemented in most database products for working with integer arithmetic. Since intervals (between two times) are simply numbers, we may use ABS() on intervals.

For instance, we might use the ABS() function to find the difference between two dates, regardless of their order:

```
SELECT ABS(DateDiff(day, date1, date2)) AS days_between
```

Even if date1 is later than date2 – in which case the difference between the dates would end up being given as a negative number – the ABS function ensures that we're given a positive result representing the difference, in days, between the two dates.

As this example depends on SQL Server's DATEDIFF function, it will have to be adjusted slightly for other DBMSs.

Aggregate Functions

Aggregate functions summarize the results of a query, rather than listing all the rows. For instance, the COUNT function will simply return the number of records produced by a particular query. The following aggregate functions are supported for date-time values:

- ❑ COUNT
- ❑ GROUPING
- ❑ MAX
- ❑ MIN

Details on using these functions may be found in Chapter 13.

Predicates

The following nine predicates are supported for the SQL TIME data type:

- ❑ BETWEEN
- ❑ DISTINCT
- ❑ EXISTS
- ❑ IN
- ❑ MATCH
- ❑ NULL
- ❑ OVERLAPS
- ❑ UNIQUE
- ❑ QUANTIFIED

The OVERLAPS predicate is the only one that is unique to the date-time data type. As it isn't supported by any of the DBMSs that we're concentrating on, we'll only briefly look at it.

The OVERLAPS function takes two spans of time, and compares them to see whether one overlaps the other. It returns TRUE if they overlap, and FALSE if they don't. For example, the following will return TRUE if and only if there is an overlap between the ten years preceding the present time, and the period from a particular person's date of birth and their thirtieth birthday. In other words, it will return TRUE for everyone whose thirtieth birthday fell in the last ten years:

```
SELECT EmployeeID, LastName, FirstName, HireDate
FROM Employees
WHERE (CURRENT_DATE, INTERVAL '-10' YEAR) OVERLAPS
(BirthDate, INTERVAL '30' YEAR)
```

With other DBMSs, we would have to devise an alternative way of achieving the same result. For instance, in SQL Server we could use the following:

```
SELECT EmployeeID, LastName, FirstName, HireDate
FROM Employees
WHERE DateAdd(yyyy, 65, BirthDate) > (GetDate() - 10)
AND DateAdd(yyyy, 65, BirthDate) < (GetDate())
```

Note that the appropriate parts of the date-time data types have to be extracted (using the DATEPART function) in order to use them in the calculations.

DBMS Date and Time Functions

The SQL 99 Date/Time functions tend to be poorly supported by most DBMSs. However, each DBMS has a number of built-in date/time functions. Let's have a look at the most common ones:

Current Date

Access	SQL Server	Oracle	DB2	MySQL
DATE	GETDATE()	SYSDATE	CURRENT_DATE	CURRENT_DATE
	GETUTCDATE()		CURRENT_TIMESTAMP	CURDATE()

Current Time

Access	SQL Server	Oracle	DB2	MySQL
TIME NOW	GETDATE()	Not Supported.	CURRENT_TIME	CURRENT_TIME
				CURTIME()

Date Addition

Access	SQL Server	Oracle	MySQL
DATEADD (Interval, Number, Date)	DATEADD (Interval, Number, Date)	ADD_MONTHS (Date, Months)	DATE_ADD (Interval, Number, Date)
			ADDDATE (Interval, Number, Date)
			PERIOD_ADD (P, N)

Date Subtraction

Access	SQL Server	Oracle	MySQL
DATEDIFF (Interval, Date1, Date2)	DATEDIFF (Interval, Date1, Date2)	MONTHS_BET WEEN (Date1, Date2)	DATE_SUB (Interval, Date1, Date2)
			SUBDATE (Interval, Date1, Date2)
			PERIOD_DIFF (P1, P2)

Extracting Date Parts

Access	SQL Server	Oracle	MySQL
DATEPART (Interval, Date[, firstdayofweek[, firstweekofyear]])	DATEPART (Interval, Date) DAY (date)	Not Supported.	DAYOFWEEK (Date) WEEKDAY (Date) DAYOFMONTH (Date) DAYOFYEAR (Date) MONTH (Date) DAYNAME (Date) MONTHNAME (Date) QUARTER (Date)
DAY (Date)	MONTH (Date)		WEEK (Date [, first]) YEAR (Date)
MONTH (Date)	YEAR (date)		YEARWEEK (Date [, first]) HOUR (Time)
YEAR (Date)			MINUTE (Time) SECOND (Time)

Remarks	MySQL has a whole **host** of Scalar functions for returning Date Parts. They fall into two basic categories – Those that work with Dates, and those that work with Times. The chart below lists these functions, and the data they return:

DAYOFWEEK (Date)

Number (1 – 7) (Sunday – Saturday)

WEEKDAY (Date)

Number (0 – 6) (Monday – Sunday)

DAYOFMONTH (Date)

Number (1 – Last day of Month)

DAYOFYEAR (Date)

Number (1 – Last day of Year)

MONTH (Date)

Number (1 –12)

DAYNAME (Date)

String (Name of day: 'Wednesday')

MONTHNAME (Date)

String (Name of Month: 'January')

QUARTER (Date)

Number (1 – 4)

WEEK (Date [, first])

Number (1 – 52) "first" is either 0 (Sunday) or 1 (Monday)

YEAR (Date)

Number (1000 – 9999)

YEARWEEK (Date [, first])

Number (1 – 52) in the format "YYYYWW" "first" is either 0 (Sunday) or 1 (Monday)

HOUR (Time)

Number (0 - 23)

MINUTE (Time)

Number (0 – 59)

SECOND (Time)

Number (0 – 59)

Syntax Variations

While most DBMS implementations of ANSI SQL are very similar (they are all at least *mostly* based upon ANSI or ANSI SQL), there are some significant differences to keep in mind when using one or another:

Date Literals

Note that the delimiter for a date literal in Access is the "#" character.

The following examples show dates being inserted into various DBMSs. In Access, we could use the following:

```
INSERT INTO Employees (EmployeeID, LastName, FirstName, HireDate)
VALUES (201, 'Smith', 'John', #12/12/2000#)
```

In SQL Server (note that we do not insert an EmployeeID here: the Northwind database in SQL Server is configured to automatically insert an appropriate EmployeeID):

```
INSERT INTO Employees (LastName, FirstName, HireDate)
VALUES ('Smith', 'John', '12/12/2000')
```

In DB2, we could use this:

```
INSERT INTO Employees (EmployeeID, LastName, FirstName, HireDate)
VALUES (201, 'Smith', 'John', '2000-12-12-00.00.00.00')
```

In Oracle, use the following:

```
INSERT INTO Employees (EmployeeID, LastName, FirstName, HireDate)
VALUES (201, 'Smith', 'John', '12-DEC-2000')
```

Format for Date and Time Literals

The following chart lists various acceptable date and time formats. In addition to showing the ANSI standard formats, it shows various formats provided by the various DBMS vendors.

SQL Version	Format	Example
ANSI SQL	yyyy-mm-dd	2001-01-25
	hh:mm:ss[.nnnnnn]	18:30:30.255
	yyyy-mm-dd hh:mm:ss[.nnn]	1998-09-24 10:02:20

Table continued on following page

SQL Version	Format	Example
SQL Server	**Locale-Specific** (Regional Settings)	1/25/01
	yyyy-mm-dd hhH:mm:ss	2001-01-25 18:30:30
	month dd, yyyy	January 25, 2001
	dd month, yyyy	25 January, 2001
	yymmdd	010125
	mm/dd/yy	01/25/01
	mm/dd/yyyy	01/25/2001
	hh:mm:ss	18:30:30
	hh:mm AM|PM	06:30 PM
Access	**Locale-Specific** (Regional Settings)	January 25, 2001
MySQL	yyyy-mm-dd hh:mm:ss	2001-01-25 18:30:30
	' yyyy-mm-dd 0	2001-01-25
	YYYYMMDDHHMMSS	20010125183030
	hh:mm:ss	18:30:30
Oracle	**Locale-Specific** (Regional Settings: Oracle Refers to these as "*National Language Settings*")	25 Jan, 2001 6:30 PM
DB2	**Locale-Specific** (Regional Settings)	1/25/01
	mm/dd/yyyy	10/27/1991
	dd.mm.yyyy	27.10.1991
	yyyy-mm-dd	1991-10-27
	hh:mm AM or PM	1:30 PM
	hh.mm.ss	13.30.05
	yyyy-mm-dd hh:mm:ss.nnnnnn	1991-03-02-08.30.00.000000

Date-time data is a morass of proprietary solutions, gradually migrating towards International Standards. Fortunately, in practice, familiarity with only a few different formats is necessary.

String and Character Data

A string is simply a sequence of characters, usually used to represent text of some sort. Such a string may contain only one character, or even none.

ANSI SQL 99 includes a lot of functionality for working with strings, and most of it is not supported by most DBMS's. Therefore, we will only touch lightly upon that functionality. We will concentrate on the commonly used functionality provided in most DBMSs.

Type Conversion (CASTing String Data Types)

Remember first that all string data types, such as char, nchar, varchar, text, and so on, are mutually compatible and comparable, as long as they belong to the same character set. Therefore, unlike some date-time data types, it is almost never necessary to CAST a string to another string data type before working with them.

In the case of strings that are from different character sets, SQL 99 specifies a TRANSLATE function, which converts the character set of one string to another.

TRANSLATE is supported by DB2 and Oracle. In Oracle, which doesn't quite conform to the ANSI SQL standards, we can use the following:

```
SELECT TRANSLATE ('ABCDEFGHIJ', 'BDE', 'bde') FROM dual;
```

to produce:

```
AbCdeFGHIJ
```

This simply checks each character in the source string ('ABCDEFGHIJ'), against characters in the second argument. If they are found there, they are replaced by the corresponding characters in the third argument.

CASTing to Other Data types

There are a few of things to remember regarding casting strings to other data types. They can be boiled down to the following simple set of rules:

1. We can CAST a string to virtually any data type. However, the string must contain data that will be valid in the data type we want to cast to. For example:

```
SELECT CAST ('12/12/2000' AS datetime)
```

The above statement returns '2000-12-12 00:00:00.000' as a date time value. However, the following will not work:

```
SELECT CAST ('today' AS datetime)
```

This will generate an error message.

2. If we CAST a string to another (fixed length) string data type for any reason, the target must contain at least enough space to hold the string. If the target contains more spaces, the string will be padded to the right with spaces to fill out the field. If the target contains less spaces, we will get an error.

299

3. Leading and trailing spaces of strings are automatically trimmed before conversion.

4. If we CAST another data type to a string data type, the target must be large enough to hold the string representation of the value that is being CAST. For example:

```
SELECT CAST 3.14 AS nvarchar(3)
```

This will return an error message, since four characters are needed to store the string representation of the number.

5. When you cast a date-time value to a string, the format of the date is determined by your computer's Regional Settings.

CONVERT

The SQL Server CONVERT function is similar to the CAST function, but with a bit more flexibility: For example, we could use the following to convert '12/12/2000' to '2000-12-12 00:00:00.000':

```
SELECT CONVERT(datetime, '12/12/2000')
```

This is functionally identical to the first CAST example, given above.

Alternatively, we may add another parameter to the CONVERT function. The '1' added in this statement specifies that the date is to be converted to the US mm/dd/yy format (style 1: a full list of all the styles supported by SQL server can be found in the help files in SQL Server's Query Analyser):

```
SELECT CONVERT(varchar(8), '12/12/2000', 1)
```

This will return '12/12'00'.

> *Note that the ANSI SQL Standard has a CONVERT function that is not the same as the SQL Server CONVERT function. The ANSI Standard CONVERT function changes a character repertoire's encoding scheme. This section refers to the SQL Server CONVERT function.*

Assignment

String values can be assigned from any string data type to any other string data type that uses the same character set.

A string value assignment will succeed if there is at least enough space in the target. If the target is longer than the source, the value will be padded with spaces on the right. If the target is shorter, the query will fail.

```
UPDATE Employees SET HomePhone = '212-555-1212' WHERE EmplooyeeID = 12
```

In SQL Server, whether or not spaces will be used to pad out the resultant string may be controlled by using SET ANSI_PADDING.

Concatenation

Strings can be strung together with one another by **concatenation**. The concatenation operator varies from one implementation to another. The ANSI SQL concatenation operator is "||". This is supported by Oracle and DB2 in the following way:

```
SELECT (FirstName || ' ' || LastName) AS Name FROM Employees
```

In SQL Server, we would use the following:

```
SELECT (FirstName + ' ' + LastName) AS Name FROM Employees
```

And in Access:

```
SELECT (FirstName & ' ' & LastName) AS Name FROM Employees
```

In MySQL, we must use the CONCAT function, in the following way:

```
SELECT CONCAT(FirstName," ",LastName) from employees
```

All of these queries do the same thing: they string the FirstName field value with a blank space followed by the LastName value. If the employee in the current row of the resulting cursor has a last name of "Smith" and a first name of "John," the resulting field would have "John Smith" in it.

Comparison

The usual comparison operators (=, <>, <, >, <=, >=) apply to SQL string data types. We can compare any string data type to any other string data type, as long as they share the same character set. The rule for the ordering of the values is alphabetical. That is, if one string is alphabetically less than (equal to, greater than, and so on.) another, the condition evaluates to TRUE.

Always keep in mind that these operators will be case sensitive in some DBMSs. SQL Server is, by default, case insensitive, but do check the case sensitivity of your DBMS.

The collation sequence of the data type being used determines how the alphabet is arranged. The collation sequence is a set of rules for working with the character set. It defines, for the most part, what alphabetical order means for that character set. A single character set can have more than one collation sequence. However, the first 127 letters of each character set are always the same, and include all the letters of the English alphabet. Therefore, we don't usually have to worry about the collation sequence.

Three **quantifiers** (ALL, SOME, and ANY) can be used with string data types subqueries. For example:

```
SELECT * FROM Employees WHERE EmployeeID = ANY
(SELECT EmployeeID FROM Orders WHERE CustomerID = 'ALFKI')
```

This query locates all Employee records in the Employees table that pertain to sales to a given customer (identified by CustomerID). The ANY quantifier means that *any* EmployeeID field in the sub query's result set will return TRUE as a test for any record in the Employees table.

In other words, all `Employee` records for `Employees` that handled `Orders` for `Customer 'ALFKI'` will be returned:

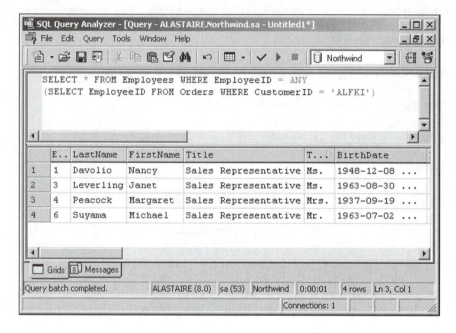

Note that MySQL doesn't support the ANY function.

Scalar Functions

A **scalar** function is a function that returns a single value, rather than a set of values (as in a result set). For example, the `DateAdd()` function we encountered earlier is a scalar function. It returns a single date value.

The following ANSI Scalar functions can be used with string data types:

❑ SUBSTRING

❑ OVERLAY

❑ TRIM

❑ FOLD

Let's look at these in some more detail.

SUBSTRING

`SUBSTRING` takes three arguments: a string, a starting point, and the length of the substring required. It returns the section of the string equal in length to the length argument, starting at the starting point argument.

In ANSI SQL, the length argument is optional. If omitted, it returns the rest of the string. In SQL Server, it is not optional.

For example, the following statement would return a string four characters long starting from the third letter of 'AMERICA':

```
SELECT SUBSTRING('AMERICA', 3, 4)
```

In other words, it will return 'ERIC'.

The SUBSTRING function differs slightly from vendor to vendor. The following table shows these variations.

SQL Version	Function	Example
Access	Mid(string, start[, length])	SELECT Mid('Americe', 3, 4)
SQL Server	SUBSTRING(string, start[, length])	SELECT SUBSTRING('AMERICA', 3, 4)
	Mid(string, start[, length])	SELECT Mid ('AMERICA', 3, 4)
Oracle	SUBSTR(string, start, length)	SELECT SUBSTR('AMERICA', 3, 4) FROM Dual;
MySQL	SUBSTRING(string, start[, length])	SELECT SUBSTRING('AMERICA', 3, 4)
	SUBSTRING(string FROM start [FOR length])	SELECT SUBSTRING('AMERICA' FROM 3 FOR 4)

OVERLAY

OVERLAY takes four arguments. The first is the target string, the second is a string that will be used to overlay part of the target string, the third specifies the point in the target string over which the new string will be overlaid, and the fourth is the length of the target that will be replaced.

For example, the following would overlay the letters 'rmeni' over 'meric' to give 'Armenia':

```
SELECT Surprise = STUFF('America', 'rmeni', 2, 5)
```

Although part of the SQL 99 standard, this isn't supported by any of the DBMSs we're concentrating on. Instead, we could us the STUFF function in SQL Server:

```
SELECT Surprise = STUFF('America', 2, 5, 'rmeni')
```

And the INSERT function in DB2:

```
VALUES CHAR(INSERT('America', 2, 5, 'rmeni'), 10)
```

MySQL also supports the INSERT function.

TRIM

The ANSI SQL TRIM specification takes two arguments. The first specifies the type of character to be trimmed. If omitted, this defaults to the space character. The second is the string being trimmed from. We can specify LEADING (trims leading characters), TRAILING (trims trailing characters) or BOTH. The default is BOTH.

For example, we could use the following to trim any spaces from the beginning and end of the notes field in the Employees table where EmployeeID is equal to 1:

```
SELECT Trim(Notes) FROM Employees WHERE EmployeeID = 1
```

The TRIM function varies from vendor to vendor. The following table summarizes the various implementations.

SQL Version	Function	Example
Access	LTrim(string)	SELECT LTrim(' trimmed ')
	RTrim(string)	SELECT RTrim(' trimmed ')
	Trim(string)	SELECT Trim(' trimmed ')
SQL Server	LTrim(string)	SELECT LTrim(' trimmed ')
	RTrim(string)	SELECT RTrim(' trimmed ')
Oracle	Trim(string)	SELECT TRIM(' trimmed ') FROM dual;
	LTRIM(string, set)	SELECT LTRIM ('XXtrimmed', 'XX') FROM dual;
	RTRIM(string, set)	SELECT RTRIM('trimmedXX', 'XX') FROM dual;
MySQL	Trim(string, string)	SELECT TRIM('XXtrimmedYXX', 'XX')
	LTRIM(string)	SELECT LTrim(' trimmed ')
	RTRIM(string)	SELECT RTrim(' trimmed ')

UPPER and LOWER

The UPPER and LOWER operators convert the case of a string. For example, the following will return the last names of the employees in the Northwind database in uppercase characters:

```
SELECT UPPER(LastName) FROM Employees
```

And the following will return the last names in lower case:

```
SELECT UPPER(LastName) FROM Employees
```

The following example is excellent for demonstrating the most common use of these functions – string comparison. Upper and lower case strings are not equal, so, when we're not sure what capitalization may or may not have been used, we can convert everything to upper or lower case, and then compare them:

```
SELECT * FROM Employees WHERE UPPER(LastName) = 'FULLER'
```

Aggregate Functions

Aggregate functions perform operations on sets of records. The following aggregate functions are supported for string values:

❑ COUNT

❑ GROUP BY

❑ MAX

❑ MIN

For details on these functions, see Chapter 13.

Predicates

In addition to the comparison operators, there are a number of other predicate expressions that can be used for comparing and working with strings:

❑ LIKE

❑ SIMILAR

❑ BETWEEN

❑ IN

❑ NULL (IS NULL, IS NOT NULL)

❑ EXISTS

❑ DISTINCT

A couple of notes would be appropriate here. LIKE and SIMILAR are similar to the "=" operator. However, the LIKE and SIMILAR operators can be used with wildcards. Of these two, only LIKE is widely supported. For this reason, we'll concentrate on this.

> By definition, the SQL 99 Standard LIKE predicate is case-sensitive for the string literals being compared. However, SQL Server and Access are both case insensitive when using LIKE, although SQL Server can be configured to be case sensitive if required.

Let's look at how LIKE functions with wildcards.

Wildcards

The underscore character (_) is the wildcard character for a single character of any kind. For example, the following query will select records from the Employees table where the first name is like 'Joan' or 'John':

```
SELECT * FROM Employees WHERE FirstName LIKE 'Jo_n'
```

The '%' wildcard stands in for any number of characters. For example, the following will return records where the first name is like "Joan2, "John", "Johann", "Jon", and "Jonathan":

```
SELECT * FROM Employees WHERE FirstName LIKE 'Jo%n'
```

Escape Character

Often, there will be a character in a string which will cause problems if inserted in a query. One of the prime culprits here is the quote character. For example, if we were to search for O'Hara in our database, we might try using the following:

```
SELECT * FROM Employees WHERE LastName = 'O'Hara'
```

However, this will cause problems, as the DBMS will take the 'O' as the string we are searching for, and take 'Hara' as being outside the single quotes.

To get round this problem, we can use an escape character. For instance, in SQL Server, we use a single quotation mark to indicate that the character following is to be interpreted as part of the string:

```
SELECT * FROM Employees WHERE LastName LIKE 'O''Hara'
```

In Oracle, the backslash character (\) is used as the escape character.

SOUNDEX

Several of these DBMSs provide support for the SOUNDEX and/or DIFFERENCE. SOUNDEX returns a SOUNDEX value for the target string. A SOUNDEX value is a four-character string that begins with a character followed by 3 digits. It represents the *phonetic sound* of the string. By comparing SOUNDEX values, we can find strings that *sound* like the search string.

Consider the following query:

```
SELECT DISTINCT Contactname, 'John Jones' AS orig,
SOUNDEX(ContactName) AS orgsound, SOUNDEX('John Jones') AS comp,
DIFFERENCE(SOUNDEX('John Jones'), SOUNDEX(ContactName))
AS difference
FROM Customers
WHERE Soundex(ContactName) IS NOT NULL
ORDER BY difference DESC
```

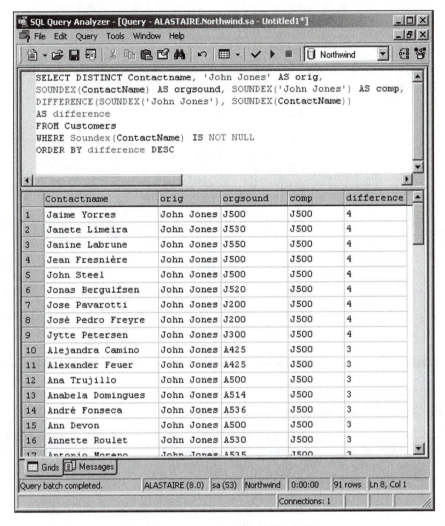

This query returns the names of those Customers who, in descending order, sound most like 'John Jones'.

Note that SOUNDEX is not widely supported.

Vendor-Specific Non-Standard String Functions

There are quite a few vendor-specific non-standard string functions for the various DBMS products. This is for the most part due to the fact that in adhering to the ANSI standards, these vendors are leaving in previous proprietary functions for backwards-compatibility, and those users who are used to older syntax. This isn't a problem, as it doesn't take away from the Standard, or change it in any way. It merely adds functionality.

Some DBMS's provide an extensive set of additional functions. These are only the most useful ones from these vendors. If you are using a different DBMS, or for more information about what is available from these vendors, consult your documentation.

Access Function	Description	Example
Asc (character)	Returns the ASCII integer value of a character.	SELECT Asc("a")
Chr (integer)	Returns the Character value for a given integer, from 0 – 255.	SELECT CHR(45)
StrComp (string1, string2)	Compares two strings numerically, and returns the difference. If the value returned is 0, the strings are identical.	SELECT StrComp("Kevin", "Spencer") AS different StrComp ("Kevin", "Kevin")
InStr ([start], string1, string2, [compare])	Returns –1 if string2 is not found in string1, or the index of the first occurrence of string2 in string1.	SELECT InStr('Kevin Spencer'," ")
Len (string)	Returns the number of characters in a string.	SELECT Len("'Kevin Spencer")
Space (Integer)	Returns a string consisting of the number of space characters specified.	SELECT "XXX" + Space(5) + "XXX"

SQL Server

Note that SQL Server also supports the Access functions

CHARINDEX (string1, string2, [start])	Like InStr(), CHARINDEX returns the index of the first occurrence of string2 in string1. The optional start parameter allows us to begin the search somewhere *inside* the target string.	SELECT CHARINDEX('e', 'Kevin Spencer', 3)
PATINDEX (string1, string2, [start])	Like CHARINDEX, PATINDEX searches for the occurrence of a string within a string. However, it can use wildcards in the string. The string1 target must be enclosed in "%" characters, and wildcards ("%" and "_") can appear anywhere inside.	SELECT PATINDEX('%e_c%', 'Kevin Spencer')

Access Function	Description	Example
REVERSE (string)	Returns the string in reverse order.	SELECT REVERSE('Kevin Spencer')
REPLACE (string, string1, string2)	Replaces all occurrences of string1 in string with string2. It can be nested!	SELECT Replace(Replace('Oh, Help me!', ' me', '!!'), 'p', 'l')
REPLICATE (string, count)	Repeats a string 'count' number of times, and returns the resulting string.	SELECT REPLICATE ('I do believe in ghosts! ', 2), REPLICATE ('I do - ', 4), 'I do believe in ghosts!'
SOUNDEX(string)	SOUNDEX returns a SOUNDEX value for the string passed.	SELECT SOUNDEX('Uncle Chutney')
DIFFERENCE(string1 ,string2)	DIFFERENCE is used with SOUNDEX to compare the sounds of two strings.	SELECT DISTINCT ContactName, 'Uncle Chutney' AS orig, SOUNDEX(ContactName) AS origsound,
	We pass it the SOUNDEX values of the two strings, and it returns the difference.	SOUNDEX('Uncle Chutney') AS comp, DIFFERENCE(SOUNDEX('Uncle Chutney'), SOUNDEX(ContactName)) AS difference FROM Customers WHERE SOUNDEX(ContactName) IS NOT NULL ORDER BY difference DESC
Oracle		
ASCII (character)	This, like the ASC function, returns the ASCII numeric value for the character passed.	SELECT ASCII('a') FROM dual;
CHR (integer)	This of course, works exactly like the CHR function in Access and SQL Server. It returns the character represented by the ASCII numeric value passed.	SELECT CHR(97) FROM dual;
CONCAT (string1, string2)	This works like the "||" concatenation operator. It concatenates (joins) 2 strings.	SELECT CONCAT ('Mick ', 'Jagger') FROM dual;

Table continued on following page

Oracle Function	Description	Example
INITCAP(string)	This function returns the string passed, with all the first letters of the words capitalized.	SELECT INITCAP('mick jagger') FROM dual;
LPAD (string1, length, string2)	This function pads string1 with 'length' of string2. We can use multiple characters in string2. However, the number of characters that are added to the left end of the string is determined by the 'length' parameter, not the number of characters in string2.	SELECT LPAD('Mick Jagger', 5, 'Concatenation') FROM dual;
INSTR (string1, string2, [start], [count])	Same as the INSTR() function of Access and SQL Server. However, it adds the optional start and count parameters, to enable us to find the *nth* occurrence of string2 in string1, starting at the count index of string1.	SELECT INSTR('Mick Jagger', 'r', 5, 2) FROM dual;
LENGTH (string)	Same as LEN in Access and SQL Server	SELECT LENGTH('Kevin Spencer') FROM dual;
MySQL		
ASCII (character)	Same as Oracle's ASCII.	SELECT ASCII('a')
CHAR (n [, ...])	Same as Oracle's implementation, except that it returns a string consisting of the characters derived from numeric values.	SELECT CHAR(75, 101, 118, 105, 110)
CONV (number, from_base, to_base)	Converts a number from one numbering system (from_base) to another (to_base).	SELECT CONV('a',16,2)
CONCAT (string1, string2 [, ...])	The CONCAT function works just like the "||" concatenation operator. However, the difference between this implementation and Oracle's, for example, is that we can concatenate as many strings with a single function as we wish.	SELECT CONCAT ('Mick', ' ', 'Jagger')

Oracle Function	Description	Example
CONCAT_WS (separator, string1, string2 [, ...])	This is just like CONCAT, except that we insert the 'separator' string in between the values we are joining.	SELECT CONCAT_WS(', ', '316 Old Wagon Rd', 'Pell City', Alabama')
LOCATE (string2, string1) POSITION string2 IN string1	Works the same as the various versions of INSTR. It returns the index of the first occurrence of string2 in string1.	SELECT LOCATE('e', 'Kevin Spencer',) SELECT POSITION 'e', 'Kevin Spencer'
LPAD (string1, length, string2)	Works just like LPAD in Oracle. We can set a string sequence to pad string1 on the left.	SELECT LPAD('Kevin Spencer', 5, 'concatenation string')
RPAD (string1, length, string2)	Works exactly like LPAD, but adds characters to the right of the string.	SELECT RPAD('Kevin Spencer', 5, 'concatenation string')
REPLACE (string, string_to_replace, replacement_string)	Works exactly like the SQL Server REPLACE function.	SELECT Replace(Replace('Oh, Help me!', ' me', '!!'), 'p', 'l')
REVERSE (string)	Exactly the same as the SQL Server REVERSE function.	SELECT REVERSE('Kevin Spencer')
REPEAT(string, count)	Returns a repeating string of the string we pass to it, repeated 'count' times.	SELECT REPEAT('I do believe in ghosts! ', 2), REPEAT ('I do - ', 4), 'I do believe in ghosts!'
SPACE(integer)	Returns a string consisting of 'integer' number of spaces.	SELECT CONCAT('XXX', SPACE(5), 'XXX')
SOUNDEX(string)	See SOUNDEX for SQL Server.	SELECT SOUNDEX('Uncle Chutney')

Now that we have looked in some detail at a number of functions that can be used on date-time data types and strings, let's look at a problem which will involve drawing on some of these functions.

Try it out – Build a Statistical Analysis Query

In this example, we will look at a specific problem. Suppose that the managers at Northwind want to implement a bonus scheme in which employees are paid a bonus on their retirement, which is based on their total earnings over their term of employment.

Note that in the following example, we will concentrate on using SQL Server. If you are using another DBMS, you will have to change the code. Alternatively, the code for MySQL, DB2, Oracle, and Access may be downloaded from the Wrox web site at www.wrox.com.

From the Northwind database, we will have to access employee IDs, names, birth dates, hire dates, and retirement dates of each employee. We will also have to show the total sales particular employees have made, and calculate the projected amount of sales they will have made by their retirement age, based on their sales to date.

Accessing employee IDs, birth dates, and hire dates will not be a problem, as these may be drawn directly from the database. However, the other information – the retirement date, total sales to date, and projected sales to retirement – will have to be calculated.

1. The name must be concatenated (combined) from information contained in the `FirstName` and `LastName` fields. We can do this using the following code. Type the following into Query Analyzer:

```
SELECT EmployeeID, (LastName + ', ' + FirstName) AS Name FROM Employees
```

This also displays the employee IDs.

2. The retirement date for each employee can be calculated by adding 65 years (the mandatory retirement age for this company) to the employees' birth dates. To do this, we can add the appropriate code to our query. As we will also be displaying the dates of birth and hire dates of the employees, we will add the appropriate code to access these from the `Employees` table:

```
SELECT EmployeeID, (LastName + ', ' + FirstName) AS Name, BirthDate, HireDate,
DateAdd(yyyy, 65, BirthDate) AS RetireDate
FROM Employees
```

If we test this now, we should get the following results:

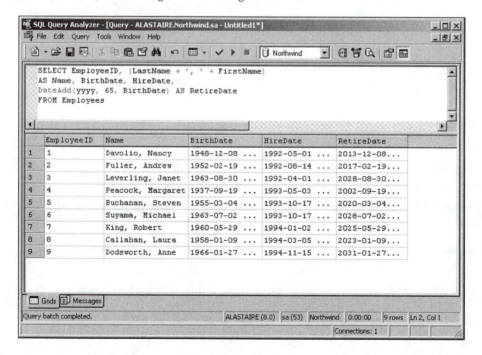

3. In order to find out the total amount of sales by each employee, we will need to access information from the `OrderDetails` and the `Orders` table. However, in order to associate information about sales with particular employees, we will have to perform a join between these two tables. The reason for this is that information relating employees with sales data in contained in the `Orders` table.

However, we also need to calculate the total sales to date for each employee. We will have to calculate this by accessing information in the UNITPRICE and QUANTITY fields of the `OrderDetails` table. The total sales for each employee may be calculated by multiplying each record's `Unit Price` and `Quantity`, and then adding up all the values associated with each employee.

We can perform all this with the following query:

```
SELECT Employees.EmployeeID AS ID,
Max((Employees.LastName +', '+ Employees.FirstName)) AS Name,
Max(Employees.BirthDate) AS BirthDate,
Max(Employees.HireDate) AS HireDate,
Max(DateAdd(yyyy,65,Employees.BirthDate)) AS RetireDate,

SUM(([Order Details].[UnitPrice] * [Order Details].[Quantity]))
AS TotalSales

FROM (Employees INNER JOIN Orders ON Employees.EmployeeID = Orders.EmployeeID)
INNER JOIN [Order Details] ON Orders.OrderID = [Order Details].OrderID
GROUP BY Employees.EmployeeID
```

Note how the information on sales for each employee necessitates performing a JOIN between the `Employees` table and the `Orders` table, and then perfoming a JOIN between the `Orders` table and the `Orders` table with the `Order Details` table. This is known as a three way join.

If we test this now, we should receive something like the following results:

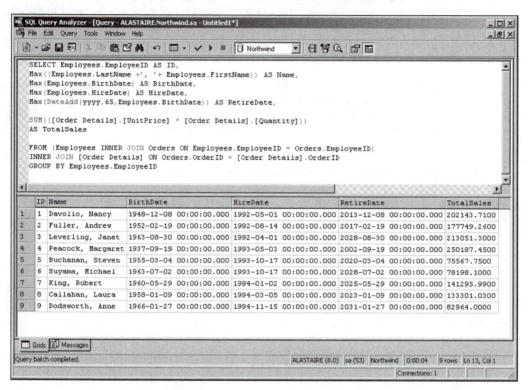

4. Next, we need to calculate the sales per employee per year. This can be done by simply dividing the total sales per employee by the number of years they've been employed.

Add the shaded code to our current query:

```
SELECT Employees.EmployeeID AS ID,
Max((Employees.LastName +', '+ Employees.FirstName)) AS Name,
Max(Employees.BirthDate) AS BirthDate,
Max(Employees.HireDate) AS HireDate,
Max(DateAdd(yyyy,65,Employees.BirthDate)) AS RetireDate,

SUM(([Order Details].[UnitPrice] * [Order Details].[Quantity])) AS TotalSales,

Max(DateDiff(yyyy, Employees.HireDate, GetDate())) AS YearsEmployed,

((SUM(([Order Details].[UnitPrice] * [Order Details].[Quantity]))) /
(Max(DateDiff(yyyy, Employees.HireDate, GetDate())))) AS SalesPerYear

FROM (Employees INNER JOIN Orders ON Employees.EmployeeID = Orders.EmployeeID)
INNER JOIN [Order Details] ON Orders.OrderID = [Order Details].OrderID
GROUP BY Employees.EmployeeID
```

Notice the use of the Max() function on the second operand in the division. This is necessary in order to satisfy the rules concerning aggregate queries. We will look at these in Chapter 13.

This should produce the following results:

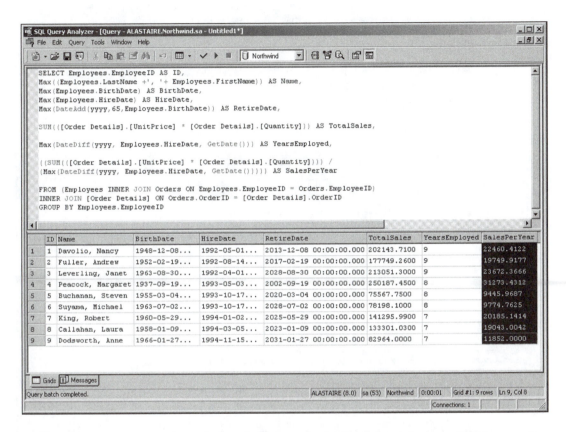

5. We now simply need to calculate the projected sales for each employee until their respective retirements. This is done by simply calculating the number of years until an employee's retirement, and multiplying this by their sales per year.

Add the shaded code to the current query. Note that, in this code – for illustrative purposes – we've duplicated the code which calculates the sales per year for each employee.

```
SELECT Employees.EmployeeID AS ID,
Max((Employees.LastName+', '+Employees.FirstName)) AS Name,
Max(Employees.BirthDate) AS BirthDate,
Max(Employees.HireDate) AS HireDate,
Max(DateAdd(yyyy,65,Employees.BirthDate)) AS RetireDate,

SUM(([Order Details].[UnitPrice] * [Order Details].[Quantity])) AS TotalSales,

Max(DateDiff(yyyy, Employees.HireDate, GetDate())) AS YearsEmployed,
```

```
((SUM(([Order Details].[UnitPrice] * [Order Details].[Quantity]))) /
(Max(DateDiff(yyyy, Employees.HireDate, GetDate())))) AS SalesPerYear,

SUM(([Order Details].[UnitPrice] * [Order Details].[Quantity])) +

(((SUM(([Order Details].[UnitPrice] * [Order Details].[Quantity]))) /
(Max(DateDiff(yyyy, Employees.HireDate, GetDate())))) *
Max(DateDiff(yyyy, Employees.HireDate, (DateAdd(yyyy,65,Employees.BirthDate)))))
AS ProjectedTotal

FROM (Employees INNER JOIN Orders ON Employees.EmployeeID = Orders.EmployeeID)
INNER JOIN [Order Details] ON Orders.OrderID = [Order Details].OrderID
GROUP BY Employees.EmployeeID
```

We should now be in a position to generate the following results:

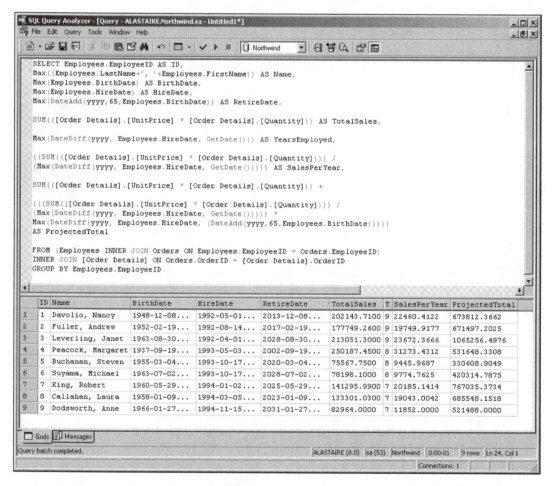

We've now generated the information requested by the Northwind manager.

Summary

In this chapter, we've looked in some detail at date and time datatypes, performing operations involving dates and times, and performing operations on character strings. We concluded with a practical example in which we built a fairly complicated query in which we put to practice some of the functions we looked at earlier in the chapter.

In the next chapter, we will look at the full range of mathematical functions available to us in SQL.

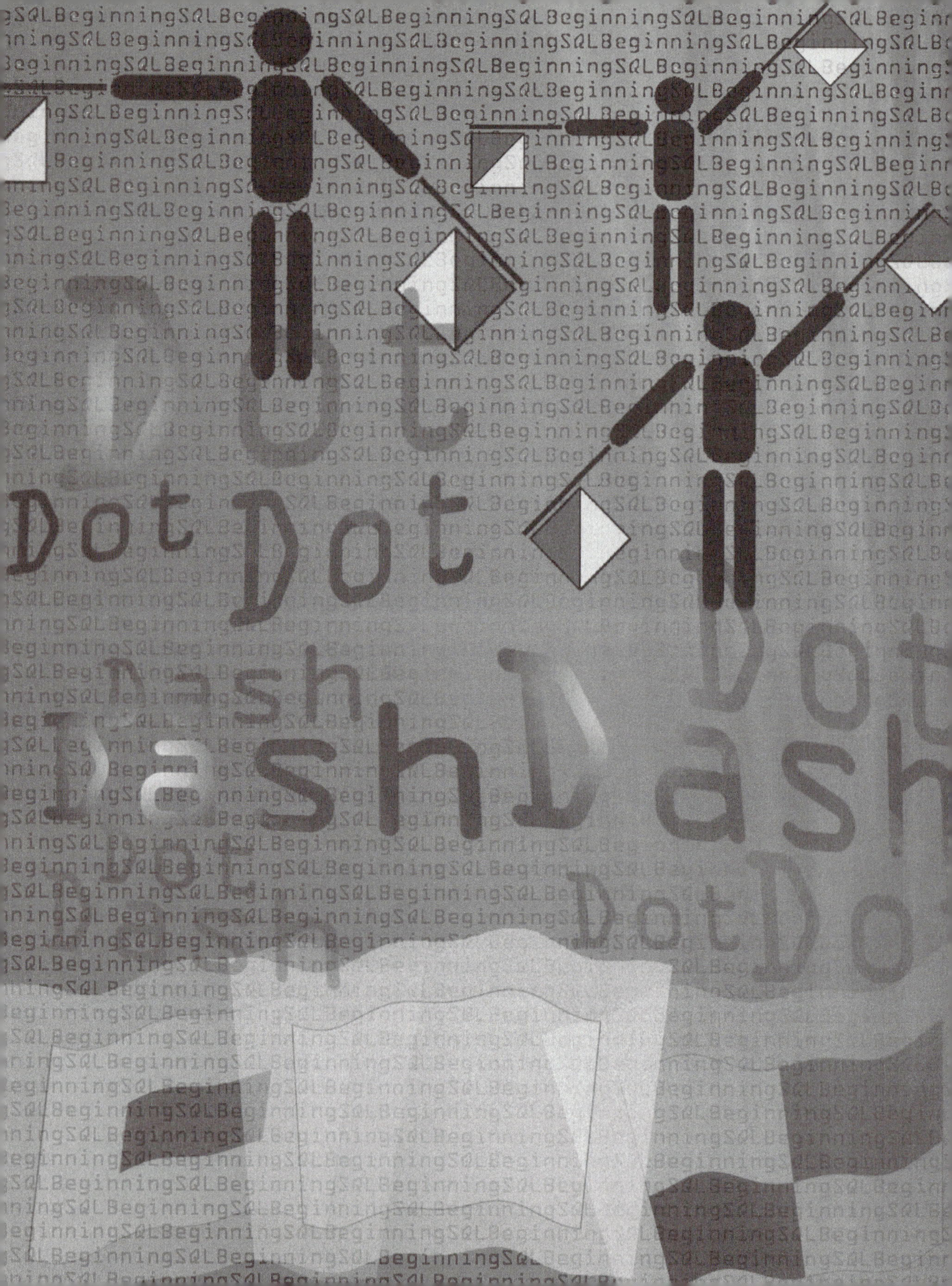

SQL Functions – Math and Data Type Conversion

Math is an integral part of everyday life – we cannot get by without it, from paying our bills, to buying items from a shop. We need math to work out all sorts of things, not least the sales figures that will allow us to claim our bonus! SQL contains many math functions and data conversion functions that can be used to build very powerful queries to allow us to get the information we want from the information we have. We can do operations such as round and approximate numbers (which can be handy for reports and displays), calculate trigonometric functions (if you need to do any distance or geometric calculations), and find several ways to convert from one data type to another. Granted, many of these functions will be of limited use on a day-to-day basis, but they do exist and can be used to create very powerful solutions to complex problems.

This chapter will, therefore, focus on the following:

- ❑ Looking at the Math Functions that SQL contains, giving their syntax
- ❑ Looking at the trigonometrical math functions that we might, some day, find useful
- ❑ Looking at converting Data Types, especially useful when dealing with Strings.

So, let's begin!

Math Functions

SQL has many built-in mathematical functions. You may not have thought that you can do trigonometry in SQL – until now!

You may never use most of the functions listed below because there are few business uses for some of them (such as the trigonometric functions), but it is important to know the capabilities of SQL and the potential of the language. You never know when you may be dealing with geographic position data and need to jump back into geometry and trigonometry to find distances and locations. It could happen!

An important note, however, before we start. Within each section, we present the basic syntax that we will need to write to use the function; however, different database vendors will have their own way of implementing the basic syntax. The examples given were written using SQL Server; as a result, other DBMSs may not be able to execute the examples as written: for example, Oracle and DB2 will not allow SELECT to be used without a FROM clause, even though the table name is arbitrary. However, the respective operators work as described with the correct syntax, which in the case of Oracle and DB2 is:

```
SELECT function_name(field_name) FROM table_name;
```

Another peculiarity with Oracle and DB2 is that they might not allow you to give your own name to the result columns – you will have to remove the AS 'x' and similar descriptions from each line of code, then add a FROM table_name; clause at the end to make the code work. Other vendors will have their own implementation, so make sure that you consult the relevant documentation if you are not using SQL Server.

ABS

The ABS function returns the absolute value of a number. The ABS function takes the parameter of a number data type (with the exception of the bit data type) and returns the positive value of the number.

```
ABS (<numeric_value>)
```

An example of the ABS function would be as follows:

```
SELECT
    ABS(-10),
    ABS(-5.234),
    ABS(0),
    ABS(10)
```

The results would all be positive numbers:

	(No column name)	(No column name)	(No column name)	(No column name)
1	10	5.234	0	10

One of the more common errors would be an overflow if you are converting a data type (a long integer to a short integer) or using a non-numeric value. For instance, if we decided that we wanted to take the absolute value of "Hello World"

```
SELECT
    ABS('Hello World')
```

we would get an error message from SQL Server:

```
Server: Msg 8114, Level 16, State 5, Line 1
Error converting data type varchar to float.
```

Be sure that you are sending numeric values to ABS (or any of the math functions for that matter) or else you will see this error.

ASCII

The ASCII function returns the ASCII value of a single character of type char or varchar. The input parameter is the character to lookup.

```
ASCII ('<character>')
```

> **Microsoft Access does not support this function; however, Access users can use the VB function, asc().**

If we needed to know what the ASCII value of A, E, I, O, and U are, then we can create a simple query that tells us:

```
SELECT
    ASCII('A') AS 'A',
    ASCII('E') AS 'E' ,
    ASCII('I') AS 'I',
    ASCII('O') AS 'O',
    ASCII('U') AS 'U'
```

Remember, if you are using Oracle or DB2 the syntax differs slightly: you may have to remove the AS 'A', and so on, from each line of code, then add a FROM table_name; clause at the end to make the code work.

The output of the query would be the five ASCII values that we had requested:

	A	E	I	O	U
1	65	69	73	79	85

Keep in mind that in ASCII terms, "A" and "a" are two different values. If you want to prevent case sensitivity issues then you should use the UPPER or LOWER functions to convert the string or the character to a common case first.

Looking at "A" versus "a", we see that there are two values that could potentially throw us off in our comparisons:

```
SELECT
    ASCII('A') AS 'A',
    ASCII('a') AS 'a'
```

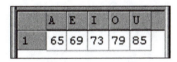

	A	a
1	65	97

One other issue with using the ASCII function is that it works on one character only. If you try to find the ASCII value of "ABC", then you will get a surprising answer:

```
SELECT
    ASCII('ABC')
```

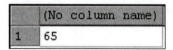

	(No column name)
1	65

Notice that the ASCII function takes only the first character and ignores the rest of the string. If you need to process an entire string then you need to loop through all of the characters and take the ASCII values individually.

CEILING

The CEILING function is a general purpose rounding function. CEILING returns the rounded-up value of the expression that is passed into the function.

```
CEILING(<numeric expression>)
```

> **The CEILING function does not exist in Microsoft Access.**

Note that the numeric expression must be a valid numeric data type with the exception of the bit data type. This function returns another numeric expression of an integer data type.

Let's look at the output of the CEILING function when used with several values.

```
SELECT
    CEILING(-10) AS '-10',
    CEILING(-5.25) AS '-5.25',
    CEILING(0) AS '0',
    CEILING(2.75) AS '2.75',
    CEILING(7) AS '7'
```

This gives us the following:

	-10	-5.25	0	2.75	7
1	-10	-5	0	3	7

Note that with the –5.25 and other negative numbers, rounding up the value will round in the positive direction. You may think that –5.25 rounded up is –6, but in actuality –5 is larger than –6, so that is why the negative numbers round in what appears to be a different manner from positive numbers.

So, what can we use the CEILING function for? Well, if we were a cellular service provider then we may use the CEILING function for call times: our service plan may need to round up to the next minute for billing purposes. We can use the CEILING function to round up all of the call times when we update the database instead of trying to do this when we calculate our bills. If we did not round the numbers first then our bills may be short due to logic (that is, adding the times and then rounding versus rounding then adding the call times).

As you can see from the above output, the CEILING function can be used as a general purpose round up function.

FLOOR

The FLOOR function is basically the opposite of the CEILING function. The purpose of FLOOR is to round down a numeric expression.

```
FLOOR (numeric_expression)
```

> Microsoft Access does not contain the **FLOOR** function.

The numeric expression must be of a numeric data type, with the exception of the bit data type.

Let's look at the same example from the CEILING function and replace the function calls with FLOOR:

```
SELECT
    FLOOR(-10) AS '-10',
    FLOOR(-5.25) AS '-5.25',
    FLOOR(0) AS '0',
    FLOOR(2.75) AS '2.75',
    FLOOR(7) AS '7'
```

The result should be:

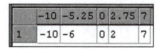

	-10	-5.25	0	2.75	7
1	-10	-6	0	2	7

Remember that FLOOR will always round down to the next whole number, so be sure that you use either FLOOR or CEILING accordingly, depending on the business need.

ROUND

The ROUND function is similar to the CEILING function, but this function is much more flexible on how the numeric expressions round the numbers. The syntax of the ROUND function is as follows:

```
ROUND(numeric_expression, length, <function>)
```

The numeric expression parameter must be any valid numeric data type, with the exception of the bit data type.

Length is the precision of the rounding operation. The length parameter must be a tinyint, smallint, or int data type. When the expression is evaluated the length is rounded to the specified number of decimal places. When length is a negative number then the expression will be rounded on the left side of the decimal point. If length is a negative number that is greater than or equal to the number of digits that exist to the left of the decimal then the result will always be zero.

The `function` parameter, which is an optional parameter, must also be a `tinyint`, `smallint`, or `int` data type. When the function parameter is 0 or omitted then the expression is rounded. If `function` has any other value, then the numeric expression is truncated (the part after the decimal point is ignored).

In order to demonstrate all of the functionality of ROUND, we will look at some expressions that cover many of the different operations.

Round a basic number (373.489)

```
SELECT
    ROUND(373.489, -3) AS '-3',
    ROUND(373.489, -2) AS '-2',
    ROUND(373.489, -1) AS '-1',
    ROUND(373.489, 0) AS '0',
    ROUND(373.489, 1) AS '1',
    ROUND(373.489, 2) AS '2',
    ROUND(373.489, 3) AS '3'
```

	-3	-2	-1	0	1	2	3
1	.000	400.000	370.000	373.000	373.500	373.490	373.489

Compare rounding and truncating

```
SELECT
    ROUND(373.489, 0, 1) AS 'Truncated',
    ROUND(1038.751, 0, 1) AS 'Truncated',
    ROUND(373.489, 0, 0) AS 'Rounded',
    ROUND(1038.751, 0, 0) AS 'Rounded'
```

	Truncated	Truncated	Rounded	Rounded
1	373.000	1038.000	373.000	1039.000

Rounding more digits than exist

```
SELECT
    ROUND(373.489, -4)
```

	(No column name)
1	.000

Comparing ROUND with CEILING

As we said earlier, ROUND is similar to CEILING – however, care must be taken when using negative numbers. Take this example comparing the ROUND of -5.75 and the CEILING of -5.75:

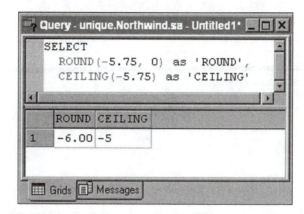

As we can see, these return greatly varying results, so bear this in mind if this should crop up in your work.

The ROUND function is a great way to do general numeric estimations on calculations with a large decimal placeholder. For instance, we may have floating-point numbers that extend to 13 or 14 decimal places. Let's say that our data is currency information from some mortgage calculations; we could use the ROUND function to make the numbers smaller (3 or 4 decimal places instead) and make the data more presentable.

This is a function that can often be used to format output of query values or for presenting currency data where only two decimals should appear.

EXP

The EXP function returns the exponential function of a numeric expression that is a float data type.

```
EXP (numeric_expression)
```

The EXP function is typically written as e^x, where e is a universal constant for many scientific equations. The short value of e is 2.718281828, but, like PI, e has an infinite number of decimal places. So, the EXP function will take the value of e and raise it to the power specified by the numeric expression:

```
SELECT
    EXP(0) AS '0',
    EXP(1) AS '1',
    EXP(2) AS '2'
```

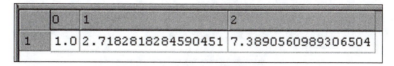

The EXP function and the following LOG function are very similar: in fact, they are called inverse functions and we will see what that means when we look at the LOG function.

LOG

The LOG function returns the natural logarithm of a numeric expression. This numeric expression must be a positive float data expression or an expression that can be converted to a float value. The return value will always be as a float value.

```
LOG (numeric_expression)
```

```
SELECT
    LOG(1) AS '1',
    LOG(5.225) AS '5.225',
    LOG(10) AS '10'
```

	1	5.225	10
1	0.0	1.6534547978508747	2.3025850929940459

The LOG function is the natural logarithm of a number; the natural logarithm is the inverse of the EXP function, so $\ln(x)$ or LOG(x) is the same as e^x or EXP(x). The cool math trick of the day is that you can execute LOG(EXP(x)) and the value is x:

```
SELECT
    EXP(1) AS 'EXP(1)',
    LOG(2.7182818284590451) AS 'LOG(2.7182818284590451)',
    LOG(EXP(1)) AS 'LOG(EXP(1))'
```

	EXP(1)	LOG(2.7182818284590451)	LOG(EXP(1))
1	2.7182818284590451	1.0	1.0

This demonstrates the relationship between the EXP and the LOG functions.

The LOG function is commonly used in financial applications where complex calculations must be performed. For example, compounded interest calculations utilize logarithms, as do many other time-based financial calculations. Unlike Microsoft Excel, SQL does not include a series of complex financial calculations and you must utilize these more basic functions to perform your calculations.

One of the more common errors that can occur when using the LOG function is that the LOG argument must be a positive value. If we attempt to execute the LOG function with 0 or a negative number then we will receive a domain error. SQL Server will report the following to us:

```
SELECT
    LOG(0)
```

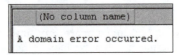

(No column name)
A domain error occurred.

Microsoft Access, on the other hand, will return an 'Invalid Procedure Call' error when trying to execute a LOG function with a 0 or negative number. All databases will return some form of error message if any zero or negative number is sent to the LOG function.

LOG10

The LOG10 function is very similar to the LOG function with one exception: unlike the LOG function, the LOG10 function returns the base-10 logarithm of a numeric expression. Like the LOG function, the LOG10 function must accept a positive float data type or a numeric expression that can be converted to a float value. The output of the function is a float value.

```
LOG10 (numeric_expression)
```

> **Microsoft Access does not contain the LOG10 function.**

```
SELECT
    LOG10(1) AS '1',
    LOG10(5.225) AS '5.225',
    LOG10(10) AS '10'
```

	1	5.225	10
1	0.0	0.71808629478309161	1.0

The LOG10 function also requires a value greater than 0 or an error will occur. In SQL Server this error is an obscure "A domain error occurred" while Access will return an "Invalid Procedure Call" error message. All databases will return some form of error if a zero or negative number is passed in.

PI

The PI function simply returns the value of PI. PI returns a float value.

> **Microsoft Access and DB2 do not contain the PI function.**

A reasonably close approximation would be (21.99/7). This would result in a value of approximately 3.1414285714285714. This approximation should be acceptable for any calculation, short of astronomical and stellar equations.

```
SELECT
    PI() AS 'PI'
```

	PI
1	3.1415926535897931

The PI function is commonly used when dealing with circular shapes such as ovals, ellipses, and circles. PI is a universal constant.

POWER

The POWER function is one of the more useful math functions in that it allows you to calculate the value of a number to a specified power. You can use this function to calculate numbers such as 2^{16} without creating a loop operation.

```
POWER (numeric_expression, value)
```

> **Although Microsoft Access does not have the POWER function, it does have a power shortcut: ^. The equivalent calculation of POWER(2, 16) in SQL would be 2^16 in Microsoft Access.**

numeric_expression is any valid numeric data type, with the exception of the bit data type. The value parameter is the power that the numeric expression should be raised to and can be any valid math data type. POWER will return the same data type as the numeric expression or a higher data type if the calculation exceeds the bounds of the data type of the numeric expression. So if we wanted to calculate 2 to the power of 16 we would use the following SQL:

```
SELECT
    POWER(2, 16) AS 'POWER'
```

The POWER function returns a float data type.

There may be times where you must take the root of a number (square root, cube root, etc). If you need to do this then you must modify the parameters of the value expression. To take the square root you would use .5, cube root .333, 4th root .25 and so on. The easiest way to take a root is to use simple division as your value: square root = 1/2, cube root = 1/3, 4th root = 1/4, and so on.

```
SELECT
    POWER(2, 4) AS '2^4',
    POWER(16, .25) AS '4th root of 16'
```

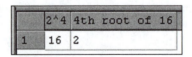

One of the more common "issues" with the POWER function is that it rounds based on the data type that is provided as the numeric expression, since the returned type is the same as the input type. Take, for instance, calculating 2^{-10} – we can do this two different ways to get two different results:

```
SELECT
    POWER(2, -10)
```

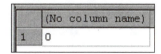

Or, we can add decimal places to the value.

```
SELECT
    POWER(2.000000000000, -10)
```

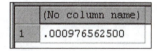

So, if you are looking for very precise values then you need to be sure that you provide a data type that will prevent any rounding problems. We can overcome this problem by using a function that we will see later in this chapter called CAST. We can use this to specify the data type that we want the numeric expression to operate as. We can change our original query to produce the second set of results just by telling the processor that the number is a float rather than an integer (as is assumed in our first example):

```
SELECT
    POWER(CAST(2 AS float), -10)
```

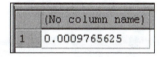

We will cover the CAST function in more detail later in this chapter.

RAND

The RAND function generates a random number from the database.

> **Oracle does not contain the RAND function.**

The RAND function returns a float value and accepts an optional seed parameter; the seed value must be an integer data type. The seed parameter is a number that tells the RAND function how it should calculate a random number. These are not actually calculated randomly, rather they are a series of known random values; thus, if you use a seed value of 10 on each calculation then you will get the same "random" number. You will see this in more detail in a few paragraphs.

Seed is used to generate a random number based on a sequence. Random numbers in computers are generally not truly random numbers: rather, a random number is one of a predefined set of numbers that are statistically random. The seed value tells the randomization engine that it should start generating numbers based on the provided sequence number. Truly random numbers must be generated with previously unknown input and must be calculated – for example, you could generate a random number based on the number of keystrokes in the last 30 seconds combined with the MAC address of the network card and the time of day. Typically you only need this level of randomness when dealing with highly scientific applications or public/private key security. You can be assured that you will not have to worry about either of these in SQL since SQL is nowhere near powerful or fast enough for these types of calculations.

The syntax of the RAND function is as follows:

```
RAND(<seed>)
```

Running the RAND function three times provides the following results (your results will vary):

```
SELECT
    RAND()
```

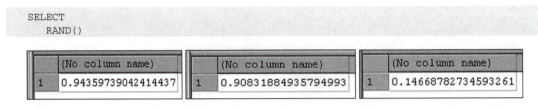

Random numbers can be used as part of an order number generating system or for picking rows of data at random intervals. An example of this would be with a quiz application where you would use the randomise function to pick a row to display.

One of the most common errors that surfaces when dealing with random numbers is that the seed value is used and not changed between function calls. If we eliminate the seed value then we will get different values upon each execution of the RAND function like the example above. On the other hand, if you add a seed value and do not make changes then you will receive the same value for each subsequent execution. Let's look at an example of using the seed value of 10 for each execution:

```
SELECT
    RAND(10)
```

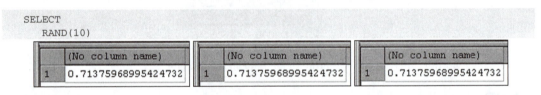

Another common mistake is that some developers try to set the seed using the RAND function, but this fails as well – by trying to randomise a value using the RAND function you get into a state of non-random values. In the example below you will see that trying to RAND a RAND value only leads to confusion:

```
SELECT
    RAND(RAND())
```

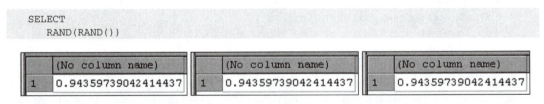

The seed value should only be used when you know a series of numbers that you want to use or you want to get the same number for each execution. The value for RAND(10) will always be the same, so this information may come in handy at some point when you need to generate and retrieve known values.

SIGN

The SIGN function is used to determine whether a number is positive, negative, or zero. The numeric expression that SIGN takes can be any numeric data type (except bit again), and returns only –1, 0, or 1 for negative, zero, or positive respectively.

Negative Number	Zero	Positive Number
-1	0	1

This is a very handy function to use since it eliminates very costly loops and numeric comparisons. You could achieve the same results using `IF` statements, but `SIGN` is much more efficient.

```
SIGN(numeric_expression)
```

For example:

```
SELECT
    SIGN(-10) AS '-10',
    SIGN(-5.225) AS '-5.225',
    SIGN(0) AS '0',
    SIGN(5.225) AS '5.225',
    SIGN(10) AS '10'
```

	-10	-5.225	0	5.225	10
1	-1	-1.000	0	1.000	1

As you can see, `SIGN` can be a handy method for evaluating the sign of a number without complex logic. Using `SIGN` you know that you will only get one of three values, so you could write a `CASE` statement to evaluate the positive or negative state of a number.

For instance, a useful `CASE` statement for using the `SIGN` function would be as follows:

```
...
CASE WHEN SIGN(Balance) = -1 THEN 'Negative Balance'
CASE WHEN SIGN(Balance) = 0 THEN 'No Balance on record'
CASE WHEN SIGN(Balance) = 1 THEN 'Positive Balance'
...
```

SQUARE

The `SQUARE` function can be considered a shortcut function since it performs the same operation as the `POWER` function with one minor difference. The `SQUARE` function only squares a number – which is the same as using 2 as the value for the exponent in the `POWER` function.

> **SQUARE is not contained in MySQL, Oracle, or DB2.**

The `SQUARE` function takes a numeric expression and returns the squared result (a float) as the output.

```
SQUARE(numeric_expression)
```

Let's demonstrate the comparison between SQUARE and POWER:

```
SELECT
    SQUARE(2) AS 'SQUARE',
    POWER(2,2) AS 'POWER'
```

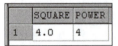

Notice the major difference between the two functions. The POWER function returns the same data type that is passed in (or the next best data type if you exceed the input data type ranges). On the other hand, the SQUARE function returns a float even if we are squaring an integer. This makes the SQUARE function less efficient than the POWER function since more memory is potentially required for the operation. SQUARE is easier to use (because it is a smaller function call) whereas POWER is more efficient with memory.

SQRT

The SQRT function takes the square root of a number. SQRT, like SQUARE, is a shortcut function to the POWER function. SQRT takes a numeric expression and returns the square root as a float value.

```
SQRT(numeric_expression)
```

As with the comparison between SQUARE and POWER, we will do the same with SQRT. Keep in mind that in order to take the square root of a number when using POWER you need to use the 1/2 power.

```
SELECT
    SQRT(4) AS 'SQRT',
    POWER(4, .5) AS 'POWER'
```

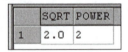

Notice once again that the POWER function returns the input data type or closest possible data type while SQRT returns a float data type causing the database to use more memory to process the results of the operation. Although in math we can take the square root of a negative number to get an imaginary number, in SQL we can't. We must use positive values for the SQRT function or an error will occur in all database systems.

Trigonometric

On top of the above math operations there is an extensive list of trigonometric functions available in SQL. We may use these infrequently, if ever at all. The times where these will really come in handy is when generating map or location information where we need to find closest points or fastest routes. These calculations come down to a bunch of triangles, arcs, squares, and other simple geometric shapes.

We will simply list the different functions and point out common usage errors since the algorithms that implement these trigonometric functions are outside the scope of this book and require a strong background in algebra and geometry.

DEGREES

The DEGREES function is used to convert radian measurements to degree measurements. The inverse trigonometric functions (ACOS, ASIN, ATAN) return radian measurements rather than degrees. The DEGREES function takes any valid numeric data type with the exception of the bit data type.

> **A radian is an angular measure. One radian equals 180/PI degrees.**

```
DEGREES(numeric_expression)
```

For instance, if we needed to know the number of degrees in PI:

```
SELECT
    DEGREES(PI())
```

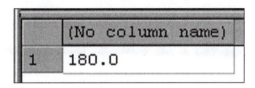

Thus, the number of degrees in PI is 180 degrees.

> **Oracle does not contain the DEGREES function.**

RADIANS

The RADIANS function is the opposite of the DEGREES function in that we are converting a degree measurement to a radian value.

> **Oracle does not contain the RADIANS function.**

RADIANS takes any valid numeric input (except the bit type) and returns a numeric value similar to the input value.

```
RADIANS(numeric_expression)
```

If we wanted to determine the number of radians in 360 degrees then we could use the RADIANS function as follows:

```
SELECT
    RADIANS(360.0)
```

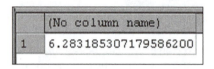

	(No column name)
1	6.283185307179586200

Note what we would get if we used an integer value instead:

```
SELECT
    RADIANS(360)
```

We would encounter a potential rounding problem since an integer was the input value and the RADIANS function will try to return an integer type back to the calling application. Use floating numbers for the highest level of precision when dealing with the trigonometric functions.

ACOS, COS

ACOS is a function that returns the angle (measured in radians) of a given numeric expression. ACOS takes a float value as input and returns a float value. Note that the numeric expression must be between –1 and 1 or an error will occur.

```
ACOS(numeric_expression)
```

COS is a complementary function that returns the cosine (measured in radians) of a numeric expression that is defined to be a float value. COS returns a float value as well, and is the opposite of ACOS.

```
COS(numeric_expression)
```

We can use the COS function to find the cosine of a given angle (in this example, 30 degrees). There is an important note to make here: COS, like the other trigonometric functions, takes measurements in radians. If you try to send the value of 30 into the COS function you will get a decimal number that looks like a valid value, but it is actually incorrect. Let's see.

```
SELECT
    COS(30)
```

	(No column name)
1	0.15425144988758405

The problem with this approach is that it looks correct, but it is actually wrong since we are getting the cosine of 30 *radians*, not degrees. In order to get degrees we need to convert 30 degrees to radians:

```
SELECT
    COS(RADIANS(30.0))
```

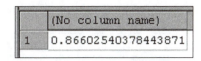

We had to convert using 30.0 rather than 30 since there would be a rounding error due to the fact that the calculations would use integer math rather than floating-point math. If we drop the decimal and rerun the query you will see the change in results.

```
SELECT
    COS(RADIANS(30))
```

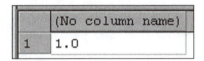

Notice that the output has been rounded to the nearest integer value. This is a big difference when dealing with cosine values, so this would be a huge math error that would be difficult to find.

The most common error with this set of trigonometric functions is that anything outside of –1 to 1 sent to ACOS will generate an error. The second most common error is that ACOS returns radians and not degrees. You must use the DEGREES function to return the proper degree angle; otherwise your other calculations must be in radians.

ASIN, SIN

ASIN and SIN are very similar to the ACOS and COS functions except that they are used for sine rather than cosine calculations. ASIN has a numeric input and radian output while SIN has a radian input and numeric output.

Valid ranges for ASIN are –1 to 1 (the same as ACOS). Any input values outside of this range will generate an input error.

```
SIN(numeric_expression)
```

```
ASIN(numeric_expression)
```

For the most accurate results be sure to use float type numbers to prevent integer rounding errors. Also, convert to radians if finding the values for a degree value.

First, let's look at the range value for ASIN:

```
SELECT
    ASIN(-1) AS '-1',
    ASIN(0) AS '0',
    ASIN(1) AS '1'
```

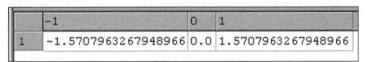

If you use these radian values as the input values for SIN, you will see that ASIN and SIN are opposites:

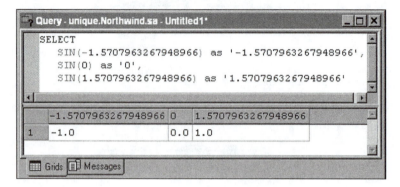

If you exceed the range of –1 to 1 then you receive the following error message from SQL Server:

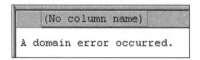

Microsoft Access will report an "Invalid Procedure Call" error message.

Remember that the SIN function takes radians as an input, so if you wanted the sine of 45 degrees then you would need to do a conversion:

```
SELECT
    SIN(RADIANS(45.0))
```

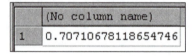

Remember that adding the .0 to the degree number changes the calculation to floating-point math. If we do not do this then our results will change dramatically:

```
SELECT
    SIN(RADIANS(45))
```

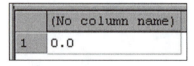

There are other ways to perform explicit floating-point math conversions that we will see later in this chapter.

ATAN, TAN, COT

ATAN, TAN, and COT are the arctangent, tangent, and cotangent functions respectively. They also function in the same manner as the previous examples. All of the rules for ASIN/SIN and ACOS/COS apply here as well. The numeric expression input parameter can be any valid number data type with the exception of the bit data type.

```
ATAN(numeric_expression)
```

```
TAN(numeric_expression)
```

```
COT(numeric_expression)
```

ATN2

The ATN2 function is a little different from the preceding functions in that it takes two input parameters. ATN2 returns the arc tangent of numeric_expression1 and numeric_expression2 (in radians), where numeric_expression1 is the length of the angle's opposite side, and numeric_expression2 is the length of the angle's adjacent side.

```
ATN2(numeric_expression1, numeric_expression2)
```

or

```
ATN2(numeric_expression1/numeric_expression2)
```

Both of these are the same and correct.

numeric_expression1 and numeric_expression2 are of the float data type – note the change from some of the prior trigonometric functions – but the returned values are in the range -PI/2 to PI/2, depending on the input values.

For instance, let's say that we need to find the arctangent between two sides, one of length 3 and one of length 5 (it might happen!!). The result we should get, when converting to degrees, is:

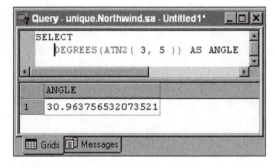

This information is used when dealing with arcs of circles. An example of this would be when dealing with pie charts. You could use the ATN2 function to determine percentages for the chart slices by determining the points in the arc.

Data Type Conversions

There will be many times through your queries where a value must be converted from one data type to another. This is most common when dealing with strings because you need to convert numbers to strings in order to put them into a varchar field. For instance, you may want to write out "Your order number is 134242" where 134242 is a numeric field in one of your tables. In order to do this operation you must be able to convert this from a number to a string or SQL will generate an error message.

We will be looking at the two ways to convert our data from one type to another using built-in SQL functions. As we will see, both of the conversion functions perform the same function and operate in very similar fashions with only a few minor differences.

CAST

The CAST function is the first data conversion function that we will look at. The reason why we have picked the CAST function first is that it is based on the SQL-92 standard and is the preferred method of converting data types. It is not always necessary to call CAST because the databases will perform implicit data conversion when possible.

> **CAST is supported by SQL Server and DB2.**

Implicit data conversions can occur between like data types within SQL. An example would be adding a float and an integer together. SQL will convert the integer to a float for the purpose of the addition operation.

There are many implicit conversions that can take place, but there are also certain conversions that can never take place. For instance, you cannot convert an image data type to an integer data type since the conversion would not make any sense the information in an image data type contains binary data that cannot convert to a meaningful number. The following graphic details what data types can be converted and which ones cannot. You can also see the implicit conversions that take place internally within SQL.

Data Type Conversion chart. Legend:

- ● Explicit Conversion
- ◐ Implicit Conversion
- ○ Conversion not allowed
- * Requires CONVERT when loss of precision or scale will occur
- — (shaded cell) same type

From: \ To:	binary	varbinary	char	varchar	nchar	nvarchar	datetime	smalldatetime	decimal	numeric	float	real	int(INT4)	smallint(INT2)	tinyint(INT1)	money	smallmoney	bit	timestamp	uniqueidentifier	image	ntext	text
binary	—	◐	◐	◐	◐	◐	◐	◐	◐	◐	○	○	◐	◐	◐	◐	◐	◐	◐	◐	◐	○	◐
varbinary	◐	—	◐	◐	◐	◐	◐	◐	◐	◐	○	○	◐	◐	◐	◐	◐	◐	◐	◐	◐	○	◐
char	●	●	—	◐	◐	◐	◐	◐	◐	◐	◐	◐	◐	◐	◐	●	●	◐	●	◐	◐	◐	◐
varchar	●	●	◐	—	◐	◐	◐	◐	◐	◐	◐	◐	◐	◐	◐	●	●	◐	●	◐	◐	◐	◐
nchar	●	●	◐	◐	—	◐	◐	◐	◐	◐	◐	◐	◐	◐	◐	●	●	◐	●	○	◐	◐	◐
nvarchar	●	●	◐	◐	◐	—	◐	◐	◐	◐	◐	◐	◐	◐	◐	●	●	◐	●	◐	◐	◐	◐
datetime	●	●	◐	◐	◐	◐	—	◐	◐	◐	●	●	●	●	●	●	●	●	●	○	○	○	○
smalldatetime	●	●	◐	◐	◐	◐	◐	—	●	●	●	●	●	◐	●	●	●	●	●	○	○	○	○
decimal	◐	◐	◐	◐	◐	◐	◐	◐	*	*	◐	◐	◐	◐	◐	◐	◐	◐	◐	○	○	○	○
numeric	◐	◐	◐	◐	◐	◐	◐	◐	*	*	◐	◐	◐	◐	◐	◐	◐	◐	◐	○	○	○	○
float	◐	◐	◐	◐	◐	◐	◐	◐	◐	◐	—	◐	◐	◐	◐	◐	◐	◐	◐	○	○	○	○
real	◐	◐	◐	◐	◐	◐	◐	◐	◐	◐	◐	—	◐	◐	◐	◐	◐	◐	◐	○	○	○	○
int(INT4)	◐	◐	◐	◐	◐	◐	◐	◐	◐	◐	◐	◐	—	◐	◐	◐	◐	◐	◐	○	○	○	○
smallint(INT2)	◐	◐	◐	◐	◐	◐	◐	◐	◐	◐	◐	◐	◐	—	◐	◐	◐	◐	◐	○	○	○	○
tinyint(INT1)	◐	◐	◐	◐	◐	◐	◐	◐	◐	◐	◐	◐	◐	◐	—	◐	◐	◐	◐	○	○	○	○
money	◐	◐	●	●	●	●	◐	◐	◐	◐	◐	◐	◐	◐	◐	—	◐	◐	◐	○	○	○	○
smallmoney	◐	◐	●	●	●	●	◐	◐	◐	◐	◐	◐	◐	◐	◐	◐	—	◐	◐	○	○	○	○
bit	◐	◐	◐	◐	◐	◐	◐	◐	◐	◐	◐	◐	◐	◐	◐	◐	◐	—	◐	○	○	○	○
timestamp	◐	◐	◐	◐	○	○	◐	◐	◐	◐	○	○	◐	◐	◐	◐	◐	◐	—	○	◐	○	○
uniqueidentifier	◐	◐	◐	◐	◐	○	○	○	○	○	○	○	○	○	○	○	○	○	○	—	○	◐	○
image	◐	◐	○	○	○	○	○	○	○	○	○	○	○	○	○	○	○	○	○	○	—	○	○
ntext	○	○	●	●	◐	◐	○	○	○	○	○	○	○	○	○	○	○	○	○	○	○	—	○
text	○	○	◐	◐	●	●	○	○	○	○	○	○	○	○	○	○	○	○	○	○	○	○	—

When calling the `CAST` function you need to provide the data type that the initial value should be cast as.

```
CAST(expression AS data type(<length>))
```

The expression can be any valid SQL expression or variable. The data type must be a valid type and will change based on the database provider that you use. The optional length parameter is used for `nchar`, `char`, `varchar`, `nvarchar`, `varbinary`, and `binary` data types.

If you attempt to make a conversion from to a number to fewer decimal places than the expression, then the value will be truncated to fit the cast data type. For example, if we wanted to cast 1.73349 as an integer:

```
SELECT
    CAST(1.73349 AS integer)
```

	(No column name)
1	1

Notice that the number was not rounded up; rather it was truncated. If we converted the same value to money, then we would get the following:

```
SELECT
    CAST(1.73349 AS money)
```

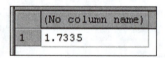

	(No column name)
1	1.7335

Here the results did round up. This seems to be a more meaningful conversion than the integer conversion since we would expect the data to be rounded appropriately. Be wary of converting floating-point numbers to integers for the reason that we just demonstrated: you will not get a rounded number, you will actually get a truncated number.

So, how is `CAST` really handy? Well, first of all, we can use `CAST` to create strings from numeric data. We can look at a more complex query where we are totalling the line item cost for each product on our orders. We want to print in plain text the line item information.

```
SELECT
    Orders.OrderID,
    Products.ProductName,
    'The total line item price is $' +
    CAST(
        CAST(
        ([Order Details].[UnitPrice]*[Quantity])*(1-[Discount])
        AS money)
    AS varchar(10))
```

```
FROM
    Products
    INNER JOIN
    (
        Orders INNER JOIN [Order Details]
        ON Orders.OrderID = [Order Details].OrderID
    )
    ON Products.ProductID = [Order Details].ProductID;
```

The results will display our custom text in the third column:

	OrderID	ProductName	(No column name)
1	10248	Queso Cabrales	The total line item price is $168.00
2	10248	Singaporean Hokkien Fried Mee	The total line item price is $98.00
3	10248	Mozzarella di Giovanni	The total line item price is $174.00
4	10249	Tofu	The total line item price is $167.40
5	10249	Manjimup Dried Apples	The total line item price is $1696.00
...	...	...	...
2151	11077	Wimmers gute Semmelknödel	The total line item price is $64.51
2152	11077	Louisiana Hot Spiced Okra	The total line item price is $17.00
2153	11077	Röd Kaviar	The total line item price is $29.70
2154	11077	Rhönbräu Klosterbier	The total line item price is $31.00
2155	11077	Original Frankfurter grüne Soße	The total line item price is $26.00

(2155 row(s) affected)

Had we not performed the CAST to a varchar(10) then we would have received an error:

```
Server: Msg 257, Level 16, State 3, Line 1
Implicit conversion from data type varchar to money is not allowed.
Use the CONVERT function to run this query.
```

This is a situation where an implicit conversion would make some sense, but SQL cannot perform this conversion and we are forced to specify the data conversion using the CAST or CONVERT functions.

Where else can the CAST function come in handy? Well, you cannot use the LIKE operator with numbers, but you can with strings. If you were looking for a product and you knew that it was $15.25, no maybe it was $15.52. OK, so you are not sure – it's either $15.25 or $15.52, but you cannot for the life of you remember. You could write a series of conditional statements to look for these ranges, but then again we can use string operations. So, we convert the price to a string and then use the LIKE to find our data:

```
SELECT
    ProductID,
    ProductName,
    UnitPrice
FROM Products
WHERE CAST(UnitPrice AS varchar(10)) LIKE '15%'
```

	ProductID	ProductName	UnitPrice
1	15	Genen Shouyu	15.5000
2	70	Outback Lager	15.0000
3	73	Röd Kaviar	15.0000

As you can see, we have applied the conversion as part of our WHERE clause. We convert the number to a string and then compare against the search criteria. Keep in mind that this will return to us any data that starts with 15, so be careful how you search since you could return more results than you bargained for.

As with our first example, we can chain multiple cast operators together to correctly format our data. We first converted to money to round our decimals then we converted to a string. Had we not added the conversion to the money data type then our results would be going past the second decimal place on our cost and you only want to show two decimal places when dealing with money.

CAST is the safe bet when you need to do a data conversion.

CONVERT

The CONVERT function is a bit more complex than the CAST operation since we can specify date styles as one of the parameters to the statement.

> **Oracle does not contain the CONVERT function; rather, it has one function for each type of conversion: TO_CHAR, TO_NUMBER, TO_DATE and so on.**

Let's first look at CONVERT to see what is in the function call:

```
CONVERT(data_ type(<length>), expression, <style>)
```

As with CAST, the length option is only used on the following data types: nchar, char, varchar, nvarchar, varbinary, and binary. The expression can be any valid SQL statement and the style is a date style for dealing with datetime and smalldatetime conversions as well as float, real, money, or smallmoney to string conversions. Below are several tables for the style values that can be used for the string conversions.

First, here is the datetime and smalldatetime to string conversion style settings:

Without century style number (yy)	With century style number (yyyy)	County Format or International Standard	Example output
-	0 or 100	Default	mon dd yyyy hh:miAM (or PM)
1	101	USA	mm/dd/yy
2	102	ANSI	yy.mm.dd

Without century style number (yy)	With century style number (yyyy)	County Format or International Standard	Example output
3	103	British/French	dd/mm/yy
	104	German	dd.mm.yy
5	105	Italian	dd-mm-yy
6	106	-	dd mon yy
7	107	-	Mon dd, yy
8	108	-	hh:mm:ss
-	9 or 109	Default + milliseconds	mon dd yyyy hh:mi:ss:mmmAM (or PM)
10	110	USA	mm-dd-yy
11	111	JAPAN	yy/mm/dd
12	112	ISO	yymmdd
-	13 or 113	Europe default + milliseconds	dd mon yyyy hh:mm:ss:mmm(24h)
14	114	-	hh:mi:ss:mmm(24h)
-	20 or 120	ODBC canonical	yyyy-mm-dd hh:mi:ss(24h)
-	21 or 121	ODBC canonical (with milliseconds)	yyyy-mm-dd hh:mi:ss.mmm(24h)
-	126	ISO8601	yyyy-mm-dd Thh:mm:ss:mmm(no spaces)
-	130	Kuwaiti	dd mon yyyy hh:mi:ss:mmmAM
-	131	Kuwaiti	dd/mm/yy hh:mi:ss:mmmAM

Note that SQL Server interprets two digit years as follows: if the year is less than 49 then the year is considered to be 20XX while anything 50 and over is considered 19XX. In order to avoid any confusion or future date issues it is recommended that you implement four digit years wherever possible.

To verify this, try the following:

```
SELECT
    CAST('1/1/50' AS smalldatetime) AS '1/1/50',
    CAST('1/1/48' AS smalldatetime) AS '1/1/48'
```

The result is what we expected:

	1/1/50	1/1/48
1	1950-01-01 00:00:00	2048-01-01 00:00:00

Let's look at some of the date conversions above. We will see some of the different styles that can be applied using the CONVERT statement.

```
SELECT
    CONVERT(varchar, getdate(), 1),
    CONVERT(varchar, getdate(), 2),
    CONVERT(varchar, getdate(), 3),
    CONVERT(varchar, getdate(), 4),
    CONVERT(varchar, getdate(), 5),
    CONVERT(varchar, getdate(), 6)
```

	(No column name)	(No column name)	(No column name)	(No column name)	(No column name)	(No column name)
1	02/14/01	01.02.14	14/02/01	14.02.01	14-02-01	14 Feb 01

For converting float or real values to strings you would have the following settings:

Value	Output
0 (default)	Six digits maximum. Use in scientific notation, when appropriate.
1	Always eight digits. Always use in scientific notation.
2	Always 16 digits. Always use in scientific notation.

Finally, for converting money or smallmoney to strings you would have these settings.

Value	Output
0 (default)	No commas and two digits to the right of the decimal point; for example, 4235.98.
1	Commas every three digits to the left of the decimal point, and two digits to the right of the decimal point; for example, 4,235.98.
2	No commas to the left of the decimal point, and four digits to the right of the decimal point; for example, 4235.9819.

Let's take a look at our price information query above and change the query to use the CONVERT function.

```
SELECT
    Orders.OrderID,
    Products.ProductName,
    'The total line item price is $' +
    CONVERT
```

```
   (varchar(10),
   CONVERT(money, ([Order Details].[UnitPrice]*[Quantity])*(1-[Discount]))))
FROM
   Products
   INNER JOIN
   (
      Orders INNER JOIN [Order Details]
      ON Orders.OrderID = [Order Details].OrderID
   )
   ON Products.ProductID = [Order Details].ProductID;
```

	OrderID	ProductName	(No column name)
1	10248	Queso Cabrales	The total line item price is $168.00
2	10248	Singaporean Hokkien Fried Mee	The total line item price is $98.00
3	10248	Mozzarella di Giovanni	The total line item price is $174.00
4	10249	Tofu	The total line item price is $167.40
5	10249	Manjimup Dried Apples	The total line item price is $1696.00
...	...	...	...
2151	11077	Wimmers gute Semmelknödel	The total line item price is $64.51
2152	11077	Louisiana Hot Spiced Okra	The total line item price is $17.00
2153	11077	Röd Kaviar	The total line item price is $29.70
2154	11077	Rhönbräu Klosterbier	The total line item price is $31.00
2155	11077	Original Frankfurter grüne Soße	The total line item price is $26.00

```
(2155 row(s) affected)
```

As you can see, the results are the same. There is very little difference (with the exception of the conversion options) between CAST and CONVERT.

A less complex example can be seen in MySQL. Here, we want to convert a hexadecimal number to a decimal number:

f represents the hexadecimal number, 16 represents the source base and 10 represents the target base.

As you can see, SQL is very flexible with conversions. It is capable of handling many conversions on its own while it provides the flexibility needed to force conversions if the developer feels that it is necessary.

Summary

In this chapter you have been exposed to the math and conversion functions provided by SQL. There are many trigonometric functions available for use, but many of the uses of those functions will be well outside the day-to-day business problems that you will see. On the other hand, functions such as CEILING and FLOOR provide quick rounding methods and SIGN evaluates the positive/negative sign of a number. A function that you may find yourself using more often than others is the POWER function that will let you perform exponential calculations on numbers.

As important as the math functions are, probably more important in day-to-day development are the CAST and CONVERT functions for performing data conversions. These functions are very powerful and can be used to format data, and to provide enhanced search capabilities and powerful string manipulation operations. Data conversions are very common in business environments and will become a fact of life at some point.

We have covered some of the more basic computational functions of SQL, but it is now time to move into an area in which SQL shines – aggregate functions. In the next chapter you will see how to move away from row-by-row calculations and into table and data-level calculations for creating summary and rollup data. You will also see how to perform statistical calculations on your data. There's much more to come and it will only get more fun and exciting from here on.

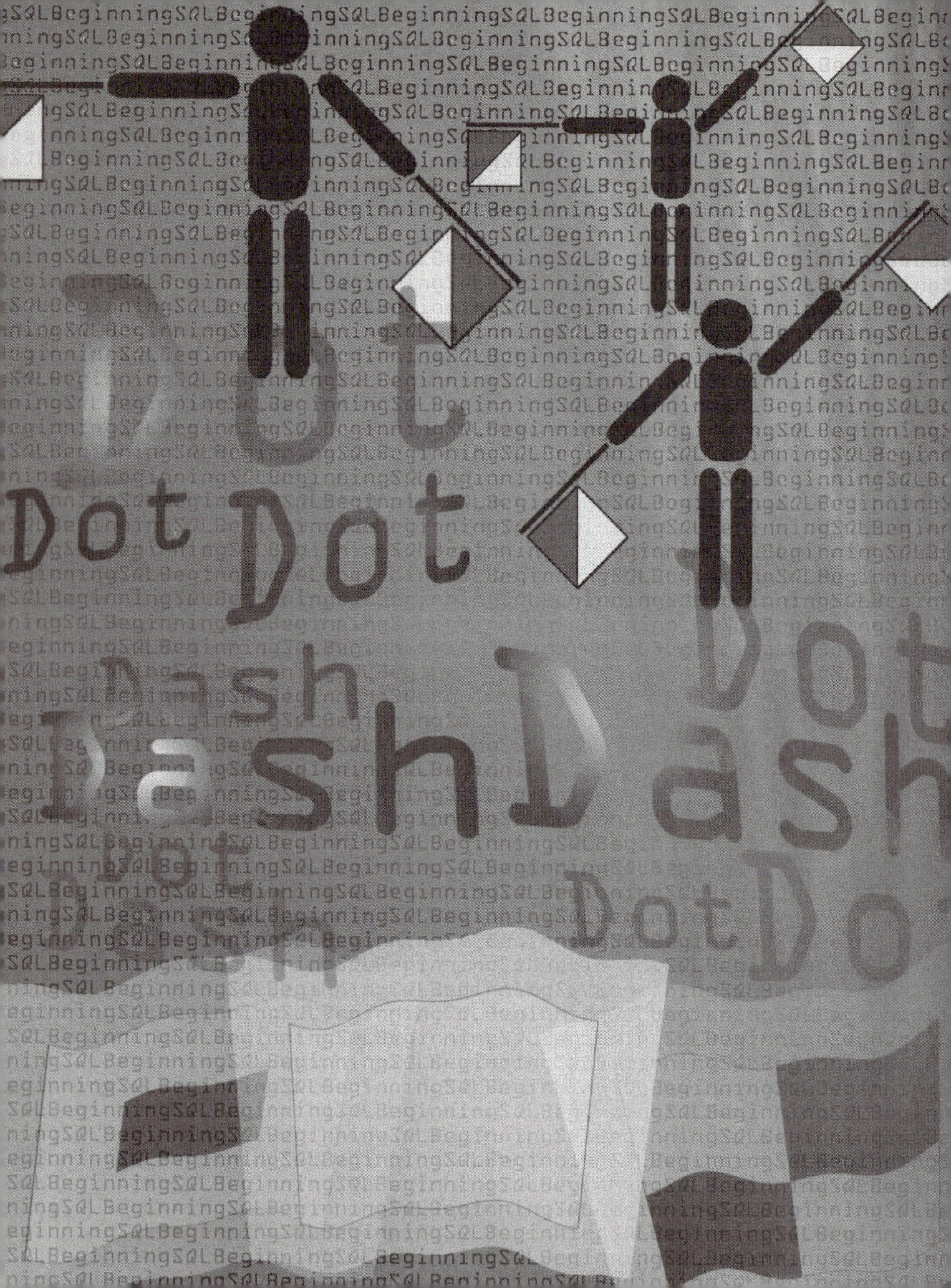

Grouping – Using Aggregate Functions

In this chapter we're going to discuss operators, functions, and clauses that work with *Sets*, or *groups* of records, fields or values. These are often called **Set operators** (or functions, clauses, etc.) or **Aggregate operators** (or functions, clauses, etc.). These pertain to *working with records as a group*.

So, this chapter will cover:

- ❑ A brief introduction to Set Theory

- ❑ Looking at the Aggregate Operators UNION, EXCEPT and INTERSECT

- ❑ Looking at the Aggregate Functions of COUNT, MAX and MIN, SUM and AVG, as well as ANY and EVERY

- ❑ Looking at the Aggregate Clauses of GROUP BY and HAVING

- ❑ Pulling all our new knowledge together to build a Sales Analysis Query

This may look like a lot, but at the end of the chapter, you will know Aggregate functions inside out.

To help us along, we're going to encounter a lot of diagrams in this chapter. Some of the concepts are extremely difficult to grasp in just words, but make themselves crystal clear when seen graphically. We'll begin with a little background, to help us understand the principles involved in what we're working with.

Set Theory

A set is a collection of *anything* that is treated as a group by some definition. This definition may be completely arbitrary. In the early 19th century, Bernard Bolzano referred to a set as:

> *"An embodiment of the idea or concept which we conceive when we regard the arrangement of its parts as a matter of indifference."*

Set Theory is important to us in so far as it forms the basis of database design.

Sets have the following general properties:

- ❑ They can have *zero* or more members: if it contains no members, it is known as a **null** set (or an empty set).

- ❑ They can be totally *disconnected* from one another (having no members in common).

- ❑ They can share *some* members with another set, and not share others.

- ❑ They can be part of a *larger* set (in which case it is a *Subset* of the larger set), or they can contain other sets (in which case, it is a *Superset*).

- ❑ They can be exactly the *same* as another set (having *all* members in common, and *no* members apart), the only difference between them being their respective *definitions*.

- ❑ They can contain anything: the *elements* in a set do not need to share *any* properties in common, other than the fact that they have been *defined* as belonging to the same set.

An "element" refers to a member of a set.

Let's take a look at how we can understand the concept of a set in the context of database design. Take a box: we will define the box by a name, calling it "The Set of Employees".

The Set of Employees

The box is empty to start with; it is a null set. We can then put a smaller box inside it, called "The Set of One Employee." And this, in turn, contains a series of smaller boxes. These are called `EmployeeID`, `LastName`, `FirstName`, and so on:

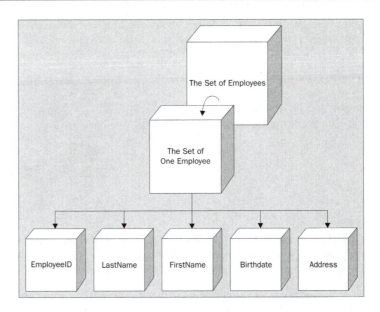

Each one of these smaller boxes is a set too. "The Set of Employees" is now defined as being a set of "The Set of One Employee" sets. It can have as many of these sets as we want to put into it, and each "The Set of One Employee" set is defined as being a set of smaller sets.

A set that is totally contained within another set is called a *subset* of the larger set. It can be up to the same size as the containing set. As long as all of its *elements* are contained within the containing set, it remains a subset. A set that contains a subset is called a *superset* of the subset.

There are other types of relationships that sets can have. Consider the following Venn diagram:

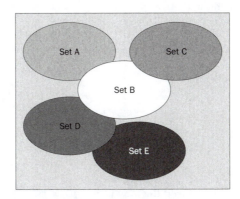

This diagram depicts five different sets. The sets share *elements* in common. Set A and set B intersect, set B intersects with sets C, D, and A, set D intersects with set B and E, and so on.

A set intersects with another set if they have elements in common.

As we can see, subsets suggest themselves. For example, the area intersected by A and B could be called "The set of elements shared by sets A and B". Now, this might not appear particularly useful, until we consider how it might be applied in a practical situation.

For example, let's rename set A "The Set of One Employee", set B "The Set of One Order", set C "The Set of One Customer", set D "The Set of One Order Detail", and set E "The Set of One Product".

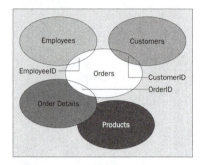

The subsets we talked about earlier (the areas that share elements in common) are those areas that lie at the intersections of the sets (where they overlap each other). At this point, you may have noticed that the sets in the diagram represent a single row from each of the tables in the Northwind database.

A table is a set of rows, and a row is a set of fields (although these aren't shown in our diagram). And even a field may be understood as a set, as it contains a lot more than just the data contained in it: it also has properties, such as data type, length, precision, etc.

The labels that point to the intersections of the sets represent particular *fields* in the rows. These fields are used to define *relationships* between the tables. If two rows in different tables share the same field, the tables are related. In effect, these fields define intersections of the sets. Here's our final "incarnation" of the illustration, showing the actual tables, fields, and relationships:

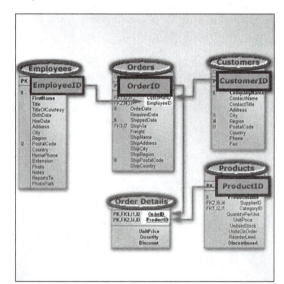

The reason that the tables are structured this way is to relate them. Let's take a look at a single Order, and its associated records in the other tables. This is a screen shot of one of the sample forms that comes with the Northwind Database. It is called "Orders" and depicts the information from a single Order Record:

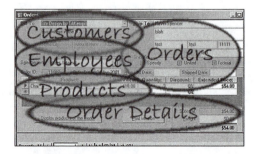

The Orders table information is found in the upper right-hand side of the form. Each Order has an OrderID, which is unique in the table to that one Order. In the upper left-hand side of the form is the related data from the Customers table. The way that this record is fetched is by using the OrderID from the Orders field. Each Customers record has a CustomerID field, and the Orders record has a CustomerID field, which is used to identify which Customer that Order belongs to.

The Orders table also has an EmployeeID field, which identifies the Employee that this particular Order belongs to. This form uses the EmployeeID field value from the Orders record to fetch the Employees record that is related to it. This information is displayed in the left-hand side of the form.

The bottom of the form is rather interesting. Notice that there is a sub-form (a form within a form) for the individual Product information for that order. As more than one Product can be included in a single Order, there may be many Products table records associated with a single Order. Therefore, the Order Details table, which stores the Product information specific to each Order, has an OrderID (Foreign Key) field, which identifies the Order that this particular Order Details record belongs to. All of the Order Details records associated with this Order are displayed in the sub-form at the bottom.

The Product Name and information for each Order Details record are fetched from the Products table. Each Order Details record has a ProductID (Foreign Key) field that "points to" (identifies) the Products table's (Primary Key) ProductID field for that record.

So, as we can see, these "intersections" are very important to not only our understanding of Set Theory in general, but to database functionality especially! These special fields that are shared in common between tables provide *links* between the tables, just as anyone who is in my Set of Friends provides a "link" to anyone who is in their Set of Friends, who doesn't happen to be in mine.

The reason for all of these links and relationships is a database concept called **normalization**, the fundamentals of which were introduced to us in Chapter 3. It is virtually the same thing as "Optimization" as we programmers would put it. As we learned, the idea is that we store information in the smallest possible space. This means that we don't duplicate information in the tables. The ultimate goal of normalization is to have just *one* copy of any piece of individual data in our database (other than primary and foreign key fields, which contain relatively small data (Unique ID values)). So, for example, rather than putting the Customer information for an Order in the Orders record (which means that each Orders record has all the Customer information, and that the Customer information is duplicated in records sharing the same Customer), we create a separate table for Customers. Then, we only have to add data to the database when a new Customer is added. By creating a primary key (CustomerID) in the Customers table, and a related foreign key (CustomerID) in the Orders table, we can always pull the right Customer information for any Order.

Subsets

Now let's take a look at subsets. A subset is a set that is *totally* encompassed by its parent set. As already mentioned, it can contain as many as *all* of the elements of the parent set; it is simply a subset by definition. And it is not the same as the parent set, even though it might contain all the same members. A SELECT query is a perfect example of creating a subset. The first part of the query (SELECT) tells the database to create a subset. The next part of the query specifies what elements will be in the subset. The next part indicates the target set from which we want to select – the table from which the data will be retrieved. And the last part contains specific instructions on how to arrange the elements in the resulting subset. For example:

```
SELECT * FROM Employees
```

This query tells the database to create a subset of the Employees table, and to populate it with *all* the fields in *all* the records in the table. This is a perfect example of a subset having the same members as the parent set.

Now let's take a look at a slightly different example:

```
SELECT EmployeeID, LastName, FirstName FROM Employees
WHERE BirthDate < '01/01/1950'
```

This query specifies that the subset should have only three fields from the parent set, and only those records which match the criterion in the WHERE clause. In this case, the subset could be much smaller – in fact, it could have zero elements, but it would still be a set (albeit an empty set), and it would still be a subset.

Finally, let's look at the same example, with the arrangement details added:

```
SELECT EmployeeID, LastName, FirstName FROM Employees
WHERE BirthDate < '01/01/1950'
ORDER BY LastName ASC
```

The last part of the query tells the database to sort the records by last name.

Sets and Aggregate Fields

Why all this talk about sets and subsets and Set Theory? Well, grasping the theory behind relational database design is important, and it becomes increasingly important to understand the logic behind the database when dealing with Aggregate functions and clauses.

How should we approach the task of constructing a list all of the employees, and the number of orders that each employee has sold? Well, we're going to have to pull information from *two tables*, and we're going to have to calculate and combine the information in some way.

We want to end up with *one* record per employee, showing the employee information as well as the number of orders. One way in which we can achieve this is through using the JOIN query, and we have already seen how to use this, in Chapter 8.

The COUNT() Aggregate function can count all of the orders for the employees, but what happens when we try to combine these results with information from the Employees table? Let's try the following SQL Statement:

```
SELECT Employees.EmployeeID, Employees.LastName, Employees.FirstName,
COUNT(Orders.OrderID) AS ct
FROM Employees INNER JOIN Orders ON Employees.EmployeeID = Orders.EmployeeID;
```

Here's what we get:

```
Server: Msg 8118, Level 16, State 1, Line 1
Column 'Employees.EmployeeID' is invalid in the select list because it is
not contained in an aggregate function and there is no GROUP BY clause.
Server: Msg 8118, Level 16, State 1, Line 1
Column 'Employees.LastName' is invalid in the select list because it is
not contained in an aggregate function and there is no GROUP BY clause.
Server: Msg 8118, Level 16, State 1, Line 1
Column 'Employees.FirstName' is invalid in the select list because it is
not contained in an aggregate function and there is no GROUP BY clause.
```

Grids Messages

Okay, what happened? Well, let's begin our analysis by splitting the results into Aggregate and non-Aggregate fields, and perform a query with each one separately:

```
SELECT Employees.EmployeeID, Employees.LastName, Employees.FirstName
FROM Employees INNER JOIN Orders ON Employees.EmployeeID = Orders.EmployeeID;
```

When we run this query in SQL Query Analyzer, we get the following results:

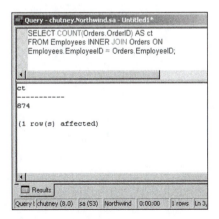

Now, this is interesting: we see "Nancy Davolio" over and over again. As we continue down the list, we come across other Employees, most of whom are listed many times, just as Nancy is. Why is that?

Well, remember, we did a `JOIN` query: the `JOIN` query creates a record for *each* of the records in the tables being `JOIN`ed. Since there are many `Orders` for each `Employee`, we see `Employee` information for each `Orders` record. If we had pulled the `OrderID` field, we would have seen this immediately. Each of the resulting records would have a unique `OrderID`.

Now for the second "part" of our query:

```
SELECT COUNT(Orders.OrderID) AS ct
FROM Employees INNER JOIN Orders ON Employees.EmployeeID = Orders.EmployeeID;
```

This results in just *one* record:

One result set has as many records as there are Orders. The other result set has only one (*Aggregate*) field. How could we possibly combine a set of many records with a set of one? How many records would the resulting set *have*?

In other words, we're trying to combine elements of two different *types* (Aggregate and non-aggregate) into the same set, and they just won't fit. An **Aggregate field** is a field that is made by combining the values of one or more other fields. When using Aggregate functions (COUNT, SUM, etc) and set operators (GROUP BY, UNION, etc), we can't combine Aggregate and non-aggregate fields in the same table, for obvious reasons.

So, let's take a look at the Aggregate Operators, and see how we might deal with the problem of combining different types of values on the same query.

Aggregate Operators: UNION, EXCEPT, INTERSECT

The ISO SQL Standard supports three set operators: UNION, EXCEPT, and INTERSECT. However, I don't plan to discuss EXCEPT and INTERSECT in detail, other than to diagram them in the following sections.

UNION

The UNION operator combines two tables (or result sets) by taking all of the records from the first table, and adding all of the records from the second table. If the DISTINCT operator is used, duplicate records (from *both* result sets) will be eliminated (combined, or grouped). If the ALL operator is used, the records are not combined in any way. Duplicates are included.

Table 1	Operator	Table 2	Result
1 Adams			1 Adams
1 Adams			
3 Cantor	UNION (DISTINCT)	3 Cantor	3 Cantor
4 Douglas		4 Douglas	4 Douglas
5		6	5 Eames

Table 1	Operator	Table 2	Result
Eames		Spencer	
		7 Blalock	6 Spencer
		8 Gosnell	7 Blalock
			8 Gosnell
1 Adams			1 Adams
1 Adams			1 Adams
3 Cantor			3 Cantor
4 Douglas		3 Cantor	4 Douglas
5 Eames	UNION ALL	4 Douglas	5 Eames
		6 Spencer	3 Cantor
		7 Blalock	4 Douglas
		8 Gosnell	6 Spencer
			7 Blalock
			8 Gosnell

EXCEPT

The EXCEPT operator SELECTs all records from the first table, EXCEPT those that are duplicated in the second table. If the DISTINCT operator is used in conjunction with EXCEPT, duplicate records in the result set are eliminated (combined, or grouped). The ALL operator allows duplicate records.

Table 1	Operator	Table 2	Result
1 Adams			1 Adams
1 Adams			
3 Cantor		3 Cantor	5 Eames
4 Douglas	EXCEPT (DISTINCT)	4 Douglas	
5 Eames		6 Spencer	
		7 Blalock	
		8 Gosnell	
1 Adams			1 Adams
1 Adams	EXCEPT ALL		1 Adams
3 Cantor		3 Cantor	
4 Douglas		4 Douglas	5 Eames

Table 1	Operator	Table 2	Result
5 Eames		6 Spencer	
		7 Blalock	
		8 Gosnell	

INTERSECT

The INTERSECT operator SELECTs only those records from the first table that *are* duplicated in the second table. In other words, it is the exact opposite of EXCEPT. When DISTINCT is used, duplicate records in the results are eliminated.

1 **Adams**			
1 **Adams**			**3** **Cantor**
3 **Cantor**	**INTERSECT** **(DISTINCT)**	**3** **Cantor**	**4** **Douglas**
4 **Douglas**		**3** **Cantor**	
5 **Eames**		**4** **Douglas**	

Table continued on following page

Table 1	Operator	Table 2	Result
		6 Spencer	
		7 Blalock	
1 Adams			
1 Adams			3 Cantor
3 Cantor		3 Cantor	3 Cantor
4 Douglas	INTERSECT ALL	3 Cantor	4 Douglas
5 Eames		4 Douglas	
		6 Spencer	
		7 Blalock	

Note: DISTINCT is implied; it is the default.

Here's another way to look at it:

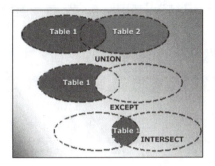

The syntax for using UNION, EXCEPT or INTERSECT is as follows:

```
SELECT [DISTINCT | ALL] Table1 UNION | EXCEPT | INTERSECT Table2
```

Using UNION

Let's suppose that the CEO of Northwind wants to send out a memo to all employees who are due to retire in 10 years, and all employees who report to Steven Buchanan (EmployeeID #5). We could use two queries to get our list, but we could also use a UNION query:

Firstly, we construct the first query: it SELECTs the Employee Information for the qualifying employees:

```
SELECT EmployeeID, LastName, FirstName FROM Employees
WHERE BirthDate < DateAdd(yyyy, -55, GetDate())
```

The result set for this is one record:

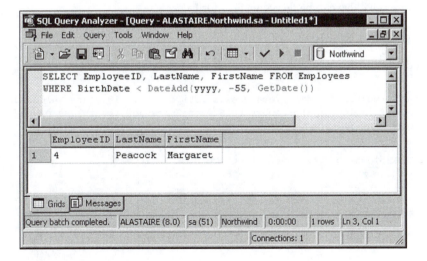

Now we construct the second query. It SELECTs the same data as the first, but uses different criteria, so that the result set contains all Employees that report to Steven Buchanan (EmployeeID # 5):

```
(SELECT EmployeeID, LastName, FirstName FROM Employees
WHERE ReportsTo = 5)
```

Here are the results from this query:

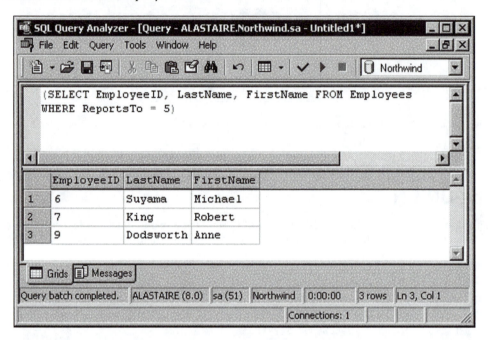

As we can see, the results from these two queries have nothing in common, *unless we say they do.* Well, they do have *one* (important!) thing in common: they both have the **exact same fields** in them. This is because we are combining these records into a *single* result set. In order to combine them, the structure of the result sets will have to be the same, field for field.

Now let's put them together:

Pseudocode:

```
Find all records for employees due to retire within 10 years, along with all
records of employees who report to Steven Buchanan, regardless of their age. Don't
duplicate any records.
```

```
SELECT EmployeeID, LastName, FirstName FROM Employees
WHERE BirthDate < DateAdd(yyyy, -55, GetDate())
UNION
(SELECT EmployeeID, LastName, FirstName FROM Employees
WHERE ReportsTo = 5)
```

This will generate the following results:

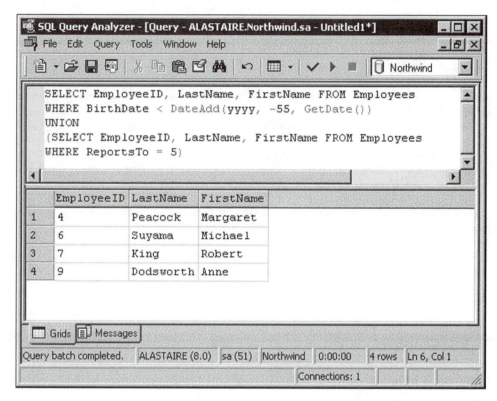

The two result sets have been combined into a single result set. If any of the elements in the set were duplicates, they would have been removed, because, as we saw earlier, DISTINCT is implied when we don't use the ALL quantifier. Also, this way of testing the queries separately before putting them together means that we can check that it is performing properly and returning the correct results.

Using EXCEPT and INTERSECT

Support for EXCEPT and INTERSECT is not present in most DBMS's: Oracle is the only database vendor that I know of which supports these. MySQL, usually the best in the compatibility department, hasn't even got support for UNION! However, it is fairly straightforward to see how they might be emulated.

For example, INTERSECT is the part of the UNION set that is shared by both tables (where the tables *intersect*). So, to get the INTERSECTION of the two tables, we would pull all records from table 1 that are duplicated in table 2:

Pseudocode for INTERSECT:

```
Find all records for employees due to retire within 10 years, who report to Steven
Buchanan.
```

```
SELECT EmployeeID, LastName, FirstName
FROM Employees
WHERE BirthDate < DateAdd(yyyy, -55, GetDate())
AND EmployeeID IN
(SELECT EmployeeID FROM Employees
WHERE ReportsTo = 5)
```

The sections of the pseudocode that pertain to the corresponding sections of the SQL have been emboldened for clarity. As we can see, there are actually two queries in this one SELECT statement. In order to perform a UNION, INTERSECT, or EXCEPT query, the database has to query both tables, whether it's (expressly) in our SQL code or not. In other words, what we are doing here is to perform both queries **explicitly**, rather than implicitly (through the syntax). By using the AND operator, we are in essence selecting only those records which match the first criteria (in essence, query number 1), *and* which are found in the result set that the second (nested) query returns.

In this case, there would be no records, because the two tables don't intersect; they have no members in common.

In the same way, an EXCEPT query gets only rows from table 1, so we could use a sub-query to eliminate the rows in table 1 that are found in table 2.

Pseudocode for EXCEPT:

```
Find all records for employees due to retire within 10 years, who do not report to
Steven Buchanan.
```

Another way of putting this, which would give us a better clue as to what syntax to use, would be:

```
Find all records for employees due to retire within 10 years, EXCEPT those
employees who report to Steven Buchanan.
```

```
SELECT EmployeeID, LastName, FirstName FROM Employees
WHERE BirthDate < DateAdd(yyyy, -55, GetDate())
AND EmployeeID NOT IN
(SELECT EmployeeID FROM Employees
WHERE ReportsTo = 5)
```

You'll notice that we don't have to include a set operator to emulate these two other operators: it's only pulling records from the first set.

If we can do this with a single WHERE clause, instead of using set operators, what are set operators useful for? Remember that the rules for set operators state that the tables must have the same data type (and length), and number and order of columns. *However*, they don't have to be derived from the same table, or even the same database. The UNION operator is excellent for combining data across tables and across databases.

Let's conclude with an example of a *useful* UNION query:

Try It out – Build a Phone Book

We need to put together a phone book of all employees and customers. There are several problems here: for one thing, the employees and customers are in separate tables, which have different structures. The `Employees` table has a `FirstName` and `LastName` field. The `Customers` table has only a `ContactName` field.

We should be able to take care of this by concatenation (joining string data – see Chapter 11). We can take the Employee's `FirstName` and concatenate it with the Employee's `LastName` (and a space in between) to build a "virtual" `ContactName` field, to match the `ContactName` field in the `Customers` table query.

1. Construct two separate queries, one to the `Customers` table, and one to the `Employees` table. We will be starting with the `ContactName` field in the `Customers` table, and the `FirstName` and `LastName` fields in the `Employees` table:

```
SELECT (FirstName + ' ' + LastName) AS ContactName
FROM Employees
```

```
SELECT ContactName
FROM Customers
```

2. Add the `Phone` and `Extension` fields to the query. The `Customers` table `HomePhone` field, and the `Employees` table `Phone` field will be `SELECT`ed. As for the `Extension`, we are going to create an `Extension` field in the result set from the `Customers` table, and populate it with some data:

```
SELECT (FirstName + ' ' + LastName) AS ContactName, Extension,
HomePhone AS Phone
FROM Employees
```

```
SELECT ContactName, 'N/A' AS Extension,
Phone
FROM Customers
```

3. We are going to create an extra field in both result sets, called `Employee`, which will identify whether the Phone Book Entry is an `Employee` (1) or a `Customer` (0):

```
SELECT (FirstName + ' ' + LastName) AS ContactName, Extension,
HomePhone, 1 AS Employee
FROM Employees
```

```
SELECT ContactName, 'N/A' AS Extension,
Phone, 0 AS Employee
FROM Customers
```

4. All that's left is adding the UNION to join the two queries, and the two result sets together:

```
SELECT (FirstName + ' ' + LastName) AS ContactName, Extension,
HomePhone, 1 AS Employee
FROM Employees
UNION
SELECT ContactName, 'N/A' AS Extension,
Phone, 0 AS Employee
FROM Customers
```

The results, when the query is run, look like this:

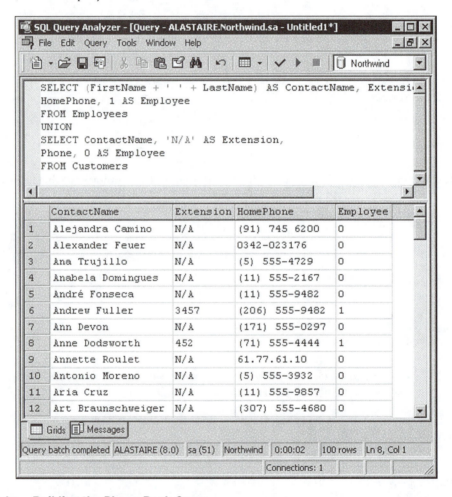

How It Works – Building the Phone Book Query

If each entry has to have all the same fields, and all the same data types for each field, (ContactName, Extension, Phone) how do we take care of the fact that the Extension field in the Employees table has no corresponding column in the Customers table? Secondly, how do we identify who is an Employee and who is a Customer? Take a look at the graphic depiction of our dilemma below:

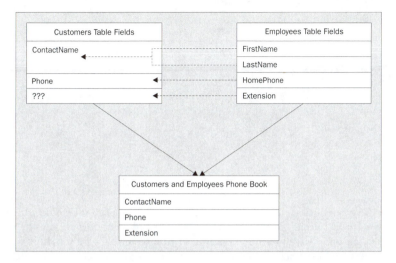

Well, it turns out that the solution is relatively simple: we know that we have to construct two *identically-structured* "tables" in our query, and we can do it by combining the values of fields to make one out of two, in the case of the Employee's `FirstName` and `LastName` fields. In the case of the missing "Extension" field in the `Customers` table, we simply create one in that query (by adding it to the `SELECT` statement's field list), and assign it a string literal value ("N/A" – Not Applicable). We could give it a `NULL` value, but I prefer "N/A", as it is more meaningful than nothing!

One last problem remains, however. How do we identify `Customers` versus `Employees` in the Phone Book? We are, after all, constructing *identical* tables in our two queries to `UNION` together.

We add a field to both queries, called `Employee`. Now, we know that an Entry in the Phone Book is going to be one of only two possible alternatives: `Customer`, or `Employee`. The smallest size that we can store one of two distinct values is, of course, a bit. In databases, a bit field has a value of either 1 or 0. In the query to the `Employees` table, we assign it a value of 1 (`True, Yes`). In the query to the `Customers` table, we assign it value of 0 (`False, Not an Employee`):

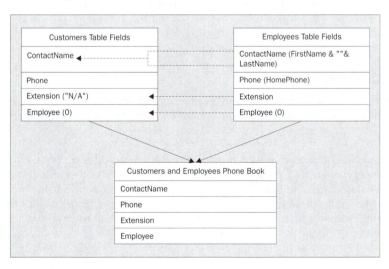

The result (recapping):

```
SELECT (FirstName + ' ' + LastName) AS ContactName, Extension,
HomePhone, 1 AS Employee
FROM Employees

UNION

SELECT ContactName, 'N/A' AS Extension,
Phone, 0 AS Employee
FROM Customers
```

Aliasing

Notice that in the first query we *alias* the ContactName field (assign it a name which we choose) to match the name of the field in the second query? Now, it isn't necessary to join the two result sets together; in fact, we don't have to use field names at all if we don't want to. However, we put them in so that the result set would have significant field names. In fact, the whole point of aliasing is to have significant field names in our result set that we can work with: if we're working with our database programmatically, that is, not directly viewing the records through any kind of interface, but writing some code (ADO, Visual Basic, whatever) that interacts with the database, our query is going to select records. However, how will we refer to them in our code? ADO does support referencing fields in a recordset by their index, or ordinal position, in the set, but that's not always an option, and it's not always convenient.

When we run a query to the database, the names given to the resulting rows are usually assigned automatically by the database. Usually, our query SELECTs fields by name, or the fields SELECTed are not manipulated (changed) in any way, such as by GROUPing, other Aggregate functions, or other operations that change the actual *structure* of the result set; the database just assigns the corresponding field names to the result set's fields.

However, when the field is derived from some operation other than simply pulling it intact from the table, such as is the case with the Employees FirstName and LastName fields, which were combined into a single field in the result set, what name does it have? The answer is, if we don't assign it a name (alias it), the database will. However, how do we find out the name the database gave the field, so that we can reference it by name? Well, there are ways, but none anywhere near as easy as simply aliasing the field during the query.

Data Type Compatibility

Also, note the way that a string literal ('N/A' in the Customers result set) is being combined with a database field (Extension, in the Employees table), which is possible because *all string data types are compatible*.

In most database operations, other than storing data, the various different types of data within a certain grouping of data types are all compatible. That is, we can use any kind of string data with any other kind of string data; we can combine char and nvarchar data in our calculations, for example. If we need to store the result, we would have to CAST or CONVERT (see Chapter 12) the value to the proper data type for the field we are storing it in. The reason for this is that when the data is stored, it is stored in a fixed format.

We can also combine any numeric data type with any other numeric data type, including money. For example, we could multiply an Integer data type value pulled from a table by a floating point decimal value. In order to UPDATE the field with the resulting data (store it back in the database), however, we would have to ROUND it down to the nearest Integer value.

Date-time values are *somewhat* compatible with each other. The rules for Date-time values are a bit more complicated, though; see the "Rules" section below for details.

In Conclusion

Note how the Extension field is either an extension or N/A, and the Employee field (the last one on the right) is either 0 or 1.

We can now see the usefulness of the UNION operator. This query could not have been constructed as a single query without it.

Rules for Aggregate Operators

These rules apply to all Aggregate operators:

❑ Columns in the two queries must have the same data type value, and be in the same order. If the names do not correspond, a random name will be assigned by the DBMS.

❑ DISTINCT is implied when we don't use the ALL quantifier.

Rules for All Aggregate Functions, Clauses, and Operators

❑ Aggregate and Non-Aggregate values may not be combined in a Result set.

❑ All numeric values are compatible. This includes derived numeric data types such as Currency.

❑ All BIT or BIT VARYING values are compatible.

❑ All BLOB (Binary Large Object) values are compatible. This would include the Access OLE and SQL Server IMAGE data types.

❑ All String values (CHAR, VARCHAR, NCHAR VARYING, CLOB and NCLOB) are compatible, providing they share the same character set. This would include the Access MEMO and SQL Server TEXT data types.

❑ All Date values are compatible.

❑ All TIME and TIME WITH TIME ZONE values are compatible.

❑ All TIMESTAMP and TIMESTAMP WITH TIME ZONE values are compatible.

❑ All Year-Month Interval values are compatible.

❑ All Day-Time Interval values are compatible.

❑ All Boolean values are compatible.

❑ All REF values of the same referenced type (UDT) are compatible.

❑ All UDT values whose most specific types have some common super-type are compatible.

Aggregate Functions

Aggregate functions are so called because they work with groups of values, and reduce them to single values. And here is where the first rule mentioned in that list above comes into play: the values returned by these functions are all Aggregate values, and so cannot be combined with non-aggregate values in a query. We'll talk more about this a little later.

The syntax for any Aggregate function is:

```
<general set function> ::=
<set function type> ([ DISTINCT | ALL ] Column expression)
```

Let's start with the ones we're more likely to run into.

COUNT

The COUNT function does exactly what we might expect: it counts records. However, with the addition of a parameter value, we can use it to count by specific columns in different ways. For example, if we omit the column expression, we are left with, for example:

```
SELECT COUNT(*) FROM Employees
```

> The "*" can be used instead of "ALL" with COUNT in ISO SQL and just about every DBMS).

This would return the count of all records in the Employees table.

Aggregates are DISTINCTly Different

However, we can be more specific in specifying the records to be counted, in the following way:

```
SELECT COUNT(DISTINCT ReportsTo) FROM Employees
```

This query counts the number of ReportsTo fields in the Employees table. However, *before* it counts the ReportsTo fields, it eliminates any records from the result set which have duplicate ReportsTo values in them. For example, if we run the following SELECT query on the Employees table for all ReportsTo fields, we get the following result set:

```
SELECT ReportsTo FROM Employees
```

Now, as we can see, if we were to do a SELECT DISTINCT on this field alone, we would end up with two records. The NULL field would not be counted. We would get the following result set:

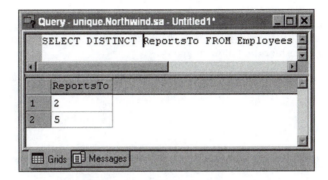

Now, that's two records. So, when we COUNT that set, we get 2.

> **NULL fields are not included in any result set which uses the DISTINCT operator with an Aggregate function, such as COUNT, SUM, AVG, UNION, INTERSECT, and EXCEPT.**

A note about aliasing and Aggregates: when running a SQL query that returns Aggregate values, it is important to alias any fields that we're going to work with in an application. These fields may be derived from fields in the table, but their names will not correspond to any in the table we fetched them from, unless we *give* them a name (alias). Therefore, if we don't alias them, we won't know how to refer to them, as the DBMS will assign them a random name. So, the query above would be better written as:

```
SELECT COUNT(*) AS NumSupervisors FROM Employees
```

The derived row (NumSupervisors) can then be accessed by its new name.

Performance Tip: The COUNT function, as well as the other Aggregate functions, is not particularly easy on performance. If we want to get the count of records returned by a query with SQL Server, we can access the @@ROWCOUNT variable, which always contains the number of rows affected by the last query of the connection. Here's an example of a query that uses @@ROWCOUNT:

```
SELECT EmployeeID FROM Employees
SELECT @@ROWCOUNT
```

This query actually returns a little MORE information than the original (SELECT COUNT(*) FROM Employees), but uses fewer resources. Depending on how we run the tests, we can get different results, but @@ROWCOUNT is faster overall. In the context of this exercise, however, we'll be better off getting the @@ROWCOUNT value, in terms of performance.

> *Remember that NULL values in Aggregate functions are ignored. For example, if we have 9 records, but one of them has a NULL value, COUNT(*) would return 9, but COUNT(ReportsTo) would return 8.*

MAX and MIN

MAX and MIN are the exact opposite of each other. These two operators compare all of the values in the fields returned by a column expression. MAX returns the maximum value, and MIN returns the minimum value. For example, consider the following query:

```
SELECT MAX(LastName) AS Last, MIN(LastName) As First
FROM Employees
```

This query yields the following results:

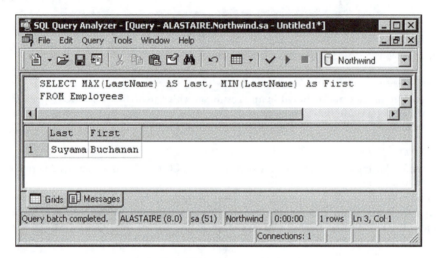

As we can see, these are the last and first LastName values from the table, ordered alphabetically. These functions can be used on any type of numeric, date, or character data type, except for CLOB and NCLOB (TEXT in SQL Server and MySQL). These exceptions are what is often referred to as "Long Text," "Long Binary," "Large Object," or "Binary" data types. They are special data types that are not of a fixed length, and are often *containers* for binary data, such as images, etc. In order to be able to sort something, we have to have some method of Collation (Rules for sorting), as we've talked about in Chapter 11, but these data types are containers, not fixed data. Therefore, there is no way to know how to "sort" them. Even if we're storing, for example, text data in a SQL Server Text field, the database has no Collation to go by.

SUM and AVG

These two functions are grouped together because they operate on the same data type: numeric. Let's start with a "simple" example. What this query does is to calculate the *totals* (SUM) for each Order in the Orders table of the Northwind database. However, since each Order can contain multiple Products, and since the Product and Price information for each Order is stored in the Order Details table, we will be querying the Order Details table.

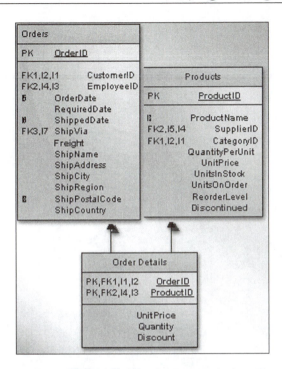

In order to do this, let's start small: the Total price for any individual Product [Order Details] in an Order is calculated using three fields: Unit Price, Quantity, and Discount. The Unit Price multiplied by the Quantity (UnitPrice * Quantity) gives us the "raw" (undiscounted) price. The Discount field stores a Real value, which is the *percentage* of discount given to that particular Order. Therefore, to calculate the Discounted Price of any Product Order, we have to subtract the Discount value from 1 (1 – Discount), divide that by 100 ((1 – Discount) / 100), and multiply that (percentage) by the calculated Price (Unit Price * Quantity):

```
SELECT SUM(
( (UnitPrice * Quantity) *
( (1 - Discount) / 100 )
) * 100)
FROM [Order Details]
```

Now, if you run this query all by itself, you'll get something like the following (depending on the contents of your tables):

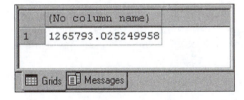

This is because, according to the query, we're calculating the SUM of the totals for the whole table. So, this is the SUM of all the totals from all the Orders together. This isn't very significant, as we want the Totals to be GROUPed by Order. So, we add a GROUP BY clause:

373

```
SELECT SUM(
( (UnitPrice * Quantity) *
( (1 - Discount) / 100 )
) * 100)
FROM [Order Details]
GROUP BY OrderID
```

This brings up:

	(No column name)
1	75.999996185302734
2	1583.9998626708984
3	2301.75
4	180.39999389648437
5	1761.9999370574951
6	537.5
7	8902.4999389648437
8	2023.3800048828125
9	48.0
10	1309.4998779296875
11	3054.0

Grids Messages

And so on. Now, this is starting to look useful, but the values we're getting are a bit too precise: we're talking about money here! So, let's CONVERT the result to get a Money value out of it. We'll also add the OrderID column, so that we can identify to whom these statistics belong:

```
SELECT OrderID,
CONVERT(money,
SUM(
( (UnitPrice * Quantity) *
( (1 - Discount) / 100 )
) * 100)
)
FROM [Order Details]
GROUP BY OrderID
ORDER BY OrderID
```

The ORDER BY clause has nothing to do with the "meat" of the query. It just seemed that it would be easier to find individual orders if we sorted the results. Note that there are now two columns in the query. This means that, since the SUM function yields an Aggregate value, the other column must also be an Aggregate.

Since we're looking for the OrderID for this SUMmed value, and we're GROUPing by OrderID, we can include the column as is, without having to use an Aggregate function to create an Aggregate value:

	OrderID	(No column name)
1	10248	440.0000
2	10249	1863.3999
3	10250	1552.6000
4	10251	654.0600
5	10252	3597.8999
6	10253	1444.7999
7	10254	556.6200
8	10255	2490.5000
9	10256	517.8000
10	10257	1119.8999

Grids Messages

DISTINCT

As SUM and AVG perform calculations, they have the same DISTINCT quirk as other Aggregate functions. Consider the following SQL, which should be run in SQL Query Analyzer against the Northwind Employees table:

```
SELECT (SUM(DateDiff(mm,HireDate, GetDate())) /
COUNT(HireDate)) AS UsingSum,
AVG(DateDiff(mm,HireDate, GetDate())) As UsingAvg
FROM Employees
```

What this yields is something like the following (according to the data in your table):

	UsingSum	UsingAvg
1	280	280

The average of any set of numbers is equal to the sum of all the numbers in the set divided by the number of elements in the set. Therefore, the two fields should have the same value, whether we use SUM or whether we use AVG.

We can use the DISTINCT operator with either of these functions, but the result set will have been grouped *before* the calculation is applied. If we try this:

```
SELECT (SUM(DISTINCT DateDiff(mm,HireDate, GetDate())) /
COUNT(HireDate)) AS UsingSum,
AVG(DISTINCT DateDiff(mm,HireDate, GetDate())) As UsingAvg
FROM Employees
```

We will get the following result set:

	UsingSum	UsingAvg
1	172	207

The discrepancy occurs because the functions do *two different things*: SUM is *summing* the number of months together from all the records, whereas AVG is *averaging* them all together. In order to get the average in the UsingSum column, we have to take that value and divide it by the number (COUNT) of Non-Null HireDate records, but the DISTINCT operator is only applied to the *dividend* in the expression (the SUM part); we also need to include it in the divisor:

```
SELECT (SUM(DISTINCT DateDiff(mm,HireDate, GetDate())) /
COUNT(DISTINCT HireDate)) AS UsingSum,
AVG(DISTINCT DateDiff(mm,HireDate, GetDate())) As UsingAvg
FROM Employees
```

Then we get the same results:

	UsingSum	UsingAvg
1	207	207

This is because the DISTINCT operator, as we may recall, eliminates duplicate records in the target set before performing the calculation. However, using the DISTINCT operator with aggregate functions is also bad for performance. Aggregate functions and operators are generally hard on performance, as each time one is used, the entire table must be scanned, and calculations performed on every record. The more Aggregates we add (DISTINCT is an Aggregate operator), the more table scans we add to our query, and the more of a performance hit we will experience.

ANY and EVERY

ANY and EVERY are new additions to the SQL Standard, and are not yet supported by many DBMS products: in fact, I know of none that do!

These functions can only be used with Boolean data type fields, and return a Boolean value of TRUE or FALSE. ANY returns TRUE if *any* of the columns in the target set have a value of TRUE. EVERY returns TRUE only if *every* value in the target set is TRUE. If any value is FALSE, EVERY will return FALSE. For example, supposing we had a table containing the following Boolean values:

```
Table1
BooleanColumn
--------------------
TRUE
TRUE
TRUE
FALSE
```

The following query :

```
SELECT ANY(BooleanColumn) FROM Table1
```

Would return TRUE and:

```
SELECT EVERY(BooleanColumn) FROM Table1
```

Would return FALSE

Aggregate Clauses: GROUP BY and HAVING

Here's where things start to get interesting, and sometimes confusing. Let's start with the HAVING clause.

HAVING

A HAVING clause acts a lot like a WHERE clause. It is a filtering clause; it evaluates a condition against a result set, and returns TRUE or FALSE for a given row in that set – that is, if the condition it specifies is TRUE for any row, that row is included in the *filtered* result set. The difference between HAVING and WHERE is that WHERE operates on a set of individual records, whereas HAVING works on an *aggregated* result set.

It is an Aggregate clause, which means that all of the Aggregate rules apply. That is, not only does the HAVING clause work on an aggregated result set, but the fields in the SELECT portion of the query must *all* be Aggregate fields, or be aggregated in a HAVING or GROUP BY clause.

This being the case, the following query is **not** going to work properly:

```
SELECT LastName FROM Employees
HAVING LastName BETWEEN 'D' AND 'F'
```

This will generate the following errors:

```
Server: Msg 8118, Level 16, State 1, Line 1
Column 'Employees.LastName' is invalid in the select list because it is
not contained in an aggregate function and there is no GROUP BY clause.
Server: Msg 8119, Level 16, State 1, Line 1
Column 'Employees.LastName' is invalid in the HAVING clause because it is
not contained in an aggregate function and there is no GROUP BY clause.
Server: Msg 8119, Level 16, State 1, Line 1
Column 'Employees.LastName' is invalid in the HAVING clause because it is
not contained in an aggregate function and there is no GROUP BY clause.
```

Grids Messages

Why is this? Well, first, let us understand how the grouping is being performed. HAVING filters a set of aggregated values. This set of aggregated values is SELECTed by the SELECT clause.
Secondly, because the HAVING clause operates on Aggregated columns, the columns in the SELECT list must *also* be aggregated somehow.

Let's take a look at the two "parts" of our query individually:

```
SELECT LastName FROM Employees
```

LastName is not aggregated, either by an Aggregate Scalar function (MIN, MAX, COUNT, etc.) on the LastName field in the SELECT list, or by a GROUP BY clause.

```
HAVING LastName BETWEEN 'D' AND 'F'
```

LastName is not aggregated, either by an Aggregate Scalar function (MIN, MAX, COUNT, etc.) on the LastName field in the HAVING clause, or by a GROUP BY clause.

Let's analyze the process of the query, to get a better understanding:

1. The LastName field is selected from the Employees table. This returns a result set of one column containing all of the LastName values in the Employees table.

2. The HAVING clause attempts to filter the result set. Whoops! No aggregated columns here!

Now, here are some that *will* work:

Try It out – HAVING Query 1

Using SQL Server Query Analyzer, or Access Query Designer, run each of the following queries to see how HAVING behaves under different conditions (your results may vary, depending on the contents of your tables):

This query returns all Last Names of Employees who have Last Names in the range of those starting with 'D' to those starting in 'E' (BETWEEN 'D' and 'F', *not* inclusive. If someone had the last name 'D' it wouldn't appear either).

```
SELECT LastName FROM Employees
GROUP BY LastName
HAVING LastName BETWEEN 'D' AND 'F'
```

The results:

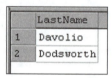

	LastName
1	Davolio
2	Dodsworth

How It Works

Remember that HAVING operates on a result set of aggregated columns. This is SELECTed by the SELECT clause. In order to aggregate the LastName column we applied a GROUP BY clause to the SELECT clause. As the LastName field was used in the HAVING clause, and it was already aggregated by the SELECT clause, there was no need to use an Aggregate function on the column reference in the HAVING clause.

Try It Out – HAVING Query 2

Let's step up a bit. This query fetches the EmployeeID and HireDate of each Employee who was hired prior to January 1, 1993. It orders them in descending order of HireDate. The result set is the set of all Employees hired prior to 1993, with the last one hired at the top.

```
SELECT EmployeeID, HireDate
FROM Employees
GROUP BY EmployeeID, HireDate
HAVING HireDate < '1993-01-01'
ORDER BY HireDate DESC
```

The results (depending on what you have in your table):

	EmployeeID	HireDate
1	2	1992-08-14 00:00:00
2	1	1992-05-01 00:00:00
3	3	1992-04-01 00:00:00
4	101	1991-02-21 00:00:00
5	100	1900-01-01 00:00:00
6	200	1900-01-01 00:00:00

How It Works

First of all, we want two pieces of data: the EmployeeID and the HireDate. That means that both columns will have to be aggregated somehow. So, let's construct our SELECT clause:

```
SELECT EmployeeID, HireDate
FROM Employees
GROUP BY EmployeeID, HireDate
```

We want a record for each Employee individually in this case (if we just wanted the last Employee hired, we could, for example, remove that column from the GROUP BY clause and use the MAX function instead). Therefore, we use the GROUP BY clause to separate out the aggregate records into individual Employee records (the EmployeeID field is the Primary Key field for the Employees table). We add the HireDate field to the GROUP BY clause as well, to aggregate it. This will not affect the records returned, since GROUPing them by the EmployeeID field already separates them into individual records.

Now we have our aggregated columns to filter, thus:

```
HAVING HireDate < '1993-01-01'
```

And this filters the result set from the SELECT clause, removing any records with HireDate on or after January 1, 1993.

HAVING Performance Issues

Actually, since this example uses individual Employees, the use of it is only for demonstration purposes. The most optimized way to write this particular query would be:

```
SELECT EmployeeID, MAX(HireDate)
FROM Employees
WHERE HireDate < '1993-01-01'
GROUP BY EmployeeID
```

> **Performance Tip:** don't use **HAVING** where you can use **WHERE**. A **WHERE** clause will generally be more optimal than a **HAVING** clause, because with a **HAVING** clause the fields must be aggregated (full table scan) *before* the filter is applied. With a **WHERE** clause, the filter is applied to the table specified in the **FROM** clause. This eliminates a full table scan from the operation.

Now, here's an excellent example of where we would have to use a HAVING clause instead of a WHERE clause:

```
SELECT EmployeeID, Count(OrderID) As NumOrders FROM Orders
GROUP BY EmployeeID
HAVING Count(OrderID) > 100
```

This query is asking for the EmployeeID and a count of the number of orders placed by each, for every Employee who has placed over 100 orders. The EmployeeID doesn't need to be Aggregated in the SELECT list because it is GROUPed in the GROUP BY clause.

The results (depending on the contents of your table):

	EmployeeID	NumOrders
1	3	127
2	1	123
3	4	156
4	8	104

We wouldn't be *able* to use a WHERE clause for this one, because the SELECT list is a list of Aggregate fields.

> **HAVING** works like **WHERE**, but filters Aggregate result sets. The **SELEC**Ted columns that the **HAVING** filter works on must all be Aggregates. All column references in the **HAVING** clause must be Aggregates.

GROUP BY

We've already seen the GROUP BY clause in action, but let's look in a little more detail at how it works. You may have figured out by now that **GROUP BY uses a field from a result set to combine (or "group") records into an Aggregate column (or "field")**. Here's an example:

```
SELECT EmployeeID, COUNT(OrderID) AS NumOrders
FROM Orders GROUP BY EmployeeID
```

This query returns the number of orders placed by each employee. When we run this query, we get the following result set (or something very similar):

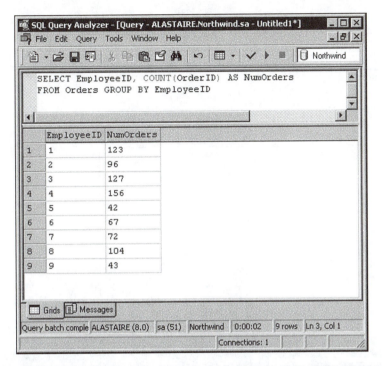

This is where the real power of a GROUP BY clause displays itself in all its glory. Notice how the result set has a different value in the NumOrders field for each EmployeeID. How did the query know from COUNT(OrderID) to count the orders for each Employee separately? The key is the GROUP BY clause.

The GROUP BY clause operates on the result set that is specified in the SELECT list (EmployeeID, COUNT(OrderID)), but also determines *how* the Aggregate results from any Aggregate functions (COUNT, in this case) in the result set should be calculated. As the EmployeeID field is specified as the field to be GROUPed by, the Aggregate functions in the select list will work with the groups of records that share the same EmployeeID field. In other words, the COUNT of Orders in each record will be the COUNT of Orders *for that Employee*.

For example, let's change the parameters of our problem slightly. Now, instead of SELECTing the COUNT of Orders for each Employee, we'll COUNT the number of Orders placed per month. To do this, we substitute a different grouping field for the EmployeeID field. Since we want to get the number of Orders per month, we'll be using the month of the order as the GROUPing field. However, in order to do this, we're going to have to use some extra coding...

Try It Out – Getting a COUNT of Orders by Month

Type the following query and run it in Query Analyzer, or whatever tool you have for running SQL queries:

```
SELECT DATENAME(mm, OrderDate) AS OrderMonth,
COUNT(OrderID) AS NumOrders
FROM Orders GROUP BY DATENAME(mm, OrderDate)
ORDER BY MAX(OrderDate)
```

This uses `OrderDate` instead of `EmployeeID` as a grouping field. However, notice that we used the `DATENAME` SQL Server function, which returns the `DATEPART` string equivalent of the part of the date specified. In this case, we return a string representing the month. This will be more informative than returning the month number. Since the string will be the same for each month, our query will group the records by month.

Here's a look at the result set:

	OrderMonth	NumOrders
1	June	30
2	July	55
3	August	58
4	September	60
5	October	64
6	November	59
7	December	79
8	January	88
9	February	83
10	March	103
11	April	105
12	May	46

How It Works

Let's start with our `SELECT` list. We want to display the Order Month and `COUNT` of Orders for that Month in each record. To do this, we need to use the `COUNT` function on the `OrderID` field (it is the Primary key for that table). We also know that the `COUNT` function, and all other aggregate functions used in a `GROUP BY` query will operate on (`COUNT`) the set of records that is `GROUP`ed `BY` in the result set. So we want to `GROUP BY` the month. One problem, though: there is no "`Month`" field in the table.

So, we look back to Chapter 11, and find a SQL Server-specific function for extracting the month from a date. In this case, we're going to use `DATENAME`. Why `DATENAME` instead of `DATEPART`? Well, we want to display the month name in our result set, so we might as well pull it in the same step, to optimize. Since all twelve months of the year have different spellings, we can use that value in our `GROUP BY` clause to separate them out by month.

```
SELECT DATENAME(mm, OrderDate) AS OrderMonth,...
```

There is one small problem with the above query that makes it not altogether useful, however: the number of Orders is correct, but there are precisely twelve months. This is because the `GROUP`ing by `DATEPART(OrderDate)` combines all records with the same Month, *regardless of Year*.

Let's try rebuilding the query to return some really useful information, `GROUP`ing the results by Month *and* Year, to get a much more "chronological" result set.

Try It Out - Getting a COUNT of Orders by Month *and* `Year`

This is going to be almost exactly the same, in terms of results, as the query above. However, as the query above only `GROUP`s records by month, and doesn't differentiate between `Year`s, we want to refine it to separate out the `Year`s. This is done by adding a new `GROUP`ing to the Query (for `Year`), and another column to the result set for the `Year` value.

Let's start by taking this thing apart and looking at the individual pieces. Copy and run each of the following queries separately in Query Analyzer or Query Designer.

1. We'll begin with our SELECT list:

```
SELECT MAX(DATENAME(mm, OrderDate)) AS OrderMonth
FROM Orders
```

Results:

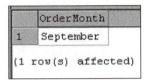

Analysis: The MAX function fetches the maximum value from a set. Unless a GROUP BY clause specifies how to group the subsets, the GROUPing is global to the table.

2. Add a GROUP BY clause:

```
SELECT DATEPART(yyyy, OrderDate) AS OrderYear
FROM Orders
```

Results:

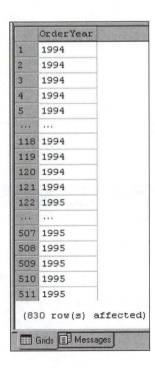

Analysis: the DATEPART function returns a non-aggregated value, simply the part of the date extracted from a date-time column. In this case, it selects the Year. The only real problem with this in regards to building our query is that we need to use an Aggregate function, clause, or operator on the value to "fit" it into the Aggregated result set.

3. Aggregate the Month value in the SELECT list:

```
SELECT COUNT(OrderID) AS NumOrders
FROM Orders
```

Results:

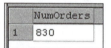

	NumOrders
1	830

Analysis: Okay, here we're looking at an Aggregate value again (COUNT(OrderID)). So, just as in the first query, we'll want to GROUP the SELECT list to calculate the Number of Orders by Month.

4. Remove the extra code and string the SELECT list together:

```
SELECT MAX(DATENAME(mm, OrderDate)) AS OrderMonth,
DATEPART(yyyy, OrderDate) AS OrderYear,
COUNT(OrderID) AS NumOrders
FROM Orders
```

5. Add our GROUP BY clause:

```
GROUP BY DATEPART(yyyy, OrderDate),
DATEPART(m, OrderDate)
```

Analysis: Here's the "tricky" part: because we want to GROUP BY Month, but keep Years in separate GROUPs, we want to GROUP BY two fields of our SELECT list – DATEPART(yyyy, OrderDate) and DATEPART(m, OrderDate) respectively. This is tricky because we have to understand the order in which the various parts of the query are executed, or we could encounter problems.

How It Works - Ordering Multiple GROUP BY Columns

When we perform a GROUP BY clause in our query, the table is scanned and GROUPed for each column in the GROUP BY clause, in order.

This means, that, for example, when we GROUP BY DATEPART(yyyy, OrderDate), and then by DATEPART(m, OrderDate), here is how the grouping happens:

The first GROUPing is applied (Year) inside the database. This divides the table (remember, there's no filtering clause in this SQL statement) up into GROUPs, like the following:

OrderYear	OrderMonth	numOrders (not calculated until all Aggregations are performed)
1995	August	1
1996	July	1
1996	July	1
...		
1996	July	1
1996	July	1
1996	July	1
1996	August	1
...		
1996	December	1
1996	December	1
1997	January	1
1997	January	1
...		
1997	February	1
...		

Now, the second pass is made against the database, and this time, the GROUP BY DATEPART(m, OrderMonth) is applied against the existing groupings, thereby creating smaller (more precise, or specific) groupings (shown by the alternating background texture):

OrderYear	OrderMonth	numOrders (not calculated until all Aggregations are performed)
1995	August	1
1996	July	1
1996	July	1
...		
1996	July	1
1996	July	1
1996	July	1

Table continued on following page

OrderYear	OrderMonth	numOrders (not calculated until all Aggregations are performed)
1996	August	1
...		
1996	December	1
1996	December	1
1997	January	1
1997	January	1
...		
1997	February	1
...		

Keeping Things Sorted

6. Add the ORDER BY clause to our query, and run it. The ORDER BY clause will work just like the GROUP BY clause, and for the same reasons (increasing precision). However, the difference is that when the GROUP BY clause finishes its calculations, it GROUPs the records in the groups it has identified, into single Aggregate records, without regard to order. The ORDER BY clause, of course, determines the order, but doesn't group any records.

```
SELECT MAX(DATENAME(mm, OrderDate)) AS OrderMonth,
DATEPART(yyyy, OrderDate) AS OrderYear,
COUNT(OrderID) AS NumOrders
FROM Orders
GROUP BY DATEPART(yyyy, OrderDate),
DATEPART(m, OrderDate)
ORDER BY DATEPART(yyyy, OrderDate),
DATEPART(m, OrderDate)
```

Results:

	UsingSum	UsingAvg
1	172	207

Analysis: The ORDER BY clause sets everything in Order. As we can see, the ordering is by Year first, with all the Years grouped together (because of the ORDER), and within those years, the individual months are ordered. The GROUP BY clause makes sure that the COUNT function is counting records by individual month.

Now we should be able to see how statistics of various kinds could be collected by grouping the Aggregated results in various ways.

Putting it All Together

This next exercise puts together everything we have learned so far.

Try It out – Build a Sales Analysis Query

Suppose that a sales account executive at Northwind has requested a report detailing the number of each Product sold by each Employee every month, showing the amount of the total sales for each product for each month.

This is going to be a bit tricky, as we're going to try to combine what we've learned so far from the book in this query. However, let's keep it to simple small steps, and we'll find that building a complex query is as easy as building a small query and adding a simple part to it at a time.

The first thing we need to do is to identify the table(s) to be used in the query. Of course, we will need the Employees table and the Products table. We need the Products table because we want to identify the product in each case, which means getting the Product Name from the Products table. Since this is a report based on sales, we will need the Orders table, which we will also need to link the Employees table to the Products table (via the [Order Details] table). We will also need to get the Product ID for the report. Therefore, we are going to have to JOIN four tables together:

- ❑ Employees
- ❑ Orders
- ❑ Order Details
- ❑ Products

A JOIN query is a SELECT query by definition (it's actually a SELECT query with a JOIN clause). Every SELECT query (against a Table or a View) has at least two parts to it: the SELECT clause and the FROM clause:

```
SELECT Employees.EmployeeID,
Employees.LastName, Employees.FirstName,
Products.ProductID, Products.ProductName

FROM Products INNER JOIN ((Employees INNER JOIN Orders ON
Employees.EmployeeID = Orders.EmployeeID) INNER JOIN [Order Details] ON
Orders.OrderID = [Order Details].OrderID) ON
Products.ProductID = [Order Details].ProductID;
```

As we can see, the JOIN part of the query *is* rather complex. This part of the query, shown in bold text, will never need to be changed. All we want to do is to make a select list of aggregated fields, and use the proper GROUP BY and ORDER BY clauses.

So, the next part of the problem is to identify:

- ❑ which fields we want to display, and in what order
- ❑ which fields we will need information from in order to derive these other fields

How It Works – Building the SELECT List

Let's start with a list of fields. The requirements want the data for each employee, for each product, for every month. They also require the number and amount of each group of products. Therefore, we will need the `EmployeeID` field, and for the purposes of ease of use, we will want to get the Employee `Name` as well. Again, for user-friendliness, we will concatenate the first and last names together in our result set. While separating Last Names and First Names is useful for sorting and searching, it is more user-friendly to *display* the name in the "typical" fashion.

We also will want the product `ID` and product name in the result set. And, because we are doing this by month, we will want the month and year in the result set as well. Finally, for each date/employee/product combination, we want a number of products, and an amount. So, we have identified seven Aggregate fields that we will need:

Derived Field Name	Derived Using	Sample Result
OrderMonth	DATENAME(mm, Orders.OrderDate) + '/' + DATENAME(yyyy, Orders.OrderDate) (GROUPed BY first)	April/1996
EmployeeID	Employees.EmployeeID (GROUPed BY second)	1
EmployeeName	MAX(Employees.FirstName + ' ' + Employees.LastName)	Steven Buchanan
ProductID	Products.ProductID (GROUPed BY third)	11
ProductName	MAX(Products.ProductName)	Queso Cabrales
NumSold	COUNT(Products.ProductID)	1
Amt	SUM(([Order Details].UnitPrice * [Order Details].Quantity))	168.0000

Let's look at each of these in detail:

❑   `OrderMonth`: We want the list to be grouped by the month, but we also want the results to look good. We could use the `DATEPART` function, but that would only return an integer. We want to be able to easily identify the month and year, so we use the SQL Server `DATENAME` function, to concatenate the month and year of the date into an easily readable format.

❑   `EmployeeID`: Since we want to group by Month, and then by Employee, and then by Product, we need to add each of these fields to the `SELECT` list. I could have used the `EmployeeName` field, but just in case any two employees shared both first and last name, we used the `EmployeeID` field. On the other hand, it isn't a bad idea to include this field anyway, since it is the unique identifier field for each employee.

❑   `EmployeeName`: This is for display purposes only, and it concatenates the `FirstName` and `LastName` fields of each Employee Record together. Since we are using it with a `GROUP BY` clause, we need to aggregate it, so we use the `MAX` function. We could also aggregate this by including this field in the `GROUP BY` clause instead, if we wanted.

❑   ProductID: the unique identifier for each Product.

❑   ProductName: Same as EmployeeName, except there isn't any need for concatenation, as it is all one field.

❑   NumSold: We use the COUNT function, and because of the grouping of the COUNT function it counts by Month, then by EmployeeID, then by ProductID, adding a total to each record. We use the [Order Details].ProductId field because there will be one record in the [Order Details] table for each Order for that Product. Note the square brackets around the name "Order Details" – this is because of a space in the name.

❑   Amt: The Amount of each order has to be calculated by multiplying the price for the product (since there is only one ProductID per record) by the quantity sold. The Amount of each aggregated record has to be the SUM of all these values added together for that Month/Employee/Product.

So, by combining all of these together, we come up with our SELECT list. We can check our syntax as we go along by adding each derived field to the query one at a time, and testing the results (as we did in our earlier exercise in this chapter). The last thing to add is an ORDER BY clause, and of course, we will want to order by date first, then by employee, then by product ID. The final query looks like this:

```
SELECT (DATENAME(mm, Orders.OrderDate) + '/' +
DATENAME(yyyy, Orders.OrderDate)) AS OrderMonth,
Employees.EmployeeID AS EmployeeID,
MAX(Employees.FirstName + ' ' + Employees.LastName) AS EmployeeName,
Products.ProductId AS ProductID,
MAX(Products.ProductName) AS ProductName,
COUNT([Order Details].ProductID) AS NumSold,
SUM(([Order Details].UnitPrice * [Order Details].Quantity)) AS Amt

FROM Products INNER JOIN ((Employees INNER JOIN Orders ON
Employees.EmployeeID = Orders.EmployeeID) INNER JOIN [Order Details] ON
Orders.OrderID = [Order Details].OrderID) ON
Products.ProductID = [Order Details].ProductID

GROUP BY  Orders.OrderDate,
Employees.EmployeeID, Products.ProductID

ORDER BY Orders.OrderDate, EmployeeID, ProductID
```

That's quite a query! Now, let's see what we get when we run it in Query Analyzer:

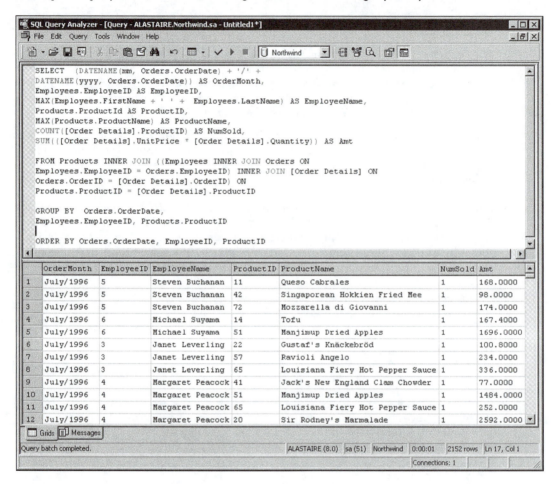

This screen shot doesn't have room for all of the fields, but as we can see, it is ordered by month, and then by employee, and then by product. The Amt field shows the total amount collected from sales of a particular product by a specific employee in that month. The Num field shows the total number of sales of a product in a particular month by a specific employee.

This query could easily be stored and used to generate a sales report. By tweaking it in a number of ways, we could also generate reports of other kinds.

Summary

In this chapter we have seen that tables and result sets may be understood as sets in the ordinary sense in which we encounter them in Set Theory.

We discussed the definition of "set" or "Aggregate" as pertaining to combining multiple values into a single value, via Aggregate operators, functions, and clauses.

We discussed the Aggregate operators UNION, EXCEPT, and INTERSECT. As EXCEPT and INTERSECT are not (yet) supported by many DBMS products (although it looks as if SQL Server is moving towards full support in SQL-99), we demonstrated how these other operators could be emulated using the available syntax.

We concentrated on UNION, which combines non-duplicate values from two result sets into a single set. We discussed the difference between UNION ALL and UNION [DISTINCT], and the effects of combining duplicate rows in result sets.

We looked at using each of the commonly available Aggregate functions:

- ❑ COUNT: Returns a count of the number of matching values in a set.
- ❑ MAX: Returns the Maximum from a set of values.
- ❑ MIN: Returns the Minimum from a set of values.
- ❑ SUM: Returns the Sum of a set of values added together.
- ❑ AVG: Returns the Average value from a set.
- ❑ ANY and EVERY: ANY returns TRUE if *any* value in the set is TRUE. EVERY returns TRUE only if every value in the set is TRUE.

We talked about the NULL rule of Aggregate functions: NULL values are always ignored.

We finished up discussing the Aggregate clauses, GROUP BY and HAVING.

Our exercise demonstrated a combination of Aggregate functions and clauses. The end product was a query useful for compiling sales statistics showing sales per month per employee.

Remember that these syntax elements are tools. This book can give you some examples of how they might be used, but the real fun begins when you become familiar enough with them to use them to write your own queries.

So far, we have looked at ways of constructing various types of SQL statements. However, it would be very useful if we could somehow store these statements in such a way that they could be continually reused. In the next chapter, we're going to look at how to do this, through constructing stored procedures.

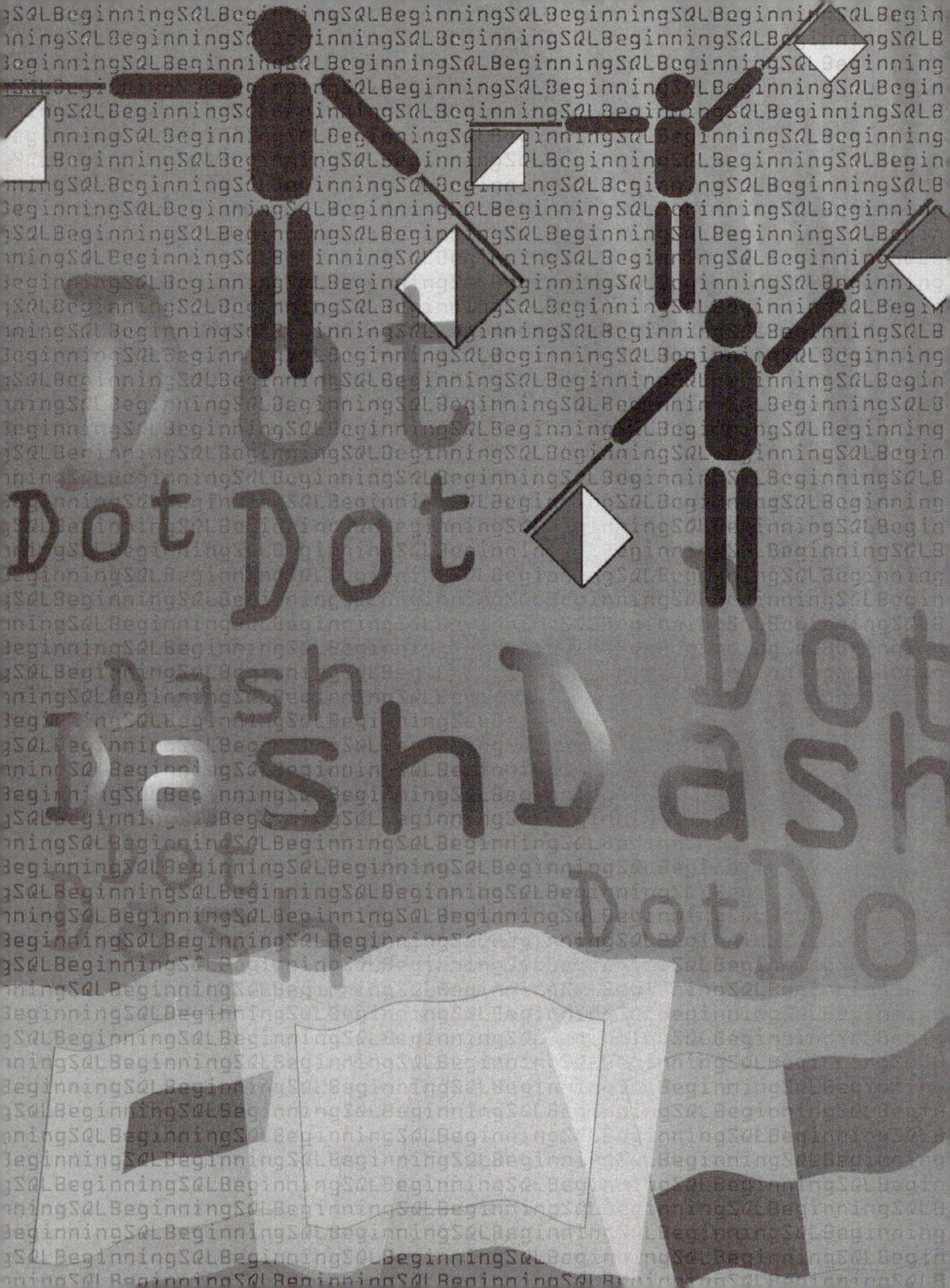

14

Stored Procedures

We can think of a stored procedure as a piece of code that runs inside the database server. This code can do things such as insert and update records, execute queries, and perform maintenance. In fact, stored procedures can do anything that we could do using SQL, for the simple reason that stored procedures are SQL functions, stored in the database, which may be reused whenever we wish.

A stored procedure can be a very powerful tool for a SQL developer since this native code in the database can be moved from applications and centralized in the database, thus building a more robust client-server architecture.

Advantages of Stored Procedures

One of the big advantages of stored procedures is that they are precompiled in the database so the database has a bit of information about what the procedure does. By pre-compiling the procedures, the database can determine the tables that will be accessed and what indexes should be used for the most efficient execution of the code. Unlike a SQL statement that has been passed from another application, the database does not have to parse this information on each function call and determine the information on the fly, so there is a large performance increase by using stored procedures. Related to this is the fact that, with stored procedures, the client-side application doesn't have to send long strings of SQL statements through the network cable, so the application can save valuable milliseconds by avoiding network traffic.

Another component of stored procedures is parameters. A stored procedure, like a VB function, can receive parameters and return results as well as output parameters. This allows us to build very powerful SQL code libraries since we can write a generic query and replace the criteria with the input parameters. For instance, we would not need to write 50 queries for an "Employees By Department" query; rather we could use one stored procedure with an input parameter called "Department" that we would use as the criteria in our SELECT statement. Later in this chapter we will see some examples of using parameters with stored procedures.

Stored procedures can also call other stored procedures. We can create very complex procedure libraries and create powerful solutions by having stored procedures access code contained in other stored procedures. This approach will make a database more complex and a little harder to maintain, but we will have a much more robust application by using this approach – this is because stored procedures can be used to act as an interface to our database. Instead of opening all of our tables for anyone to see, stored procedures can be used to read and write data into the system.

For instance, let's assume that we are working on an accounting package. If you have ever seen an accounting system you know it can be very complex and very dependent on multiple updates for any event. If we want to add inventory to our database we may need to read and/or update four or five tables for this to appear "correct" in the system. A stored procedure could handle all of the logic that a novice developer may not know; rather than providing direct access to the individual tables, the developers must use the stored procedure to update the data. This protects our system from wayward SQL code that can compromise the integrity of our data, as well as simplifying the use of our system for developers that may not be as familiar with the business logic of the system as the database designer may have been.

Additionally, putting all of the primary SQL code into the database through stored procedures will reduce the maintenance on applications that would otherwise use embedded SQL for queries. Let's assume that we have ten applications that use the same inline SQL code to access our database. One day we realize that our logic is incorrect and the SQL must be updated. Now let's also assume that a total of 15 users access each of the applications; we must now update the equivalent of 150 desktops to make one change. On the other hand, if we utilize stored procedures we will have no deployment and application changes to make: if all ten of the applications accessed one stored procedure then only the content of the stored procedure would need to be changed. This is a huge advantage in the development world since we will have reduced our work from 150 application updates (and all of the deployment issues associated with those) and taken the complexity down to one change that will be completely transparent to both the users and the application developers.

There is not only an overall increase in speed in using stored procedures, but they also enable us to write modular code in a database, passing parameters to and between them. Also, an often-overlooked use for stored procedures is for implementing additional security. Let's look at these advantages in more detail.

Stored Procedures and Performance

Firstly, moving logic from components and applications into stored procedures will greatly improve performance and reduce network traffic. All processing of stored procedures is performed at the database server, so no data is physically transferred until the stored procedure has finished executing. Imagine a scenario where we had to scan 50,000 records and return 1,000 records of summarized data. If we executed this code in a component, then all 50,000 records would be transferred over the network while a stored procedure would only send 1,000 records over the network. Not only will your applications run faster, but also there is a benefit to network traffic due to the reduced amount of data that is being sent.

Stored Procedures and Modularization

One of the key advantages for developers is that we can modularize database code into stored procedures for better organization and more efficient design. Think of a stored procedure as a function in Visual Basic. With Visual Basic, you would not put all of your code into one or two functions; rather you use many functions to implement the features and functionality of your application. Stored procedures are treated in the same way since we can create thse smaller sets of code to make an application more manageable.

For instance, we could create a stored procedure to add an employee. We could design this procedure to insert information into an employee table, make a record in the salary table, and then update the department table. Doing all of this might require a lot of code for one procedure, so we could break it up so that we call one procedure (let's suppose we call it sp_AddEmployee), and, in turn, that procedure calls three other procedures: sp_AddEmployeeRecord, sp_UpdateEmployeeSalary, and sp_UpdateDepartmentList, for instance.

> Note that the names of these procedures can be anything that we want – we will look at naming conventions later on in the chapter.

Notice that the stored procedures are more manageable and modular with this approach. Instead of one large procedure, we now have several small ones that can be reused in other locations. Later, if we need to maintain department lists, we already have code (sp_UpdateDepartmentList) that we can use. This also provides a single point of maintenance for our core logic. Rather than maintaining all of the department code throughout the database you can instead modify just the sp_UpdateDepartmentList procedure to make common changes to the logic. This will greatly reduce maintenance effort during the life of an application. This concept is referred to as encapsulation and is a very common technique used in object-oriented programming.

Stored Procedures and Security

Security is a very important feature of a database. We would typically not give everyone full access to every item in the database, so some level of internal database security would be implemented to keep people out of the database completely, or to limit the capabilities of the user in the database.

On the other hand, we may want to give people the ability to modify, add, and delete data from tables, but want to maintain a level of control over how they make the table modifications. For instance, in the above example of adding an employee to a database, we need to update three tables. If we wanted to delete an employee, we would also have to delete information from the three tables. If we just gave users delete privileges on the employee table then they could delete an employee record but not delete the related data. This is a very bad thing; so bad that a term has been coined to refer to the records that correspond to the now deleted employee record: they are known as **orphaned records**.

> **Orphaned records** – records that exist in tables after the parent or key record in a parent table has been deleted. One example is when order details (in the Order Details table) exist after the order header (in the Orders table) has been deleted: we delete order number 12048 from the Order table, but leave all of the entries in the Order Details table for order 12048. The Order Detail records no longer refer to any valid order, so these are considered orphaned records.

Using stored procedures, we can prevent this issue from occurring while securing our database. We could create a special procedure for this delete operation (sp_DeleteEmployee) and allow the appropriate users to execute this function. At the same time, we would not let them directly delete information from the three key tables. The stored procedures act as a gateway to direct table modifications. One of the advantages to implementing stored procedures and security on an enterprise database is that you can give users access to the stored procedure and disallow access to the table. This makes the stored procedures the *only* way that a user can get to data.

> **Stored procedures are not the only way to ensure data integrity and prevent orphaned records. Using primary and foreign key relationships in your database will also prevent this from occurring. Stored procedures will add an additional layer into preventing any problems by implementing the correct logic to delete the child records when a parent record is deleted. Remember that this is one of the key uses of stored procedures – implementing business logic.**

It is not unusual to find, in an enterprise scale database, that each table has a specific procedure for inserts, updates, and deletes. This is to ensure that core relation logic must be maintained. Stored procedures provide a means of implementing robust error checking.

Stored Procedures and Parameters

Finally, stored procedures have the distinct advantage that they can take parameters: this allows us to open a whole new way to modularize our queries. We can use the input parameters for query criteria; this will provide much more flexibility within our stored procedures and allows for very complex queries that return common resultsets. We will look at an example of building a parameterized query later in this section.

As a simple example, suppose we wanted to generate a state-by-state list of customers. We could write a query for each state, but it would be much easier to create one statement with a WHERE clause to filter by state. We can use parameters for input into the WHERE clause such that we will retrieve only the state of choice based on the parameter. Instead of fifty queries, we now have one stored procedure.

So, we have an idea about why we should use a stored procedure:

- ❑ Reduced network traffic
- ❑ Increased security
- ❑ Modular programming
- ❑ Faster processing due to logic executing on the database server rather than within the client application
- ❑ More complex data processing on data manipulation operations

Now that we know why stored procedures are used, let's look at how they're used. The next section will discuss how to create a stored procedure.

Creating a Stored Procedure

The CREATE PROCEDURE statement is used to create a stored procedure. This statement looks very simple on the surface, and for the most part it is – so long as we understand all of the parts of the statement.

Let's take a look at the SQL CREATE PROCEDURE statement:

```
CREATE PROCEDURE procedure_name
[parameter data_type attributes][,...n]
AS
code block
```

This is the basic implementation of this function, but different vendors have added different things to it. For example, if we look at the SQL Server version, we will see:

```
CREATE PROC[EDURE] <procedure_name>
[{@parameter_name data_type} [VARYING] [= default_value] [OUTPUT] [,...n]
[WITH {RECOMPILE | ENCRYPTION | RECOMPILE, ENCRYPTION}]
[FOR REPLICATION]
AS
SQL_statement
```

This may look complex, but the procedure is not as difficult as it looks – understanding the individual components is the key. Remember that all of the items in brackets ([ ]) are optional, so a very simple stored procedure can be built using only the following:

```
CREATE PROC <procedure_name>
AS
SQL_Statement
```

The first item is the procedure name (`procedure_name`). We can create local-temporary and global-temporary stored procedures using a prefix of # for local and ## for global, or we can create a permanent stored procedure by using a standard name without a prefix to it.

The recommended naming prefix for a stored procedure is `sp` or `sp_`. Of course, we can call it whatever we want, but sticking with a common naming convention will make the database much more manageable than a haphazard approach to naming objects. Some of the stored procedures in SQL Server are named `xp_` because they are considered extended stored procedures and are part of the system-level stored procedure library.

The next part of the statement is the parameter list. We do not have to declare any parameters, but if we have any, then this is the section to which they would belong. This part of the stored procedure declaration may seem a bit more complex than the others due to the number of parameters, so let's look at each aspect of it in turn.

`@parameter_name` is the name of the parameter that is passed to the stored procedure. Once again, we need to follow all of the database naming rules that have been defined.

> **In SQL Server, but not in any other DBMS, it is necessary to use the @ to declare a parameter; it is NOT an optional character. When referring to the parameter in a stored procedure, it is also necessary to use the @ declaration for naming variables.**

The next part is the data type. If we declare a parameter, then we must declare a data type for it. The `data_type` value will be any of the valid SQL data types. There is also an optional default value that we can place on a parameter. The parameter will be initialized with this value if no value is specified when the stored procedure is called.

Finally, the `OUTPUT` option will declare the parameter as input/output rather than the default of input only. By default, the parameter is an input only item.

A Closer Look at Parameters

Using SQL Server, let's take a look at the Northwind stored procedure SalesByCategory (notice the lack of a naming convention). If we look at the declaration (seen here as bold), we will see that there are two parameters declared:

```
CREATE PROCEDURE SalesByCategory
    @CategoryName nvarchar(15),
    @OrdYear nvarchar(4) = '1998'
AS
IF @OrdYear != '1996' AND @OrdYear != '1997' AND @OrdYear != '1998'
BEGIN
    SELECT @OrdYear = '1998'
END

SELECT ProductName,
    TotalPurchase=ROUND(SUM(CONVERT(decimal(14,2), OD.Quantity *_
                                (1-OD.Discount) * OD.UnitPrice)), 0)
FROM [Order Details] OD, Orders O, Products P, Categories C
WHERE OD.OrderID = O.OrderID
    AND OD.ProductID = P.ProductID
    AND P.CategoryID = C.CategoryID
    AND C.CategoryName = @CategoryName
    AND SUBSTRING(CONVERT(nvarchar(22), O.OrderDate, 111), 1, 4) = @OrdYear
GROUP BY ProductName
ORDER BY ProductName
```

We have declared a parameter named @CategoryName that is an nvarchar(15). The next parameter is @OrderYear which is an nvarchar(4) with a default value of 1998. Thus, if we called this procedure as follows:

```
EXEC SalesByCategory "condiments"
```

We will get the following results:

	ProductName	TotalPurchase
1	Aniseed Syrup	1080.00
2	Chef Anton's Cajun Seasoning	1502.00
3	Chef Anton's Gumbo Mix	3042.00
4	Grandma's Boysenberry Spread	3917.00
5	Gula Malacca	1136.00
6	Louisiana Fiery Hot Pepper ...	2023.00
7	Louisiana Hot Spiced Okra	17.00
8	Northwoods Cranberry Sauce	4592.00
9	Original Frankfurter grüne Soße	3755.00
10	Sirop d'érable	5261.00
11	Vegie-spread	6453.00

On the other hand, if we changed the call to:

```
exec SalesByCategory "condiments", 1997
```

Then we will use the year of 1997 for the execution of the stored procedure.

	ProductName	TotalPurchase
1	Aniseed Syrup	1724.00
2	Chef Anton's Cajun Seasoning	5215.00
3	Chef Anton's Gumbo Mix	374.00
4	Genen Shouyu	1475.00
5	Grandma's Boysenberry Spread	2500.00
6	Gula Malacca	6738.00
7	Louisiana Fiery Hot Pepper ...	9373.00
8	Louisiana Hot Spiced Okra	2958.00
9	Northwoods Cranberry Sauce	4260.00
10	Original Frankfurter grüne Soße	4761.00
11	Sirop d'érable	9092.00
12	Vegie-spread	6899.00

In the first example, we did not declare a year and the stored procedure used the default of 1998 for the `@OrderYear` variable.

So, the parameter list is not really that difficult. If you have a parameter then you have `@parameter_name` and `data_type` attributes that are required.

There is an optional default value that you can specify by using the = operator.

Finally, there is the optional `OUTPUT` attribute that declares the property to be capable returning a value to the calling statement. If the stored procedure contains more than one parameter then you must separate the list of parameters with a comma.

The WITH Option

The next item in the `CREATE PROCEDURE` statement is the `WITH` option:

```
[
    WITH {RECOMPILE | ENCRYPTION | RECOMPILE, ENCRYPTION}
]
```

The options that this provides are:

RECOMPILE	The `RECOMPILE` option tells SQL Server that it should rebuild the execution plan for the procedure upon each execution. Without this option SQL Server will pre-compile the procedure and build an execution plan for the procedure. This plan tells the database the best methods of execution including the dependant objects and appropriate indexes to use.
ENCRYPTION	The encryption option will encrypt the contents of the procedure declaration in the `syscomments` table. Without this setting you can see the full text of the stored procedure in the table (and may be able to modify the text as well).
RECOMPILE, ENCRYPTION	This combines both the `RECOMPILE` and the `ENCRYPTION` options.

The FOR REPLICATION option in the CREATE PROCEDURE statement marks the stored procedure as a special replication procedure. This stored procedure can then only be executed as part of a replication package. If you use FOR REPLICATION then you cannot use WITH RECOMPILE at the same time. This is more detail than we need in this book already, but for more information on SQL Server replication see *Professional SQL Server 2000*, by Rob Vieira, ISBN 1-861004-48-6.

The SQL Statement

The last part of the CREATE PROCEDURE statement is the AS keyword followed by the SQL code of the procedure.

Try It Out – Creating a Basic Stored Procedure

Before we go any further in this chapter, let's look at creating a series of stored procedures. The first procedure will be a basic customer list: we will simply return the CustomerID, CompanyName, and Region of each customer. The next example will modify this to use a parameter to look up customers by region.

1. Firstly, we need to generate the SQL statement that we want to use. Since we know that we will be outputting the CustomerID, CompanyName, and Region we can determine that this is a basic SELECT from the Customers table.

```
SELECT
    CustomerID,
    CompanyName,
    Region
FROM
    Customers
```

This provides the correct results that we need to see:

	CustomerID	CompanyName	Region
1	ALFKI	Alfreds Futterkiste	NULL
2	ANATR	Ana Trujillo Emparedados y ...	NULL
3	ANTON	Antonio Moreno Taquería	NULL
4	AROUT	Around the Horn	NULL
5	BERGS	Berglunds snabbköp	NULL
...	...	...	...
87	WARTH	Wartian Herkku	NULL
88	WELLI	Wellington Importadora	SP
89	WHITC	White Clover Markets	WA
90	WILMK	Wilman Kala	NULL
91	WOLZA	Wolski Zajazd	NULL

```
(91 row(s) affected)
```

2. Now, we need to create the procedure declaration. We will call this sp_GlobalCustomerList; we have no parameters, so this is a pretty straightforward stored procedure.

```
CREATE PROCEDURE sp_GlobalCustomerList
AS

SELECT
    CustomerID,
    CompanyName,
    Region
FROM
    Customers
```

3. When we execute this statement we get the following message telling us that the syntax is correct and that the stored procedure has been added to the system catalog:

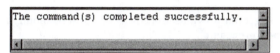

The command(s) completed successfully.

4. We can test this procedure by executing the procedure from Query Analyzer:

```
EXEC sp_GlobalCustomerList
```

When we run this, we get the results of the SELECT statement from the procedure:

	CustomerID	CompanyName	Region
1	ALFKI	Alfreds Futterkiste	NULL
2	ANATR	Ana Trujillo Emparedados y ...	NULL
3	ANTON	Antonio Moreno Taquería	NULL
4	AROUT	Around the Horn	NULL
5	BERGS	Berglunds snabbköp	NULL
...	...	...	...
87	WARTH	Wartian Herkku	NULL
88	WELLI	Wellington Importadora	SP
89	WHITC	White Clover Markets	WA
90	WILMK	Wilman Kala	NULL
91	WOLZA	Wolski Zajazd	NULL

```
(91 row(s) affected)
```

You have successfully created and tested your first procedure – Congratulations!

In Oracle, we would use the following. Note the use of a cursor, and note that specific commands have to be entered to output the results in the SQL+ editor.

```
CREATE OR REPLACE
PROCEDURE sp_GetEmployees IS
CURSOR GetEmp IS
SELECT CustomerID, CompanyName, Region FROM Customers;
```

401

```
BEGIN
FOR GetEmp_cur IN GetEmp Loop
DBMS_OUTPUT.PUT_LINE(GetEmp_cur.customerid);
DBMS_OUTPUT.PUT_LINE(GetEmp_cur.CompanyName);
DBMS_OUTPUT.PUT_LINE(GetEmp_cur.Region);
END LOOP;
END sp_GetEmployees;
/
```

Try It Out – Adding Parameters to a Stored Procedure

OK, now let's make this procedure a little more complex. While it is a useful procedure it does not do everything for us; we are more likely to have a need to get customers by region. Also, we see above that the international customers do not have a region code – it is only for the US and Canada. We will make an additional modification to filter the non-US and non-Canadian customers from the result set.

1. First, we need to get our previous procedure – we will be modifying the text of that procedure to create our new procedure.

```
CREATE PROCEDURE sp_GlobalCustomerList
AS

SELECT
    CustomerID,
    CompanyName,
    Region
FROM
    Customers
```

2. The next step is to change the name from sp_GlobalCustomerList to sp_NACustomerListByRegion and change the SELECT statement to filter for the US and Canadian customers:

```
CREATE PROCEDURE sp_NACustomerListByRegion
AS

SELECT
    CustomerID,
    CompanyName,
    Region
FROM
    Customers
WHERE
  Country IN ('USA', 'Canada')
```

3. Now, we want to add the parameter for the region. We will call the parameter @Region so that we can easily remember the name and the field that it is associated with. If we look at the structure of the Customer table we will see that the Region field is declared as an nvarchar(15), so we need to use the same declaration to avoid any input errors with the parameters. It is always a good idea to use the same data type declaration for a parameter as appears in the table. We want this parameter to be an input only field and there will be no defaults.

```
CREATE PROCEDURE sp_NACustomerListByRegion
   @Region nvarchar(15)
AS

SELECT
   CustomerID,
   CompanyName,
   Region
FROM
   Customers
WHERE
   Country IN ('USA', 'Canada')
   AND Region = @Region
```

4. We have added our input parameter of `@Region` and the additional criteria in the `WHERE` clause of the SQL statement. We execute the statement to add the stored procedure to the catalog.

5. Now, let's test this stored procedure. This time, we need to send in the parameter for `@Region` – we will look for the customers in the state of Washington:

```
EXEC sp_NACustomerListByRegion 'WA'
```

This yields a much smaller result set than our first example:

	CustomerID	CompanyName	Region
1	LAZYK	Lazy K Kountry Store	WA
2	TRAIH	Trail's Head Gourmet Provis...	WA
3	WHITC	White Clover Markets	WA

As you can see, we have used a parameter to increase the usefulness and functionality of our stored procedure. While this example may be fairly basic in its utility, the concepts applied here will apply to any number of parameters that we use.

Alternatively, we could have used the `ALTER PROCEDURE` command. The `ALTER PROCEDURE` statement will create the procedure if it does not exist or will modify the procedure if it does exist. If we try to execute previous `CREATE PROCEDURE` code again, we will get an error that a stored procedure with that name already exists.

In Oracle, we would use the following:

```
CREATE OR REPLACE PROCEDURE sp_ListByRegion (p_Region IN Customers.Region%TYPE)
IS

Cursor GetInfo IS

SELECT
   CustomerID,
   CompanyName,
   Region
```

```
FROM
  Customers
WHERE
  (Country = 'USA' OR Country ='Canada')
  AND Region = p_Region;

BEGIN
FOR GetInfo_cur IN GetInfo LOOP
DBMS_OUTPUT.PUT_LINE(GetInfo_cur.CustomerID);
DBMS_OUTPUT.PUT_LINE(GetInfo_cur.CompanyName);
DBMS_OUTPUT.PUT_LINE(GetInfo_cur.Region);

END LOOP;
END;
/
```

```
Oracle SQL*Plus                                                    _ □ ×
File  Edit  Search  Options  Help
PL/SQL procedure successfully completed.

SQL> CREATE OR REPLACE PROCEDURE sp_ListByRegion (p_Region IN Customers.Region%TYPE)
  2  IS
  3
  4  Cursor GetInfo IS
  5
  6  SELECT
  7     CustomerID,
  8     CompanyName,
  9     Region
 10  FROM
 11     Customers
 12  WHERE
 13     (Country = 'USA' OR Country ='Canada')
 14     AND Region = p_Region;
 15
 16  BEGIN
 17  FOR GetInfo_cur IN GetInfo LOOP
 18  DBMS_OUTPUT.PUT_LINE(GetInfo_cur.CustomerID);
 19  DBMS_OUTPUT.PUT_LINE(GetInfo_cur.CompanyName);
 20  DBMS_OUTPUT.PUT_LINE(GetInfo_cur.Region);
 21
 22  END LOOP;
 23  END;
 24  /

Procedure created.

SQL> exec sp_ListByRegion('CA');
LETSS
Let's Stop N Shop
CA
LETSS
Let's Stop N Shop
CA
LETSS
Let's Stop N Shop
CA
LETSS
Let's Stop N Shop
CA
LETSS
Let's Stop N Shop
CA

PL/SQL procedure successfully completed.

SQL>
```

The SQL Server CREATE PROCEDURE Template

Microsoft includes a series of templates that we can use in Query Analyzer. We can access the templates by going to Edit | Insert Template. From here we will get a series of templates that we can use for many of the routine DDL functions. Below is the dialog that we will see for selecting templates:

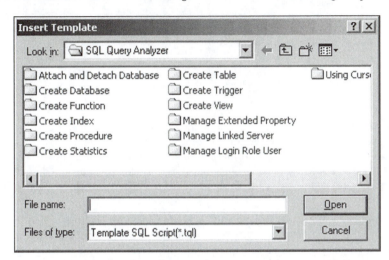

If we go to the Create Procedure folder we will get the predefined list of Create Procedure templates:

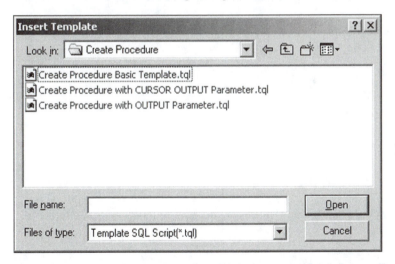

One of these is the Create Procedure Basic Template that has a very handy piece of code for managing stored procedures. Notice that this template uses a slightly different approach to editing the procedure than we have seen up to this point. First, it checks to see if the procedure already exists: if the procedure does exist then it is dropped using a DROP PROCEDURE statement. Then, we proceed to create the statement again. This is just another way to handle the editing of stored procedures and this is the format that many of the Microsoft stored procedures will look like (though, of course, we could always use ALTER PROCEDURE instead):

405

```
-- ================================================
-- Create procedure basic template
-- ================================================
-- creating the store procedure
IF EXISTS (SELECT name
    FROM  sysobjects
        WHERE name = N'sp_GetCustomerList'
        AND type = 'P')
    DROP PROCEDURE sp_GetCustomerList
GO

CREATE PROCEDURE sp_GetCustomerList
AS
```

Of course, we have changed the template file to look at our stored procedure –
sp_GetCustomerList. What this does is look for a procedure called sp_GetCustomerList from
the system table called sysobjects. If there is an entry for this item then we will drop the procedure
using the DROP PROCEDURE statement. Once the stored procedure is dropped, and we determine that
there is no existing procedure, we can proceed to our CREATE PROCEDURE statement.

> *This declaration contains the coding conventions, headers, and flow that are standard between our
> procedures. We want this level of consistency in our coding so that we will be familiar with what to
> look for and at, and you will also begin to integrate the standards into your daily practice so that it
> becomes as much of the process as typing CREATE PROCEDURE. However, for the sake of
> simplicity, this section of code will not appear again in this chapter.*

If we look at the complete text of our stored procedure now, we will see that there is a lot more going
on:

```
CREATE PROCEDURE sp_GetCustomerList
AS

SELECT
    CustomerID,
    CompanyName,
    ContactName
FROM
    Customers
```

We can now handle any situation that may arise by modifying our procedures.

Calling a Stored Procedure

We have gone through the process of creating a stored procedure, but how do we call a stored
procedure? We use the EXECUTE or EXEC statement to achieve this. EXEC will run the contents of a
stored procedure. If the procedure returns a result set, then we will be able to process or display the
data in the calling module.

Since we have no parameters to send to the `sp_GetCustomerList` stored procedure, all we have to do is call the stored procedure by name in Query Analyzer:

```
EXEC sp_GetCustomerList
```

This will return a result set of data back to us:

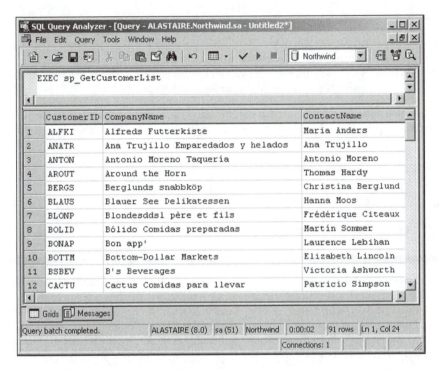

This differs a bit when using parameters. Before we go into calling a procedure with parameters, let's look at how we might change our stored procedure so that it accepts parameters. Once we've looked at this, we'll be in a position to create more advanced procedures.

Using Parameters

We have seen the basic declaration of a stored procedure using the CREATE PROCEDURE statement, and we have looked at the requirements and procedures for adding parameters to a stored procedure, but we want to take a little more time to look at parameters in more detail.

Using INPUT Parameters

By default, all parameters are input only parameters. Any changes that we make to the value of the parameter within the stored procedure will not change the underlying value of the parameter. To better demonstrate this, let's look at an example. We will create a procedure called `sp_ChangeParams`. This is a very basic stored procedure that will take two input parameters and perform some minor calculations. What we will see is that with a standard parameter declaration (input only) none of the values passed into the stored procedure change externally. The values we send in as parameters will be the same before and after execution, but inside the procedure itself the values will change.

```
CREATE PROCEDURE sp_ChangeParams
    @number1 int,
    @number2 int
AS

    SET @number1 = @number1 * 2
    SET @number2 = 0

    SELECT @number1, @number2
```

Now that we have created this procedure, let's examine what it does. First, we pass in two integer parameters (@number1 and @number2). We use the SET command to set the value of @number1 to twice the parameter value. We then set the value of @number2 to zero. Once this is complete, we run a SELECT statement to access the values of @number1 and @number2.

If we write some code to call this, we can demonstrate that whatever happens to the parameter values inside the stored procedure do not affect the original values of these variables outside the procedure.

```
DECLARE @num1 int
DECLARE @num2 int

SET @num1 = 8
SET @num2 = 11

EXEC sp_ChangeParams @num1, @num2

SELECT @num1, @num2
```

We are declaring two local variables – @num1 and @num2. We set the initial values to 8 for @num1 and 11 for @num2. Then the EXEC statement is used to call the procedure and pass in the values for the parameters using @num1 and @num2 for the parameter values. The stored procedure will display the contents of the parameters; but we want to compare the changes (if any), so we execute a SELECT statement to output the values of the variables after the execution of the stored procedure to see if the values have been modified or not.

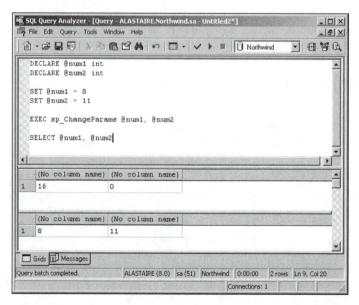

Notice that the stored procedure thinks that @num1 is 16 and @num2 is 0, but when we get back to the calling statement and print @num1 and @num2 we get the original values of the variables before the stored procedure was executed.

Try It Out – More with Parameters

We will be creating another stored procedure in this example, except this time we will be using two parameters and we will add the twist that they can be optional parameters. Our procedure should print the order number and amount from the Order Subtotal view. We also want to filter the information based on a range of values (orders between $100 and $110 for example). We will have two parameters called LowAmount and HighAmount. These parameters will be optional to allow us to automatically select the minimum or maximum value for the subtotal.

1. OK, one step at a time. We first need to build the base query for the procedure.

```
SELECT
    OrderID,
    Subtotal
FROM
    [Order Subtotals]
```

2. We then want to put this into a stored procedure called sp_GetOrdersByRange.

```
CREATE PROCEDURE sp_GetOrdersByRange
AS
SELECT
    OrderID,
    Subtotal
FROM
    [Order Subtotals]
```

3. This will get our base information from the view, but we want to do a filter. We need to add our two optional parameters of LowAmount and HighAmount. We also want to add this as a filter in a WHERE clause to limit the amount of the order information. In order to make a parameter optional we need to give it a default value. We will assign a default value of NULL in order to check if the amount has been set in our procedure a little later.

```
CREATE PROCEDURE sp_GetOrdersByRange
    @LowAmount decimal(19,4) = NULL,
    @HighAmount decimal(19,4) = NULL
AS
SELECT
    OrderID,
    Subtotal
FROM
    [Order Subtotals]
WHERE
    Subtotal BETWEEN @LowAmount AND @HighAmount
```

4. This will work, but will not account for a situation where we want the lowest amount in the view or the highest amount in the view. We need to add some SQL to find the correct low and high amounts if necessary. We will be using an IF statement that we will see in more detail a little later in this chapter. We will also add an ORDER BY clause just to make the data look a little cleaner. We will order by the Subtotal column.

```
ALTER PROCEDURE sp_GetOrdersByRange
   @LowAmount decimal(19,4) = NULL,
   @HighAmount decimal(19,4) = NULL
AS

IF @LowAmount IS NULL
BEGIN
    SELECT @LowAmount = MIN(Subtotal) FROM [Order Subtotals]
END

IF @HighAmount IS NULL
BEGIN
    SELECT @HighAmount = MAX(Subtotal) FROM [Order Subtotals]
END

SELECT
    OrderID,
    Subtotal
FROM
    [Order Subtotals]
WHERE
    Subtotal BETWEEN @LowAmount AND @HighAmount
ORDER BY
    Subtotal
```

Some of the techniques here are just a bit ahead of what we have already covered, but the important concept to keep at the forefront of this demonstration is the use of the parameters within the procedure.

5. Now we can execute the statement and add it to the library.

6. In order to test the procedure, we will try with parameters and by using the dynamically generated values for @LowAmount and @HighAmount. First, let's try with known values of $100 and $110 for the subtotal information:

```
EXEC sp_GetOrdersByRange 100, 110
```

This results in the following seven rows:

	OrderID	Subtotal
1	10259	100.8000
2	10415	102.4000
3	10378	103.2000
4	10969	108.0000
5	10907	108.5000
6	10950	110.0000
7	10531	110.0000

7. On the other hand, if we wanted to see all of the orders up to $20 we could do the following:

```
EXEC sp_GetOrdersByRange NULL, 20
```

By sending a NULL value we are telling the stored procedure to determine the value of the @LowAmount parameter at run time. When we execute this we get only two rows of data:

	OrderID	Subtotal
1	10782	12.5000
2	10807	18.4000

8. We can then do the same with all orders from $10,000 and up. We can execute this in two different ways – the first is like this:

```
EXEC sp_GetOrdersByRange 10000, NULL
```

Here we are specifying that the second parameter is NULL. We could also execute this by sending only the first parameter:

```
EXEC sp_GetOrdersByRange 10000
```

This also works because the second parameter will automatically default to NULL since that is how we defined the parameter. If you execute either of these statements you will get the ten rows of the highest sales that have been placed:

	OrderID	Subtotal
1	10691	10164.8000
2	10540	10191.7000
3	10479	10495.6000
4	10897	10835.2400
5	10817	10952.8400
6	10417	11188.4000
7	10889	11380.0000
8	11030	12615.0500
9	10981	15810.0000
10	10865	16387.5000

Using OUTPUT Parameters

What if we did want to alter the contents of the variables? Well, we need to add the OUTPUT attribute to the appropriate parameters. Let's look at what lines must be modified for this to work:

```
ALTER PROCEDURE sp_ChangeParams
  @number1 int OUTPUT,
  @number2 int OUTPUT
AS


SET @number1 = @number1 * 2
SET @number2 = 0

SELECT @number1, @number2
```

Now, if we re-execute our calling code block, we will see that the results do change a bit. We need to make a minor modification to our calling code to define the parameter as an output parameter. The changed lines are highlighted.

```
DECLARE @num1 int
DECLARE @num2 int

SET @num1 = 8
SET @num2 = 11

EXEC sp_ChangeParams @num1 OUTPUT, @num2 OUTPUT

SELECT @num1, @num2
```

Now, if we execute this we get the following output:

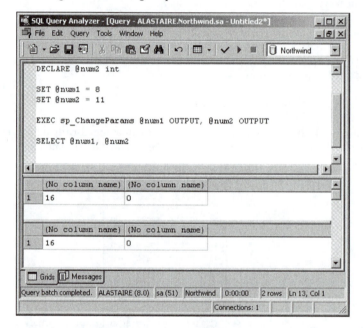

Unlike the first example, this example does modify the values of the input variables. Now when the stored procedure is executed the initial values are modified and @num1 no longer contains the number 8, rather it contains the number 16. A common error with this is to leave out the OUTPUT declaration in the EXEC statement.

If we executed the new function with the original code of:

```
DECLARE @num1 int
DECLARE @num2 int

SET @num1 = 8
SET @num2 = 11

EXEC sp_ChangeParams @num1, @num2

SELECT @num1, @num2
```

We would get the same output as the original stored procedure that used only input parameters:

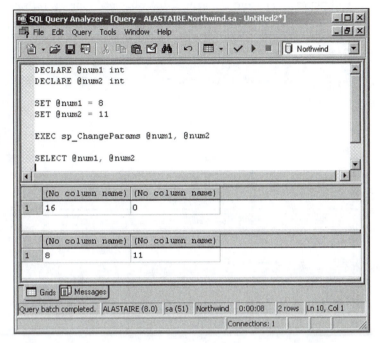

It is very important to be consistent with the use of the OUTPUT attribute. Without this attribute specified in the EXEC call, we will, by default, end up with input only parameters.

Let's change our stored procedure declaration so that @number1 will default to 15 if there is no value specified:

```
CREATE PROCEDURE sp_ChangeParams
    @number1 int = 15 OUTPUT,
    @number2 int OUTPUT
AS

    SET @number1 = @number1 * 2
    SET @number2 = 0

    SELECT @number1, @number2
```

If we call this stored procedure without sending in a value for @number1 the stored procedure will default the value of @number1 to 15. Let's see this in action:

```
DECLARE @num1 int
DECLARE @num2 int

SET @num1 = 8
SET @num2 = 11

EXEC sp_ChangeParams @number2 = @num1

SELECT @num1, @num2
```

Notice that we are now sending a value for @number2 only. What will happen when this executes? The stored procedure will run as normal and will assume the value of 15 for our missing parameter.

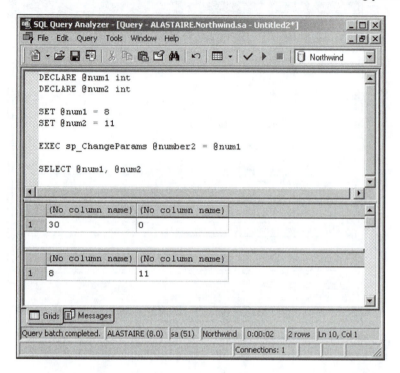

Notice in the first output the value for @number1 is 30 since our procedure multiplies the value of @number1 by 2. Since @number1 defaulted to 15 then we know our logic is correct and that the stored procedure is functioning properly.

This type of function calling can get a bit messy since we may or may not send in all of the parameters to a stored procedure. A cleaner method of calling a stored procedure is to use the DEFAULT keyword. This keyword tells the stored procedure to take any default value associated with a parameter –exactly the same thing that happens when the parameter is not sent. The main difference in this technique is that you maintain the placeholder for the parameter even though we are not sending in a value. This will keep your stored procedure calls more consistent between procedures.

Let's change our code so that we use the DEFAULT keyword rather than named parameters.

```
DECLARE @num1 int
DECLARE @num2 int

SET @num1 = 8
SET @num2 = 11

EXEC sp_ChangeParams DEFAULT, @num2

SELECT @num1, @num2
```

When we run this, we get the exact same results as we did when we used named parameters:

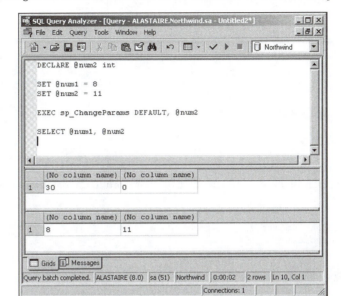

The main difference between the two now is a bit of readability. We can look at this function call and see that there are two parameters to the stored procedure whereas before we didn't know how many parameters there were in the stored procedure. Using the DEFAULT as a placeholder will take us one step closer to more readable code.

That covers the many ways to use parameters when calling stored procedures. That was a lot of ground to cover, but there are many ways to use a stored procedure. Understanding the different ways to utilize parameters will not only build a general understanding of the process but it will provide us with the background to read the code of other developers – and that is critical when doing any form of development.

Updating Data

Updating existing information in a table is very straightforward. Problems arise when users send in data that does not exist. You have an option of generating an error message, or inserting the data when necessary.

Try It Out – Updating Existing Data

Here, we will create a procedure that will update the basic customer data, but will add a record if the CustomerID field does not exist.

1. Firstly, we need to write the declaration and include our parameters:

```
CREATE PROCEDURE sp_UpdateCustomerData
    @CustomerID nchar(5),
    @CompanyName nvarchar
AS
```

2. Now, we test to see if the `CustomerID` already exists.

```
IF EXISTS
    (
    SELECT
        CustomerID
    FROM
        Customers
    WHERE
        CustomerID = @CustomerID
    )

BEGIN
```

3. If it does, then we need to update the existing record in the database. We do this with the following code:

```
-- We need to update the customer data
UPDATE Customers
    SET CompanyName = @CompanyName
FROM
    Customers
WHERE
    CustomerID = @CustomerID
END
```

Here we update the `CompanyName` based on the `@CustomerID` value that was sent in as a parameter for the stored procedure.

4. If the record does not exist then we need to add the new customer into the `Customers` table. This occurs in the `ELSE` portion of the logical `IF` statement.

```
ELSE

BEGIN
    -- The customer does not exist, so we will add
    INSERT INTO Customers(CustomerID, CompanyName)
        VALUES (@CustomerID, @CompanyName)
END
```

Here we call the SQL `INSERT` statement to add the new record.

5. Once the stored procedure has been constructed, we can test it with the following line:

```
exec sp_UpdateCustomerData 'TROTT', 'Trotter inc'
```

In Oracle, we could use the following stored procedure to achieve the same results:

```
CREATE OR REPLACE PROCEDURE sp_UpdateCust
(p_custid IN Customers.CustomerID%TYPE,
p_CompanyName IN Customers.CompanyName%TYPE)
```

```
IS
   Cursor GetCust IS
   SELECT
   CustomerID,
   CompanyName
FROM
   Customers
WHERE
   p_custid = CustomerID;

   custintable NUMBER :=0;

BEGIN
   FOR GetCust_cur IN GetCust LOOP
     IF GetCust_cur.CustomerID = p_custid THEN
       UPDATE Customers SET CompanyName = p_CompanyName;
       custintable := 1;
     END IF;
   END LOOP;
   IF custintable = 0 THEN
     INSERT INTO Customers(CustomerID, CompanyName)
     VALUES (p_custid, p_CompanyName);
   END IF;
END;
/
```

This might be called by using:

```
exec sp_UpdateCustomerData ('TROTT', 'Trotter Inc');
```

Summary

You have been exposed to one of the most powerful features of SQL Server – stored procedures. A stored procedure will not only help you to create modular code, it will help you to solve some of the most complex business problems that you can face in a business application.

You now have the base knowledge required to create a procedure, implement control flow statements, and implement transactional items within your code. While there is much more to stored procedures, you now know enough to begin writing your basic procedures and implementing these modular functions in an enterprise database.

One of the best ways to proceed with stored procedures is to read the procedures created by other developers. There are many ingenious solutions to business problems sitting at the end of your fingertips. One of the most valuable resources to any new developer is the work of the developers that came before you. It will take some time to become very proficient with stored procedures, so take it slow and start with small blocks of code. Soon you will find that you are writing very powerful solutions using SQL.

In the next chapter you will look at other key components of SQL – views and indexes. You will see that these objects can be easily integrated into your stored procedures and provide another level of database development and access in an enterprise database.

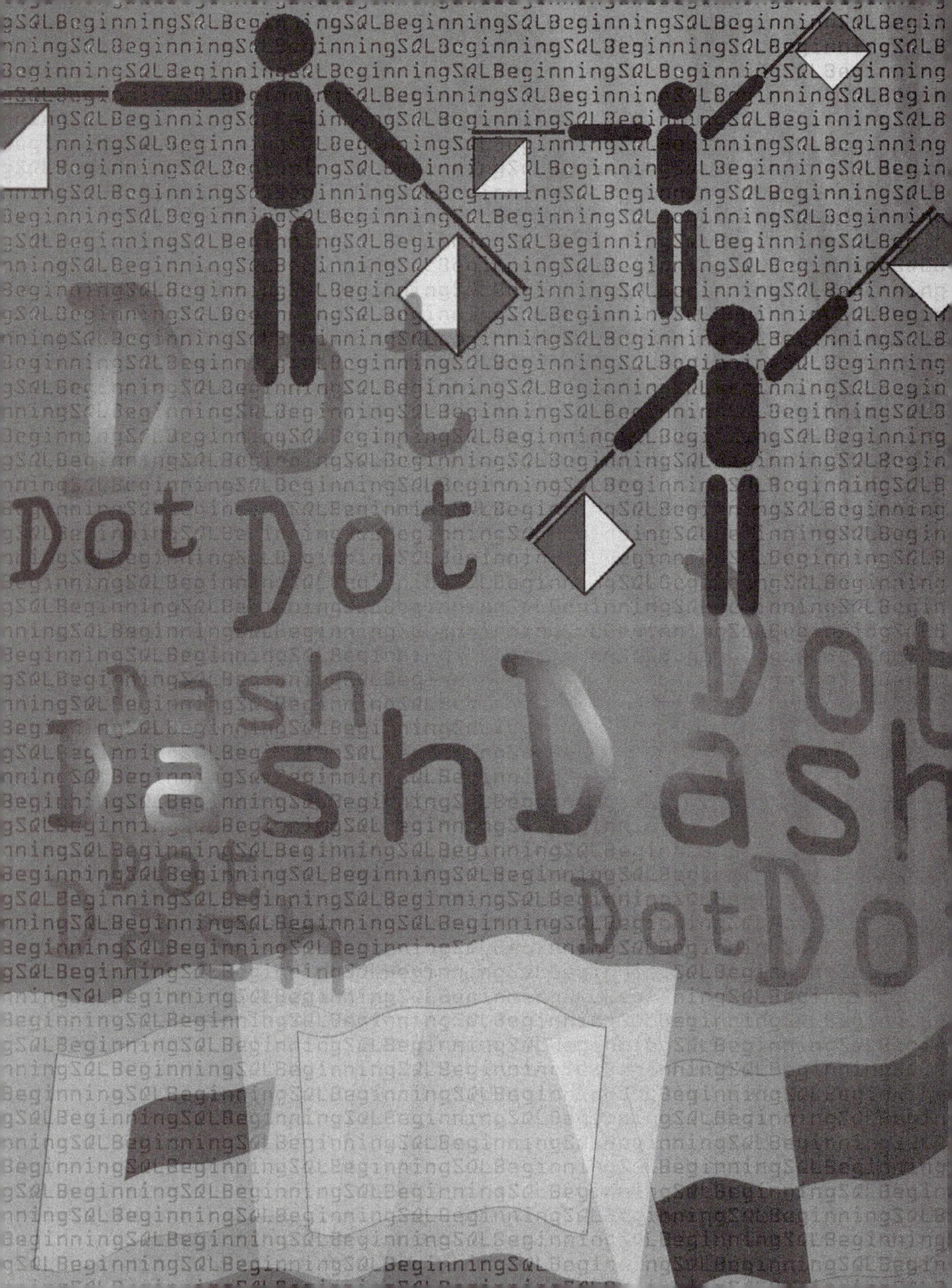

Views and Indexes

Most of the queries that we have looked at up to this point can be reused over and over again. Frequently, these queries will combine information from more than one table. Instead of rewriting these queries every time we want to access data in a particular way, we can create a **view**. In many respects, a view is just like a table, in that it contains fields from which information can be accessed. However, it is very unlike a table in that it isn't stored in the same way – the information it contains is really stored in tables. In some respects, it can be thought of as a **stored procedure**.

What is a View?

Views do not store data in the database; rather, a view stores a query definition. However, the data which is accessed via this query is accessible *as if* the view were just another table. We can run SELECT queries against a view, perform Joins with other tables, and even use the view as the basis of another view.

The key here is that we are only storing the definition of the view, not the data within the view. Thus, whenever we do a SELECT from a view, we actually execute the query and return the results. When we execute the view we get the results from the underlying tables as they were at the time of execution. If the data in the table changes after we get our results, then our view data will be incorrect. At no point does the view reset the data unless we re-execute the view again.

Note that MySQL does not currently support views.

Advantages to Using Views

There are two chief advantages to using views rather than tables:

❑ Views can ease data access: on many occasions, the information we require from a database can involve accessing data from many tables, and this can mean having to construct long and complex queries. When such information is required frequently, using a view can help insofar as it can present data from numerous tables, performing calculations and filters, where necessary, in one place.

❑   Views can increase security: in some situations, we would want people to access information from one field of a table, but deny access to another field of the same table. With a view, we can allow users to access just particular information, by presenting it in a view. We can also assign appropriate permissions to the view. This is known as **partitioning**.

Creating Views

Views are created using the CREATE VIEW statement. This defines a SQL query as a view in the database. Once we execute the CREATE VIEW statement, then the contents of the view will be accessible as a *virtual table*, against which we can run ordinary queries.

Creating a View in SQL Server

The CREATE VIEW statement is a very straightforward SQL command for creating views. Let's take a look at an example of a simple CREATE VIEW statement:

```
CREATE VIEW vw_Contacts AS
SELECT CustomerID,
    ContactName
FROM customers
```

In this simple example, we have created a view called vw_Contacts which contains two columns: CustomerID and ContactName. The contents of these fields have been taken directly from the customers table.

> *Note how the part of the statement which specifies how the view is to be structured, is just like an ordinary SELECT query.*

Creating a View in Oracle

In Oracle, we could create the same view with the following:

```
CREATE VIEW vw_Contacts AS
SELECT CustomerID, ContactName
FROM customers;
```

As we can see, the syntax is identical to the SQL Server CREATE VIEW statement.

Creating a View in DB2

Similarly, creating a view in DB2 is an identical process:

```
CREATE VIEW vw_Contacts AS
SELECT CustomerID, ContactName
FROM customers;
```

If we were now to access the contents of this view using:

```
SELECT * FROM vw_Contacts
```

We would receive the following:

Restrictions

Note, however, that the following restrictions apply to using a query with a view:

- ❑ We cannot use COMPUTE or COMPUTE BY in the query.
- ❑ The ORDER BY clause can only be used when the TOP operator is specified.
- ❑ The INTO clause may not be used.
- ❑ Temporary tables cannot be used in a view.

Outside of these basic rules, most valid SELECT statements can be used with views.

Creating a view such as this is called **vertical partitioning** because we are filtering columns from a table or tables.

> **Vertical partitioning – creating a view to modify the number of columns returned from a table (or tables) in a SELECT statement.**

We can also use a WHERE clause to create **horizontal partitioning** of a table. We could change our view to only display customers from the state of Washington:

```
CREATE VIEW Contacts AS
SELECT CustomerID,
    CompanyName,
    ContactName,
    ContactTitle,
    Phone
FROM customers
WHERE Region = 'WA'
```

This would reduce (or filter) the number of rows that are returned. Actually, this view is partitioning both horizontally (with the WHERE clause) and vertically (using a restricted column list).

If we were to access the contents of this view, we would receive the following:

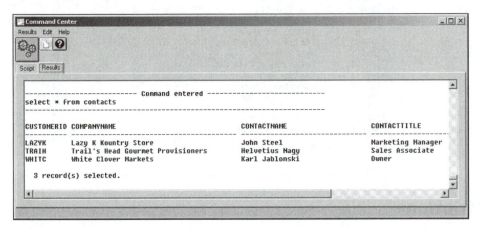

Note that this screenshot has been taken from the DB2 Command Center, and that – due to the small size of the window – not all the returned records can be seen.

Inserting Data Into a View

In many cases, we can insert data into a view, just as though it were an ordinary table. This data will automatically be entered in the relevant places in the tables from which the view has been derived. However, data cannot be entered into all types of view. We will encounter views later in the chapter that will not allow us to enter data into them.

> Note that, due to the structure of many types of views, data cannot be entered into them.

However, if we create a view which is horizontally partitioned in some way – for instance, if it is designed to present information about employees who earn more than $100,000 per year – we can set it up in such a way that entries that conflict with its scope – in this case, salary entries of less than $100,000 – will not be allowed.

We do this using the WITH CHECK OPTION. This may simply be appended to our previous view in the following way:

```
CREATE VIEW Contacts AS
SELECT CustomerID,
    CompanyName,
    ContactName,
    ContactTitle,
    Phone
FROM customers
WHERE Region = 'WA'
WITH CHECK OPTION
```

In this case, we will not be able to insert records into the view where the Region is not 'WA'.

Try it Out – Creating a Partitioned View

Let's create a view that displays the list of products that are priced between $10 and $15. We will horizontally partition the view using a where clause, and we will vertically partition the view using a specific column list. Finally, we will add the WITH CHECK OPTION to prevent any updates that would make the prices fall outside the scope of the view.

The following example will work with SQL Server, Oracle, and DB2.

1. First, let's create the SQL query for generating the result set. We want to display the ProductID, ProductName, and UnitPrice from the Products table:

```
SELECT
  ProductID,
  ProductName,
  UnitPrice
FROM
  Products
```

This returns all of the data.

2. Our view should be based on the price of $10 to $15, so we need to add a WHERE clause to get the filtered results:

```
SELECT
  ProductID,
  ProductName,
  UnitPrice
FROM
  Products
WHERE
  UnitPrice BETWEEN 10 AND 15
```

If we test this query, we see that this is correctly filtering and displaying the data that we want.

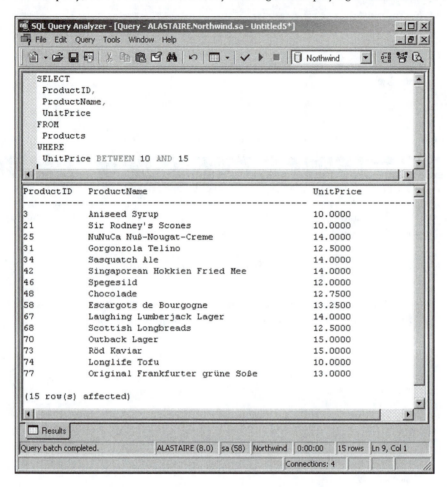

3. Now we need to create the view. We will add a CREATE VIEW statement, and add the WITH CHECK OPTION to preserve the data range:

```
CREATE VIEW vw_FilteredProductList
AS
SELECT
 ProductID,
 ProductName,
 UnitPrice
FROM
 Products
WHERE
 UnitPrice BETWEEN 10 AND 15

WITH CHECK OPTION
```

4. After executing this query, we can test that it is working properly by executing the following code:

```
SELECT * FROM vw_FilteredProductList
```

We should have the following results returned:

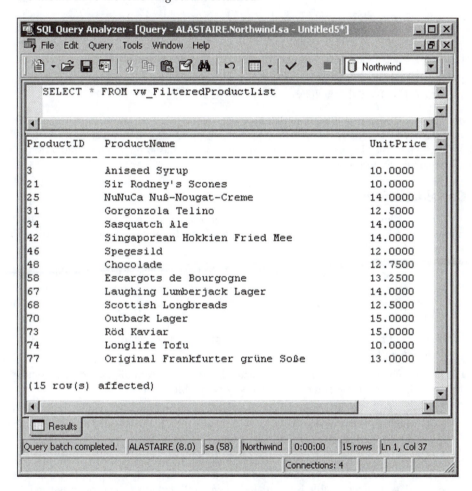

As we have the WITH CHECK OPTION specified, we should not be able to enter data into this view which has a price tag lying outside the $10 - $15 range. For instance, if we were to try to execute the following command:

```
UPDATE vw_FilteredProductList
SET UnitPrice = 20
WHERE ProductID = 3
```

We will encounter an error message.

Updateable Views

Some views can be updated (like a regular table), but not all views. The following list contains the rules for updateable views:

❑ The SELECT statement cannot have any Aggregate functions in the SELECT list (SUM, MIN, MAX, etc).

❑ The TOP operator cannot be used.

❑ The GROUP BY operator cannot be used.

❑ Any SELECT statement that uses the UNION operator cannot be used.

❑ There can be no derived columns in the SELECT list. An example of a derived column would be a calculated field (such as Quantity * Price).

Another general design rule is that the database must know what tables must be updated. If, for instance, we have a key value that we are updating, and it is an ambiguous field reference, then the view will not be updateable. Typically this occurs when a view is based on a one-to-many Join (such as a Join between customers and orders).

View Considerations

When creating a view, there are several design guidelines that we must keep in mind. There are some limitations to creating views, and not knowing some of the design rules can be frustrating and time consuming.

❑ First, we can only create a view in the current database. The SELECT statement of the view, on the other hand, can reference tables in other databases or servers. Thus, we can only create a view in the current database, but the contents of the view can come from other distributed locations.

❑ We cannot have two views with the same name. This is a general naming rule that must be followed with all SQL objects.

❑ Rules such as defaults cannot be associated with views. Although a view acts much like a table, it is not a table and cannot access certain table objects.

❑ We cannot use INTO, COMPUTE, COMPUTE BY, or ORDER BY in a view. ORDER BY can only be used when the TOP operator is also used. A stored procedure would be more appropriate for using the above operators.

❑ The SQL Server full text search capability cannot be used on a view. If you need full text search capability, then you may need to create another table and populate that table with the query data. Once the table is populated, then a full text search can be initialised. SQL Server full text search is covered in more detail in *Professional SQL Server 2000* by Wrox Press.

❑ Temporary tables cannot be accessed in a view, and we cannot create temporary views. A view must be declared with the CREATE VIEW statement and the object is then global to everyone in the database or the user – depending on security settings.

Using JOINS in Views

As we've seen, one of the useful aspects of views is that we can use them to access information from more than one table, presenting data which is distributed over many tables in one place. We can do this using a JOIN (we explored the use of JOINs back in Chapter 8).

Supposing we wanted to create a view which would display information from both the `Customers` and `Orders` tables, we could use the following.

```
CREATE VIEW vw_customerorders
AS
SELECT
 Orders.OrderID,
 Customers.CompanyName
FROM
 Orders
 INNER JOIN Customers ON Orders.CustomerID = Customers.CustomerID
```

This will simply create a view in which order IDs are matched up with particular customers. It will work exactly the same in SQL Server and DB2.

Creating Joined Views in Oracle

We saw back in Chapter 8 that Oracle doesn't support the `JOIN` statement. However, creating a `Join` is very straightforward. To create the equivalent joined view in Oracle, we would use the following:

```
CREATE VIEW vw_customerorders
AS
SELECT
 Orders.OrderID,
 Customers.CompanyName
FROM
 Orders, Customers
 WHERE Orders.CustomerID = Customers.CustomerID;
```

Note how *both* tables from which data is accessed have to be specified in the query, unlike the query in SQL Server.

Try It Out – Creating a JOIN

Suppose that we want to create a view that displays customer's names, the order number and date of a particular order, and the employee responsible for the order.

First, we can think about how to create a query to do this. Let's select the relevant data from the `Orders` table to start with.

```
SELECT
 OrderID,
 CustomerID,
 EmployeeID,
 OrderDate
FROM
 Orders
```

We know that we will want to join the `employee` table and the `Customers` table to the `Orders` table. This is to correlate information about particular orders with information from the `Customers` and `Employees` tables.

First, we'll join the `Orders` and `Customers` tables on the `CustomerID` field:

```
SELECT
  Orders.OrderID,
  Customers.CompanyName,
  Orders.EmployeeID,
  Orders.OrderDate
FROM
  Orders
  INNER JOIN Customers ON Orders.CustomerID = Customers.CustomerID
```

We have also prefixed the field names with the appropriate table names. This can be a useful way of avoiding problems when more than one table contains the same field name.

Now that we have that part working, we need to add the employee information into the query. We will be using the first and last name fields from the `Employee` table. Note how we have concatenated the last and first names of the employees into one field in our view:

```
SELECT
  Orders.OrderID,
  Customers.CompanyName,
  Employees.LastName + ', ' + Employees.FirstName as Employee,
  Orders.OrderDate
FROM
  Orders
  INNER JOIN Customers ON Orders.CustomerID = Customers.CustomerID
  INNER JOIN Employees ON Orders.EmployeeID = Employees.EmployeeID
```

Now, if we execute the query we get the correct results:

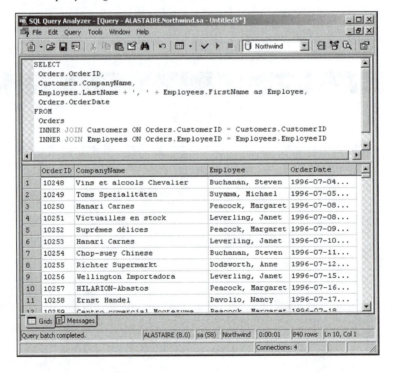

Now we simply need to add `CREATE VIEW` to our query. Let's call it `vw_ExpandedOrderInfo`.

```
CREATE VIEW vw_ExpandedOrderInfo
AS
SELECT
 Orders.OrderID,
 Customers.CompanyName,
 Employees.LastName + ', ' + Employees.FirstName as Employee,
 Orders.OrderDate
FROM
 Orders
 INNER JOIN Customers ON Orders.CustomerID = Customers.CustomerID
 INNER JOIN Employees ON Orders.EmployeeID = Employees.EmployeeID
```

From now on we can use the `vw_ExpandedOrderInfo` view in much the same way that we would use the `Order` table. We now have associated information presented in one place.

DB2 Variation

In DB2, we can construct this view in almost exactly the same way. We saw back in Chapter 11 how DB2 conforms to the ANSI SQL standards for concatenation, using the (||) operator, so note the slight difference in the following:

```
CREATE VIEW vw_ExpandedOrderInfo
AS
SELECT
 Orders.OrderID,
 Customers.CompanyName,
 Employees.LastName || ', ' || Employees.FirstName as Employee,
 Orders.OrderDate
FROM
 Orders
 INNER JOIN Customers ON Orders.CustomerID = Customers.CustomerID
 INNER JOIN Employees ON Orders.EmployeeID = Employees.EmployeeID
```

Oracle Variation

In Oracle, we would use the following:

```
CREATE VIEW vw_ExpandedOrderInfo
AS
SELECT
 Orders.OrderID,
 Customers.CompanyName,
 Employees.LastName || ', ' || Employees.FirstName as Employee,
 Orders.OrderDate
FROM
 Orders, Customers, Employees
WHERE Orders.CustomerID = Customers.CustomerID
AND Orders.EmployeeID = Employees.EmployeeID;
```

Views from Views

Views allow us to consolidate data and calculate values based on one or more tables. We can then take that view and base a new view on it. Views can be the basis for other views, so we can make very complex calculations and summaries using easy to debug intermittent views.

Problems with Views

One of the primary problems with views is that a view is a virtual table. Each time we execute a view, the query must be processed, and the results are then returned. When we are dealing with tables the data already exists in the database. If we do complex calculations or many joins, then performance will suffer since the output must be evaluated each time we execute the statement.

Using a Table Instead of a View

The performance overhead involved with some views can prevent the view from being very useful. There is a workaround for this – use a real table. If we have data that is calculated but does not change often, then we may be better off using a real table to store the values.

For instance, if we have sales rollup data (such as the total sales for a particular year) then we can create this as a table and populate the table with the appropriate data. Since it is very unlikely that we will change the sales data for a previous year, the table will easily suffice for a lookup. Instead of dynamically determining the result set from the view, we can look directly to the table. Not only does this give us a speed increase since we do not have to filter rows of sales data, we now skip the additional step of calculating the values as well.

If, on the other hand, we had values that changed hourly, then this will not be the best approach.

Problems Ordering Data in Views

Another problem with a view is the inability to order the data. We can only use the ORDER BY clause with the TOP clause, so we would have to write an additional SQL statement based on the view in order to view sorted information. This extra layer of SQL coding may be frustrating since there will be additional statements for each column that must be sorted.

Still, the view is handy since it does encapsulate much of the logic of a statement as well as allow for the reuse of SQL code. While this is an annoyance, it is something that all SQL developers learn to live with.

As we saw above, one of the other problems associated with using views is that many of them aren't updateable.

Modifying Existing Views

Of course, we may well encounter situations in which we need to change the structure of a given view. As we will see, this is a relatively straightforward matter.

Checking for Existing Views

Once we have created a view, we cannot simply overwrite it by using a CREATE statement with the same view name. If we wish to recreate a view using the CREATE keyword, then we have to check whether a particular view exists, remove it, and recreate it, using a different specification.

Using SQL Server, information about views may be found in the INFORMATION_SCHEMA object. We delve into the INFORMATION_SCHEMA object in more detail in Chapter 16. We can check whether or not a particular view exists here and, if it does, we can delete it using the DROP command:

```
IF EXISTS (SELECT TABLE_NAME FROM INFORMATION_SCHEMA.VIEWS
              WHERE TABLE_NAME = 'vw_ExpandedOrderInfo')
   DROP VIEW vw_ExpandedOrderInfo
```

The DROP VIEW command is supported in SQL Server, Oracle, and DB2.

Modifying Views

A second option for views is to use ALTER VIEW rather than CREATE VIEW. Like the CREATE VIEW statement, the ALTER VIEW statement takes as parameters a name of a view and a SQL statement. For example, we could alter our vw_ExpandedOrderInfo view so that it no longer displays the order ID in the following way:

```
ALTER VIEW vw_ExpandedOrderInfo
AS
SELECT
 Customers.CompanyName,
 Employees.LastName + ', ' + Employees.FirstName as Employee,
 Orders.OrderDate
FROM
 Orders
 INNER JOIN Customers ON Orders.CustomerID = Customers.CustomerID
 INNER JOIN Employees ON Orders.EmployeeID = Employees.EmployeeID
```

Note that the only difference between this and our earlier CREATE VIEW command is that we're here not selecting the OrderID field.

Modifying a View in Oracle

In Oracle, we have to make some slight changes to this statement. Basically, the main difference, apart from the fact that Oracle doesn't support the JOIN statement, is that we have to explicitly recompile it:

```
ALTER VIEW vw_ExpandedOrderInfo COMPILE
AS
SELECT
 Customers.CompanyName,
 Employees.LastName || ', ' || Employees.FirstName as Employee,
 Orders.OrderDate
FROM
 Orders, Customers, Employees
WHERE Orders.CustomerID = Customers.CustomerID
AND Orders.EmployeeID = Employees.EmployeeID;
```

In DB2, the ALTER VIEW command operates in a very different way to the other DBMS, and it is more straightforward to drop and create a new view.

What is an Index?

One of the most important steps in designing and implementing a database system is creating and properly configuring an **index**. An index is primarily useful in improving performance. An index consists of a series of pointers which identify particular blocks of data in the database. We will look at how an index actually works a little later in this section.

Supposing we frequently use the `LastName` field of the employees table for searching using a `WHERE` clause. In such a situation, we could build an index based on the `LastName` field in the table. Now, when we run our query, the records of the last names in the index are scanned, and, as scanning these requires less resources than scanning the actual contents of a table, our query will run much faster.

However, indexing can be a double-edged sword. When entering data into an indexed table, not only does the table have to be updated, but the index also has to be updated. This requires resources, so, if we are in a situation where a lot of updates have to be done, having the table indexed can actually slow down performance.

Let's look at how we actually construct an index.

Creating an Index

An index is created using the `CREATE INDEX` statement. This is a more complex statement than the `CREATE VIEW` statement, since there are several options that you can choose when building a database index.

There are three different types of index that we can create: unique, clustered, or non-clustered. We will be discussing each one of these in more detail in the next section. For now, just note that the default is non-clustered, but we can override that option by explicitly stating the index type.

In creating an index, we would also specify an index name, the tables or views which the index is to be built for, and the fields which are to act as the basis of the index. Although we can index a view, there are many issues associated with doing so. We would be better served to properly index the underlying tables rather than the view itself.

> *If you want more information on creating indexed views then you should take a look at the SQL Server Books Online for more information. Search on "Creating an Indexed View" for the details and pitfalls of indexed views.*

The general structure of an index declaration is:

```
CREATE CLUSTERED INDEX index_name ON table_name (field_name)
```

As we have seen, there are three different types of index. Let's take a look at these in turn.

Creating an Index on MySQL

In MySQL, we can create a simple index using the following:

```
CREATE INDEX ix_Prod ON Products (ProductName);
```

Creating an Index on Oracle

In Oracle, we could use the following to create a simple index:

```
CREATE INDEX ix_Prod ON Products (ProductName);
```

Creating an Index on DB2

And in DB2, we could also use the following:

```
CREATE INDEX ix_Prod ON Products (ProductName);
```

Index Types

There are three distinct index types that we can create: clustered, non-clustered, and unique. Each index type has its particular uses within the database system. As with other aspects of indexing, it is important to note how each index type works and when to use the individual types.

Clustered

A **clustered** index is a special type of index because it physically reorders the data in the table to conform to the new index definition. For this reason, creating a clustered index may take a good bit of time if you have a lot of data in your table already.

A clustered index is the fastest type of index to use on a table for the simple fact that the data is physically sorted and eliminates the lookup pages of a non-clustered index. Inserts can be slow on a clustered index because the entire table may need to be resorted to preserve the index.

There is one major caveat to a clustered index – a table may only have one clustered index at a time. The reason that a table can only have one clustered index is because the data is physically sorted.

A good example would be a telephone directory. The names of each person are listed in alphabetical order with the phone number after the name.

A clustered index is not the default index type. For this reason, a clustered index must be explicitly specified when creating the index:

```
CREATE CLUSTERED INDEX ix_Prod ON Products (ProductName)
```

Note that in this example, we try to create a clustered index on a table in the Northwind database which already has a clustered index. In order for it to run, we would have to DROP the existing index. We see how to do this a little later.

Depending on its size, a clustered index is broken down into three different parts:

- ❑ Root node
- ❑ Intermediate level
- ❑ Leaf nodes (or data pages)

The root level contains the coarsest breakdown of the index. For example, if the index specifies last names, this node would consist of entries such as 'Ab – Bo', 'Bp – Ck', and 'Cl – Em'. These will point to intermediate level nodes, where more fine grained entries will point to data in the leaf nodes.

For example, entries in the intermediate level nodes might consist of entries such as 'Abra – Adri'. These will point to leaf nodes, which contain the actual records corresponding to particular last names.

The purpose of having such intermediate nodes is to minimize the total amount of rows the DBMS has to search through. There may be more than one level of intermediate nodes.

The following diagram illustrates this structure:

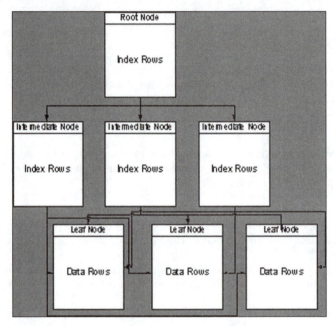

When data is added to the system all of the nodes must be checked to see if any changes need to be made to the index. For this reason, a clustered index may take longer to update.

In practice, we don't generally have to worry about the structuring of such an index: the DBMS will look after it for us. However, it is important to understand how indexes work, because understanding their structure helps us understand their effect on performance.

NonClustered

A **non-clustered** index is an index that does not physically reorder the pages. Instead, it consists of pages of pointers which allow us to trace rows in particular data pages. We can think of it as the index of a book.

A non-clustered index is much less efficient than a clustered index because it does not reorder the data in a table. Instead, it creates a page of lookup information, and points us to a relevant page number.

Such an index may be structured in a similar way to a clustered index, including intermediate nodes. Where the non-clustered index differs from the clustered index is that the leaf and data pages are not sorted, so there is some additional scanning that is required to locate data. This means that it is generally slower than a clustered index.

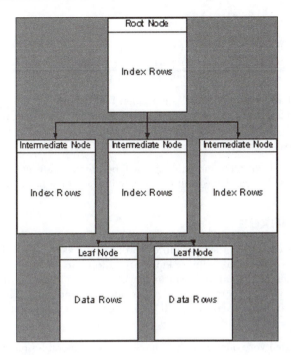

Notice that this graphic of a non-clustered index is much more complex than the example of a clustered index. Any of the intermediate pages can point to any of the leaf pages. Since there is no physical reordering of a page, we may need to scan multiple intermediate pages to find the information that will lead us to the data page. Likewise, notice that a data page can be associated with any of the intermediate pages. This index is much less efficient than the same clustered index, but the tradeoff is that we can have more than one of these indexes on a table. Also, as complex as this may seem, it is much more efficient than not having an index at all.

Also, non-clustered indexes are much faster to maintain. If we have a large number of updates on a table with few queries, then a non-clustered index may be the most useful type of index to use.

A non-clustered index may be created in the following way:

```
CREATE NONCLUSTERED INDEX ix_Prod ON Products (ProductName)
```

In SQL Server, indexes will be created as non-clustered indexes by default. However, when in doubt, specify. If we are not sure of the current system configuration and want to be sure that the index is non-clustered, then we should specify the non-clustered parameter. This is an example of where we could make cleaner SQL code. Rather than assume the system defaults, we explicitly state the index type. Someone coming along later can look at the index and determine exactly what sort of index it is. There is no guarantee that future releases of SQL Server will assume that the non-clustered index is the default index type.

There is no ALTER INDEX functionality in SQL, so indexes must be dropped and re-added if we want to change the index structure or type.

Unique

A **unique** index is used when we do not want any duplicate values in the field or fields within the index. An example of a unique index would be a part number, employee number, or any key value that must be unique within the table. This is used most often for primary keys.

We can have more than one unique index on a table. For instance, an employee number is an auto-generating number that is used as the primary key of the `Employees` table. Alternatively, we could use a *Social Security Number* field (or *National Insurance Number* field) as the basis of a unique index, as these will be unique to individuals.

As we saw, if we create a clustered index, then it will be unique. However, a unique index does not have to be a clustered index. We can have multiple unique indexes on a particular table.

Composite Indexes

A composite index is where an index has more than one field as the key value. Composite indexes can be very handy since we can break primary key information into multiple columns. This would allow us to build what are called **intelligent keys**. For instance, if we had inventory information, then we could create a composite key based on manufacturer, part number, and color. This would assure us that there is a level of uniqueness in our data, while still being able to search information based just on color or manufacturer.

Such a technique is used very often in large databases, since the tables have been so normalized that keys carry over to other tables. Through using composite keys, we could create more efficient joins between tables, since the composite key would have enough information contained within it that we would not need to join a large number of tables to get from table A to table E. Instead, table E would contain enough key information from A that we could join directly between A and E without needing to include tables B, C, and D just for the join information.

Composite indexes are larger than most other indexes due to the fact that they contain information based on two or more columns of data. We need to be careful when creating large composite indexes, since each index is limited to 900 bytes of information per row. If we had three columns of `varchar(300)`, `varchar(300)`, and `varchar(400)` then we could not create the index.

Now, this would (in most situations) be a bad index in any case since there would be too much data. However, on the other hand, if we carry composite indexes between tables, then our indexes may grow very large.

> **A SQL Server index cannot exceed 900 bytes of information per row of data.**

A Simple Example of a Composite Index

Let's take a look at an example of composite keys that carry between tables.

Suppose we have a `conference` table which contains `ConferenceID` and `ConferenceName` fields, the `ConferenceID` being the primary key. Also, we have a `session` table with `SessionID`, `ConferenceID`, and `SessionName` fields.

The composite key in this situation could include `SessionID` and `ConferenceID`. This would allow us to have the same session name, but for difference conferences.

Suppose also that we have a third table: the `presentation` table. This table contains `PresentationID`, `SessionID`, `ConferenceID`, and `PresentationName`.

The composite key could now consist of the `PresentationID`, `SessionID`, and `ConferenceID`.

Using composite keys, we could find all of the presentations for a given conference without using either the `conference` table or the `session` table. We have eliminated the need for several joins, and thus speeded up our query.

The following diagram illustrates these relationships:

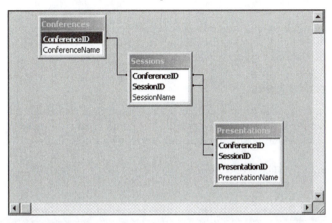

We could now write a `SELECT` statement to find all of the presentations at conference number 1 without the need to include any tables other than the `Presentation` table:

```
SELECT
  *
FROM
  Presentations
WHERE
  ConferenceID = 1
```

If we had a structure that did not include any composite keys, then our query would be a bit more complex. The following diagram shows the table structure without the composite keys:

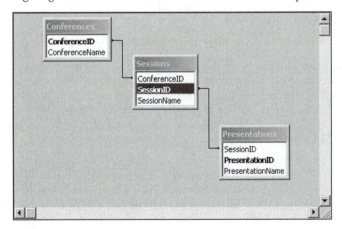

Now, if we wanted to do the same query as before it would be more complex, since we would need to add one or more tables to the query:

```
SELECT
  Presentations.*
FROM
  Sessions
  INNER JOIN Presentations ON Sessions.SessionID = Presentations.SessionID
WHERE
  Sessions.ConferenceID=1
```

Composite keys are not for every situation. They can be very handy when dealing with large numbers of tables. On the other hand, they can be difficult to maintain since we need to know information about other tables that may not be readily available.

Creating Composite Keys

In order to create a composite key we need to specify more than one column in the column list of the CREATE INDEX statement. In our above example, we could create the index for the presentation table using the following statement (assuming that we wanted a clustered index):

```
CREATE CLUSTERED INDEX ix_Presentation_Comp ON
Presentation (PresentationID, SessionID, ConferenceID)
```

Note that the order in which the fields are specified can affect performance. We want the fields to appear in the most common search order, since part of an index is not only the type and the field, but the order as well. We would still be able to search using the fields out of order, but there would be a performance hit on our queries.

Another important thing to note is that a search on just PresentationID would use the composite key: we would not have to create a separate non-clustered index to cover this. This is referred to as a covered index. On the other hand, a search that uses only SessionID would not utilize the index due to the order of the fields. If PresentationID and SessionID were used, then the index would cover the search. This is the reason that field order is so important.

As we have seen, creating a composite index is straightforward.

Guidelines to Writing Indexes

When creating an index, there are several items to keep in mind:

❑   First, create an index on rows that have a high degree of uniqueness. If we create an index on the gender column of an employee table, then the index will not be as efficient as creating the index on the last name column. If there are too many like values (sex, state, etc.) then the index will require multiple leaf pages for the record pointers. On an efficient index the root should be read, the leaf should then be read, and finally the data page should be scanned for the data. On a limited value index, we may have to scan multiple leaf or data pages for the results.

❑   Second, only index columns that are frequently used as search criteria. If we rarely search on the employee badge number, for instance, then this probably should not be an index. An index requires extra space to maintain the page data and resources to maintain the information in the index.

❑ Third, we should base your indexes on our criteria. If we usually search for the employee department and division at the same time, then we would be better served to create a composite index of the two columns rather than two individual indexes. SQL will respond faster to the composite since the composite key looks more like the actual criteria. Granted, two indexes would also work, but they would not be as efficient.

❑ Fourth, we should only create a clustered index if we need to reorder the data. A clustered index is typically used for a primary key where it will be used as join criteria between tables. The fastest type of index is a clustered index, but there can only be one clustered index on a table. There are also more overheads involved with a clustered index since the data must be ordered. If the table has a high number of additions and deletions, then we may find ourselves rebuilding an index as often as once a week (maybe even sooner). Clustered indexes, while fast, require more overhead from the system. When possible, we should use a non-clustered index.

Problems with Indexing

If we do not have enough indexing on our tables, then our queries may run slowly. If we have too many indexes on our tables then the queries may still run slow, and updates will be very slow. Whenever we add a new record or delete a record, the indexes must be updated to reflect the changes. I have actually seen databases that were so over-indexed that a simple insert took over a minute to complete (this is just ONE row of data).

There is a fine line between under-indexing and over-indexing. Where is that line? Generally, experience will dictate the best way to index our tables, but the general rule of thumb is to only index what is frequently searched on.

> **Only index what is searched most often!**

Checking for Existing Indexes

Indexes cannot be directly edited. We must first check to see if an index already exists under the name we are trying to save as. We must use the DROP INDEX and CREATE INDEX statements in order to make modifications to the index.

The primary way to check for the existence of an index – in SQL Server – is to first check the sysindexes table. The following code can be used at the beginning of an index to drop any pre-existing indexes:

```
IF EXISTS (SELECT name FROM sysindexes
    WHERE name = ' ix_Prod')
   DROP INDEX ix_Prod
```

Remember that, within SQL Server, to check for the existence of a view, we need to check the Information_Schema.Tables table, while to check for the existence of an index, we need to look at the sysindexes table.

Summary

This chapter has introduced two topics: views and indexes. We saw that views are primarily useful in two ways:

- ❑ They can increase security.
- ❑ They can present frequently accessed data from multiple tables in one place.

We saw that indexes can help us:

- ❑ Speed up queries.
- ❑ Obviate the need for multiple joins.

In the next chapter we will look at the database structure in more detail: specifically, we will concentrate on schemas.

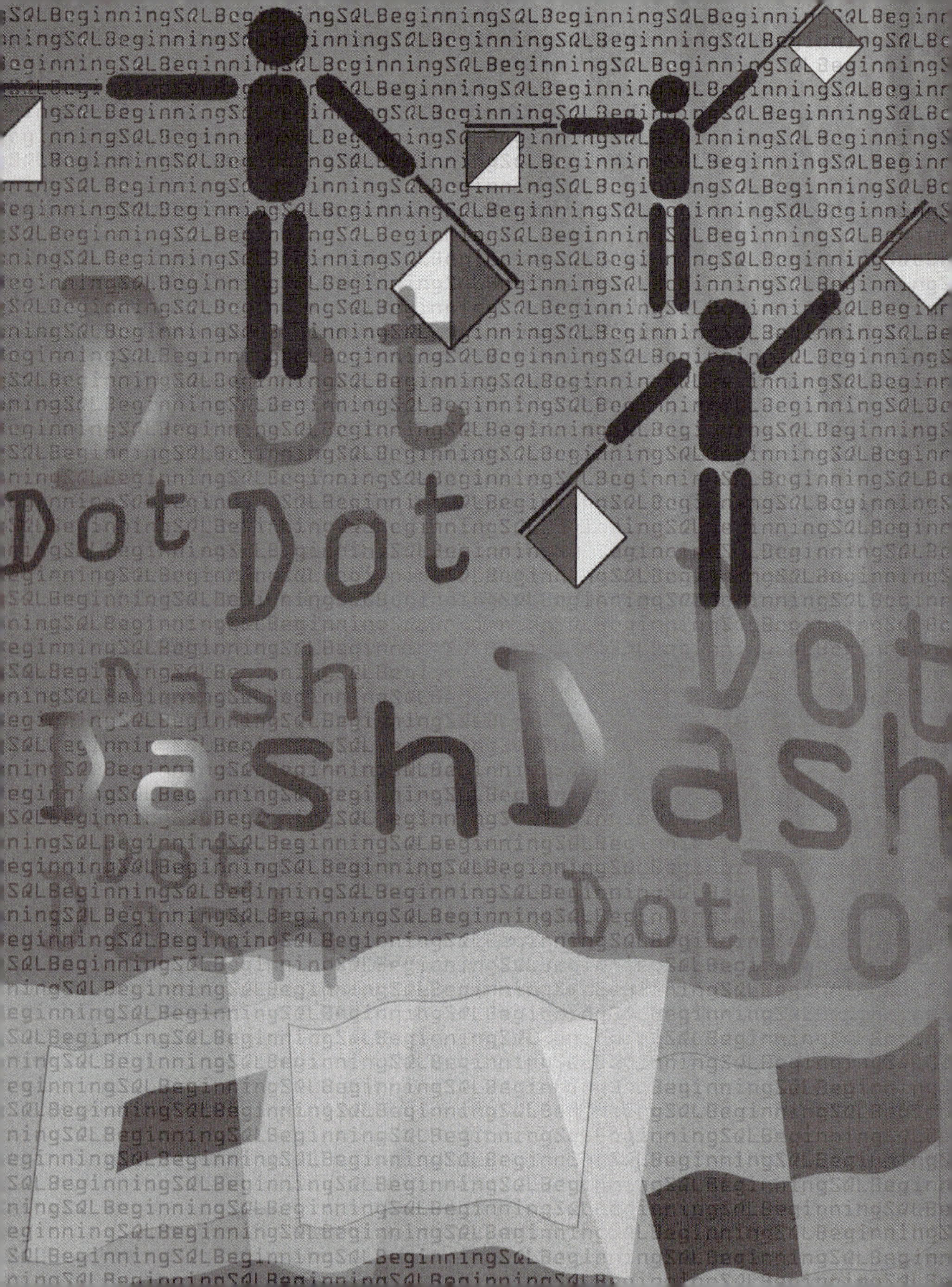
Dot
Dot
Dash
Dash
Dot
Dash
Dot
Dot

Schemas

So far, we have looked in some depth at the basics of the SQL language and how it is used in DBMS products. We should now be in a position to be able to use SQL to retrieve records from a database table, or a combination of tables, insert new records in a table, update or delete table records, and build many of the database structures, such as tables, views, and stored procedures.

In this chapter, we will look at a container object that contains most of the other database objects, and helps organize them in terms of ownership and access privileges. This container object is called the **schema** object. We will look at how to find out which schemas certain objects, such as tables, belong to. This is particularly important if we want to decide who can access these objects, and what kinds of permissions they have when doing so. We will be covering the following topics:

- ❑   What is a schema, and when do we need to use it?
- ❑   What are the various objects that comprise a schema?
- ❑   What is INFORMATION_SCHEMA and how is it implemented in major SQL dialects?
- ❑   How to use INFORMATION_SCHEMA to view information about a database and its objects.
- ❑   How to find out what schema certain database objects belong to.

As with other chapters in the book, the Northwind sample database will be used as the basis for examples.

What are Schemas?

The database **schema** is a high-level container object defined by the SQL standard to contain other database objects. This object is implemented differently among different Relational Database Management Systems (RDBMS or more commonly DBMS). In some of these implementations, such as Microsoft SQL Server, the schema becomes synonymous with the catalog or database owner. In other implementations, such as Oracle, a database can include more than one schema, and a schema denotes a group of database objects belonging to one user.

A schema is a named entity with the name usually following the owner, or the person who creates it. Some of the objects a schema contains are:

❑   tables

❑   views

❑   stored procedures

❑   domains

❑   assertions

❑   privileges

❑   character sets

❑   collations

❑   translations

❑   triggers

❑   SQL modules

❑   SQL routines

❑   roles

We have already encountered some of these objects, such as tables, views, and stored procedures. A description of some of the other schema objects that have not yet been covered in the book will follow later in the chapter, but first, let's take a closer look at SQL schemas.

Creating Schemas

The SQL standard provides a statement to help create a schema. There are no surprises here: the statement is called CREATE SCHEMA. The general syntax of this statement is:

```
CREATE SCHEMA <Schema name> |
            AUTHORIZATION <AuthorizationID>
            [DEFAULT CHARACTER SET <character set name>]
            [<Schema Element List>]
```

The [<Schema Element List>] list includes optional CREATE statements for all the objects within the schema. In other words, we can create all the objects within the schema at the time we create the schema. Alternatively, we can just create some at that time, and add the rest of the objects later on using their own CREATE statements. The following code shows how such a list is defined in SQL:

```
<Schema Element List> ::=
   CREATE DOMAIN statement(s) |
   CREATE TABLE statement(s) |
   CREATE VIEW statement(s) |
   CREATE ASSERTION statement(s) |
   CREATE CHARACTER SET statement(s) |
   CREATE COLLATION statement(s) |
   CREATE TRANSLATION statement(s) |
   CREATE TRIGGER statement(s) |
   CREATE TYPE statement(s) |
   CREATE PROCEDURE statement(s) |
   CREATE FUNCTION statement(s) |
   CREATE ROLE statement(s) |
   GRANT statement(s)
```

A schema name is identified by the **catalog name**. This is the name of the database that contains the schema. If the catalog name is left out in the CREATE SCHEMA statement, the schema is created in the catalog of the SQL session. A schema name must be unique within the catalog it belongs to.

> When you log into a database, a session is created on the database server that holds the credentials that you used to log in, a current database (the one you logged into), and all the data relating to your work, such as any global variables, and so on. The session will belong to you as a user, and any objects created during the session, such as a schema object, will be placed in the session's database unless the name of such objects indicated otherwise. For instance, if you log into the Northwind database in Query Analyzer in SQL Server, you create a session on the database server with Northwind as the session database. If you create a schema or a table, for example, during this session in a statement like: **CREATE SCHEMA myschema** ... then the new schema **myschema** will be located in the Northwind database.

The AuthorizationID is the name of the owner of the schema. A CREATE SCHEMA statement must include the schema name, the authorization, or both. If the schema name is not included in the CREATE SCHEMA statement, then the AuthorizationID must be included, and the schema name will default to that authorization ID. If the statement does not include an AUTHORIZATION clause, then the authorization defaults to the name of the owner of the module containing the statement, or, if that does not exist, it defaults to the session authorization ID (the ID used to log into the SQL session).

> As mentioned earlier, a schema, like any other database object, has an owner. For instance, when you log into a database as SCOTT and create some objects, these objects will be owned by SCOTT. This user will have owner privileges to these objects, in other words more power to deal with them than other users. Privileges are authorization levels that determine what parts of the database a user can access and what type of access they have on it. For instance, privileges can determine that a certain user or group of users can only **SELECT** (read) from a certain table without inserting, updating, or deleting records. An owner privilege to an object allows the user with such a privilege to do virtually anything they want with the object, even altering (modifying) it, or deleting it altogether.

As an example, the following statement creates a schema called myschema and sets the owner as dave:

```
CREATE SCHEMA myschema AUTHORIZATION dave
```

The following statement creates a schema and calls it myschema. The authorization defaults to the session authorization, which we assume is dave.

```
CREATE SCHEMA myschema
```

The following statement creates a schema called dave with an authorization ID as dave.

```
CREATE SCHEMA AUTHORIZATION dave
```

Note that creating a schema does not make it the current schema, and does not make the schema authorization the current authorization. For instance, if a user is logged into a DBMS with AUTHORIZATION john, *and issues the first* CREATE SCHEMA *statement shown above, the current schema remains whatever it was before, and the current authorization remains* john.

> **Each database comes with a character set and may support more than one. Character sets express what locale the database supports, for instance the language: English versus Japanese; currency: US Dollars versus Japanese Yen, and time zone used to create timestamps.**

The DEFAULT CHARACTER SET clause sets a default character set for the newly created schema. If it is not included, the default character set for the schema defaults to that of the INFORMATION_SCHEMA. Well, you may ask, what is this INFORMATION_SCHEMA thing? The answer is that every SQL standard catalog (database) comes with a schema called INFORMATION_SCHEMA. As the name implies, this schema includes data about all of the objects in the catalog. In some implementations, such as SQL Server, it is expanded and called the system tables, in others, such as Oracle, it is vastly expanded and called the data dictionary. We will see how we can use the INFORMATION_SCHEMA to retrieve information about our schema and its objects.

As an example of creating a schema with some of its listed objects, the following statement creates a schema called myself in a SQL Server 2000 environment. The statement applies to the Northwind sample database. Along with the schema, the statement creates three tables: Customers, Employees, and Products, as well as a view called ProductList. In SQL Server, the schema name is always the same as the authorization name; therefore, there is no schema name defined in the statement. Also, notice that a SELECT privilege is granted to the public system login within the CREATE SCHEMA statement.

```
CREATE SCHEMA AUTHORIZATION myself
CREATE TABLE Customers (
    CustomerID nchar (5) PRIMARY KEY ,
    CompanyName nvarchar (40) NOT NULL ,
    ContactName nvarchar (30)  NULL ,
    ContactTitle nvarchar (30)  NULL ,
    Address nvarchar (60)  NULL ,
    City nvarchar (15)  NULL ,
    Region nvarchar (15)  NULL ,
    PostalCode nvarchar (10)  NULL ,
    Country nvarchar (15)  NULL ,
    Phone nvarchar (24)  NULL ,
    Fax nvarchar (24)  NULL
)
GO

CREATE TABLE Employees (
    EmployeeID int IDENTITY (1, 1) PRIMARY KEY ,
    LastName nvarchar (20)  NOT NULL ,
    FirstName nvarchar (10)  NOT NULL ,
    Title nvarchar (30)  NULL ,
    TitleOfCourtesy nvarchar (25)  NULL ,
    BirthDate datetime NULL ,
    HireDate datetime NULL ,
```

```
        Address nvarchar (60)  NULL ,
        City nvarchar (15)  NULL ,
        Region nvarchar (15)  NULL ,
        PostalCode nvarchar (10)  NULL ,
        Country nvarchar (15)  NULL ,
        HomePhone nvarchar (24)  NULL ,
        Extension nvarchar (4)  NULL ,
        Photo image NULL ,
        Notes ntext  NULL ,
        ReportsTo int NULL ,
        PhotoPath nvarchar (255)  NULL
)
GO

CREATE TABLE Products (
        ProductID int IDENTITY (1, 1) PRIMARY KEY ,
        ProductName nvarchar (40)  NOT NULL ,
        SupplierID int NULL ,
        CategoryID int NULL ,
        QuantityPerUnit nvarchar (20)  NULL ,
        UnitPrice money NULL ,
        UnitsInStock smallint NULL ,
        UnitsOnOrder smallint NULL ,
        ReorderLevel smallint NULL ,
        Discontinued bit NOT NULL
)
GO

create view "ProductList" AS
SELECT Product_List.ProductID, Product_List.ProductName
FROM Products AS Product_List
WHERE (((Product_List.Discontinued)=0))
GO
GRANT SELECT on ProductList TO public
```

SQL Domains

Domains serve as **extended data types** to define columns within tables of a schema. They are basically named, user-defined sets of values. A schema may contain zero or more domains. Domains are created according to the SQL standard with the CREATE DOMAIN statement. Not all SQL flavors implement this statement as the standard dictates. For instance, in SQL Server, domains are closely related to user-defined data types, but there is no CREATE DOMAIN statement; instead, they are considered system objects that are created and maintained by SQL Server when the user creates user-defined types.

The general syntax for the CREATE DOMAIN statement is:

```
CREATE DOMAIN <domain name> [AS]
            <data type>
            [<DEFAULT default value>]
            [<Domain Constraint> List]
            [COLLATE <collation name>]
```

The domain name identifies the domain and schema to which it belongs. If the schema name is included in the name specification, the domain will belong to the schema with that name. If a schema name is not included, the domain will belong to the session's schema. A domain name must be unique within the schema that contains it.

447

Domain Examples

A good example of using a domain in a schema would be a generic NAME field. Many tables include a derivative of the name field. For instance, the Customer table may include a First_Name and Last_Name field; the Employee table may include the same, and so on. Defining a generic name field will save time when creating these tables. For example:

```
CREATE DOMAIN GenericName AS VARCHAR(30);
```

The created domain can then be used in the CREATE TABLE statement for both the Employee and Customer table without being worried about specifying the length and data type of name fields in these tables:

```
CREATE TABLE Employee (
        Emp_ID     INTEGER,
        FirstName  GenericName,
        LastName   GenericName, …);

CREATE TABLE Customer (
        Cust_ID    INTEGER,
        FirstName  GenericName,
        LastName   GenericName, …);
```

Another example would be creating some numeric fields that have certain characteristics and are not defined in the SQL implementation. For instance, we can define a domain to represent a MONEY data type as a decimal with two decimal digits, or an INTEREST data type as a decimal with three decimal digits and a constraint that it has to be greater or equal to zero:

```
CREATE DOMAIN MyMoney AS DECIMAL(8,2);
CREATE DOMAIN INTEREST AS DECIMAL(5,3);
ALTER DOMAIN INTEREST ADD CONSTRAINT PositiveValue
        CHECK (VALUE >= 00.000);

CREATE TABLE Transactions (
        Trans_ID   INTEGER,
        Discount   INTEREST,
        Amount     MyMoney, …)
```

Notice in the example above how we used the ALTER DOMAIN statement to add the constraint PositiveValue that restricts the values of this domain to zero or greater.

Try It Out – Creating a Domain in SQL Server

This section will create a domain that represents a social security number as a character field with a length of 11. Use the domain in the date/time fields of the Order table in the Northwind database, but remember that in SQL Server, there is no CREATE DOMAIN statement, and that domains are basically user-defined data types.

In SQL Server, the concept of domains is very narrow and is labeled as user-defined data types (UDTs). You can create a UDT in one of two ways: within Enterprise Manager or using Transact SQL (the SQL flavor that ships with SQL Server). Let's see how we can create such a UDT using Transact SQL.

To do this, we need to be familiar with a system stored procedure in SQL Server, sp_addtype. This procedure allows you to add new data types by passing to it four parameters: name, definition, null type (whether it accepts NULL values), and the owner of the UDT.

```
EXEC sp_addtype SocialSecurityNum, 'VARCHAR(11)', 'NOT NULL'
```

The code above will create a new user-defined data type, called SocialSecurityNum of varchar(11) specification. The new type does not accept NULL values and is owned by whoever is logged into the session.

Assertions (Constraints)

Assertions are expressions that cause an error if their logical value is not obtained when evaluated by the database engine. Assertions are practical constraints that are placed on schema objects, such as tables and domains, based on some business logic. These constraints are available in virtually all DBMSs and they could include: CHECK constraints, DEFAULT constraints, UNIQUE constraints, PRIMARY KEY constraints, and FOREIGN KEY constraints.

The SQL standard provides the statement CREATE ASSERTION to create such assertions. For instance, to create a CHECK assertion that ensures that the value of start_date is smaller than that of end_date in a table, we could write something like:

```
CREATE ASSERTION correct_date_sequence
    CHECK (end_date >= start_date)
```

Constraints in SQL Server

SQL implementations use their own syntax most of the time. Creation of the assertion becomes part of the creation (or alteration) of the schema of the object to which it applies. For instance, to add a UNIQUE constraint on a newly added social security field to the Customers table in the SQL Server database, Northwind, we can write:

```
ALTER TABLE Customers ADD SSN NCHAR(11) NULL
    CONSTRAINT cust_unique UNIQUE
```

However, be aware that this example will only work if the table is empty beforehand. If there are already records in the table, when you add a new field, the value of this field takes the default (if defined) or NULL (this case): if all the values in the table for that field are NULL, then they are not unique any more, which defeats the purpose of the unique constraint.

Constraints in Oracle

In Oracle, a similar syntax is used whereby constraint creation is part of the creation or alteration of the table or object to which it applies. For instance, to create a CHECK constraint in Oracle, we would use the following type of statement. This constraint applies to the department table and will ensure that the department ID (deptid) is between 10 and 99, that its name is always entered in upper case, and that the department is located in one of a list of specific cities:

```
CREATE TABLE department
    (deptid NUMBER  CONSTRAINT check_deptid
        CHECK (deptid BETWEEN 10 AND 99),
```

```
deptname VARCHAR2(9)  CONSTRAINT check_deptname
   CHECK (deptname = UPPER(deptname)),
location VARCHAR2(10)  CONSTRAINT check_location
   CHECK (location IN ('DETROIT','LOS ANGELES',
   'NEW YORK','CHICAGO','SEATTLE'))
);
```

Try It Out – Writing a Check Constraint

Create a table called `tblSportingEvent`. This will hold data for a sporting event. In this table, we have two fields, `team1` and `team2`, that represent the opposing teams in the event. Write a table-level check constraint that ensures that the two teams do not have the same value.

```
CREATE TABLE tblSportingEvent (
   Team1 varchar(50),
   Team2 varchar(50),
CONSTRAINT chk CHECK  (Team1 <> Team2))
```

How It Works

In the code above, a table was created with two fields in it. A table-level check constraint was also added to the statement to ensure that the two fields cannot have the same value. The check constraint is table-level because a field-level check constraint cannot reference another field in the table. A table-level check constraint, on the other side, can reference any fields within that table.

Privileges

Privileges are actions that can be performed on schema objects. These actions depend on the type of object they are applied to. For instance, table privileges may include: ALTER, DELETE, INDEX, INSERT, REFERENCES, SELECT, and UPDATE privileges. A procedure, function, or package, on the other hand, may have a privilege called EXECUTE. Privileges are granted with the GRANT statement, and they are granted to users and roles (we looked at users and roles back in Chapter 3). There are usually system privileges that control access to the system data, such as system tables, and schema object privileges, such as those granted to schema tables, views, and procedures.

Granting Privileges in Oracle

As an example on granting privileges in Oracle, the following statement grants SELECT and UPDATE privileges on the view vwListProducts to all users (this is done by using the special user, **public**, in Oracle):

```
GRANT SELECT, UPDATE
ON golf_ vwListProducts TO PUBLIC;
```

Granting Privileges in SQL Server

In SQL Server, we can do something similar to grant SELECT privilege to all users on the Orders table:

```
GRANT SELECT, UPDATE
ON Orders
TO public
```

Try It Out – Granting Privileges

Create a role in SQL Server and grant it the SELECT, INSERT, and UPDATE privileges on a table you create, tblTest. Insert some values into the table, create a user, and add it as a member of the role you have just created. Log on as the new user and try to insert a record into the tblTest table. Then, try to delete a record in the same table. What error message do you get in the later case?

In SQL Server:

1. Create a table and call it tblTest:

```
CREATE TABLE tblTest(Field1 int, Field2 nvarchar(20))
GO
```

2. Create a new login in SQL Server and call it newuser:

```
sp_addlogin 'newuser'
GO
```

3. Create a new role in SQL Server and call it testRole:

```
Sp_addrole 'testRole'
GO
```

4. Grant SELECT, INSERT, and UPDATE privileges on the created table (tblTest) to the created role (testRole):

```
GRANT SELECT, INSERT, UPDATE on tblTest TO testRole
GO
```

5. Create a new SQL Server database user, calling it newuser:

```
sp_adduser 'newuser'
GO
```

6. Assign the created role testRole to the new user:

```
sp_addrolemember 'testRole', 'newuser'
GO
```

7. Log in as the new user 'newuser' with password "" (empty string), and insert some values into the new table tblTest using the statements:

```
insert into tbltest VALUES(1, 'test1')
GO

insert into tbltest VALUES(2, 'test2')
GO

insert into tbltest VALUES(3, 'test3')
GO
```

8. To view the inserted values, issue the statement:

```
SELECT * FROM tblTest
GO
```

The result of the above statement is:

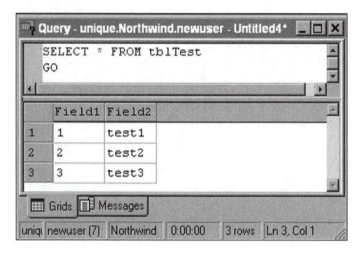

9. Try to delete the values in the new table:

```
delete tbltest
GO
```

This gives us the following error message:

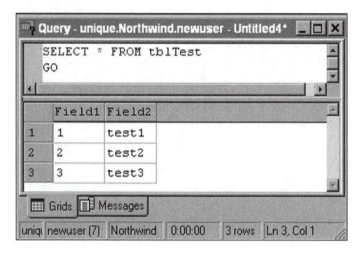

How It Works

This series of SQL statements simply creates a new table, user, and role and grants some privileges to the new user. However, nowhere do we mention that the `newuser` user has DELETE privileges on the new table `tblTest`, which is why we get an error message when we try to delete the `tblTest` table when we are logged in as `newuser`.

Character Sets and Collations

Databases can contain Greek characters, or Latin characters, or even Chinese or Japanese characters. They may also include characters that have special accents that can be found in only particular languages, such as Romanian, or Turkish and so on. Even with well-known West European languages such as French, German, and Spanish, there are special rules of collation (how to sort) that make it a challenge for SQL DBMSs.

The letter 'A', for instance, is represented by the ASCII number 65, or HEX 41; also, we know that 'A' comes before 'B' in English. Therefore, a character set is a series of statements about what symbols exist and what code values they have. For instance, in our example, the statement that the letter 'A' is represented by the ASCII code 65 is part of such a character set.

On the other hand, when we say that the letter 'B' comes after the letter 'A', we are actually using a collation statement. Most European languages behave in this way; however, there are many languages that behave differently, so SQL allows for the creation of separate collations for such languages. These collations include different types of sorts for each of these languages, such as binary sort, case-sensitivity (or insensitivity) sorting, and so on. The detail of collations is really beyond the scope of this book, and so we will not attempt to cover any more information here.

Translations

Translations are SQL objects that allow for the transliteration from one character set to another. For instance, we can have a translation that controls how to convert the character set support in a database from the US English character set to the French character set. I am not aware of any SQL implementation that supports these objects at this time, and discussing them in detail is beyond the scope of this book.

Roles

One of the great security advances in SQL is its allowance of the creation of **roles**. Roles are logical groupings of privileges. Users that have similar security characteristics, such as rights to access the same data in a similar manner, are then assigned to these groups. Roles make administration of users and user security easier.

For instance, we can create a role that represents a large number of users, and grant a privilege (access right) to a schema object to the role, instead of granting it to each and every user who is a member of the role. We can even grant a role to another role. This allows us to immediately add a set of new privileges to users who are members of the original role.

Creating roles is done with the CREATE ROLE statement. Again, SQL implementations create roles differently.

Creating a Role in Oracle

In Oracle, to create a role called insert_customers, we can write:

```
CREATE ROLE insert_customers
   IDENTIFIED BY mypassword;
```

The optional IDENTIFIED BY clause indicates that granting the role to users requires entering the password mypassword.

453

Creating a Role in SQL Server

IN SQL Server, adding a new role in the current database is done by executing the system stored procedure `sp_addrole`. This procedure requires the name of the new role and, optionally, an owner of it:

```
EXEC sp_addrole 'insert_customers'
```

INFORMATION_SCHEMA

There is no sense in discussing the standard SQL's schemas objects without discussing `INFORMATION_SCHEMA`. This actually builds the grounds for understanding many things about how to find information about other schema objects in the database. Therefore, the following sections may seem overwhelming and very theoretical, but the information within them is more for reference than study – if you are more interested in the practical side of this topic, you may skip part of this section and proceed directly to the SQL Server or Oracle, sub-sections, whichever interests you, where you can find practical implementations of this topic.

As we saw earlier, every SQL catalog includes a schema called the `INFORMATION_SCHEMA`. This schema includes a series of views, assertions, and domains. These objects are read-only: in other words, they allow us to view the description of every object in the catalog as though it were regular SQL data.

Using the objects in this schema, we can view the properties and attributes of all catalog objects to which we have privileges. Conversely, we should not be able to view the details of objects for which we do not have privileges. In some cases, the `INFORMATION_SCHEMA` is labeled as the data dictionary, or even metadata repository.

Each database management system adopts a list of the standard `INFORMATION_SCHEMA` views and objects. In all cases, a subset of the views in the standard set exists in each DBMS along with some DBMS-specific views. In this section, we will see the standard `INFORMATION_SCHEMA` views along with their implementation in SQL Server and Oracle.

SQL-99 Standard INFORMATION_SCHEMA Views

The following table shows the definitions of the views in the `INFORMATION_SCHEMA` according to the SQL-99 standard. Brief descriptions of each of the schema views are also given:

> `INFORMATION_SCHEMA.ADMINISTRABLE_ROLE_AUTHORIZATIONS`: As the name indicates, this view allows you to retrieve data about roles that can be administered by the database administrator.
>
> `INFORMATION_SCHEMA.APPLICABLE_ROLES`: This view allows you to retrieve a list of the system and administrable roles in the database schemas.
>
> `INFORMATION_SCHEMA.ASSERTIONS`: This view allows you to retrieve a list of assertions in the database.

INFORMATION_SCHEMA.ATTRIBUTES: This view shows you the attributes of the database schemas.

INFORMATION_SCHEMA.CHARACTER_SETS: This view allows you to retrieve the list of character sets supported by the database.

INFORMATION_SCHEMA.CHECK_CONSTRAINTS: This view retrieves a list of all CHECK constraints in the database.

INFORMATION_SCHEMA.COLLATIONS: This view allows you to retrieve information about all the collations in the database.

INFORMATION_SCHEMA.COLUMNS: This view allows you to retrieve information about the columns in the tables of the database schemas.

INFORMATION_SCHEMA.COLUMN_DOMAIN_USAGE: This view presents a list of domains used by columns in the database schemas. For instance, a domain that defines a US Dollar data type may be used in several table columns; this view allows you to retrieve a list of such columns.

INFORMATION_SCHEMA.COLUMN_PRIVILEGES: This view presents a list of all privileges of all columns in the database.

INFORMATION_SCHEMA.COLUMN_USER_DEFINED_TYPE_USAGE: This view shows you how the user-defined data types are used in database columns.

INFORMATION_SCHEMA.CONSTRAINT_COLUMN_USAGE: This view presents a list of constraints and what columns they are used for in the database.

INFORMATION_SCHEMA.CONSTRAINT_TABLE_USAGE: This view shows you a list of tables in the database schemas.

INFORMATION_SCHEMA.DIRECT_SUPERTABLES: This view applies to database management systems that support nested tables and object types. It allows you to list the supertables (tables that include other tables nested within) in a database.

INFORMATION_SCHEMA.DIRECT_SUPERTYPES: similar to the view above, this view applies to database management systems that support supertypes. It shows a list of such supertypes in the database. A supertype is a type that can include subtypes derived from it. For instance, the integer data type in SQL Server is a supertype that includes subtypes, such as: tinyInt, smallInt, int, and bigInt.

INFORMATION_SCHEMA.DOMAINS: As the name of this view suggests, it presents a list of domains in the database.

INFORMATION_SCHEMA.DOMAIN_CONSTRAINTS: This view shows the domain constraints in the database.

INFORMATION_SCHEMA.DOMAIN_USER_DEFINED_TYPE_USAGE: This view shows a list of domains in the database and the user-defined data types used in these domains. For instance, you may have a domain that defines an employee address. The address includes a street address, city, state, and phone number. It also includes an optional component called CompanyAddress of a special user-defined data type that may include something like phone, fax, web page, etc. in addition to the other address parameters.

Table continued on following page

INFORMATION_SCHEMA.ENABLED_ROLES: This view shows the list of active roles in the database that can be assigned users by the administrators.

INFORMATION_SCHEMA.KEY_COLUMN_USAGE: This view shows you a list of the key columns in tables (primary, foreign, alternate) in the specified database schemas.

INFORMATION_SCHEMA.METHOD_SPECIFICATIONS: This view shows the specifications (parameters, attributes, text, etc.) of the methods (procedures and functions) in the database schemas.

INFORMATION_SCHEMA.METHOD_SPECIFICATION_PARAMETERS: This view shows you a list of methods in the database and their parameters (all types of parameters: in, out, and in/out).

INFORMATION_SCHEMA.PARAMETERS: This view shows you a list of parameters used in the database's stored procedures and functions.

INFORMATION_SCHEMA.REFERENTIAL_CONSTRAINTS: This view presents a list of referential integrity constraints (foreign key constraints) in the database schemas.

INFORMATION_SCHEMA.ROLE_COLUMN_GRANTS: This view presents a list of roles and privileges granted on the column level.

INFORMATION_SCHEMA.ROLE_ROUTINE_GRANTS: This view shows a list of roles granted on the stored procedures/functions level.

INFORMATION_SCHEMA.ROLE_TABLE_GRANTS: This view shows a list of privilege grants for all tables in the database.

INFORMATION_SCHEMA.ROLE_USAGE_GRANTS: This view shows a list of roles in the database and how they are used (on what objects).

INFORMATION_SCHEMA.ROLE_USER_DEFINED_TYPE_GRANTS: This view shows a list of user-defined data types and the privileges granted on them in the database.

INFORMATION_SCHEMA.ROUTINES: This view shows a list of stored procedures and functions in the database.

INFORMATION_SCHEMA.ROUTINE_COLUMN_USAGE: This view shows a list of routines in the database and the table columns used in them, and how they are used.

INFORMATION_SCHEMA.ROUTINE_PRIVILEGES: This view shows the privileges granted on stored procedures and functions in the database.

INFORMATION_SCHEMA.ROUTINE_TABLE_USAGE: This procedure shows a list of stored procedures and functions in the database and the tables used in such routines.

INFORMATION_SCHEMA.SCHEMATA: This view shows information about the schemas in the database that have permissions for the current user.

INFORMATION_SCHEMA.SQL_IMPLEMENTATION_INFO: This view shows information about the implementation and deployment of the database, such as locale information, character set, etc.

INFORMATION_SCHEMA.SQL_PACKAGES: This view applies to DMBS systems that support grouping stored routines in packages (such as Oracle). The view shows a list of such SQL packages.

`INFORMATION_SCHEMA.SQL_LANGUAGES`: This view shows a list of the languages supported in the database.

`INFORMATION_SCHEMA.TABLES`: This view lists all the user and system tables in the database schemas.

`INFORMATION_SCHEMA.TABLE_CONSTRAINTS`: This view lists the table constraints in the database schemas.

`INFORMATION_SCHEMA.TABLE_METHOD_PRIVILEGES`: This view shows a list of tables and what stored procedures and functions can access these tables through privileges set on them.

`INFORMATION_SCHEMA.TABLE_PRIVILEGES`: This view shows a list of tables and their privileges in the database.

`INFORMATION_SCHEMA.TRANSFORMS`: This view lists the transforms in the database.

`INFORMATION_SCHEMA.TRANSLATIONS`: This view shows a list of translations in the database schemas.

`INFORMATION_SCHEMA.TRIGGERED_UPDATE_COLUMNS`: This view shows a list of columns in the database that are updated as a result of triggers.

`INFORMATION_SCHEMA.TRIGGERS`: This view shows a list of all triggers in the database.

`INFORMATION_SCHEMA.TRIGGER_COLUMN_USAGE`: This view shows a list of triggers in the database and the table columns they are applied to.

`INFORMATION_SCHEMA.TRIGGER_TABLE_USAGE`: This view shows a list of triggers and tables they are applied to in the database.

`INFORMATION_SCHEMA.TYPE_INFO`: This view shows a list of supported data types and information on these types.

`INFORMATION_SCHEMA.USER_DEFINED_TYPES`: This view shows a list of user-defined data types in the database.

`INFORMATION_SCHEMA.VIEWS`: This view shows a list of user views in the database.

`INFORMATION_SCHEMA.VIEW_COLUMN_USAGE`: This view shows the list of user views in the database and the columns used in these views.

`INFORMATION_SCHEMA.VIEW_TABLE_USAGE`: This view lists user views and the tables used in these views in the database.

SQL Server INFORMATION_SCHEMA Views

After looking at the long list of standard `INFORMATION_SCHEMA` views, we may be left wondering how those views are implemented in some of the most popular DBMSs.

In this section, we will see how those views are implemented in Microsoft SQL Server, and in the next section we will see how some of those views are implemented in Oracle. We will also get a chance to see how to use these views to obtain information on database schemas to which we have access privileges.

SQL Server INFORMATION_SCHEMA is SQL-92-compatible. In other words, it still follows the SQL-92 standard rather than the new SQL-99 standard. However, the views in the SQL-92 standard are a subset of those in the new standard. Therefore, it was important to list the new SQL standard INFORMATION_SCHEMA views in the previous section.

With SQL Server, a schema maps to a database owner or catalog owner. Therefore, the schema name and catalog owner fields are the same when we use some of these views to obtain information about such databases. The following table lists the specific INFORMATION_SCHEMA views that SQL Server supports:

INFORMATION_SCHEMA.CHECK_CONSTRAINTS
INFORMATION_SCHEMA.COLUMN_DOMAIN_USAGE
INFORMATION_SCHEMA.COLUMN_PRIVILEGES
INFORMATION_SCHEMA.COLUMNS
INFORMATION_SCHEMA.CONSTRAINT_COLUMN_USAGE
INFORMATION_SCHEMA.CONSTRAINT_TABLE_USAGE
INFORMATION_SCHEMA.DOMAIN_CONSTRAINTS
INFORMATION_SCHEMA.DOMAINS
INFORMATION_SCHEMA.KEY_COLUMN_USAGE
INFORMATION_SCHEMA.PARAMETERS
INFORMATION_SCHEMA.REFERENTIAL_CONSTRAINTS
INFORMATION_SCHEMA.ROUTINE_COLUMNS
INFORMATION_SCHEMA.ROUTINES
INFORMATION_SCHEMA.SCHEMATA
INFORMATION_SCHEMA.TABLE_CONSTRAINTS
INFORMATION_SCHEMA.TABLE_PRIVILEGES
INFORMATION_SCHEMA.TABLES
INFORMATION_SCHEMA.VIEW_COLUMN_USAGE
INFORMATION_SCHEMA.VIEW_TABLE_USAGE
INFORMATION_SCHEMA.VIEWS

The views that SQL Server supports are all based on system tables in SQL Server. Such system tables include, but are not limited to: sysobjects, syscolumns, sysreferences, spt_values, and sysindexes. I am not going to go into the details of each of the views; however, I will present how some of them can be used and what type of data we can expect to see in them.

> System tables are tables that ship with the DBMS. In SQL Server, there are system tables in the **master** database and others in each database. System tables include data about the database server, the database objects, and so on. Basically, they are used internally by SQL Server to keep track of the activities and objects on the server.

INFORMATION_SCHEMA.SCHEMATA View

This view returns a list of schemas and catalogs in the database server along with their owners, and character sets. The view includes the following columns:

Column name	Data type	Description
CATALOG_NAME	Sysname	Name of the database where the current user has permissions
SCHEMA_NAME	nvarchar(128)	Returns name of the schema owner in SQL Server
SCHEMA_OWNER	nvarchar(128)	Schema owner name
DEFAULT_CHARACTER_SET_CATALOG	varchar(6)	Returns master, the database where the default character set is defined in SQL Server
DEFAULT_CHARACTER_SET_SCHEMA	varchar(3)	Returns dbo, indicating the name of the default character set owner
DEFAULT_CHARACTER_SET_NAME	Sysname	Returns the name of the default character set

To query this view, we can write:

```
SELECT Catalog_Name,
    Schema_Name,
    Schema_Owner,
    DEFAULT_CHARACTER_SET_NAME
FROM  INFORMATION_SCHEMA.SCHEMATA
```

The result of the query above is shown below (assuming that you do not have any user-created databases on your SQL server):

	Catalog_Name	Schema_Name	Schema_Owner	DEFAULT_CHARACTER_SET_NAME
1	master	dbo	dbo	iso_1
2	tempdb	dbo	dbo	iso_1
3	model	dbo	dbo	iso_1
4	msdb	dbo	dbo	iso_1
5	Pubs	dbo	dbo	iso_1
6	Northwind	dbo	dbo	iso_1
7	Archive	dbo	dbo	iso_1

Grids Messages

INFORMATION_SCHEMA.KEY_COLUMN_USAGE View

This view returns a list of columns with key constraints in the database. The view shows a list of objects the user has permission to. The view includes the following columns, which are retrieved from the system tables listed earlier:

Column Name	Data Type	Description
CONSTRAINT_CATALOG	nvarchar(128)	Constraint qualifier
CONSTRAINT_SCHEMA	nvarchar(128)	Constraint owner name
CONSTRAINT_NAME	nvarchar(128)	Constraint name
TABLE_CATALOG	nvarchar(128)	Table qualifier
TABLE_SCHEMA	nvarchar(128)	Table owner name
TABLE_NAME	nvarchar(128)	Table name
COLUMN_NAME	nvarchar(128)	Column name
ORDINAL_POSITION	int	Column ordinal position

As an example, we can obtain a list of constraints in the current database (assuming it is Northwind) for the `Orders` table, and what fields they are applied to by issuing the SQL statement:

```
SELECT CONSTRAINT_NAME,
    TABLE_NAME,
    COLUMN_NAME
FROM INFORMATION_SCHEMA.KEY_COLUMN_USAGE
WHERE TABLE_NAME = 'Orders'
```

The result of the query would be something like:

	CONSTRAINT_NAME	TABLE_NAME	COLUMN_NAME
1	FK_Orders_Customers	Orders	CustomerID
2	FK_Orders_Employees	Orders	EmployeeID
3	FK_Orders_Shippers	Orders	ShipVia
4	PK_Orders	Orders	OrderID

Grids Messages

Try It Out – Stored Procedures

INFORMATION_SCHEMA is not the only way you find information on schema objects in SQL Server: you can also use system stored procedures and system tables to do so. It is not recommended, though, to use system tables to retrieve schema information since these tables could change in structure (as Microsoft warns) in the next releases of SQL Server. One of the system stored procedures that you can use to retrieve the constraints of a particular table is sp_helpconstraint.

1. Try to execute the procedure sp_helpconstraints, passing to it the Orders table and compare the result to what we have already found out from the INFORMATION_SCHEMA.KEY_COLUMN_USAGE view.

```
EXEC sp_helpconstraint 'Orders'
```

2. If you insist on using system tables to obtain information on the schema you are working with in SQL Server, try to query the system tables sysobjects and sysforeignkeys and examine the results and what you can get out of them.

3. As another example of finding out information about SQL Server objects, you can use the statement below to retrieve information about a particular stored procedure in the database:

```
EXEC sp_help 'CustOrderHist'
```

The result is something like:

	Name	Owner	Type	Created_datetime	
1	CustOrderHist	dbo	stored procedure	2000-08-06 01:34:52.967	

	Parameter_name	Type	Length	Prec	Scale	Param_order	Collation
1	@CustomerID	nchar	10	5	NULL	1	Latin1_General_CI_AS

If you execute the system stored procedure sp_helptext, you can even get the text of the stored procedure.

```
EXEC sp_helptext 'CustOrderHist'
```

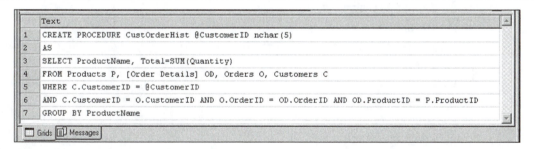

	Text
1	CREATE PROCEDURE CustOrderHist @CustomerID nchar(5)
2	AS
3	SELECT ProductName, Total=SUM(Quantity)
4	FROM Products P, [Order Details] OD, Orders O, Customers C
5	WHERE C.CustomerID = @CustomerID
6	AND C.CustomerID = O.CustomerID AND O.OrderID = OD.OrderID AND OD.ProductID = P.ProductID
7	GROUP BY ProductName

Grids Messages

Oracle Implementation of INFORMATION_SCHEMA (the Data Dictionary)

Oracle implements the INFORMATION_SCHEMA in a different way from SQL Server. Oracle (at least 7.x and beyond) has a huge data dictionary that includes views that allow the user to view information about virtually any object in the database schema. The dictionary is divided into static views, which correspond more or less to the standard INFORMATION_SCHEMA views, with many extensions, as we will see, and dynamic views. The static views are also divided by their scope as ALL, USER, or DBA, where ALL refers to objects belonging to all users of the database (all schemas, including DBA), DBA refers only to objects owned by a user with DBA role, and USER refers to schema objects owned by a certain user. The later one is the one that interests us and is the one we will discuss briefly here.

The following is a partial list of static dictionary views belonging to the user schema:

- ❑ USER_ALL_TABLES
- ❑ USER_ARGUMENTS
- ❑ USER_ASSOCIATIONS
- ❑ USER_CATALOG
- ❑ USER_CLUSTERS USER_CLUSTER_HASH_EXPRESSIONS
- ❑ USER_CLU_COLUMNS
- ❑ USER_COL_COMMENTS
- ❑ USER_COL_PRIVS
- ❑ USER_COL_PRIVS_MADE
- ❑ USER_COL_PRIVS_RECD
- ❑ USER_COLL_TYPES
- ❑ USER_CONSTRAINTS
- ❑ USER_CONS_COLUMNS
- ❑ USER_ERRORS
- ❑ USER_EXTENTS
- ❑ USER_FREE_SPACE
- ❑ USER_INDEXES
- ❑ USER_IND_COLUMNS
- ❑ USER_IND_EXPRESSIONS
- ❑ USER_IND_PARTITIONS
- ❑ USER_IND_SUBPARTITIONS
- ❑ USER_INDEXTYPES
- ❑ USER_INDEXTYPE_OPERATORS
- ❑ USER_JOBS
- ❑ USER_LIBRARIES
- ❑ USER_LOBS
- ❑ USER_LOB_PARTITIONS
- ❑ USER_LOB_SUBPARTITIONS
- ❑ USER_METHOD_PARAMS
- ❑ USER_NESTED_TABLES
- ❑ USER_OBJECT_TABLES
- ❑ USER_OBJECTS
- ❑ USER_OBJECT_SIZE
- ❑ USER_PART_TABLES
- ❑ USER_POLICIES

- ❑ USER_ROLE_PRIVS
- ❑ USER_SEQUENCES
- ❑ USER_SYNONYMS
- ❑ USER_SYS_PRIVS
- ❑ USER_TAB_COLUMNS
- ❑ USER_TAB_COMMENTS
- ❑ USER_TAB_PARTITIONS
- ❑ USER_TAB_PRIVS
- ❑ USER_TAB_PRIVS_MADE
- ❑ USER_TABLES
- ❑ USER_TABLESPACES
- ❑ USER_TRIGGERS
- ❑ USER_TRIGGER_COLS
- ❑ USER_TYPES
- ❑ USER_TYPE_ATTRS
- ❑ USER_TYPE_METHODS
- ❑ USER_USERS
- ❑ USER_VIEWS

This is just a subset of the user views in the static dictionary in Oracle. As an example of using it, let's look at the following Try It Out sections:

Try It Out – Tables Owned by the Current User

In this Try It Out, you will find all the tables that are owned by the current user.

1. Identify the view that includes information on the user's tables: USER_TABLES. In SQL*Plus, or any other Oracle SQL editing tool, type the statement:

```
SELECT TABLE_NAME FROM USER_TABLES;
```

The result of the statement is:

```
TABLE_NAME
------------------------------
BONUS
CUSTOMER
DEPT
EMP
LINEITEMS
ORDERS
SALGRADE
STOCKITEMS
```

How It Works

The USER_TABLES view includes information on the tables and users owning them. If you want to examine the structure of such view, you can type the SQL*Plus command (no need to include a semi colon),

```
DESC USER_TABLES;
```

The result is:

Name	Null?	Type
TABLE_NAME	NOT NULL	varchar2(30)
TABLESPACE_NAME		varchar2(30)
CLUSTER_NAME		varchar2(30)
IOT_NAME		varchar2(30)
PCT_FREE		number
PCT_USED		number
INI_TRANS		number
MAX_TRANS		number
INITIAL_EXTENT		number
NEXT_EXTENT		number
MIN_EXTENTS		number
MAX_EXTENTS		number
PCT_INCREASE		number
FREELISTS		number
FREELIST_GROUPS		number
LOGGING		varchar2(3)
BACKED_UP		varchar2(1)
NUM_ROWS		number
BLOCKS		number
EMPTY_BLOCKS		number
AVG_SPACE		number
CHAIN_CNT		number
AVG_ROW_LEN		number
AVG_SPACE_FREELIST_BLOCKS		number
NUM_FREELIST_BLOCKS		number
DEGREE		varchar2(10)

Name	Null?	Type
INSTANCES		varchar2(10)
CACHE		varchar2(5)
TABLE_LOCK		varchar2(8)
SAMPLE_SIZE		number
LAST_ANALYZED		date
PARTITIONED		varchar2(3)
IOT_TYPE		varchar2(12)
TEMPORARY		varchar2(1)
SECONDARY		varchar2(1)
NESTED		varchar2(3)
BUFFER_POOL		varchar2(7)
ROW_MOVEMENT		varchar2(8)
GLOBAL_STATS		varchar2(3)
USER_STATS		varchar2(3)
DURATION		varchar2(15)
SKIP_CORRUPT		varchar2(8)
MONITORING		varchar2(3)

So, as you can see, you can get a ton of information about the user tables, or a particular user table, using this static view. As for our Try It Out, we were only concerned with the name of the tables, hence we selected only the field TABLE_NAME from this view.

Try It Out – Current User Triggers

Find the current user triggers in the database schema.

1. Identify the static dictionary view to be used for this purpose. The view is USER_TRIGGERS. Write the following statement:

```
SELECT TRIGGER_NAME FROM USER_TRIGGERS;
```

```
The result is:

TRIGGER_NAME
-------------------------------
TD_CUSTOMER
TD_ORDERS
TD_STOCKITEMS
TI_LINEITEMS
TI_ORDERS
TU_CUSTOMER
TU_LINEITEMS
TU_ORDERS
TU_STOCKITEMS
```

Try It Out – Constraints

Now, list all constraints on a certain table, and what is the statement used to do so?

The statement would use the view USER_CONSTRAINTS as follows:

```
SELECT CONSTRAINT_NAME,
    CONSTRAINT_TYPE AS TYPE,
    TABLE_NAME
FROM USER_CONSTRAINTS
WHERE TABLE_NAME = 'CUSTOMER';
```

```
CONSTRAINT_NAME                    TYPE TABLE_NAME
------------------------------     ---- ------------------------------
SYS_C001234                        C    CUSTOMER
SYS_C001235                        P    CUSTOMER
```

Try It Out – Table Structure

Find the structure of a particular table in an Oracle database.

This is an easy one; all you need to do is issue a SQL*Plus command, DESC[RIBE] to find the table structure. In the first Try It Out of this section, we already used this command to view the structure of the static view, USER_TABLES. I will leave it to you to examine the structure of the Customer table. However, another way to do this is by querying the USER_TAB_COLUMNS static view in the data dictionary.

1. Issue the following statement:

```
SELECT TABLE_NAME,
    COLUMN_NAME,
    DATA_TYPE
FROM USER_TAB_COLUMNS
WHERE TABLE_NAME = 'CUSTOMERS';
```

2. The result is:

```
TABLE_NAME                     COLUMN_NAME                    DATA_TYPE
------------------------------ ------------------------------ --------------
CUSTOMERS                      CUSTNO                         NUMBER
CUSTOMERS                      CUSTNAME                       VARCHAR2
CUSTOMERS                      STREETADDRESS                  VARCHAR2
CUSTOMERS                      CITY                           VARCHAR2
CUSTOMERS                      STATE                          VARCHAR2
CUSTOMERS                      POSTALCODE                     VARCHAR2
CUSTOMERS                      PHONE                          VARCHAR2
CUSTOMERS                      CREDITCARD                     VARCHAR2
8 rows selected.
```

Summary

In this chapter, you have learned about SQL schemas, what they are, and how they are implemented in some of the major SQL implementations. You also learned about some of the schema objects that were not covered in previous chapters, such as domains and assertions. Also, you learned why you need to learn about SQL schemas and how you can find information about schema objects when you inherit a database that you did not design and create. Basically, the SQL standard's INFORMATION_SCHEMA and its implementations in SQL Server and Oracle were presented to show you how you can find such valuable information when you need it most. In the next chapter, you will read about a case study that goes through the design process, creation, and use of a database schema.

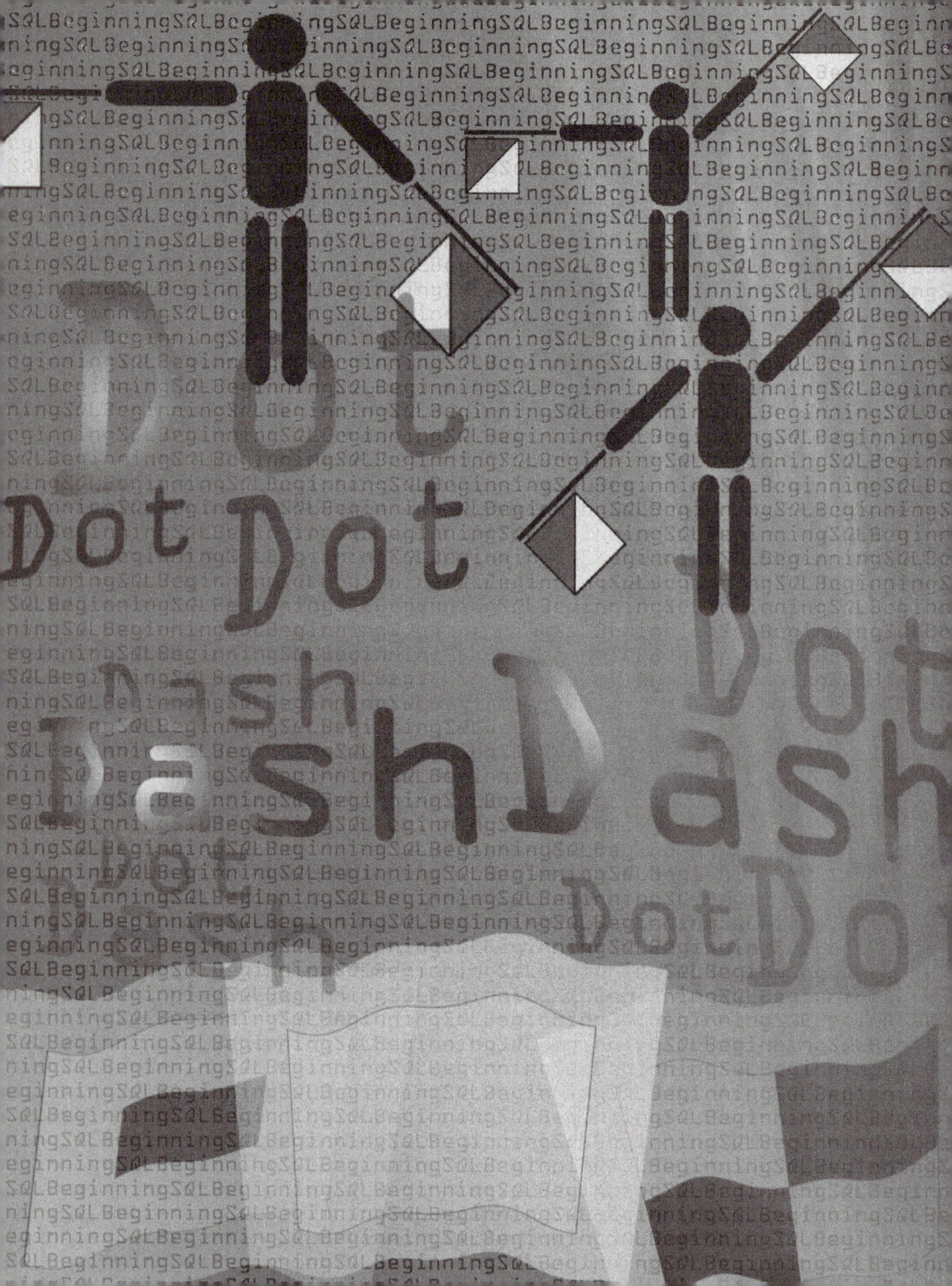

Case Study: Creating a Database and its Schema

Right, you've seen the basic concepts of SQL, and used it to build database objects and manipulate the data in such databases. You may be thinking, well that's all well and good, but when it comes to real-life situations, these books rarely show me what I really need. This is exactly why this chapter is here. It is to show, to some extent, how the information gathered in the previous chapters can be used in the context of a real-life situation.

An example problem is stated along with the client requirements. These requirements are then translated into a specification to be used in designing and building the database that will serve as the backend for the client's application. The sample case study will use SQL Server 2000 as the database management system.

In this chapter we will look at:

- ❑   The business description and client requirements
- ❑   A database design specification
- ❑   An approach for designing the database
- ❑   Good programming practices
- ❑   Building the database schema objects
- ❑   QA testing the database design
- ❑   Finalizing the database design

If you are a reader who has children who participate in many community sporting events, you will easily identify with the sample database in this case study!

Problem Statement

As you were watching your daughter play soccer in the Community Athletic Club (CAC), you started to chat with the athletic club director who was also watching his daughter play on the same team. The director said: "With the athletic club becoming more popular and participation of local families and their children increasing, wouldn't it be wonderful if we could organize these athletic events better than the way we are doing now?" Of course, as you chatted with him, you realized that these events are organized in a very crude and time-consuming way, and that if this did not change, the club would not be able to accommodate many more events in the future.

As you are telling the director that you design and architect databases used for business applications for a living, he asks if you could help them build a system that would organize sports programs for the children in the community.

The broad requirement of such a system is that CAC staff and local families want to be able to view athletic event schedules, schedule events, and even view the results of past events using a simple web browser. The system staff also want to be able to generate reports, printed or on the screen, of other important information. What made this idea float so quickly is that the club has just bought a few high-caliber workstations that can be used as servers to house such a system. These broad requirements hide many details and complexities underneath them, as we will see in the next sections.

Gathering the Requirements

What started as a casual conversation between you and the CAC director is now quickly evolving into a real business problem that you need to solve. As a good database designer and architect, you know that a good system should always be built on sufficient and well-gathered requirements. Therefore, you set out to collect requirements from the athletic club staff and the families who will also be eventually accessing the system. In this section, we're going to see how the detailed requirements ended up and how they can be used to create a data model that represents the business processes.

Since the idea of developing a system to organize the CAC's sporting activities came about, you started to collect requirements from the CAC staff and other families who were attending these events. As you asked more questions, you were able to learn more about the "business" processes. For instance, you learned that to the CAC, each sport for a particular age group is considered a league, such as the CAC Basketball League for children between 7 and 8, CAC Ice Hockey League for children between 8 and 11, and so on. Within each league there are two to twenty teams (Sharks, Raptors, etc.). Families, of course, may have several children who are athletes as well as parents that coach.

Learning about the "business rules" of the sports club enables us to layout the basic requirements of the system. The primary requirements are as follows:

- ❑ Ability to list families and their contact information
- ❑ Ability to get contact information for one family
- ❑ Ability to list athletes in various orders (by age, by last name, etc.)
- ❑ Ability to list teams within one league
- ❑ Ability to list all members and coaches of one team

- Ability to list some basic team statistics such as average age of players, total weight or height of players
- Ability to list players with same postal codes for help in organizing transportation
- Ability to list players in a league who are at extremes: tallest, youngest, etc.
- Ability to list players who are most active in the league
- Ability to list players who are in the league but not in a certain postal code
- Ability to add: new family, new athlete or coach, new sport, new team
- Ability to register an athlete as a player in a team of a given league
- Ability to edit or delete any of the above, especially if the event is a present or future event, and only to view it if it is a past event.

Design Approach and Specifications

As we gather the requirements, we can start to juggle ideas of what physical entities should be represented as tables in the database. The following entities seem to be the likely contenders (notice in the list below that we look for nouns):

- League
- Team
- Family
- Schedule
- Sporting Event
- Child/Player
- Coach
- Age group
- Staff Member
- Event Location

These are the entities that will make up the required system for the CAC. They will be represented as tables in our schema. The next sections discuss each one of these entities and present the fields and properties that they might contain.

Naming Conventions

Before we go any further, we need to decide on a naming scheme that we can stick with for the next sections when we design our schema objects. The rules we set for ourselves can be summarized as:

- Physical table names will be pre fixed with `tbl`; for example, the league table would be named `tblLeague`.
- View names will be prefixed with `vw`; for instance, a view showing all families and their children in a certain city would be called `vwCityFamilyChildren`.

❑ If the name is composed of more than one word, we'll use upper case for the **first** letter of each of these component words. For example, the table storing team players would be called `tblTeamPlayer`.

❑ Use **singular**, not plural for object names, for instance, `tblTeam`, not `tblTeams`.

❑ For column names, use the table name with the first **ID (primary key)** column when appropriate, but not with subsequent columns. For instance, in the `tblPlayer` table, the `PlayerID` field includes the entity name (`Player`); the remaining fields should not include the entity name: `FirstName`, not `PlayerFirstName`

❑ For field names also, we will not prefix the names with something that shows its data type; for instance, we'll call a field `Height`, not `numHeight`

❑ Names will not include any whitespace .

Design Tools

Luckily some products we are familiar with already allow us to design databases and build schemas. For instance, Microsoft Visual Studio provides the ability to design database schemas. Microsoft Access also provides similar capabilities. Finally, SQL Server Enterprise Manager (EM) also allows us to build the schema objects for our case study.

As well as the tools included with products that we are likely to be familiar with already, there are actually a number of database design tools available. The most notable and popular of database design tools is CA Associate's ERwin (formerly Platinum Technology's ERwin). This tool can be used to create a logical design of the database, along with a physical design, then generate a script to create the database in many database management systems, including SQL Server, MS Access, Oracle, DB2, etc. We will look at how we could use either Enterprise Manager or a tool such as ERwin now in the database design phase of this case study, before we move on to look at the specific details for each table that will allow us to build our database.

> **So, the next sections will briefly run through the creation of database diagrams as an aid to designing a schema for our database. After that we'll analyse the relationships we want to build and then we'll present each table in turn so that you can follow the database creation and use SQL to build the database for yourself.**

Using SQL Server Enterprise Manager to Build the Schema Tables

Here we'll see how to use SQL Server Enterprise Manager to create tables and relationships in order to build an entity-relationship diagram.

In SQL Server EM, create a blank database called CAC. We can do this by right-clicking the Databases tree item in the tree pane and selecting New Database:

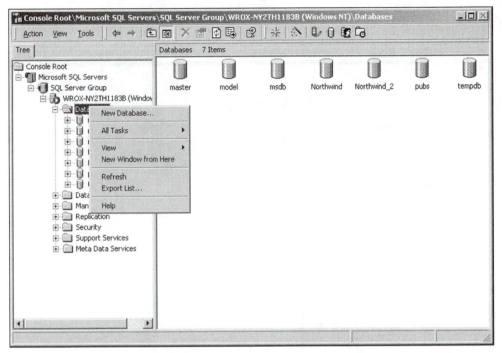

or by clicking on the New Database button on the tool bar:

The dialog below will then be presented:

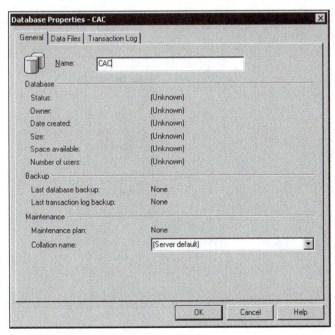

Enter the database name as **CAC** and click **OK**. This will create a blank database for us to contain the tables and other schema objects.

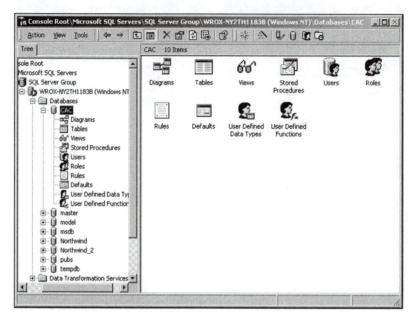

To design your database, expand the **CAC** database node and right-click the **Diagrams** tree item. Select **New Database Diagram**. This will launch a wizard that will lead you through creating a database diagram. Click the **Cancel** button on the wizard screen, and you will be left with a blank diagram, as shown in the figure below:

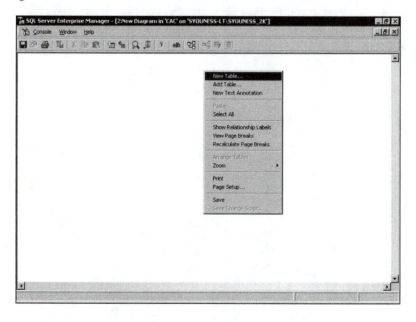

Use the tool bar, or right-click to show the context-sensitive menu, which includes the commands that you can use in your design (see figure above). For instance, to create a new table, you may want to select New Table from the context-sensitive menu, or from the tool bar. This will present you with a dialog that allows you to choose a physical name for the new table as shown below.

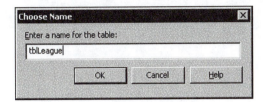

After entering the table name and clicking OK, you will see your table in design mode. You can enter field names, and their data types right on the diagram. You can even assign the primary key field(s), add annotations, and even define the Null constraint using this diagram (see figure below).

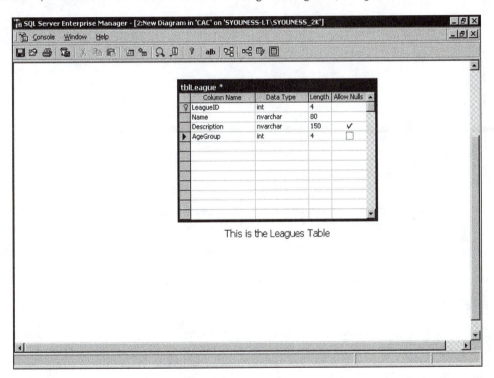

This is the Leagues Table

Building Schema Tables with ERwin

Computer Associate's (CA) ERwin Model Mart Client is considered one of the best and most widely used products for database design and creation. It is up to you, however, to use ERwin, EM or any other tool that you like to build the tables that we are going to build in the following sections.

In this section, I will only show how ERwin can be used to build an entity-relation diagram (ERD). I will, specifically show how to create a table and a relationship between two tables. The sections that follow will walk you through building the data model for our case study.

When you first start ERwin you get the screen below. You can see the screen below:

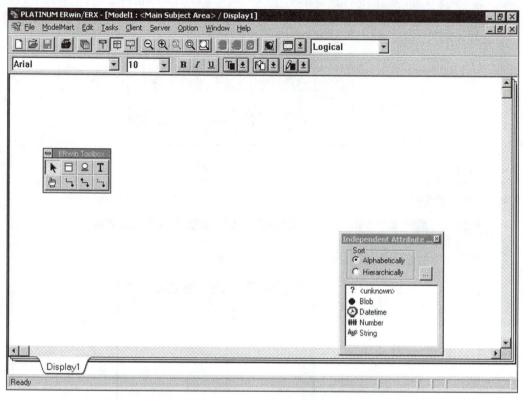

You can use the toolbox shown in the figure above to create entities (tables) and relationships. You can create three types of relationships with these tools: an identifying relationship (represented with a solid line with one dark circle at one end) , a many-to-many relationship (represented with a solid line with a dark circle at either end) , and a non-identifying relationship (represented with a dashed line with one dark circle at one end) . You will see what these relationships mean as you continue to read on. Clicking on the entity (table) tool in the toolbox , will allow you to create a representation of an entity (table) on your data model. You can enter the field names and assign the primary key on this representation, or you can select the Table Editor by double-clicking the new table or selecting it from the Edit menu. The Table Editor is shown in the figure opposite:

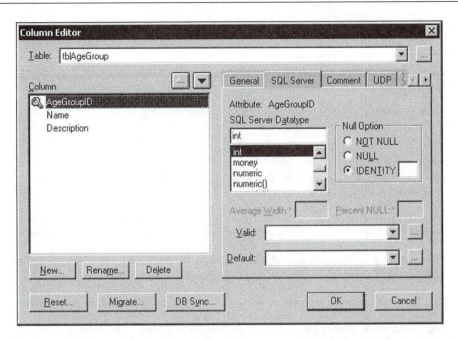

After building two tables that are related to each other, you can build a relationship between the two tables by selecting the relationship tool that matches your requirement, clicking on the first table, and then clicking on the second table. You can double-click the relationship on the data model to open the Relationship Editor (shown in the figure below), which you can use to further design your relationship attributes.

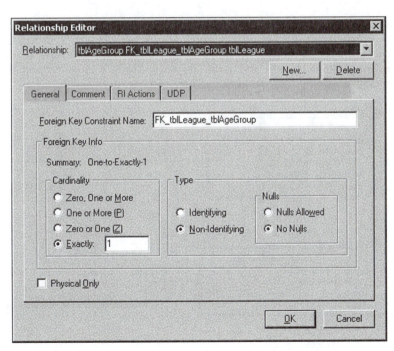

The following sections will walk you through building the data model for our case study. It is up to you whether you want to use SQL Server EM or a tool such as ERwin or to build this diagram. Either way, the result will be the same for our purposes.

The ERD Diagram

Based on the requirements gathered so far, we need to keep track of leagues, teams, family members, players, coaches, events, event locations, etc. Let's take a closer look at how these entities relate to each other.

> Before moving on, let's introduce the concept of identifying and non-identifying relationships:
>
> A non-identifying relationship is a relationship between two tables where the foreign key relating one of them to the other is not part of the primary key of that table.
>
> An identifying relationship is a relationship between two tables where the foreign key relating one of them to the other *is* part of the primary key of that table.
>
> As a generic example, if we were to link two tables, `employee` and `department`, the `department_id` field in the `department` table will be a foreign key in the `employee` table. If the primary key of the employee table is composed of one field, `employee_id`, then the relationship between the two tables is non-identifying; however, if the primary key in the `employee` table were comprised of the `employee_name` and `department_id` fields, then the relationship would be an identifying one, because the foreign key, `department_id` is part of the primary key of the `employee` table.

Each league can have many teams in it, which defines a one-to-many relationship between the league entity and the team entity. On the other hand, each league represents a specific age group. For instance, you can find a Soccer league for children below 5 years of age, one for children between 6 and 8, and another league for children above 9, and so on. The diagram below shows how the relationships between the league, age group, and team entities are represented:

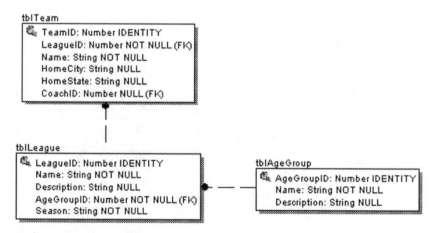

The ERDs here happen to be drawn using ERwin. As we said earlier, this is purely to show that although you may wish to use SQL Server's Enterprise Manager to build relationship diagrams, you don't have to. You can select any design tool of your choice.

In the diagram above, the broken lines indicate a "non-identifying relationship". We learned just before that a non-identifying relationship is a relationship between two tables where the foreign key relating one of them to the other is not part of the primary key of that table.

For instance, in our example, the field `AgeGroupID` is a foreign key in the `tblLeague` table and links this table to the `tblAgeGroup` table. However, this foreign key is not part of the primary key, nor an alternate key in the table `tblLeague`. Therefore, the relationship between the two tables, `tblLeague` and `tblAgeGroup`, is non-identifying.

The dark dots on the one end of the relationship line indicate the "many" side of the one-to-many relationship. For instance, the relationship between `tblLeague` and `tblTeam` is a one-to-many relationship with the `tblTeam` on the "many" side; therefore, we see that the dark dot is located at the `tblTeam` side. This relationship can be expressed in English as: "one league may have many teams in it, but any single team can only be a member of only one league".

The event entity, represented physically by the table `tblEvent`, represents the schedule of the sporting events for each of the leagues. It is in this table where the time and location of each event is kept along with the teams playing in the event. For instance, a record in this table would include something like:

- ❑ Date of event is January 2

- ❑ Teams involved: Tigers and Sharks

- ❑ League: Soccer junior league

- ❑ Time of event: 2:00 PM

- ❑ Location of event: Troy Sports Center

- ❑ Event scheduler: CAC staff member Mike

Based on this data, the table will include a pointer to the League, another one to the Location entity, and a pointer to the Staff entity.

The diagram overleaf shows how these relationships are represented. You may notice that this representation may not be the only way to model such information. For instance, you may want to link the Event entity to the Team entity. This is valid, but at this stage would make our example too complex for this book. This is because there should be two links from the Team entity to the Event entity, since we may have two teams in an event. In this case study we will stick with the simpler method of establishing the relationship between the League entity and the Event entity, and not enforce that between the Event and Team entities.

Notice on the diagram overleaf that the relationship between the Location entity and the Event entity is a one-to-one relationship. In other words, an event must have one and only one location.

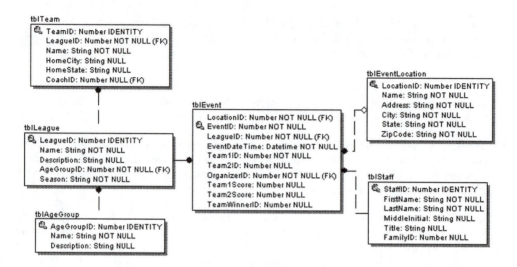

Let's now look at another subject area of the schema. As you may expect, teams have players, and this whole schema is about organizing these players and their activities in the leagues. This area includes entities like Family, Player, and Coach. These entities are related directly or indirectly to the Team entity.

Let's first look at the relationship between the team and the player. In general, unless it is an individual sport, a team can have several players; and on the other hand, a player can play for more than one team. For instance, my daughter can play in both the soccer league and the softball league; however, she can only play for one team in one league. Therefore, the relationship between a team and a player is a many-to-many relationship. Such a relationship is usually resolved by converting it to two one-to-many relationships. This is done by adding a "normalizing or intersection" table in the middle between the two sides of the relationship. This table should include the primary keys of both tables as an alternate key at a minimum (if not a primary key).

So, in our case, the many-to-many relation between the Team entity and the Player entity is resolved by adding an entity, TeamPlayer, as the diagram below shows. This table will also include specific attributes that identify the player on that team. For instance, it would include the start date and end date of the period during which the player played for the team, the role she was playing, and the shirt number of the player.

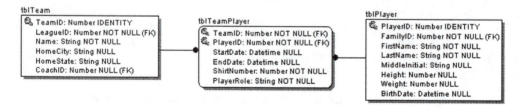

Building on the diagram above, we can add the Family and Coach entities, which would give us the diagram opposite:

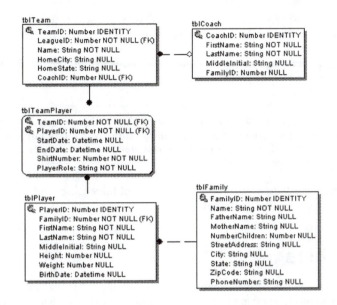

The Complete Schema

Finally, putting it all together, we arrive at the diagram below for all the entities in our case study:

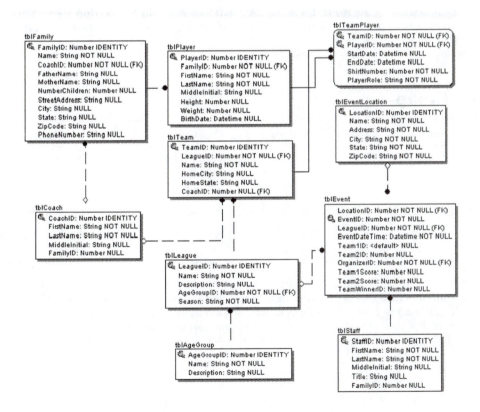

This diagram includes the physical structure of the CAC schema in which the table structure shows their fields, and even some of the constraints on these tables and fields. For instance, the table tblCoach shows that the FirstName and LastName fields cannot be NULL, and the table tblTeam shows that the field LeagueID is a foreign key and cannot be NULL. It also shows that the primary key (shown next to the key icon) is an identity field.

> If you wish to build an ERD yourself, remember that in SQL Server, identity fields are fields whose values are incremented automatically by the database engine. When these fields are defined, a seed value is assigned along with an increment.

In the next section, we will go over the creation of each of these tables and we will list all the fields in them along with any constraints that apply to them.

Schema Tables

This section presents all schema tables in more detail showing the fields in each table, along with their data types, and any constraints that apply to them or to the tables as a whole. The script needed to create the tables in SQL Server 7.0 or SQL Server 2000 is also presented for each table.

> Remember to create the tables in the CAC database using the SQL scripts shown later in this section, or whatever method you like, if you wish to follow the creation of the CAC system as we present it.

tblAgeGroup

Field Name	Data Type (and Size)	Constraints	Description
AgeGroupID	Int	Primary Key – Identity with Seed = 1 and Increment = 1	Primary Key
[Name]	NVarchar(30)	Not NULL	Name of the age group
Description	Nvarchar(80)	None	Brief description of age group

> Notice the field [Name] is surrounded by square brackets. Usually, it is not a good idea to use reserved key words as names for your fields, and if you do want to use them, it is recommended that you use the square brackets in SQL Server.

The script to create this table is:

```
CREATE TABLE tblAgeGroup (
    AgeGroupID int IDENTITY (1, 1) PRIMARY KEY,
    [Name] nvarchar (30)  NOT NULL ,
    Description nvarchar (80)  NULL
)
```

tblCoach

Field Name	Data Type (and Size)	Constraints	Description
CoachID	int	Primary Key – Identity with Seed = 1 and Increment = 1	Primary key
FamilyID	int	Points to the family in the tblFamily table (if the coach happens to be a member of the league families)	A pointer to the table tblFamily
FirstName	nvarchar(30)	Not NULL	First name of the coach
LastName	nvarchar(30)	Not NULL	Last name of coach
MiddleInitial	nchar(1)	None	Middle initial of coach

The script to create this table is:

```
CREATE TABLE tblCoach (
    CoachID int IDENTITY (1, 1) PRIMARY KEY ,
    FirstName nvarchar (30)  NOT NULL ,
    LastName nvarchar (30)  NOT NULL ,
    MiddleInitial nchar (1)  NULL ,
    FamilyID int NULL
)
```

tblEvent

Field Name	Data Type (and Size)	Constraints	Description
EventID	int	Primary Key – Identity with Seed = 1 and Increment = 1	Primary key
LeagueID	int	Foreign Key for tblLeague	A pointer to the table tblLeague

Table continued on following page

Field Name	Data Type (and Size)	Constraints	Description
OrganizerID	int	Foreign key for tblStaff	A pointer to the table tblStaff
TeamWinnerID	int	None	Points to the ID of the team that won the event
Team1ID	int	Not NULL	Points to the ID of the first team in the event
Team2ID	int	None	Points to the ID of the second team in the event (if needed)
LocationID	int	Foreign key	Pointer to table tblEventLocation
EventDateTime	datetime	Not NULL	Date and time of event
Team1Score	smallInt	None	Final score of Team1
Team2Score	smallInt	None	Final score of Team2

The SQL script needed to create this table is:

```
CREATE TABLE tblEvent (
    EventID int IDENTITY (1, 1) PRIMARY KEY ,
    LeagueID int NOT NULL ,
    EventDateTime datetime NOT NULL ,
    Team1ID int NOT NULL ,
    Team2ID int NULL ,
    LocationID int NULL ,
    OrganizerID int NOT NULL ,
    Team1Score smallint NULL ,
    Team2Score smallint NULL ,
    TeamWinnerID int NULL
)
```

tblEventLocation

Field Name	Data Type (and Size)	Constraints	Description
LocationID	int	Primary Key – Identity with Seed = 1 and Increment = 1	Primary key
[Name]	nvarchar(30)	Not NULL	Event location name
Address	nvarchar(50)	Not NULL	Event location street address

Field Name	Data Type (and Size)	Constraints	Description
City	nvarchar(50)	Not NULL	Event location city
State	nchar(2)	Not NULL	Event location state (two letters)
ZipCode	nvarchar (10)	Not NULL	Event location zip code

The script to create this table is:

```
CREATE TABLE tblEventLocation (
    LocationID int IDENTITY (1, 1) PRIMARY KEY ,
    [Name] nvarchar (30)  NOT NULL ,
    Address nvarchar (50)  NOT NULL ,
    City nvarchar (50)  NOT NULL ,
    State nchar (2)  NOT NULL ,
    ZipCode nvarchar (10)  NOT NULL
)
```

tblFamily

Field Name	Data Type (and Size)	Constraints	Description
FamilyID	int	Primary Key – Identity with Seed = 1 and Increment = 1	Primary key
[Name]	nvarchar(30)	Not NULL	Family name
FatherName	nvarchar(50)	None	Name of father
MotherName	nvarchar(50)	None	Name of mother
NumberChildren	smallint	None	Number of children in the family
StreetAddress	nvarchar(50)	NULL	Family street address
City	nvarchar(50)	NULL	Family city
State	nchar(2)	NULL	Family state (two letters)
ZipCode	nvarchar (10)	NULL	Family zip code
PhoneNumber	nvarchar(13)	NU overleaf LL	Family phone number

The script to create this table is:

```
CREATE TABLE tblFamily (
    FamilyID int IDENTITY (1, 1) PRIMARY KEY ,
    [Name] nvarchar (30)  NOT NULL ,
    FatherName nvarchar (50)  NULL ,
    MotherName nvarchar (50)  NULL ,
    NumberChildren smallint NULL ,
    StreetAddress nvarchar (80)  NULL ,
    City nvarchar (50)  NULL ,
    State nchar (2)  NULL ,
    ZipCode nvarchar (10)  NULL ,
    PhoneNumber nvarchar (13)  NULL
)
```

tblLeague

Field Name	Data Type (and Size)	Constraints	Description
LeagueID	int	Primary Key – Identity with Seed = 1 and Increment = 1	Primary key
AgeGroupID	int	Foreign Key for tblAgeGroup	A pointer to the table tblAgeGroup
Name	nvarchar(80)	Not NULL	Name of the league
Description	nvarchar(150)	None	Brief description of league
Season	nvarchar(30)	Not NULL	The season in which the league is held

The script to create this table is:

```
CREATE TABLE tblLeague (
    LeagueID int  IDENTITY (1, 1) PRIMARY KEY,
    [Name] nvarchar (80) NOT NULL ,
    Description nvarchar (150) NULL ,
    AgeGroupID int NOT NULL ,
    Season nvarchar (30) NOT NULL
)
```

tblPlayer

Field Name	Data Type (and Size)	Constraints	Description
PlayerID	int	Primary Key – Identity with Seed = 1 and Increment = 1	Primary key
FamilyID	int	Foreign Key for tblFamily	A pointer to the table tblFamily

Field Name	Data Type (and Size)	Constraints	Description
FirstName	nvarchar(30)	Not NULL	First name of player
LastName	nvarchar(30)	Not NULL	Last name of player
MiddleInitial	nchar(1)	None	Middle initial of player
Height	numeric(18,2)	None	Height of player
Weight	numeric(18,2)	None	Weight of player
Birthdate	smalldatetime	None	Birth date of player

The script to create this table is:

```
CREATE TABLE tblPlayer (
    PlayerID int IDENTITY (1, 1) PRIMARY KEY,
    FamilyID int NOT NULL ,
    FirstName nvarchar (30)  NOT NULL ,
    LastName nvarchar (30)  NOT NULL ,
    MiddleInitial nchar (1)  NULL ,
    Height numeric(18, 2) NULL ,
    Weight numeric(18, 2) NULL ,
    BirthDate smalldatetime NULL
)
```

tblStaff

Field Name	Data Type (and Size)	Constraints	Description
StaffID	int	Primary Key – Identity with Seed = 1 and Increment = 1	Primary key
FamilyID	int	None	A pointer to the table tblFamily if the CAC staff member happens to be a member of one of the families
FirstName	nvarchar(30)	Not NULL	First name of staff member
LastName	nvarchar(30)	Not NU overleaf LL	Last name of staff member
MiddleInitial	nchar(1)	None	Middle initial of staff member
Title	nvarchar(50)	None	Title of staff member

The script to create this table is:

```
CREATE TABLE tblStaff (
    StaffID int IDENTITY (1, 1) PRIMARY KEY,
    FirstName nvarchar (30)  NOT NULL ,
    LastName nvarchar (30)  NOT NULL ,
    MiddleInitial nchar (1)  NULL ,
    Title nvarchar (50)  NULL ,
    FamilyID int NULL
)
```

tblTeam

Field Name	Data Type (and Size)	Constraints	Description
TeamID	int	Primary Key – Identity with Seed = 1 and Increment = 1	Primary key
LeagueID	int	Foreign Key for tblLeague	A pointer to the table tblLeague
[Name]	nvarchar(50)	Not NULL	Name of team.
HomeCity	nvarchar(50)	Not NULL	Home city of the team
HomeState	nchar(2)	Not NULL	Home state of the team
CoachID	int	Foreign key for tblCoach	A pointer to the table tblCoach

The script to create this table is:

```
CREATE TABLE tblTeam (
    TeamID int IDENTITY (1, 1) PRIMARY KEY ,
    LeagueID int NOT NULL ,
    [Name] nvarchar (50)  NOT NULL ,
    HomeCity nvarchar (50)  NOT NULL ,
    HomeState nchar (2)  NOT NULL ,
    CoachID int NULL
)
```

tblTeamPlayer

Field Name	Data Type (and Size)	Constraints	Description
TeamID	int	Foreign key for tblTeam	Pointer to tblTeam and part of the primary key in tblTeamPlayer
PlayerID	int	Foreign key for tblPlayer	Pointer to tblPlayer and part of the primary key in tblTeamPlayer

Field Name	Data Type (and Size)	Constraints	Description
StartDate	smallDatetime	NULL	Start date of player with team
EndDate	smallDatetime	NULL	End date of player with team
ShirtNumber	smallInt	Not NULL	Number of player on the team
PlayerRole	nvarchar(30)	Not NULL	A pointer to the table tblCoach

The script to create this table is:

```
CREATE TABLE tblTeamPlayer (
    TeamID int NOT NULL ,
    PlayerID int NOT NULL ,
    StartDate smalldatetime NULL ,
    EndDate smalldatetime NULL ,
    ShirtNumber smallint Not NULL ,
    PlayerRole nvarchar (30)  NOT NULL
)
```

Creating the Table Constraints

As you already saw in the scripts above, we have already taken care of the primary key constraints of all of the tables except for the table tblTeamPlayer. In this section, we will create the remaining constraints as described in the schema design.

Let's start with the primary key for the tblTeamPlayer. The script used to create this key is:

```
ALTER TABLE tblTeamPlayer WITH NOCHECK ADD
    CONSTRAINT PK_tblTeamPlayer PRIMARY KEY CLUSTERED (TeamID, PlayerID)
```

Notice that the primary key in this case is a composite key that includes two foreign keys that point to two tables: tblTeam and tblPlayer. Also notice that the naming for the key: we used a prefix that indicates the type of the constraint (PK for primary key) followed by the table name on which the primary key is defined, thus, the name of the primary key constraint is PK_tblTeamPlayer.

The table tblEvent has several foreign key constraints. These constraints reference the tables tblEventLocation, tblLeague, and tblStaff. The script needed to create these constraints is:

```
ALTER TABLE tblEvent ADD
    CONSTRAINT FK_tblEvent_tblEventLocation FOREIGN KEY
        (LocationID) REFERENCES
            tblEventLocation (LocationID),
    CONSTRAINT FK_tblEvent_tblLeague FOREIGN KEY
        (LeagueID) REFERENCES
            tblLeague (LeagueID),
    CONSTRAINT FK_tblEvent_tblStaff FOREIGN KEY
        (OrganizerID) REFERENCES
            tblStaff (StaffID)
```

489

Notice in the script above, the naming scheme for the foreign key constraint: it starts with a prefix that indicates what type of constraint it is (FK for foreign key), followed by the table that has the foreign key, and then the table that has the referenced primary key. For instance, FK_tblEvent_tblEventLocation is the name of the foreign key constraint that links the tables tblEvent and tblEventLocation. In this relationship, the primary key in the tblEventLocation is referenced by the field LocationID, the foreign key in the tblEvent table.

Also notice that we are using the data definition language (DDL) command ALTER TABLE to add the foreign key. We could have included the foreign key constraint in the CREATE TABLE statement, but deferring it until all the tables have been created is a safer way to do it, since the success of the foreign key creation depends on both tables in the relationship having been created.

The table tblLeague has the foreign key constraint that references the table tblAgeGroup. The script needed to create this constraint is:

```
ALTER TABLE tblLeague ADD
    CONSTRAINT FK_tblLeague_tblAgeGroup FOREIGN KEY
        (AgeGroupID) REFERENCES tblAgeGroup (AgeGroupID)
```

The table tblPlayer has a foreign key constraint that links it to the table tblFamily. The script used to create this foreign key constraint and the foreign key constraints in the remaining tables is shown below:

```
--Foreign key constraint for tblPlayer
ALTER TABLE tblPlayer ADD
    CONSTRAINT FK_tblPlayer_tblFamily FOREIGN KEY
        (FamilyID) REFERENCES
        tblFamily (FamilyID)

--Foreign key constraints for tblTeam
ALTER TABLE tblTeam ADD
    CONSTRAINT FK_tblTeam_tblCoach FOREIGN KEY
        (CoachID) REFERENCES
        tblCoach (CoachID),
    CONSTRAINT FK_tblTeam_tblLeague FOREIGN KEY
        (LeagueID) REFERENCES
        tblLeague (LeagueID)

--Foreign key constraints for tblTeamPlayer
ALTER TABLE tblTeamPlayer ADD
    CONSTRAINT FK_tblTeamPlayer_tblPlayer FOREIGN KEY
        (PlayerID) REFERENCES
        tblPlayer (PlayerID),
    CONSTRAINT FK_tblTeamPlayer_tblTeam FOREIGN KEY
        (TeamID) REFERENCES
        tblTeam (TeamID)
```

Populating the Tables with Sample Data

Well, now we have the physical structure of the database all ready for us, how do we use it? First, we need to populate some sample data in the database before we can even think about using it. There are many ways to do so. For instance, we could write a quick graphical interface to enter the data, use Enterprise Manager to directly enter data in the table, or use SQL data manipulation language (DML) commands, namely the INSERT statement, to populate the tables.

If we use DML commands there are some issues that we need to be aware of. We'll look at those next. After that we'll present the sample values with which we will work for the remainder of this case study.

Populating the Database using DML

One thing to be careful of before we try to populate the database: we need to do so in a particular order. The order of the table population is determined by the foreign key relationships or referential integrity. Try, for instance, to insert a record in the table tblLeague before having any records in the table tblAgeGroup:

```
INSERT INTO tblLeague ([Name],
     Description,
     AgeGroupID,
     Season)
   VALUES ('Junior Soccer',
     'Junior Soccer League for ages 8 to 10',
     1,
     'Spring 2001')
```

You will be faced with the error message:

```
Server: Msg 547, Level 16, State 1, Line 1
INSERT statement conflicted with COLUMN FOREIGN KEY constraint
'FK_tblLeague_tblAgeGroup'. The conflict occurred in database 'CAC',
table 'tblAgeGroup', column 'AgeGroupID'.
The statement has been terminated.
```

Of course, the error message will look different according to which DBMS you are using, but, no matter how it looks, it will reflect the foreign key violation error.

If we did not try to enter a value for the AgeGroupID field (left it at NULL):

```
INSERT INTO tblLeague ([Name],
     Description,
     Season)
   VALUES ('Junior Soccer',
     'Junior Soccer League for ages 8 to 10',
     'Spring 2001')
```

We would get a different error message, saying that the foreign key field in tblLeague does not allow NULL values:

```
Server: Msg 515, Level 16, State 2, Line 1
Cannot insert the value NULL into column 'AgeGroupID', table 'CAC.dbo.tblLeague';
column does not allow nulls. INSERT fails.
The statement has been terminated.
```

491

So, keeping this in mind, we should populate the tables in an order similar to the following, and always use valid values for the foreign key fields that already exist in their referenced tables.

1. `tblAgeGroup`

2. `tblLeague`

3. `tblFamily`

4. `tblPlayer`

5. `tblStaff`

6. `tblCoach`

7. `tblEventLocation`

8. `tblTeam`

9. `tblEvent`

10. `tblTeamPlayer`

Another thing to watch for when populating the tables with DML statements is to remember not to enter a value for identity columns. These columns get their values automatically from the database engine and if we have an identity field in our table, we cannot skip the list of fields being populated in the INSERT statement. In other words, we cannot write:

```
INSERT INTO tblLeague
    VALUES ('Junior Soccer',
        'Junior Soccer League for ages 8 to 10',
        1,
        'Spring 2001')
```

Nor can we write (unless we have IDENTITY INSERT set to ON in SQL Server):

```
INSERT INTO tblLeague
    VALUES (3, --for LeagueID field
        'Junior Soccer',
        'Junior Soccer League for ages 8 to 10',
        1,
        'Spring 2001')
```

Instead, we need to write:

```
INSERT INTO tblLeague tblLeague (
        [Name],
        Description,
        AgeGroupID,
        Season)
    VALUES ('Junior Soccer',
        'Junior Soccer League for ages 8 to 10',
        1,
        'Spring 2001')
```

In other words, in most cases, we need to include the list of fields in the INSERT statement if we have an identity column in the table. The only exception is when IDENTITY INSERT is set to ON in SQL Server.

> *To learn more about identity fields and how they are treated in SQL Server, you may want to read the Wrox book:* Professional SQL Server 2000 Programming *by Robert Vieira ISBN 1-861004-48-6.*

Updating Values

Similar to the INSERT statement, you can use Enterprise Manager or any other graphical interface to change the data values in the tables. However, in this case study we're going to be using DML statements, namely UPDATE statements, to do so. Be careful with foreign key values so that you do not update a value of a foreign key field to something that does not exist in the referenced table. For instance, if a record in the table tblLeague references a value in the table tblAgeGroup with the ID of 4, you cannot change it to a value, say 13, that does not exist in tblAgeGroup.

An example of the UPDATE statement is:

```
UPDATE tblLeague
SET Season = 'Summer 2001'
WHERE LeagueID = 34
```

Deleting Values

Similar to updating and inserting, we will be using SQL DML statements for deleting data, namely DELETE statements. You should also be careful here when you delete a record in a table that is referenced by another table through a foreign key in the other table. The foreign key constraint will not let you do so because no "orphan" records can be left in the referencing table. So if you try to delete an age group from the table tblAgeGroup that is referenced in the table tblLeague, you will get an error message:

```
DELETE FROM tblAgeGroup WHERE AgeGroupID = 2

Server: Msg 547, Level 16, State 1, Line 1
DELETE statement conflicted with COLUMN REFERENCE constraint
'FK_tblLeague_tblAgeGroup'. The conflict occurred in database 'CAC', table
'tblLeague', column 'AgeGroupID'.
The statement has been terminated.
```

Therefore, if you want to delete a value in the table tblAgeGroup (without having the CASCADE DELETE set to ON), you need to delete the records referencing it in the child table tblLeague first.

> **With relational database management systems, such as SQL Server, tables are linked with relations and such relations create what is called referential integrity. Referential Integrity, as the name implies, helps to maintain the integrity of the data in the database. Such relations ensure that no "orphan" records exist in a table after the related tables in the parent table are deleted. This last point is referred to as cascading deletes. In other words, if you delete a record in a table, all related records in tables linked to it in foreign key relationships will be deleted. The same rule applies for updates as well.**

Chapter 10 looked at the principals of deleting and updating.

Sample Data

This section presents the values used to populate the database tables. These values will be used in the examples in the following sections of the chapter. Although we've discussed the issues involved in using DML, you could populate the values in any way you like. You can import them from a text file, an Excel file, or even type them into the tables using EM or use INSERT SQL statements, as we've just talked about, to do so.

> You will be able to download an Excel file that includes the data, as well as a database dump file of the database from www.wrox.com. Once you restore the file to your SQL server, you will have the database already populated with values.

tblCoach

CoachID	FirstName	LastName	MiddleInitial	FamilyID
1	John	Smiths	A	1
2	Dave	Jones	B	2
3	Mike	Shaw	L	
4	Gloria	Friday	O	7

tblEvent

EventID	1	2	3
LeagueID	1	1	1
EventDateTime	5/20/2000	5/20/2000	5/20/2000
Team1ID	1	3	5
Team2ID	2	4	6
LocationID	1	1	1
OrganizerID	4	4	4
Team1Score	7	4	12
Team2Score	9	11	8
TeamWinnerID	2	4	5

tblEventLocation

LocationID	Name	Address	City	State	ZipCode
1	Troy Civic Center	1234 Big Beaver Rd.	Troy	MI	48084
2	Troy High	333 Long Lake Rd.	Troy	MI	48098
3	Troy Sports Center	3451 Livernois	Troy	MI	48084
4	Rochester Civic Center	1234 Rochester Rd.	Rochester	MI	48101

tblAgeGroup

AgeGroupID	Name	Description
2	Juniors	6 – 8 years old
3	MiddleGroup	9 – 11 years old
4	Seniors	12 or above years old
5	Preschool	Less than 6 years old

tblFamily

FamilyID	1	2	3	4	5	6	7	8
Name	Smiths	Jones	Jaris	Jordan	James	Smith	Friday	Bowers
Father Name	John	Dave	Yohan	Michael	Jim	Scott	Bob	Larry
Mother Name	Ledia	Mary	Alice	Cindy	July	Freda	Gloria	Lisa
Number Children	2	3	1	4	2	3	2	3
Street Address	1234 Main Street	234 Main Ave	2345 Address Blvd	1234 Anywhere St.	376 James Ct.	123 Main	2345 Rochester Blvd	54 N. Rolly Cr.
City	Troy	Troy	Troy	Troy	Troy	Rochester	Rochester	Rochester
State	MI	MI	MI	MI	MI	MI	MI	MI
ZipCode	48084	48932	48098	48099	48085	48100	48100	48101
Phone Number								

tblLeague

League ID	Name	Description	AgeGroup ID	Season
1	2000 Juniors Softball	Softball for junior age group	2	2000 Summer
2	2000 Outdoor Junior Soccer	Soccer for Junior age group for year 2000 season	2	2000 Summer
3	2000 Indoor Junior Soccer	Soccer for Junior age group for 2000 winter	2	2000 Winter
4	2000 Senior Soccer	Soccer for senior ages for 2000	3	2000 Summer
5	2000 Senior Hockey	Ice Hockey	3	2000 Winter

tblStaff

StaffID	First Name	Last Name	MiddleInitial	Title	FamilyID
1	Jim	Jamison	J	Director	
2	Karl	Chavez	Y	Leagues Manager	
3	Ledia	Smiths	P	Soccer Event Coordinator	1
4	Cindy	Jordan	R	Softball Event Coordinator	4
5	Steve	Collin	S	Ice Hockey Coordinator	
6	Wendy	Warren	W	Secretery	
7	Jeff	Ray	R	Travel Coordinator	

tblPlayer

Player ID	Family ID	First Name	Last Name	Middle Initial	Height	Weight	BirthDate
1	1	Dave	Smiths	A	4.4	60	1/1/1996
3	1	Mike	Smith	S	4.9	76	2/3/1992
4	2	Lisa	Jones	B	5.4	96	3/23/1987
5	2	Scott	Jones	S	4.5	58	10/2/1995
6	2	Julia	Jones	W	3.8	40	1/23/1997
7	3	Philip	Jaris	S	5.2	80	2/1/1990

Player ID	Family ID	First Name	Last Name	Middle Initial	Height	Weight	BirthDate
9	4	Mark	Jordan	K	5.3	98	1/22/1991
10	4	Melissa	Jordan	F	5	78	9/4/1992
11	4	Judy	Jordan	L	4.1	48	6/13/1996
12	4	Carla	Jordan	R	3.6	30	7/17/1998
13	5	Marla	James	G	3.8	30	9/13/1998
14	5	Andy	James	T	4.3	40	8/19/1996
15	6	Sam	Smith	V	3.9	34	7/2/1997
16	6	Sarah	Smith	M	4.1	42	2/8/1996
17	6	Steve	Smith	T	4.4	48	11/21/1994
18	7	Amanda	Friday	H	4.8	58	1/4/1994
19	7	Carl	Friday	C	5.4	85	12/1/1992
20	8	Salma	Bowers	Y	4	40	12/31/1996
21	8	Jack	Bowers	R	5.2	53	9/10/1995
22	8	Dawn	Bowers	L	5.4	59	5/3/1993

tblTeam

TeamID	LeagueID	Name	HomeCity	HomeState	CoachID
1	1	Rochester Lions	Rochester	Michigan	
2	1	Troy Lizards	Troy	Michigan	
3	1	Dearborn Titans	Dearborn	Michigan	
4	1	Farmington Bulldogs	Farmington	Michigan	
5	1	Livonia Rockets	Livonia	Michigan	
6	1	Warren Tigers	Warren	Michigan	

tblTeamPlayer

TeamID	PlayerID	StartDate	EndDate	ShirtNumber	PlayerRole
1	5	2/1/2000		4	Catcher
1	18	2/1/2000		6	Pitcher
1	21	2/1/2000		23	Batter

Building Supporting Queries, Views, and Stored Procedures

Now that we have built the database structure and populated it with some sample data to test our application, let's build the views and stored procedures that can be used to satisfy the customer requirements. Did we say requirements? Yes – remember early in the chapter when we listed the requirements that the CAC members wanted from this database? In case you do not remember, here they are again:

- ❑ Ability to list families and their contact information
- ❑ Ability to get contact information for one family
- ❑ Ability to list athletes in various orders (by age, by last name, etc.)
- ❑ Ability to list teams within one league
- ❑ Ability to list all members and coaches of one team
- ❑ Ability to list some basic team statistics such as average age of players, total weight or height of players
- ❑ Ability to list players with same postal codes for help in organizing transportation
- ❑ Ability to list players in a league who are at extremes: tallest, youngest, etc.
- ❑ Ability to list players who are most active in the league
- ❑ Ability to list players who are in the league but not in a certain postal code

There isn't room in this chapter to address all of these requirements, so in the next few sections, we will look at how we could build stored procedures to satisfy the first three.

Obtain a List of Families and Their Contact Information

Let's create a stored procedure that returns all families and their contact information in a particular city. In this procedure, you can just enter the first few characters of the city name. For instance, you can enter "Pa" and that would return all families in cities that start with "Pa", such as Paris, Panama, etc.

The script to do so is:

```
CREATE PROCEDURE GetFamiliesInCity @City NVarchar(50)
AS
SELECT
    [Name],
    FatherName,
    NumberChildren,
    StreetAddress,
    City,
    State,
    ZipCode,
    PhoneNumber
FROM tblFamily
WHERE City LIKE @City + '%'

RETURN
```

We use the following command to invoke the stored procedure:

```
EXEC GetFamiliesInCity @City='Tr'
```

Testing the procedure would yield the following results:

```
Name     FatherName NumberChildren StreetAddress City   State  ZipCode PhoneNumber
--------------------------------------------------------------------------------
Smiths   John       2              1234 Main      Troy   MI     48084   NULL
Jones    Dave       3              234 Main Ave   Troy   MI     48932   NULL
Jaris    Yohan      1              2345 Address   Troy   MI     48098   NULL
Jordan   Michael    4              1234 Anywhere  Troy   MI     48099   NULL
James    Jim        2              376 James Ct.  Troy   MI     48085   NULL
```

Getting Contact Information for One Family

To ensure that the returned result set from the query is one family (one record), we have to pass the primary key value as a parameter in the WHERE clause. This means that this value must be known before the query is executed. Therefore, the stored procedure will take the FamilyID as a parameter and use it in the WHERE clause.

Of course we do not expect the end users to know families by their IDs in the database. Usually, what happens is that a graphical user interface (GUI) is used to present the user with a list that shows other attributes of the family, such as the name or father's name, etc. the selection of the item from the list in the GUI triggers the execution of the stored procedure in the backend database passing to it the mapped ID from the GUI.

```
CREATE PROCEDURE GetFamilyInfo @FamilyID Int
AS
SELECT
    [Name],
    FatherName,
    NumberChildren,
    StreetAddress,
    City,
    State,
    ZipCode,
    PhoneNumber
FROM tblFamily
WHERE FamilyID = @FamilyID

RETURN
```

Listing Players in Various Orders

This is an interesting problem to resolve. We can build a stored procedure that accepts a parameter indicating the name of the field to sort by. Such a procedure would look like this (in SQL Server):

```
CREATE PROCEDURE SortPlayers @SortOrder nVarchar(30)
AS

If @SortOrder = 'Weight'
    SELECT PlayerID,
        FirstName + ' ' + LastName AS PlayerName,
        Height,
        Weight,
```

499

```
            BirthDate
     FROM tblPlayer
        ORDER BY Weight
Else If @SortOrder = 'Height'
    SELECT PlayerID,
        FirstName + ' ' + LastName AS PlayerName,
        Height,
        Weight,
        BirthDate
    FROM tblPlayer
        ORDER BY Height

Else If @SortOrder = 'LastName'
    SELECT PlayerID,
        FirstName + ' ' + LastName AS PlayerName,
        Height,
        Weight,
        BirthDate
    FROM tblPlayer
        ORDER BY LastName

Else If @SortOrder = 'BirthDate'
    SELECT PlayerID,
        FirstName + ' ' + LastName AS PlayerName,
        Height,
        Weight,
        BirthDate
    FROM tblPlayer
        ORDER BY BirthDate

ELSE
    SELECT PlayerID,
        FirstName + ' ' + LastName AS PlayerName,
        Height,
        Weight,
        BirthDate
    FROM tblPlayer
        ORDER BY FirstName

RETURN
```

In the procedure above, we are concatenating the first and last names and presenting them as a player name. We are also sorting by one of four parameters. If the passed value of the procedure parameter is not one of the four values, we default to sort by the players' first name.

Another way to write the procedure is to use dynamic SQL. In this scenario, we would build the SQL statement as a string and store it in a variable that we would then execute. This gives us the ability to concatenate the parameter passed to the procedure with the SQL statement. The procedure would then look like:

```
CREATE PROCEDURE SortPlayers @SortOrder nVarchar(30),
@AscDesc nchar(3) = 'ASC'
AS
DECLARE @sql NVARCHAR(1000)

If @SortOrder NOT IN('FirstName', 'LastName', 'Weight', 'Height', 'BirthDate')
    RETURN 1
```

```
SET @sql = 'SELECT PlayerID,' +
           'FirstName + '' '' + LastName AS PlayerName,' +
           'Height,' +
           'Weight,' +
           'BirthDate  ' +
           'FROM tblPlayer ' +
           'ORDER BY ' +  @SortOrder

IF @AscDesc = 'DESC'
SET @sql = @sql + ' DESC'

EXEC (@sql)

RETURN
```

To execute this procedure, we write:

```
EXEC SortPlayers 'BirthDate', 'ASC'
```

Part of the results would look like this:

```
PlayerID    PlayerName      Height   Weight    BirthDate
----------  --------------  -------  --------  ------------------------
4           Lisa Jones      5.40     96.00     1987-03-23 00:00:00
7           Philip Jaris    5.20     80.00     1990-02-01 00:00:00
9           Mark Jordan     5.30     98.00     1991-01-22 00:00:00
3           Mike Smith      4.90     76.00     1992-02-03 00:00:00
```

Listing Teams Within One League

This problem requires that you join two tables if the league name is being passed in the WHERE clause. The query would look like:

```
SELECT     t.[name]   Team
FROM       tblTeam t,
           tblLeague l
WHERE      t.leagueid=l.leagueid AND
           l.name LIKE '2%'
```

The result of the query would look like:

```
Team
------------------------
Rochester Lions
Troy Lizards
Dearborn Titans
Farmington Bulldogs
Livonia Rockets
Warren Tigers
```

To make this query more usable, we can make it the basis for a stored procedure as follows:

```
CREATE PROCEDURE getLeagueTeams @League NVARCHAR(50)
AS
SELECT      t.name Team,
            l.name League
FROM        tblTeam t,
            tblLeague l
WHERE       t.leagueid=l.leagueid AND
            l.name LIKE @League + '%'
RETURN
```

Executing the procedure can be done as follows:

```
--Find all teams in League with LeagueID = 2.
EXEC getLeagueTeams '2'
```

```
Team                        League
------------------------------------------------
Rochester Lions             2000 Juniors Softball
Troy Lizards                2000 Juniors Softball
Dearborn Titans             2000 Juniors Softball
Farmington Bulldogs         2000 Juniors Softball
Livonia Rockets             2000 Juniors Softball
Warren Tigers               2000 Juniors Softball
```

Listing Members and Coaches of One Team

To list all members and coaches of one team, we can create a view and use it to select based on the team name as follows:

```
CREATE VIEW vwTeamPlayersANDCoach
AS
SELECT    p.firstname + ' ' + p.lastname Player,
          c.firstname + ' ' + c.lastname Coach,
          t.Name Team
FROM tblTeam t,
tblPlayer p,
tblCoach c,
tblTeamPlayer tp
WHERE t.teamID = tp.TeamID AND
          p.PlayerID = tp.PlayerID AND
          c.CoachID = t.CoachID
```

To use the view, we can just issue a statement like:

```
SELECT * FROM vwTeamPlayersANDCoach
```

Listing Average Age of Team Players

To list the average age of team players, we can use the following view:

```
CREATE VIEW vwAVGTeamAge
AS
SELECT      t.Name Team,
            AVG(CONVERT(INT,GetDate() - p.BirthDate)/365) AvgAge
FROM        tblTeam t,
            tblPlayer p,
            tblTeamPlayer tp
WHERE       t.TeamID = tp.TeamID AND
            p.PlayerID = tp.PlayerID
GROUP BY    t.Name
```

Using the view would be like:

```
SELECT      *
FROM        vwAVGTeamAge
WHERE       Team Like 'Roch%'
```

The result of the query above would look like:

```
Team                     AvgAge
------------------------------
Rochester Lions          5
```

How Can I Access the Database from a Web Application?

This is the question that many developers ask when they start learning SQL. Well, we now know the basic commands of SQL and how it can be used, but, as far as the end user is concerned, they should not worry about SQL and writing SQL queries to get the data they want. We developers must make it transparent to them and easy to do these functions. This is where client-server, multi-tier, and web applications that we discussed at the start of this book come into play. Such applications present a GUI to the end user where they select their query parameters and criteria without writing a single line of SQL. As an example, suppose in this case study that parents want to see which players live in the same postal code as they do so that they can organize shared rides among them and their children. To do so, they could create the following view and use it in our GUI:

```
CREATE VIEW vwPlayerInPostalArea
AS
SELECT p.FirstName + ' ' + p.LastName Player,
       f.[Name] Family,
       f.ZipCode
FROM tblPlayer p, tblFamily f
WHERE p.FamilyID = f.FamilyID
```

Now, to get the players in a particular postal area, we can write the query:

```
SELECT Family,
       Player,
       ZipCode
FROM vwPlayerInPostalArea
WHERE ZipCode = '48084'
```

The result of the query would be:

```
Family        Player                ZipCode
-----------   -------------------   -------
Smiths        Dave Smiths           48084
Smiths        Mike Smith            48084
Jones         Sam Jones             48084
Jones         Sally Jones           48084
```

Of course, Dave's mother or father do not want to issue such queries, nor do they have access to the database from their home through Query Analyser or a similar SQL Server tool; instead, they can go to the CAC home page and enter a zip code into a text box. The entry they make will then be used to display all the families and players living in that postal area. The code that allows this to happen, assuming that the CAC application uses Active Server Pages (ASP) is:

```
<%
OPTION EXPLICIT
dim conn
dim rs
dim strConnect
dim strSQL
dim strZip


on error resume next

strZip = "" & Request.Form("txtZip")
SET conn = server.CreateObject("ADODB.Connection")
strConnect="PROVIDER=SQLOLEDB; Data Source=SYOUNESS-LT\SYOUNESS_2K;" &_
           "INITIAL CATALOG=CAC; User ID=sa;Password=;"
conn.Open strConnect
if err.number <> 0 then
   raiseError err.number, err.description, err.source
   Response.End
end if

FUNCTION raiseError(ErrNo, ErrDesc, ErrSrc)
   Response.Write "ERROR: " & ErrNo & "(" & ErrSrc & "):<BR>" & ErrDesc
END Function

Function buildResult (strZip)
   set rs=server.CreateObject("ADODB.Recordset")
   strSQL = "SELECT Family, Player, ZipCode FROM vwPlayerInPostalArea " & _
            " WHERE ZipCode = '" & strZip & "'"
   rs.Open strSQL,conn
```

```
    if not rs.EOF and not rs.BOF then                    ,
        Response.Write
            "<Table><TR><th>Family</th><th>Player</th><th>ZipCode</th></tr>"
        do while not rs.EOF
        Response.Write "<TR><td>" & rs("Family") & "</td>" & _
            "<td>" & rs("Player") & "</td>" & _
            "<td>" & rs("ZipCode") & "</td></tr>"
        rs.MoveNext
        loop
        Response.Write "</table>"
    else
        Response.Write "No families or players found in this area code..."
        end if
        set rs=nothing
End Function

%>
<HTML>
<HEAD>
<TITLE>CAC Sample...</TITLE>
</HEAD>
<BODY>
Enter Zip Code:
<Form METHOD=POST ACTION=CAC.ASP NAME=frmMain ID=frmMain>
<INPUT type="text" id=txtZip name=txtZip VALUE=<%=strZip%>>
<INPUT type="submit" value="Submit" id=submit1 name=submit1>
<BR><BR>
<%Call buildResult(strZip)%>

</Form>
<P> </P>
</BODY>
</HTML>
<%Set conn=nothing%>
```

If you are an ASP programmer, you will find the example above useful and you will be able to understand it. One thing to keep in mind here is that the connection string in the example above will differ on your machines from what appears in the example. The names of the data source and the initial catalog may be different, as well as the user ID and password.

Don't worry if you have difficulty in following this ASP code. We've included it to demonstrate how you can use an interface to shield everyday users who want to access data from having to write SQL statements themselves. ASP is a vast subject with many books dedicated to teaching it; it would be well beyond the scope of this book to start trying to teach ASP here. To help you through the ASP code in this case study and the next one, which demonstrates how SQL is used in a basic e-commerce application, we have included an ASP primer that you'll find in Appendix E at the back of the book.

If you want to learn more about ASP, check out: *Beginning Active Server Pages 3.0* **which is also published by Wrox Press ISBN 1-861003-38-2.**

In the end, this example shows you how you can establish a connection to the database that includes your data, run a query against a view that we had already created, and present the results to the end user in a web page format. Explaining the details of the example above is beyond the scope of this chapter. Thereforewe will just focus on the area where we used our view in the ASP code. That is in the function buildResult():

```
set rs=server.CreateObject("ADODB.Recordset")
strSQL = "SELECT Family, Player, ZipCode FROM vwPlayerInPostalArea " & _
         " WHERE ZipCode = '" & strZip & "'"
rs.Open strSQL,conn
```

In the code excerpt above, we used the ADO connection object and a query that uses the view we created earlier in the chapter, to build a recordset. The recordset was then used to build the table with the query results. The output of this query would look like:

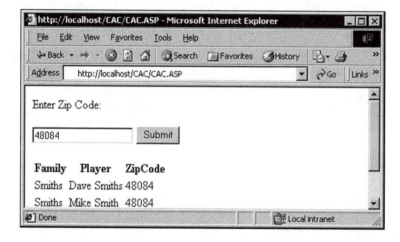

This web page is called CAC.asp. You will find this sample web page for download at **www.wrox.com**. In order to render it in your browser, you will need Microsoft Personal Web Server or Internet Information Server as we discussed in the section on ASP in Chapter 2.

Summary

By the time you get to this summary, you should have learned about how to gather requirements for a good database design, how to go about designing and building the database, and how to use SQL to populate the database with data, retrieve information from its tables, and even create and alter the structure of some of its objects. We've also seen how it is possible to incorporate our SQL statements within ASP so that end users can query the database via a graphical interface.

The next chapter presents another case study demonstrating a basic web application that uses SQL to allow users to browse products in a catalog (database) and order them on-line from their browser, again from an interface in the form of a web page.

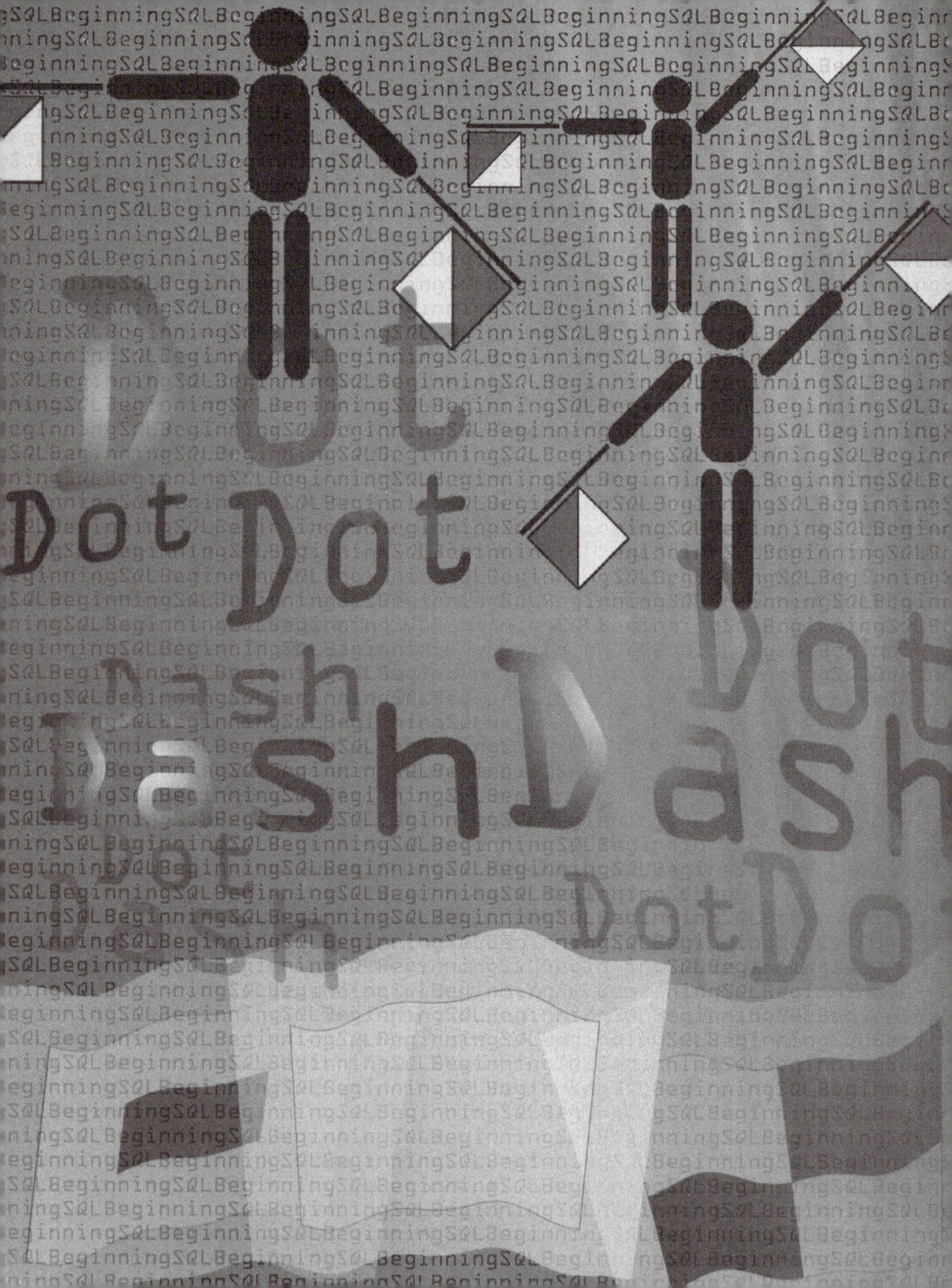

Case Study: Northwind Online Product Catalog

As with the last case study we are going to pull all of the varoius aspects of SQL together in a typical real-world situation: building an online application. In doing this, we'll have to get to grips with a fair amount of Active Server Pages (ASP) coding. More general information about ASP may be found in Appendix E.

> **This case study is primarily intended to show one way in which SQL code may be used in the context of developing an Internet Application. The explanation of the application itself is, of necessity, quite cursory. If you would like to find out more about ASP, a wealth of information can be found in *Wrox's Beginning Active Server Pages 3.0*, ISBN 1-861003-38-2.**

We will be using the Microsoft Northwind database for this case study. For those who are not using SQL Server or Access, information about migrating the Northwind database to Oracle, MySQL and DB2 may be found in Appendix D.

In this chapter, we will:

❑ Investigate the structure of an Internet Application

❑ Look at the role of a DBMS and SQL in such an application

❑ Overview ASP technology

❑ Build the application, making use of ASP and SQL stored procedures

The Northwind database is a good approximation to the way in which many databases in real-world situations are built. It stores information about products, sales, employees, and customers in such a way that useful information may be stored, retrieved, and operated upon.

In this case study, we will be building an online product catalog. In order to build it, we will be working directly with five tables in the Northwind database: `Orders`, `Order Details`, `Products`, `Categories`, and `Customers`.

The following diagram, taken from SQL Server's Enterprise Manager, shows these tables and the relationships between them:

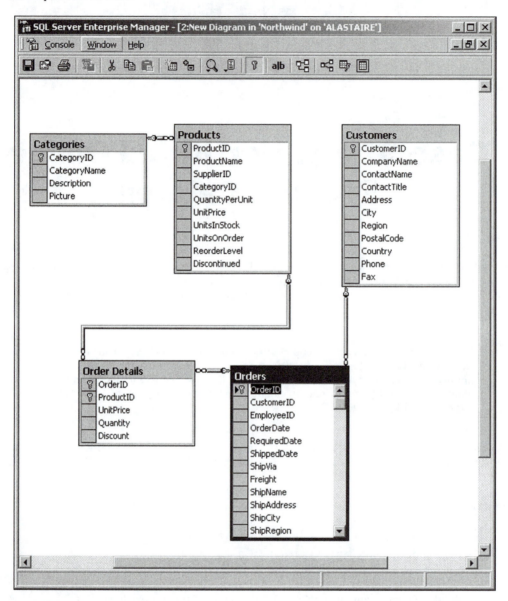

Our application will allow users to:

1. Browse and Search the Product Catalog database online

2. Purchase multiple items in a single purchase (this entails implementing some kind of shopping cart functionality)

What We Will Need

1. The Microsoft Northwind sample database. This comes with Access and SQL Server. If you don't have SQL Server, but you *do* have Access 2000, you can use the `NorthindCS.adp` Microsoft Data Engine (MSDE) sample database which comes with Acesss 2000. MSDE is a fully SQL Server compatible database engine that can be worked with directly through Access 2000.

2. Microsoft Access 2000 with MSDE or SQL Server. Note that you cannot use Access in isolation for this project: you must use Access with MSDE.

3. A web server on the machine you plan to run this on. Windows 98 comes with Microsoft **Personal Web Server**, and NT/Windows 2000 comes with **Internet Information Server** (called **Internet Information Services** on Windows 2000). Any of these will do.

4. A text editor for creating the web pages: either Notepad, Microsoft FrontPage, or any other HTML editor. ASP pages are scripted HTML pages, which means that their contents are nothing but plain text.

5. A web browser. Any web browser will do, so long as it supports JavaScript and Cookies.

Building a Web Application

In order to access information from the database from our ASP pages, we will have to have some way of connecting to the database. This is achieved by an appropriate **data provider**. Depending on the type of database we're using, we'll need to use a different data provider.

If using SQL Server, we'll use the SQL Server **ODBC** provider (**Open DataBase Connectivity**) or the SQL Server **OLE DB** provider (**Object Linking and Embedding Database**). If Access, we'll use the **Jet ODBC** provider or the **Jet OLE DB** provider. Information about the providers required for Oracle, DB2 and MySQL is supplied in text documents contained in the relevant code downloads.

What we are going to develop is not a web site, it is a **Web Application**. Unlike the static web sites of yore, a web application allows a high degree of interactivity.

Before we go any further in our planning process, it's going to be important here to explain a bit about the underlying technologies we're going to be working with. Although this isn't a book on ASP, SQL is a language that is almost always used with some sort of front end or interface. The Web Interface is one of the fastest-growing areas of development right now, so a little bit of background about these three technologies not only won't hurt, but should help you to build your own prototype on your local machine.

The Internet and n-tiered Applications

A web application has multiple *tiers*, or areas of operation, due to the distributed nature of such an application. You may or may not have come across references to *n*-tier applications. Such a locution refers to the number of tiers in a web application.

The web browser comprises one tier of the application. This is sometimes referred to as the **client tier**. This interacts, over the Internet, with a **web server**.

The web server is another tier of the application. It manages requests for the ASP pages from the client. These pages contain the scripting code of the application, and control both the information that is passed back to the client tier, and accessing and manipulating data in a database. As we've already seen, in order for an ASP page to interact with a database, some sort of data provider is needed. Such a provider consists of a number of objects that expose particular methods and properties, and interact directly with a database. We don't have to worry about the intricate mechanics of how a data provider interacts with a given database. All we have to concern ourselves with is how we can interact with a data provider from an ASP page. We will see later how this can be done.

The third tier of the application is the data tier. This consists of the database, and may include such items as **stored procedures**, which may be used by the application to interact with the database in particular ways.

Planning

The first step in developing an application is to outline the business rules. The business rules of a database application define both what the application should do, and the rules for maintaining data integrity, relationships, triggers, and other aspects of the database. So, let's begin by describing exactly what we want our online catalog to do:

1. Display up to date lists of products in the database, organized by category

2. Enable the user to search for particular products

3. Display individual product information

4. Add products to shopping cart

5. Examine and change the shopping cart's contents

6. Buy the selected products

We now have the basic functionality of our application specified, but it will be necessary to examine each aspect of the application in more detail, as well as the application as a whole, and specify exactly *how* each part of the application will work.

1. Display a list of products by category.

We need there to be a default or home page. The home page should display a list of categories with the appropriate information and picture from each category. This will involve querying the Categories table in the Northwind database. It would be good to be able to navigate to these product lists from any page in the web, so we will provide an appropriate navigation bar.

2. Enable the user to search for particular products

The search engine will consist of a single multiple-field search form, which will allow a user to search for a product by any combination of category, product name, and price. The results page will be a list of matching products. In order to display these, we can use the same page as that used to display the category lists of products.

3. **Display information about particular products**

This entails adding an individual product page, which will be accessed via the product listings. It will contain all of the pertinent information for a product, as well as a link that will allow the user to add the product to the shopping cart.

4. **Add product to the shopping cart**

The Add to Cart link on the product page will activate a stored procedure in the DBMS, which will add the particular product to the user's cart (information about which will be stored in the database).

5. **Examine and change the cart's contents**

Standard for most shopping carts, this page will enable the user to review the cart's contents, and change or remove items from the cart. It will also contain a link to check out.

6. **Buy Products**

Information about the customer's order will be stored in the database.

Setting Up The Web Application

Before we start constructing the ASP pages, we need to construct a **Web Application**. To do this, we will need to use the **Internet Services Manager** tool. This is simply an interface that makes the task of creating and managing web sites and web applications easier.

Try It Out – Set up a Virtual Web Application

On Windows 2000 Professional, the Internet Services Manager tool can be found under Settings | Control Panel | Administrative Tools. After opening, if we click on the server name (this will be the name of your computer), we will see the Default Web Site:

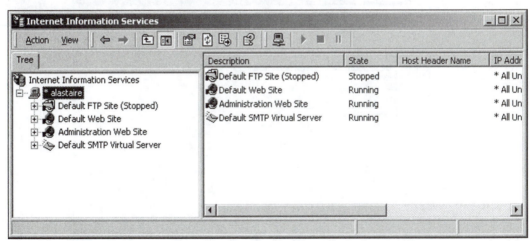

If we now expand the Default Web Site, we will see the **child** web sites that already exist on the machine. These will almost certainly be different on your machine from those shown here:

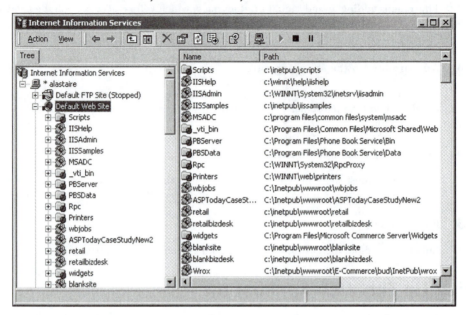

We will need to create a new child web site, in order to contain our application. To do this, we simply right-click on the Default Web Site icon, and select New | Server Extensions Web. This starts the New Subweb Wizard. We first have to specify the name for our new site – this will be the name given to the new virtual directory which will contain our site. The title is simply a 'friendly' name we can give the site.

Give the Directory name as Northwind, and the Title as Northwind product Catalog:

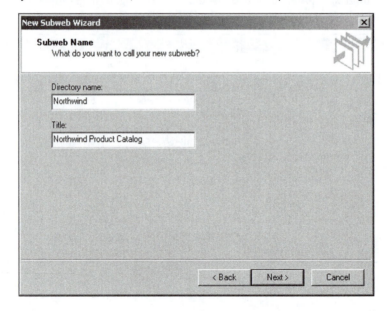

On the next screen, we will simply stay with the default: using the same administrator as the parent site. After clicking on Next, we are presented with a final screen in which we confirm what we want by clicking Finish.

We've now created a new child site. However, we still need to designate our new child site as an application. This basically means that it will be independent of the parent site in every way, so that it has its own application memory space. In many contexts, it is essential that an application has its own application memory space. Otherwise, various types of problems may be encountered.

In order to do this. We will have to right-click on the Northwind virtual folder. As this has just been created, in order to see it you will have to click on the refresh button at the top of the screen. After right-clicking, select Properties. This will bring up the following screen:

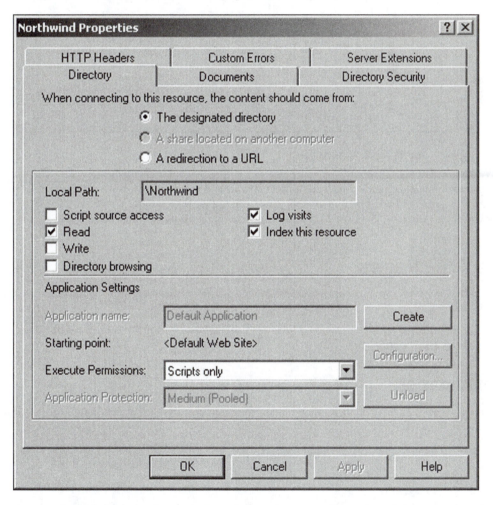

All we have to do is click on the Create button. Our application will now have been created, and we can close the dialog box by clicking OK. Back in the Internet Services Manager window, we should see that the Northwind virtual folder has become an application. This is shown by the different icon:

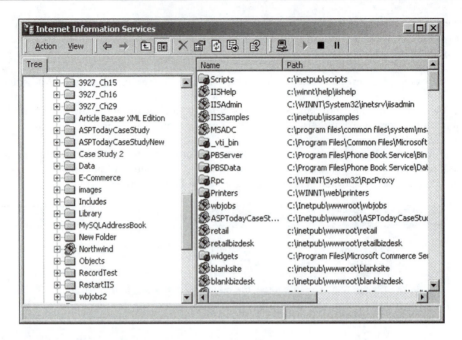

How it Works – An IIS Web Application

We have created an IIS Web Application in order to ensure that our application will have its own application memory space. This was done in a two stage process. First, we created the child site. This created a virtual folder, which maps onto a corresponding folder under C:\Inetpub\wwwroot\. Secondly, we ensured that this child site would operate as an independent web application.

The ASP Pages

Now that we've created our application, we're in a position to start building our ASP pages. We can use Notepad or any other text editor in order to view and revise our pages.

Note that all of the code for this appliation can be downloaded from the Wrox web site at www.wrox.com.

Preliminaries

Initially, we'll look at a few pages that contain functions and formatting that may be accessed from any of the main pages of the application. These are:

- ❑ Global.asa
- ❑ Settings.asp
- ❑ String.asp
- ❑ Template1.asp
- ❑ Template2.asp

Let's look at these in turn.

Global.asa

The `global.asa` file is used in an ASP Application for several important reasons. It can contain a number of subroutines (called subs) that are activated by certain events in the application. It must reside in the application root: in our case, the `C:\Inetpub\wwwroot\Northwind` folder.

In the first section, various variables are declared:

```
' ** global.asa file - located in the /northwind Root folder.


<SCRIPT LANGUAGE=VBScript RUNAT=Server>

Sub Application_OnStart
    Dim cn, rs, arycats, rows    ' ** Variables used to get Categories
                                 ' **   into Array
            ' ** cn is the Connection Object
            ' ** rs is the RecordSet
            ' ** arycats - a copy of Application("arycats")
            ' ** rows - a copy of Application("rows")
```

The following contains both the information required to connect to the database, and the code which will create the connection. The data provider is specified. In this case, we're using the SQL OLEDB provider. The datasource specifies the name of the server on which the database is running. If your database is on another machine, you will have to change this. Otherwise, by default, 'localhost' will be adequate. `Initial Catalog` specifies the name of the database we will use. By default, with SQL Server, the `User` can be 'sa' (system administrator). However, you may have to change this if your database has been reconfigured. Also, by default, we can leave the password blank. But again, this may have been changed on your DBMS, in which case you will have to change this.

The code that is critical in making the connection is the last two lines of the application. Basically, these create an instance of the appropriate object, and tell it to establish a connection to the database, using the information provided in the connection string (the `cstring`).

We don't have to concern ourselves with the details of what is happening here. All we have to understand is that a connection from our application to the relevant database has been established. If, when running the application, you encounter an error message that states that a connection cannot be established, or the server doesn't exist, it is very likely that the problem will lie in the connection string.

```
Application("cstring") = "Provider=sqloledb;Data Source=localhost; " &_
"Initial Catalog=Northwind;User Id=sa;Password=;"

' ** Change this to your Contact Name
Application("contactname") = "xxxxx"

' **  change this to your Contact email address
Application("companyemail") = xxxxx@xxxxx.com

Set cn = Server.CreateObject("ADODB.Connection")
cn.Open Application("cstring")
```

The following accesses information from the `categories` table. This is the first point at which we can see how SQL code is passed from an ASP application to the database. Basically, it is passed as a string to the `Execute` method of the connection object (called `cn` in this case). This will execute the SQL code, and the results will be returned as a **recordset**. This is just a set of records, which we access using the `GetRows` method.

In the next couple of lines, we transfer the records from the record set into an **array** which is stored in the `Application` object. An array is like a variable, except it can contain multiple values.

```
    Set rs = cn.Execute("SELECT CategoryID, CategoryName, Description FROM
categories")
    if NOT rs.EOF then
        Application("arycats") = rs.GetRows()
        Application("rows") = UBound(Application("arycats"),2)
    else
        Application("rows") = -1
    end if
    rs.Close
Set rs = Nothing
cn.close
Set cn = Nothing
End Sub

Sub Session_OnStart
    Session.Timeout = 30
    Session("ct") = -1
End Sub

</SCRIPT>
```

Settings.asp

The `settings.asp` page contains a few sub functions, which will be used repeatedly throughout the application. This page will be accessible from all the other pages of the application. We can ensure this by including the following line in our other pages:

```
<!--#INCLUDE FILE="settings.asp" -->
```

It contains one subfunction for opening a connection to the database, and another for closing it. Note that the connection string does not have to be included here. This is because it is already contained in the `Application` object as 'cstring'. Also, various variables, which are used throughout the application, are stored here. This is a useful way of keeping track of variables. The alternative would be to pass values between different ASP pages, and that can become unnecessarily complex.

```
<%

' ** These variables are copies of the Application variables,
' ** mostly for the purpose of making our coding easier to
' ** write. Rather than referring to 'Application("cstring"),
' ** we simply write "cstring"
```

```
Dim cstring, cn, rs, q, cmd, numrecords, testmode, rows, arycats, title

cstring = Application("cstring")
testmode = Application("testmode")
rows = Application("rows")
arycats = Application("arycats")

Sub openconn()
  Set cn = Server.CreateObject("ADODB.Connection")
  cn.Open cstring
End Sub

Sub closeconn()
  cn.close
  Set cn = Nothing
End Sub
```

The following section simply checks what page has called this page, and dynamically assigns a title to each page the user will see.

```
Select Case LCase(Request.ServerVariables("PATH_INFO"))
  Case "/northwind/default.asp"
    title = "Northwind Product Catalog"
  Case "/northwind/catalog.asp"
    title = "Search the Product Catalog"
  Case "/northwind/viewcart.asp"
    title = "View Your Cart"
  Case "/northwind/checkout.asp"
    title = "Check Out"
  Case "/northwind/checkout2.asp"
    title = "Thank You For Your Order!"
  Case Else
    title = "An Error Occurred in Processing Your Shopping Cart"
End Select
%>
```

string.asp

The `string.asp` page is also an 'include' file, insofar as it is 'included' in other pages, so that the functions it contains can be called from anywhere else in the application. The functions it contains are all intended to manipulate strings in various ways.

This first function, `sqlencode`, is used to encode quotation marks in strings that are to be inserted into SQL queries. As we saw in Chapter 11, when a string which contains a single quotation mark is passed to an DBMS, it can cause problems. This function inserts an extra quotation mark in front of the existing quotation mark, which ensures that the quotation mark is counted as part of the string by SQl Server (rather than marking the end of the string).

Users of Oracle should note that the forward slash character (/) is used as an escape character in Oracle.

```
<%
Function sqlencode(str)
   sqlencode = Replace(Replace(str, "'", "''"), CHR(34), CHR(34) & CHR(34))
End Function
```

The `breakstring()` function is used when we want to display data from a text field. It simply replaces the ASCII character for a line break (vbCrLf) with the HTML tag for a line break (<br>). This ensures that the text is displayed properly when presented in the browser.

```
Function breakstring(str)
   breakstring = Replace(str, VbCrLf, "<br>")
End Function
```

The `formencode()` function takes two parameters: `val` is the value being passed, `obj` is the name of the form object the string is being modified for. Basically, this function ensures that no illegal characters interfere with a text form field.

```
' ** Can be used with text, textarea, checkbox
Function formencode(v, o)
   if o = "checkbox" then
      if ((CStr(v) = "0") OR (Cstr(v) = "")) then
         formencode = ""
      else
         formencode = " checked "
      end if
   else
      formencode = Server.HTMLEncode(Replace(v, "&quot;", CHR(34)))
   end if

End Function
```

The Template Files

The template files simply provide a common format for all the ASP pages in our application, specifying colors, styles, and layout. The first contains most of this code, and ends, note, with a <td> tag. This marks the beginning of a table box, and it is in this that the other ASP pages of the application will display information. The second template file begins begins the corresponding closing tag of the table (</td>).

Template1.asp

```
<!--#INCLUDE FILE="settings.asp" -->
<html>

<head>
<meta http-equiv="Content-Type" content="text/html; charset=iso-8859-1">
<title><%=title%></title>
</head>
```

```
<body bgcolor="#B9B9FF">

<p align="center"><img src="images/northwindlogo.jpg"
alt="Northwind Traders" border="2"
width="468" height="162"></p>

<table border="0" width="100%">
  <tr>
    <td width="150" valign="top"><table border="0" cellpadding="2">
      <tr>
        <td><strong><font face="Arial" size="2">Categories</strong>
<br>(Click to view)</font></td>
      </tr>
```

At this point, something interesting happens. The categories contained in the Northwind database file are accessed and displayed. Note that this is done by calling the catalog.asp page. We will be looking at this page later.

```
<%if rows >= 0 then
for i = 0 to rows%>
      <tr>
        <td><%
Response.Write "<p><a href='catalog.asp?catid=" & arycats(0, i) &_
  "cat=" & Server.URLEncode(arycats(1, i)) & "'>" &_
  "<font face='Arial' size='2'><strong>" & arycats(1, i) &_
  "</strong><br>" &  arycats(2, i) & "</font></p>"%>
</td>
      </tr>
<%next
end if%>
```

The following provides hyperlinks to other pages in our application: default.asp, viewcart.asp, and checkout.asp.

```
    <tr>
      <td><strong><font face="Arial" size="2"><a
href="default.asp">Search</a></font></strong></td>
    </tr>
    <tr>
      <td><strong><font face="Arial" size="2"><a
href="viewcart.asp">View Your Cart</a></font></strong></td>
    </tr>
    <tr>
      <td><strong><font face="Arial" size="2"><a
href="checkout.asp">Checkout</a></font></strong></td>
    </tr>
  </table>
  </td>
  <td valign="top">
```

template2.asp

The second template file simply provides the necessary closing tags:

```
</td>
  </tr>
</table>
</body>
</html>
```

The Application

We can now move on to the pages that make up the bulk of the application. These are:

- ❑ `default.asp`
- ❑ `catalog.asp`
- ❑ `viewcart.asp`
- ❑ `checkout.asp`
- ❑ `checkout2.asp`
- ❑ `error.asp`

We'll start by looking at the `default.asp` page.

default.asp

The appearance of this page, like all the others, is determined by the template page. The content provided by this page is contained in the main central section. Once the application is up and running, it will look like this:

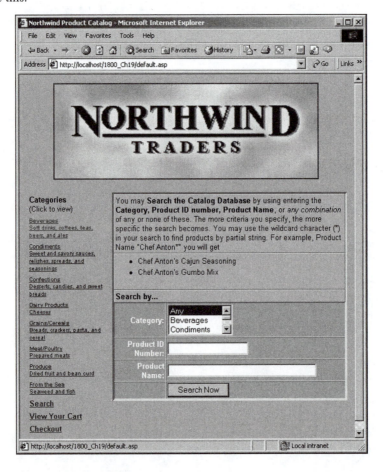

Note how the categories in the box correspond to the categories in the list on the left.

Let's take a look at the code for this page.

Initially, we 'include' the `template1.asp` file:

```
<!--#INCLUDE FILE="template1.asp" -->
```

Next, a function is specified. This function, called `validator`, is the form validation function for the form on the page. Form validation is important when submitting data in an SQL Statement to a database. The format of the data must match the data type that it will be used against in the query.

For example, the **Product ID Number** form field data will be used against the `ProductID` field in the `Products` table, in order to search for individual Products records. However, the `ProductID` field in the table is *numeric* in type. This is a text box. We can type anything we want into it. If some characters were passed to the SQL query instead of a number, it would generate an error.

So, when this form is submitted, the `validator` function will test the input, and only if it is of the appropriate kind (numeric) will it be passed to the SQL query.

Note that the `validator` function has been written in javascript.

```javascript
<script Language="JavaScript"><!--
function Validator(theForm)
{
  var checkOK = "0123456789-";
  var checkStr = theForm.ProductID.value;
  var allValid = true;
  var decPoints = 0;
  var allNum = "";
  for (i = 0;  i < checkStr.length;  i++)
  {
    ch = checkStr.charAt(i);
    for (j = 0;  j < checkOK.length;  j++)
      if (ch == checkOK.charAt(j))
        break;
    if (j == checkOK.length)
    {
      allValid = false;
      break;
    }
    allNum += ch;
  }
  if (!allValid)
  {
    alert("Please enter only digit characters in the \"Product ID Number\"
        field.");
    theForm.ProductID.focus();
    return (false);
  }
  return (true);
}
//--></script>
```

Next, we have the code that builds the form. Note the `onsubmit` event. This ensures that when the form is submitted, the submitted values are passed to the `validator` function.

```
<form action="catalog.asp" method="POST" onsubmit="return Validator(this)">
  <table border="3" width="100%" bordercolorlight="#7A59DB"
  bordercolordark="#E8E8FF"
  bgcolor="#AEAEFF" cellspacing="0" cellpadding="2">
    <tr>
      <td colspan="2"><font face="Arial" size="2">You may <strong>Search the
      Catalog Database</strong> by using entering the <strong>Category,
      Product ID number, Product Name</strong>, or <em>any combination</em>
      of any or none of these. The more criteria you specify,
      the more specific the search becomes. You may use the wildcard character
      (*) in your search to find products by partial string. For example,
      Product Name &quot;Chef Anton*&quot; you will get</font></td>
    </tr>
    <tr>
      <td colspan="2"><ul>
        <li><font face="Arial" size="2">Chef Anton's Cajun
        Seasoning</font></li>
        <li><font face="Arial" size="2">Chef Anton's Gumbo Mix</font></li>
      </ul>
      </td>
    </tr>
    <tr>
      <td><strong><font face="Arial" size="2">Search
      by...</font></strong></td>
      <td> </td>
    </tr>
```

The following builds a drop-down list box of product categories. It is populated dynamically by an ASP script that accesses the category names from the array in which we earlier stored the category names (called `arycats`).

```
    <tr>
      <td align="right"><strong><font face="Arial" size="2">Category:
      </font></strong></td>
      <td><select name="catid" size="3" multiple>
        <option value="Any" selected>Any</option>
<%for x = 0 to rows%>
<option value="<%=arycats(0,x)%>">
<%=arycats(1,x)%>
</option>
<%next%>
</select>
</td>
    </tr>
```

Note that the option to select products from any category is provided for by including `Any` in the drop-down list box.

The `ProductID` and `ProductName` fields are very similar to the category drop-down list box. They are both text objects. The only real difference is the form validation for the `ProductID` field, which ensures that the data entered into it is numeric:

```
<tr>
  <td align="right"><strong><font face="Arial" size="2">Product ID Number:
  </font></strong></td>
  <td><strong><font face="Arial" size="2"><input type="text"
  name="ProductID" size="20"></font></strong></td>
</tr>
<tr>
  <td align="right"><font face="Arial" size="2"><strong>Product Name:
  </strong></font></td>
  <td><strong><font face="Arial" size="2"><input type="text"
  name="ProductName" size="40"></font></strong></td>
</tr>
<tr>
  <td align="right"> </td>
  <td><strong><font face="Arial" size="2"><input type="submit"
  value="Search Now" name="B1"></font></strong>
  </td>
</tr>
</table>
</form>
```

And finally, the second half of the template page:

```
<!--#INCLUDE FILE="template2.asp" -->
```

catalog.asp

Now that we've looked at default.asp, we need to know what do do with the data that it passes. default.asp passes data to another page via one of two different methods. The first is via the navigation menu on the left (which is actually part of tempate1.asp), which has parameterized hyperlinks in it. All of the hyperlinks in the navigation bar point to one page: catalog.asp.

Here's an example of one of these URLs, from the top link in the menu (Query String in bold):

```
http://chutney/northwind/catalog.asp?catid=1&cat=Beverages
```

We can see from this that there are 2 parameters being passed to the catalog.asp page: catid and cat. The first of these, catid, is the CategoryID of the relevant category from the Categories table. The second, cat, is the CategoryName of that same category.

Parameters may also be passed to the catalog.asp page from the form in the default.asp page. As we just saw, this form has three form fields: catid, ProductID, and ProductName. The catid field corresponds to the CategoryID field in the Categories table. The other two fields correspond to the similarly named fields in the Products table (ProductID and ProductName).

So, on being passed particular parameters, the catalog.asp page operates as a search results page. It is designed to receive data, perform a SQL query against the Northwind database, and display the results. It can search on any combination of CategoryID, ProductID, and ProductName.

It will generate results that appear like this:

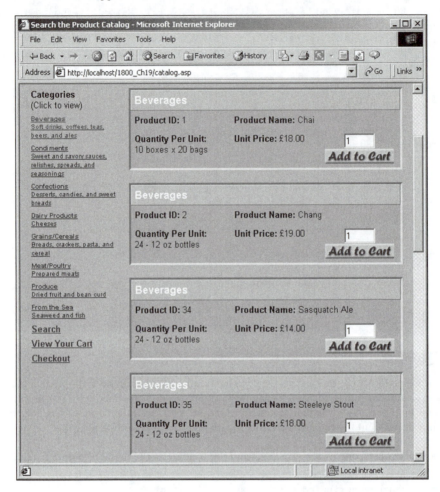

Note the Add to Cart buttons. These submit information from this form to the addtocart.asp page. addtocart.asp will be designed to add an item to the User's cart, and then return to this page. This means that we will have to pass the data received *by* this page *to* the addtocart.asp page, and then pass it *back* when we return.

Note also that only ten records at a time will be presented on this page. If more records are to be displayed, the user will have to click on a Next 10 Records button.

Thus, there are four different ways in which this page can be accessed:

❑ Hyperlink from Navigation bar

❑ Search Form from default.asp

❑ Coming back from addtocart.asp

❑ From this very page, when more records are requested

Therefore, we will need to be able to identify each of these situations in our code and be able to act accordingly:

1. Hyperlink from Navigation bar (menu): get `catid` and `cat` values, and perform a category search.

2. Search Form from `default.asp`: get `catid`, `ProductName`, and `ProductID` values from the form, and perform a search.

3. Next Ten Records (same query, different set of records): get the query parameters from the last search, along with the current result set's last record's `ProductID` (`prodid`) and `CategoryID` (`rscatid`) fields, as well as the current `Product ID` and `Product Name` to pass to this same form (which will be its' own form handler), in order to get the next ten records from the same result set.

4. Coming back from `addtocart.asp`: replace all the information that was currently in this form with the data returned from `addtocart.asp`.

Let's look at the actual code that builds this page.

We begin by specifying the files we wish to include. The `adovbs.inc` file is a Microsoft file that contains information tha, basically, allows us to use some names instead of numerical values in passing information to the data provider. We don't have to worry about the content, as far as building this case study is involved.

```
<!--#INCLUDE FILE="template1.asp" -->
<!--#INCLUDE FILE="adovbs.inc" -->
<!--#INCLUDE FILE="string.asp" -->
```

Next, we delare various variables. They contain the following information:

❑ productid: the `ProductID` passed as a search criteria to the application

❑ prodid: the last `ProductID` in the current result set

❑ productname: the `ProductName` passed as search criteria to the application

❑ catid: the `CategoryID` passed as search criteria to the application

❑ rscatid: the last `CategoryID` in the current result set

❑ maxrecords: the maximum number of records to display per page

❑ i: a count variable, for general purpose counting

```
<%
Dim productid, prodid, productname, catid, rscatid, catname
Dim maxrecords, i

maxrecords = 10
```

We then create and open the connection to the database, create the command object, and populate its `Parameters` collection with the form input data. This data is then passed to the SQL Server stored procedure `sp_searchproducts`. We will be looking at the stored procedures we use a little later.

```
openconn()
Set cmd = Server.CreateObject("ADODB.Command")
cmd.CommandType = adCmdStoredProc
cmd.CommandText = "sp_searchproducts"
cmd.ActiveConnection = cn

' ** This will hod the return Value from the Stored Procedure
cmd.Parameters.Append(cmd.CreateParameter("@RETURN_VALUE", 3, 4, 0, 0))

' ** Add the ProductID Search criteria. If no ProductID was entered,
' ** make it zero. The Stored Procedure will ignore it if it is zero.
productid = Trim(Request.Form("ProductID"))
if productid = "" then productid = 0
cmd.Parameters.Append(cmd.CreateParameter _
   ("@productid", 3, 1, 0, CInt(productid)))

' ** Add the prodid (last record in current result set).
' **  This is used if we are getting the "Next 10 Records"
' ** Otherwise, make it zero (ignored BY THE sp)
prodid = Trim(Request.Form("prodid"))
if prodid = "" then prodid = 0
cmd.Parameters.Append(cmd.CreateParameter("@prodid", 3, 1, 0, CInt(prodid)))

' ** Add the ProductName Search Criteria. We are allowing a wildcard
' ** search by allowing the use of the asterisk (*), which we substitute the
' ** SQL wildcard character (%) for. If it's a blank string, it will be
' ** ignored
productname = Replace(Trim(Request.Form("ProductName")), "*", "%")
if productname = "" then productname = "%"
cmd.Parameters.Append(cmd.CreateParameter("@productname", 202, 1, 40,
Left(productname, 40)))
```

If necessary, we might have to fetch the next ten records from the table. In this case, we will need to pass a unique value to the query, to indicate the precise record we stopped at (the last record in the current result set). However, since we don't know whether there will be more products from the same category in the next result set, we need to test for one of *two* possible conditions:

5. Whether the `CategoryID` of the record is higher than the `CategoryID` of the last record in our current result set.

6. Whether the `CategoryID` is the *same* as the `CategoryID` of the last record of the current result set, *and* the `ProductID` number is higher.

Although we're selecting products using the `categoryID` as the search criteria, we also need to use the `ProductID` of each product in order to keep track of what products we've already displayed.

```
catid = Split(Request("catid"), ",")
i = UBound(catid)

' ** if there is more than one CategoryID to search...
if i > 0 then    ' ** More than one Category

' ** 4 possible input parameters
  For x = 0 to 4
    if x <= i then   ' ** We are still using the array
          ' ** from the Request.

' ** Test for a number or " (no catid)
      if IsNumeric(catid(x)) then
        cmd.Parameters.Append(cmd.CreateParameter _
          ("@catid" & (x + 1), 3, 1, 0, CInt(catid(x))))
      else
        cmd.Parameters.Append(cmd.CreateParameter _
          ("@catid" & (x + 1), 3, 1, 0, 0))
      end if
    else
      cmd.Parameters.Append(cmd.CreateParameter _
        ("@catid" & (x + 1), 3, 1, 0, 0))
    end if
  Next
else

' ** if no value, fill the Parameters (@catid1 - @catid4) with zeros
  For x = 0 to 4
    cmd.Parameters.Append(cmd.CreateParameter("@catid" & (x + 1), 3, 1, 0, 0))
  Next
end if

' ** rscatid is the CategoryID of the last record in the RecordSet.
' ** It is used for a "Next 10 records" operation. The SP will get
' **  records only higher than this one in the result set.
rscatid = Request("rscatid")

' ** if the rscatid is blank, we're starting from the beginning (0)
if rscatid = "" then rscatid = 0

' ** if CategoryIDs were input, load them into the Parameters Collection
if i >= 0 then
  if IsNumeric(catid(0)) then
    cmd.Parameters.Append(cmd.CreateParameter _
      ("@catid", 3, 1, 1, CInt(catid(0))))
  elseif catid(0) = "Any" then
      cmd.Parameters.Append(cmd.CreateParameter("@catid", 3, 1, 1, -1))
  elseif i > 0 then
    cmd.Parameters.Append(cmd.CreateParameter("@catid", 3, 1, 1, 0))
  else
    cmd.Parameters.Append(cmd.CreateParameter("@catid", 3, 1, 1, -1))
  end if
else
  cmd.Parameters.Append(cmd.CreateParameter("@catid", 3, 1, 1, -1))
```

```
      end if
      cmd.Parameters.Append(cmd.CreateParameter("@rscatid", 3, 1, 1, CInt(rscatid)))


      ' ** Execute the search, via the Stored Procedure, and place the results
      ' ** in our RecordSet object
      Set rs = cmd.Execute


      ' ** Debugging code. You can use statements like this to see values
      ' ** That don't ordinarily appear on the page, for debugging.
      ' ** When you are finished, comment them out (like this one) or delete them.
      'For Each p in cmd.Parameters
      '  Response.Write p.Name & ": " & p.Value & "<br>"
      'Next


      if NOT rs.EOF then%></p>   ' ** Check to see if there are any records

<table border="0" width="100%">
  <tr>
    <td valign="top"><%x = 0

      ' ** Here's our loop through the RecordSet. It breaks when the RecordSet
      ' ** reaches EOF, or when the maximum number of records is displayed.
      DO WHILE (NOT rs.EOF) and (x < maxrecords)

      ' ** each record has a form for adding that item to the Shopping Cart.
      ' ** The form repeats once per record.
%>
<form method="POST" action="addtocart.asp">
      <input type="hidden" name="cat" value="<%=Request("cat")%>">
      <input type="hidden" name="catid" value="<%=Request("catid")%>">
      <input type="hidden" name="prodid" value="<%=prodid%>">
      <input type="hidden" name="ProductID" value="<%=ProductID%>">
      <input type="hidden" name="ProductName"
      value="<%=formencode(ProductName, "hidden")%>">
      <input type="hidden" name="quantityperunit"
      value="<%
   =formencode(rs("QuantityPerUnit").value, "hidden")%>">
      <input type="hidden" name="rsproductid"
      value="<%=rs("productid").value%>">
      <input type="hidden" name="rsproductname"
      value="<%=formencode(rs("ProductName").value, "hidden")%>">
      <input type="hidden" name="unitprice"
      value="<%=rs("Unitprice").value%>">
    <table border="3" width="100%" bordercolordark="#E8E8FF"
    bordercolorlight="#7A59DB" height="51" cellspacing="0"
    cellpadding="5">
        <tr>
          <td bordercolorlight="#AEAEFF" bordercolordark="#AEAEFF"
          width="100%" colspan="3" bgcolor="#AEAEFF"><font face="Arial"
          size="3" color="#FFFFFF"><strong><%=rs("CategoryName").value%>
          </strong></font></td>
        </tr>
        <tr>
          <td bordercolorlight="#AEAEFF" bordercolordark="#AEAEFF"
```

```
                    width="37%" valign="top" bgcolor="#AEAEFF"><font face="Arial"
                    size="2"><strong>Product ID:</strong>
                    <%=rs("ProductID").value%> </font></td>
                    <td width="63%" bordercolorlight="#AEAEFF"
                    bordercolordark="#AEAEFF" colspan="2" valign="top"
                    bgcolor="#AEAEFF"><font face="Arial" size="2"><strong>Product
                    Name:</strong> <%=rs("ProductName").value%></font></td>
                </tr>
                <tr>
                    <td bordercolorlight="#AEAEFF" bordercolordark="#AEAEFF" width="37%"
                    valign="top" bgcolor="#AEAEFF"><font face="Arial"
                    size="2"><strong>Quantity Per Unit: </strong><br>
                    <%=rs("QuantityPerUnit").value%> </font></td>
                    <td width="33%" bordercolorlight="#AEAEFF" bordercolordark="#AEAEFF"
                    valign="top" bgcolor="#AEAEFF"><font face="Arial"
                    size="2"><strong>Unit Price:</strong>
                    <%=FormatCurrency(rs("UnitPrice").value)%> </font></td>
                    <td width="30%" bordercolorlight="#AEAEFF" bordercolordark="#AEAEFF"
                    align="center" valign="top" bgcolor="#AEAEFF"><font face="Arial"
                    size="2"><input type="text" name="qty" size="4" value="1">
                    <input src="images/addtocart.jpg" name="I4" alt="Add to Cart"
                    type="image" border="0" align="absmiddle"> </font></td>
                </tr>
            </table>
        </form>
        <p><%

' ** end of our loop. We set the rscatid and prodid values from the last
' ** record in the set (it gets them each time, but stops at the last)
rscatid = rs("CategoryID").value
prodid = rs("ProductID").value
rs.Movenext
x = x + 1
Loop

' ** Clean up and go on home.
rs.Close
Set rs = Nothing
closeconn

' ** If there are more records, our Count variable (x) will be
' ** equal to maxrecords
if x = maxrecords then%>
```

This last part of the page consists of two forms. The first form is repeated for each record returned, and contains the information needed to pass to the addtocart.asp page.

The second form is used to re-run the query, getting the next ten records. It submits the last ProductID (prodid), the last CategoryID (rscatid), and all of the original search criteria back to this same page:

```
<form method="POST" action="catalog.asp">
    <input type="hidden" name="cat" value="<%=Request("cat")%>">
    <input type="hidden" name="catid" value="<%=Request("catid")%>">
    <input type="hidden" name="prodid" value="<%=prodid%>">
    <input type="hidden" name="ProductID" value="<%=productid%>">
    <input type="hidden" name="ProductName"
    value="<%=formencode(productname, "hidden")%>">
```

```
            <input type="hidden" name="rscatid" value="<%=rscatid%>">

        <p><input type="submit" value="Next <%=maxrecords%> Records"
        name="B1"></p>

    </form><%
' ** This is the Else from the check for more records.
' ** If there are no more records, this displays "End of List."
else
Response.Write "<font face='Arial' color='#FF0000'>End of List.</font>"
end if%></td>
    </tr>
</table>

<%
' ** this is the Else statement for the initial check for records in
' ** the current RecordSet. If there are none, it displays a message
' ** to that effect.
else%>
<p> </p>

<p align="center"><font face="Arial" size="2"><strong><font color="#FF0000">Sorry.
No matching Products found</font>.</strong></font></p>

<p><%end if%>
```

And then the rest of the page:

```
<!--#INCLUDE FILE="template2.asp" -->
```

sp_searchproducts

In order to run as nearly optimally as possible, we will use a stored procedure to search for the products in the Products table. As we saw, information is passed to this, from the catalog.asp.

We begin by declaring our input parameters. Note the parameters catid1 – catid5. These will hold the values of the split CategoryID field from the ASP form.

```
SET QUOTED_IDENTIFIER OFF
GO
SET ANSI_NULLS ON
GO

CREATE PROCEDURE sp_searchproducts
@productid int,           /* Product ID Passed as search criteria */
@prodid int,              /*Product ID of last Product in last result set */
@productname nvarchar(40),  /* Product Name Passed as search criteria */
@catid1 int,              /* Up to 5 Category IDs may be passed */
@catid2 int,              /* from the Application. They must be */
@catid3 int,              /* passed individually */
@catid4 int,
@catid5 int,
@catid int,               /* Category ID passed as search criteria */
@rscatid int              /* Category ID of last Product in last result set */

AS
```

Next comes the actual query. The first part is our SELECT list. Because we want to include the category name for each product, and this is not stored in the Products table, we perform an INNER JOIN query to combine the data from the two tables.

```
SELECT Products.ProductID AS ProductID, Products.ProductName AS ProductName,
Products.QuantityPerUnit AS QuantityPerUnit,
Products.UnitPrice AS UnitPrice,
Categories.CategoryID AS CategoryID, Categories.CategoryName AS CategoryName
FROM Products INNER JOIN Categories ON Products.CategoryID = Categories.CategoryID
```

Our WHERE clause comes next. Since we do not know for sure what fields (from the form) and their corresponding input parameters) will be used, any empty value must be accounted for.

```
WHERE Discontinued = 0

AND
```

If the value is 0, it compares the value of the variable against itself. Why? Because the CASE clause only allows us to substitute one value for another in the query. It doesn't give us the option of not including this part of the WHERE clause. All we can do is compare equal values if we don't want to include this field in the search. Since equal values always equate to TRUE, this will eliminate any filtering by this field.

```
CASE @productid
   WHEN 0 THEN @productid
   ELSE Products.ProductID
END
= @productid

AND ProductName LIKE @productname

AND  (((Categories.CategoryID = @catid1)
OR (Categories.CategoryID = @catid2)
OR (Categories.CategoryID = @catid3)
OR (Categories.CategoryID = @catid4)
OR (Categories.CategoryID = @catid5))
OR ((@catid = -1) OR (Categories.CategoryID = @catid)))

AND
((Categories.CategoryID > @rscatid)
OR
((Categories.CategoryID = @rscatid)
AND
(Products.ProductID > @prodid)))

ORDER BY CategoryID, ProductID

GO
SET QUOTED_IDENTIFIER OFF
GO
SET ANSI_NULLS ON
GO
```

addtocart.asp

As its name would suggest, the `addtocart.asp` page adds particular products to the shopping cart.

In order to store information about what is in the cart, we use an array which is contained in ASP's `session` object. This object is associated with a particular user, so information about the contents of a particular cart can be associated with a particular user.

When an item is added to the cart, the `session` array is checked to see whether that item has already been added to the cart. If it has, the application simply increments the quantity and price. Otherwise, it generates a new element in each array and populates them with the necessary information. Such information is stored in the array in the following way:

session("ct")	aryproductid	aryqperu	aryproductname	aryunitprice	aryqty
0	1	"10 boxes x 20 bags"	"Chai"	18	2
1	2	"24 - 12 oz bottles"	"Chang"	19	1
2	3	"12 - 550 ml bottles"	"Aniseed Syrup"	10	1

Let's take a look at the code. Initially, we declare the 'include' files and declare various variables:

```
<!--#INCLUDE FILE="settings.asp" -->
<!--#INCLUDE FILE="string.asp" -->
<%
Dim qty, qperu, unitprice, rsproductname, rsproductid  ' ** For Shopping Cart

Dim productid, prodid, cat, catid, rscatid, productname ' ** To pass back to
                                                        ' ** calling page
Dim x, len, mess

' ** Get the values to pass back in the form (if any)
productid = Request.Form("productid")
prodid = Request.Form("prodid")
cat = Request.Form("cat")
catid = Request.Form("catid")
rscatid = Request.Form("rscatid")
productname = Request.form("productname")

' ** Get the values for the cart
rsproductid = Request.Form("rsproductid")
rsproductname = Request.form("rsproductname")
qperu = Request.form("qperu")
unitprice = CDbl(Request.Form("unitprice"))
qty = CInt(Request.Form("qty"))
```

Then we test to see whether the cart is empty. If the cart is empty, we need to create a new session array to hold the contents of the cart. In order to do this, we create a new local array, work with that, and then copy it to the session object.

```
' ** If there are no items in cart
' ** (no cart - Session("ct") initialized to -1)
if Session("ct") < 0 then
   Dim aryproductid()
   Dim aryqperu()
   Dim aryproductname()
   Dim aryunitprice()
   Dim aryqty()
   Session("ct") = 0
   Redim Preserve aryproductid(0)
   aryproductid(0) = rsproductid
   Redim Preserve aryqperu(0)
   aryqperu(0) = qperu
   Redim Preserve aryproductname(0)
   aryproductname(0) = rsproductname
   Redim Preserve aryunitprice(0)
   aryunitprice(0) = unitprice
   Redim Preserve aryqty(0)
   aryqty(0) = qty
```

If the Session("ct") value is 0 or greater, we know that there are already items in the cart. In that case, we want to copy the Session array to a local array, work with this, and then copy it back to the session object array (Session("aryqty")) when we're finished.

```
else
   aryproductid = Session("aryproductid")
   aryqperu = Session("aryqperu")
   aryproductname = Session("aryproductname")
   aryunitprice = Session("aryunitprice")
   aryqty = Session("aryqty")
```

We next check to see whether the particular item is already in the cart. If it is, we increment the number of items required and the price accordingly:

```
' ** See if that item is already in the cart
len = UBound(aryproductid)
for x = 0 to len
   if rsproductid = aryproductid(x) then
      aryqty(x) = aryqty(x) + qty
      Exit For
   end if
next
if x > len then
   Redim Preserve aryproductid(x)
   aryproductid(x) = rsproductid
   Redim Preserve aryqperu(x)
   aryqperu(x) = qperu
   Redim Preserve aryproductname(x)
   aryproductname(x) = rsproductname
   Redim Preserve aryunitprice(x)
   aryunitprice(x) = unitprice
   Redim Preserve aryqty(x)
   aryqty(x) = qty
   Session("ct") = Session("ct") + 1
   end if
end if
```

Next, we copy the contents of the local array to the session object arrays:

```
" ** Now we recopy the arrays to the Session
Session("aryproductid") = aryproductid
Session("aryqperu") = aryqperu
Session("aryproductname") = aryproductname
Session("aryunitprice") = aryunitprice
Session("aryqty") = aryqty
mess = qty & " '" & Replace(rsproductname, CHR(34), "'") & "' added to Cart."
%>
```

The following HTML code controls the appearance of the page, and builds the appropriate forms:

```
<html>

<head>
<meta http-equiv="Content-Type" content="text/html; charset=iso-8859-1">
<title><%=mess%></title>
</head>

<body bgcolor="#B9B9FF">

<p> </p>

<p> </p>

<p> </p>

<p> </p>

<p align="center"><font face="Arial" size="2"><strong><%=mess%></strong></font>
<br>
<font face="Arial" size="2"><strong>Please Stand by...</strong></font></p>

<%
" ** Here's the form that passes the data back to catalog.asp}
' ** Note the "action" property of the form, pointing to
' ** Request.ServerVariables("HTTP_REFERER"). This is the ServerVariable that
' ** indicates the URL of the page that "called" this one.%>
<form method="POST" action="<%=Request.ServerVariables("HTTP_REFERER")%>">
  <input type="hidden" name="cat" value="<%=formencode(cat,
  "hidden")%>"><input
  type="hidden" name="catid" value="<%=catid%>"><input type="hidden"
  name="prodid" value="<%=prodid%>"><input type="hidden"
  name="ProductID" value="<%=productid%>"><input type="hidden"
  name="ProductName" value="<%=formencode(productname, "hidden")%>">
  <input type="hidden" name="rscatid" value="<%=rscatid%>"><p> </p>
</form>
```

The following function lets the user know that an item has been added to the cart. The message is contained in the mess variable. This was generated a little earlier.

```
<script language="JavaScript">
<!--
confirm("<%=Replace(mess, CHR(34), "\" & CHR(34))%>");
document.forms[0].submit();
// --></script>
</body>
</html>
```

Notice that any double-quotes in the `mess` variable have been replaced with the JavaScript escape sequence for double-quote literals. In HTML, double-quotes are delimiters for strings, and this is also the case with JavaScript. If we use a JavaScript function, therefore, which works with a string, and the string has double-quotes in it, it may cause an error, depending on how the extra quotes make this turn out. In JavaScript, we can escape problem characters by placing a backslash (`"\"`) in front of them. So we escape any possible double-quotes in the message.

viewcart.asp

The `viewcart.asp` page doesn't interact with the database. Instead, it accesses information about which objects are in a cart from the arrays stored in the `session` object. It then displays this information, and allows the user to update it.

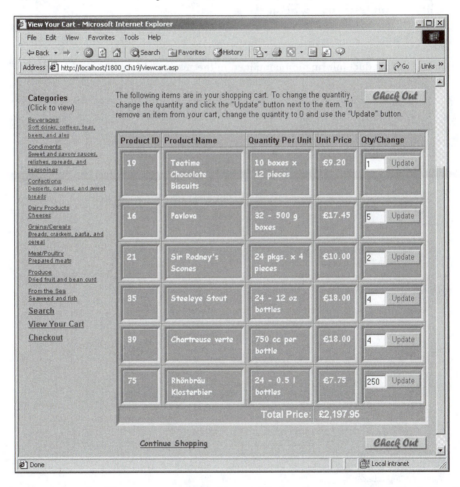

Let's look at how it works. We start, as usual, with our include references and variable declarations:

```
<!--#INCLUDE FILE="template1.asp" --><!--#INCLUDE FILE="string.asp" --><%
Dim total
```

After a predetermined amount of time, if a session object has not been utilized, it will be erased. This is known as 'timing out'. This means that, if the user has been idle for a while, yet has decided to view the contents of their cart and check out, the cart will now be empty. However, the form that submits to this page will not be empty. In this rare case, there's nothing to do but inform the user that their shopping cart data has been lost, and to start over again with a new cart.

```
if Request.Form("productid") <> "" then   " ** An Update was submitted
  if Session("ct") = -1 then    " ** The cart is empty?!
    Response.Redirect "error.asp"
  else
    Dim productid, qty, x, y, z
    Dim aryqty()
    productid = CInt(Request.Form("productid"))
    qty = CInt(Request.Form("qty"))
    if qty < 0 then qty = 0
```

We now find the product information contained in the session object arrays:

```
' ** Find the "record" (in the Session) containing the product

    For x = 0 to UBound(Session("aryproductid"))
      if productid = CInt(Session("aryproductid")(x)) then
```

If the number of a particular product has been set to zero, then it is removed completely:

```
' ** If they have set to zero, remove the item completely.

        if qty = 0 then
          Dim aryqperu()
          Dim aryproductid()
          Dim aryproductname()
          Dim aryunitprice()
          z = 0

" ** Read the Session items into the new arrays, one at a time,
" ** omitting the one we're removing
          For y = 0 to UBound(Session("aryproductid"))
            if y <> x then
              Redim Preserve aryqperu(y - z)
              aryqperu(y - z) = Session("aryqperu")(y)
              Redim Preserve aryproductid(y - z)
              aryproductid(y - z) = Session("aryproductid")(y)
              Redim Preserve aryproductname(y - z)
              aryproductname(y - z) = Session("aryproductname")(y)
              Redim Preserve aryunitprice(y - z)
              aryunitprice(y - z) = Session("aryunitprice")(y)
              Redim Preserve aryqty(y - z)
              aryqty(y - z) = Session("aryqty")(y)
            else
              z = 1
            end if
          Next
```

```
" ** Copy the arrays back over the Session arrays

        Session("aryqperu") = aryqperu
        Session("aryproductid") = aryproductid
        Session("aryproductname") = aryproductname
        Session("aryunitprice") = aryunitprice
        Session("aryqty") = aryqty
        Session("ct") = Session("ct") - 1
        Session("mess") = "Item removed from Cart"
        Exit For
    else

" ** If qty > 0, update the array with the new qty
        For y = 0 to UBound(Session("aryqty"))

" ** Find the element index containing the Product, and update it
        Redim Preserve aryqty(y)
        if y = x then
          aryqty(y) = qty
        else
          aryqty(y) = Session("aryqty")(y)
        end if
        Next
" ** Copy the •aryqty• array back over the Session array
        Session("aryqty") = aryqty
        Session("mess") = Session("mess") & "Your Cart has been updated."
      end if
    end if
  Next
  end if
end if
%>
```

Again, we present any appropriate messages to the user. These are stored in the `mess` variable.

```
<script language="JavaScript"><!--
<%if Session("mess") <> "" then%>
alert("<%=Session("mess")%>");
<%Session("mess") = ""
end if%>
// --></script>
```

We check to see whether the shopping cart is empty:

```
<%
" ** If the Shopping Cart is now empty (after removing the item)
" ** It is not an error. Just display message that cart is now empty
if Session("ct") < 0 then%>
<p> </p>

<blockquote>
  <p><font face="Arial" size="2" color="#FF0000"><strong>Your Shopping Cart is
empty.</strong></font><%else%></p>
</blockquote>
```

We then display the contents of the shopping cart:

```
<p align="left"><a href="checkout.asp"><img src="images/checkout.jpg" alt="Check
Out"
border="0" align="right"></a></p>

<p><font face="Arial" size="2">The following items are in your shopping cart. To
change
the quantitiy, change the quantity and click the &quot;Update&quot; button next to
the
item. To remove an item from your cart, change the quantity to 0 and use the
&quot;Update&quot; button.</font></p>

<table border="4" width="100%" bgcolor="#AEAEFF" bordercolorlight="#7A59DB"
bordercolordark="#E8E8FF" cellspacing="0" cellpadding="3">
  <tr>
    <td width="12%" bordercolorlight="#7A59DB" bordercolordark="#E8E8FF"
    bgcolor="#C1C1FF" nowrap><font face="Arial" size="2"><strong>Product
    ID</strong></font></td>
    <td width="33%" bordercolorlight="#7A59DB" bordercolordark="#E8E8FF"
    bgcolor="#C1C1FF" nowrap><font face="Arial" size="2"><strong>Product
    Name</strong></font></td>
    <td width="25%" bordercolorlight="#7A59DB" bordercolordark="#E8E8FF"
    bgcolor="#C1C1FF" nowrap><font face="Arial" size="2"><strong>Quantity Per
    Unit</strong></font></td>
    <td width="10%" bordercolorlight="#7A59DB" bordercolordark="#E8E8FF"
    bgcolor="#C1C1FF" nowrap><font face="Arial" size="2"><strong>Unit
    Price</strong></font></td>
    <td width="20%" bordercolorlight="#7A59DB" bordercolordark="#E8E8FF"
    bgcolor="#C1C1FF" nowrap><font face="Arial"
    size="2"><strong>Qty/Change</strong></font></td>
  </tr>
```

Next, we loop through the contents of the session object shopping cart arrays. Note that we initialize total to 0, and add to it with each product displayed in the table. This is how we compute the total, by adding to total each time we pass through the loop. It also displays the elements from the arrays in the process.

```
<%total = 0
For x = 0 to UBound(Session("aryproductid"))
  total = total + (Session("aryunitprice")(x) * Session("aryqty")(x))%>
  <tr>
    <td width="12%" valign="top" bordercolorlight="#7A59DB"
    bordercolordark="#E8E8FF"><font face="Arial"
    size="2"><%=Session("aryproductid")(x)%>  </font></td>
    <td width="33%" valign="top" bordercolorlight="#7A59DB"
    bordercolordark="#E8E8FF"><font face="Arial"
    size="2"><%=Session("aryproductname")(x)%>  </font></td>
    <td width="25%" valign="top" bordercolorlight="#7A59DB"
    bordercolordark="#E8E8FF"><font face="Arial"
    size="2"><%=Session("aryqperu")(x)%>  </font></td>
    <td width="10%" valign="top" bordercolorlight="#7A59DB"
    bordercolordark="#E8E8FF"><font face="Arial"
    size="2"><%=FormatCurrency(Session("aryunitprice")(x))%>
     </font></td>
    <td width="20%" valign="top" bordercolorlight="#7A59DB"
    bordercolordark="#E8E8FF">
```

Following this is a JavaScript form validation function. This is used to check the form input when changing shopping cart data. The `qty` field in the form must be numeric:

```javascript
<script Language="JavaScript"><!--
function Validator(theForm)
{
  if (theForm.qty.value == "")
  {
    alert("Please enter a value for the \"Quantity\" field.");
    theForm.qty.focus();
    return (false);
  }

  var checkOK = "0123456789-";
  var checkStr = theForm.qty.value;
  var allValid = true;
  var decPoints = 0;
  var allNum = "";
  for (i = 0;  i < checkStr.length;  i++)
  {
    ch = checkStr.charAt(i);
    for (j = 0;  j < checkOK.length;  j++)
      if (ch == checkOK.charAt(j))
        break;
    if (j == checkOK.length)
    {
      allValid = false;
      break;
    }
    allNum += ch;
  }
  if (!allValid)
  {
    alert("Please enter only digit characters in the \"Quantity\" field.");
    theForm.qty.focus();
    return (false);
  }
  return (true);
}
//--></script>
```

Next is a 'hidden' form (one that the user never sees) that submits updated quantities for the products in the shopping cart back to this same page. This occurs when the user updates the fields. It repeats once per record.

```asp
<form method="POST" action="viewcart.asp" onsubmit="return Validator(this)">
      <input type="hidden" name="productid"
      value="<%=Session("aryproductid")(x)%>"><p>
      <input type="text" name="qty" size="2"
      value="<%=Session("aryqty")(x)%>">
      <input type="submit" value="Update" name="B1"></p>
    </form>
    </td>
  </tr>
<%next%>
```

And finally, we can display the total cost of items in the cart:

```
<tr>
  <td width="70%" valign="top" colspan="3" align="right"
  bordercolorlight="#E8E8FF"
  bordercolordark="#7A59DB" bgcolor="#9B9BFF">
  <font face="Arial" size="2" color="#FFFFFF"><strong>Total
  Price:</strong></font></td>
  <td width="30%" valign="top" colspan="2" bordercolorlight="#E8E8FF"
  bordercolordark="#7A59DB" bgcolor="#9B9BFF"><font face="Arial"
  size="2" color="#FFFFFF"> <strong>
  <%=FormatCurrency(total)%></strong></font></td>
  </tr>
</table>

<p><a href="checkout.asp"><img src="images/checkout.jpg" alt="Check Out"
border="0"
align="right"></a></p>
<%end if%>
<blockquote>
  <p><font face="Arial" size="2"><a href="default.asp"><strong>Continue
Shopping</strong></a></font></p>
</blockquote>
<!--#INCLUDE FILE="template2.asp" -->
```

checkout.asp

The checkout.asp page gets customer and shippping information from the user and submits it to the next page (checkout2.asp). It also recaps the order by showing the user the same table as seen on the addtocart.asp page. The reason for this is that we cannot know whether the user has been to the viewcart.asp page, and it is convenient for the user to have the order information laid out here for a final review.

This is another page that doesn't interact with the database, but uses the session arrays to display the order, and to populate the customer information form at the bottom with the order data (in hidden fields). When the customer information form is submitted (to checkout2.asp), the order information is submitted with it.

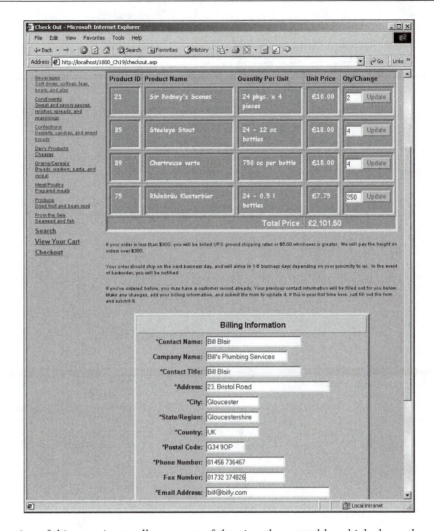

The first section of this page is actually a repeat of the view the cart table, which shows the user what they are ordering:

Include pages and variable declarations start the page, as usual:

```
<!--#INCLUDE FILE="template1.asp" -->
<%Dim total, x
```

Then Session("ct") is checked to see that it hasn't been erased (for instance, if it has been left for too long):

```
if Session("ct") = -1 then
   Response.Redirect "error.asp"
end if
```

Then we display any pertinent messages (again, contained in the `mess` variable):

```
%><script language="JavaScript"><!--
<%if Session("mess") <> "" then%>
alert("<%=Session("mess")%>");
<%Session("mess") = ""
end if%>
// --></script>
```

Then the contents of the cart are displayed. As we've seen, this uses almost exactly the same code as the order display table in `addtocart.asp` for this section:

```
<p><font face="Arial" size="2">You have the following item(s) in your cart.
To process your order, please fill out the form below:</font></p>

<table border="4" width="100%" bgcolor="#AEAEFF" bordercolorlight="#7A59DB"
bordercolordark="#E8E8FF" cellspacing="0" cellpadding="3">
  <tr>
    <td width="12%" bordercolorlight="#7A59DB" bordercolordark="#E8E8FF"
    bgcolor="#AEAEFF" nowrap><font face="Arial" size="2"><strong>Product
    ID</strong></font></td>
    <td width="33%" bordercolorlight="#7A59DB" bordercolordark="#E8E8FF"
    bgcolor="#AEAEFF"
    nowrap><font face="Arial" size="2"><strong>Product
    Name</strong></font></td>
    <td width="25%" bordercolorlight="#7A59DB" bordercolordark="#E8E8FF"
    bgcolor="#AEAEFF"
    nowrap><font face="Arial" size="2"><strong>Quantity Per
    Unit</strong></font></td>
    <td width="10%" bordercolorlight="#7A59DB" bordercolordark="#E8E8FF"
    bgcolor="#AEAEFF"
    nowrap><font face="Arial" size="2"><strong>Unit Price</strong></font></td>
    <td width="20%" bordercolorlight="#7A59DB" bordercolordark="#E8E8FF"
    bgcolor="#AEAEFF" nowrap><font face="Arial"
    size="2"><strong>Qty/Change</strong></font></td>
  </tr>
```

Again, the same loop as in `addtocart.asp`:

```
<%total = 0
For x = 0 to UBound(Session("aryproductid"))
total = total + (Session("aryunitprice")(x) * Session("aryqty")(x))%>
  <tr>
    <td width="12%" valign="top" bordercolorlight="#7A59DB"
    bordercolordark="#E8E8FF" height="100%"><table border="3" width="100%"
    cellspacing="0" bordercolorlight="#7A59DB"
    bordercolordark="#E8E8FF" bgcolor="#C1C1FF" cellpadding="6" height="100%">
      <tr>
        <td width="100%" valign="top" height="100%" bgcolor="#B3B3FF"><font
        face="Arial" size="2"><%=Session("aryproductid")(x)%></font></td>
      </tr>
    </table>
    </td>
    <td width="33%" valign="top" bordercolorlight="#7A59DB"
    bordercolordark="#E8E8FF"
    height="100%"><table border="3" width="100%" cellspacing="0"
```

```
    bordercolorlight="#7A59DB"  bordercolordark="#E8E8FF" bgcolor="#B3B3FF"
    cellpadding="6" height="100%">
      <tr>
        <td width="100%" valign="top" height="100%"><font face="Arial"
        size="2"><%=Session("aryproductname")(x)%></font></td>
      </tr>
    </table>
    </td>
    <td width="25%" valign="top" bordercolorlight="#7A59DB"
    bordercolordark="#E8E8FF" height="100%"><table border="3" width="100%"
    cellspacing="0" bordercolorlight="#7A59DB"
    bordercolordark="#E8E8FF" bgcolor="#B3B3FF" cellpadding="6" height="100%">
      <tr>
        <td width="100%" valign="top" height="100%"><font face="Arial"
        size="2"><%=Session("aryqperu")(x)%></font></td>
      </tr>
    </table>
    </td>
    <td width="10%" valign="top" bordercolorlight="#7A59DB"
    bordercolordark="#E8E8FF" height="100%"><table border="3" width="100%"
    cellspacing="0" bordercolorlight="#7A59DB"
    bordercolordark="#E8E8FF" bgcolor="#B3B3FF" cellpadding="6" height="100%">
      <tr>
        <td width="100%" valign="top" height="100%"><font face="Arial"
        size="2"><%=FormatCurrency(Session("aryunitprice")(x))%></font></td>
      </tr>
    </table>
    </td>
    <td width="20%" valign="top" bordercolorlight="#7A59DB"
    bordercolordark="#E8E8FF" height="100%"><table border="3" width="100%"
    cellspacing="0" bordercolorlight="#7A59DB"
    bordercolordark="#E8E8FF" bgcolor="#B3B3FF" cellpadding="0">
      <tr>
        <td width="100%" valign="top" height="100%">
<script Language="JavaScript"><!--
function Validator(theForm)
{

  if (theForm.qty.value == "")
  {
    alert("Please enter a value for the \"Quantity\" field.");
    theForm.qty.focus();
    return (false);
  }

  var checkOK = "0123456789-";
  var checkStr = theForm.qty.value;
  var allValid = true;
  var decPoints = 0;
  var allNum = "";
  for (i = 0;  i < checkStr.length;  i++)
  {
    ch = checkStr.charAt(i);
    for (j = 0;  j < checkOK.length;  j++)
      if (ch == checkOK.charAt(j))
        break;
    if (j == checkOK.length)
    {
      allValid = false;
      break;
    }
```

```
      allNum += ch;
   }
   if (!allValid)
   {
     alert("Please enter only digit characters in the \"Quantity\" field.");
     theForm.qty.focus();
     return (false);
   }
   return (true);
}
//--></script>
```

Then we build the form that allows the user to change the contents of their cart:

```
            <form method="POST" action="viewcart.asp" onsubmit="return
            Validator(this)" name="FrontPage_Form1">
            <input type="hidden" name="productid"
            value="<%=Session("aryproductid")(x)%>"><p><font
            face="Arial" size="2">
            <input type="text" name="qty" size="2"
            value="<%=Session("aryqty")(x)%>">
            <input type="submit" value="Update" name="B1"
            style="background-color: rgb(193,193,255);
            font-family: Forte, sans-serif; font-size: 10pt; color:
            rgb(77,40,183); border-left: thin solid rgb(232,232,255);
            border-right: thin solid rgb(122,89,219);
            border-top: thin solid rgb(232,232,255);
            border-bottom: thin solid rgb(122,89,219)"></font></p>
            </form>
            </td>
        </tr>
      </table>
      </td>
   </tr>
<%next%>
   <tr>
     <td width="70%" valign="top" colspan="3" align="right"
     bordercolorlight="#E8E8FF" bordercolordark="#7A59DB"
     bgcolor="#9B9BFF"><font face="Arial" size="3"
     color="#FFFFFF"><strong>Total Price:</strong></font></td>
     <td width="30%" valign="top" colspan="2" bordercolorlight="#E8E8FF"
     bordercolordark="#7A59DB" bgcolor="#9B9BFF"><font face="Arial" size="3"
color="#FFFFFF"> <strong><%=FormatCurrency(total)%></strong></font></td>
   </tr></table>
```

We then present some information about shipping:

```
<p><font face="Arial" size="1">If your order is less than $300, you will be
billed UPS ground shipping rates or $5.00 whichever is greater.  We will
pay the freight on orders over $300.</font></p>

<p><font face="Arial" size="1">Your order should ship on the next business
day, and will arrive in 1-6 business days depending on your proximity to
us.  In the event of backorder, you will be notified.</font></p>
```

```
<p><font face="Arial" size="1">If you've ordered before, you may have a
customer record already. Your previous contact information will be filled out
for you below. Make any changes, add your billing information, and submit the
form to update it. If this is your first time here, just fill out the form and
submit it.</font></p>
```

Then we build the form, into which the user enters billing information. Note the hidden form fields with the order data. We begin with the form validation script. Note that we have a lot more validation to perform here:

```
<script Language="JavaScript"><!--
function Validator2(theForm)
{

// Make sure the required fields are filled out
// And the data is not too long (or short)
  if (theForm.contactname.value == "")
  {
    alert("Please enter a value for the \"Contact Name\" field.");
    theForm.contactname.focus();
    return (false);
  }

  if (theForm.contactname.value.length > 30)
  {
    alert("Please enter at most 30 characters in the \"Contact Name\" field.");
    theForm.contactname.focus();
    return (false);
  }

  if (theForm.address.value == "")
  {
    alert("Please enter a value for the \"Address\" field.");
    theForm.address.focus();
    return (false);
  }

  if (theForm.address.value.length > 60)
  {
    alert("Please enter at most 60 characters in the \"Address\" field.");
    theForm.address.focus();
    return (false);
  }

  if (theForm.city.value == "")
  {
    alert("Please enter a value for the \"City\" field.");
    theForm.city.focus();
    return (false);
  }

  if (theForm.city.value.length > 15)
  {
    alert("Please enter at most 15 characters in the \"City\" field.");
    theForm.city.focus();
    return (false);
  }
```

547

```
if (theForm.region.value == "")
{
  alert("Please enter a value for the \"region\" field.");
  theForm.region.focus();
  return (false);
}

if (theForm.region.value.length > 15)
{
  alert("Please enter at most 15 characters in the \"region\" field.");
  theForm.region.focus();
  return (false);
}

if (theForm.country.value == "")
{
  alert("Please enter a value for the \"Country\" field.");
  theForm.country.focus();
  return (false);
}

if (theForm.country.value.length > 15)
{
  alert("Please enter at most 15 characters in the \"Country\" field.");
  theForm.country.focus();
  return (false);
}

if (theForm.postalcode.value == "")
{
  alert("Please enter a value for the \"Postal Code\" field.");
  theForm.postalcode.focus();
  return (false);
}

if (theForm.postalcode.value.length > 10)
{
  alert("Please enter at most 10 characters in the \"Postal Code\" field.");
  theForm.postalcode.focus();
  return (false);
}

if (theForm.phone.value == "")
{
  alert("Please enter a value for the \"Phone Number\" field.");
  theForm.phone.focus();
  return (false);
}

if (theForm.phone.value.length > 24)
{
  alert("Please enter at most 24 characters in the \" _
    Phone Number\" field.");
  theForm.phone.focus();
  return (false);
}

if (theForm.email.value == "")
{
  alert("Please enter a value for the \"Email Address\" field.");
  theForm.email.focus();
```

```
      return (false);
    }

  if (theForm.email.value.length > 100)
  {
    alert("Please enter at most 100 characters in the \"Email Address\" field.");
    theForm.email.focus();
    return (false);
  }
  return (true);
}
//--></script>
```

Again, note the hidden form fields with the Order data. Also, note that we are giving "default" values to the text fields with the Customer information. This is for the convenience of returning Customers.

When this form is successfully submitted, the customer information will be stored in a cookie. The next time the customer returns, the information will be pre-filled-out in the form. They can change it, but it is already there if they just want to submit the form without changing anything. The value of a cookie is "" if it doesn't exist, so these fields will be blank the first time the customer fills out the form:

```
<form method="POST" action="checkout2.asp" onsubmit="return Validator2(this)">
  <input type="hidden" name="customerid"
  value="<%=Request.Cookies("customerid")%>">
<div align="center"><center>
<table border="4" cellspacing="3" bgcolor="#C1C1FF"
  bordercolorlight="#E8E8FF" bordercolordark="#7A59DB" width="500"
  height="655">
    <tr>
      <td align="center" colspan="2" valign="middle"
      bordercolorlight="#724FD9"  bordercolordark="#E8E8FF" bgcolor="#CECEFF"
      height="30"><img src="images/spacer.gif"  width="2" height="30"
      alt="spacer.gif (834 bytes)" align="absmiddle"><strong><font
      face="Arial" size="3">Billing Information</font></strong></td>
    </tr>
    <tr>
      <td align="right" bordercolorlight="#C1C1FF" bordercolordark="#C1C1FF"
      height="23"><font
      face="Arial" size="2"><strong>*Contact Name: </strong></font></td>
      <td bordercolorlight="#C1C1FF" bordercolordark="#C1C1FF"
      height="23"><strong><font face="Arial" size="2">
      <input type="text" name="contactname" size="30" maxlength="30"
      value="<%=Request.Cookies("contactname")%>"></font></strong></td>
    </tr>
    <tr>
      <td align="right" bordercolorlight="#C1C1FF" bordercolordark="#C1C1FF"
      height="23"><font face="Arial" size="2"><strong>Company Name:
      </strong></font></td>
      <td bordercolorlight="#C1C1FF" bordercolordark="#C1C1FF"
      height="23"><strong><font face="Arial" size="2"><input type="text"
      name="companyname" size="25" maxlength="40"
      value="<%=Request.Cookies("companyname")%>"></font></strong></td>
    </tr>
    <tr>
      <td align="right" bordercolorlight="#C1C1FF" bordercolordark="#C1C1FF"
      height="23"><font face="Arial" size="2"><strong>*Contact Title:
      </strong></font></td>
      <td bordercolorlight="#C1C1FF" bordercolordark="#C1C1FF"
```

```
      height="23"><strong><font face="Arial" size="2"><input type="text"
   name="contacttitle" size="30" maxlength="30"
   value="<%=Request.Cookies("contacttitle")%>"></font></strong></td>
</tr>
<tr>
   <td align="right" bordercolorlight="#C1C1FF" bordercolordark="#C1C1FF"
   height="23"><font face="Arial" size="2"><strong>*Address:
   </strong></font></td>
   <td bordercolorlight="#C1C1FF" bordercolordark="#C1C1FF"
   height="23"><strong><font face="Arial" size="2">
   <input type="text" name="address" size="40"
   value="<%=Request.Cookies("address")%>"
   maxlength="60"></font></strong></td>
</tr>
<tr>
   <td align="right" bordercolorlight="#C1C1FF" bordercolordark="#C1C1FF"
   height="23"><font face="Arial" size="2"><strong>*City:
   </strong></font></td>
   <td bordercolorlight="#C1C1FF" bordercolordark="#C1C1FF"
   height="23"><strong><font face="Arial" size="2">
 <input type="text" name="city" size="15"
   value="<%=Request.Cookies("city")%>"
   maxlength="15"></font></strong></td>
</tr>
<tr>
   <td align="right" bordercolorlight="#C1C1FF" bordercolordark="#C1C1FF"
   height="23"><font face="Arial" size="2"><strong>*State/Region:
   </strong></font></td>
   <td bordercolorlight="#C1C1FF" bordercolordark="#C1C1FF"
   height="23"><strong><font face="Arial" size="2">
   <input type="text" name="region" size="15"
   value="<%=Request.Cookies("region")%>"
   maxlength="15"></font></strong></td>
</tr>
<tr>
   <td align="right" bordercolorlight="#C1C1FF" bordercolordark="#C1C1FF"
   height="23"><font face="Arial" size="2"><strong>*Country:
   </strong></font></td>
   <td bordercolorlight="#C1C1FF" bordercolordark="#C1C1FF"
   height="23"><strong><font face="Arial" size="2">
   <input type="text" name="country" size="15"
   value="<%=Request.cookies("country")%>"
   maxlength="15"></font></strong></td>
</tr>
<tr>
   <td align="right" bordercolorlight="#C1C1FF" bordercolordark="#C1C1FF"
   height="23"><font
   face="Arial" size="2"><strong>*Postal Code: </strong></font></td>
   <td bordercolorlight="#C1C1FF" bordercolordark="#C1C1FF"
   height="23"><strong><font
   face="Arial" size="2"><input type="text" name="postalcode"
   size="10" value="<%=Request.Cookies("postalcode")%>"
   maxlength="10"></font></strong></td>
</tr>
<tr>
   <td align="right" bordercolorlight="#C1C1FF"
   bordercolordark="#C1C1FF" height="23"><font
   face="Arial" size="2"><strong>*Phone Number: </strong></font></td>
   <td bordercolorlight="#C1C1FF" bordercolordark="#C1C1FF"
   height="23"><strong><font
```

```
      face="Arial" size="2"><input type="text" name="phone" size="24"
      value="<%=Request.Cookies("phone")%>"
      maxlength="24"></font></strong></td>
    </tr>
    <tr>
      <td align="right" bordercolorlight="#C1C1FF"
      bordercolordark="#C1C1FF" height="23"><font
      face="Arial" size="2"><strong>Fax Number: </strong></font></td>
      <td bordercolorlight="#C1C1FF" bordercolordark="#C1C1FF"
      height="23"><strong><font face="Arial" size="2"><input type="text"
      name="fax" size="24" maxlength="24"
      value="<%=Request.Cookies("fax")%>"></font></strong></td>
    </tr>
    <tr>
      <td align="right" bordercolorlight="#C1C1FF" bordercolordark="#C1C1FF"
      height="23"><font face="Arial" size="2"><strong>*Email Address:
      </strong></font></td>
      <td bordercolorlight="#C1C1FF" bordercolordark="#C1C1FF"
      height="23"><strong><font face="Arial" size="2"><input type="text"
      name="email" size="40" value="<%=Request.Cookies("email")%>"
 maxlength="100"></font></strong></td>
    </tr>
    <tr>
      <td align="center" colspan="2" bordercolorlight="#6D49D8"
      bordercolordark="#E8E8FF" bgcolor="#CCCCFF" height="30"><img
      src="images/spacer.gif" width="2" height="30"
      alt="spacer.gif (834 bytes)" align="absmiddle"><font face="Arial"
      size="3"><strong>Shipping Information (<font
      color="#0000A0"><em>only</em></font> if different from
      Billing)</strong></font></td>
    </tr>
    <tr>
      <td align="right" bordercolorlight="#C1C1FF" bordercolordark="#C1C1FF"
      height="23"><font face="Arial" size="2"><strong>Name:
      </strong></font></td>
      <td bordercolorlight="#C1C1FF" bordercolordark="#C1C1FF"
      height="23"><strong><font face="Arial" size="2"><input type="text"
      name="shipname" size="30" value="<%=Request.Cookies("shipname")%>"
      maxlength="30"></font></strong></td>
    </tr>
    <tr>
      <td align="right" bordercolorlight="#C1C1FF" bordercolordark="#C1C1FF"
      height="23"><font face="Arial" size="2"><strong>Address:
      </strong></font></td>
      <td bordercolorlight="#C1C1FF" bordercolordark="#C1C1FF"
      height="23"><strong><font face="Arial" size="2"><input type="text"
      name="shipaddress" size="40" maxlength="60"
      value="<%=Request.Cookies("shipaddress")%>"></font></strong></td>
    </tr>
    <tr>
      <td align="right" bordercolorlight="#C1C1FF" bordercolordark="#C1C1FF"
      height="23"><font face="Arial" size="2"><strong>City:
      </strong></font></td>
      <td bordercolorlight="#C1C1FF" bordercolordark="#C1C1FF"
      height="23"><strong><font
      face="Arial" size="2"><input type="text" name="shipcity" size="15"
      maxlength="15"
      value="<%=Request.Cookies("shipcity")%>"></font></strong></td>
    </tr>
    <tr>
```

```
        <td align="right" bordercolorlight="#C1C1FF" bordercolordark="#C1C1FF"
        height="23"><font
        face="Arial" size="2"><strong>State/Region: </strong></font></td>
        <td bordercolorlight="#C1C1FF" bordercolordark="#C1C1FF"
        height="23"><strong><font
        face="Arial" size="2"><input type="text" name="shipregion" size="15"
        maxlength="15"
        value="<%=Request.Cookies("shipregion")%>"></font></strong></td>
    </tr>
    <tr>
        <td align="right" bordercolorlight="#C1C1FF" bordercolordark="#C1C1FF"
        height="23"><font
        face="Arial" size="2"><strong>Country: </strong></font></td>
        <td bordercolorlight="#C1C1FF" bordercolordark="#C1C1FF"
        height="23"><strong><font
        face="Arial" size="2"><input type="text" name="shipcountry" size="15"
        maxlength="15"
        value="<%=Request.Cookies("shipcountry")%>"></font></strong></td>
    </tr>
    <tr>
        <td align="right" bordercolorlight="#C1C1FF" bordercolordark="#C1C1FF"
        height="23"><font face="Arial" size="2"><strong>Postal Code:
        </strong></font></td>
        <td bordercolorlight="#C1C1FF" bordercolordark="#C1C1FF"
        height="23"><strong><font face="Arial" size="2"><input type="text"
        name="shippostalcode" size="10" maxlength="10"
        value="<%=Request.Cookies("shippostalcode")%>"></font></strong></td>
    </tr>
    <tr>
        <td align="right" bordercolorlight="#C1C1FF" bordercolordark="#C1C1FF"
        height="44"></td>
        <td bordercolorlight="#C1C1FF" bordercolordark="#C1C1FF"
        height="44"><strong><font face="Arial" size="2"><input type="submit"
        value="Submit" name="B1"></font></strong><br>
        </td>
    </tr>
  </table>
  </center></div>
</form>
```

And finally, the second Template include page:

```
<!--#INCLUDE FILE="template2.asp" -->
```

when the Customer finishes filling out the form, it submits the Customer and Order information to `checkout2.asp`.

checkout2.asp

This page is designed to perform the following:

1. Enter a new `Customers` table record, or update an existing one, with the information supplied by the customer when filling out the customer information form in `checkout.asp`. Because the `CustomerID` is a primary key, *and* a string, it must also be checked against the database for duplicates. If there are duplicates, the application needs to make up a new `CustomerID` that is unique, and return it to the customer.

2. Enter a new `Orders` table record with the new order information. This includes the `CustomerID`, so this operation is dependent on Step 1.

3. Enter new `Order Details` records for each product in the order. The way the database is set up, we can have multiple products in a single order. Each `Order Details` record contains the pertinent product information for that order. The `Order Details` records are related to the `Orders` records by the `OrderID` of the order it belongs to. So this operation is dependent upon Step 2.

To do all of this, this page uses a combination of ASP and ADO code, and stored procedures, written in SQL.

As usual, we start with our include pages and variable declarations:

```
<!--#INCLUDE FILE="adovbs.inc" -->
<!--#INCLUDE FILE="template1.asp" -->
<%
Dim total, x, customerid, companyname, contactname
Dim newcustomer, existingorderid
Dim contacttitle, address, city, region, country
Dim postalcode, phone, fax, email
Dim shipname, shipaddress, shipcity, shipregion
Dim shipcountry, shippostalcode, b, d, sp
```

We then initialize the variables that we will use. `total`, again, will be used to keep track of the total price for the order:

```
total = 0
b = ""
sp = "sp_onlineorder"
existingorderid = 0
```

This sub function, `getform`, gets the form input data, assigns the values to their respective local variables, and then sets cookies to hold the customer information for future orders.

```
' ** Sub to assign form values to local variables
Sub getform()
   customerid = Request.Form("customerid")
   contactname = Request.Form("contactname")
   contacttitle = Request.Form("contacttitle")
   companyname = Request.Form("companyname")
   address = Request.Form("address")
   city = Request.Form("city")
   region = Request.Form("region")
   country = Request.Form("country")
   postalcode = Request.form("postalcode")
   phone = Request.Form("phone")
   fax = Request.Form("fax")
   email = Request.Form("email")
```

```
    shipname = Trim(Request.Form("shipname"))
    if shipname = "" then shipname = contactname
    shipaddress = Trim(Request.Form("shipaddress"))
    if shipaddress = "" then shipaddress = address
    shipcity = Trim(Request.Form("shipcity"))
    if shipcity = "" then shipcity = city
    shipregion = Trim(Request.Form("shipregion"))
    if shipregion = "" then shipregion = region
    shipcountry = Trim(Request.Form("shipcountry"))
    if shipcountry = "" then shipcountry = country
    shippostalcode = Trim(Request.Form("shippostalcode"))
    if shippostalcode = "" then shippostalcode = postalcode
    d = DateAdd("yyyy", 2, Date)

' ** For the convenience of the customer, and to keep the data more
' ** accurate, we store the information entered in a Cookie.
' ** The expiration date for the Coookie is set to 2 years. Plenty
' ** of time, since each visit refreshes the Cookie, and resets
' ** the expiration date to 2 years.
    Response.Cookies("customerid") = customerid
    Response.Cookies("contactname") = contactname
    Response.Cookies("contacttitle") = contactname
    Response.Cookies("companyname") = companyname
    Response.Cookies("address") = address
    Response.Cookies("city") = city
    Response.Cookies("region") = region
    Response.Cookies("country") = country
    Response.Cookies("postalcode") = postalcode
    Response.Cookies("phone") = phone
    Response.Cookies("fax") = fax
    Response.Cookies("email") = email
    Response.Cookies("shipname") = shipname
    Response.Cookies("shipaddress") = shipaddress
    Response.Cookies("shipcity") = shipcity
    Response.Cookies("shipregion") = shipregion
    Response.Cookies("shipcountry") = shipcountry
    Response.Cookies("shippostalcode") = shippostalcode
    Response.Cookies("customerid").Expires = d
    Response.Cookies("contactname").Expires = d
    Response.Cookies("contacttitle").Expires = d
    Response.Cookies("companyname").Expires = d
    Response.Cookies("address").Expires = d
    Response.Cookies("city").Expires = d
    Response.Cookies("region").Expires = d
    Response.Cookies("country").Expires = d
    Response.Cookies("postalcode").Expires = d
    Response.Cookies("phone").Expires = d
    Response.Cookies("fax").Expires = d
    Response.Cookies("email").Expires = d
    Response.Cookies("shipname").Expires = d
    Response.Cookies("shipaddress").Expires = d
    Response.Cookies("shipcity").Expires = d
    Response.Cookies("shipregion").Expires = d
    Response.Cookies("shipcountry").Expires = d
    Response.Cookies("shippostalcode").Expires = d
End Sub
```

Next, we check for a lost Session (empty cart). Assuming that all is well with the Session, we continue, by using getform to get the form data, and then openconn to open the database connection (remember that this was contained in the global.asa file):

```
' ** If the Session has been lost, so has the Cart.
if Session("ct") = -1 then
  Response.Redirect "error.asp"
else
  b = ""
  getform()
  openconn()

' ** If an existing customer (customerid Not blank), update their record

  if customerid <> "" then
    newcustomer = 0
    candidate = customerid

  else
    newcustomer = 1
    candidate = LEFT(Right(contactname, Len(contactname) - InStrRev(contactname, "
")), 5)

  end if
```

Remember that we need to enter a new `CustomerID` in the `Customers` table (if this isn't a return visit). The `CustomerID` field in the `Customers` table is a 5-character nvarchar (string) field. It is a primary key field, so it must be a unique string. The `CustomerID` in the Northwind database is actually derived from the `CompanyName` of the `Customers` record. However, we'll base ours on the customers' last names (it doesn't matter how we derive the `customerID`, so long as it's unique):

The following code sends values from the form that was posted to this page from the `checkout.asp` page to the `sp_onlineorder` stored procedure:

```
    openconn()
    Set cmd = Server.CreateObject("ADODB.Command")
    cmd.CommandType = adCmdStoredProc
    cmd.CommandText = sp
    cmd.ActiveConnection = cn
    cmd.Parameters.Append(cmd.CreateParameter _
      ("@RETURN_VALUE", 3, 4, 0, 0))

if customerid <>"" then
    cmd.Parameters.Append(cmd.CreateParameter("@newcustomer", 11, 1, 0, 0))
else
    cmd.Parameters.Append(cmd.CreateParameter("@newcustomer", 11, 1, 0, 1))
end if

' ** initialize @existingorderid to 0.
' ** It will revert to the first orderid you get when you place an order

    cmd.Parameters.Append(cmd.CreateParameter("@existingorderid", 3, 1, 0, 0))
    cmd.Parameters.Append(cmd.CreateParameter_
      ("@candidate", 202, 1, 30, candidate))
    cmd.Parameters.Append(cmd.CreateParameter _
      ("@companyname", 202, 1, 40, companyname))
    cmd.Parameters.Append(cmd.CreateParameter _
      ("@contactname", 202, 1, 30, contactname))
    cmd.Parameters.Append(cmd.CreateParameter _
      ("@contacttitle", 202, 1, 30, contacttitle))
    cmd.Parameters.Append(cmd.CreateParameter _
      ("@address", 202, 1, 60, address))
```

```
cmd.Parameters.Append(cmd.CreateParameter _
   ("@city", 202, 1, 15, city))
cmd.Parameters.Append(cmd.CreateParameter _
   ("@region", 202, 1, 15, region))
cmd.Parameters.Append(cmd.CreateParameter _
   ("@postalcode", 202, 1, 10, postalcode))
cmd.Parameters.Append(cmd.CreateParameter _
   ("@country", 202, 1, 15, country))
cmd.Parameters.Append(cmd.CreateParameter _
   ("@phone", 202, 1, 24, phone))
cmd.Parameters.Append(cmd.CreateParameter _
   ("@fax", 202, 1, 24, fax))
cmd.Parameters.Append(cmd.CreateParameter _
   ("@shipname", 202, 1, 30, shipname))
cmd.Parameters.Append(cmd.CreateParameter _
   ("@shipaddress", 202, 1, 60, shipaddress))
cmd.Parameters.Append(cmd.CreateParameter _
   ("@shipcity", 202, 1, 15, shipcity))
cmd.Parameters.Append(cmd.CreateParameter _
   ("@shipregion", 202, 1, 15, shipregion))
cmd.Parameters.Append(cmd.CreateParameter _
   ("@shippostalcode", 202, 1, 10, shippostalcode))
cmd.Parameters.Append(cmd.CreateParameter _
   ("@shipcountry", 202, 1, 15, shipcountry))
cmd.Parameters.Append(cmd.CreateParameter _
   ("@productid", 3, 1, 0, 0))
cmd.Parameters.Append(cmd.CreateParameter _
   ("@unitprice", 6, 1, 0, 0))
cmd.Parameters.Append(cmd.CreateParameter _
   ("@quantity", 2, 1, 0, 0))
```

Unlike the sp_searchproducts stored procedure, the sp_onlineorder includes two output parameters: @customerid and @orderid. The purpose of these two parameters is to return to the ASP application the customer ID and order ID for the new customer. This has to be done because, even though we're simply using the customer's last name as the basis of the new customer ID, if their last name has already been used in the database, a new one will have to be generated. This is looked after by the sp_onlineorder stored procedure.

```
' ** Output parameters
cmd.Parameters.Append(cmd.CreateParameter _
("@customerid", 202, 3, 5, customerid))
cmd.Parameters.Append(cmd.CreateParameter("@orderid", 3, 3, 0, orderid))
```

Next, we enter information about the order into the Order Details table, and calculate the total amount of the order.

We start by looping through the session arrays to get the values we want to send to our stored procedure:

```
total = 0
For x = 0 to UBound(Session("aryproductid"))

  total = total + (Session("aryunitprice")(x) * Session("aryqty")(x))
  cmd.Parameters("@productid").value = Session("aryproductid")(x)
  cmd.Parameters("@unitprice").value = Session("aryunitprice")(x)
  cmd.Parameters("@quantity").value = Session("aryqty")(x)
  cmd.Execute
```

```
      cmd.Parameters("@existingorderid").value = cmd.Parameters("@orderid").value
      cmd.Parameters("@newcustomer").value = 0
      cmd.Parameters("@candidate").value = cmd.Parameters("@customerid").value
      cmd.Parameters("@customerid").value = cmd.Parameters("@customerid").value
    Next

  Response.Cookies("customerid") = cmd.Parameters("@customerID").value

  end if
  %>
```

Then we generate the part of the screen that the user will see after the order is processed:

```
<p align="center"> </p>

<p align="center"> </p>
<div align="center"><center>

<table border="3" cellpadding="2" cellspacing="0" bgcolor="#AEAEFF"
bordercolorlight="#724FD9" bordercolordark="#E8E8FF" width="460">
  <tr>
    <td width="100%"> <p align="center">
    <font face="Arial" size="4"><strong>Your Order has been
    processed.</strong></font></p>
    <p align="center"><font face="Arial" size="4">
    <strong>Thank you for your Order!</strong></font></p>
    <p align="center"> </td>
  </tr>
</table>
</center></div>

<p> </p>

<p><!--#INCLUDE FILE="template2.asp" --> </p>
```

Now that we've looked at the construction of the ASP pages, albeit in very general terms, let's look in a little more detail at the stored procedures we've mentioned.

sp_newcustomer

A Primary Key field, as you know by now, is a uniquely-valued indexed field in a table. It is used as the primary identifier column for the table in which it resides. The most commonly-used primary key column is the Identity column, which is a long integer, and is *autoincremented* (automatically incremented) to create a new unique primary key column value whenever a new record is entered into the table. If we were to use that as a CustomerID field, we wouldn't even have to assign a value to it; we'd just get the value after the new record was entered.

But because the CustomerID field it is a string data type field, and it must be unique, we are going to have to come up with a way of automatically assigning a unique CustomerID string for each new record. In addition, by observing the records in the Customers table, we can see that the CustomerID field values are all 5 characters long, all capital letters, and derived from the last name of the Customer. These rules concerning our data are what are termed **business rules** in the programming business. Business rules are the rules that your business, and hence, your database application, employ in their storage organization. Our job is to translate them into SQL. Much of the stored procudre is concerned with doing just this.

The strategy we have adopted here is as follows:

❑   We convert each letter in the string to its numerical counterpart.

❑   We add these together to get the total value of the string.

❑   We add one to this value to get the next highest numerical value.

❑   We convert the number back to the corresponding characters.

❑   We place the characters their appropriate places in the string.

As we can see, the SQL code that achieves this is fairly complex. However, it shows just how complex an operation can be implemented in SQL.

Once the new CustomerID value is obtained, the rest of the input parameters for the new customer record, along with the new CustomerID are inserted into the database. The new CustomerID is returned to the application calling the stored procedure as the output parameter @newid.

```
CREATE PROCEDURE sp_newcustomer
@candidate nvarchar(30),
@companyname nvarchar(40) = 'Site Design by TAKempis',
@contactname nvarchar(30) = 'Kevin Spencer',
@contacttitle nvarchar(30) = 'Grand Poobah',
@address nvarchar(60) = 'Somewhere in the U.S.',
@city nvarchar(15) = 'Some City',
@region nvarchar(15) = 'Around Here',
@postalcode nvarchar(10) = '1234567890',
@country nvarchar(15) = 'USofA',
@phone nvarchar(24) = '123-456-7890',
@fax nvarchar(24) = '123-456-7890',
@newid nvarchar(5) = ' ' OUTPUT

AS
DECLARE @lastname nvarchar(5), @hold nvarchar(40)
DECLARE @fill nvarchar(5), @lenfill int
DECLARE @ct int, @col int,  @b26 int
DECLARE @alpha int, @omega int, @num int, @rows int

/* @candidate is the value being passed.*/
/* @lastname is the "abridged" value  */
/* of @candidate (max 5 characters). */
/* @hold is the portion of @candidate  */
/* that we are currently testing. */
/* @fill is the calculated "end portion" of the test  */
/* value for each query. */

SET @alpha = 65  /* ASCII value of 'A')*/
SET @omega = 90  /*ASCII value of 'Z') */
SET  @num = 48  /* ASCII value of '1' */

/* @lastname is initialized to the value*/
/* of the first (up to) 5 chars of the candidate  */
/* @hold is initialized to the value of @lastname   */

SET @lastname =LTRIM(RIGHT(UPPER(@candidate), 5))

SET @hold = @lastname

/* @fill is initialized to the character representation*/
/* of our base 26 number (0),  */
SET @fill = LEFT('AAAAA', 5 - LEN(@hold))
```

```
/* @lenfill holds the number of characters that @fill will hold. */
/* This is derived initially by getting the length of @hold. */
/* During the loop, it's length is    */
/* increased if the length of space to hold*/
/* @b26 in a character string  increases.    */
SET @lenfill = 5 - LEN(@hold)

/*   @b26 is the decimal numeric value of*/
/* the base 26 number we're working on  */
SET    @b26 = 0

SET @rows = 1
WHILE @rows > 0
BEGIN
  SET @hold = LEFT(@hold, 5 - LEN(@fill)) +  @fill
  SELECT @rows = COUNT(*) FROM Customers
  WHERE CustomerID LIKE @hold


  IF @rows = 0 GOTO found_newid

  /* Calculate the rest of the new candidate id, then calculate the next  */
  /* @fill and @lenfill values to use in our query.    */
  /* We start by setting @lenfill to the length of the current value of */
  /* fill We will determine whether to increase it*/
  /* based upon the number  of columns necessary*/
  /* to hold our base 26 number.        */
  SET @ct = 0
  SET @col = 1
  WHILE @lenfill > 0
  BEGIN
    PRINT 'char converted: ' + SUBSTRING(@fill, @lenfill, 1)
    SET @ct = @ct + (@col * (ASCII(SUBSTRING(@fill, @lenfill, 1)) - @alpha))
PRINT '@ct(value): ' + STR(@ct)
SET @lenfill = @lenfill - 1
SET @col = @col * 26
  END

  /* Increment the result by 1 and convert it back to a string      */
  SET    @b26 = @ct + 1
  SET @ct = @b26
  SET @fill = ''
  SET @col = 5
  SET @lenfill = 5
  WHILE @lenfill >= 0
  BEGIN
    IF @ct  >= POWER(26, @lenfill)
    BEGIN
      SET @fill = @fill + (CHAR((@b26 / POWER(26, @lenfill)) + @alpha))
      SET @b26 = (@b26 % POWER(26, @lenfill))
    END
    SET @lenfill = @lenfill - 1
  END
  SET @lenfill = LEN(@fill)
  SET @lenfill = 5 - LEN(@lastname)
  IF @lenfill < LEN(@fill)
    SET @lenfill = LEN(@fill)
  SET @fill = LEFT('AAAAA', @lenfill - LEN(@fill)) + @fill

END
found_newid:
```

At this point, we actually insert the appropriate information into the Customers table:

```
INSERT INTO Customers (CustomerID, CompanyName, ContactTitle,
   ContactName, Address, City, Region, Country, PostalCode,
   Phone, Fax)
VALUES (@hold, @companyname, @contacttitle, @contactname,
   @address, @city, @region, @country, @postalCode,
   @phone, @fax) SELECT @newid = @hold

RETURN @@ERROR

GO
SET QUOTED_IDENTIFIER OFF
GO
SET ANSI_NULLS ON
GO
```

sp_onlineorder

The sp_onlineorder stored procedure is designed to insert a new customer record (if necessary), and add appropriate information, about an order, to the Order Details table.

Initially, the procedure has to determine whether the customer is new, or whether they are a returning customer. This is determined by the @newcustomer variable. If the customer is already recorded, then @candidate is used to store information about the customer. Otherwise, the value of @candidate is used to calculate a unique CustomerID and insert a new customer record into the Customer table (using the sp_newcustomer stored procedure).

An interesting point about this stored procedure is that it implements **transactions**.

> **A transaction is a series of database operations that are carried out as a single operation. The changes made are not committed until all of the operations in the transaction are successfully carried out. If at any point something goes wrong, the entire series of operations is "rolled back," or reversed.**

Because we have to insert three different records in three different tables to complete the transaction, we want to make sure that all three operations are carried out without error, or we should roll them back (not implement any of the changes). If any one operation fails, the error code for that operation will be returned. So, we can check the success of the transaction by looking at the value of the @@ERROR variable, which the store procedure returns, along with the output parameters @customerid and @ordered, both of which are generated during the insertion of the new records. If @@ERROR is anything but 0, an error has occurred, and we know that no changes have been implemented.

Let's have a look at this in sections. We start with parameter declarations:

```
CREATE PROCEDURE sp_onlineorder

/* @newcustomer indicates whether a new Customer record should be   */
/* created for the order, or whether the Customer ID supplied in    */
/* the @candidate variable should be used as a reference to an      */
/* existing Customer record. The @existingorderid parameter         */
/* has the dual purpose of inmdicating whether or not to add a new  */
/* Orders Record to the table, or to use the value of @existingorderid */
/* to insert only a new Order Details record. If it is zero, a new  */
/* Order Details Record is created.            */
@newcustomer bit = 1,
@existingorderid int = 0,

/* Customers table*/
@candidate nvarchar(30) = 'SPENC',
@companyname nvarchar(40) = 'Site Design by TAKempis',
@contactname nvarchar(30) = 'Spencer',
@contacttitle nvarchar(30) = 'Grand Poobah',
@address nvarchar(60) = 'Somewhere in the U.S.',
@city nvarchar(15) = 'Some City',
@region nvarchar(15) = 'Around Here',
@postalcode nvarchar(10) = '1234567890',
@country nvarchar(15) = 'USofA',
@phone nvarchar(24) = '123-456-7890',
@fax nvarchar(24) = '123-456-7890',
@shipname nvarchar(30) = 'Ship to Kevin Spencer',
@shipaddress nvarchar(60) = 'Ship Somewhere in the U.S.',
@shipcity nvarchar(15) = 'Ship Some City',
@shipregion nvarchar(15) = 'Ship Around Here',
@shippostalcode nvarchar(10) = '1234567890',
@shipcountry nvarchar(15) = 'USofA',

/* Order_Details table*/
@productid int = 1,
@unitprice money = 10,
@quantity smallint = 2,
```

Again, this procedure returns two output parameters, @customerid (the new CustomerID value) and @orderid (the new OrderID value):

```
/* OUTPUT parameters */
@customerid nvarchar(5) = ' ' OUTPUT,
@orderid int = 0 OUTPUT

AS

/* "Constants" - You can change these manually, but they don't change.*/
DECLARE @discount int
SET @discount = 0

DECLARE @employeeid int
SET @employeeid = 1
```

```
/* Used internally*/
DECLARE @orderdate datetime
SET @orderdate = GetDate()
```

We next implement the beginning of the transaction. We're going to enter three records in three tables in the same transaction. We start with the new `Customers` table record, using the stored procedure `sp_newcustomer`. Then we take the `CustomerID` received from that, and enter it into a new `Orders` table record, along with the order data in our parameters. Finally, we take the new `OrderID` from *that* record, and enter the `Order Details` record for the product included in this order:

```
BEGIN TRAN
```

We enter the new `Customers` record with the `sp_newcustomer` stored procedure (or update the existing `Customers` record):

```
/* If it's a New Customer, run the sp_newcustomer Stored Procedure, */
/* passing it the new Customer information, and getting back    */
/* the CustomerID.                    */
  IF @newcustomer = 1
  BEGIN
    EXEC sp_newcustomer @candidate = @candidate,
    @newid = @customerid OUTPUT
  END

/* Otherwise, it's an existing Customer. Use the @candidate value */
/* and update the Customer table with the data from the form    */
  ELSE
    SET @customerID = @candidate
    UPDATE Customers SET CompanyName = @companyname,
      ContactName = @contactname,
      ContactTitle = @contacttitle, Address = @address,
      City = @city, Region = @region, Country = @country,
      PostalCode = @postalcode, Phone = @phone,
      Fax = @fax
    WHERE CustomerID = @customerid
```

Here, we enter a new `Orders` record, or, if we are simply continuing to enter products, we use the existing order:

```
/* If @existingorderid = 0, it means that a new Order must be created.*/
/* The OrderID is SELECTed back immediately as part of the    */
/* transaction. If @existingorderid is greater than 0, the value is */
/* used in the insertion of the new Order Detail record.    */
  IF @existingorderid = 0
  BEGIN
    INSERT INTO Orders (CustomerID, EmployeeID, OrderDate,
      ShipName, ShipAddress, ShipCity, ShipRegion,
      ShipPostalCode, ShipCountry)
    VALUES (@customerid, @employeeid, @orderdate,
```

```
        @shipname, @shipaddress, @shipcity, @shipregion,
        @shippostalcode, @shipcountry)
   IF (@@ERROR <> 0)
   BEGIN
      ROLLBACK TRAN
      GOTO failed
   END
   SELECT @orderid = MAX(OrderID) FROM Orders
   IF (@@ERROR <> 0)
   BEGIN
      ROLLBACK TRAN
      GOTO failed
   END
 END
 ELSE
   SET @orderid = @existingorderid
/* Below is some debugging code I commented out.      */
   /* PRINT @orderid */
```

And finally, the `Order Details` record:

```
/* Now we insert the Order Details record, using the information  */
/* we have gathered thus far.              */
   INSERT INTO [Order Details] (OrderID, ProductID,
      UnitPrice,  Quantity, Discount)
       VALUES (@orderid, @productid,
      @unitprice, @quantity, @discount)
   IF (@@ERROR <> 0)
   BEGIN
      ROLLBACK TRAN
      GOTO failed
   END
COMMIT TRAN
failed:
RETURN @@ERROR
```

It's always useful to test code as it is developed, and this applies equally when we are developing stored procedures using SQL. Once the stored procedures have been built, it is worthwhile testing them in some way. To do this, we could use the following code. This passes appropriate parameters to the `sp_onlineorder` procedure, and prints out the returned values. It also prints out any error messages that might be returned. In this case, we received a zero, which means that no errors occurred.

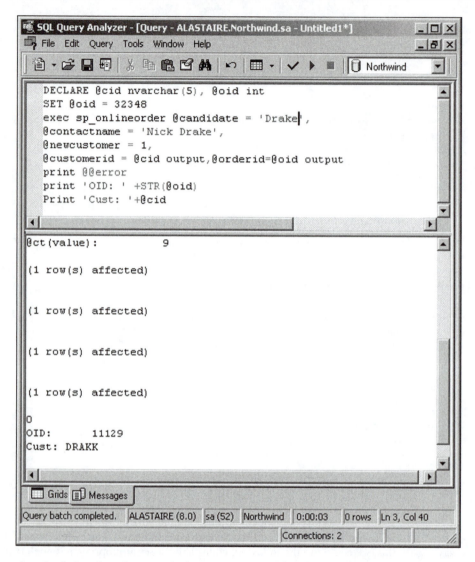

We can also check that the relevant information was entered into the appropriate tables. The following three SELECT statements return the records that we just stored, via the sp_onlineorder stored procedure:

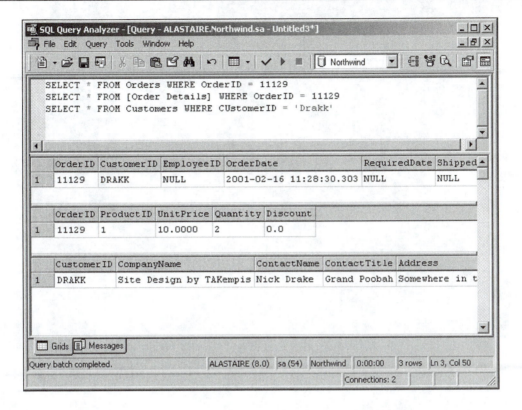

Summary

In this chapter, we've looked at the way in which SQL may be used in the context of developing an Internet Appplication. We've covered a great deal of ground, but those of you not familiar with ASP development needn't worry about not following everything. The intention of looking at such a case study has been to present some serious, and rather complex, SQL code in the kind of context in which SQL is becoming increasingly important.

We've looked at the typical structure of a multi-tiered Internet Application, seen the role that data access technologies such as OLEDB and ODBC play, covered the basics of creating an ASP application, and, most importantly, seen where the DBMS and SQL play a role within such a framework.

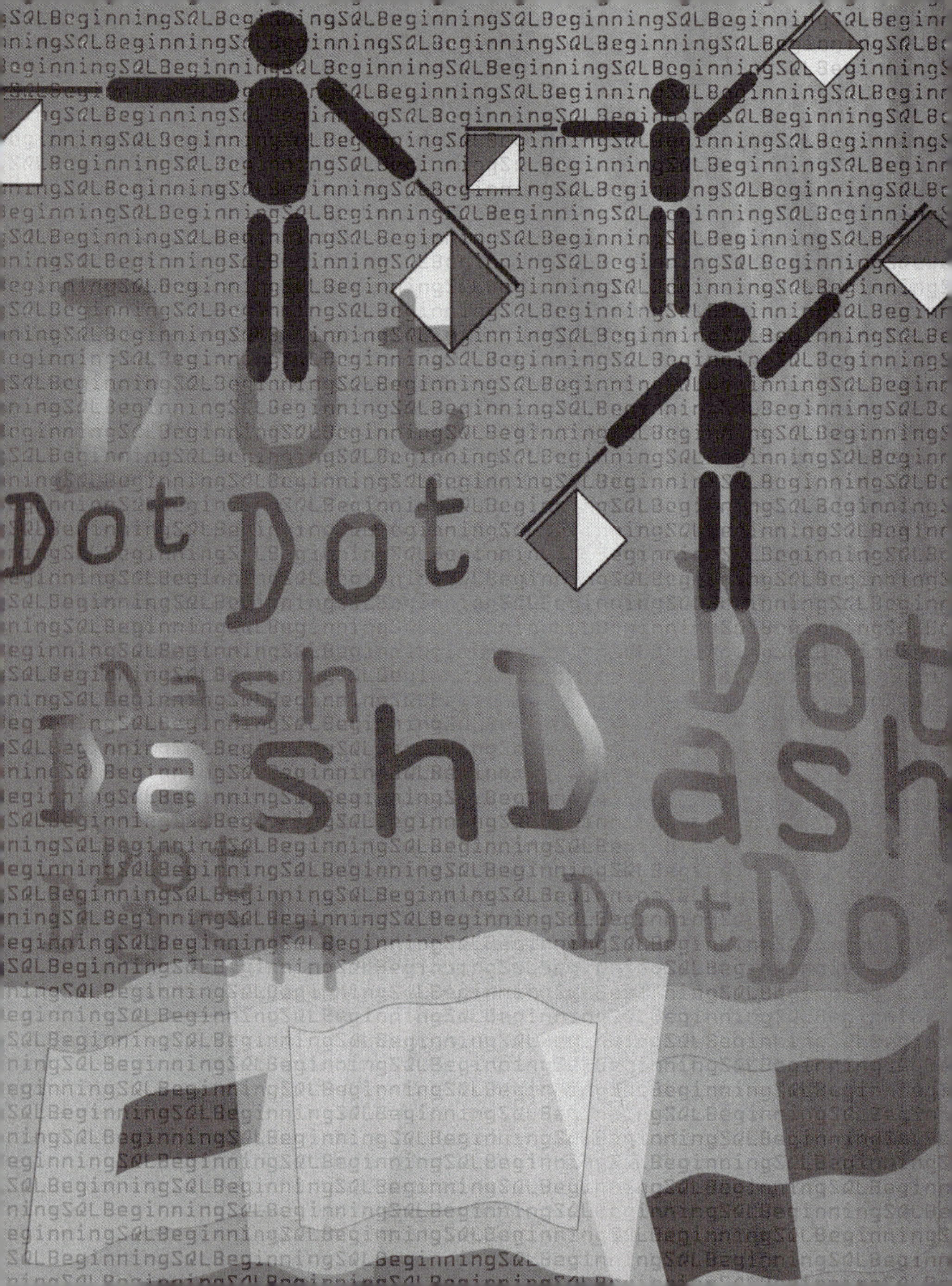
BeginningSQL
Dot
Dot
Dash
Dash
Dot
Dot

The Northwind Database

This appendix is designed to acquaint you with the Northwind database from a perspective that is probably already familiar – Microsoft Access.

In this appendix, we look in some detail at the structure of Microsoft's Northwind database. The Northwind database has formed the basis of many of the SQL examples throughout the book, and a thorough understanding of its structure will help us understand the rationale behind database design in general.

To this end, we begin by introducing the concept of the database schema. We then delve more deeply into the schema of Northwind, placing particular emphasis on how its organization and structure help us to access and manipulate data in the way we want using SQL. For most of the time, we will be using Microsoft Access to investigate the Northwind database, but will occasionally refer to features that are particular to the SQL Server version. We will also take a quick look at one or two of the **forms** that come with the Microsoft Access version of Northwind. The reason for this is not particularly to learn more about these particular user interfaces, but to learn more about the importance of SQL in the design of elegant user-interfaces.

To spice things up a bit, a significant part of this appendix will cover a short case study built around the Northwind database. In this case study, we'll add some search functionality to the database using some simple and straightforward SQL statements. The search functionality will be presented to the end user as a Microsoft Access search form. In working through this case study, we will be able to apply our knowledge of Northwind to good effect. Along the way, we'll also learn some useful (and simple!) VBA skills.

The Northwind Database

There are several reasons for using Northwind as our example database:

❑ It is a well designed relational database

❑ It is not too complex

❑ It already has some useful objects built into it from which we can learn, such as **views** (known as **queries** in Access).

❑ It comes with a useful help file

❑ It is populated with a reasonable amount of data

Of all these reasons, the first and last are the most important. The fact that the database contains a reasonable amount of data is especially beneficial for us. Why? Because it means we don't have to go to the trouble of typing in lots of data before we get started. Also, having plenty of data in the database ensures that most of our queries will actually return data: if there were little data in the database, perfectly sensible queries would frequently fail to return any results. Note, however, that Northwind is nowhere near large enough to be able to test the performance of the database in terms of how quickly and efficiently we can interrogate it.

How to Open Northwind

To open Northwind with Microsoft Access 2000:

1. Start Microsoft Access.

2. On the opening dialog screen, check that 'Open an existing file' is selected (this is the default):

3. If you haven't used Access very much before, 'Northwind' may already be displayed in the file list. If so, simply highlight and click on OK. Northwind should now open.

4. If it is not displayed in the list, highlight 'More Files ...', then click **OK**.

5. From the standard file '**Open**' dialog that now appears, we need to navigate to the file `northwind.mdb` (or `NWIND.mdb`). If you have a standard installation of Microsoft Office, this will be located in the folder `C:\Program Files\Microsoft Office\Office\Samples`.

6. Once you've located the `northwind.mdb` file, highlight it and click **Open**.

You may find it useful to keep a "clean" copy of the file `Northwind.mdb` *that you can revert to in case you accidentally delete something (e.g. a table!) that you should have kept. Use Windows Explorer to do this:* `Northwind.mdb` *can be found in the folder* `C:\Program Files\Microsoft Office\Office\Samples`.

You can also find the appropriate file as `Nwind.mdb` *on the Office 2000 CD in the folder* `\Pfiles\Msoffice\Office\Samples`. *If you copy the file from here to your hard drive, remember to right-click on the copied file in Explorer, click on* **Properties**, *then uncheck the file's* **Read-Only** *attribute, otherwise you won't be able to modify any data in the database.*

In Access, Northwind will normally open by displaying a pretty "splash" screen. Click **OK** to close this form. You will now see the Access Database Window for Northwind. This Database Window is part of the Access user-interface and allows us to see all of the objects that make up the Access database. We'll come back to this in a moment, but first we need a brief introduction to the Northwind database schema.

The Database Schema

The subject of the database schema has been discussed back in Chapter 16. Here, we can just content ourselves with a brief description of the concept before examining Northwind in more detail.

What's in a schema??

The Oxford English Dictionary defines the word *schema* as "synopsis, outline, diagram, proposed arrangement" and this proves a good starting point for discussion when it comes to the schema for a database.

The database schema is essentially a synopsis or outline of the database structure, sometimes displayed in the form of a diagram. However, the schema is like a skeleton of the database, in that it isn't concerned with the actual data that might be stored in it. So what kinds of things does it include? Primarily, a database schema will contain information on the following objects:

- ❑   Tables
- ❑   Views (or Queries)
- ❑   Stored Procedures

It may also include other information, such as who is allowed to use the database, that is, information on users and groups, their roles, their permissions, and their logins. Importantly, and as mentioned above, a schema does not contain any of the attendant data. Instead, it is a summary of how that data is organized and manipulated. It's also worth pointing out that Access objects such as forms and reports are not part of a database schema. These objects are really part of the user interface or front end and have no bearing on the structure of the database.

At this point, we need to say a little bit more about queries, Views, and Stored Procedures:

❑ The term "query" is a generic term used to describe a SQL statement that is used to query a database.

❑ Views (or Queries, as they're called in Access), may be thought of as virtual tables, their contents defined by a query.

❑ Stored Procedures are objects that generally comprise a set of SQL statements that allow us to control access to and manipulation of data programmatically (stored procedures are not supported by Access).

The information about views and stored procedures is stored in a schema as text: essentially, they are SQL code.

In the case of tables (without which, of course, our database would not be very useful) the information stored on these in a schema is somewhat richer and will include:

❑ Field or column names

❑ Data types for each field or column, for example, number, text, date

❑ Constraints, such as:

❑ Relationships and information on referential integrity

❑ Primary keys

❑ Default values for each field or column, whether null or empty values are allowed, and so on

❑ Indexes

In essence, therefore, a schema describes the fundamental structure of a database.

Why is the schema important?

There are several reasons why the database schema is important. At the outset, the schema provides us with a starting point for understanding how an existing database works. At a very trivial level, imagine a database with a table containing details of all the products sold by a food store. Now, suppose that we want to look up the price of a box of cornflakes. We might struggle to do this quickly if we didn't know that the field (or column) names in this Products table were, say, ProductName and UnitPrice. At a less basic level, say we now want to see how many boxes of cornflakes we have in stock. Again, this might be quite difficult unless we knew both that our database contained a table called StockMovements and that this table contained a field ProductID that is related to the primary key of our Products table. It is only when we are armed with this information that we can start to make proper sense of things.

Now that we've recapped on what a schema actually is, we can return to the Northwind database and start examining its schema in some more detail.

The Northwind Schema

As might be anticipated from the recent digression, initially we are going to be concerned more with the structure of Northwind than the actual data that it contains. So where's the best place to start examining the schema of Northwind?

Northwind Tables & Relationships

Given the fundamental importance of tables in any database, we could start by examining the design of each table object in turn. However, this could be quite laborious and it might be difficult to keep track of the various table relationships. Fortunately, Access offers us a tool for viewing a diagram of the database tables and their relationships. First, then, let's take a look at the diagram using Access.

> *You may have noticed that, when you have Northwind open in Access, there is an extra item on the Access menu bar labeled* Show Me. *This links you to a Help file specific to Northwind database. You may find it useful to explore this before proceeding.*

The Relationships Window in Access

To view a diagram of Northwind, we can either click on the Relationships toolbar button, or select Relationships from the Tools menu. The Relationships window for Northwind will appear as shown in the screenshot below. It's worth mentioning that Access does not generate these diagrams automatically: it is up to the developer to add and arrange the tables in the Relationships window. Fortunately for us, though, Northwind comes with a ready-built diagram of its relationships, which saves us some effort here.

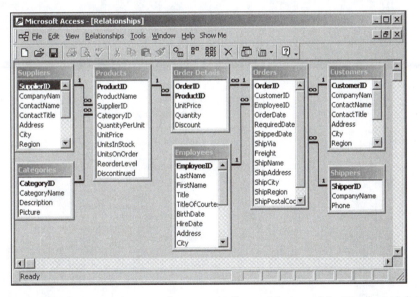

This Relationships window provides us with an especially useful view of the Northwind database. Not only does it show us all of the table objects in the database, it also shows us all of the fields in each table. Moreover, the lines that link the tables depict the relationships in the database. Let's take a look at some of the features of this diagram:

- ❑ Eight tables are depicted in the diagram. The Employees table has several fields, such as EmployeeID, FirstName, LastName, and so on (we'll need to use the scroll bar on this table to see all the fields).

- ❑ Primary key fields are displayed in bold font. For instance, the primary key for the Employees table is the EmployeeID field.

571

❑ The Employees table is in a one-to-many relationship with the Orders table, as shown by the line linking the two tables. We can tell that Employees is on the *one* side of this relationship because of the number 1 adjacent to this table. Similarly, Orders is on the *many* side of the relationship, as indicated by the infinity symbol (∞) adjacent to this table.

❑ The relationship, or **join**, between Employees and Orders is based on the primary key EmployeeID in the Employees table, and the foreign key EmployeeID in the Orders table. In Access, we can tell this from the positioning of the relationship line between the two tables. Note that there is no necessity for the primary and foreign key fields to have the same name. However, it's usually a good idea if they do, since it's then much easier to follow the relationships.

Clearly, this diagram shows us the key aspects of the Northwind schema, and is therefore an especially useful tool in documenting that schema. Even better, Access allows us to examine the objects in the diagram in more detail. For example, right-clicking the mouse anywhere on Employees table in the diagrams, and selecting Table Design from the pop-up menu, will open up the table design view for the Employees table, allowing us to see the table schema (the field names, the data types associated with these fields, and so on). We're not going to examine the detail of any of the table schemas here, suffice to say that we know where to find the information when required:

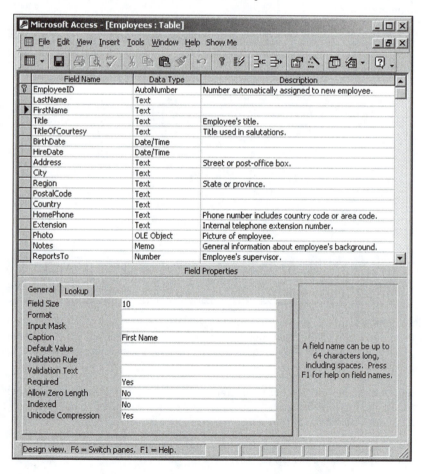

Similarly, double-clicking on one of the lines representing a relationship opens up a pop-up dialog showing us details of the relationship. We can achieve the same thing by right-clicking on a relationship line and selecting the Edit Relationship... option from the context menu that appears. Here we can see the detail for the one-to-many relationship between Employees and Orders:

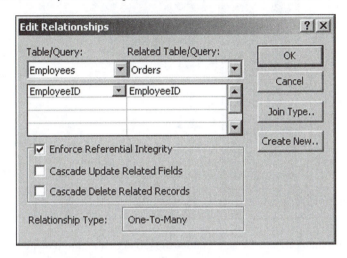

This dialog tells us the tables linked by the relationship and the fields upon which the relationship is based. In addition, we have several other options. In this particular example, the Enforce Referential Integrity box is checked. When this property is set, we cannot add a new order to the Orders table without entering a valid value for EmployeeID. That is, the EmployeeID foreign key field in the Orders table must correspond to one of the EmployeeID primary key values in the Employees table. This is very sensible: we don't want to enter Orders that refer to a non-existent employee!

The Process of Placing an Order

OK, so we've taken a look at a view of the tables and relationships in Northwind. We now need to get down to the nitty-gritty of seeing how the database works. We'll concentrate on the eight tables shown in the database diagrams above. Note that the Northwind database in SQL Server has slightly more tables. We won't be concerned with these here.

We'll start the discussion by examining the process of a customer placing an order with Northwind Traders. The easiest way to explain things will be to use some of the front-end functionality that has been built into Access for us. First, however, we're going to take a quick look at the data that's actually in the Orders table.

Try It Out – Accessing and Entering Data

1. We'll assume that Access is running and that Northwind is loaded. If you still have the Relationships window open, you can close this down.

2. You should see the Database window which shows all the objects in the database.

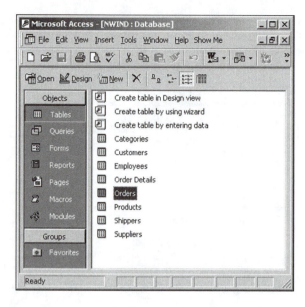

3. Make sure that Tables is selected under the Objects menu to left side of the database window.

4. Open the table Orders, either by double-clicking its name, or by highlighting it and clicking on the Open button on the database window toolbar.

5. Go to the last record in the table, either by using the scroll bar or the navigation buttons to the bottom left of the table window. Make a note of the OrderID for the last record in the table. If this is the first time that the database has been used, there should be 830 records in the table and the last record should have an OrderID of 11077. However, if you have previously been entering or removing records from the database, this will be different.

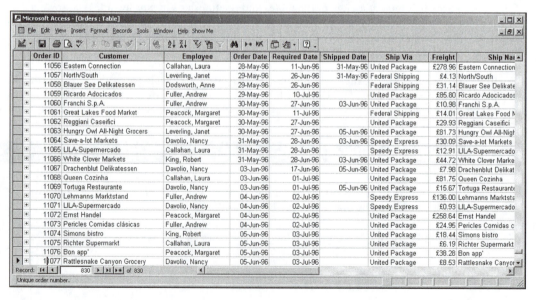

6. Close the `Orders` table.

7. Now we're going to add an order using a built-in Access form. On the database window, select **Forms** on the object menu on the left-hand side of the window.

8. Double-click on the form called **Main Switchboard**. We can consider this the main form in Northwind since it is the entry point into the Access application that has been built around the Nortwind tables. We can use this form to explore Northwind more fully later. For the moment, however, click on the button labeled **Orders**.

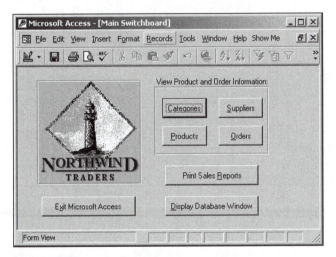

9. The Orders form will now be displayed:

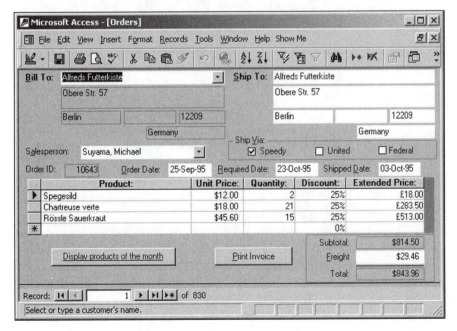

10. We want to add a new order, so click on the navigation button labeled with an arrowhead and asterisk at the bottom of the form. We are then presented with a blank form:

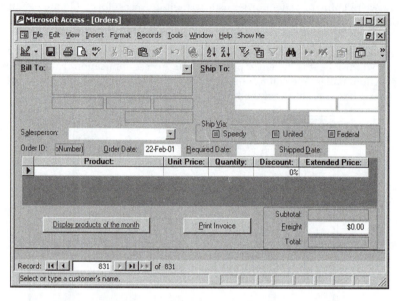

11. Start entering some information for the new order. In the screenshot below, I've set up an order from Alfreds Futterkiste for the products Aniseed Syrup and Boston Crab Meat, the salesperson was Anne Dodsworth, and the order is to be shipped via United. Where appropriate, use the drop-down lists (known as combo boxes) to make data entry easy:

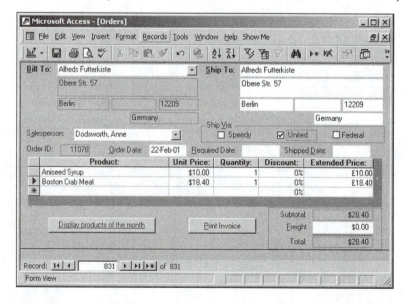

12. When you've finished entering the order details, close the Orders form and Main Switchboard.

How It Works

So what's actually happening to the data in the Northwind tables when we place this order? All of the action is taking place in two tables, Orders and Order Details: these are key tables in the Northwind database. Let's run through things:

❑ As soon as we selected the company Alfreds Futterkiste from the **Bill To:** drop-down list, a new row was created in the Orders table. This was automatically given the an OrderID number 11078 (the primary key). OrderID is an "autonumber" field – that is, its value is automatically generated by Access.

❑ The company name, **Alfred Futterkiste,** was not stored in the table! Instead, the Orders table simply stored a number in the CustomerID field corresponding to the CustomerID primary key field in the Customers table. Remember that this is a relational database, and we don't want to keep duplicating the same information in a table over and over again, such as customer names and addresses. By storing the CustomerID number only, we can look up all the information we want from the Customer table simply by taking advantage of the one-to-many relationship between Customers and Orders.

❑ Similarly, when we entered **Anne Dodsworth** as the saleperson, all that was stored in the Orders table was her EmployeeID number rather than all the rest of her details. It's a similar story for the company selected to ship the order (**United** in this case): a ShipperID number is stored rather than the actual name of the shipper, which can be looked up from the Shippers table as required.

❑ Some of the other information that was stored in the table got there automatically, the process being driven by the Access form (via some underlying Visual Basic for Applications code) rather than by anything that we did. In particular, most of the shipping information (such as ShipName, ShipAddress) was pulled from the Customer table. This information can be overwritten by the user if the shipping address happens to be different from the customer's address.

Now that we've been through the process, let's re-open the Orders table to check that our new order is there. We should see that the last order in the table now has an OrderID one higher than previously (11078 if it's the first time that you've used the Northwind sample):

In this table view, Access actually tricks us into believing that we're really storing some information from other tables. For example, in the order we've just entered, Anne Dodsworth is shown as the Employee. In fact, the table has only stored Anne's `EmployeeID:` *and looks up her name in the* `Employees` *table based on her* `EmployeeID`. *This is performed by a join between the* `Orders` *and* `Employees` *tables.*

The OrderDetails Table

OK, so we've confirmed that our order we entered has appeared in the *Orders* table. But hang on a minute! Didn't we actually place an order for two products? What's happened to the information that we entered for these? If you scroll across the `Orders` table or look at the `Orders` table schema, there are no fields at all that refer to any product information. Instead, the information on the products ordered gets stored in another table, `OrderDetails`, which is related to both the `Orders` table and the `Products` table.

If we think about this in a bit more detail, it does all start to make some sense. If we wanted to use the `Orders` table to store the product details, we'd have two options, neither of which is very satisfactory:

❑ We could put a new row in the `Orders` table for each product ordered. This is not a very good idea since each product ordered would have a different `OrderID`. In addition, we'd be duplicating customer and shipping information in the table each time.

❑ We could have several `Product` fields in the `Orders` table, for example, `ProductID1`, `ProductID2`, `ProductID3`, etc. Again, this is not acceptable since we wouldn't know how many product fields to include.

The actual solution, whereby the required information is stored in the related `OrderDetails` table, is much more elegant and, importantly, much more efficient. For every product in a given order, there will be a row in the `OrderDetails` table, which holds both the `OrderID` and the `ProductID` (displayed as the product name). Moreover, both of these fields are keys in the `OrderDetails` table (and taken together they actually form the primary key for the table).

The Relationship between Orders and Products

Consider the relationship between `Orders` and `Products`. A single order can have as many products as we wish. Likewise, a single product can appear in as many different orders as we wish. Thus, the relationship between the two tables is known as a **many-to-many** relationship.

The only way to establish this type of relationship is to use an **intersection**, **cross-reference**, or **junction** table that links the two tables. `OrderDetails` is exactly this type of table. This intersection table has a one-to-many relationship with `Orders` (using the `OrderID` key field) and a one-to many relationship with `Products` (using the `ProductID` key). Taken together, this provides a many-to-many relationship between `Orders` and `Products`.

To see how it relates `Orders` and `Products`, it's useful to refer back to the Access Relationships diagram. Northwind also uses this intersection table to store information about each product order, such as quantity ordered and unit price of the product at the time of ordering.

To finish our examination of the ordering process, it's worth taking a look at the `OrderDetails` table for the order we placed where the `OrderID` = 11078. Open up the `OrderDetails` table and scroll down to the last few rows.

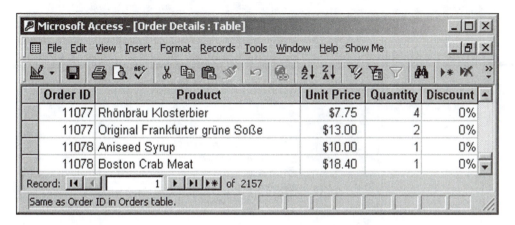

As we can see, there are two rows for this OrderID since we ordered two different products.

To summarize, the key tables in the database are, in effect, Orders and OrderDetails. It is the information in these that is updated every time an order is placed. The other tables hold fairly static information that is used by way of look-up data. Of course, some of the data in these other tables will change from time to time: for instance, a new product may come on the market, or a new employee may join the company, but not at the same frequency as in Orders and OrderDetails. To gain a bit more familiarity with Northwind, you might find it useful to open up each table in turn to take a look at the kinds of information that they each contain.

Access Queries in Northwind

As mentioned previously, Access Queries are essentially SQL statements that allow us to extract and manipulate the data in our tables in whichever way is appropriate for the task at hand. We can think of an Access Query simply as a request on the database. The database responds to this request by generating a table of results. An Access Query (or View) is often referred to as a virtual table since the results aren't stored physically within the database.

Let's look at some of the Access Queries that come ready made as part of the Northwind database.

In the Database window, click Queries in the Objects menu on the left-hand side. We should now see a list of the Queries that come as part of Northwind:

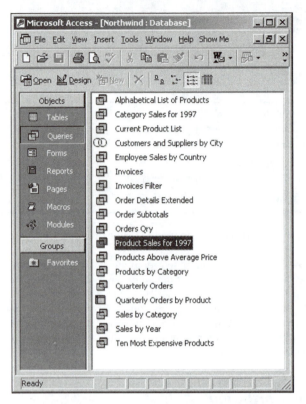

We'll look at a very simple one. Single-click on the Query called **Current Product List** so that it is highlighted, then click on the **Design** button on the Database window. This opens up the Query Design Grid, which is a very useful tool in Access:

The top half of this design grid shows us tables used as the basis for the Query. In this particular case, only the Products table is being used. The lower half of the grid shows the fields that are included in the Query, along with other information such as criteria and sort orders. Here's what the grid shows us:

❑ The results table will show only ProductID, and ProductName.

❑ The results table will be sorted by ProductName, in ascending order.

❑ Only products where the Discontinued field is **No** will be shown.

❑ The Discontinued field will not appear in the results view (the reason for having this field in the Query is so that we can select only those products that have not been discontinued).

In other, words, we are using the Query to select only certain sets of data. When we add tables and fields using the design grid, Access actually constructs the underlying SQL statements for us. To view the SQL for this Query, click on **View** on the Access menu bar, then select **SQL View**. We will see the following SQL statement:

```
SELECT [Product List].ProductID, [Product List].ProductName
FROM Products AS [Product List]
WHERE ((([Product List].Discontinued)=No))
ORDER BY [Product List].ProductName;
```

Note that this is fairly straightforward SQL: not nearly as complex as some of the examples we've looked at in the body of the book. We simply select the ProductID and ProductName from the Product List table where the product is not discontinued, give the results an alias, and order them by name.

We can view the results table for the Query by selecting **Datasheet View** from the View menu:

As expected, we only see `ProductID` and `Product` Name in our results table. Moreover, the Query shows 69 records. If we take a look at the `Products` table, we will see that there actually 77 products altogether. The reason we only see 69 products is because the Query only selects those records where the `Discontinued` field is `No`.

Orders Qry and 'Order Details Extended

We're now going to examine of couple of slightly more complicated queries. You may not have realized it, but the `Orders` form that we used earlier actually comprises two forms. The main form displays information based not on the `Orders` table but on a query called `Orders Qry`. Embedded in the main form is a sub-form that displays information concerning the actual products ordered: again, this is not based directly on the `Order Details` table, but on a query called `Order Details Extended`. It's instructive to take a closer look at both of these queries.

Open up the `Orders Qry` Query in Design View. We'll see that the query is based on both the `Orders` table and the `Customers` table, and selects fields from both, making use of the relationship between the two tables. We'll need to scroll across a little to see all of the fields that are selected.

Note that we can improve viewablilty by dragging the tables to a new location in the display window. To drag a table, simply click on its name bar and hold the mouse button down while moving it. When we rearrange the tables in this way, the relationships between them rearrange themselves automatically.

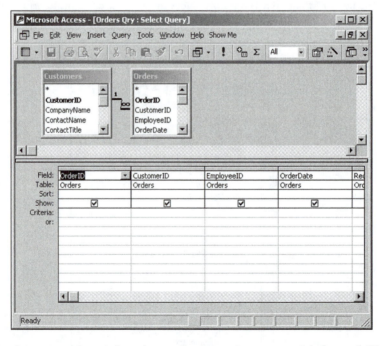

The reason why the `Orders` form is based on such a query is pretty straightforward. The form needs to display customer information for every order as well as the order information. That is, it needs to pull in the customer address information from `Customers` based on the `CustomerID`, and this is stored in the `Orders` table. The best way to do this is to base the form on a query that does this automatically.

Now switch to **SQL View** for this query. Although the SELECT part of the statement looks a bit complicated, it's really just a list of field or column names that the query is going to display. For the time being, ignore the DISTINCTROW predicate that comes after the SELECT: we'll take a closer look at this later on. The key part of the query is the last line:

```
SELECT DISTINCTROW Orders.OrderID, Orders.CustomerID, Orders.EmployeeID,
Orders.OrderDate, Orders.RequiredDate, Orders.ShippedDate, Orders.ShipVia,
Orders.Freight, Orders.ShipName, Orders.ShipAddress, Orders.ShipCity,
Orders.ShipRegion, Orders.ShipPostalCode, Orders.ShipCountry,
Customers.CompanyName, Customers.Address, Customers.City, Customers.Region,
Customers.PostalCode, Customers.Country
FROM Customers INNER JOIN Orders ON Customers.CustomerID = Orders.CustomerID;
```

The last line tells the DBMS that the rows of data are to be selected from both Customers and the Orders table and that the data from the two tables are to be joined by the CustomerID fields. For example, if one the rows of data selected from the Orders table has a CustomerID of 5, the query looks up all the address fields from the Customers table where Customers.CustomerID is also 5.

We can inspect the results table for this query by switching to **Datasheet View**. The screenshot below shows part of the results table generated by Orders Qry. Notice that I've scrolled across a bit for the purposes of this example:

The Ship_Country and Ship_Postal_Code fields both come from the Orders table. In contrast, the Address field for each order is taken from the Customers table.

This ability to combine information from more than one table is, of course, an extremely powerful feature of SQL and is exploited in many of the queries within Northwind and, of course, in other databases.

The Order Details Extended Query, which is the record source for the Orders sub-form, provides the sub-form with information about products being ordered. The reason why this sub-form is based on a query rather than directly on an Order Details Extended table is that the query returns a calculated field called ExtendedPrice. Take a look at the query in **SQL View:**

```
SELECT DISTINCTROW
[Order Details].[OrderID],
[Order Details].[ProductID],
[Products].[ProductName],
[Order Details].[UnitPrice],
[Order Details].[Quantity],
[Order Details].[Discount],
CCur([Order Details].[UnitPrice]*[Quantity]*(1-[Discount])/100)*100 AS
ExtendedPrice
FROM Products INNER JOIN [Order Details] ON [Products].[ProductID]=[Order
Details].[ProductID]
ORDER BY [Order Details].[OrderID];
```

An interesting aspect of this SELECT statement is:

```
CCur([Order Details].[UnitPrice]*[Quantity]*(1-[Discount])/100)*100 AS
ExtendedPrice
```

Essentially, this field calculates the price of the products ordered in each row in Order Details, based on UnitPrice multiplied by Quantity less the Discount. As the math here might seem a touch complicated, let's take a closer look at what's going on. The central part of the calculation is:

```
UnitPrice * Quantity * (1 - Discount)
```

Note that in the actual calculation used in the Query, square brackets are used around the column names. Moreover, the UnitPrice column is referred to as [Order Details].[UnitPrice]. As the two tables that make up the Order Details Extended (Products *and* Order Details*)* both have a UnitPrice column, it is essential to specify which table column is being used in the calculation.

Clearly, UnitPrice * Quantity gives us a basic price to work with. This is then multiplied by 1-Discount to work out a price with any discount applied.

Why do we have to subtract the discount from one? Well, the discount is stored in the Order Details table as a proportion of one. Thus, a discount of 15% will be stored as 0.15.

The CCur function is used to force the calculated price into a currency format.

As calculations of this type are sometimes prone to rounding errors, the calculated price is divided by 100 before being converted with the CCur function, and then multiplied by 100 again to give a correctly-rounded result.

Now that we have discussed Northwind in some detail, we can turn our attention to a Case Study where we see how to build some search functionality into the application using some simple SQL statements.

Case Study: Adding Search Functionality to Northwind

If we spend some time navigating through the various forms and reports in Northwind (the form `Main Switchboard` is a good starting point), we will begin to realize that the application is quite poor in terms of being able to search for information. As it stands, the system is obviously pretty good for entering orders, maintaining employee, supplier, customer, and product records, producing invoices, and summarizing sales data.

Suppose that we've just joined Northwind Traders, and have been given responsibility for looking after the database. Think of a couple of Northwind scenarios that we might be presented with:

- ❑ A supplier contacts us to tell us that they're replacing one of their products with a new, low-fat variety. We decide to mail our customers to tell them about the substitution. However, to keep costs down, we are only going to contact those customers that buy this product.

- ❑ A customer phones to find out much they've ordered from us over the last few years – their records are in a bit of a mess and they want to try to see where they are spending their money (or maybe they want to negotiate a bigger discount)!

We might think of building a custom query for each of these scenarios. However, if we were to get a few such queries, writing queries for each such request would become cumbersome and time consuming. It would be better to build a user-friendly front end form so that employees could carry out such searches.

This is exactly what we are going to in this Case Study. We are going to build on our knowledge of Northwind to develop search and results forms in Access. In doing this, we are going to see how easy it is to exploit the power of SQL in a front end. To make our task easier, we're going to break things down into stages.

Stage 1: Building a Simple Search Form

In this Case Study, there are three key steps that we need take:

- ❑ Provide the user with a form or interface that allows them to select their search criteria with the minimum of effort.

- ❑ Translate the user's selected search criteria into a SQL statement that will be used to perform the search.

- ❑ Present the results of the search to the user in an intelligible and useful format and, where appropriate, link these results back into the existing Northwind application.

In this first stage, we're actually going to do all of these three things, but we'll keep everything very simple to start with. Even better, we'll cheat a little on step 3 by using an existing form for our results.

To begin with, our search form will simply offer us the ability to search for orders by `CompanyName`.

A modified version of Northwind, which includes all the Access objects created in this case study, can be found on the Wrox web site at www.wrox.com.

Try It Out – Build a Simple Search Form in Access

1. Open up the Northwind database in Access.

2. In the database window, select Forms from the Objects menu on the left-hand side.

3. In the Forms window, locate the object labeled Create Form in Design View. This opens up an empty form in design view:

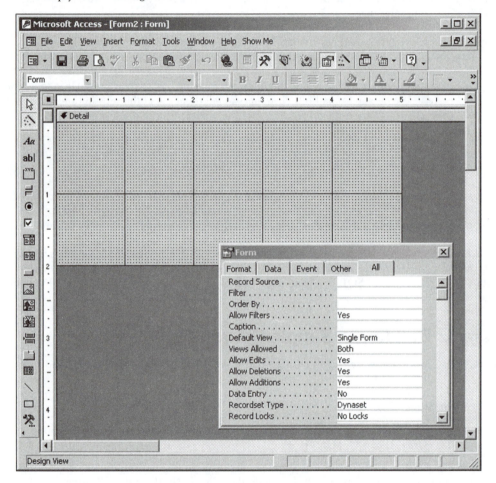

4. Hopefully, you'll also see a toolbox, either floating or docked (in the screenshot above, this is docked to the left side of the Access application window). If you don't see it, right-click on the Access menu bar and click on Toolbox in the pop-up menu.

It's also useful to display the Properties window when designing forms (this is displayed to the right of the form in the above screenshot). If you don't see this, click the Properties button on the Form Design toolbar. If you don't see the Form Design toolbar, right-click the mouse on a blank part of any of the toolbar and select Form Design.

5. In the Properties window, select the All tab. The top line, corresponding to Record Source, is blank and we want it to remain that way. The reason for this is that we want to create an unbound form. This is a form that is not linked to any record source (such as a Table or Query). This contrasts with most of the forms in Northwind that are normally bound to a record source. Bound forms allow us to read, edit, add, and delete data directly from the form. This is great if we want to enter a new contact address or change someone's telephone number. However, in the Search form that we are about to create, we want users to able to select a variety of search criteria, not to be able to edit, add, or delete things. Later on, we will be creating a couple of forms to display the search results: as these will be displaying data from the Orders and Order Details tables, these will be bound forms, so that the user can update data from them.

Adding a Combo Box

1. We're now going to add a combo box control to our blank form to allow the user to search by customer name. On the toolbox toolbar, make sure that Control Wizards is selected – this is the second item on the toolbox and depicts a magic wand. Now click on the combo box icon– this is normally the control immediately after the checkbox icon.

2. Move the mouse pointer to the empty form – when it's over the form, the pointer will change to a + sign along with a combo box icon. Click the mouse button to add the combo box to the form. Almost immediately, the Combo Box Wizard should start.

Select has the first option that the combo box will look up its values in a table or query, then click next.

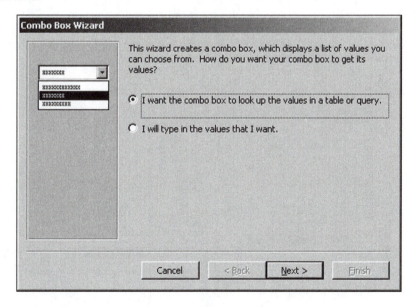

3. As we're setting up this combo box to allow the user to search by customer name, select the Customers table as the source for the combo box, then click Next.

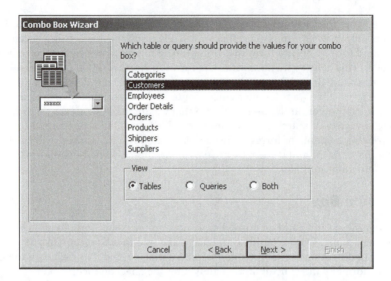

4. Now select the fields we want as the combo box columns by highlighting each field in turn and clicking on the right arrowhead – we're going to select CustomerID and CompanyName.

The reasons why we're selecting two columns for the combo box are as follows. First, we want it to display CompanyName to help the user select the desired company for their search. If we just chose CustomerID, this might be a bit difficult. Second, we actually want the combo box to take on the value of CustomerID for the CompanyName that's been selected. This is because the Orders form that we are going to be searching has CustomerID, not CompanyName, as a foreign key. It's important to make sure that we select these fields in the order shown. Putting CustomerID first ensures that the combo box takes the value of CustomerID corresponding to the selected CompanyName.

Now click Next.

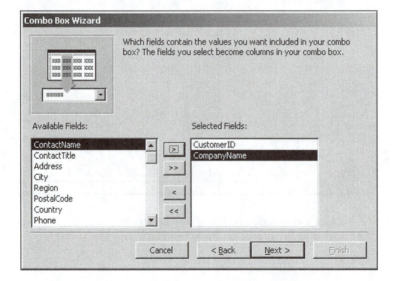

5. In the next screen, make sure that Hide key column is selected, then click Next.

6. In the final wizard screen, type in the label name 'Company', then click Finish.

7. We should now see a combo box and its label on the new form. To reposition the combo box and its label, hover the mouse pointer over the combo box – when you see a hand symbol, click and drag the box to the desired position. If you don't see the hand symbol, make sure that the combo box is selected by clicking on it – it will have some resize handles if it is. Your form should look something like this:

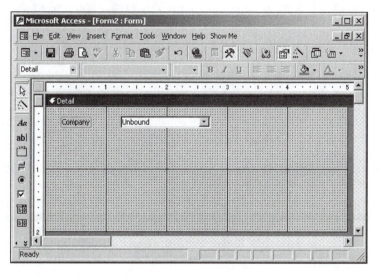

8. As we will want to refer to our combo box in code in a moment, it is worth giving it a meaningful name, rather than the default that Access gives it. The Name property for the combo can be found on the Other tab (or the All tab) in the Properties window. We'll call it cmbCustomerID.

There are various conventions for naming Access objects and form elements. It doesn't really matter which system we use: the key thing is to try to be consistent. I generally use the prefix 'cmb' to name combo-boxes followed by the name of the column whose value the combo box takes, hence 'cmbCustomerID'.

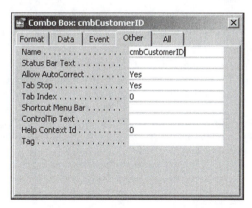

If you need to know a little bit more about Access combo boxes, try the Access Help menus. Using the Office assistant, search on 'add a combo box' then select 'Create a bound or unbound combo box, drop-down list box, or list box'.

9. Let's take a quick look at our handiwork in form view. Right-click the title bar of the form and select **Form View** from the context-sensitive menu. Try out the combo box: you should see all of the company names of the Northwind customers displayed in alphabetical order.

10. Switch back to Design view – right-click the form's title bar and select **Design View** from the context-sensitive menu. At this stage, it is a good idea to save the form. Click on the floppy disk icon on the Access toolbar (or use the menu **File | Save As**) and save the form as `Search`.

OK, so we've added a combo box to our form and, using a wizard, set it up so that it will display `CompanyName`. It is instructive to see how Access does this. Make sure that you've switched back to Form Design view. With our combo box still selected, take a look at its **Row Source** property on the **Properties** window under the **Data** tab. You'll see that the wizard actually created the following statement as its row source, which again demonstrates the importance of SQL:

```
SELECT [Customers].[CustomerID], [Customers].[CompanyName] FROM Customers;
```

There are a couple of additional and important things that we need to note about this combo box:

❑ First, its row source has two columns (or fields): `CustomerID` and `CompanyName`, but only `CompanyName` is displayed. Remember that we told the wizard to hide the key column: Access achieves this simply by setting the display width for the first column to zero.

❑ Second, as we said before, the value of the combo box is set by `CustomerID`, not `CompanyName`. Thus, if we select the customer '**Alfreds Futterkiste**' in the combo box, its value will actually become `'ALFKI'`. `'ALFKI'` is the `CustomerID` for the company named `'Alfreds Futterkiste'`. In other words, the first column in our combo box is the bound column. We can see this by inspecting the **Bound Column** property for the combo box: it is set to **1**. We could change it to the second column if we wished but it is normally better to set it to the primary key of the row source.

Adding a Command Button

We now need to add a command button to our form for the user to click on to initiate a search based on the `CustomerID` of the `CompanyName` selected in the combo box.

1. With our form in Design View, turn off **Control Wizards** on the toolbox toolbar (deselect the magic wand icon). We want to generate our own Visual Basic code for this command button rather than letting the wizard do it.

2. Click on the command button icon on the toolbox, then click on the form to place the button. You can use the handles to resize the button as appropriate; you can move it by dragging it whenever a hand icon is displayed.

3. Now we need to change the button's caption and give it a meaningful name. With the button still selected, locate its Caption property in the Properties window (on the Format tab) and set to Search, then locate its Name property (on the Other tab) and set to cmdSearch. If we don't bother to set the Name property for the button, Access will set a default name. For a simple form such as the one we're building here, that's not too much of an issue. However, if you have several buttons on a form, it's a good idea to give each one a name that says something about what it does. If you add event procedures to these buttons using Visual Basic for Applications (as we're going to do in a moment), it helps you to keep track of which piece of code belongs to which button. In this particular case, I'm using the prefix 'cmd' to show that 'cmdSearch' is a command button; some people use the prefix 'btn' instead. As I said earlier, it doesn't really matter which system you use as long as you are consistent.

4. We are now ready to add a Visual Basic for Applications (VBA) event procedure to our search button: this procedure will launch when the user clicks on the button (the click on the button counts as an event, hence the name event procedure).

VBA is a programming language that is available in all Microsoft Office products. In Access, VBA is a very powerful way of not only accessing and manipulating the data in a database, but also making user-interface components work, such as our search form.

5. Make sure that the Search button is still selected (it should have handles – if not, click on it once in design view). Select the Event tab on the Properties window, then click in the box labeled On Click. Now click on the ellipsis that appears to the right-hand side of the On Click box:

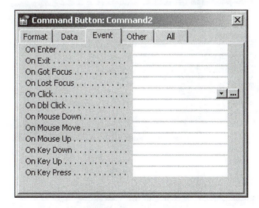

6. Select Code Builder from the Choose Builder dialog that appears, then click OK.

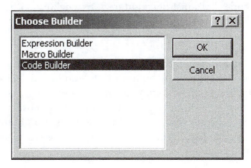

7. This launches the Visual Basic editor and conveniently sets up a sub procedure declaration for us by automatically adding the start and end lines of code for us.

There are two types of procedure in VBA, the **Sub procedure** and the **Function procedure**:

❑ Sub procedures contain a series of statements and methods that perform a particular operation.

❑ Function procedures also contain a series of statements but return a value – hence, they're often used in calculations.

For the search functionality, we're not going to return any values so we use a sub procedure. This sub procedure will run each time a user clicks on the Search button. Of course, we now put VBA code in the subroutine to get it to do something. This is the second step in building some simple search functionality: that is, translating the selected search criteria into a SQL statement. The screenshot below shows the code that we now need to enter to do this.

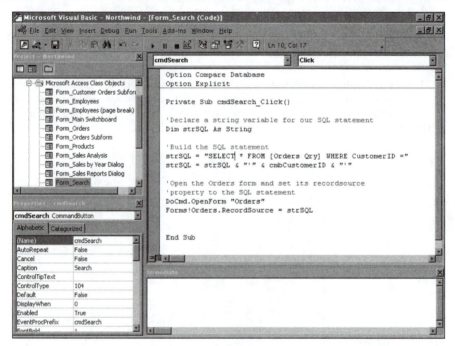

8. We'll finish off here, then come back to take a look at how the code works. First, it's a good idea to save the code that's just been entered, by clicking on the save icon. Now close the VB Editor, and click on the save icon again to make sure that any other changes that we've made to the form have been saved.

9. Now let's take a look at the search form in its normal Form View by selecting Form View from the View menu or using the View button on the toolbar. Select a customer name from the combo box, then click on the Search button. If everything has been set up correctly, the Northwind Orders form should open, displaying only those records for the customer that you selected. You can confirm this by using the navigation buttons at the bottom of the Orders form. For example, if you choose 'Around the Horn' as the customer, you should see the 13 orders that this company has placed.

How It Works – Adding a Command Button

Let's take a look at how the simple code behind our Search button works.

```
Private Sub cmdSearch_Click()

'Declare a string variable for our SQL statement
Dim strSQL As String

'Build the SQL statement
strSQL = "SELECT * FROM [Orders Qry] WHERE CustomerID = "
strSQL = strSQL & "'" & cmbCustomerID & "'"

'Open the Orders form and set its recordsource
'property to the SQL statement
DoCmd.OpenForm "Orders"
Forms!Orders.RecordSource = strSQL

End Sub
```

In case you're not familiar with VBA, all lines preceded by a single quotation mark are comment lines. The first statement after the comment line in the procedure simply declares a string variable to store the SQL statement that we are going to build to perform the search. We then commence to build this string.

As it's a string, it needs to be in quotation marks. Because we're using the Orders form to display the search output, we need to make sure that our SQL statement is based on the record source used for this form. That is, it needs to be a sub-set of the Access query Orders Qry.

> You can find out the record source for an Access form by inspecting the form's **RecordSource** property using the **Properties** window. If the form is in Design View, use the scroll bars to scroll below the bottom of the form, then click on a blank area of the window. This ensures that you see the form's properties.

Thus, the first part of our SQL statement is simply to select all the fields or columns from Orders Qry. Note that we need to enclose the query name in square brackets: this is because the name contains a space.

We then add a WHERE clause to the statement to limit the results to those where CustomerID is equal to the value selected in the combo box, cmbCustomerID. There are two things to note here. First, the value of CustomerID that we get from the combo box needs to be in (single) quotation marks. This is because CustomerID is actually a string variable (it's more normal to use integer variables for ID fields). Second, we're using the '&' symbol to concatenate (or link together) the different parts of our SQL statement.

Finally, the code then opens the Orders form and sets its RecordSource property to the SQL statement that has just been built.

The Recordsource Property

The RecordSource property is used to specify the source of the data for a form (or report). It can be a table name, a Query name, or a SQL statement. Normally, RecordSource property for the Orders form is set as the Access Query name, Orders Qry. Using our VBA procedure, we're setting the RecordSource property to a SQL statement instead, albeit one still based on Orders Qry.

In essence, the search is being carried out simply by us setting the RecordSource property of the Orders form to our SQL statement. It's worth noting that the change to the Orders RecordSource property via our search form is only temporary. If we subsequently open Orders from the main switchboard, its RecordSource property will revert to Orders Qry.

By way of example, if 'Alfreds Futterkiste' is selected as the customer to search on, the VB code generates the following string for strSQL:

```
SELECT * FROM [Order Qry] WHERE CustomerID = 'ALFKI'
```

'ALFKI' is, of course, the CustomerID for 'Alfreds Futterkiste'.

OK, so we've managed to build some very simple search functionality into Northwind using SQL in VBA code. We're now going to step up the pace significantly and exploit the skills we've learnt to build a more sophisticated search capability. This will allow us to cater for some of the more complex search scenarios that we discussed at the start of this Case Study.

Stage 2: Increasing the Search Sophistication

Here's a quick summary of what we are going to do next:

- ❑ Extend the search form so that it will allow users to search either Orders or Order Details, based on:
    - ❑ The customer who placed the order
    - ❑ The employee who took the order
    - ❑ The date of the order
    - ❑ The product ordered
    - ❑ The city that the order was shipped to
    - ❑ Any combination of the above
- ❑ Build two output forms to present the search results to the user: these will be built using the form wizard to minimize the need to spend too much time designing forms
- ❑ Link the output forms to the existing Northwind Orders form in the application

Try It Out - Extending the Search Form

1. Open up the search form in Design View. At this stage, you may want to autoformat it to a style of your liking. Use the Autoformat button on the Format menu toolbar to do this. It's also a good idea to remove the navigation buttons and dividing lines from the form, since they're not really needed: you can change these settings via the Format tab of the form's Properties window.

2. Add the controls shown in the table opposite to the form, starting underneath the cmbCustomerID control. In the case of the combo boxes, make sure that the controls wizard is activated on the toolbox; in the case of the control buttons, make sure that the controls wizard is de-activated. The form has three text boxes: we select these controls from the toolbox, then click on the form and position/resize them as appropriate. Note that there is no text box wizard.

Control Type	Name	Label	Columns	Special Instructions / Properties
Combo box	cmb EmployeeID	Employee	EmployeeID LastName	Hide key column
Combo box	cmbProduct ID	Product	ProductID ProductName	Hide key column
Text box	BeforeDate	Order Date Before	n/a	Format = Short Date Input Mask = 00/00/00;0;_
Text box	AfterDate	Order Date After	n/a	Format = Short Date Input Mask = 00/00/00;0;_
Text box	City	Ship City	n/a	
Button	cmdSearch1	View Order Summary	n/a	
Button	cmdSearch2	View Order Details	n/a	

3. As we no longer require the original **Search** button, this can be deleted from the form. Arrange the form so that it looks something like the one shown in the screenshot below:

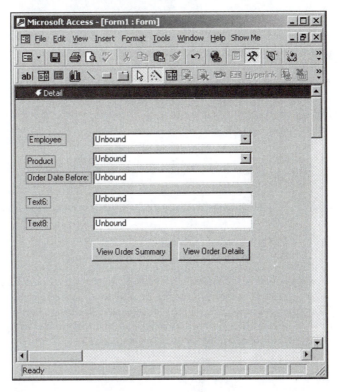

4. Now go to the Form View on the view menu.

5. We should find that the two combo boxes are populated. However, you'll see that the entries are not in alphabetical order. The reason for this is that, by default, the rows are sorted by the combo box's bound columns, `EmployeeID` and `ProductID` respectively.

6. To change their sort order, switch back to Design View. Select the `Empoyee` combo box and select its Row Source property from the Properties window.

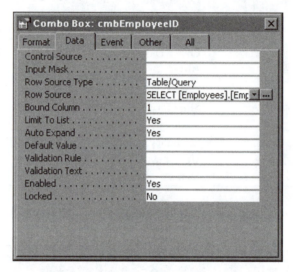

7. At the moment, the Row Source is set to the SQL statement:

```
SELECT Employees.EmployeeID, Employees.LastName FROM Employees;
```

We need to add an `ORDER BY` clause to end of this after `FROM Employees` and before the closing semicolon, as follows:

```
SELECT Employees.EmployeeID, Employees.LastName FROM Employees
ORDER BY Employees.LastName;
```

8. Similarly, change the Row Source property for the Product combo box to:

```
SELECT Products.ProductID, Products.ProductName FROM Products
ORDER BY Products.ProductName;
```

Note that we don't need to change the sort order for the `Customer` combo box. Recall that its bound column (`CustomerID`) happens to be a text field based on the company name, rather than an ID number. Strictly, this will not necessarily give proper ordering of `CompanyName` values. `CustomerID` values do not follow exactly the same order as `CompanyName` values. However, for the purposes of this chapter, we can ignore this.

9. Now close the Search form, saving your changes when prompted.

We still need to add some code to our new command buttons to make the form function, but we'll come back to this task a little later. For the moment, we're going to look at designing some output forms.

The Results Forms

In Stage 1, we simply took advantage of one of Northwind's built-in forms to present our simple search results. However, this is not an especially convenient way of presenting search results, since we can only see one result at a time. It would be much better if users were to see a list of results from their search, from which they could then link into the rest of Northwind.

As well as thinking about the format of the results, we also need to consider the actual data that we want to display in the results. In many cases, a list of orders will be sufficient. In other cases, however, we might want to see the order/product details, for example, when we want to know how much a particular customer has spent with us. We can't simply do this by looking at the Orders table because all of the pricing information is contained in the Order Details table. Our simplest strategy, therefore, is to design two results forms, one based on Orders and the other on Order Details. We can then let the user choose the output that they require. In both cases, we still need to take advantage of the fact that these source tables are related via the OrderID field. We'll see how we exploit this when to code up the all-important SQL statement that actually performs the search for us.

Unfortunately, none of the forms provided with Northwind are quite suitable for our needs, so we need to build some. Fortunately, Access comes with some fairly powerful wizards that make this task a breeze.

Try It Out – Building the Order Summary Form

1. The first form that we're going to build is simply based on the Orders table. From the Database Window, select **Tables** under the **Object** menu, then highlight the Order table.

2. From the menu bar, select **Insert | Form**. This opens the **New Form** wizard (there's also a toolbar button that launches the wizard).

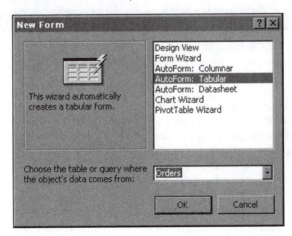

3. Make sure that the Orders table is selected in the drop-down list at the bottom of the dialog box, then select **Autoform: Tabular** and click **OK**. The wizard will now create a tabular form based on the Orders table.

4. Close the form (you may want to inspect it first, though), saving it as `OrderSummary`, when prompted for a name.

That's almost all there is to it! The wizard has done all the hard work for us. The reason that we've chosen a tabular form is so that we'll see a list of orders as the search results rather than one at a time. Of course, the layout may not be quite to your liking: in a real-life example, we might want to modify some of the wizard's design work. We're actually going to add one line of code to the form to allow the user to open up the built-in `Orders` form from `OrderSummary`.

5. Open up `OrderSummary` in **DesignView**. In the **Properties** window for the form, locate the 'Has Module' property (it's on the 'Other' tab) and make sure that this is set to 'Yes'. Without this, we can't add any code to the form.

6. With the form still selected, locate and select the form's 'On Dbl Click' property (on the **Event** tab). Click on the ellipsis to the right-hand side and select **Code Builder**. The VB editor will open. Add the following code:

```
Private Sub Form_DblClick(Cancel As Integer)
DoCmd.OpenForm "Orders", , , "OrderID = " & Me!OrderID
End Sub
```

7. To test the form, go to **Form View** on the **View** drop-down list.

8. Re-open `OrderSummary` in Form View. To the left of each record, there's a gray box, known as a record selector. If you click on one of these, an arrow head will be displayed in the box, showing you which record is selected. Try double-clicking a record selector! The `Orders` form should open, displaying information for the selected record.

We can now move on to designing our second results form.

Try It Out – Building the Order Details Summary Form

Again, we're going to use the Form Wizard to build this form. However, we're going to base our form on an Access Query. Recall the earlier discussion on Northwind Queries and, in particular, the Query `Order Details Extended`.

This query is used in a sub-form that resides within the `Orders` form to show product information. In particular, remember that the query contains a calculated field that works out the extended price of each product ordered based on `Unit Price`, `Quantity`, and `Discount`. As we want to be able to display this information in our search results, we need to base our results form on a similar query. `Order Details Extended` is actually slightly too complex for our needs since it displays information from `Products` as well, so we'll take a copy of it and modify it a little bit first.

1. From the Database Window, select **Queries** from the **Objects** menu and highlight the query Order Details Extended. Now select **Copy**, either from the **Edit** menu or using the toolbar **Copy** button. Next, select **Paste**. Access will prompt you for a new name for the copy: call it OrderDetailsExt (don't use any spaces).

2. Open up the copied query, OrderDetailsExt, in Design View. The top half of the query design grid shows two tables, Products and Order Details but we only need information from the latter. Click somewhere on the Products table, then press the *Delete* key on your keyboard. The Products table will disappear. Before exiting, it's worthwhile inspecting the SQL statement that forms this query (remember that you can do this by switching to **SQL View** from the **View** menu or toolbar button):

```
SELECT DISTINCTROW [Order Details].OrderID, [Order Details].ProductID,
[Order Details].UnitPrice, [Order Details].Quantity, [Order Details].Discount,
CCur([Order Details].[UnitPrice]*[Quantity]*(1-[Discount])/100)*100 AS
ExtendedPrice
FROM [Order Details] ORDER BY [Order Details].OrderID;
```

Bascially, we are selecting all the fields in the Order Details table and generating a calculated field called ExtendedPrice. Details of the ExtendedPrice calculation were given earlier in the chapter. The DISTINCTROW predicate used after the SELECT keyword is Access-specific and was probably introduced because early versions of Access did not support sub-queries. It should not be confused with the DISTINCT predicate, which is available in most versions of SQL. It is only significant when the Access Query includes a join and does not include output columns from all tables. In the above case, therefore, it could be removed without making any difference to the results.

3. Close the query, saving changes when prompted.

4. With this query still highlighted, fire up the form wizard via **Insert** menu or the toolbar button. Select **Autoform: Tabular**, just as we did when creating the OrderSummary form above.

5. If you inspect the form, you will see that it contains the Extended Price field. Save the form, calling it OrderDetailsSummary (again, don't use any spaces).

6. As it would be extremely useful to display a "totals" field for Extended Price, we need to do a little bit of modification to the form. Open the form in Design View. At the bottom of the form, you will see a form footer bar. Hover the mouse pointer near the bottom of this until you see a double-headed arrow, then click the mouse and drag down a little to display a portion of the footer.

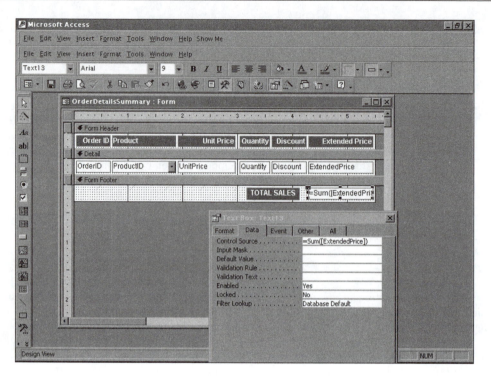

7. We now need to add a text box to the footer for our totals field. The easiest way to do this is to click on **Extended Price**, then **Text Box** in the **Detail** section of the form and click the **Copy** button on the Access toolbar. Now click back into the footer region and click **Paste**.

8. Drag the text box so that it lines up underneath **Extended Price**. We now need to change the `Control Source` property for the text box from `ExtendedPrice` to `=sum(ExtendedPrice)`. You can either do this from the **Properties** window for the text box or simply by clicking on the text box when it's already selected.

9. It's useful to add a label to the footer, either using the toolbox or by copying an exisiting label from the **Form Header** section to the **FormFooter** section. Set the label's **Caption** property to **Total Sales**.

10. As with the `OrderSummary` form, we can add a line of VB code so that the users can open up the `Orders` form by double-clicking on a record selector. We'll go through the instructions for this here again. In the **Properties** window for the Form, locate the **Has Module** property (it's on the **Other** tab) and make sure that this is set to 'Yes'. Without this, you can't add any code to the form.

11. With the form still selected, locate and select the form's **On Dbl Click** property (on the **Event** tab). Click on the ellipsis to the right-hand side and select **Code Builder**. The VB editor will open. Add the single line of code, as shown below:

```
Private Sub Form_DblClick(Cancel As Integer)
DoCmd.OpenForm "Orders", , , "OrderID = " & Me!OrderID
End Sub
```

12. Close the VB editor, then close the form, saving changes as you go.

13. Re-open `OrderDetaislSummary` in form view. Try double-clicking a record selector! The `Orders` form should open, displaying information for the selected record.

We've now finished designing our results forms and can turn our attention to coding the SQL statement that makes the link between the search criteria selected by the user and the output of the results.

The Final Step – Adding the Visual Basic Code

First of all, we'll show the code that needs to be added to the search form to make the search routine function, then we'll run through the code to show how works. The focus will be on the SQL statements that it constructs.

1. Open up our Search form in Design View.

2. Select the first of our command buttons, called cmdSearch1 and labeled View Order Summary. In the Properties window for the button, click on the On Click property under the Event tab, then click on the ellipsis that appears to the right-hand side, and select Code Builder.

3. Add the following lines of code in the VB Editor (recall that the VB Editor automatically puts in the first and last lines of the code shown).

```
Private Sub cmdSearch1_Click()

'Declare a string variable for our SQL statement
Dim strSQL As String

'Assign first part of SQL to string variable
strSQL = "SELECT Orders.* FROM Orders WHERE "

'Call the BuildWhereClause function to add the
'WHERE clause to the SQL statement
strSQL = strSQL & BuildWhereClause

'If something's been selected from the Product combo box
'add the ProductID sub-query to the statement
If Not IsNull(cmbProductID) Then
   strSQL = strSQL & "OrderID IN (SELECT OrderID FROM [Order Details]" & _
           " WHERE ProductID = " & cmbProductID & ")"
End If

'Tidy up the SQL statement by removing any residual AND
'Use some standard string functions to do this
If Right(strSQL, 4) = "AND " Then
   strSQL = Left(strSQL, Len(strSQL) - 4)
End If

'If our SQL string ends in WHERE then no search criteria have been selected
'Tell the user and exit without doing a search
If Right(strSQL, 6) = "WHERE " Then
   MsgBox "No search criteria selected!", vbInformation
   Exit Sub
End If
```

```
'Show the user the SQL statement that's been constructed
'based on their Search criteria
MsgBox strSQL

'Open the OrderSummary form and set its recordsource
'property to the SQL statement that's been built
DoCmd.OpenForm "OrderSummary"
Forms!OrderSummary.RecordSource = strSQL

End Sub
```

4. Exit the VB Editor, then repeat instruction 2, this time for the other command button, named cmdSearch2, and labeled View Order Details.

5. Add the following lines of code in the VB editor:

```
Private Sub cmdSearch2_Click()
'Declare a string variable for our SQL statement
Dim strSQL As String

'Start building SQL statement using INNER JOIN between
'OrderDetailsExt query and Orders table
strSQL = "SELECT OrderDetailsExt.* FROM Orders" & _
    " INNER JOIN OrderDetailsExt ON " & _
    "Orders.OrderID = OrderDetailsExt.OrderID WHERE "

'Call the BuildWhereClause function to add the
'WHERE clause to the SQL statement
strSQL = strSQL & BuildWhereClause

'If something's been selected from the Product combo box
'add include it as part of the WHERE clause
If Not IsNull(cmbProductID) Then
  strSQL = strSQL & "ProductID = " & cmbProductID
End If

'Tidy up the SQL statement by removing any residual AND
'Use some standard string functions to do this
If Right(strSQL, 4) = "AND " Then
  strSQL = Left(strSQL, Len(strSQL) - 4)
End If

'If our SQL string ends in WHERE then no search criteria have been selected
'Tell the user and exit without doing a search
If Right(strSQL, 6) = "WHERE " Then
  MsgBox "No search criteria selected!", vbInformation
  Exit Sub
End If

'Show the user the SQL statement that's been constructed
'based on their Search criteria
MsgBox strSQL

'Open the OrderDetailsSummary form and set its recordsource
'property to the SQL statement
DoCmd.OpenForm "OrderDetailsSummary"
Forms!OrderDetailsSummary.RecordSource = strSQL

End Sub
```

6. Before closing the VB editor, we now need to add some code for the `BuildWhereClause` function that both of the above sub-procedures call. Click the mouse at the end of the last `End Sub` statement, then press the *Enter* key a couple of times. Now add the following code:

```
Private Function BuildWhereClause() As String

'This function builds a WHERE clause for SQL statement
'based on selections made on Search form. Uses AND to combine
'selections
'Declare string variable to store the WHERE bits
Dim strWHERE As String

'If a Customer has been selected, add this to WHERE clause
If Not IsNull(cmbCustomerID) Then
  strWHERE = "CustomerID = '" & cmbCustomerID & "' AND "
End If

'And now with Employee
If Not IsNull(cmbEmployeeID) Then
  strWHERE = strWHERE & "EmployeeID = " & cmbEmployeeID & " AND "
End If

'Add Date criteria
If Not IsNull(BeforeDate) Then
  strWHERE = strWHERE & "OrderDate < #" & BeforeDate & "# AND "
End If

If Not IsNull(AfterDate) Then
  strWHERE = strWHERE & "OrderDate > #" & AfterDate & "# AND "
End If

'Add ability to search on ShipCity field
'Uses LIKE to allow partial string search
If Not IsNull(City) Then
  strWHERE = strWHERE & "ShipCity LIKE '" & City & "' AND "
End If

BuildWhereClause = strWHERE

End Function
```

7. Finally, close down the VB editor and close the **Search** form, making sure that you save your changes when prompted.

Our Northwind search functionality is now built and ready to go! Before we explain how the code works, perhaps it's a good idea to test out the search form.

Testing the Search Functionality

Open the search form in **Form View**. Select **Around the Horn** on the **Customer** combo box and click on **View Order Summary**. First, a message box is displayed that shows you the SQL statement that is about to be used as the record source for the `OrderSummary` form, as shown:

When you click **OK** , the `OrderSummary` form will open and you should see 13 records listed, all relating to orders for **Around the Horn**. Note that two of the orders shown, 10768 and 10793 were taken by Janet Leverling.

Close the results form. Now search for orders where the customer is again 'Around the Horn' and the Employee is 'Leverling':

This time the `OrderSummary` form only displays two orders, as expected.

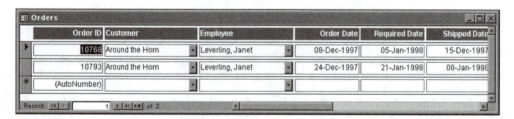

Test out other search criteria, for example, looking for orders that fell between certain dates, or orders that were shipped to London. The **Ship City** search criterion was included to demonstrate the use of wildcards in SQL using the `LIKE` keyword (we'll see more on this in a moment).

For example, we can use the * character as a wildcard. Thus, if we enter 'L*' in the **Ship City** box, we will see results for all orders that were shipped to places beginning with the letter L. (Note that in SQL Server, we use the % sign as the wildcard in `LIKE` clauses rather than an asterisk).

So far, so good! But what about the two search scenarios we discussed at the start of the case study? Let's take a quick look at these.

Customers and Products

In the first scenario, we wanted to see a list of all the customers who had ordered a particular product. We'll take a look to see who's ordered Aniseed Syrup in the past. Simply select this product from the appropriate combo box (make sure all other boxes are cleared), then click on View Order Summary. In the results form, we should see 13 records, as shown in the following screenshot:

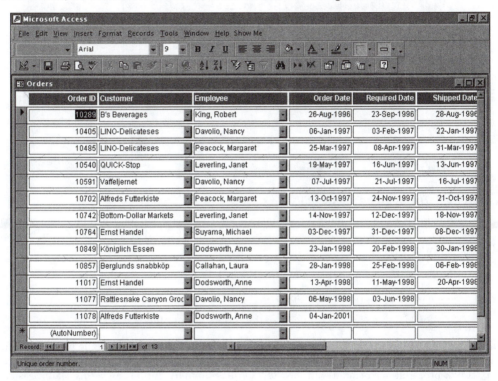

Don't forget that we can double-click on the record selector for any of the orders listed to open up the Orders form. From here, you'll be able to confirm that Aniseed Syrup was, indeed, part of the order. OK, perhaps there's nothing too surprising in this. But then remember that we're displaying information here from the Orders table and that table doesn't contain any product information. The trick here, of course, is in the SQL statement that we've used. When searching the Orders table, it actually carries out what's known as a sub-query on the OrderDetails table looking for every OrderID where the product was Aniseed Syrup. We'll say a bit more about this methodology in a moment.

Money Spent

In the second scenario, a customer wanted to know how much money they'd spent with us. Here, we'll select Alfreds Futterkiste as the customer. To make things a bit more interesting, let's say we only want to see what's been spent from 1998 onwards, so enter 12/31/97 in the Order Date After box. Once you've made your selection, click on the View Order Details button. You should now see eight records listed in the output form, along with a Total Sales value at the bottom of the form:

How It Works – The Search Functionality

It's now time to take a look at the VB code that we added to our search form via the two command buttons! As in the very simple example that we started with, this code is really very straightforward. In effect, this is what it does:

❑ Builds a SQL statement based on the criteria selected on the search form

❑ Opens the appropriate results form

❑ Sets the RecordSource property of the results form to the SQL statement

In the first step, we saw that the second two steps are easy and only take a couple of lines of code. It's the first step that's the most complex part of the operation, so let's take a closer look. We'll start with the On_Click procedure associated with the View Order Summary button, since this is a bit easier, at least to start with.

The View Order Summary Code

The first line of code in the procedure is simply to set up a string variable, strSQL, to hold the SQL statement as we build it up.

```
'Declare a string variable for our SQL statement
Dim strSQL As String

'Assign first part of SQL to string variable
strSQL = "SELECT Orders.* FROM Orders WHERE "

'Call the BuildWhereClause function to add the
'WHERE clause to the SQL statement
strSQL = strSQL & BuildWhereClause
```

Next, we assign some text to `strSQL`. This text forms the first part of the SELECT statement and simply states that we're going to select all the fields from the Orders table. Hopefully, nothing too complicated here. It makes sense to get records from this table since our OrderSummary results form was derived from it initially. Note that the code also adds a WHERE clause to the SELECT statement. Clearly, we need this condition as we are carrying out a search.

In the third line of code, we add the missing bits of the WHERE clause by calling the function `BuildWhereClause`. Remember that we added the code for this after we'd added code for the two command buttons. This function returns a string value, which has the form:

```
Criterion1 = x AND Criterion2 = y AND Criterion3 = z ...
```

The use of AND means that all the selected criteria need to be met. For example, depending on what's been selected on the **Search** form, it might return:

```
CustomerID = 'ALFKI' AND EmployeeID = 3 AND
```

Ultimately, when this string has been added to the rest of the SQL statement and has been tidied up, the **OrdersSummary** form will open to display only those records where both CustomerID is ALFKI and EmployeeID = 3. Thus, the BuildWhereClause function returns the missing bits of our WHERE clause and these get added on to our strSQL string. We'll examine the code for this function in a few moments.

The next three lines of code in our `cmdSearch1_Click` procedure are probably the most complicated to understand.

```
'If something's been selected from the Product combo box
'add the ProductID sub-query to the statement
If Not IsNull(cmbProductID) Then
  strSQL = strSQL & "OrderID IN (SELECT OrderID FROM [Order Details]" & _
          " WHERE ProductID = " & cmbProductID & ")"
End If
```

The first line, the If statement, checks to see if a Product has been selected on the **Search** form (remember that the Product combo box is called cmbProductID). If nothing's been selected (that is, the value of this combo box is Null), then nothing is done and the procedure moves on to the next statement. On the other hand, if something has been selected in the Product combo box, another chunk of SQL is added to the WHERE clause of our existing SELECT statement.

Here's something in VB that may cause confusion. If you look at the line of code between the If
... End If construction in the snippet above, it actually looks like there are two lines of code!
To make it easier to read long lines of code, the VB editor allows you to chop them up into two or
more shorter lines, as long as you use a space followed by the underscore character at the end of each
line that you've broken. The next line doesn't need any special characters in front of it.

However, if it's a string that we're breaking up, as in the above example, we need to terminate and
restart the string using quotation marks and place an ampersand (&) character before the
underscore. Things can get a bit confusing when then string variable that we're building up already
contains quotation marks!

But hang on a minute, part of it looks remarkably like another SELECT statement! Well, in fact it is. Indeed, it's part of the sub-query that we mentioned when we tested out the Search form earlier on. To help us understand what's happening, let's look back at the 'Aniseed Syrup' order search again.

Before the results form opened, we will have seen the following message box:

Let's take a quick look at how this has worked:

❑ First, take a look at the part in parentheses. This is a straightforward SELECT statement that returns all the OrderID values from the Order Details table where the ProductID is 3 (that is, the ProductName is 'Aniseed Syrup'). Think of this result as a 'set' of OrderID values or, if you prefer, a virtual table containing OrderID values.

❑ Second, consider the main SELECT statement. This returns records from Orders where the OrderID is in the set of OrderID values returned by the bracketed part of the SQL statement. In other words, it returns all of the records from Orders where the OrderID has the same values of those in the virtual table.

Using this methodology, therefore, we can select the appropriate order information from the Orders table based on a ProductID even though Orders contains no product information. We might wonder why we couldn't use a join to do this instead! Well, we could have done but this was a good opportunity to see a sub-query in action. The 'View Order Details' button, which we'll look at in a minute, does use a join to build its SQL statement.

The next three lines of code in the procedure use some standard string functions to check if there is a rogue AND at the end of strSQL: if there is, this gets stripped out.

```
'Tidy up the SQL statement by removing any residual AND
'Use some standard string functions to do this
If Right(strSQL, 4) = "AND " Then
  strSQL = Left(strSQL, Len(strSQL) - 4)
End If
```

There are then three further lines of code to see if strSQL ends with WHERE. If it does, this means that no search criteria have been selected, so the routine is exited, and the user informed. Otherwise, a message box opens that shows the value of strSQL. This is useful since we can see the SQL statement that's being used. In a real-life example, we probably wouldn't want to include this.

Finally, the procedure opens the OrderSummary form and sets its record source property to strSQL.

```
'If our SQL string ends in WHERE then no search criteria have been selected
'Tell the user and exit without doing a search
If Right(strSQL, 6) = "WHERE " Then
  MsgBox "No search criteria selected!", vbInformation
  Exit Sub
End If
```

```
'Show the user the SQL statement that's been constructed
'based on their Search criteria
MsgBox strSQL

'Open the OrderSummary form and set its recordsource
'property to the SQL statement that's been built
DoCmd.OpenForm "OrderSummary"
Forms!OrderSummary.RecordSource = strSQL
```

The BuildWhereClause Function

We need to take a quick look at the code for the `BuildWhereClause` function. We won't examine all of it since it's quite repetitive. We'll just take a look at a couple of snippets.

Recall the function builds up the various criteria in for the WHERE clause based on selections made by the user on the Search form. The string variable `strWHERE` is used to store the WHERE clause as it is built up. From the following snippet, we can see that `OrderDate > some date` will be added to the WHERE clause if something has been entered in the `AfterDate` box. The actual format that needs to be used is `OrderDate > '#31/12/00#'`. Note the use of the # marks around date: the use of these symbols is an Access peculiarity!

```
If Not IsNull(AfterDate) Then
    strWHERE = strWHERE & "OrderDate > #" & AfterDate & "# AND "
End If
```

Similarly, if something's been entered in ShipCity, the SQL WHERE clause will include `ShipCity LIKE 'Birmingham'`. The word LIKE has been used rather than = to allow the use of wildcards when searching for information. The use of wildcards is not limited to Access.

```
'Add ability to search on ShipCity field
'Uses LIKE to allow partial string search
If Not IsNull(City) Then
    strWHERE = strWHERE & "ShipCity LIKE '" & City & "' AND "
End If
```

Finally, the `BuildWhereClause` function is assigned the value `strWHERE` in order to return the WHERE clause to the calling procedure:

```
BuildWhereClause = strWHERE
```

The Code for View Order Details Summary

We now finish the case study by taking a look at the code behind the command button labeled View Order Details. As the bulk of the code is very similar to that used for the View Order Summary button, we'll only examine the differences.

```
'Start building SQL statement using INNER JOIN between
'OrderDetailsExt query and Orders table
strSQL = "SELECT OrderDetailsExt.* FROM Orders" & _
    " INNER JOIN OrderDetailsExt ON " & _
    "Orders.OrderID = OrderDetailsExt.OrderID WHERE "
```

In this case, the output form, `OrderDetailsSummary`, is based on the query `OrderDetailsExt`. Thus, our `SELECT` statement needs to be selecting columns or fields from this query. Further, as some of the fields we're searching on actually come from the `Orders` table, we need to use an inner join between the `OrderDetailsExt` query and the `Orders` table.

The procedure then uses the `BuildWhereClause` function as previously before adding a `ProductID` criterion (if required). Unlike the previous sub-procedure, there's no need to use a sub-query as `ProductID` is one of the columns in the `OrderDetailsExt` query:

```
'Call the BuildWhereClause function to add the
'WHERE clause to the SQL statement
strSQL = strSQL & BuildWhereClause

'If something's been selected from the Product combo box
'add include it as part of the WHERE clause
If Not IsNull(cmbProductID) Then
  strSQL = strSQL & "ProductID = " & cmbProductID
End If
```

The remainder of the sub-procedure is almost identical to one used for the **View Order Summary** button, with the exception that the name of the form it opens is, of course, different.

Finally, it is worth mentioning that much of the VBA that we have covered in this case study is not limited to Access. The coding of SQL statements, in particular, is readily transferable to other frontends such as Visual Basic and Active Server Pages.

Summary

In this appendix, we have examined the schema for the Northwind database in some detail, and gained insight into how the process of placing an order in the Access version of Northwind actually works. We also looked at the importance of intersection tables, and looked at the intersection table between the `Orders` and `Products` tables.

Next, we turned our attention to some of the queries that are used in Northwind. Further, we delved into the SQL statements behind these objects.

Finally, we exploited some of the things we had learned about Northwind by developing a search engine for the database. This gave us further exposure to the power of even fairly simple SQL statements. Along the way, we learned some Access skills. The most important of these was how to use VBA to code and to apply SQL statements within Access.

BeginningSQLBeginningSQLBeginningSQL
Dot Dot
Dash
Dash
Dot
DotDo

Introduction to DCL
Data Control/Security

SQL has three divisions of language elements:

- ❑ **DDL** (Data Definition Language) – used to create tables, database objects, and so on (CREATE TABLE, ALTER TABLE, etc.)
- ❑ **DML** (Data Manipulation Language) – used, as the name implies, to *manipulate* data in your database (SELECT, INSERT, UPDATE, etc.)
- ❑ **DCL** (Data Control Language) – used to control *access* to data.

It is the third of these, DCL, that we will be focusing on in this appendix.

I was watching a television program the other night about the National Security Agency (NSA). It caught my eye because I, like many of us who work daily on the Internet, am concerned about the issues of freedom and privacy on the Internet, and what my government might plan to do about it. Of course, many people have heard the various rumors of "domestic espionage". You may have heard that the NSA listens in on Internet traffic; in fact, they admit that they do. And they add that it is necessary to National Security. Why is this? Because of what the Internet is.

The Internet has had effects that are only just beginning to be felt in the world. One of these effects is that the infrastructure of developed nations now includes a large portion that is comprised of computer networks linked to, and linked through, the Internet. The nature of the Internet is one of sharing; that is, that machines have *access* to one another. Now, millions of computers all over the world have access to computer systems all over the rest of the world. Within a ten-year span of time, the doors to the computing infrastructures of the world have been opened wide.

Who hasn't, in some way, been affected by an Internet virus? How often do you hear, or read in the papers, about some white-collar criminal who broke into a computer system and stole a whole bunch of money, simply by changing some numbers? Most money in the world today exists only as numbers stored in computers, and most of these computers are connected to the Internet, at least in some way. Not only that, but a sizeable (and rapidly growing) portion of the world economy is dependent upon the Internet. There are plenty of hackers out there who like to break into systems and play around with them, for lots of reasons. So, you can certainly see that security has become of paramount importance.

As an Internet server may host as many as millions of user sessions a day, the traditional client-server way of handling things has had to be re-designed. For example, prior to the advent of the World-Wide Web, the typical network database application served a relatively small number of clients, and security was handled largely from the Operating System. Permissions were much simpler: they could be broadly assigned to individual users, as in the illustration below:

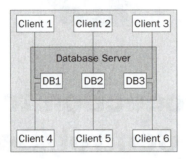

In this model, each client had a separate logon, and permissions could be assigned individually to the user, according to that user's *Role* in the organization. The number and kind of permissions were relatively small – after all, the network was physically self-contained, in most instances. Nobody could break in unless they were physically on one of the machines in that network.

The Internet changed everything, though. Within a short period of time, millions of computers worldwide were linked together, sharing data and files in a variety of ways. There were a whole slew of forthcoming new technologies for sharing information and *access* to a server computer. Along with these came a host of new kinds of permissions, and as security issues arose and were dealt with, the permissions became both more complex, and more specific. You could assign more and more specific and detailed kinds of permissions on more and more objects and services on your computer, for a larger and more varied group of logins.

The capability of sharing logins was still a viable method for a large variety of Internet services, and is still used, in fact. For example, when you use your browser to view a web page, your browser has to log on to the web server. It uses the Anonymous Internet User account on the server, for which specific permissions are granted. However, new technologies and methods have had to be developed to handle the ever-growing load of clients and users accessing the servers.

Finally, the Internet is a large network of small networks, made up of smaller networks, and so on. Remote management technologies such as Microsoft Active Directory have made it possible to manage every aspect of a subnet (a Network within a Network), and even an entire Domain (a group of computers and subnets that are networked together in such a way that all permissions and messaging services for the network are managed centrally) from a single location, *or* from multiple locations. In fact, not only the computers, but also the entire Business Organization/Enterprise can be managed "remotely" – "remotely" is becoming a meaningless term very quickly.

Put all of these requirements together, and you're left with a security nightmare of monumental proportions. Take Windows 2000 Server, for example. *Every* aspect of the Operating System, from the files and folders to the individual portions of the System Registry, is highly configurable regarding security. To get to the Security settings for a *single file* on my computer, I have to right-click on the file, select **Properties**, click the **Security** tab, and bring up the **Access Control Settings** dialog. From here, I am able to view the individual login permissions for the file, as shown opposite.

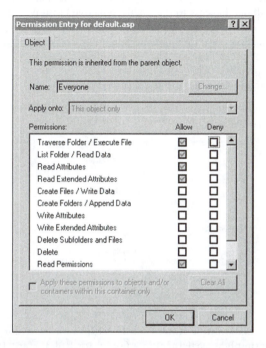

Now, in order to deal with such a complexity of security rules and regulations, and such a large variety and type of users who might be accessing a server, the concept of *grouping* individual user accounts into groups that represented *Roles*, and shared the same set of permissions came into being. After all, the types of activity that an individual user might perform could be fairly easily categorized, depending on the *Role* of the user in the organization.

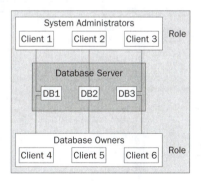

Users and Roles

The idea of Roles is born out of Set Theory (see Chapter 13 for more on Set Theory). Just as the computers of the Internet, which share the same backbone, can be divided and sub-divided into subnets, which are *sets* of computers, users and logins in an organization can also be divided and sub-divided into logical sets of related functionality, and therefore, security.

By this, we mean that roles can be defined by the activities the members can carry out. For instance, the financial department will need access to the highly sensitive employee salary information, whereas the sales department and customer service department should not be able to view this information. So, there is a role that allows access to the financial data, allocated only to those with the authority to see the sensitive information, and other roles that do not allow access to the financial data for those who do not have the authority to view it. This further enforces security, as the "wrong" people should never be allocated to the role that allows access to the sensitive information.

Consider the following chart, depicting the same database application as the one above, but with the users grouped into logical Roles:

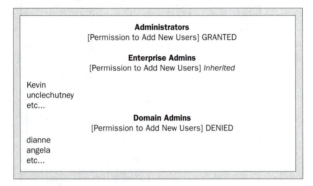

By assigning a set of permissions to a Role, security settings for individual logins don't have to be explicitly set. A User is simply a participant in a Group (or Role). Here, for example, is a screenshot of a listing of Users and Groups on my local machine:

Each Group has a specific set of permissions set for that Group. A Group can have as many members as desired. When a User login is joined to a Group, it inherits the permission settings of that Group. A single User login can belong to as many Groups as desired, and inherits the permissions granted/denied to those groups.

Even Groups can be joined to other Groups. When a Group is joined to another Group, it inherits the permissions of that Group, along with its own. In this way, an entire hierarchy of Groups and Users can be created, and tweaked in any way that you wish, as conveniently as possible. For example, the built-in Windows 2000 Administrators group has a broad variety of permissions assigned to it. When a Windows 2000 server is promoted to Domain controller, several new Groups are created, such as Domain Admins, and Enterprise Admins. Rather than reassigning this broad range of permissions to these new groups, Windows 2000 simply joins them to the Administrators group, thereby endowing them with all the privileges afforded to the Administrators. Then additional permissions for these groups are added if desired. Consider the following chart, which shows three different Security Groups on my local system:

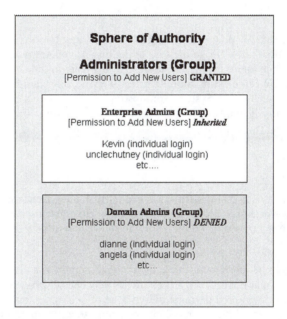

OK, I'm introducing a new concept here. Notice that the Administrators group has two child groups: **Domain Admins** and **Enterprise Admins**. Permission to Add new Users is GRANTED to the Administrators group. This means that the Enterprise Admins group *inherits* the permission from the Administrators group. The Domain Admins group has this permission DENIED, but they also belong to the Administrators group, for which this permission is GRANTED. So, what is their permission setting regarding this? DENIED.

Now, operating systems have quite a bit more to them in terms of Security and Permissions than a database server, so we're not going to go into that any deeper. What I've been trying to do is to show you a model to which you can relate database security and DCL. If, for instance, you change the above chart to read like the following:

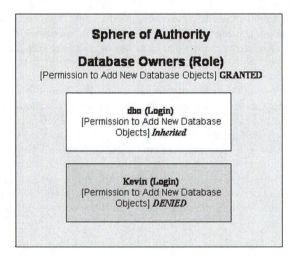

Of course, the biggest obvious difference is that there aren't any Groups inside other Groups (sure makes things easier, doesn't it?). No, in the case of databases, you are dealing with **Roles** and **Logins**. A Role can support multiple logins (as the Database Owners Role in the chart above supports the dbo and Kevin logins), and a login can exist in multiple roles: "Kevin", for example, might exist in both the "Database Owners" Role, and the "System Administrators" Role. Again, however, note the **precedence of Authorization**: if a user is in a Role that explicitly GRANTS permission to do something, the user inherits that right, unless it is explicitly DENIED. Also, if the user's individual permissions GRANT a privilege, belonging to a Role that doesn't GRANT it doesn't restrain the permission; however, DENYing it would. In other words:

> **Permissions are inherited, unless they are explicitly denied. DENIED always overrides GRANTED. However, *unless otherwise DENIED*, inherited permissions and explicit permissions (those granted on an individual basis) remain intact.**

Let's go through it again: all permissions must be *explicitly granted* to a given login, or that login doesn't have them. That means that if a user doesn't explicitly *have* certain privileges, and that user is added to a Role that does, that user *is* granted permission by virtue of belonging to that Group. However, if that User is either explicitly denied that permission, or belongs to any Group that explicitly denies that permission, it doesn't matter if that User belongs to a Group that has that permission: that User is denied. In other words, **the more restrictive permissions acting upon a user login are the ones that apply.**

Special Users and Roles

In SQL, Roles and Logins are referred to as **AuthorizationID**s. The "Special Users and Roles" that this section refers to are not actually Users or Roles, but *Scalar Functions* in SQL that return values, just as, for example, the Temporal Scalar function CURRENT_TIMESTAMP returns a Timestamp data type with a value of the current date/time. It may be easier to think of them as Users and Roles, rather than functions, in this case, as that is what they return:

User or Role (Scalar Function)	Definition
USER	The Current User.
CURRENT_USER	The Current User – Same as USER.
SESSION_USER	The SQL-Session User – the differences between this and CURRENT_USER are highly technical, and really beyond the scope of this book. In almost all cases, this is functionally the same as CURRENT_USER.
SYSTEM_USER	The Operating System user login that logged on to use the SQL Server. This varies from one provider to another.
CURRENT_ROLE	The AuthorizationID of the Current Role. If the user is not logged in as a Role, it returns NULL.

Note: You're not likely to be using any of these other than the first two; these are synonymous. The other three are for more specialized purposes, and not used often, mostly because the value of each of them can change from one provider to another.

Privileges and Objects

At this point, then, we are talking about Users and Roles. We now also need to talk about *permissions*, or *privileges*, which belong to those Users or Roles. Those permissions pertain to certain kinds of *actions* on certain kinds of *objects*.

A **Privilege Specification** consists of the name of the Privilege, which describes an action, such as SELECT, INSERT, DELETE, and so on, and the name of the *Object* for which the Privilege is granted.

```
<privileges> ::=
<object privileges> ON <Object Name>

    <Object Name> ::=
    [ TABLE ] <table name> |
    DOMAIN <Domain name> |
    CHARACTER SET >Character set name> |
    COLLATION <Collation name> |
    TRANSLATION <Translation name> |
    TYPE {<UDT name> | typed <table name> |
    <specific routine designator>

    Object Privileges ::=
    ALL PRIVILEGES |
    <action> [ {, <action>}... ]

        <action> ::=
        DELETE |
        SELECT [ (<Column name> [ {,<Column name>}... ]) ] |
        INSERT [ (<Column name> [ {,<Column name>}... ]) ] |
        UPDATE [ (<Column name> [ {,<Column name>}... ]) ] |
        REFERENCES [ (<Column name> [ {,<Column name>}... ]) ] |
        TRIGGER |
        UNDER |
        USAGE |
        EXECUTE
```

619

For example, consider the following SQL statement:

```
GRANT SELECT
ON Products
TO Kevin
```

The Privilege being granted is SELECT. The object it is being granted for is the table Products. It is being granted to the Kevin login account. The Privilege Specification is SELECT ON Products. If you were to think of this SQL statement as an English sentence, the GRANT part would be an imperative (command) verb, with the object of the verb being SELECT ON Products, and the indirect object being Kevin. And, as you may remember from the first section of this appendix, Kevin is a User login. Now, let's try that in plain English:

"Grant the privilege to SELECT data from the Products table to Kevin."

And that brings us to the next section.

Data Control Language Syntax

Most Data Control SQL statements have three basic parts to them:

- ❑ **Action** – GRANT, REVOKE
- ❑ **Privilege Specification** – SELECT, INSERT, DELETE, UPDATE, etc.
- ❑ **User Login** – User or Role

As you can see, the second and third bullet points correspond to the first two sections of this Appendix – hopefully by now you should be able to understand exactly what they're doing.

GRANT

Obviously, this is used to grant privileges to a User or Role. Let's take a look at the basic syntax:

```
<grant privilege statement> ::=
GRANT <privileges> TO <grantee> [ {,<grantee>}... ]
[ WITH HIERARCHY OPTION ] [WITH GRANT OPTION]
[ FROM grantor ]

    <grantee> ::= PUBLIC | <AuthorizationID>
    <grantor> ::= CURRENT_USER | CURRENT_ROLE
```

As you can see, it is basically the same as our earlier example, but with the addition of a couple of *options*:

```
GRANT SELECT
ON Products
WITH GRANT OPTION
TO Kevin
```

I've modified our earlier example to include the WITH GRANT OPTION optional clause. This enables Kevin to GRANT this privilege to others.

The WITH HIERARCHY OPTION option is not yet widely supported, but what it does is to cascade the privilege granted on a given typed table to all of its subtables.

The GRANT ROLE statement does the same thing as the GRANT PRIVILEGE statement, but grants a role rather than a privilege.

```
<grant role statement> ::=
GRANT <Role Name> [ {,<Role Name>}... ] TO <grantee> [ {,<grantee>}... ]
[ WITH ADMIN OPTION ]
[ FROM grantor ]

   <grantee> ::= PUBLIC | <AuthorizationID>
   <grantor> ::= CURRENT_USER | CURRENT_ROLE
```

The WITH ADMIN OPTION option is the equivalent of the WITH GRANT OPTION for the GRANT PRIVILEGES statement; it enables the grantee to grant that role to other users.

REVOKE

The REVOKE statement is nearly identical to the GRANT statement, as it revokes the same privileges from the same User/Role that the GRANT Statement GRANTs to them. One important note: only the original grantor of the privileges can REVOKE them.

```
<revoke privilege statement> ::=
REVOKE [ {GRANT OPTION FOR | HIERARCHY OPTION FOR} ]
<privileges> FROM <grantee> [ {,<grantee>}... ]
[ FROM {CURRENT_USER | CURRENT_ROLE} ]
{RESTRICT | CASCADE}

<revoke role statement> ::=
REVOKE [ {ADMIN OPTION FOR } ] <Role Name> [ {,<Role Name>}... ]
FROM <grantee> [ {,<grantee>}... ]
[ FROM {CURRENT_USER | CURRENT_ROLE} ]
{RESTRICT | CASCADE}

REVOKE SELECT
ON Products
FROM Kevin
RESTRICT
```

The above statement revokes all SELECT ON Products permissions for Kevin.

Notice that you can revoke either the privilege itself, or just an option.

```
REVOKE GRANT OPTION FOR SELECT
ON Products
TO Kevin
CASCADE
```

This one only revokes the right for Kevin to GRANT this permission to someone else.

The last part of the statement (RESTRICT | CASCADE) requires a bit of introduction. As you recall, you can GRANT privileges with the option to allow the grantee the privilege of being able to grant these privileges to others. But what happens when you GRANT a privilege to a given User, and that User GRANTS the same privilege to another User, and you go to REVOKE the privilege from the first user?

What happens to the second user? Well, it all depends on which of these two options you use in your SQL Statement.

CASCADE indicates that the revocation of the privilege will CASCADE to all users who were GRANTed that privilege *by* the grantee. In other words, if I GRANT you SELECT privilege for the Products table of the Northwind product catalog, and you GRANT it to Joe Beets, when I REVOKE the privilege FROM you, it REVOKES Joe Beets' privilege as well.

RESTRICT indicates that if there are any "orphaned" Users or Roles as a result of my revocation, it will not succeed. If RESTRICT is used, you must REVOKE all "dependent" privileges before you can REVOKE the privileges of the immediate "target." In our example, for instance, I would not be able to REVOKE your privilege until Joe Beets' privilege was revoked as well.

Let's first take a look at a couple of SQL Statements (versions of the earlier ones) that use these terms, and what happens as a result:

```
REVOKE SELECT
ON Products
FROM Kevin
RESTRICT
```

The above statement revokes all SELECT ON Products permissions for Kevin. If Kevin has GRANTed this privilege to others, the query would fail. Only if Kevin hasn't GRANTed SELECT ON Products permission to anyone else may this permission be revoked.

```
REVOKE GRANT OPTION FOR SELECT
ON Products
TO Kevin
CASCADE
```

In this case, the privilege to GRANT SELECT On Products permission is taken away (revoked) from Kevin. If Kevin has GRANTed this permission to others, the revocation will CASCADE to the others, and their privileges will also be revoked.

The reason for this last part of the statement is obvious when you think about it: only the grantor can REVOKE a privilege that he/she has granted. If his/her permission to GRANT/REVOKE privileges is removed, the privilege for the dependent Users (those to whom he/she granted the privilege) would never lose it. In fact, the only way that the privilege could be REVOKED would be if their User account were deleted, in which case the database would "clean up all the leftovers" (remove all privileges and options granted by the User that was removed) So, the REVOKE statement requires you to either CASCADE the revocation, or not be able to perform it until all dependencies are resolved.

Creating/Dropping Users and Roles

There are a couple of other syntactical elements of the Data Control Language of SQL which bear mentioning at least. These are the CREATE ROLE and DROP ROLE statements. Neither of these statements are parts of core SQL, nor are they well supported by any DBMS that I know of, except for Oracle. The reason for this is that how Users and Roles are created and managed by a given DBMS varies widely. This is also the reason that there is no such thing as a CREATE USER or DROP USER function in SQL.

Most DBMSs that support SQL and have security built into them also support some localized flavor of these statements.

SQL Server

SQL Server has a number of built-in Stored Procedures for managing Logins:

- **sp_addlogin 'login'** – Add a new SQL Server login
- **sp_droplogin login'** – Drop (remove) a login created by sp_addlogin
- **sp_grantlogin 'login'** – Grant SQL Server login privilege to an NT User or Group
- **sp_denylogin 'login'** – Deny SQL Server login privilege to an NT User or Group

For example, the following adds a login with the name 'Kevin'

```
EXEC sp_addlogin 'Kevin'
```

Oracle

Oracle is the closest to ANSI SQL in this regard:

```
CREATE_ROLE 'role' { [ NOT ] IDENTIFIED | IDENTIFIED BY 'password'| IDENTIFED
GLOBALLY | EXTERNALLY } - Creates a new DB role.
DROP ROLE 'role' - Drops a DB role.
```

For example, the following creates a new role named 'Kevin' with a password of 'mypassword'

```
CREATE ROLE 'Kevin' IDENTIFIED BY 'mypassword'
```

MySQL

MySQL is just as bad as SQL Server when it comes to creating and dropping Roles in SQL. In fact, there is no direct syntax in MySQL for creating and dropping roles. To do so in MySQL, you can use the GRANT statement, with a new Login name, which creates a new user. Or, you can perform an INSERT statement on the Database's Users table.

The following creates a new login (User) from an OS login account named 'Kevin'. The login account has all privileges for all database objects, but must log in with the password 'mypassword.'

```
GRANT ALL PRIVILEGES ON *.* TO Kevin@localhost IDENTIFIED BY 'mypassword' WITH
GRANT OPTION
GRANT ALL PRIVILEGES ON *.* TO Kevin@"%" IDENTIFIED BY 'mypassword' WITH GRANT
OPTION;
```

Access

Even Access can be manipulated in this way, although it's not easy to do. For example, to use SQL to create a User or Role in Access (or actually, to perform any DCL function in Access), you would have to be using the Jet Data Provider directly, not via ODBC, and you have to use ADO. Don't ask me why, but the syntax is fairly simple:

```
CREATE USER (or CREATE GROUP) username password
```

The following also creates a User (Login) with the name 'Kevin' and the password 'mypassword':

```
CREATE USER 'Kevin' 'mypassword'
```

You won't find this in the Access product documentation, but you will find it in the MSDN Library.

At any rate, the conclusion of the matter is, creating and dropping Users and Roles is implementation-defined. In other words, it varies from one data source to another.

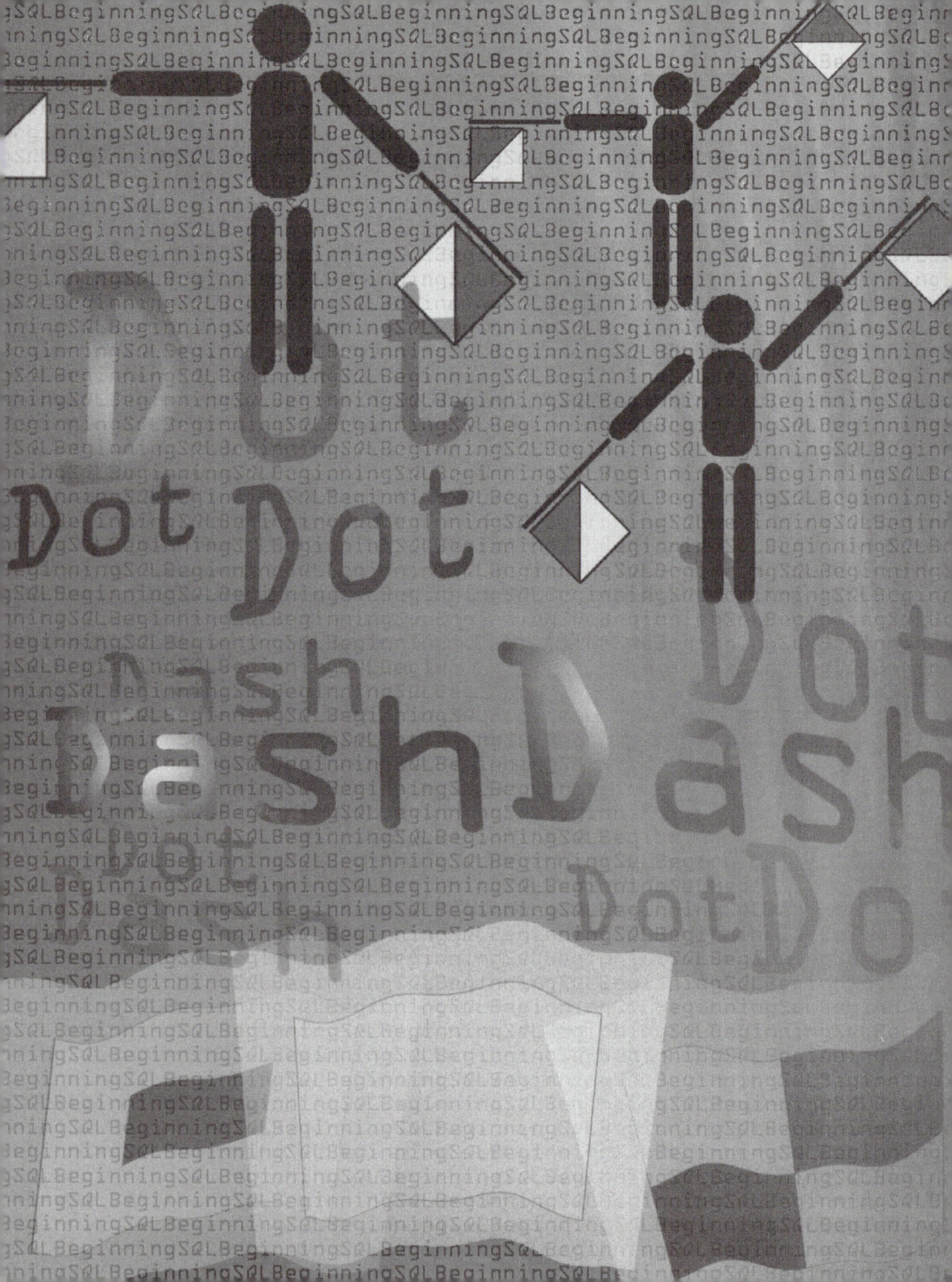
BeginningSQL
Dot Dot
Dash
Dot Dash

Notes on the "Flavors" of SQL

Structured Query Language, or SQL, was originally developed by IBM in the 1970's. It didn't take long for other software companies to see the advantages of using a "universal" programming language for databases (and now for other data sources as well, such as email servers, newsgroup servers, file systems, and so on), which could be used by any messaging system, such as TCP/IP. These other software companies (starting with Oracle) began to "adopt" SQL to their database software. In the mid-1980's, ANSI (American National Standards Institute) and ISO (International Organization for Standardization) released the first International SQL Standard. Of course, about 10 years had gone by since IBM initially released SQL, and there were, by now, quite a few "flavors" of it in existence.

Up until recently the structure of databases and database servers, and the way they store and retrieve data, has been pretty much proprietary from one software manufacturer to another. Relational databases, developed initially in the early 1970's, are really a fairly recent addition to the group. In fact, it was the development of the Relational database model by E. F. Codd, an IBM researcher, which led to the development of SQL by IBM in the first place.

The purpose of a database is to store, retrieve, and manipulate data in a meaningful way. How this is achieved can vary greatly from one solution to another. For example, the File System on any computer uses a database to create, delete, and manipulate files (which are collections of data) and folders (which are containers, or organizers for files). And, as you may know, there are a number of different file systems that you can use, even within the Microsoft family. Each of these file systems, like any database software, has different capabilities, particularly regarding the amount and kind of data about files and folders that is stored. NTFS (NT File System), for example, stores a huge variety of data about a file in its database, including security, attributes, sharing, and so on, whereas FAT (File Allocation Table) stores only a limited set of properties about the file or folder itself, such as name, size, last modified date, and so on.

However, at the bottom level, these file systems (and databases) hold certain functionality in common. Each of them is used to (at least) INSERT new "records", UPDATE (modify) existing "records", DELETE "records", and SELECT (retrieve) "records". The beauty of SQL is that it has syntax to cover all of the possible things that you can do with data sources, *whether a given data source supports those functions or not*. Now, as we mentioned, all of these software companies, with all of their proprietary software, had embraced SQL and "adapted" it to their system. This meant that when ANSI and ISO released their specification, a whole lot of software and SQL was already in place and adapting any software to meet the standard would at least take a sizable amount of time. In turn, that meant expense, and so there wasn't all that much incentive to standardize database software or SQL Syntax. After all, it wasn't as if these proprietary systems were actually going to talk to *each other*.

Of course, the Internet changed all that. And, at the same time that the World Wide Web was being born, Microsoft's **UDA** (Universal Data Access) strategy was also being born. Microsoft began by looking at SQL, a text-based, cross-platform compatible database language (at least in so far as language elements were shared by the two databases communicating). SQL, Microsoft observed, had wonderful potential, but how do you actually connect the two proprietary databases together? Even a cursor (record set) returned by a given query would be proprietary in structure. What was needed was a "universal translator" for databases, where each database could function in its proprietary way, and pass data back and forth using an intermediate interface.

Well, Microsoft had been doing just that for years with their Operating Systems. Proprietary hardware is connected to a non-proprietary Operating System by means of *Device Drivers*; small packets of software which "translate" between the hardware and the Operating System. This model would clearly solve this inter-Database communication problem, and **ODBC** (Open DataBase Connectivity) was born. ODBC uses ODBC drivers to translate between one data source and another.

However, ODBC wasn't *really* the first technology that Microsoft invented along these lines; thee first was OLE DB (Object Linking and Embedding for DataBases). OLE DB, along with ODBC, ADO, and a number of other similar database-connective technologies are part of Microsoft's UDA (Universal Data Access) initiative. OLE DB is a low-level programming interface for working with a large variety of data sources. ODBC is a high-level "user-friendly" *layer* for working with OLE DB in the most common ways that it is used.

Then the World Wide Web sprang into being almost overnight, and began linking all the computers of the world together into a unified network. Suddenly, proprietary (non-standardized) software and syntax was becoming a more important issue. The need to adhere to some form of standard for database communication became much more acute.

Just about every database software manufacturer is now scrambling to adapt to the standards, as adherence to international standards makes software more cross-platform compatible, and thereby able to interact more powerfully with remote data sources. In other words, the closer a database's structure and SQL syntax are to the international standard, the more *competitive* it is. The name of the game today is *interaction*. Now that these computers are linked, we are working on making them more able to work in concert, and therefore, much more powerfully. In the meantime, however, we are stuck with an ever-dwindling (thankfully) variance in syntax from one data provider to another.

We are now going to take a look at some of the most common differences among various data providers, and the SQL syntax that they support. For the most part, we are going to try to remain as general as possible, but we will use specific examples from SQL Server, Access, MySQL, and Oracle.

Databases, Data Sources, and Data Providers

We've been throwing around some terminology in this section that we really need to define before we go any further. You may have wondered about these three terms, and exactly what they mean. We hope so at any rate, because this is the section where they really become important, especially as the lines between databases and other non-relational data management systems continue to blur.

A **Data Source** is a broad definition, which was originally used to describe databases, their DBMS's, and the Platform on which they reside. The definition has grown way beyond the scope of its original purpose, as the various "non-database" data storage structures and methods have been incorporated (logically) into the Universal Data Access model. A Data Source can be a relational or non-relational database (spreadsheet, email server, new server, etc.), a file system, the System Registry, in fact, any container used to store, fetch, and manipulate data of any kind. However, remember that the software that comprises a Data Source is, for the most part, proprietary.

A **Data Provider** is very similar to a Device Driver, which we discussed earlier. The Data Provider is the actual software that connects two Data Sources and communicates between them. It provides a **Programming Interface** for the Data Source. The Programming Interface is the same, regardless of the software at the other end. It is a "universal translator" for data sources.

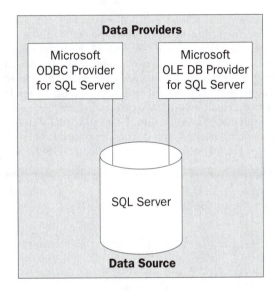

The reason that we make this distinction is that the Data Provider is the real entity that you have to take into consideration when it comes to your SQL syntax. For example, in the illustration above, you'll notice that the Data Source is SQL Server. However, the Data Provider could be either Microsoft OLE DB provider for SQL Server, or it could be the ODBC provider for SQL Server. The syntax supported can vary from one provider to another, even when using the same Data Source. In the case of SQL Server this is not true, but is true of many other Data Sources, such as Access.

Don't be too worried about this at this point, though. For one thing, the programming syntax for the provider itself doesn't vary when using the same Data Source. The only thing that varies is what syntax you can *use*, that is, what functionality is available through that provider. The sorts of differences that occur between one provider for the same data source and another are not appropriate to the scope of this book. However, we do want you to be aware that these things exist, as you will probably encounter a few of them as you continue to work with SQL and move to more advanced types of operations. At this point, knowing the terminology, and what it represents, is enough.

You shouldn't have to be too worried for too much longer about differences in syntax as well. For now, though, here are some significant ones that we will want to be aware of.

Primary Differences in Syntax

SELECT Statement

Believe it not, there is one primary difference in SQL with the SELECT statement. Actually, it's not the SELECT statement, but the SELECT ... INTO statement. This is not part of ANSI SQL, but is supported by a number of vendors, including most of the Microsoft database products. Oracle has no support for this specifically, and neither does MySQL. MySQL does support its own "flavor" of SELECT INTO, but in the case of MySQL, you can only SELECT INTO a file, not a table.

```
SELECT <select clause> INTO <new table name>
```

The SELECT ... INTO statement selects a record set from a table, and inserts it into a new table, which is created by the statement. It probably isn't supported by the standard because it doesn't really define the new table: it uses the data types of the fields in the result set to determine the data types for the new table, but doesn't allow you to configure the new table, nor specify the length of string columns, etc. Furthermore, the new table is born without permissions, other than the Creator/Owner of the table. It may be useful for creating a table on the fly, and is, in fact, useful for Transact-SQL (SQL Server) scripts that require data to be kept in temporary cursors (tables) during execution. With Transact-SQL, you can create a temporary cursor and treat it as if it were a "real" table, such as using it in a SELECT ... INTO query. When you're finished with it, you can return it as an OUTPUT parameter, or destroy it (remove it from memory). Let's take a look at an example of the SQL Server version:

The following Transact-SQL script creates a temporary table named #products from the Products table of the Northwind database (after first dropping it if a version already exists). It then resets the Discontinued field to 1 (True) for all products under $20:

```
DROP TABLE #products
SELECT ProductID, ProductName, UnitPrice, Discontinued INTO #products
FROM Products
UPDATE #products
SET Discontinued = 1
WHERE UnitPrice < 20
SELECT ProductID, ProductName, UnitPrice, Discontinued
FROM #products
```

When this script is run in Query Analyzer, the results look something like the following:

	ProductID	ProductName	UnitPrice	Discontinued
1	1	Chai	18.0000	1
2	2	Chang	19.0000	1
3	3	Aniseed Syrup	10.0000	1
4	4	Chef Anton's Cajun Seasoning	22.0000	0
5	5	Chef Anton's Gumbo Mix	21.3500	1
6	6	Grandma's Boysenberry Spread	25.0000	0
7	7	Uncle Bob's Organic Dried Pears	30.0000	0
8	8	Northwoods Cranberry Sauce	40.0000	0
9	9	Mishi Kobe Niku	97.0000	1
10	10	Ikura	31.0000	0
11	11	Queso Cabrales	21.0000	0

Grids Messages

This returns a result set that contains different values in the Discontinued field than the original table. Note the "#" symbol in the front of the new Cursor's variable name. This indicates that it is a temporary table. In the new temporary table, all products under $20 are listed as Discontinued.

With ANSI SQL, you would have to create the new table with a CREATE TABLE statement, and then execute an INSERT INTO query, with the new table as the target, and a SELECT query to get the records from the first table:

```
IF EXISTS
    (SELECT * from dbo.sysobjects
    WHERE id = object_id(N'[dbo].[SpecialProducts]')
        AND OBJECTPROPERTY(id, N'IsUserTable') = 1)

BEGIN
DROP TABLE SpecialProducts
END
CREATE TABLE SpecialProducts (
    ProductID int NOT NULL ,
    ProductName nvarchar (40) NOT NULL ,
    UnitPrice money NULL,
    Discontinued bit NOT NULL
)
GO

INSERT INTO SpecialProducts
    (ProductID, ProductName, UnitPrice, Discontinued)

SELECT ProductID, ProductName, UnitPrice, Discontinued
FROM Products
GO

UPDATE SpecialProducts
SET Discontinued = 1
WHERE UnitPrice < 20
GO

SELECT * FROM SpecialProducts
```

As you can see, this does not create a temporary table, but a permanent one. However, it can be as easily DROPped as it can be CREATEd. In general, we would recommend that when you have a choice, you do things the standard way. In the future, this will require fewer rewrites of your code!

WHERE Clause

The WHERE clause itself, and the syntax for it, is not a problem, but the filtering conditions can be in certain cases, and especially with Dates.

Dates

Just about every DBMS supports the standard date-time storage method of storing dates as the number of days that have elapsed between their specific base date and the 'current' date, plus the number of seconds that have elapsed since midnight.

Vendor	Base Date	End Date
SQL Server	01/01/1753 00:00:00	12/31/9999 23:59:59
MySQL	01/01/1000 00:00:00	12/31/9999 23:59:59
Oracle	01/01/4712BC 00:00:00	12/31/9999 23:59:59

As we can see, this gives rise to a large range of dates, larger than the amount that it would seem, as negative numbers can also be used to represent dates prior to the base date. However, the way that dates and times are worked with can vary significantly.

Strangely enough, Oracle leads the way in regards to date-time variations from the standard. Oracle, which was the first database to adopt SQL, has never upgraded its date-time syntax to the standard. While it works with date literals in the standard format, it uses a proprietary function (sysdate) to return the current date and time. Date arithmetic in Oracle is also proprietary. When adding and subtracting intervals from dates, they are not specified; that is, the interval is implied.

Access comes in second in this area, with the Visual Basic Date-time functions being the only ones available (Date, DateDiff(), DateAdd()). While SQL Server also supports the DateDiff() and DateAdd() functions, the syntax is different! The difference between Access and SQL Server regarding the DateDiff() and DateAdd() functions is that Access uses a string to represent the Interval that is being used in the query, while SQL Server uses a *token*. A string is a string of characters. It can be represented as a literal ("my string") or a variable (strMystring). A token, while a string of characters, is not a string. It is a *symbol*, represented in characters, like a variable, but with constant values.

SQL Server Date Interval Tokens	
Datepart (Interval)	Abbreviations
Year	yy, yyyy
quarter	qq, q
Month	mm, m
dayofyear	dy, y

SQL Server Date Interval Tokens	
Datepart (Interval)	**Abbreviations**
Day	dd, d
Week	wk, ww
Hour	hh
minute	mi, n
second	ss, s
millisecond	ms

One of these days we sure would like to see these 2 versions get together!

Access Date Interval Strings	
Interval	**Description**
'yyyy'	Year
'q'	Quarter
'm'	Month
'y'	Day of year
'd'	Day
'w'	Weekday
'ww'	Week of year
'h'	Hour
'n'	Minute
's'	Second

SQL Server supports the scalar CURRENT_TIMESTAMP ANSI SQL function, which returns the same value as the SQL Server proprietary GetDate() function; that is, it returns the current date and time. Most DBMS's use a single date-time data type, which corresponds to the ANSI TIMESTAMP data type. Even though it is not yet cross-platform, we would advise you to stick to the standard.

Oracle has only one built-in function for date arithmetic: ADD_MONTHS (see Chapter 11 for details). Other than that, the unary operator "+" is used, with DAY Interval implied. MySQL uses the ANSI SQL standard for date arithmetic (see Chapter 11 for details).

Also, Access delimits date literals with the "#" character. Access is the only DBMS that I know of that does not use the standard single-quote date literal delimiter. Again, you'll find much more detailed information about Date-time syntactical differences in Chapter 11.

LIKE

MySQL uses LIKE with numeric data types as well as with strings. This is the only one of the DBMS products that we have looked at which does this rather strange thing. I know of no other that does; but that doesn't mean that there isn't.

Other than that, the LIKE operator is a funny one in just one respect: Case. Some providers use a case-sensitive approach to LIKE, and some do not. SQL Server is case-insensitive (by default) when using LIKE. Access is case-insensitive. Oracle is also case-sensitive, as is ANSI SQL. Access is also funny when it comes to wildcards. The ANSI SQL wildcard characters are "_" for a single character and "%" for multiples. This is generally used by most DBMS's. However, Access uses the asterisk (*) for multiple characters, and the "?" for single characters. But wait! There's more! Here's where the provider comes in. If you connect to Access via ODBC, or via the Jet OLE DB provider for Access, the wildcard characters are the same as the ANSI standard!

CREATE TABLE

While the syntax for this generally adheres to the standard, the structure of databases does not. Therefore, some of the options may not be present in the Data provider you're working with, such as certain kinds of indexing, constraints, and so on. The bottom line on this one is, find out what your Data Provider supports in so far as the schema creation for a table is concerned, and develop your SQL statements accordingly.

Every DBMS has its own documentation.

❑ The MSDN Library at http://msdn.microsoft.com/library/default.asp has documentation for every Microsoft DBMS.

❑ Documentation for MySQL can be found at http://www.mysql.com/doc/R/e/Reference.html

❑ Oracle's reference can be found at http://technet.oracle.com/doc/server.815/a67779/toc.htm You need to register for this service, but it is free.

JOINs

The rules for JOINs are rather complex to say the least. ANSI SQL allows a number of different ways to perform the various types of JOINs, and some DBMS's support some of them while not supporting others. Some vendors come very close to ANSI SQL, and some vendors seem to almost totally ignore the standard almost completely.

In fact, even those vendors who adhere rather strictly to the standard have trouble deciding how to handle OUTER JOINs especially, not to mention nested JOINs and combinations of JOINs (for example: Table1 INNER JOIN Table 2 OUTER JOIN Table3).

Chapter 8 covers this subject in detail, but here is a chart to help you understand how confusing this all can be:

SQL Flavor	JOIN Type	Syntax	Definition
ISO	Cartesian, INNER, CROSS	`Table1, Table2` `Table1 CROSS JOIN Table2`	Returns all combinations of rows from both tables.[1]

Access	Cartesian, INNER	`Table1, Table2`
		`Table1 INNER JOIN Table2`
		`ON...`
			Returns all combinations of rows from both tables.[1]

SQL Server	Cartesian, INNER, CROSS	`Table1, Table2` `Table1 CROSS JOIN Table2`	Returns all combinations of rows from both tables.[1]

MySQL	Cartesian, INNER, JOIN, CROSS, STRAIGHT	`Table1, Table2`
		`Table1 INNER JOIN Table2`
		`ON...`
		`Table1 JOIN Table2`
		`Table1 CROSS JOIN Table2`
		`Table1 STRAIGHT JOIN Table2`
			Returns all combinations of rows from both tables. `STRAIGHT JOIN` indicates `LEFT` rather than `RIGHT` always.[1]

Oracle	Cartesian	`Table1, Table2`	Returns all combinations of rows from both tables.[1]

[1] The Cartesian `JOIN` may be used as an `INNER JOIN` with the correct `WHERE` clause in most DBMS's. `INNER JOIN` was not part of ANSI SQL until SQL-92, when `JOIN...ON` (ISO SQL also supports `JOIN...USING`) was introduced, and there had to be some way of differentiating between a `JOIN` (`INNER`) and an `OUTER JOIN`. Oracle does not yet support the `INNER JOIN` syntax. `LEFT` and `RIGHT` can be used in most DBMS products, with both `INNER` and `OUTER JOIN`s to specify whether fields in the second table which do not exist in the first are included. Also, in general, when `LEFT` or `RIGHT` is not specified, `LEFT` is implied. However, in Oracle, this is handled entirely proprietarily.

SQL Flavor	JOIN Type	Syntax	Definition
ISO	OUTER	`Table1 OUTER JOIN Table2`	Returns all rows from one table, and fields in the other table that don't exist are included and given a `NULL` value.
Access	OUTER	`Table1 OUTER JOIN Table2`	Returns all rows from one table, and fields in the other table that don't exist are included and given a `NULL` value.
SQL Server	OUTER	`Table1 OUTER JOIN Table2`	Returns all rows from one table, and fields in the other table that don't exist are included and given a `NULL` value.
MySQL	OUTER	`Table1 OUTER JOIN Table2`	Returns all rows from one table, and fields in the other table that don't exist are included and given a `NULL` value.

Table continued on following page

QL Flavor	JOIN Type	Syntax	Definition
Oracle	Cartesian + WHERE + (+)	`Table1, Table2 WHERE Table1.field1 (+) = Table2.field1`	Returns all rows from one table (indicated by the "(+)" operator), and fields in the other table that don't exist are included and given a NULL value.

[2] The difference between INNER and OUTER JOIN is whether records are *combined* from both tables. In Oracle, this is handled with the proprietary "(+)" operator.

SQL Flavor	JOIN Type	Syntax	Definition
ISO	NATURAL JOIN	`Table1 NATURAL JOIN Table2`	Same thing as an INNER JOIN without the ON clause. Equivalent to `Table1 INNER JOIN Table2 ON Table1.primarykey = Table2.Foreignkey`.
Access	NA (See INNER JOIN)	NA	NA
SQL Server	NA (See INNER JOIN)	NA	NA
MySQL	NATURAL [RIGHT [OUTER]] JOIN	`Table1 NATURAL [RIGHT [OUTER]] JOIN Table2`	Same thing as an INNER JOIN without the ON clause. Equivalent to `Table1 INNER JOIN Table2 ON Table1.primarykey = Table2.Foreignkey`. In addition, MySQL allows additional operators in the clause.
Oracle	NA (See INNER JOIN)	NA	NA

[3] The NATURAL JOIN only works when naming conventions are formal and enforced, because it doesn't specify the JOIN condition.

Let me give you a tip for working with JOINs: most DBMS products include some form of visual tool for constructing SQL statements; Access has one, Visual InterDev has one, even Visual FoxPro has one. And SQL Server 2000 has several, built into its various tools. If you have some software for working with your queries in this fashion, use it.

Here's what we do: using Access Query Designer, for example, we open a new Query in Design view. We then drag the tables that we want to JOIN into the top window. If the primary and foreign keys are obvious enough, your software may even at this point create a JOIN for you, in essence performing a NATURAL JOIN internally. Query Designer certainly will in most cases. If not, simply drag from the primary key of one to the foreign key of another:

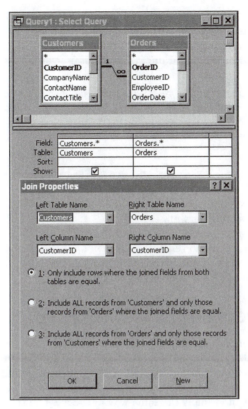

You can create a very simple query, and the syntax for the SELECT clause and the WHERE condition don't *have* to be correct, as we are using the utility to get the JOIN (FROM clause) syntax. However, this doesn't particularly matter, as in this example we want to edit the SELECT clause and the WHERE clause separately. Here's the SQL our simple query generated:

```
SELECT Customers.*, Orders.*
FROM Customers INNER JOIN Orders
ON Customers.CustomerID = Orders.CustomerID;
```

Now, because this is a JOIN query, using the "*" (ALL) operator would generate an error if the fields in the tables were not all the same, or we didn't use an OUTER JOIN to get all fields from the tables that don't have them, and include them in the result set.

Note that we have here everything we need to modify or customize this query. We have the syntax for the SELECT list (minus aliases). We have the proper format for the JOIN syntax. All we need to do is plug in some actual field names, aliases, and optionally a WHERE clause. Let's start with some field names:

```
SELECT Customers.ContactName AS Name, Orders.OrderDate AS Date,
Orders.OrderID AS OrderID, Customers.CustomerID AS CustomerID

FROM Customers INNER JOIN Orders
ON Customers.CustomerID = Orders.CustomerID;
```

Following the pattern laid down in the first query, we've substituted some actual field names and appropriate aliases for the original placeholders. Note that each reference to a field is preceded by the table name. Since we're selecting from multiple tables, we have to tell the program *which* table a given field is being SELECTed from. Now for the WHERE clause:

```
SELECT Customers.ContactName AS CustomerName, Orders.OrderDate AS OrderDate,
Orders.OrderID AS OrderID, Customers.CustomerID AS CustomerID

FROM Customers INNER JOIN Orders
ON Customers.CustomerID = Orders.CustomerID

WHERE Customers.City = 'Madrid' AND Orders.ShippedDate > 06/01/1995
```

Again note that we are using the table names in the WHERE clause. Also note that you could use conditions that check *both* tables as well.

Isn't that a lot easier than having to remember or look up the individual rules? Actually, in most cases, you're not going to have any problem writing a JOIN query unless it's a particularly tricky one. Most JOINs are simply INNER JOINs, and involve only two tables.

Data Type Conversion

This is an area where there is a fair amount of variation from one Data Source and Provider to another. SQL-99 supports two data type conversion operators, CAST and CONVERT. SQL Server also provides CAST and CONVERT functions, but the CONVERT function is entirely different to the ANSI standard. The ANSI standard CONVERT function uses a stored Schema to convert the object. The SQL Server CONVERT function works in virtually the same way as CAST. You simply pass the data type (and length when it's a string data type) to the function, and the data type is changed to the type you specify.

Access uses Visual Basic functions to convert data types, and as yet has no support for the SQL Standard CAST and CONVERT functions. This includes the following:

Conversion Function	Converts to Data type
CByte	Byte
CCur	Currency
CDate	Date-time
CDbl	Double Numeric
CInt	Integer Numeric
CLng	Long Numeric
CSng	Single Numeric
CStr	String

Oracle has its own proprietary conversion functions as well:

Conversion Function	Converts to Data type
CHARTOROWID	Character to ROWID
ROWIDTOCHAR	ROWID to Character
CONVERT*	Character to Different Character Set
HEXTORAW	Hexadecimal to RAW
RAWTOHEX	RAW to Hexadecimal
TO_CHAR	Number or Date to Character
TO_DATE	Character to Date
TO_LOB	LONG or LONG RAW to LOB
TO_MULTI_BYTE	Single-Byte Character to Multi-byte Character
TO_SINGLE_BYTE	Multi-byte Character to Single-Byte Character
TO_NUMBER	Character to Number

Note that the Oracle CONVERT function is entirely different to ANSI SQL: it changes the Character Set *only* of a Character data type.

MySQL is also lacking in conformance to the standard conversion functions. Numeric and Character data types are implicitly converted (no conversion necessary). In addition, the following proprietary functions are supported:

Conversion Function	Converts to Data type
CONV(N, base x, base y)	Base x number converted to Base y
BIN(N)	BIGINT to Binary (Base 2) Equivalent to CONV(N, 10, 2)
OCT(N)	BIGINT to Octal (Base 8) Equivalent to CONV(N, 10, 8)
HEX(N)	BIGINT to Hexadecimal (Base 16) Equivalent to CONV(N, 10, 16)
CHAR(N,...)	A comma-delimited string of Numeric values to a string of their (comma-delimited) ASCII Character values
BINARY	Character to Binary value

Primary Differences Between Vendors

Every vendor, with a few unimportant exceptions, has proprietary syntax in their SQL. However, proprietary syntax isn't half as important as support for standard syntax. This is true for any programming language. Why? Consider the C programming language. No, we didn't say C++, we said C. C is the "father" of C++, meaning that C++ is *derived* from C; that is, all C++ objects are built using C. More than that, the complete ANSI/ISO C standard specification is included in the C++ language. What that means is that you can write *any* C++ program in C. The C++ language specification (now long-since standardized as well) is a superset of the C language specification. Remember back in the chapter on Grouping and Aggregates when we talked about Set Theory? A superset is the opposite of a subset. A subset is entirely contained within its superset. The superset almost always, however, includes *additional* elements that are *not* in the subset.

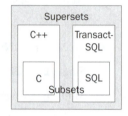

What we're getting at here is that some DBMS vendors are working very diligently to include full support for the ANSI standard in their products. However, additional syntax and functionality doesn't cause any problems with existing standard syntax, as long as full support for standard syntax is at least there. We will be talking in this context when it comes to our evaluation of the support for standard SQL in DBMS vendor products, next.

SQL Server

SQL Server uses Transact-SQL, which is one of those supersets we mentioned earlier. Microsoft is leading the way in bringing their products in line with International standards, as they did with browser software and support for DHTML and XML. Of course, this could be expected from a maker of Operating Systems, which always seek to be as cross-platform-compatible as possible. However, any software company that is bringing their software in line with international standards is to be commended, both because of the practicality of such software, and because they recognize that competition in the Internet marketplace means flexibility of use, when it comes to software. The Internet is a conglomeration of virtually every hardware and software platform imaginable in the world. To bring them together effectively, we need to standardize as much as possible.

Let me begin by saying that, at this point, Transact-SQL is not fully compliant with the ANSI standard. However, on closer examination, a look at the history of SQL Server shows it is the history of a DBMS product that has been gradually becoming increasingly "universal" in its functionality and behavior. Also, you will note that the standard SQL functions that SQL Server does not yet support are all earmarked by SQL Server as "reserved words" that are reserved for future use. Therefore, we can logically assume that not only is each generation of SQL Server more ANSI-compliant than the previous, but that it will eventually, and in the no-so-distant future, become fully compliant.

In addition to the nearly complete compliance with ANSI standard SQL, Transact-SQL offers additional proprietary syntax for performing a large variety of server and database functions, in fact, just about everything that you can do.

If you've ever used SQL Server Enterprise Manager, you have probably built databases, created logons for them, assigned permissions, scheduled execution of stored procedures, and a variety of other "administrative" functions. When you did so, you used the increasing slew of visual tools that the SQL Server Enterprise Manager offers. What you may not have been aware of was, that, underneath it all, rather than executing simple machine code for all of this, SQL Server Enterprise Manager is writing and executing SQL Statements against the Master database. Most of these SQL Statements are executing Stored Procedures in the Master database.

> It's a great idea to take a look at the Master Database Stored Procedures in SQL Server. You can learn a lot about both SQL and Transact-SQL from studying them. These Transact-SQL scripts perform almost all of the actual work performed by SQL Server, and are written by some of the best SQL programmers in the world.

Oracle

Oracle is the most popular database software in the world, and in fact, the second largest software company in the world. The fact that Microsoft has been catching up with their SQL Server product says more about Microsoft's ability to develop technology rapidly than it does about Oracle. Oracle is arguably the world's most powerful database server, depending on how you benchmark it. SQL Server is running a close second now, and still gaining.

Oracle, like SQL Server, is not fully ANSI-compliant. In fact, Oracle has yet to catch up with the ANSI SQL-99 standard at all. However, like SQL Server, Oracle is both very close to the standard, and offers additional functionality in its implementation of the language. Oracle's superset of SQL is called PL/SQL, and offers much the same additional functionality as SQL Server's Transact-SQL. Both are capable of creating rather long and complex "scripts" containing multiple queries and database operations in a single script.

MySQL

While MySQL is generally very conformant to the ANSI SQL-92 standard, at this time of writing it has not yet adapted the ANSI SQL-99 standard. Most probably this will happen shortly.

There are some significant differences:

- ❑ Non-standard data types: MEDIUMINT, SET, ENUM.

- ❑ **All** string comparisons are case insensitive by default, regardless of the operator ("=" or "LIKE").

- ❑ MySQL databases are folders, and tables within a database are filenames in the database folders. Due to this, you can work directly with the files if you are brave enough (or foolish enough!), and you can use standard system commands to backup, rename, move, delete, and copy tables.

- ❑ Non-standard SELECT syntax: SQL_SMALL_RESULT, INTO, OUTFILE, and STRAIGHT_JOIN in a SELECT statement.

- ❑ EXPLAIN SELECT to get a description on how tables are joined.

❑ RENAME TABLE to rename a table.

❑ You can drop multiple tables with a single DROP TABLE statement.

❑ The non-standard LIMIT clause of the DELETE statement to restrict deletions.

❑ The DELAYED clause of the INSERT and REPLACE non-standard SQL statements.

❑ The ANALYZE TABLE, CHECK TABLE, OPTIMIZE TABLE, and REPAIR TABLE non-standard SQL statements.

❑ GROUP BY allows you to not specify all of the columns GROUPed BY.

❑ CONCAT() and CHAR() may take any number of arguments.

MySQL also has a number of syntactical elements and functions that have been added to the standard, and provide extra functionality, without detracting from the standard.

MSDE

Microsoft Data Engine is basically a Database Management System for SQL Server 7.0-compatible databases, without a front-end. It was developed by Microsoft as an "intermediate" solution between Access and the far more expensive SQL Server. A "Database Engine" is the set of core processes that work with databases. It provides a programming interface, but no user interface (GUI).

The great thing about MSDE is that it can be used as an alternative Database Engine for Access. That is, you can create an MSDE project in Access, with the complete Access familiar front-end. The default, and,until Access 2000, the only Access Database engine up to this point was Jet, which is incompatible with SQL Server (although it too is moving towards standardization, at a slower pace).

You can also use MSDE as a programming interface (Provider) via ADO (ActiveX Data Objects) and DAO (the nearly obsolete Data Access Objects, created originally for the proprietary Access database format only).

The same syntax rules that apply for SQL Server apply to MSDE.

Access

Even the most popular desktop database solution in the world is coming in line with the standards. Why? Well, let's face it. Everything is going to the Internet. At least, that's how Microsoft is betting. A lot of people are employing Access databases on the Internet, despite Microsoft's warnings about its lack of scalability. It is, after all, currently a lot cheaper than SQL Server.

Still, it is far behind the major players, such as SQL Server and Oracle. However, at this stage of the SQL "game", you won't really run into the differences: In any "flavor" of SQL, the basic syntax is going to be the same.

So, what do we need to be concerned with regarding Access? Well, first of all, there are dates. While Access stores dates in the same standardized way as any other DBMS, like almost every other DBMS, it has that set of proprietary Date-time functions. That was covered in the earlier section of this chapter.

In addition, like SQL Server and Oracle, Access has additional proprietary functionality above and beyond the scope of standardized SQL. Most of these are in the form of Visual Basic functions, all of which are supported by the Jet database provider. That's right, we said, *all*. This can come in quite handy in your Access SQL statements, but it is highly proprietary.

Remember that Access Modules, Macros, and user-defined Stored Procedures and Functions can not be used via ADO or any other remote database technology. You *can* store parameterized Queries in Access. Parameterized Queries are simply Stored Queries that have parameters in them, and can be accessed via ADO and the Command Object, using the ADO Command Object's Parameters Collection. A parameterized query in Access is very easy to create: in fact, a lot of people create them *by accident*! To create a parameterized query in Access, you just insert a parameter name in the query somewhere. When Access can't find a reference to an object by that name (make sure you don't use the name of an existing object!), it assumes that it is a parameter name, and will take whatever parameter value for that parameter that you pass to it. For example:

```
SELECT * FROM Products WHERE CustomerID = [Insert CustomerID]
```

Now, the reason we used the name [Insert CustomerID] was because in the Access front-end, when you run this query, it will put up a prompt box, with the name of the parameter in it. In this case, the box would prompt you with Insert CustomerID. In Microsoft products, when you give a database object a name with spaces in it, you indicate that the entire string is a name by enclosing it in square brackets ([]).

Much of the Access advanced SQL functionality, including DCL (Data Control Language – see Appendix A), some of the DDL (Data Definition Language), and some advanced Data Manipulation syntax for Access are not "available through regular channels". That is, the **Jet ODBC Provider** for Access doesn't support them. The **Jet OLE DB Provider** for Access does, when used in conjunction with ADO (ActiveX Data Objects).

Summary

The issue of SQL "Flavors" is a rapidly-dying one, as almost every DBMS vendor out there is scrambling to adopt the standards to their software, and thus make it more portable and cross-platform compatible. For the time being, though, we will have to continue to grapple with it every once in a while.

Most of the time, the minor differences in syntax don't even manifest themselves, as you aren't likely to be, for instance, trying to programmatically change a User's permission settings for an Access database. However, when they do, it's important to be able to identify the syntactical differences between one Data Provider and another. Date and Time issues are the most troublesome and the most frequently encountered, but the differences, as we have pointed out, are minor.

At this point, we would not recommend trying to memorize all of these differences, but keep this book handy, and remember that they exist. When you need to, look them up.

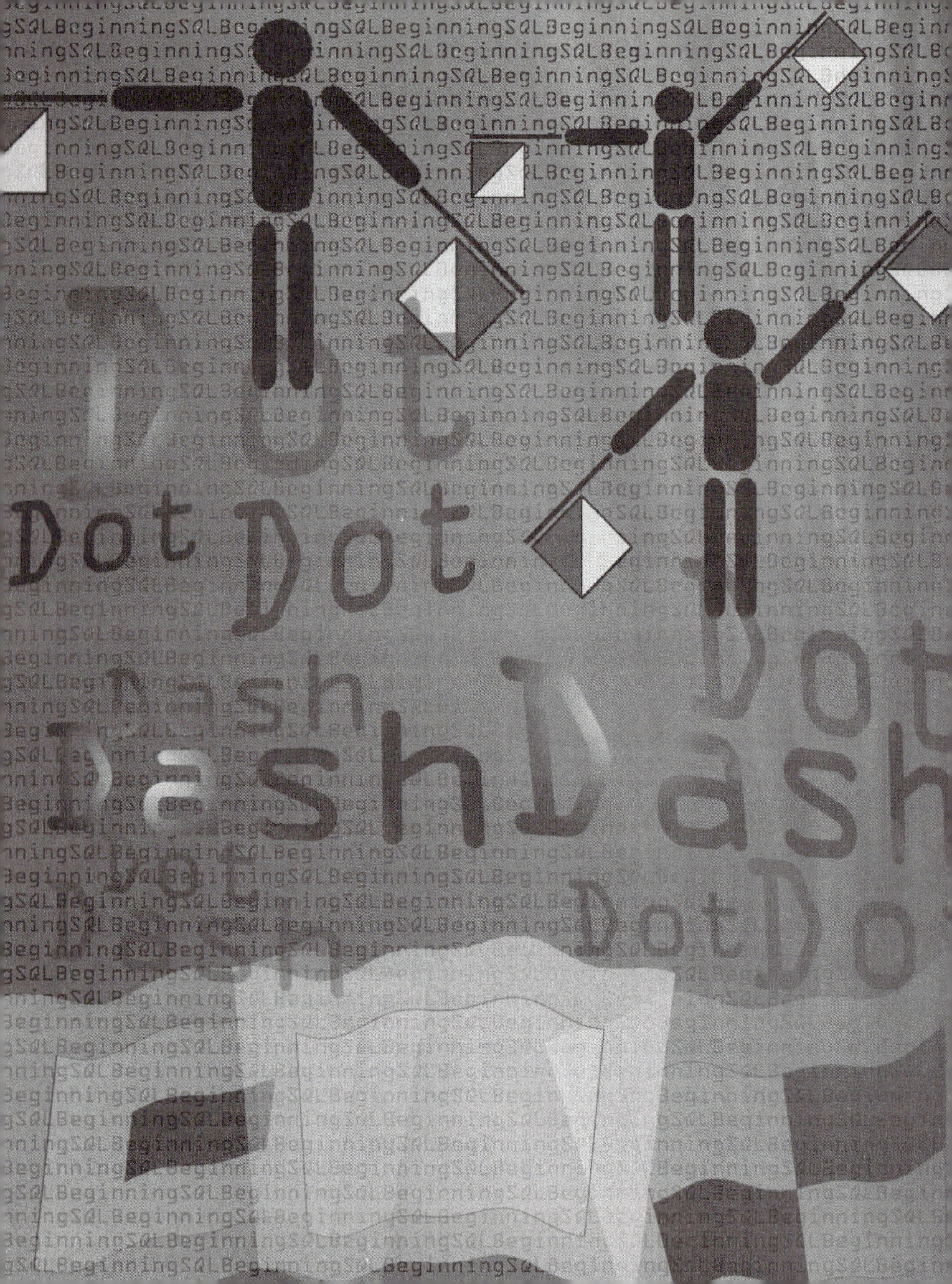

Migrating the Northwind Database

This book comes with an evaluation edition of SQL Server 2000, and its examples use the Northwind database, which is shipped with SQL Server. But what if you use another database system, and you want to try out the same examples with that? No problem – SQL Server is shipped with a wizard which allows us easily to migrate data between any two database systems, as long as they both support OLE DB or ODBC. In the first section of this appendix, we'll look at the steps we need to take to export the Northwind database to Oracle, and in the next two sections, we'll look at the same process for IBM's DB2, and for the open source database MySQL.

Migrating the Northwind Database to Oracle

There are actually three steps required for the migration to Oracle:

❑   Firstly, we need to install Oracle client components on the SQL Server machine, so that the Import and Export Data wizard can connect to our Oracle server. If the client components are already installed, or if the evaluation edition of SQL Server was installed on the Oracle server, this step can be omitted.

❑   Next, we need to create a schema in the Oracle database where we can store the exported data.

❑   Finally, we can run the Import and Export Data wizard itself to move the data into the Oracle database.

In this section, we'll explain each of these three steps in turn. We'll run through the process with Oracle 8i, but the steps will be very similar with other versions of Oracle.

> If you don't have access to an edition of SQL Server (for example, if you're using a Windows 95/98 machine and can't install the evaluation edition of SQL Server 2000), you can still migrate the data in the Access `Nwind.mdb` database using the Data Migration Tool available with the source code for the book. We'll look at using this utility in the next section, on migrating the database to a DB2 server. You will still need to follow the first two steps of this chapter.

Installing Oracle Client Components

Our first step, then, is to install Oracle's client components onto our SQL Server machine. Unlike SQL Server, we can't just access an Oracle database from any computer on the network armed only with an OLE DB provider – we also need to install various client-side components of the Oracle database system. These include data access components, such as Oracle's own ODBC driver, and OO4O (Oracle's answer to OLE DB); Net8, which allows us to make the network connection to the Oracle server; and optional database administration and developer components, such as DBA Studio and SQL*Plus. Be warned that the smallest standard configuration of Oracle client components takes up around 100 MB of disk space, so make sure there's lots of spare room on your hard drive!

Selecting the Installation Options

The client installation of Oracle uses the same installation program as the database server itself, so you'll need to get the Oracle CD from your System Administrator and start up the Oracle Universal Installer:

Click **Next** on this screen to start the installation process. The next screen allows us to specify the folder where the Oracle installation files reside, the folder where we want to install the Oracle components, and the Oracle home name (the name which we want to give to this installation of Oracle):

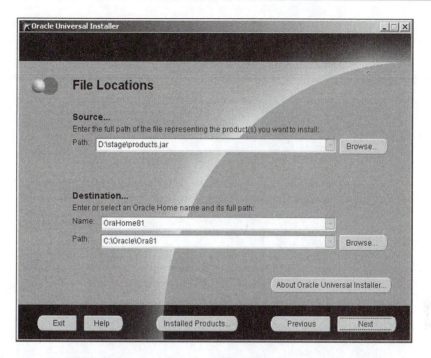

The default settings should be fine unless you need to change the drive letter to install Oracle on another partition, so click on the **Next** button. This will take us to the Available Products screen, where we can choose to install the full Oracle database server or just the client components:

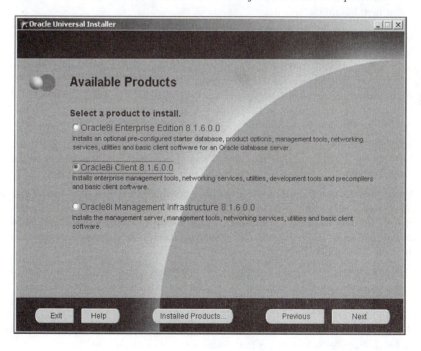

In this case, we only need the client components, so click on the radio button next to the client option (in this case, Oracle8i Client 8.1.6.0.0), and then click on Next.

This takes us to the Installation Types screen, where we can specify what sort of installation we need, and which components we want to install:

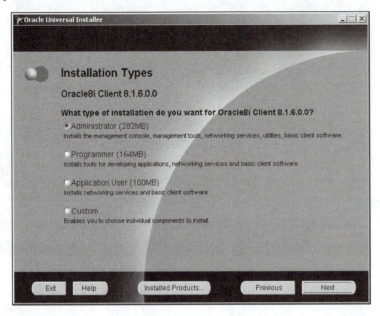

There are four installation options here:

❑   Administrator – This option will install pretty well everything we need for accessing the Oracle server from the local machine, including DBA Studio, a Graphical User Interface for carrying out administrative tasks against the database, such as creating tables, entering data, etc., and roughly equivalent to SQL Server's Enterprise Manager; and SQL*Plus, a text editor which allows us to execute SQL statements against the Oracle database. This is the best option if you can afford the 280-odd MB of disk space, since we'll be using DBA Studio to create the schema for the Northwind database.

❑   Programmer – This option gives us all the necessary components for programmatic access to the database including SQL*Plus, but it doesn't give us administrative tools such as DBA Studio.

❑   Application User – This type of installation contains all the networking and data access components we need to access the database, and is all we really need. However, it doesn't include the administrative components such as DBA Studio. If you have limited disk space and direct access to the Oracle server, and can carry out administrative tasks on that machine, this may be a good option.

❑   Custom – This allows us to choose precisely which components we want to install. This is a good option if you are familiar with Oracle, but otherwise it is probably safer to stick to one of the standard configurations.

After you've selected the appropriate installation type for your needs, click on the Next button. The Oracle Universal Installer will then present a summary of your choices:

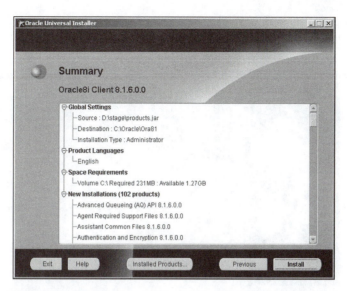

Clicking on the Install button will begin the installation proper. This process requires no user input, so you can go and have a cup of tea while the Universal Installer gets on with it.

Configuring Net8

After Oracle has finished installing the selected client components, you will be given the option of configuring Net8. Net8 is the network software which the Oracle client will use to connect to the database server.

> **Net8 configuration options may depend on your network setup. Here we will run through a common setup using Oracle 8i and TCP, but you may need to consult with your System Administrator to check how your Oracle database is configured.**

When asked, you should select Yes to run the Net8 Configuration Assistant:

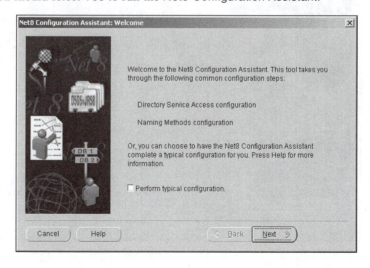

The first choice presented to us is whether we wish to perform a typical installation. We'll go through the standard configuration, so don't check this box, just click on the Next button.

In order to access an Oracle database server, we will need a net service name. This is simply a name given to a set of connection details which our client will use to connect to the server. These names can be stored in a directory service, or in a file on the local machine. The former option is easier to configure, but requires the pre-configured service names to be stored in an available directory already. We will therefore run through the second option, since we can use this option whether or not a directory service is available. So, make sure the lower radio button is checked, and click on Next.

The next screen asks us to specify the version of the Oracle database we wish to connect to:

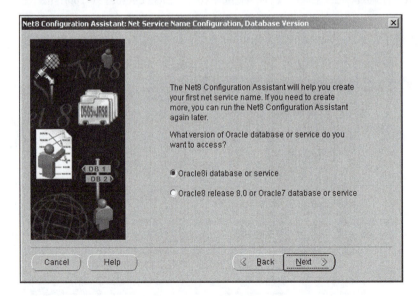

Here we may select whether we want to connect to an Oracle 8i database, or an Oracle 8 or Oracle 7 database. In this example, we're using Oracle 8i, so we've selected the first option.

After clicking on **Next**, we are asked to provide the service name for the Oracle 8i database:

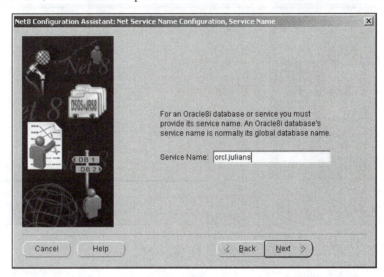

The service name distinguishes an Oracle database from other available instances of Oracle. This is usually in the form *service_name.domain_name*, but you will need to ask your System Administrator or Database Administrator to find out the service name for the database you want to connect to. Entering this and clicking on **Next** brings up the **Select Protocols** screen:

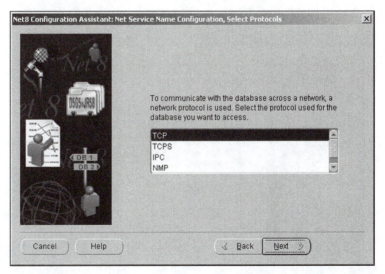

The most common networking protocol on Microsoft networks is TCP/IP (Transmission Control Protocol/Internet Protocol) (strictly, this is actually a set of protocols). It is very likely that your Oracle server will support this, although it may also support other protocols. Therefore, select the first option (**TCP**) and click on **Next**. You will now be prompted to provide more information about the server computer:

649

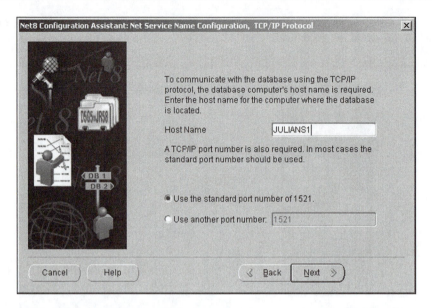

Here we must enter two pieces of information. Firstly, we must specify the hostname (or machine name) of the computer on which the Oracle server is running (in this case, JULIANS1). Again, you may need to ask your System Administrator to find this. Next, we need to specify the TCP/IP that Oracle is using. By default, this is port 1521, and it is very likely that your Oracle server will be running on this port. However, if another application is running on port 1521 on the server, you will need to find out from your System Administrator which port Oracle is using.

The next screen asks us whether we want to test this setup:

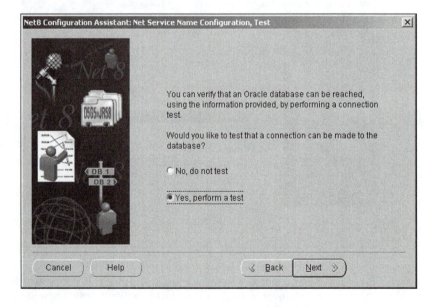

It is highly advisable to perform the test to ensure that the configuration information you have supplied is correct, so ensure the bottom radio button is checked and click on <u>N</u>ext. The Net8 Configuration Assistant will now attempt to connect to the database using the information you supplied, and hopefully you will be presented with the screen below:

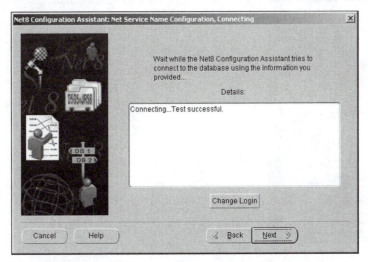

If the test wasn't successful first time round, check with your System Administrator to make sure that all the details you supplied were correct (in particular, check that you specified the correct service name). It may also be necessary to change the username/password combination used to connect to the database, so if you're sure that all the details are correct, click on the Change Login button, and enter a username and password combination which you know to be correct, and perform the test again.

Once we've verified our connection, we have only one more step – to assign a name to this net service:

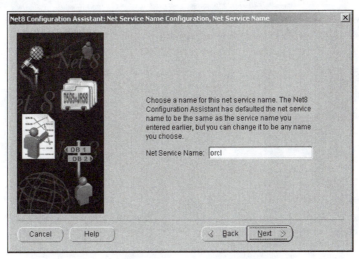

We will use this net service name when we want to connect to the database from this machine, so make a note of whatever you enter here. By default, the Net8 Configuration Assistant will use the service name minus its domain component as the net service name, so in our case the name is orcl. However, you can enter a completely different name, if you wish.

This completes the configuration of our net service name; the next screen of the wizard simply asks us if we wish to configure another net service name:

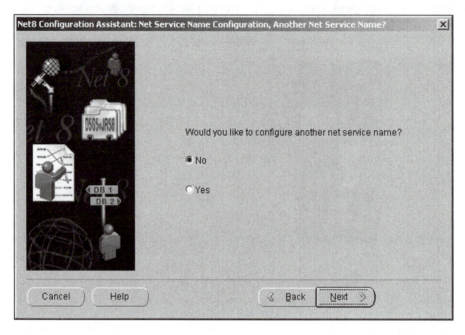

Unless you want to connect to another database from your machine, you can select No here. This will finish the Net8 Configuration Assistant:

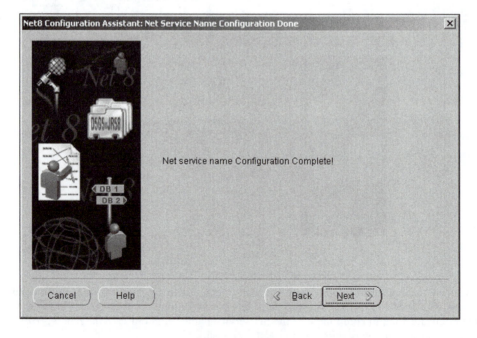

Selecting <u>N</u>ext returns us to the Oracle Universal Installer. You should now see the screen below:

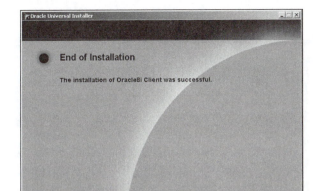

We're finally done with installing the client components, and we can select Exit to leave the installation program.

Creating a Schema

Our next task is to create a schema where we can store the data which we are going to export from SQL Server. Oracle stores tables and other database objects in **schemas**. Each schema represents a specific security configuration, containing access rights to the objects within the schema. The schema name also serves as a username, which we can use to log into the database, and is associated with a specific password.

In this section, we will look at the steps we need to take to create a schema for our Northwind data using DBA Studio. If you chose the Administrator installation type during the installation of the client components, you will be able to use this program from your local machine. Otherwise, you will need to follow these steps on the Oracle server itself, or on another Administrator client.

Start up DBA Studio by selecting Programs | Oracle – OraHome81 | Database Administration | DBA Studio from the Start menu. (This assumes that you are using Oracle 8i and accepted the default Oracle Home name of OraHome81.) We are first asked whether we want to log in to a management server or launch DBA Studio standalone:

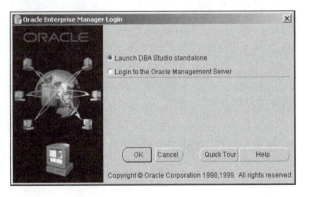

Select the standalone option and click on Next. Once DBA Studio has loaded, you will see a tree view in the left-hand pane:

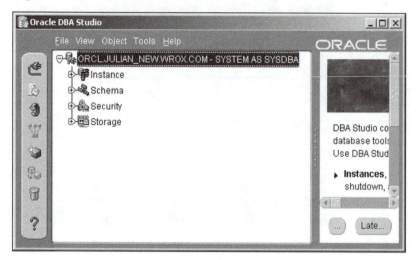

Open up the node which represents our net service (ORCL.*domain_name*). You may now be asked for a username and password to log in to the database:

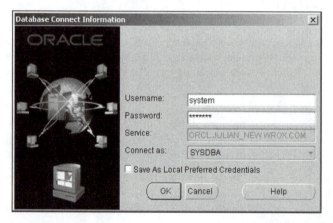

We need DBA (Database Administrator) privileges to create a schema, so select **SYSDBA** from the **Connect as** drop-down list. By default, Oracle has a user called system (with the password manager) with DBA privileges, so we will use this username to log on. The password should have been changed for security reasons, so check with your DBA if you can't log on with this combination.

The service node has four sub-nodes (**Instance**, **Schema**, **Security**, and **Storage**). Open up the **Security** sub-node; this has sub-nodes named **Users**, **Roles**, and **Profiles**. To create a new schema, we must create a new user, so open up the **Users** node.

Oracle is shipped with a number of sample schemas, including one named SCOTT which contains some tables and sample data. This schema has the permissions needed for connecting to the database and accessing its objects, so we will create our new schema by copying this one. This saves us from having to assign privileges ourselves. To do this, right-click on the **SCOTT** node, and select **Create Like...** from the context menu:

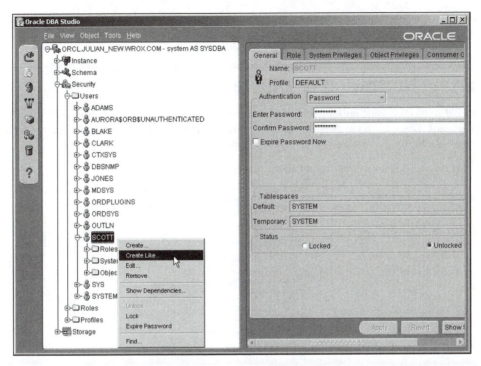

Copying the SCOTT user gets us up and running with the absolute minimum of fuss. All we need to do is enter a name for the new user (let's call it NORTHWIND), and type and confirm a password:

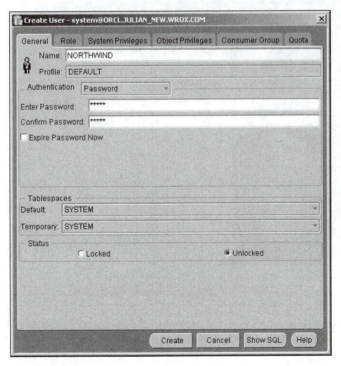

When you've entered this information, just click on **Create**. This will create the new user and the associated schema, so we will have somewhere to put our Northwind tables. We can now close DBA Studio – we're ready to begin actually migrating the database.

Exporting Northwind to Oracle

The final step is the most important one – this is where we actually run SQL Server's **Import and Export Data** wizard. The wizard has two functions: we will use it both to create the tables in our Oracle database, and to populate these tables with the data from the Northwind database.

To start the wizard, select **Import and Export Data** from the SQL Server start menu:

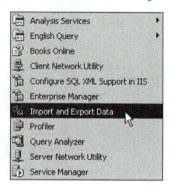

The first screen is simply a splash screen:

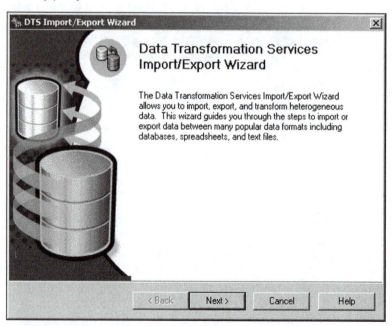

After clicking on the **Next >** button, we are asked to choose a data source from which we want to copy the data:

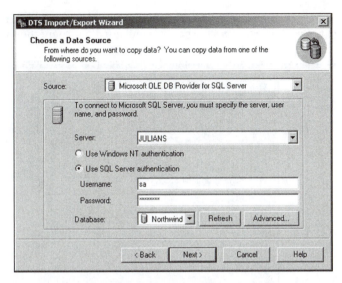

On this screen, ensure that the Microsoft OLE DB Provider for SQL Server is selected as the source, specify the name of the SQL Server from which you want to export the data (this will be the machine where you installed the evaluation version, unless you have access to another SQL Server), and select either Windows NT or SQL Server authentication mode. If you select Windows NT authentication, SQL Server will attempt to authenticate the Windows user account that you are currently using; if you choose SQL Server authentication, you will need to supply a username and password for an account which has access to the Northwind database.

Finally, select Northwind from the Database drop-down list, and click on Next >. We can now specify the database into which we want to export the data.

This screen is initially similar to the preceding one, but select Microsoft OLE DB Provider for Oracle from the Destination drop-down list, and, this time, the inner frame will be replaced with one containing just a single button labeled Properties...:

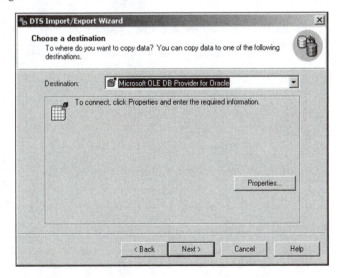

Clicking on this button brings up a **Data Link Properties** dialog box where we can specify the details we will use to connect to the Oracle database. Since we configured our connection when we installed the client components, all we need to do here is enter our net service name (ORCL), the username (NORTHWIND), and whatever password we assigned when we created this user:

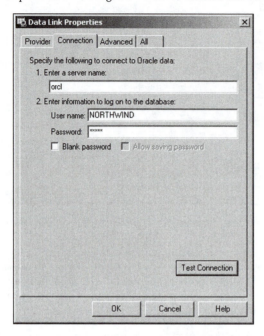

Click on **Test Connection** to check that the information we've given is correct and that we can access the Oracle server, then click on **OK** to close the **Data Link Properties** dialog, and click on **Next >** back on the **DTS Import/Export Wizard**.

The next screen asks us whether we want to copy entire tables to Oracle, or whether we want to run a SQL query to specify which data to copy:

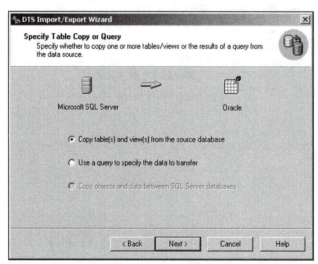

We want to recreate the database as closely as possible in Oracle, so leave the first option checked, and click on **Next >**. The next screen lets us select the tables and views that we want to export to Oracle. We've got quite a bit of work to do here, so it probably isn't worth exporting the views. We'll also leave out the tables `CustomerCustomerDemo` and `CustomerDemographics`, since these contain no data. Select all the remaining tables; the wizard will fill in the **Destination** column for each table selected:

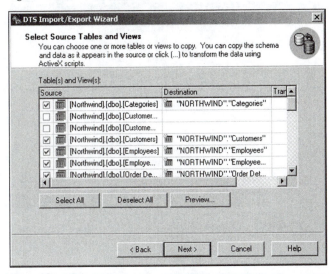

The default table names are in the form `"schema_name"."table_name"`. If we don't modify the default table names, the quotation marks will be included, so we'll have to use, for example, `SELECT * FROM "Categories"`, rather than `SELECT * FROM Categories`. There are a couple of things we'll have to do to rectify this. Firstly, in the **Destination** column, remove the schema name (an error will be generated because the table names are too long if we don't do this) and the quotation marks from each of the table names. We also need to remove the space from the `Order Details` table, so rename this `OrderDetails`:

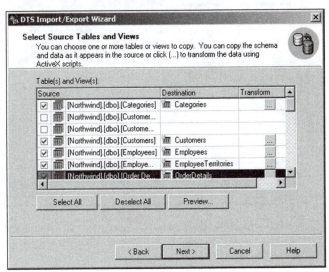

Unfortunately, there's still more to do. The wizard creates the tables in the Oracle database by executing SQL CREATE TABLE statements, and we'll also need to modify these to remove the quotation marks. To do this, click on the ... button in the Transform column for each table. This allows us to refine how the table is created:

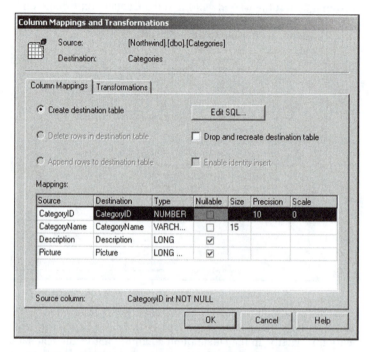

To edit the SQL statement used to create the table, click on the Edit SQL... button:

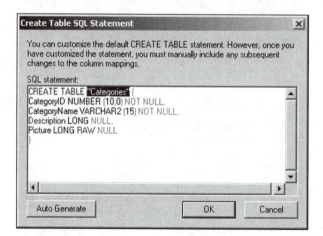

Remove the quotation marks round the table name in this CREATE TABLE statement (for example, replace CREATE TABLE "Categories" with CREATE TABLE Categories), and repeat this step for each of the tables that we're exporting.

The second change we have to make is due to the fact that Oracle doesn't allow two long fields in a single table. Two of the tables in Northwind (Categories and Employees) have both image fields and long text fields, so we will remove the image fields to prevent an error being generated. There are two steps to this; firstly, in the CREATE TABLE statement for each of these tables, delete the field from the list of fields. For the Categories table, this is the Picture field:

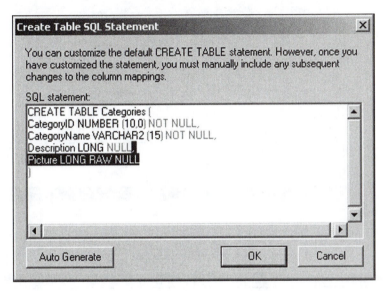

And for the Employees table, this is the Photo field. Don't forget to remove the preceding or following comma in both cases.

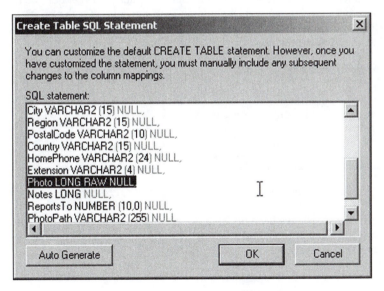

The next step is to alter the column mappings in the Column Mappings and Transformations dialog:

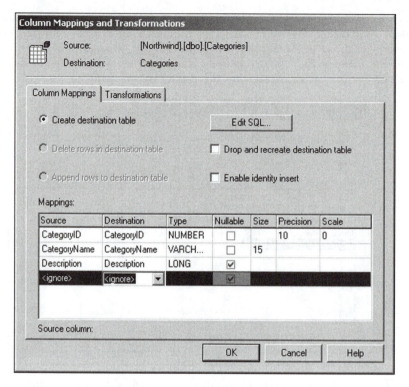

Altering the CREATE TABLE statement will prevent the field being included when the table is created, but we also need to tell the wizard to ignore this field the data itself is exported. To do this, select <ignore> from both the **Source** and **Destination** drop-down lists for the two fields we want to ignore. When you click on **OK** after updating each of these fields, a message will be displayed asking if you want to update the SQL statement:

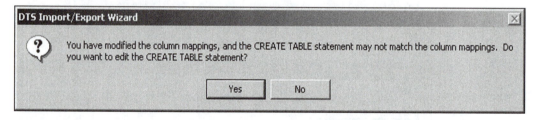

It's safe to select **No** here, since we've already updated the SQL statements.

When both of these tables have been updated, we're now ready to move on to the actual data migration, so click on **Next >**. The next screen asks us whether we want to migrate the data immediately, or save our settings as a DTS package:

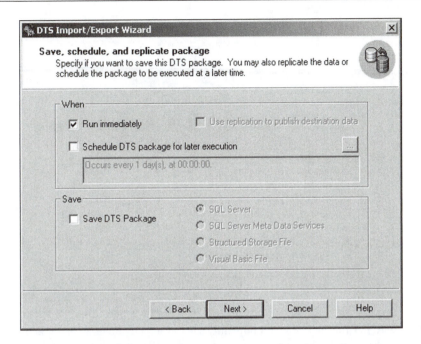

We want to run the migration package straight away, so just click on Next > here. A summary of our settings will be displayed:

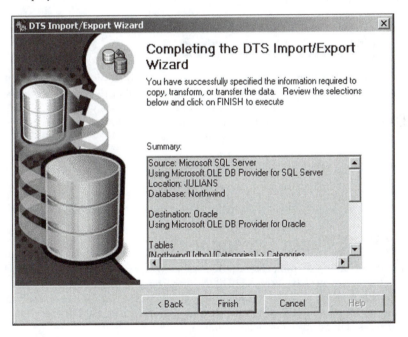

When we click on Finish, DTS will run, creating the tables and exporting the data. This may take a while, but the wizard keeps us informed of the status of operation as it progresses:

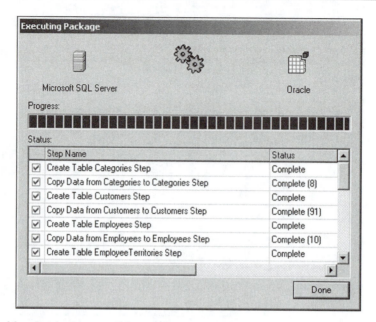

When the wizard has finished, you will hopefully see the screen above, with a green tick next to each of the steps, and you should get a message saying that eleven tables were successfully copied. And that's it – just click on Done to close the wizard. You can now access the Northwind data in Oracle by logging on to the database with the username Northwind.

Migrating Northwind to DB2

In this middle section, we'll see how to migrate the database to IBM's DB2 Universal Database, so you can use the examples in this book even if you're using DB2 rather than SQL Server as your database system. The process is similar to that for Oracle, but in this case, we won't use SQL Server's Import and Export Data wizard, but our own utility, which can be downloaded, along with the book's source code, from http://www.wrox.com. The steps we need to take are:

- ❑ Installing DB2 client components
- ❑ Creating a DB2 database for the Northwind data
- ❑ Running our data migration tool to import the data

Installing DB2 Client Components

As with Oracle, we can't just connect to a DB2 database server without first installing DB2's client components. If you can already access the DB2 server from the machine where you installed the SQL Server Evaluation Edition, or if you installed this on the DB2 server itself, you can omit this step. You can also omit this step if you plan to run the data migration tool on the DB2 server and you don't need to be able to access DB2 from your own machine.

Again, the process for installing these client components is similar to that for a full installation of the database server, so you'll need to get the DB2 CD from your system administrator.

Alternatively, a one-client personal developer's edition of the full database server can be downloaded free of charge from IBM's web site at
`http://www6.software.ibm.com/dl/db2pde/db2pde-p`.

When you run the setup program, you will be presented with several options:

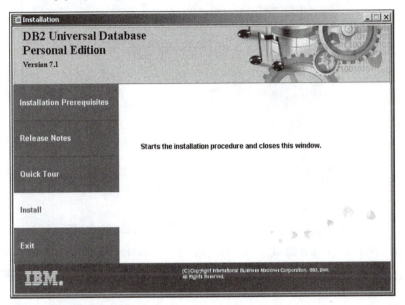

Select Install, and you'll be given the choice of installing either the database server, the Application Development Client, or the Administration Client:

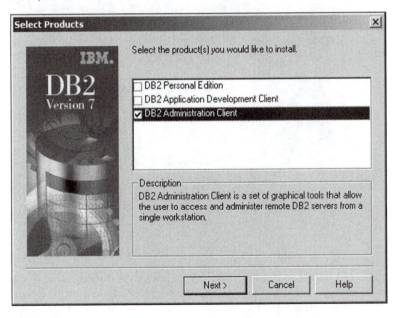

We will use the administrative tools to create a database on the remote DB2 server, so select the third of these options (**DB2 Administration Client**) and click on **Next**. We are now asked to select an installation type:

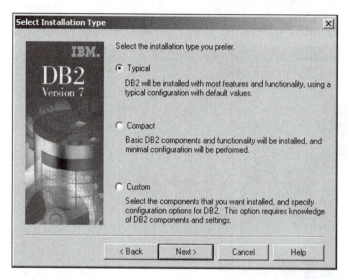

If you're very familiar with DB2, it's a good idea to select **Custom** to choose exactly which components are to be installed. However, here we'll take the simplest option and select a **Typical** installation, which will give us the functionality we need. However, be aware that this option requires over 200MB free space on your hard drive.

When we click on **Next**, we are asked to choose the folder where DB2 will be installed:

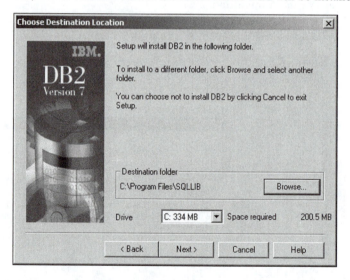

The default folder is \Program Files\SQLLIB, and it's a good idea to accept this default, since choosing another may require some configuration should you later choose to install additional DB2 components (such as the DB2 XML Extender).

When we click on the Next button, we are asked to enter a username and password which DB2 will use to log on to our operating system:

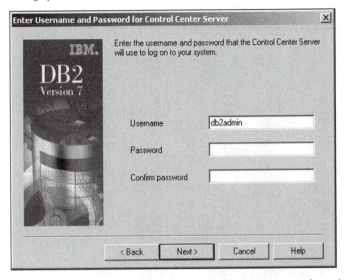

This is the username for the Windows account under which DB2 will run, and can be a new or existing account. If the specified username does not already exist, DB2 will ask whether it should create it for us:

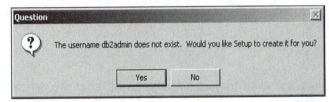

Select Yes to create the account. DB2 has now finished gathering the information it needs to install, and will present a summary of the settings:

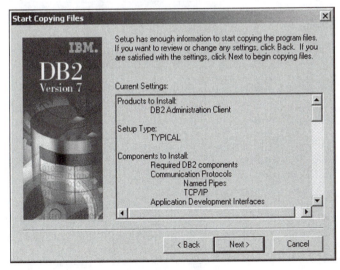

Click on **Next** to start the installation process itself. This may take some time, but it is the final step in the installation of the client components. When the setup has finished, you should be presented with the following message:

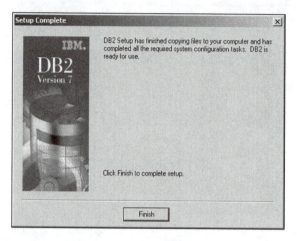

Creating a DB2 Database

Now we can access the DB2 server from our machine, we can create the database where we will store the data from Northwind. To do this, we will use Control Center (the DB2 equivalent of SQL Server's Enterprise Manager, or Oracle's DBA Studio). Start this up by selecting Programs | IBM DB2 | Control Center from your Start menu.

When this loads, we are presented with a tree view showing the DB2 servers and databases available on your system:

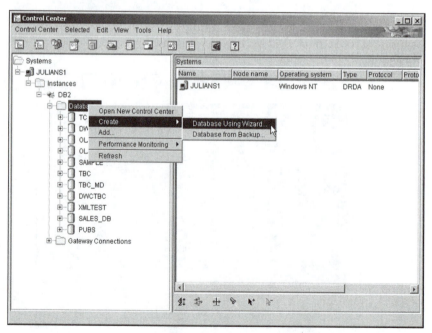

Each DB2 server can have a number of **instances** of DB2 installed on it. Each of these instances can have different configuration settings (e.g. they can use different data transfer protocols such as TCP/IP, or Named Pipes); you should be able to use any of the instances visible to your system, but if in doubt consult your database administrator.

Right-click on the Database node under the DB2 instance where you want to create the database, and select Create | Database Using Wizard... from the context menu. You will now be asked for a username and password to connect to the DB2 server:

You will need to enter the username and password of a user who already has access rights to the DB2 server – ask your DBA to give you the details of a suitable account, or to create a new account for the purpose.

> **Control Center doesn't always give us a lot of time to enter a username and password before hiding the dialog box, so if you have any difficulty running the Create Database Wizard, try minimizing and then maximizing the Control Center Window.**

We will now be asked to enter a name for our new database and the alias which we will use to access it:

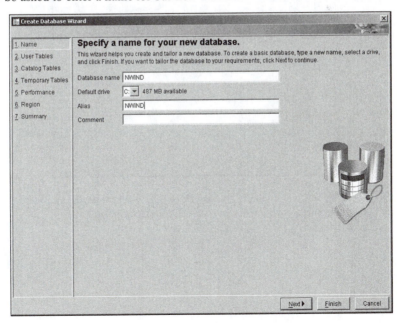

DB2 only supports database names of up to eight characters, so enter NWIND for both the name and alias. We don't want to create any tables at this time, so just click on the Finish button. You should now see a dialog box stating that DB2 has created the new NWIND database. Close this down, and then shut down the Control Center. We're now very nearly ready to run the Database Migration Tool to export the Northwind data to DB2.

The Data Migration Tool

However, there's just one more thing we have to do before we export the data – we need to ensure we've got the latest version of IBM's OLE DB provider for DB2. This can be downloaded from http://www-3.ibm.com/software/data/db2/udb/ad/v71/oledb.html. Unzip the downloaded file IBMDADB2.dll into a temporary directory, and find the file of the same name in the Program Files | SQLLIB | bin folder, and rename it IBMDADB2.bak (this is your existing OLE DB provider). Now copy the new file to this directory, and register it by selecting Run... from the Windows Start menu, typing Regsvr32 "C:\Program Files\SQLLIB\bin\IBMDADB2.dll" in the Run dialog box, and clicking on OK. We should now receive a message box informing us that the DLL registered successfully.

We're now all ready to run the Data Migration Tool. Double-click on the file in Windows Explorer, and the tool will start up:

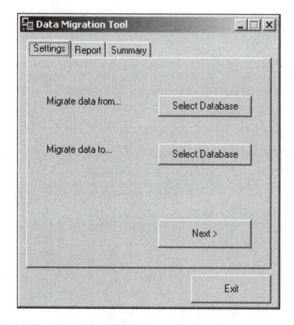

First, we need to specify the Northwind database from which we want to export the data, so click on the upper Select Database button. This will open up a Data Link dialog box:

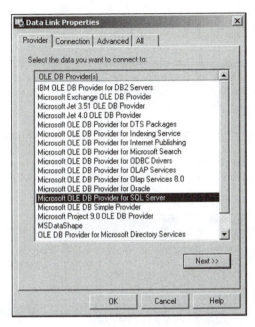

Ensure that Microsoft OLE DB Provider for SQL Server is selected on the Provider tab, and click on Next.

> *The utility can also migrate data from the Access Northwind database. If you wish to use this data, select either the Microsoft Jet 3.51 OLEDB Provider or Microsoft Jet 4.0 OLEDB Provider, and on the Connection tab browse to the NWIND.mdb file.*

The Connection tab allows us to specify the connection details for our database:

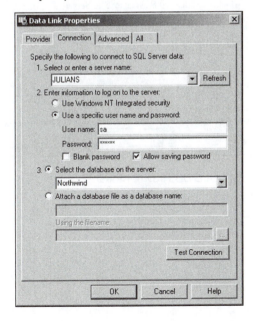

On this tab, specify the name of the SQL Server you want to connect to, the user ID and password to connect with, and specify the Northwind database.

> Make sure that the **Allow saving password** box is ticked, or the password won't be passed back to the utility, and it won't be able to open the connection.

Finally, click on the Test Connection button to ensure that the program can connect to the database.

Click on OK to return to the Data Migration Tool, and click on the lower Select Database button to select the DB2 database to which we'll be exporting the data. This will bring up another Data Link dialog box:

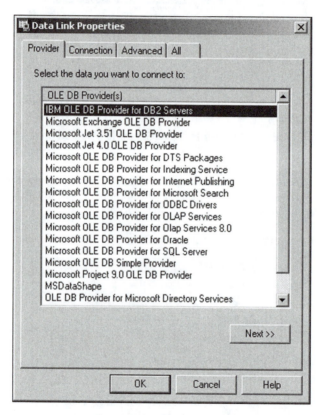

This time, make sure that IBM OLE DB Provider for DB2 Servers is selected on the Provider tab, and click on Next to move to the Connection tab:

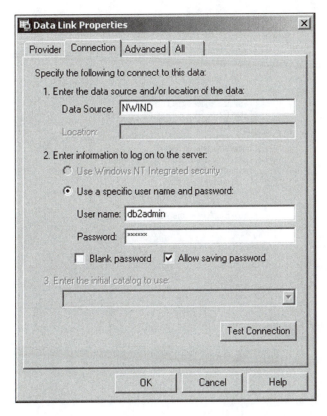

Specify **NWIND** in the **Data Source** box; this is the alias we used when we set up the NWIND database on DB2.

> *If you're familiar with ADO connection strings, note that, unlike a connection to SQL Server, the data source in a DB2 connection is not the server name.*

Specify the user name and password that was used to create the database, and again ensure that the **Allow saving password** box is checked. Click on the **Test Connection** button to ensure that the connection details are correct, and then on **OK** to return to the Data Migration Tool.

Clicking on the **Next >** button on the **Settings** tab will start the migration process. As the process continues, a progress report will be compiled on the **Report** tab, indicating if any errors occurred (if an entry doesn't fit in the listbox, you can double-click on that line to read the whole entry):

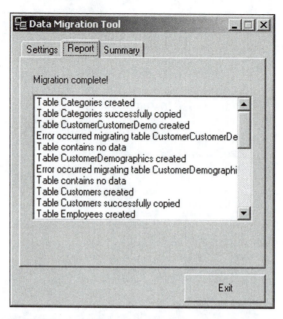

When the entire database has been exported, a final report will be displayed on the Summary tab:

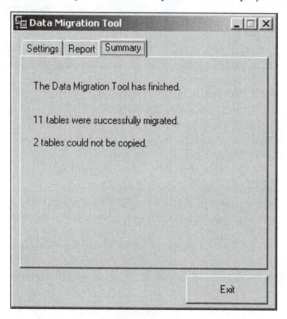

Don't worry if there are two tables which couldn't be copied – this is because the CustomerCustomerDemo and the CustomerDemographics tables contain no data. The tables themselves should be created without problems.

And that's it – your DB2 NWIND database should now have been populated with the data from the SQL Server Northwind database.

Migrating Northwind to MySQL

The last two sections demonstrated how to migrate the Northwind database to Oracle 8i and DB2. In this final section, we'll see how to migrate the database to the open-source database MySQL. For this, we will use the same custom data migration tool which we used to migrate to DB2, and which can be downloaded, along with the book's source code, from `http://www.wrox.com`. The process involves four steps:

- ❑ Installing the ODBC driver for MySQL (MyODBC)
- ❑ Creating a MySQL database for the Northwind data
- ❑ Creating an ODBC Data Source Name (DSN) to access this database
- ❑ Running our data migration tool to import the data

The current version (at the time of writing) of the MySQL database server can be downloaded under the GNU Public License from `http://www.mysql.com/downloads/mysql-3.23.html`.

Installing MyODBC

Like SQL Server, but unlike DB2 and Oracle, MySQL doesn't require any special components to be installed on the client-side before a MySQL database can be accessed on a remote server. However, if we want to access a MySQL database via ADO (which is what our utility does internally), we need to install the ODBC driver for MySQL: MyODBC.

MyODBC can be downloaded free of charge from the MySQL website at `http://www.mysql.com/downloads/api-myodbc.html`. The current version (at the time of going to press) is 2.50.36. It is available in versions for both Windows NT/2000 (`myodbc-2.50.36-nt.zip`) and Windows 95/98 (`myodbc-2.50.36-win95.zip`), as well as various Linux and Unix operating systems. Download the appropriate version for your platform, create a new directory (such as `C:\MyODBC`) and extract all the files in the Zip archive to this folder. When you have extracted all the files, you should find a file named `setup.exe` in the MyODBC folder. Double-click on this in Windows Explorer to start the installation process:

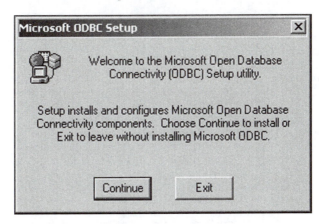

After clicking on Continue on this introductory screen, we are asked which ODBC drivers we want to install:

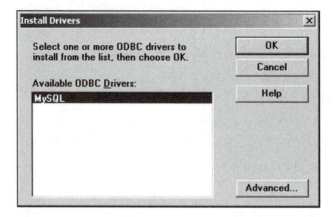

There will only be one driver in this list – the MySQL driver, which we want to install. Ensure this is selected, and click on OK.

The next screen displays a list of ODBC data sources already available on your machine:

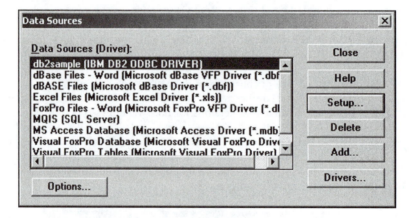

We need to create our Northwind database on the MySQL server before we create the DSN which will access it, so just click on Close here. You should now see a message informing you that the ODBC driver has been correctly installed:

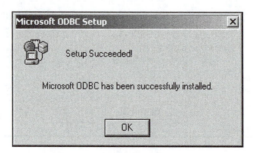

Creating a MySQL Database

We're now ready to create the MySQL database which will hold the Northwind data. To do this, we just need to execute the simple SQL statement CREATE DATABASE Northwind against the MySQL server. There are different ways of doing this, depending on the platform which the MySQL server is running on.

Windows Installations

The easiest way of doing this on a Windows platform is to run the MySQLManager.exe program on the MySQL server itself. This is a fairly simple GUI used for managing databases and is supplied with Windows distributions of MySQL. It is found in the \bin subfolder of the MySQL installation folder:

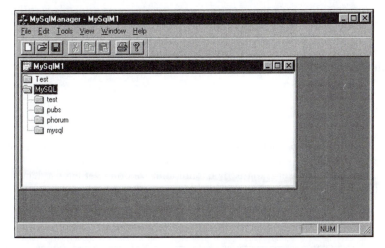

Open up this application, and you will see two nodes in the open MySqlManager document, called **Test** and **MySQL**. The live data on the server is accessed through the **MySQL** node, so select this node by clicking on it. To execute our CREATE DATABASE SQL statement, right-click on this node, and select **SQL Query** from the context menu. This will bring up a dialog box where we can enter SQL statements:

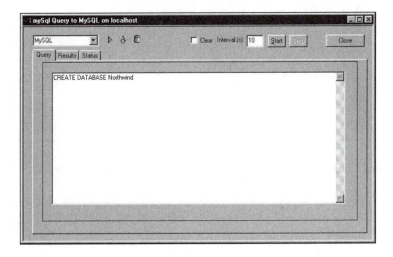

677

Type CREATE DATABASE Northwind into the **Query** box, and click on the little green arrow (towards the right-hand side at the top of the window) to execute the query. MySqlManager will now switch to the **Results** tab. If the query was unsuccessful, the error message will be displayed in the textbox on this tab. Otherwise, the database has been created successfully, and we're ready to move on to the next step.

Note that the new database won't appear in MySqlManager unless we open up a new document (by selecting File | New from the menu).

Linux and Unix Installations

Since Linux and Unix installations of MySQL aren't supplied with the MySqlManager program, we need to create the database using the console. However, the basic principle is still the same – we'll be executing exactly the same SQL statement against MySQL.

Navigate to the | bin directory under the MySQL installation directory (for example, | usr | local | mysql | bin). We will use the mysql program to execute our CREATE DATABASE statement. The command to start this takes the basic form:

```
mysql [-u username] [-p=password] [database]
```

MySQL uses a combination of username and machine name to authenticate users. By default, the user root on the MySQL server (root@localhost) is the system administrator and has full privileges. The password for the root user is blank by default, and we don't yet have a database to log on to, so we will start the mysql program using the command:

```
./mysql -u root
```

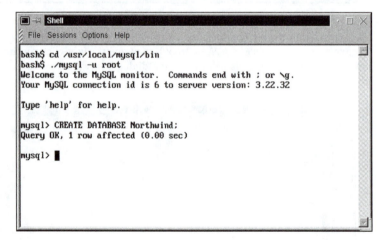

The initial . / just indicates that the mysql program is in the current directory.

When you've logged in, just type the SQL command CREATE DATABASE Northwind;. Note that when entering SQL statements via the mysql console, we need to end the statement with a semi-colon (;).

Assigning Database Privileges

Our next step is to assign permissions on the MySQL database to our user. By default, Windows installations of MySQL grant full privileges, to all databases, to the user `root` on any machine. You may find that these privileges aren't granted on other installations, so we'll assign privileges ourselves to a new user. To do this, we use the SQL `GRANT` statement:

```
GRANT privileges ON database.table TO user@host IDENTIFIED BY 'password';
```

In our case, we absolutely need `CREATE`, `SELECT`, and `INSERT` privileges (or the data migration utility won't work), and we'll add `UPDATE` and `DELETE` privileges for good measure. We will grant these privileges on all tables in all databases. The wild card to indicate 'all' (databases or tables) is the asterisk (`*`), so to assign privileges on all tables in all databases, we use `*.*`. We'll call our user `JULIAN`, and allow access from any machine. Note that the wild card we use here is the percentage sign (`%`), and *not* the asterisk, so the full user plus host name is `JULIAN@%`. Finally, we'll use the (admittedly feeble) password `password`. So our full SQL statement will look like this:

```
GRANT SELECT, CREATE, INSERT, UPDATE, DELETE ON *.* TO
JULIAN@% IDENTIFIED BY 'password';
```

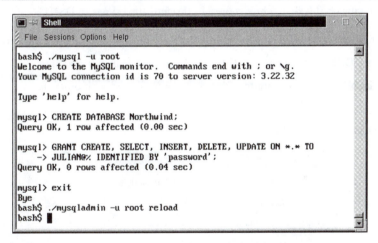

Finally, we need to reload the database to ensure that these changes take effect. Type `exit` to leave the `mysql` program, then type the line:

```
./mysqladmin -u root reload
```

And we can now use our new username to access the MySQL database.

Creating an ODBC DSN

Once we've created the `Northwind` database, we can create an ODBC Data Source Name (DSN) to connect to it from our client computer. A DSN is simply a name given to a set of connection information, which we can use to connect to a specific database. To create a new DSN, open up the **ODBC Data Source Administrator**; this is found as **Data Sources (ODBC)** under the **Administrative Tools** folder on a Windows 2000 machine, or as **ODBC Data Sources (32bit)** on a Windows 95/98 machine:

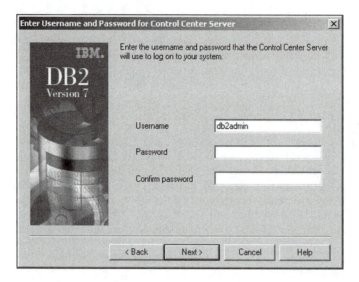

The first three tabs on this dialog box represent three distinct types of DSNs:

- ❑ User DSN – These are usable only by the current user, and only on the current machine.

- ❑ System DSN – These are usable by any user on the current machine.

- ❑ File DSN – These are stored as files, and can be shared with other users.

Our Northwind data isn't sensitive, so we'll create a System DSN which any user on the current machine can use, so click on the second tab:

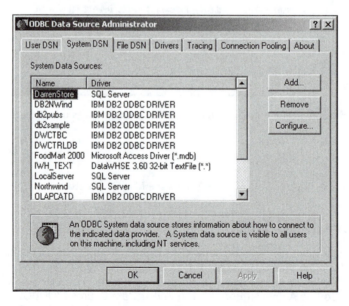

We need to create a completely new DSN, so now click on the Add... button towards the top right of the dialog box. We're now presented with a list of the available ODBC drivers on the computer:

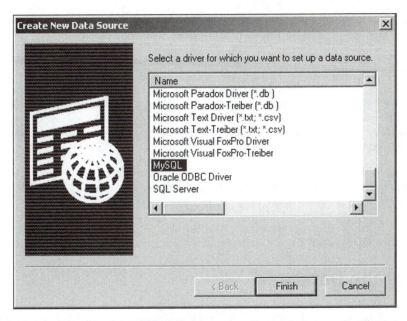

Scroll down the list until you find the **MySQL** driver, select that and click on the **Finish** button. The MyODBC data source configuration dialog will now be displayed:

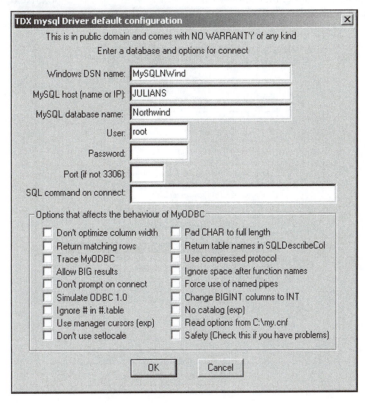

Enter a name for this DSN in the top box (e.g. MySQLNWind), the name or IP address of the MySQL server in the second box, and Northwind in the MySQL database name box.

In the next two boxes, we need to enter the username and password of a user who has access permissions to our database. As we mentioned above, MySQL uses a combination of username plus hostname (that is, the name or IP address of the user's computer). By default, Windows installations of MySQL allow full access to all databases to the root user on any machine, so we will enter root in the User box. The password for this user is blank by default, but should have been changed – you need to ask your DBA for this. For Linux/Unix installations, enter the username and password which we created when we created the Northwind database.

You probably won't need to alter any of the other fields, but if the MySQL server is running on a TCP port other than 3306, you will need to enter the appropriate port number in the fifth box. Your system administrator should be able to tell you the correct port.

When you've filled out this information, click on the OK button to create the DSN, and then click on OK to close the ODBC Data Source Administrator. We're now ready to run the data migration utility.

Migrating the Database

This final step is essentially the same as for migrating to DB2, as discussed in the previous section, so we'll go over it very quickly. Load up the migrate.exe program, and click on the top Select Database button. This will bring up a Data Links dialog box; use this to connect to the SQL Server or Access Northwind database. Remember to check the Allow saving password box. Next, click on the lower Select Database button. This will bring up another Data Links dialog box, which we will use to connect to our MySQL database:

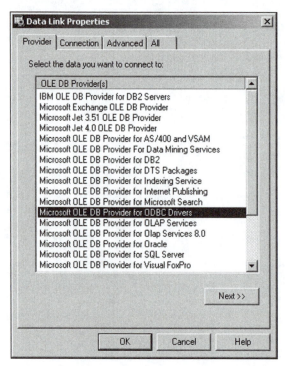

On the first tab, Provider, ensure that the Microsoft OLE DB Provider for ODBC Drivers is selected, then click on the Next button to move to the next tab:

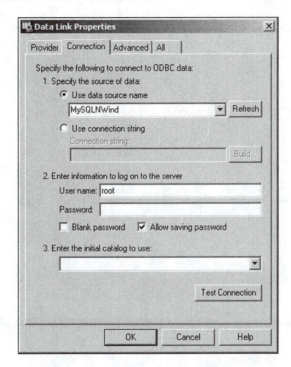

Click on the Refresh button next to the Use data source name radio button to refresh the list of DSNs available, and then select the DSN you've just created from the drop-down list. In the second section, enter the same username and password that you used when you created the DSN, and again ensure that the Allow saving password box is checked. Note that we do *not* need to select the initial catalog in the third section. Finally, click on the Test Connection button to ensure that all the connection information is correct. If this succeeds, click on OK to close the Data Links dialog.

Clicking on the Next > button now on the Data Migration Tool will start the migration process; this requires no more user input, but see the DB2 section for a description of the process. When the utility has finished running, the Northwind data should have been successfully migrated to MySQL.

> **There's just one more word of warning – note that table names in MySQL on Linux/Unix are case-sensitive.**

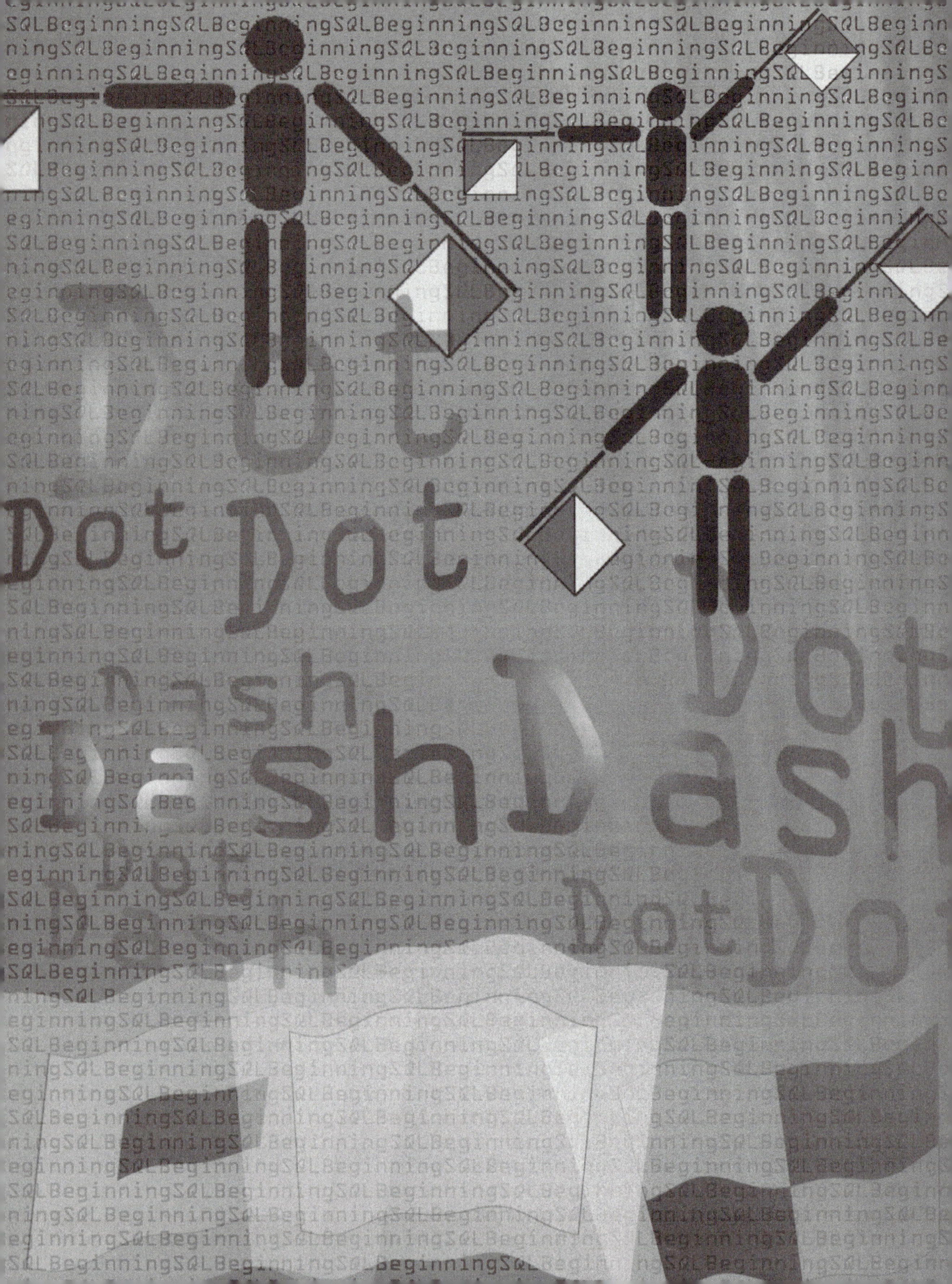
Dot Dot
Dash
Dash
Dot
Dot

ASP Quick Start Tutorial

This appendix is intended to help if you have *limited* previous ASP experience, or simply need a refresher. It is not intended to teach you everything there is to know about ASP – this is the subject of many other books, such as *Beginning ASP 3.0* (ISBN 1-861003-38-2) from Wrox Press. However, it should give you enough of an understanding to be able to follow along with our examples of ASP, such as in Chapter 18.

ASP is a great tool for creating dynamic web pages. It is a Microsoft technology, which works by allowing us the functionality of a programming language, using the programming code to dynamically generate HTML for our web pages. Using ASP you can do many things. You are able to draw upon the wealth of data available to you on the server and across the enterprise in various databases. You are able to customize pages to the needs of each different user that comes to your web site. In addition, by keeping your code on the server-side you can build a library of functionality. This library can be drawn upon again and again to further enhance other web sites. Best of all, using server-side script libraries will allow your web sites to scale to multi-tier, or distributed, web applications.

ASP can be used to create everything from simple, static web pages, to database-aware dynamic sites, using HTML and scripting. Its other important use is as programming *glue*. Through the use of ASP, you can create and manipulate server-side components. These components can perhaps provide data to your application such as graphic image generation, or maybe link to a mainframe database. ASP does nothing but facilitate the use of these components on the web. ASP comes with some built-in objects that are important to understand before their full potential can be unleashed. We will cover each of these objects in depth. Finally, we'll look at some real-world examples of using ASP on a web site.

Introducing Active Server Pages

When a web page is viewed over the Internet, there are a lot of things going on behind the scenes. For instance, when we type in a URL, what actually happens is that the client makes a request to the server, and the server provides the response to the client. What we're looking at here is really the foundation of client/server computing. A client makes a request from a server and the server fulfills that request. We see this pattern of behavior throughout the programming world today, not only in web programming.

Microsoft recognized this pattern and developed a new technology that rendered web programming a much more accessible technique. This technology is Active Server Pages or ASP for short. ASP is a server-side scripting environment that comes with Microsoft's Internet Information Services. ASP allows you to embed scripting commands inside your HTML documents. The scripting commands are interpreted by the server and translated into the corresponding HTML and sent back to the server. This enables the web developer to create content that is dynamic and fresh. The beauty of this is that it does not matter which browser your web visitor is using, because the server returns only pure HTML. Sure you can extend your returned HTML with browser specific programming, but that is your choice. By no means is this all that ASP can do, but we'll cover more of its capabilities, such as form validation and data manipulation, later in this appendix.

Although you can use languages such as JavaScript or even Perl, by default the ASP scripting language is VBScript.

InASP.Net, VBscript has been replaced by pure VB.Net.

How the Server Recognizes ASPs

ASP pages do not have an `html` or `htm` extension; they have a `.asp` extension instead. The reason for this is twofold. First, in order for the web server to know to process the scripting in your web page, it needs to know that there is some in there. Well, by setting the extension of your web page to `.asp`, the server can assume that there are scripts in your page.

A nice side effect of naming your ASP pages with the `asp` *extension is that the ASP processor knows that it does not need to process your HTML files. It used to be the case, as in ASP 2.0, that any page with the* `.asp` *extension, no matter whether it contained any server side scripting code or not, was automatically sent to the server, and would thereby take longer to process. With the introduction of ASP 3.0 in Windows 2000, the server is able to determine the presence of any server side code and process or not process the page accordingly. This increases the speed of your HTML file retrieval and makes your web server run more efficiently.*

Secondly, using an `asp` extension (forcing interpretation by the ASP processor every time your page is requested) hides your ASP scripts. If someone requests your `.asp` file from the web server, all he is going to get back is the resultant processed HTML. If you put your ASP code in a file called `mycode.scr` and request it from the web server, you'll see all of the code inside.

ASP Basics

ASP files are really just HTML files with scripting embedded within them. When a browser requests an ASP file from the server, it is passed on to the ASP-processing DLL for execution. After processing, the resulting file is then sent on to the requesting browser. Any scripting commands embedded from the original HTML file are executed and then removed from the results. This is excellent in that all of your scripting code is hidden from the person viewing your web pages. That is why it is so important that files containing ASP scripts have an `.asp` extension.

The Tags of ASP

To distinguish the ASP code from the HTML inside your files, ASP code is placed between `<%` and `%>` tags. This convention should be familiar to you if you have ever worked with any kind of server-side commands before in HTML. The tag combination implies to the ASP processor that the code within should be executed by the server and removed from the results. Depending on the default scripting language of your web site, this code may be VBScript, JScript, or any other language you've installed.

All of our ASP scripts in this appendix will be in VBScript, since that is the default.

In the following snippet of HTML, you'll see an example of some ASP code between the `<%` and `%>` tags:

```
<TABLE>
<TR>
<TD>
<%
    x = x + 1
    y = y - 1
%>
</TD>
</TR>
</TABLE>
```

<SCRIPT> Blocks

You may also place your ASP code between `<SCRIPT></SCRIPT>` blocks. However, unless you direct the script to run at the server level, code placed between these tags will be executed at the client as normal client-side scripts. To direct your script block to execute on the server, use the `RUNAT="Server"` command within your `<SCRIPT>` block as follows:

```
<SCRIPT Language="VBScript" RUNAT="Server">
… Your Script …
</SCRIPT>
```

The Default Scripting Language

As stated previously, the default scripting language used by ASP is VBScript. However, you may change it for your entire site, or just a single web page. Placing a special scripting tag at the beginning of your web page does this. This tag specifies the scripting language to use for this page only:

```
<%@ LANGUAGE=ScriptingLanguage%>
```

ScriptingLanguage can be any language for which you have the scripting engine installed. ASP comes with JScript, as well as VBScript.

If you are using the `<SCRIPT>` tags, you can specify which language to use by adding the `Language` attribute as shown:

```
<SCRIPT Language="VBScript" RUNAT="Server">
```

You can set the default scripting language for the entire application by changing the Default ASP language field in the Internet Service Manager on the App Options tab.

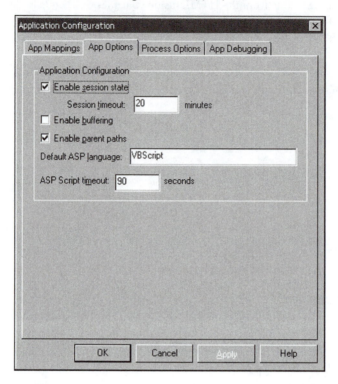

Mixing HTML and ASP

You've probably guessed by now that one can easily mix HTML code with ASP scripts. VBScript has all of the control flow mechanisms like If Then, For Next, and Do While loops. However, with ASP you can selectively include HTML code based on the results of these operators. Let's look at an example.

Suppose you are creating a web page that greets the viewer with a "Good Morning", "Good Afternoon", or "Good Evening" depending on the time of day. This can be done as follows:

```
<HTML>
<BODY>
<P>The time is now <%=Time()%></P>
<%
    Dim iHour

    iHour = Hour(Time())

    If (iHour >= 0 And iHour < 12 ) Then
%>
Good Morning!
<%
```

```
        ElseIf (iHour > 11 And iHour < 5 ) Then
%>
Good Afternoon!
<%
    Else
%>
Good Evening!
<%
End If
%>
</BODY>
</HTML>
```

First we print out the current time. The <%= notation is shorthand to print out the value of an ASP variable or the result of a function call. We then move the hour of the current time into a variable called iHour. Based on the value of this variable we write our normal HTML text.

Notice how the HTML code is outside of the ASP script tags. When the ASP processor executes this page, the HTML that lies between control flow blocks that aren't executed is discarded, leaving you with only the correct code. Here is the source of what is returned from our web server after processing this page (at 19:48:37):

```
<HTML>
<BODY>
<P>The time is now 7:48:37 PM</P>

Good Evening!

</BODY>
</HTML>
```

As you can see, the scripting is completely removed leaving only the HTML tags and text.

The other way to output data to your web page viewer is using one of ASP's built-in objects called Response. We'll cover this approach in the next section as you learn about the ASP object model.

Commenting Your ASP Code

As with any programming language, it is of the utmost importance to comment your ASP code as much as possible. However, unclear comments are not worth putting in your code.

Comments in ASP are identical to comments in VBScript. When ASP comes across the single quote character it will graciously ignore the rest of the line:

```
<%
Dim iLumberJack

'I'm a comment and I'm O.K.
iLumberJack = iLumberJack + 1
%>
```

The Active Server Pages Object Model

ASP, like most Microsoft technologies, utilizes a Component Object Model, or COM, to expose functionality to consumer applications. ASP is actually an extension to your web server that allows server-side scripting. At the same time it also provides a compendium of objects and components, which manage interaction between the web server and the browser. These objects form the **Active Server Pages Object Model**. These objects can be manipulated by scripting languages. Take a look at the following diagram:

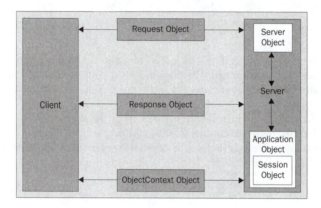

ASP 3.0 neatly divides into objects, which manage their own part of the interaction between client and server. As you can see in the diagram, at the heart of the interaction between client and server are the Request and Response objects, but we will be taking a quick tour through the major objects and components that are part of ASP.

The object model consists of six core objects, each one with distinct properties and methods. The objects are:

- ❑ Request
- ❑ Response
- ❑ Application
- ❑ Session
- ❑ Server
- ❑ ObjectContext

There are other objects within ASP 3.0, but the ones above are the ones you will use more frequently, and so we will not cover the other objects here.

Request

When your web page is requested, much information is passed along with the HTTP request, such as the URL of the web page requested and format of the data being passed. It can also contain feedback from the user such as the input from a text box or drop down list box. The Request object allows you to get at information passed along as part of the HTTP request. The corresponding output from the server is returned as part of the Response.

The `Request` object has five collections. Interestingly, they all act as the default property for the object. That is to say, you may retrieve information from any of the five collections by using the abbreviated syntax, for example:

```
ClientIPAddress = Request("REMOTE_ADDR")
```

> *Collections in ASP are very similar to their VBScript namesakes. They act as data containers that store their data in a manner close to that of an array. The information is stored in the form of name/value pairs.*

ASP searches through the collections in the following order:

- ❑   `QueryString`
- ❑   `Form`
- ❑   `Cookies`
- ❑   `ClientCertificate`
- ❑   `ServerVariables`

If there are variables with the same name, only the first is returned when you allow ASP to search. This is another good reason for you to fully qualify your collection.

QueryString

Contains a collection of all the information attached to the end of a URL. When you make a URL request, the additional information is passed along with the URL to the web page, appended with a question mark. This information takes the following form:

```
URL?item=data[&item=data][...]
```

The clue to the server is the question mark. When the server sees this, it knows that the URL has ended, and variables are starting. So an example of a URL with a query string might look like this:

```
http://www.buythisbook.com/book.asp?bookname=BeginningSQL
```

We stated earlier that the collections store information in name/value pairs. Despite this slightly unusual method of creating the name/value pair, the principle remains the same. `bookname` is the name and `BeginningSQL` is the value. When ASP gets hold of this URL request, it breaks apart all of the name/value pairs and places them into this collection for easy access. This is another excellent feature of ASP. Query strings are built up using ampersands to delimit each name/value pair so if you wished to pass the user information along with the book information, you could pass the following:

```
http://www.buythisbook.com/book.asp?bookname=BeginningSQL&buyer=JohnSmith
```

Query strings can be generated in one of three ways. The first is, as discussed, by a user-typed URL. The second is as part of a URL specified in an anchor tag:

```
<A HREF="book.asp?bookname=BeginningXML">Go to book buying page</A>
```

So when you click on the link, the name/value pair is passed along with the URL. The third and final method is via a form sent to the server with the GET method:

```
<FORM ACTION="book.asp" METHOD="GET">
Type your name: <INPUT TYPE="TEXT" NAME="buyer"><BR>
Type your requested book:  <INPUT TYPE="TEXT" NAME="bookname" SIZE=40><BR>
<INPUT TYPE=SUBMIT VALUE=Submit>
</FORM>
```

You input the information into the text boxes on the form. The text is submitted when you click on the Submit button and two query strings are generated.

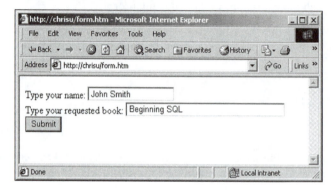

Next you need to be able to retrieve information, and you use this technique regardless of which of the three methods were used to generate the query string:

```
Request.QueryString("buyer")
Request.QueryString("bookname")
```

Note that these lines won't display anything by themselves, you need to add either the shorthand notation (equality operator) to display functions in front of a single statement, or when a number of values need displaying then use Response.Write to separately display each value in the collection.

e.g. <%=Request.QueryString("buyer")%> or
Response.Write(Request.QueryString("bookname"))

The first of the two Request object calls should return the name of John Smith on the page and the second of the two should return Beginning SQL. Of course you could always store this information in a variable for later access:

```
sBookName = Request.QueryString("bookname")
```

Form

Contains a collection of all the form variables posted to the HTTP request by an HTML form. Query strings aren't very private as they transmit information via a very visible method, the URL. If you want to transmit information more privately then you can use the Form collection to do so – it sends its information as part of the HTTP Request body. This easy access to form variables is one of ASP's best features.

If we go back to our previous example, the only alteration we need to make to our HTML form code is to change the METHOD attribute. Forms using this collection must be sent with the POST method and not the GET method. It is actually this attribute that determines how the information is sent by the form. So if we change the method of the form as follows:

```
<FORM ACTION="book.asp" METHOD="POST">
Type your name: <INPUT TYPE="TEXT" NAME="buyer"><BR>
Type your requested book:  <INPUT TYPE="TEXT" NAME="bookname" SIZE=40><BR>
<INPUT TYPE=SUBMIT VALUE=Submit>
</FORM>
```

Once the form has been submitted in this style, then we can retrieve and display the information using the following:

```
<%=Request.Form("buyer")%>
```

Cookies

Contains a read-only collection of cookies sent by the client browser along with the request. Because the cookies were sent from the client, they cannot be changed here. You must change them using the Response.Cookies collection. A discussion of cookies can be found a little later on when we look at the Response object.

ClientCertificate

When a client makes a connection with a server requiring a high degree of security, either party can confirm who the sender/receiver is by inspecting their digital certificate. A digital certificate contains a number of items of information about the sender, such as the holder's name, address and length of time the certificate is valid for. A third party, known as the Certificate Authority or CA, will have previously verified these details.

The ClientCertificate collection is used to access details held in a client side digital certificate sent by the browser. This collection is only populated if you are running a secure server, and the request was via an https:// call instead of an http:// call. This is the preferred method to invoke a secure connection.

ServerVariables

When the client sends a request and information is passed across to the server, it's not just the page that is passed across, but information such as who created the page, the server name, and the port that the request was sent to. The HTTP header that is sent across together with the HTTP request also contains information of this nature, such as the type of browser, and type of connection. This information is combined into a list of variables that are predefined by the server as environment variables. Most of them are static and never really change unless you change the configuration of your web server. The rest are based on the client browser. Server variables are merely informative, but they do give you the ability to customize page content for specific browsers, or to avoid script errors that might be generated.

Request Object Property and Method

The Request object contains a single property and a single method. They are used together to transfer files from the client to the server. Uploading is accomplished using HTML forms.

TotalBytes Property

When the request is processed, this property will hold the total number of bytes in the client browser request. Most likely you'd use it to return the number of bytes in the file you wish to transfer. This information is important to the `BinaryRead` method.

BinaryRead Method

This method retrieves the information sent to the web server by the client browser in a `POST` operation. When the browser issues a `POST`, the data is encoded and sent to the server. When the browser issues a `GET`, there is no data other than the URL. The `BinaryRead` method takes one parameter, the number of bytes to read. So if you want it to read a whole file, you pass it the total number of bytes in the file, generated by the `TotalBytes` property.

It's very rarely applied because `Request.QueryString` and `Request.Form` are much easier to use. That's because `BinaryRead` wraps its answer in a safe array of bytes. For a scripting language that essentially only handles variants, that makes life a little complicated. However this format is essential for file uploading when the file contains something other than pure text. You can find full details on how to upload files and then decode a safe array of bytes in an excellent article at: http://www.15seconds.com/Issue/981121.htm.

The Response Object

After you've processed the request information from the client browser, you'll need to be able to send information back. The `Response` object is just the ticket. It provides you with the tools necessary to send anything you need back to the client.

The Response Object's Collection

The `Response` object contains only one collection: `Cookies`. This is the version of the `Request` object's `Cookies` collection that can be written to.

If you've not come across them before, cookies are small (limited to 4kb of data) text files stored on the hard drive of the client that contain information about the user, such as whether they have visited the site before and what date they last visited the site. There are lots of misapprehensions about cookies being intrusive as they allow servers to store information on the user's drive. However you need to remember that firstly the user has to voluntarily accept cookies or activate an Accept Cookies mechanism on the browser for them to work, secondly this information is completely benign and cannot be used to determine the user's e-mail address or such like. They are used to personalize pages that the user might have visited before. Examples of things to store in cookies are unique user ids, or user names; then, when the user returns to your web site, a quick check of cookies will let you know if this is a return visitor or not.

You can create a cookie on the user's machine as follows:

```
Response.Cookies("BookBought") = "Beginning SQL"
```

You can also store multiple values in one cookie using an index value key. The cookie effectively contains a VBScript `Dictionary` object and using the key can retrieve individual items. The way it functions is very similar to an array.

```
Response.Cookies("BookBought")("1") = "Beginning SQL"
Response.Cookies("BookBought")("2") = "Professional ASP 3.0"
```

A cookie will automatically expire – disappear from the user's machine – the moment a user ends their session. To extend the cookie beyond this natural lifetime, you can specify a date with the Expires property. The date takes the following format: *WEEKDAY DD-MON-YY HH:MM:SS*, for example:

```
Response.Cookies("BookBought").Expires = #31-Dec-99#
```

The # sign can be used to delimit dates in ASP (as in VBScript).

Other properties that can be used in conjunction with this collection are:

- ❑   Domain: a cookie is only sent to pages requested within the domain from which it was created
- ❑   Path: a cookie is only sent to pages requested within this path
- ❑   HasKeys: specifies whether the cookie uses an index/Dictionary object or not
- ❑   Secure: specifies whether the cookie is secure – a cookie is only deemed secure if sent via the HTTPS protocol

You can retrieve the cookie's information using the Request object's Cookies collection, mentioned earlier. To do this you could do the following:

```
You purchased <%=Request.Cookies("BookBought")%> last time you visited the site.
```

If there were several cookies in the collection you could iterate through each cookie and display the contents as follows:

```
For Each cookie in Request.Cookies
    Response.Write (Request.Cookies(cookie))
Next
```

The Response Object's Methods

To understand what the Response object's methods and properties do, we need to examine in more detail the workings of how ASP sends a response. When an ASP script is run, an **HTML output stream** is created. This stream is a receptacle in which the web server can store details and create the dynamic/interactive web page. As mentioned before, the page has to be created entirely in HTML for the browser to understand it (excluding client-side scripting, which is ignored by the server).

The stream is initially empty when created. New information is added to the end. If any custom HTML headers are required then they have to be added at the beginning. Then the HTML contained in the ASP page is added next to the script, so anything not encompassed by <% %> tags is added. The Response object provides two ways of writing directly to the output stream, either using the Write method or its shorthand technique.

Write

Probably the most frequently used method of all the built-in objects, Write allows you to send information back to the client browser. You can write text directly to a web page by encasing the text in quotation marks:

```
Response.Write "Hello World!"
```

Or to display the contents of a variant you just drop the quotation marks:

```
sText = "Hello World!"
Response.Write sText
```

For single portions of dynamic information that only require adding into large portions of HTML, you can use the equality sign as shorthand for this method, as specified earlier, for example:

```
My message is <% =sText %>
```

This technique reduces the amount of code needed, but at the expense of readability. There is nothing to choose between these techniques in terms of performance.

AddHeader

This method allows you to add custom headers to the HTTP response. For example, if you were to write a custom browser application that examined the headers of your HTTP requests for a certain value, you'd use this method to set that value. Usage is as follows:

```
Response.AddHeader "CustomServerApp", "BogiePicker/1.0"
```

This would add the header `CustomServerApp` to the response with the value of `BogiePicker/1.0`. There are no restrictions regarding headers and header value.

AppendToLog

Calling this method allows you to append a string to the web server log file entry for this particular request. This allows you to add custom log messages to the log file.

BinaryWrite

This method allows you to bypass the normal character conversion that takes place when data is sent back to the client. Usually, only text is returned, so the web server cleans it up. By calling `BinaryWrite` to send your data, the actual binary data is sent back, bypassing that cleaning process.

Clear

This method allows you to delete any data that has been buffered for this page so far. See the discussion of the `Buffer` property for more details.

End

This method stops processing the ASP file and returns any currently buffered data to the client browser.

Flush

This method returns any currently buffered data to the client browser and then clears the buffer. See the discussion of the `Buffer` property for more details.

Redirect

This method allows you to relinquish control of the current page to another web page entirely. For example, you can use this method to redirect users to a login page if they have not yet logged on to your web site:

```
<%
If (Not Session("LoggedOn") ) Then
    Response.Redirect "login.asp"
End If
%>
```

The Response Object's Properties

Buffer

You may optionally have ASP buffer your output for you. The `Buffer` property tells ASP whether or not to buffer output. Usually, output is sent to the client as it is generated. If you turn buffering on (by setting this property to `True`), output will not be sent until all scripts have been executed for the current page, or the `Flush` or `End` methods are called.

`Response.Buffer` has to be inserted after the language declaration, but before any HTML is used. If you insert it outside this scope you will most likely generate an error. A correct use of this method would look like:

```
<@ LANGUAGE = "VBSCRIPT">
<% Response.Buffer = True %>
<HTML>
...
```

The `Flush` method is used in conjunction with the `Buffer` property. To use it correctly you must set the `Buffer` property first and then at places within the script you can flush the buffer to the output stream, while continuing processing. This is useful for long queries, which might otherwise worry the user that nothing was being returned.

The `Clear` method erases everything in the buffer that has been added since the last `Response.Flush` call. It erases only the response body however and leaves the response header intact.

CacheControl

Generally when a proxy server retrieves an ASP web page, it does not place a copy of it into its cache. That is because by their very nature ASP pages are dynamic and, most likely, a page will be stale by the next time it is requested. You may override this feature by changing the value of this property to `Public`.

Charset

This property will append its contents to the HTTP content-type header that is sent back to the browser. Every HTTP response has a content-type header that defines the content of the response. Usually the content-type is `"text/html"`. Setting this property will modify the type sent back to the browser.

ContentType

This property allows you to set the value of the content-type that is sent back to the client browser.

Expires

Most web browsers keep web pages in a local cache. The cache is usually kept as long as you keep your browser running. Setting the Expires property allows you to limit the time the page stays in the local cache. The value of the Expires property specifies the length of time in minutes before the page will expire from the local cache. If you set this to zero, the page will not be cached at all.

ExpiresAbsolute

Just like the Expires property, this property allows you to specify the exact time and date on which the page will expire.

IsClientConnected

This read-only property indicates whether or not the client is still connected to the server. Remember that the client browser makes a request then waits for a response? Well, imagine you're running a lengthy script and during the middle of processing, the client disconnects because he was waiting too long. Reading this property will tell you if the client is still connected or not. Unfortunately in ASP 2.0, this property doesn't seem to function correctly, and has only been repaired within ASP 3.0 in Windows 2000.

Status

This property allows you to set the value returned on the status header with the HTTP response.

The Application and Session Objects

The Application and Session objects, like Request and Response, work very closely together. Application is used to tie all of the pages together into one consistent application, while the Session object is used to track and present a user's series of requests to the web site as a continuous action, rather than as an arbitrary set of requests.

Scope Springs Eternal

Normally, you will declare a variable for use within your web page. You'll use it, manipulate it, then perhaps print out its value, or whatever. But when your page is reloaded, or the viewer moves to another page, the variable, with its value, is gone forever. By placing your variable within the Contents collection of the Application or Session objects, you can extend the life span of your variable!

Any variable or object that you declare has two potential scopes: procedure and page. When you declare a variable within a procedure, its life span is limited to that procedure. Once the procedure has executed, your variable is gone. You may also declare a variable at the web page level but like the procedure-defined variable, once the page is reloaded, the value is reset.

Enter the Application and Session objects. The Contents collections of these two objects allow you to extend the scope of your variables to session-wide, and application-wide. If you place a value in the Session object, it will be available to all web pages in your site for the life span of the current session (more on sessions later). Good session scope variables are user ids, user names, login time, etc, things that pertain only to the session. Likewise, if you place your value into the Application object, it will exist until the web site is restarted. This allows you to place application-wide settings into a conveniently accessible place. Good application scope variables are font names and sizes, table colors, system constants, etc; things that pertain to the application as a whole.

The global.asa File

Every ASP application may utilize a special script file. This file is named global.asa and it must reside in the root directory of your web application. It can contain script code that pertains to the application as a whole, or each session. You may also create ActiveX objects for later use in this scripting file.

The Application Object

ASP works on the concept that an entire web site is a single web application. Therefore, there is only one instance of the Application object available for use in your scripting at all times. Note that it is possible to divide up your web site into separate applications, but for the purposes of this discussion we'll assume there is only one application per web site.

Collections

The Application object contains two collections: Contents and StaticObjects. The Contents collection was discussed earlier. The StaticObjects collection is similar to Contents, but only contains the objects that were created with the <OBJECT> tag in the scope of your application. This collection can be iterated just like the Contents collection.

You cannot store references to ASP's built-in objects in Application*'s collections.*

Methods

The Application object contains two methods:

❑ The Lock method is used to "lock-down" the Contents collection so that it cannot be modified by other clients. This is useful if you are updating a counter, or perhaps grabbing a transaction number stored in the Application's Contents collection.

❑ The Unlock method "unlocks" the Application object thus allowing others to modify the Contents collection.

Events

The Application object generates two events: Application_OnStart and Application_OnEnd. The Application_OnStart event is fired when the first view of your web page occurs. The Application_OnEnd event is fired when the web server is shut down. If you choose to write scripts for these events they must be placed in your global.asa file.

The most common use of these events is to initialize application-wide variables. Items such as font names, table colors, database connection strings, perhaps even writing information to a system log file. The following is an example global.asa file with script for these events:

```
<SCRIPT LANGUAGE=VBScript RUNAT=Server>
Sub Application_OnStart
    'Globals…
    Application("ErrorPage") = "handleError.asp"
    Application("SiteBanAttemptLimit") = 10
    Application("AccessErrorPage") = "handleError.asp"
    Application("RestrictAccess") = False

    'Keep track of visitors…
    Application("NumVisits") = Application("NumVisits") + 1
End Sub
</SCRIPT>
```

The Session Object

Each time a visitor comes to your web site, a `Session` object is created for the visitor if the visitor does not already have one. Therefore, there is an instance of the `Session` object available to you in your scripting as well. The `Session` object is similar to the `Application` object in that it can contain values. However, the `Session` object's values are lost when your visitor leaves the site. The `Session` object is most useful for transferring information from web page to web page. Using the `Session` object, there is no need to pass information in the URL.

The most common use of the `Session` object is to store information in its `Contents` collection. This information would be session-specific in that it would pertain only to the current user.

Many web sites today offer a "user personalization" service, that is, to customize a web page to their preference. This is easily done with ASP and the `Session` object. The user variables are stored in the client browser for retrieval by the server later. Simply load the user's preferences at the start of the session and then, as the user browses your site, utilize the information regarding the user's preferences to display information.

For example, suppose your web site displays stock quotes for users. You could allow users to customize the start page to display their favorite stock quotes when they visit the site. By storing the stock symbols in your `Session` object, you can easily display the correct quotes when you render your web page.

This session management system relies on the use of browser cookies. The cookies allow the user information to be persisted even after a client leaves the site. Unfortunately, if a visitor to your web site does not allow cookies to be stored, you will be unable to pass information between web pages within the `Session` object.

Collections

The `Session` object contains two collections: `Contents` and `StaticObjects`. The `Contents` collection we discussed earlier. The `StaticObjects` collection is similar to `Contents`, but only contains the objects that were created with the <OBJECT> tag in your HTML page. This collection can be iterated just like the `Contents` collection.

Properties

The following table contains the properties that the `Session` object exposes for your use:

Property	Description
CodePage	Setting this property will allow you to change the character set used by ASP when it is creating output. This property could be used if you were creating a multi-national web site.
LCID	This property sets the internal locale value for the entire web application. By default, your application's locale is your server's locale. If your server is in the U.S., then your application will default to the U.S. Much of the formatting functionality of ASP utilizes this locale setting to display information correctly for the country in question. For example, the date is displayed differently in Europe versus the U.S. So based on the locale setting, the date formatting functions will output the date in the correct format.

Property	Description
LCID (*Continued*)	You can also change this property temporarily to output data in a different format. A good example is currency. Let's say your web site had a shopping cart and you wanted to display totals in U.S. dollars for U.S. customers, and Pounds Sterling for U.K. customers. To do this you'd change the LCID property to the British locale setting, and then call the currency formatting routine.
SessionID	Every session created by ASP has a unique identifier. This identifier is called the SessionID and is accessible through this property. It can be used for debugging ASP scripts.
Timeout	By default, ASP sessions will timeout after 20 minutes of inactivity. Every time a web page is requested or refreshed by a user, the internal ASP time clock starts ticking. When the time clock reaches the value set in this property, the session is automatically destroyed. You can set this property to change the timeout period if you wish.

Methods

The Session object contains a single method, Abandon. This instructs ASP to destroy the current Session object for this user. This method is what you would call when a user logs off your web site.

Events

The Session object generates two events: Session_OnStart and Session_OnEnd. The Session_OnStart event is fired when the first view of your web page occurs. The Session_OnEnd event is fired when the web server is shut down. If you choose to write scripts for these events they must be placed in your global.asa file.

The most common use of these events is to initialize session-wide variables – items like usage counts, login names, real names, user preferences, etc. The following is an example global.asa file with script for these events:

```
<SCRIPT LANGUAGE=VBScript RUNAT=Server>
Sub Session_OnStart
    Session("LoginAttempts") = 0
    Session("LoggedOn") = False
End Sub

Sub Session_OnEnd
    Session("LoggedOn") = False
End Sub
</SCRIPT>
```

The Server Object

The next object in the ASP object model is the Server object. The Server object enables you to create and work with ActiveX controls in your web pages. In addition, the Server object exposes methods that help in the encoding of URLs and HTML text.

Properties

ScriptTimeout

This property sets the time in seconds that a script will be allowed to run. The default value for all scripts on the system is 90 seconds. Or, if a script has run for longer than 90 seconds, the web server will intervene and let the client browser know something is wrong. If you expect your scripts to run for a long time, you will want to use this property.

Methods

CreateObject

This method is the equivalent to VBScript's `CreateObject`, or using the `New` keyword – it instantiates a new instance of an object. The result can be placed into the `Application` or `Session Contents` collection to lengthen its life span.

Generally you'll create an object at the time the session is created and place it into the `Session.Contents` collection. For example, let's say you've created a killer ActiveX DLL with a really cool class that converts Fahrenheit to Celsius and vice versa. You could create an instance of this class with the `CreateObject` method and store it in the `Session.Contents` collection like this:

```
Set Session("MyConverter") = Server.CreateObject("KillerDLL.CDegreeConverter")
```

This object would be around as long as the session is and will be available for you to call. This method is invaluable when working with database connections.

ASP comes with its own built in set of components that you can create instances of using the `CreateObject` method. These are:

- ❑ **AdRotator** – used to display a random graphic and link every time a user connects to the page
- ❑ **Browser Capabilities** – manipulates a file called `browscap.ini` contained on the server computer to determine the capabilities of a particular client's browser
- ❑ **Content Linker** – provides a central repository file from where you manage a series of links and their URLs, and provides appropriate descriptions about them
- ❑ **ContentRotator** – a cut down version of the Ad Rotator that provides the same function but without optional redirection
- ❑ **PageCounter** – counts the number of times a page has been hit
- ❑ **PermissionChecker** – checks to see if a user has permissions before allowing them to access a given page
- ❑ **Counters** – counts any value on an ASP page from anywhere within an ASP application
- ❑ **MyInfo** – can be used to store personal information about a user within an XML file
- ❑ **Status** – used to collect server profile information
- ❑ **Tools** – a set of miscellaneous methods that are grouped under the generic heading of Tools
- ❑ **IISLog** – allows you to create an object that allows your applications to write to and otherwise access the IIS log

Execute

This method executes an ASP file and inserts the results into the response. You can use this call to include snippets of ASP code, like subroutines.

GetLastError

This method returns an ASPError object that contains all of the information about the last error that has occurred.

HTMLEncode

This method encodes a string for proper HTML usage. This is useful if you want to actually display HTML code on your web pages.

MapPath

This method returns a string that contains the actual physical path to the file in question. Subdirectories of your web site can be virtual. That is to say that they don't physically exist in the hierarchy of your web site. To find out the true whereabouts of a file, you can call this method.

Transfer

The Transfer method allows you to immediately transfer control of the executing page to another page. This is similar to the Response.Redirect method except for the fact that the Transfer method makes all variables and the Request collections available to the called page.

URLEncode

This method, as the title suggests, encodes a URL for transmission. This encoding includes replacing spaces with a plus sign (+) and replacing unprintable characters with hexadecimal values. You should always run your URLs through this method when redirecting.

The ObjectContext Object

The final object we shall consider is the ObjectContext object, which comes into play when you use transactions in your web page. When an ASP script has initiated a transaction, it can either be committed or aborted by this object. It has two methods to do this.

SetAbort

SetAbort is called when the transaction has not been completed and you don't want resources updated.

SetComplete

SetComplete is called when there is no reason for the transaction to fail. If all of the components that form part of the transaction call SetComplete, then the transaction will complete.

Using Active Server Pages Effectively

Is it true that a little bit of knowledge is a bad thing? In the realm of ASP, I think not. A little bit of knowledge is probably just piquing your interest. For the final part of this appendix we're going to build a web site to demonstrate some of the features of ASP. This sample site will demonstrate many of the ASP features and principles described earlier.

Designing the Site

Before we start creating our new web site, we should discuss the design. For your first ASP application, we'll keep it quite simple. What we want to create is an HTML form that accepts for input the following information: first name, last name, and e-mail address. After the user submits the form, our ASP page will reformat the first and last name, and check the e-mail address for proper syntax.

The user will be given three attempts to enter the information correctly or else a warning message will display at the bottom of the screen. The input page will look like this:

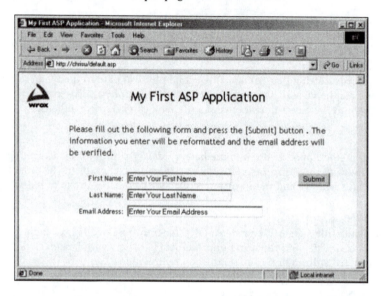

Creating the global.asa File

The first step in creating a new ASP application is to create your `global.asa` file. This is the file that houses your event handlers for the `Application` and `Session` objects. In addition, in this file you may set application-wide and session-wide variables to their default values. To create this file, in the root of your web server directory create a file called `global.asa`. Here is the content of our sample `global.asa`:

```
<SCRIPT LANGUAGE=VBScript RUNAT=Server>
Sub Application_OnStart
    Application("AllowedErrorsBeforeWarning") = 3
End Sub

Sub Session_OnStart
    Session("ErrorCount") = 0
End Sub

Sub Session_OnEnd
    'Nothing to do here...
End Sub
```

```
Sub Application_OnEnd
    'Nothing to do here...
End Sub
</SCRIPT>
```

Our file has handlers defined for `Application_OnStart`, `Application_OnEnd`, `Session_OnStart`, and `Session_OnEnd`. The `Application_OnEnd` and `Session_OnEnd` events are not used in this example, but are shown above for completeness.

We want to set a limit on the number of submissions the user can make before a warning message is shown. Since this is a feature of the application and affects all users, we will store this constant in the `Application.Contents` collection. This is done in the `Application_OnStart` event. We add to the collection an item named `AllowedErrorsBeforeWarning` and set its value to 3.

Now that we know how many times a user can *try* to get it right, we need a place to store the number of times the user has *tried* to get it right. Since this counter is different for each user, we'll place this into the `Session.Contents` collection. We initialize our variable to 0. This is done in the `Session_OnStart` event. We add to the collection an item named, appropriately, `ErrorCount`, with a value of 0.

Creating our Main Page

Now that we've laid the groundwork for our ASP application, it's time to build the main page. Since this is a simple example, we will only utilize a single web page. Let's begin by creating this single page.

Create a new web page on your site and name it `default.asp`. This is the file name used by IIS as the default web page. The default web page is the page that is returned by a web server when no web page is specified. For example, when you call up http://www.wrox.com/, you aren't specifying a web page. The server looks through its list of default file names and finds the first match in the web site's root directory.

The page is quite long. But it breaks logically into two distinct sections: the ASP/VBScript portion, and the HTML portion. Let's examine each section individually.

The ASP/VBScript Section

The top half of our file is where the ASP code lives. This is the code that is executed by the server before the page is returned to the browser that requested it. As you've seen, any code that is to be executed on the server before returning is enclosed in the special `<%` and `%>` tags.

For clarity (and sanity!), the ASP code has been divided into subroutines. This not only makes the code more readable, but also will aid in its reuse. Our code has two routines: `Main`, and `InitCap`.

Before we do anything else however, we declare some variables:

```
<%@ Language=VBScript %>
<%
Dim txtFirstName, txtLastName, txtEmailAddr
Dim sMessage
```

When variables are declared outside of a subroutine in an ASP page, the variables retain their data until the page is completely processed. This allows you to pass information from your ASP code to your HTML code, as you'll see.

After our variables have been declared, we have our `Main` routine. This is what is called by our ASP code every time a browser retrieves the page. The `Main` subroutine is not called automatically: we must explicitly call it ourselves.

```
'*************************************************************************
'* Main
'*
'* The main subroutine for this page...
'*************************************************************************

Sub Main()
    ' Was this page submitted?
   if ( Request("cmdSubmit") = "Submit" ) Then
    ' Reformat the data into a more readable format...
      txtFirstName = InitCap(Request("txtFirstName"))
      txtLastName = InitCap(Request("txtLastName"))
      txtEmailAddr = LCase(Request("txtEmailAddr"))
      ' Check the email address for the correct components...
      if ( Instr(1, txtEmailAddr, "@") = 0 or Instr(1, txtEmailAddr, ".") = 0 ) Then
        sMessage = "The email address you entered does not appear to be valid."
      Else
         ' Make sure there is something after the period..
         if ( Instr(1, txtEmailAddr, ".") = Len(txtEmailAddr) & _
            or Instr(1, txtEmailAddr, "@") = 1 or & _
            (Instr(1, txtEmailAddr, ".") = Instr(1, txtEmailAddr, "@") + 1) ) Then
            sMessage = "You must enter a complete email address."
         end if
      End If

      'We passed our validation, show that all is good...
      if ( sMessage = "" ) Then
        sMessage = "Thank you for your input. All data has passed verification."
      else
         Session("ErrorCount") = Session("ErrorCount") + 1

       if ( Session("ErrorCount") > Application("AllowedErrorsBeforeWarning") ) then
           sMessage = sMessage & "<P><Font Size=1>You have exceeded the" & _
                  " normal number of times it takes to get this right!</Font>"
        end if
      End If
   Else
      ' First time in here? Set some default values...
      txtFirstName = "Enter Your First Name"
      txtLastName = "Enter Your Last Name"
      txtEmailAddr = "Enter Your Email Address"
   End If
End Sub
```

First we see if the form was actually submitted by the user, otherwise we initialize our variables. To determine if the page has been submitted, we check the value of the `cmdSubmit Request` variable. This is the button on our form. When pressed, the form calls this page and sets the value of the `cmdSubmit` button to `Submit`. If a user just loads the page without pressing the button, the value of `cmdSubmit` is blank (`" "`). There are other ways to determine if a web page was submitted, but this method is the simplest.

After we have determined that the page was in fact submitted, we run the names through the second function on this page: `InitCap`. `InitCap` is a quick little function that will format a word to proper case. That is to say that the first letter will be capitalized, and the rest of the word will be lower case. Here is the function:

```
'****************************************************************
'* InitCap
'*
'* Capitalizes the first letter of the string
'****************************************************************

Function InitCap(sStr)
    InitCap = UCase(Left(sStr, 1)) & LCase(Right(sStr, Len(sStr) - 1))
End Function
```

Now that we've cleaned up the names, we need to check the e-mail address for validity. To do this we ensure that it contains an "@" sign and a period (.). Once past this check, we make sure that there is data after the period and that there is data before the "@" sign. This is 'quick and dirty' e-mail validity checking.

If either of these checks fail, we place a failure message into the string sMessage. This will be displayed in our HTML section after the page processing is complete.

Now, if our e-mail address has passed the test, we set the message (sMessage) to display a thank you note. If we failed our test, we increment our error counter that we set up in the global.asa file. Here we also check to see if we have exceeded our limit on errors. If we have, a sterner message is set for display.

Finally, the last thing in our ASP section is our call to Main. This is what is called when the page is loaded:

```
'****************************************************************
'* Call our main subroutine
'****************************************************************

Call Main()
```

The HTML Section

This section is a regular HTML form with a smattering of ASP thrown in for good measure. The ASP that we've embedded in the HTML sets default values for the input fields, and displays any messages that our server side code has generated:

```
<HTML>
<HEAD>
    <META NAME="GENERATOR" Content="Microsoft FrontPage 3.0">
    <TITLE>My First ASP Application</TITLE>
</HEAD>

<BODY>
<TABLE border="0" cellPadding="0" cellSpacing="0" width="600">
```

```
<TBODY>
  <TR>
    <TD width="100"><A href="http://www.wrox.com" target="_blank"
    border=0 alt><IMG border=0 title="Check out the Wrox Press Web Site!"
    src="images/wroxlogo.gif" WIDTH="56" HEIGHT="56"></A></TD>
    <TD width="500"><CENTER><FONT size="5" face="Trebuchet MS">My First
    ASP Application</FONT></CENTER></TD>
  </TR>

  <TR>
    <TD width="100"> </TD>
    <TD width="500" align="left"><FONT face="Trebuchet MS"><BR>
    Please fill out the following form and press the [Submit] button. The
    information you enter will be reformatted and the email address will
    be verified.</FONT>
    <FORM action="default.asp" id="FORM1" method="post" name="frmMain">
     <TABLE border="0" cellPadding="1" cellSpacing="5" width="100%">
      <TR>
        <TD width="100" nowrap align="right">
          <FONT size="2" face="Trebuchet MS">First Name:</FONT>
        </TD>
        <TD width="350"><FONT size="2" face="Trebuchet MS">
          <INPUT title="Enter your first name here" name="txtFirstName"
          size="30" value="<%=txtFirstName%>" tabindex="1"></FONT></TD>
        <TD width="50"><DIV align="right"><FONT size="2" face="Trebuchet MS">
          <INPUT type="submit" title="Submit this data for processing..."
          value="Submit" name="cmdSubmit" tabindex="4"></FONT></TD>
      </TR>

      <TR>
        <TD width="100" nowrap align="right">
          <FONT size="2" face="Trebuchet MS">Last Name:</FONT></TD>
        <TD width="400" colspan="2">
          <FONT size="2" face="Trebuchet MS">
          <INPUT title="Enter your last name here" name="txtLastName"
          size="30" value="<%=txtLastName%>" tabindex="2"></FONT></TD>
      </TR>

      <TR>
        <TD width="100" nowrap align="right">
          <FONT size="2" face="Trebuchet MS">Email Address:</FONT>
        </TD>
        <TD width="400" colspan="2"><FONT size="2" face="Trebuchet MS">
        <INPUT title="Enter your valid email address here"
        name="txtEmailAddr" size="40" value="<%=txtEmailAddr%>"
        tabindex="3"></FONT></TD>
      </TR>
      <TR>
        <TD nowrap width=500 colspan="3" align="center">
        <FONT face="Trebuchet MS"><BR>
        <STRONG><%=sMessage%></STRONG> </FONT></TD>
      </TR>
    </TABLE>
  </FORM>
  <P> </TD>
  </TR>
</TBODY>
</TABLE>
</BODY>
</HTML>
```

The most important part of the HTML is where the ASP code is embedded. The following snippet illustrates this:

```
<INPUT title="Enter your first name here" name="txtFirstName" size="30"
 value="<%=txtFirstName%>" tabindex="1">
```

Here we see a normal text input box. However, to set the value of the text box we use the `Response.Write` shortcut (`<%=`) to insert the value of the variable `txtFirstName`. Remember that we dimensioned this outside of our ASP functions so that it would have page scope. Now we utilize its value by inserting it into our HTML. We do exactly the same thing with the Last Name and Email Address text boxes.

The last trick in the HTML section is the display of our failure or success message. This message is stored in the variable called `sMessage`. At the bottom of the form, we display the contents of this variable like so:

```
<TD nowrap width=500 colspan="3" align="center">
    <FONT face="Trebuchet MS">
    <BR>
    <STRONG>
    <%=sMessage%>
    </STRONG>
    </FONT>
</TD>
```

The beauty of this code is that if `sMessage` is blank then nothing is shown, otherwise the message is displayed.

Summary

In this ASP Quick Start tutorial we discussed Active Server Pages, or ASP. You learned how ASP pages are created, and what special HTML tags you need to include in your files to use ASP. We looked through the ASP object model and saw that the `Request` and `Response` objects are used to manage details of the HTTP request and responses. We saw that the `Application` object is used to group pages together into one application and we saw that the `Session` object is used to create the illusion that the interaction between user and site is one continuous action. Finally, we created a small application that demonstrates two uses for ASP: form validation and data manipulation.

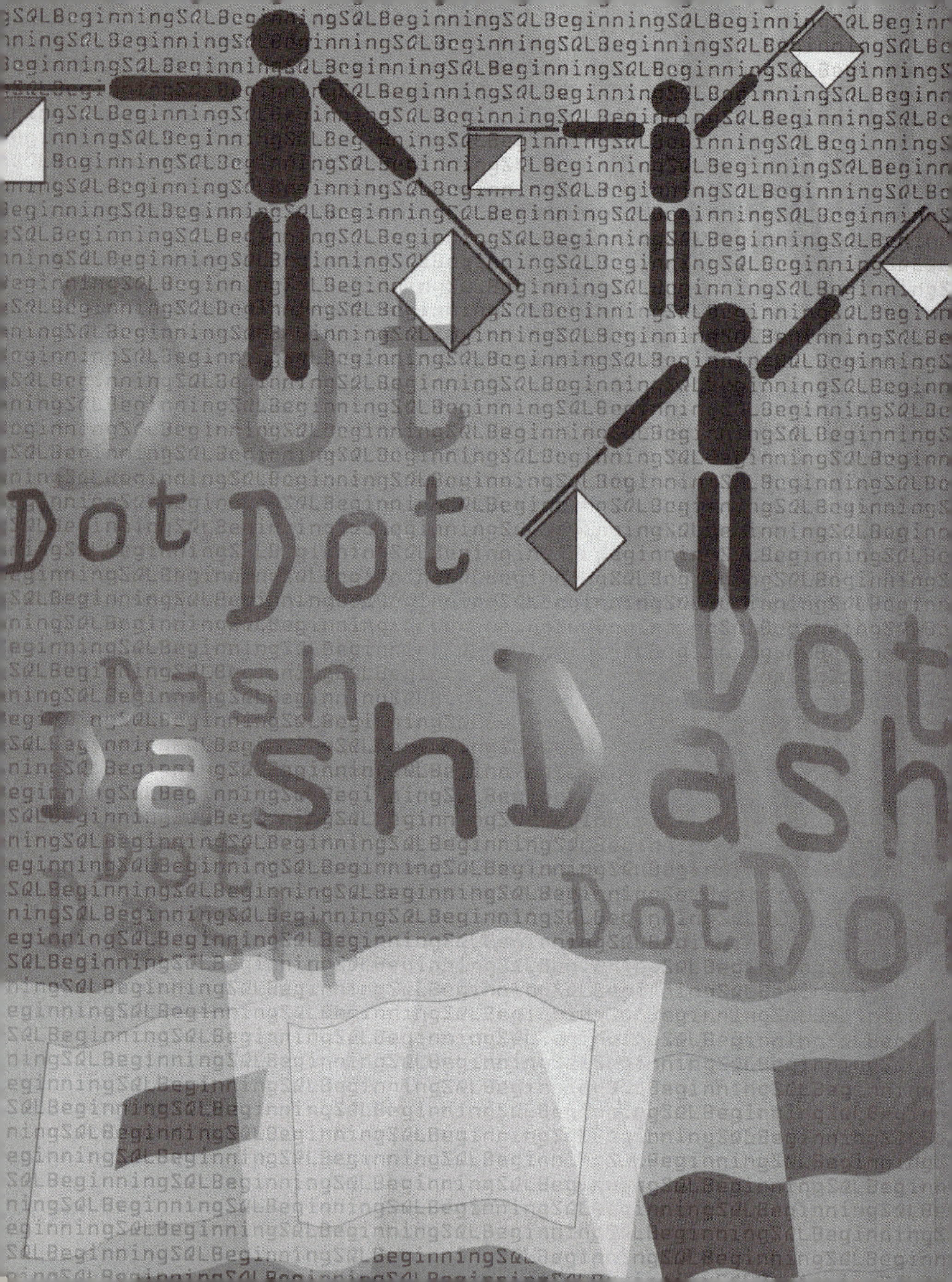
BeginningSQL
Dot Dot
Dash
Dash
Dot
DotDot

Support, Errata and P2P.Wrox.Com

One of the most irritating things about any programming book is when you find that bit of code you've just spent an hour typing simply doesn't work. You check it a hundred times to see if you've set it up correctly and then you notice the spelling mistake in the variable name on the book page. Of course, you can blame the authors for not taking enough care and testing the code, the editors for not doing their job properly, or the proofreaders for not being eagle-eyed enough, but this doesn't get around the fact that mistakes do happen.

We try hard to ensure no mistakes sneak out into the real world, but we can't promise that this book is 100% error free. What we can do is offer the next best thing by providing you with immediate support and feedback from experts who have worked on the book, and try to ensure that future editions eliminate these gremlins.

We also now commit to supporting you not just while you read the book, but once you start developing applications as well, through our online forums, where you can put your questions to the authors, reviewers, and fellow industry professionals.

In this appendix we'll look at how to:

❑   Enroll in the peer to peer forums at http://p2p.wrox.com

❑   Post and check for errata on our main site, http://www.wrox.com

❑   E-mail technical support with a query or feedback on our books in general

Between all three of these support procedures, you should get an answer to your problem very quickly.

The Online Forums at P2P.Wrox.Com

You can join the SQL mailing list (or any others which are of interest to you) for author and peer support. Our system provides **programmer to programmer™ support** on mailing lists, forums and newsgroups all in addition to our one-to-one e-mail system, which we'll look at in just a while. Be confident that your query is not just being examined by a support professional, but by the many Wrox authors and other industry experts present on our mailing lists.

How to Enroll for Online Support

Just follow this four-step system:

1. Go to p2p.wrox.com in your favorite browser. Here you'll find any current announcements concerning P2P – new lists created, any removed and so on.

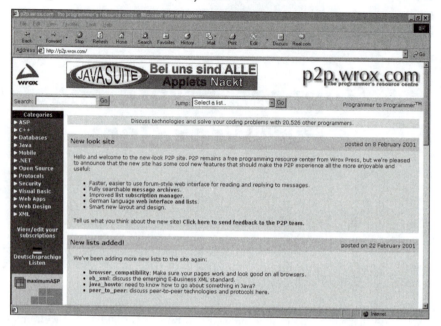

2. Click on the Databases button in the left hand column.

3. Choose to access the sql_language list.

4. If you are not a member of the list, you can choose to either view the list without joining it or create an account in the list, by hitting the respective buttons.

5. If you wish to join, you'll be presented with a form in which you'll need to fill in your e-mail address, name and a password (of at least 4 digits). Choose how you would like to receive the messages from the list and then hit Save.

6. Congratulations. You're now a member of the sql_language mailing list.

Why this System Offers the Best Support

You can choose to join the mailing lists and you can receive a weekly digest of the list. If you don't have the time or facility to receive the mailing list, then you can search our online archives. You'll find the ability to search on specific subject areas or keywords. As these lists are moderated, you can be confident of finding good, accurate information quickly. Mails can be edited or moved by the moderator into the correct place, making this a most efficient resource. Junk and spam mail are deleted, and your own e-mail address is protected by the unique Lyris system from web-bots that can automatically hoover up newsgroup mailing list addresses. Any queries about joining, leaving the lists or any query about the list should be sent to: listsupport@p2p.wrox.com.

Support and Errata

The following section will take you step by step through the process of finding errata on our web site to get book-specific help. The sections that follow, therefore, are:

- ❑ Finding a list of existing errata on the web site
- ❑ Adding your own errata to the existing list

There is also a section covering how to e-mail a question for technical support. This comprises:

- ❑ What your e-mail should include
- ❑ What happens to your e-mail once it has been received by us

Finding an Erratum on the Web Site

Before you send in a query, you might be able to save time by finding the answer to your problem on our web site – http:\\www.wrox.com.

Each book we publish has its own page and its own errata sheet. You can get to any book's page by clicking on the Books link on the left hand side of the page.

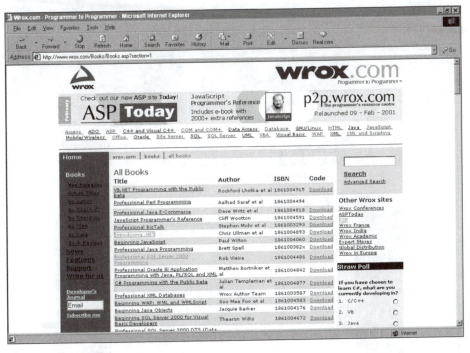

From here, find the book you are interested in and click the link. Towards the bottom of the page, underneath the book information at the right hand side of the central column is a link called Book Errata.

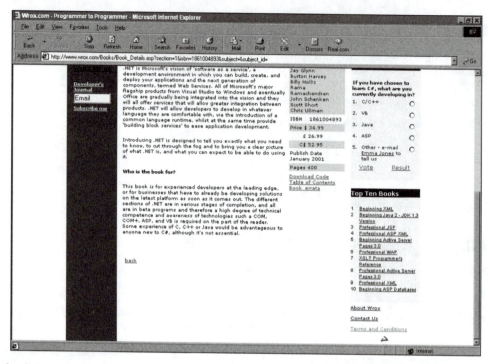

Simply click on this and you will be able to view a list of errata for that book:

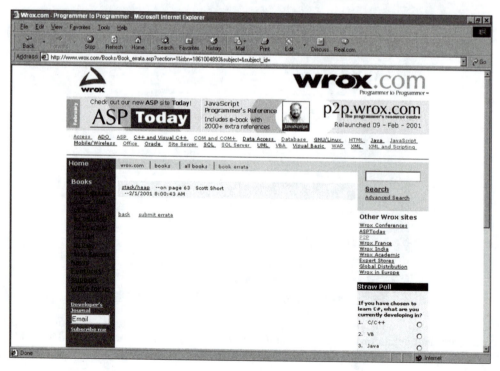

Add an Erratum: E-mail Support

If you wish to point out an erratum to put up on the web site, or directly query a problem in the book with an expert who knows the book in detail, then e-mail support@wrox.com. A typical e-mail should include the following things:

- ❑ The **book name**, **last four digits of the ISBN** and **page number** of the problem in the Subject field

- ❑ Your **name**, **contact info** and details of the **problem** in the body of the message

We won't send you junk mail. We need the details to save your time and ours. When you send us an e-mail it will go through the following chain of support.

Customer Support

Your message is delivered to one of our customer support staff, who are the first people to read it. They have files on most frequently asked questions and will answer anything general immediately. They answer general questions about the book and the web site.

Editorial

Deeper queries are forwarded to the technical editor responsible for that book. They have experience with the programming language or particular product and are able to answer detailed technical questions on the subject, directly related to the book's contents. Once an issue has been resolved, the editor can post errata to the web site or reply directly to your e-mail as appropriate.

The Authors

Finally, in the unlikely event that the editor can't answer your problem, s/he will forward the request to the author. We try to protect the author from any distractions from writing. However, we are quite happy to forward specific requests to them. All Wrox authors help with the support on their books. They'll mail the customer and the editor with their response, and again all readers should benefit.

What We Can't Answer

Obviously with an ever-growing range of books and an ever-changing technology base, there is an increasing volume of data requiring support. While we endeavor to answer all questions about the book, we can't solve bugs in your own programs that you've adapted from our code. However, do tell us if you're especially pleased with the routine you developed with our help.

How to Tell Us Exactly What You Think

We understand that errors can destroy the enjoyment of a book and can cause many wasted and frustrated hours, so we seek to minimize the distress that they can cause.

You might just wish to tell us how much you liked or loathed the book in question. Or you might have ideas about how this whole process could be improved. In which case you should e-mail feedback@wrox.com. You'll always find a sympathetic ear, no matter what the problem is. Above all you should remember that we do care about what you have to say and we will do our utmost to act upon it.

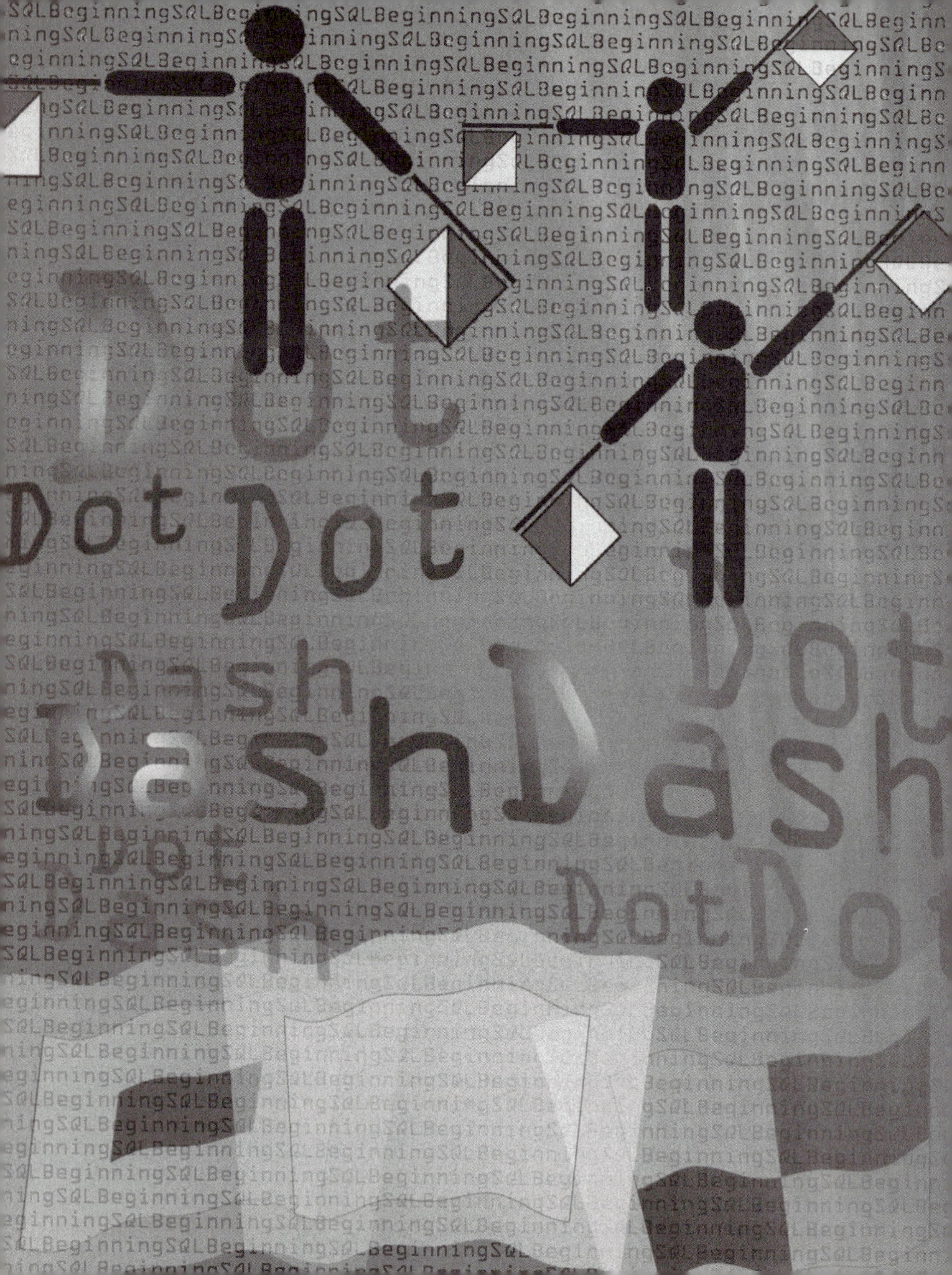
Dot Dot
Dash
Dash
Dot
Dot

Index

A Guide to the Index

This index covers numbered chapters but not the Appendices. It is arranged alphabetically, word-by-word, with Symbols and numerals preceding the letter A in the order:

- ! # $ % & (" * , . / : ; ? @ [\ ^ _ ` { | ~ + < = > 0 1 2 3 4 5 6 7 8 9

(although a hyphen immediately followed by another character is ignored so that –a option appears under a).

Where a main heading has both page references and subheadings, the unmodified page references will include any major treatment of the topic, while the sub headings identify passages dealing with specific aspects only.

Acronyms, rather than their expansions, have been selected as main entries on the grounds that unfamiliar acronyms are easier to construct than to expand.

Dot Dot

Dash Dash

Dot Dot